Supreme

수능 영어
듣기 모의고사
20+3회 실전

Supreme 수프림은

내신과 수능을 한 번에 잡아주는

프리미엄 고등 영어 브랜드입니다.

학습자의 마음을 읽는 동아영어콘텐츠연구팀

동아영어콘텐츠연구팀은 동아출판의 영어 개발 연구원, 현장 선생님, 그리고 전문 원고 집필자들이
공동연구를 통해 최적의 콘텐츠를 개발하는 연구조직입니다.

원고 개발에 참여하신 분들

Christian Kim   권혜경   오건석   이승옥   장정근   최진영

수능·내신 프리미엄 고등 영어 시리즈

수능 영어
듣기 모의고사
20+3회 실전

Structures 구성과 특징

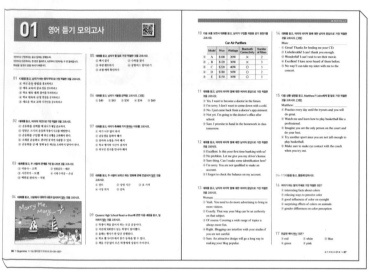

영어 듣기 모의고사 20+3회

- 수능 수준의 난이도 20회와 고난도 추가 3회를 더하여, 총 23회의 수능 영어 듣기 모의고사를 수록하였습니다. 최신 수능을 분석하여 문제 유형, 소재, 난이도 등을 동일하게 구성함으로써 수능을 완벽히 대비할 수 있게 했습니다.

- 편리한 QR 코드 스캔으로 바로 녹음 대본 음원 청취가 가능합니다.

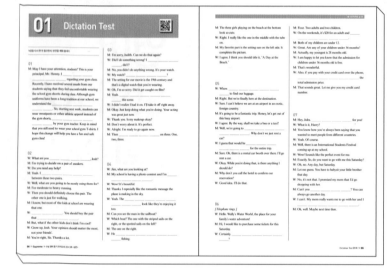

Dictation Test 받아쓰기

'23회 모의고사를 다시 한 번 들으면서 잘 안 들렸던 부분을 체크하고 핵심 단어와 표현을 받아쓰면서, 듣기 실력을 향상시키고 수능 실전을 대비할 수 있습니다.

부록 OMR 카드

OMR 카드 작성 요령을 숙지할 수 있도록 수능 영어 영역의 OMR 카드 예시를 수록했습니다.

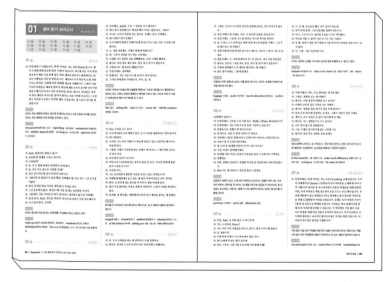

정답 및 해설

- 23회 모의고사에 대해 문항별로 대화·담화 해석과 문제 해결 전략, 어휘·표현을 자세히 정리했습니다.

- Dictation Test에 대한 정답을 마지막 페이지에 모아 수록했습니다.

Contents 목차

Supreme

Part 1 듣기 모의고사

수능 영어 듣기 모의고사 20+3회 실전

1번부터 17번까지는 듣고 답하는 문제입니다.
1번부터 15번까지는 한 번만 들려주고, 16번부터 17번까지는 두 번 들려줍니다.
방송을 잘 듣고 답을 하시기 바랍니다.

01 다음을 듣고, 남자가 하는 말의 목적으로 가장 적절한 것을 고르시오.
① 최신 운동 방법을 홍보하려고
② 체육 교육의 중요성을 강조하려고
③ 학교 체육 대회 참여를 독려하려고
④ 학교 체육복 규정 변경을 공지하려고
⑤ 새로운 학교 교복 디자인을 공모하려고

02 대화를 듣고, 여자의 의견으로 가장 적절한 것을 고르시오.
① 운동화를 선택할 때 용도가 제일 중요하다.
② 알맞은 크기의 운동화 착용이 사고를 예방한다.
③ 운동화를 구입할 때 최신 유행을 고려해야 한다.
④ 오래된 운동화도 관리만 잘 하면 사용할 수 있다.
⑤ 운동화를 살 때 정해 놓은 예산을 초과하지 말아야 한다.

03 대화를 듣고, 두 사람의 관계를 가장 잘 나타낸 것을 고르시오.
① 미용사 – 고객
② 영화감독 – 배우
③ 사진작가 – 모델
④ 시계 수리공 – 손님
⑤ 백화점 관리자 – 직원

04 대화를 듣고, 그림에서 대화의 내용과 일치하지 않는 것을 고르시오.

05 대화를 듣고, 남자가 할 일로 가장 적절한 것을 고르시오.
① 택시 잡기
② 수하물 찾기
③ 차량 렌트하기
④ 공항버스 알아보기
⑤ 호텔 예약 확인하기

06 대화를 듣고, 남자가 지불할 금액을 고르시오. [3점]
① $40 ② $45 ③ $50 ④ $54 ⑤ $60

07 대화를 듣고, 여자가 축제에 가지 못하는 이유를 고르시오.
① 비가 너무 많이 와서
② 남동생을 돌봐야 해서
③ 엄마와 쇼핑을 가야 해서
④ 학교 행사와 시간이 겹쳐서
⑤ 외국인 친구를 만나야 해서

08 대화를 듣고, 두 사람이 보려고 하는 영화에 관해 언급되지 않은 것을 고르시오.
① 장르
② 상영 시간
③ 표 가격
④ 극장 위치
⑤ 감독

09 Queens High School Read-a-thon에 관한 다음 내용을 듣고, 일치하지 않는 것을 고르시오.
① 학생이 책을 읽어서 하는 모금 운동이다.
② 작년에 500명이 넘는 학생이 참여했다.
③ 올해는 행사가 한 달간 진행된다.
④ 학교 웹 사이트에서 참가 등록을 할 수 있다.
⑤ 책을 가장 많이 모은 학생에게 상품이 주어진다.

10 다음 표를 보면서 대화를 듣고, 남자가 구입할 차량용 공기 청정기를 고르시오.

Car Air Purifiers

	Model	Price	Wattage	Bluetooth Connectivity	Number of Filters
①	A	$100	20W	×	2
②	B	$120	30W	×	3
③	C	$220	40W	○	3
④	D	$180	50W	○	2
⑤	E	$150	30W	○	3

11 대화를 듣고, 남자의 마지막 말에 대한 여자의 응답으로 가장 적절한 것을 고르시오.

① Yes. I want to become a doctor in the future.
② I'm sorry. I don't want to come down with a cold.
③ No. I just came back from a doctor's appointment.
④ Not yet. I'm going to the doctor's office after school.
⑤ Sure. I promise to hand in the homework in class tomorrow.

12 대화를 듣고, 여자의 마지막 말에 대한 남자의 응답으로 가장 적절한 것을 고르시오.

① Excellent. Is this your first time banking with us?
② No problem. Let me give you my driver's license.
③ Sure thing. Can I make some identification here?
④ I'm sorry. You are not qualified to make an account.
⑤ I forgot to check the balance on my account.

13 대화를 듣고, 남자의 마지막 말에 대한 여자의 응답으로 가장 적절한 것을 고르시오.

Woman: _____
① Yeah. You need to do more advertising to bring in more visitors.
② Exactly. That way your blog can be an authority on that subject.
③ Of course. Covering a wide range of topics is always more fun.
④ Right. Blogging can interfere with your studies if you are not careful.
⑤ Sure. An attractive design will go a long way in making your blog popular.

14 대화를 듣고, 여자의 마지막 말에 대한 남자의 응답으로 가장 적절한 것을 고르시오. [3점]

Man: _____
① Great! Thanks for lending me your CD.
② Unbelievable! I can't thank you enough.
③ Wonderful! I can't wait to see their movie.
④ Excellent! I have never heard of them before.
⑤ No way! I can take my sister with me to the concert.

15 다음 상황 설명을 듣고, Matthew가 John에게 할 말로 가장 적절한 것을 고르시오. [3점]

Matthew: _____
① Practice every day until the tryouts and you will do great.
② Watch me and learn how to play basketball like a professional.
③ Imagine you are the only person on the court and do your best.
④ Try another sport since you are not tall enough to play basketball.
⑤ Make sure to make eye contact with the coach when you try out.

[16-17] 다음을 듣고, 물음에 답하시오.

16 여자가 하는 말의 주제로 가장 적절한 것은?
① interesting facts about colors
② relaxing ways to perceive color
③ good influences of color on eyesight
④ surprising effects of colors on animals
⑤ gender differences on color perception

17 언급된 색이 아닌 것은?
① red   ② white   ③ blue
④ green   ⑤ pink

02 영어 듣기 모의고사

1번부터 17번까지는 듣고 답하는 문제입니다.
1번부터 15번까지는 한 번만 들려주고, 16번부터 17번까지는 두 번 들려줍니다.
방송을 잘 듣고 답을 하시기 바랍니다.

01 다음을 듣고, 여자가 하는 말의 목적으로 가장 적절한 것을 고르시오.
① 세탁용 세제를 판매하려고
② 뉴스의 헤드라인을 전하려고
③ 후원 업체가 만든 제품을 홍보하려고
④ 시청자들에게 새로운 프로그램을 소개하려고
⑤ 시청자들에게 방송사의 새 홈페이지 방문을 독려하려고

02 대화를 듣고, 남자의 의견으로 가장 적절한 것을 고르시오.
① 특수 효과의 도입으로 영화 산업이 발전했다.
② 영화에 더 많은 슈퍼 영웅들이 등장해야 한다.
③ 모든 슈퍼 영웅 영화는 줄거리가 잘 구성되어 있다.
④ 캐릭터 변화는 모든 슈퍼 영웅 영화에 꼭 필요하다.
⑤ 슈퍼 영웅 영화 때문에 영화의 다양성이 부족해지고 있다.

03 대화를 듣고, 두 사람의 관계를 가장 잘 나타낸 것을 고르시오.
① 소방관 – 시민   ② 간호사 – 환자
③ 경찰관 – 학생   ④ 자동차 정비사 – 고객
⑤ 자동차 판매원 – 고객

04 대화를 듣고, 그림에서 대화의 내용과 일치하지 않는 것을 고르시오.

05 대화를 듣고, 남자가 여자에게 부탁한 일로 가장 적절한 것을 고르시오.
① 문구점에서 봉투 사기
② 조간신문을 가져다 주기
③ 우체국에서 편지 부치기
④ 정육점에서 스테이크 사기
⑤ 세탁소에서 원피스 찾아 오기

06 대화를 듣고, 여자가 지불할 금액을 고르시오. [3점]
① $120   ② $220   ③ $320   ④ $350   ⑤ $420

07 대화를 듣고, 여자가 동영상을 보는 이유를 고르시오.
① 남편의 생일을 축하하기 위해서
② 스테이크 식당을 개업하기 위해서
③ 남편에게 멋진 식사를 만들어 주기 위해서
④ 여동생의 고등학교 졸업을 축하하기 위해서
⑤ 부모님의 기념일에 음식을 요리하기 위해서

08 대화를 듣고, Summer Seminar에 관해 언급되지 않은 것을 고르시오.
① 개최 요일   ② 활동   ③ 옷차림
④ 모이는 장소   ⑤ 토론 주제

09 Pets for Vets 모임에 관한 다음 내용을 듣고, 일치하지 않는 것을 고르시오.
① Aloha 경기장에서 열린다.
② 목표는 유기 동물을 은퇴한 군인들에게 배정해 주는 것이다.
③ 고양이 기르기에 관한 짧은 강연이 있을 예정이다.
④ 대회의 일등에게는 애완동물의 사료가 평생 제공된다.
⑤ 이번 주말에 끝난다.

10 다음 표를 보면서 대화를 듣고, 두 사람이 구입할 텐트를 고르시오.

Outdoor Tents

	Model	Price	Size	Shape	Number of Doors
①	A	$150	4-person	Pyramid	2
②	B	$250	2-person	Dome	1
③	C	$190	4-person	Dome	2
④	D	$180	6-person	Pyramid	1
⑤	E	$199	4-person	Dome	1

11 대화를 듣고, 남자의 마지막 말에 대한 여자의 응답으로 가장 적절한 것을 고르시오.

① I'll be there early in the week.
② Will the doctor be very upset?
③ The appointment time is near.
④ Tomorrow is a perfect time for me.
⑤ Yes. How does Thursday afternoon sound?

12 대화를 듣고, 여자의 마지막 말에 대한 남자의 응답으로 가장 적절한 것을 고르시오.

① Of course. I'm sure you'll enjoy it.
② Don't worry. I'll return it to the library.
③ How can I become a mystery writer?
④ Why don't we get Steven King's autograph?
⑤ You really have a talent for writing.

13 대화를 듣고, 여자의 마지막 말에 대한 남자의 응답으로 가장 적절한 것을 고르시오.

Man: _____
① Hurry up. I'm really hungry.
② Did you find a gift for Mom?
③ Don't worry. I'm sure it's still there.
④ Do you know what you want to order?
⑤ I don't know. This roller coaster is scary.

14 대화를 듣고, 남자의 마지막 말에 대한 여자의 응답으로 가장 적절한 것을 고르시오. [3점]

Woman: _____
① Order me a cup of coffee please.
② Just be yourself and don't overthink it.
③ Tell your parents that dinner was great.
④ I can't wait. I'll see you at the show tonight.
⑤ Who knows? Maybe the band will come back.

15 다음 상황 설명을 듣고, Jimmy가 Sunny에게 할 말로 가장 적절한 것을 고르시오. [3점]

Jimmy: _____
① People nowadays love to read classic novels.
② This contemporary author has upset many critics.
③ We should move our inventory to the online store.
④ I think we should spend more money on newer authors.
⑤ I think adding magazines to our selection might help our sales.

[16-17] 다음을 듣고, 물음에 답하시오.

16 남자가 하는 말의 주제로 가장 적절한 것은?
① health hazards of cycling
② features of a new hybrid bicycle
③ components needed on a bicycle
④ benefits of puncture resistant tires
⑤ advantages of a new drive-train system

17 언급된 특징이 아닌 것은?
① lightweight body
② comfortable seat
③ foldable body
④ drive-train
⑤ puncture resistant wheels

1번부터 17번까지는 듣고 답하는 문제입니다.
1번부터 15번까지는 한 번만 들려주고, 16번부터 17번까지는 두 번 들려줍니다.
방송을 잘 듣고 답을 하시기 바랍니다.

01 다음을 듣고, 남자가 하는 말의 목적으로 가장 적절한 것을 고르시오.
① 음악 교육의 중요성을 강조하려고
② 청취자들에게 희망곡 신청 방법을 공지하려고
③ 클래식 음악 프로그램의 첫 방송을 홍보하려고
④ 새로운 라디오 공동 진행자의 합류를 안내하려고
⑤ 클래식 음악 프로그램에 적합한 진행자를 추천하려고

02 대화를 듣고, 여자의 의견으로 가장 적절한 것을 고르시오.
① 학창 시절에 사귄 친구들을 소중히 여겨야 한다.
② 친구를 사귀는 것은 학교생활에 적응하는 데 도움이 된다.
③ 자신과 다른 생각을 가진 친구들의 의견도 존중해야 한다.
④ 학교에서 스트레스를 받지 않도록 노력하는 것이 중요하다.
⑤ 다양한 동아리에 가입하여 활동하는 것은 좋은 경험이 된다.

03 대화를 듣고, 두 사람의 관계를 가장 잘 나타낸 것을 고르시오.
① 학생 – 교수   ② 교사 – 교장
③ 환자 – 의사   ④ 후원자 – 과학자
⑤ 간병인 – 간호사

04 대화를 듣고, 그림에서 대화의 내용과 일치하지 않는 것을 고르시오.

05 대화를 듣고, 남자가 여자에게 부탁한 일로 가장 적절한 것을 고르시오.
① 앱 다운로드하기
② 회의 스케줄 조정하기
③ 스마트폰 업데이트하기
④ 생일 축하 메시지 보내기
⑤ 생일 파티 날짜와 시간 알려 주기

06 대화를 듣고, 남자가 지불할 금액을 고르시오. [3점]
① $20   ② $30   ③ $40   ④ $50   ⑤ $60

07 대화를 듣고, 여자가 뮤지컬을 보러 갈 수 없는 이유를 고르시오.
① 표를 예매하지 못해서
② 사진 촬영을 해야 해서
③ 오디션에 참가해야 해서
④ 춤 연습을 하러 가야 해서
⑤ 친구의 결혼식에 가야 해서

08 대화를 듣고, Eco-Friendly Night에 관해 언급되지 않은 것을 고르시오.
① 개최 일시   ② 신청 방법   ③ 기념품 종류
④ 후원 업체   ⑤ 개최 장소

09 화재경보기 점검에 관한 다음 내용을 듣고, 일치하지 않는 것을 고르시오.
① 이틀간 이루어질 것이다.
② 관리 사무소도 점검 대상에 포함된다.
③ 지역 소방서의 소방관에 의해 진행된다.
④ 점검 기간 동안 경보음이 울릴 수 있다.
⑤ 점검을 위해 각 가구의 방의 문은 모두 열어 두어야 한다.

10 다음 표를 보면서 대화를 듣고, 두 사람이 구매할 애완동물 이동 장을 고르시오.

Pet Carriers

	Model	Height	Shoulder Strap	Ventilation Slots	Door Material
①	A	35 cm	○	2 sides	plastic
②	B	40 cm	○	3 sides	plastic
③	C	44 cm	×	3 sides	steel
④	D	47 cm	×	3 sides	plastic
⑤	E	50 cm	×	2 sides	steel

11 대화를 듣고, 남자의 마지막 말에 대한 여자의 응답으로 가장 적절한 것을 고르시오.

① Yes. We need more club members.
② Sorry. I have choir practice tomorrow.
③ Sure. I'll show you my new performance.
④ Okay. I'll go with you and see what it's like.
⑤ No thanks. I already joined the school choir.

12 대화를 듣고, 여자의 마지막 말에 대한 남자의 응답으로 가장 적절한 것을 고르시오.

① Of course. We can buy her a new printer.
② No thanks. I already printed out my pictures.
③ No, I'm afraid you can't. We're out of ink right now.
④ Good idea. Let's go to Jeju Island with Grandma.
⑤ I understand. It's not easy to make a photo album.

13 대화를 듣고, 남자의 마지막 말에 대한 여자의 응답으로 가장 적절한 것을 고르시오. [3점]

Woman: _____

① I agree. We should support our local supermarket.
② No problem. Our campsite is far away from the lake.
③ Of course. I scratch a lot when I get a mosquito bite.
④ All right. I'll go to the pharmacy after school and get one.
⑤ That's okay. This insect repellent is made from organic ingredients.

14 대화를 듣고, 여자의 마지막 말에 대한 남자의 응답으로 가장 적절한 것을 고르시오.

Man: _____

① Thank you. Then, I'll volunteer at the school library.
② That's nice. You can help me organize these books.
③ Yes. I have some experience of raising cats and dogs.
④ I agree. We need more volunteering programs at school.
⑤ You're right. Sign me up for the animal hospital program.

15 다음 상황 설명을 듣고, Emma가 Janice에게 할 말로 가장 적절한 것을 고르시오. [3점]

Emma: _____

① How about hanging out with some new friends?
② Don't forget that I'm on your side no matter what.
③ You need to stick to your idea even if she disagrees.
④ Why don't you ask her to help you with your art project?
⑤ I think you should calm down and try to make up with her.

[16-17] 다음을 듣고, 물음에 답하시오.

16 여자가 하는 말의 주제로 가장 적절한 것은?

① interesting features of animals
② idioms that are related to body parts
③ common ways of expressing emotions
④ functions of different parts of the body
⑤ use of body language in conversations

17 언급된 신체 부위가 아닌 것은?

① head
② ears
③ eyes
④ arms
⑤ feet

1번부터 17번까지는 듣고 답하는 문제입니다.

1번부터 15번까지는 한 번만 들려주고, 16번부터 17번까지는 두 번 들려줍니다.

방송을 잘 듣고 답을 하시기 바랍니다.

01 다음을 듣고, 남자가 하는 말의 목적으로 가장 적절한 것을 고르시오.

① 은퇴 후에 구직을 안내하려고

② 고령 직원 채용을 권유하려고

③ 실업률 증가 원인을 설명하려고

④ 고령화 사회의 문제점을 알리려고

⑤ 직원 교육의 필요성을 강조하려고

02 대화를 듣고, 남자의 의견으로 가장 적절한 것을 고르시오.

① 일상용품을 재활용 및 재사용해야 한다.

② 분리수거를 통해 재활용을 생활화해야 한다.

③ 쓰레기를 줄이는 것이 환경 보호의 핵심이다.

④ 캠페인을 통해 사람들의 환경 보호 참여를 독려할 수 있다.

⑤ 교육을 통해 환경에 대한 사람들의 인식을 개선해야 한다.

03 대화를 듣고, 두 사람의 관계를 가장 잘 나타낸 것을 고르시오.

① 환자 – 의사

② 연출자 – 공연장 관리자

③ 고객 – 이삿짐센터 직원

④ 세입자 – 부동산 중개업자

⑤ 상점 주인 – 소방 시설 점검원

04 대화를 듣고, 그림에서 대화의 내용과 일치하지 않는 것을 고르시오.

05 대화를 듣고, 여자가 남자에게 부탁한 일로 가장 적절한 것을 고르시오.

① 캠핑 요리 해 주기

② 텐트 빌려주기

③ 캠핑 일정 조정하기

④ 침낭 빌려주기

⑤ 캠핑 장소 추천하기

06 대화를 듣고, 여자가 지불할 금액을 고르시오. [3점]

① $30   ② $40   ③ $50   ④ $60   ⑤ $80

07 대화를 듣고, 여자가 생일 파티에 갈 수 없는 이유를 고르시오.

① 이사를 도와야 해서

② 컨디션이 좋지 않아서

③ 발표 준비를 해야 해서

④ 아르바이트를 해야 해서

⑤ 부모님을 모시러 가야 해서

08 대화를 듣고, Ontario Sheep Farms 주최 행사에 관해 언급되지 않은 것을 고르시오.

① 행사 일시   ② 행사 종류   ③ 행사장 교통편

④ 입장료   ⑤ 행사장 위치

09 Auburn Student Council Election에 관한 다음 내용을 듣고, 일치하지 않는 것을 고르시오.

① 온라인으로 이틀에 걸쳐 진행된다.

② 후보자 지명은 선거일 두 달 전에 끝내야 한다.

③ 스스로를 후보자로 추천할 수는 없다.

④ 후보자로 지명되었음이 당사자에게 이메일로 공지된다.

⑤ 새롭게 선출된 후보자들은 선거 직후에 임기를 시작한다.

10 다음 표를 보면서 대화를 듣고, 남자가 구매할 자외선 차단 크림을 고르시오.

Sunblocks

	Model	SPF	Volume	Price	Delivery Fee
①	A	15	50 ml	$15	○
②	B	15	75 ml	$23	×
③	C	30	50 ml	$19	×
④	D	30	100 ml	$25	×
⑤	E	50	75 ml	$22	○

11 대화를 듣고, 남자의 마지막 말에 대한 여자의 응답으로 가장 적절한 것을 고르시오.

① Of course. It's impolite to visit someone so late.
② I don't think so. She must be a morning person.
③ No way. You'd better call her first before visiting her.
④ You should visit her now. Ask for her address first.
⑤ I see your point. You have to get up early next time.

12 대화를 듣고, 여자의 마지막 말에 대한 남자의 응답으로 가장 적절한 것을 고르시오.

① Good. Cooking always makes me happy.
② Why not. We should visit the grocery store first.
③ I'm happy that we finally arrived at the destination.
④ Of course. It was the best restaurant I've ever been to.
⑤ Good idea. Let's get some sandwiches and orange juice.

13 대화를 듣고, 여자의 마지막 말에 대한 남자의 응답으로 가장 적절한 것을 고르시오. [3점]

Man: _____
① Of course. She must be proud of her presentation.
② Right. You should have presented the project for her.
③ Forget it. Try not to be late for the meeting next time.
④ Don't worry. I think you will do the presentation very well.
⑤ Don't be so harsh on yourself. I'm sure you did a good job.

14 대화를 듣고, 남자의 마지막 말에 대한 여자의 응답으로 가장 적절한 것을 고르시오.

Woman: _____
① It's too late. You should have renewed your library card first.
② Don't worry. I can talk about it because I already read the book.
③ I'm sorry. The book you want to check out is already being borrowed.
④ In that case, you can check out the book when you return the overdue one.
⑤ No problem. You can renew your card later.

15 다음 상황 설명을 듣고, James가 점원에게 할 말로 가장 적절한 것을 고르시오. [3점]

James: _____
① I'm sorry, but you are not allowed to enter now.
② Pardon me. I want to get a refund for these tickets.
③ I understand. I think we can watch a movie next time.
④ Excuse me, but are there any popular movies you can recommend?
⑤ I know we are late, but can I buy two tickets for the 7 p.m. movie showing now?

[16-17] 다음을 듣고, 물음에 답하시오.

16 여자가 하는 말의 주제로 가장 적절한 것은?
① guidelines about adopting pets
② how pets benefit our mental health
③ tips on choosing pets according to age
④ how raising pets makes children more responsible
⑤ importance of giving pets enough exercise

17 언급된 동물이 아닌 것은?
① dog　② fish　③ rabbit
④ snake　⑤ kitten

1번부터 17번까지는 듣고 답하는 문제입니다.
1번부터 15번까지는 한 번만 들려주고, 16번부터 17번까지는 두 번 들려줍니다.
방송을 잘 듣고 답을 하시기 바랍니다.

01 다음을 듣고, 남자가 하는 말의 목적으로 가장 적절한 것을 고르시오.
① 혼자 여행을 떠나 볼 것을 권유하려고
② 청년에게 인기 있는 여행지를 광고하려고
③ 여행 칼럼니스트가 되는 법을 안내하려고
④ 현재 유행하고 있는 여행 방식을 비판하려고
⑤ 배낭여행을 잘 할 수 있는 방법을 조언하려고

02 대화를 듣고, 여자의 의견으로 가장 적절한 것을 고르시오.
① 건강 관리를 위해서는 정기 검진이 필요하다.
② 간암은 조기 발견 시 완치가 가능한 질병이다.
③ 암에 걸린 사람이 병가를 신청하는 것은 당연하다.
④ 직장에서 받는 스트레스가 암 발병의 가장 큰 원인이다.
⑤ 간암 치료를 위해서는 의사를 절대적으로 신뢰해야 한다.

03 대화를 듣고, 두 사람의 관계를 가장 잘 나타낸 것을 고르시오.
① 환자 – 치과 의사   ② 손님 – 서점 직원
③ 공항 이용객 – 공항 직원   ④ 승객 – 비행기 승무원
⑤ 기자 – 추리 소설 작가

04 대화를 듣고, 그림에서 대화의 내용과 일치하지 <u>않는</u> 것을 고르시오.

05 대화를 듣고, 남자가 할 일로 가장 적절한 것을 고르시오.
① 영화 표 예매하기   ② 동호회 회원 소개하기
③ 식당 약도 그려 주기   ④ 종이와 연필 가져오기
⑤ 자동차로 시청에 데려다주기

06 대화를 듣고, 여자가 지불할 금액을 고르시오. [3점]
① $72   ② $81   ③ $108   ④ $110   ⑤ $120

07 대화를 듣고, 남자가 여자의 태블릿 PC를 구입하지 <u>않는</u> 이유를 고르시오.
① 용량이 적어서
② 판매 가격이 비싸서
③ 보증 기간이 지나서
④ 사용한 지 오래 되어서
⑤ 디자인이 마음에 들지 않아서

08 대화를 듣고, 남자가 여자에게 권유한 아파트에 관해 언급되지 <u>않은</u> 것을 고르시오.
① 위치   ② 층수   ③ 거실 전망
④ 월 임대료   ⑤ 편의 시설

09 Seattle Pet Fair에 관한 다음 내용을 듣고, 일치하지 <u>않는</u> 것을 고르시오.
① 5월 1일에 시작해서 3주간 지속된다.
② 작년과 같은 장소에서 개최된다.
③ 100개가 넘는 애완동물 관련 회사가 참가한다.
④ 올해 관람객은 약 200,000만 명으로 예상된다.
⑤ 5달러의 입장료는 동물 복지 증진에 사용된다.

10 다음 표를 보면서 대화를 듣고, 남자가 구입할 세탁기를 고르시오.

Washing Machines

	Model	Manufacturer	Capacity	Price	Warranty Period
①	A	Queen Electronics	6 kg	$530	1 year
②	B	Sun Star	7 kg	$450	1 year
③	C	Queen Electronics	9 kg	$710	2 years
④	D	Techno	8 kg	$690	2 years
⑤	E	Techno	6 kg	$570	2 years

11 대화를 듣고, 남자의 마지막 말에 대한 여자의 응답으로 가장 적절한 것을 고르시오.

① Right. I didn't know the house was so clean.
② I'm sorry, but I forgot to clean the house today.
③ Yeah. You'd better park your car in the garage.
④ Sure. The cleaning service was very convenient.
⑤ Good. Then I'll be in charge of the living room.

12 대화를 듣고, 여자의 마지막 말에 대한 남자의 응답으로 가장 적절한 것을 고르시오.

① I think the monthly fee is too expensive.
② It's $50 and it includes a personal locker.
③ I'm sorry, but I'm not interested in swimming.
④ Don't worry about the monthly fee. I'll lend you $50.
⑤ If you practice, you can move up to the advanced course.

13 대화를 듣고, 남자의 마지막 말에 대한 여자의 응답으로 가장 적절한 것을 고르시오.

Woman: _____

① Don't worry. I'll give you a new remote control.
② Okay. I'll send someone to your room right away.
③ It's up to you. Please make your own password.
④ Right. I want to have my computer connected to the Wi-Fi.
⑤ Thanks to your Wi-Fi network service, I finished my job on time.

14 대화를 듣고, 여자의 마지막 말에 대한 남자의 응답으로 가장 적절한 것을 고르시오. [3점]

Man: _____

① Actually, I already registered my name.
② Good! Let's go see the children right away.
③ Simple! Donate the stuff you don't use.
④ Right. My volunteer experience was rewarding.
⑤ I think so. Volunteer work is not as easy as you think.

15 다음 상황 설명을 듣고, Brian이 김 교수님에게 할 말로 가장 적절한 것을 고르시오. [3점]

Brian: _____

① Could you check my novel for grammatical mistakes?
② I'm sorry, but I don't feel like visiting professor Kim's office.
③ Why don't you become one of the judges for the competition?
④ I'm wondering why you decided to major in Korean grammar.
⑤ If you don't mind, can you submit my novel to the Korean Embassy?

[16-17] 다음을 듣고, 물음에 답하시오.

16 여자가 하는 말의 주제로 가장 적절한 것은?

① the effect of electricity on our lives
② benefits of power-saving appliances
③ how to save electricity in the home
④ the need for sustainable alternative energy
⑤ how electricity harms the environment

17 언급된 제품이 아닌 것은?

① computers   ② washing machines
③ air conditioners   ④ televisions
⑤ electric heaters

1번부터 17번까지는 듣고 답하는 문제입니다.
1번부터 15번까지는 한 번만 들려주고, 16번부터 17번까지는 두 번 들려줍니다.
방송을 잘 듣고 답을 하시기 바랍니다.

01 다음을 듣고, 남자가 하는 말의 목적으로 가장 적절한 것을 고르시오.
① 교내 무료 아침 식사 프로젝트를 공지하려고
② 교내 학생 식당 사용 시간 변경을 안내하려고
③ 지역 사회와 연계된 식습관 개선 프로그램을 권유하려고
④ 아침 식사 여부와 학교 출석률의 상관관계를 확인하려고
⑤ 학생들의 의견을 반영한 새로운 학교 급식 메뉴를 홍보하려고

02 대화를 듣고, 여자의 의견으로 가장 적절한 것을 고르시오.
① 직업 선택 시 반드시 자신의 적성을 고려해야 한다.
② 다양한 분야에 관심을 갖는 것은 바람직한 태도이다.
③ 올바른 진로 결정을 위해서는 교사와의 상담도 필요하다.
④ 직업 체험 센터 방문은 효과적인 진로 탐색에 도움이 된다.
⑤ 관심 분야를 좁힌 뒤 체험할 구체적인 직업을 선택하는 게 좋다.

03 대화를 듣고, 두 사람의 관계를 가장 잘 나타낸 것을 고르시오.
① 동물학자 – 학생   ② 구조대원 – 기자
③ 수의사 – 동물 훈련가   ④ 수족관 안내원 – 관람객
⑤ 반려동물 미용사 – 반려동물 주인

04 대화를 듣고, 그림에서 대화의 내용과 일치하지 <u>않는</u> 것을 고르시오.

05 대화를 듣고, 여자가 남자에게 부탁한 일로 가장 적절한 것을 고르시오.
① 박스에 구호물품 담기
② 우체국에서 택배 보내기
③ 봄맞이 대청소 도와주기
④ 보건소에서 자원봉사하기
⑤ 학교로 아이들 데리러 가기

06 대화를 듣고, 남자가 지불할 금액을 고르시오. [3점]
① $15   ② $20   ③ $25   ④ $30   ⑤ $35

07 대화를 듣고, 여자가 요리 수업을 들을 수 <u>없는</u> 이유를 고르시오.
① 치과 예약이 있어서
② 안내문을 받지 못해서
③ 요리를 잘 하지 못해서
④ 조리 기구를 준비하지 못해서
⑤ 할머니의 정원 일을 도와드려야 해서

08 대화를 듣고, Book Festival에 관해 언급되지 <u>않은</u> 것을 고르시오.
① 행사 일시   ② 행사 장소
③ 교통편   ④ 참가비
⑤ 반입 가능 물품

09 Multicultural Day에 관한 다음 내용을 듣고, 일치하지 <u>않는</u> 것을 고르시오.
① 학생회관에서 열린다.
② 금요일 오후 강의는 모두 취소될 것이다.
③ 다양한 문화권의 예술 전시와 춤 공연이 준비되어 있다.
④ 행사에 참가하기 위해서는 소정의 기부금을 내야 한다.
⑤ 행사에 가족과 친구들을 동반할 수 있다.

10 다음 표를 보면서 대화를 듣고, 여자가 구입할 캠핑용 탁자를 고르시오.

Camping Tables

	Model	Weight	Material	Cup Holders	Price
①	A	0.8 kg	aluminum	0	$20
②	B	1 kg	aluminum	4	$45
③	C	2 kg	aluminum	2	$30
④	D	3 kg	wood	0	$60
⑤	E	5 kg	wood	2	$665

11 대화를 듣고, 남자의 마지막 말에 대한 여자의 응답으로 가장 적절한 것을 고르시오.

① Yes. Those are your books.
② Sure, I can do that for you.
③ Right. I'll tell her you're coming.
④ No. Her office is far from the library.
⑤ Too bad. The library is not open today.

12 대화를 듣고, 여자의 마지막 말에 대한 남자의 응답으로 가장 적절한 것을 고르시오.

① Sure. You can have my sandwich.
② No thanks. I'm allergic to cheese.
③ That's okay. I don't need a drink.
④ Great. I'll bring your food right away.
⑤ I'm sorry. Our coffee machine broke down.

13 대화를 듣고, 여자의 마지막 말에 대한 남자의 응답으로 가장 적절한 것을 고르시오. [3점]

Man: _____

① You're right. She likes jokes a lot.
② That's okay. I don't like yellow sneakers.
③ All right. I'll apologize to her after school.
④ Good idea. I like practicing in the music room.
⑤ I'm not sure. She doesn't seem to like bananas.

14 대화를 듣고, 남자의 마지막 말에 대한 여자의 응답으로 가장 적절한 것을 고르시오.

Woman: _____

① Of course. All the volunteers are art major students.
② I'm sorry. Children under 7 are not allowed in this exhibit.
③ Yes. You have to make a reservation at the information desk.
④ I hope they're displaying works by your favorite illustrator.
⑤ I'm not sure, but I think the City Art Center closes every Sunday.

15 다음 상황 설명을 듣고, Teresa 선생님이 George에게 할 말로 가장 적절한 것을 고르시오. [3점]

Ms. Teresa: _____

① If I were you, I would focus on developing my own program.
② I think knowing the history of computer programming is very important.
③ You should get some valuable experience by taking the national examination.
④ Why don't you participate in the competition after you graduate from high school?
⑤ How about asking your history teacher if you can do your presentation in advance?

[16-17] 다음을 듣고, 물음에 답하시오.

16 남자가 하는 말의 주제로 가장 적절한 것은?

① various types of animal camouflage
② natural enemies in the animal kingdom
③ common behaviors of animals in the wild
④ effects of the environment on animal evolution
⑤ differences of natural and artificial camouflage

17 언급된 동물이 아닌 것은?

① snowy owl   ② zebra
③ sea horse   ④ stick insect
⑤ scarlet kingsnake

1번부터 17번까지는 듣고 답하는 문제입니다.
1번부터 15번까지는 한 번만 들려주고, 16번부터 17번까지는 두 번 들려줍니다.
방송을 잘 듣고 답을 하시기 바랍니다.

01 다음을 듣고, 여자가 하는 말의 목적으로 가장 적절한 것을 고르시오.
① 새로운 팟캐스트를 홍보하려고
② 지역 내 기부 활동을 독려하려고
③ 스트레스 해소 방법을 안내하려고
④ 프로그램 편성표 변경을 공지하려고
⑤ 일상에서 겪는 스트레스에 관해 설명하려고

02 대화를 듣고, 남자의 의견으로 가장 적절한 것을 고르시오.
① 행복은 성적순이 아니다.
② 독서는 모든 배움의 첫 걸음이다.
③ 외국어 교육은 일찍 시작할수록 좋다.
④ 아이들의 상상력을 자극하는 것이 중요하다.
⑤ 글을 늦게 배우는 아이들이 더 창의적인 경향이 있다.

03 대화를 듣고, 두 사람의 관계를 가장 잘 나타낸 것을 고르시오.
① 학생 – 경찰관
② 환자 – 간호사
③ 건물주 – 소방관
④ 손님 – 자동차 정비공
⑤ 학부모 – 영양사

04 대화를 듣고, 그림에서 대화의 내용과 일치하지 않는 것을 고르시오.

05 대화를 듣고, 여자가 할 일로 가장 적절한 것을 고르시오.
① 짐 싸기
② 택시 부르기
③ 안경집 찾기
④ 강아지 산책 시키기
⑤ 도그 시터가 할 일 목록 작성하기

06 대화를 듣고, 여자가 지불할 금액을 고르시오. [3점]
① $46 ② $50 ③ $81 ④ $82 ⑤ $90

07 대화를 듣고, 남자가 책을 읽고 있는 이유를 고르시오.
① 엄마가 시켜서
② 가산점을 받으려고
③ 학교 과제를 해야 해서
④ 책을 쓴 작가를 좋아해서
⑤ 고전 문학 소설을 좋아해서

08 대화를 듣고, Summer Jamboree에 관해 언급되지 않은 것을 고르시오.
① 날짜
② 장소
③ 활동 내용
④ 입장료
⑤ 진행 시간

09 교내 에어컨 사용에 관한 다음 내용을 듣고, 일치하지 않는 것을 고르시오.
① 오늘부터 오후 4시 30분 이후에는 에어컨이 자동으로 꺼진다.
② 정규 수업 후 에어컨을 사용하려면 하루 전에 Miller 선생님에게 알려야 한다.
③ 에어컨의 온도는 중앙 통제에 의해 28도로 설정된다.
④ 이번 주 토요일에 에어컨 필터가 교체될 예정이다.
⑤ 이번 주 토요일에 체육관에서 하는 스포츠 동아리 활동은 오후부터 가능하다.

10 다음 표를 보면서 대화를 듣고, 남자가 구입할 등산화를 고르시오.

Hiking Boots

	Model	Price	Weight	Waterproof	Color
①	A	$63	1 kg	No	Green
②	B	$46	900 g	Yes	Yellow
③	C	$59	1.1 kg	Yes	Blue
④	D	$49	950 g	No	White
⑤	E	$57	975 g	Yes	Black

11 대화를 듣고, 남자의 마지막 말에 대한 여자의 응답으로 가장 적절한 것을 고르시오.

① Fine. Please put your package on the scales.
② You wrap the package. I'll go to the post office.
③ Of course. I really want to see my daughter.
④ This Friday? It's impossible to send it by ship.
⑤ In fact, I'm very busy because of work this Friday.

12 대화를 듣고, 여자의 마지막 말에 대한 남자의 응답으로 가장 적절한 것을 고르시오.

① Let's visit her this weekend.
② She'll be back in a few days.
③ Her flight came in yesterday.
④ I want a vacation to Hawaii too.
⑤ We'll be taking our trip next week.

13 대화를 듣고, 여자의 마지막 말에 대한 남자의 응답으로 가장 적절한 것을 고르시오.

Man: _____

① No way. My coffee is too hot.
② Okay, I'm ready. Let's go to lunch.
③ This scuba diving tour is real exciting.
④ The aquarium is closing now. We should go.
⑤ I'm so excited about going on our honeymoon.

14 대화를 듣고, 남자의 마지막 말에 대한 여자의 응답으로 가장 적절한 것을 고르시오. [3점]

Woman: _____

① What time is the dinner?
② I'll buy two tickets for 9:30 p.m.
③ Lunch is going to be lots of fun.
④ Should we eat the salmon or tuna?
⑤ I'm looking forward to pasta tonight.

15 다음 상황 설명을 듣고, Charles가 Gina에게 할 말로 가장 적절한 것을 고르시오. [3점]

Charles: _____

① I think hiring a new employee is a great idea.
② How about buying an espresso machine instead?
③ We need to develop a new drink for lunch time.
④ Do you want me to make you an espresso?
⑤ Maybe we should buy a new cash register.

[16-17] 다음을 듣고, 물음에 답하시오.

16 남자가 하는 말의 주제로 가장 적절한 것은?

① ways to build apps using Antunes
② developers' needs when building apps
③ how to use a new development kit
④ new apps for novice smartphone users
⑤ improvements to an app development kit

17 언급된 기능이 아닌 것은?

① Fast App Building
② Memory Management
③ AI Helper
④ Battery Consumption Viewer
⑤ User Interface

1번부터 17번까지는 듣고 답하는 문제입니다.
1번부터 15번까지는 한 번만 들려주고, 16번부터 17번까지는 두 번 들려줍니다.
방송을 잘 듣고 답을 하시기 바랍니다.

01 다음을 듣고, 남자가 하는 말의 목적으로 가장 적절한 것을 고르시오.
① 에너지 절약 방법을 안내하려고
② 새 보일러 설치 기간을 알리려고
③ 물을 아껴서 사용할 것을 권장하려고
④ 아파트 내 온수 공급 중단을 공지하려고
⑤ 수리가 필요한 아파트 시설물 신고를 받으려고

02 대화를 듣고, 여자의 의견으로 가장 적절한 것을 고르시오.
① 시험 결과에 너무 좌지우지되어서는 안 된다.
② 학습 시간이 늘수록 학업 성취도를 높일 수 있다.
③ 계획을 세울 때는 실천 가능성을 따져 봐야 한다.
④ 충분한 시간의 수면은 건강을 유지하는 데 중요하다.
⑤ 효율적인 시간 사용을 위해 세부적인 계획을 세워야 한다.

03 대화를 듣고, 두 사람의 관계를 가장 잘 나타낸 것을 고르시오.
① 모델 – 감독
② 기자 – 소설가
③ 사진작가 – 편집장
④ 여행사 직원 – 고객
⑤ 환경 운동가 – 학생

04 대화를 듣고, 그림에서 대화의 내용과 일치하지 않는 것을 고르시오.

05 대화를 듣고 여자가 남자에게 부탁한 일로 가장 적절한 것을 고르시오.
① 냅킨 사 오기
② 접시 사 오기
③ 식료품 장 보기
④ 보드게임 꺼내 놓기
⑤ 참석 확인 문자 보내기

06 대화를 듣고, 여자가 지불할 금액을 고르시오. [3점]
① $180   ② $190   ③ $210   ④ $220   ⑤ $250

07 대화를 듣고 남자가 제주도행 비행기표를 취소한 이유를 고르시오.
① 날씨가 좋지 않아서
② 친구가 못 가게 되어서
③ 과제를 끝내지 못해서
④ 다른 여행지로 변경해서
⑤ 비행기표 가격이 부담되어서

08 대화를 듣고, Amateur Chess Tournament에 관해 언급되지 않은 것을 고르시오.
① 개최 기간
② 개최 장소
③ 참가비
④ 리그 종류
⑤ 우승 상품

09 미세 먼지가 심한 날의 학교생활에 관한 다음 내용을 듣고, 일치하지 않는 것을 고르시오.
① 야외 체육 수업이 취소된다.
② 마스크는 가급적 실내에서도 쓴다.
③ 환기 시간은 짧게 유지한다.
④ 손을 자주 씻고 입안을 헹군다.
⑤ 보건실에서 안약을 받을 수 있다.

10 다음 표를 보면서 대화를 듣고, 남자가 구매할 케이크를 고르시오.

Camellia's Bakery

	Cake	Flavor	Shape	Price	Writing
①	A	fruit	round	$18	○
②	B	cheese	heart	$22	○
③	C	cheese	animal	$24	×
④	D	chocolate	round	$28	○
⑤	E	chocolate	animal	$32	×

11 대화를 듣고, 여자의 마지막 말에 대한 남자의 응답으로 가장 적절한 것을 고르시오.

① No. You cannot have my laptop.
② Sorry, I don't know how to fix it.
③ Yes. We can buy a new one this weekend.
④ Okay. This is the latest model you asked for.
⑤ Sure. It might take a couple of days to fix it.

12 대화를 듣고, 남자의 마지막 말에 대한 여자의 응답으로 가장 적절한 것을 고르시오.

① Not really. My car is not that old yet.
② I know. Careless driving is really dangerous.
③ That's very kind of you. But I think I'll rent a car.
④ You're right. Sometimes traffic signs are confusing.
⑤ I agree. A regular vehicle check-up is very important.

13 대화를 듣고, 남자의 마지막 말에 대한 여자의 응답으로 가장 적절한 것을 고르시오. [3점]

Woman: _____

① You should figure out which style and color suits you.
② You will save money by buying suits in a second-hand store.
③ You should wear appropriate clothes depending on the occasion.
④ You can give a professional impression to people by wearing suits.
⑤ You can enter our address on its homepage and it will send you a box.

14 대화를 듣고, 여자의 마지막 말에 대한 남자의 응답으로 가장 적절한 것을 고르시오.

Man: _____

① Absolutely! You know I love trying exotic food!
② No problem. I know how to keep plants healthy.
③ Sure. There is a plant shop on the way to Maple Street.
④ Sorry. I don't know what gift will be good for your friend.
⑤ Don't worry. The new Mexican restaurant offers take-out food.

15 다음 상황 설명을 듣고, Amelia가 Jason에게 할 말로 가장 적절한 것을 고르시오. [3점]

Amelia: _____

① How about consulting with teachers about your situation?
② You need to focus on your study, rather than club activities.
③ Why don't you build your career on film making with your talents?
④ You should quit the broadcasting club and do what you want to do.
⑤ You should tell the members how you feel and ask them to share the work.

[16-17] 다음을 듣고, 물음에 답하시오.

16 남자가 하는 말의 주제로 가장 적절한 것은?

① why plastic pollution is dangerous
② how microplastics affect our bodies
③ how we can reduce plastic pollution
④ what kinds of products are made of plastic
⑤ how the plastic industry became so successful

17 언급된 물건이 <u>아닌</u> 것은?

① reusable water bottles ② stainless steel straws
③ bamboo toothbrushes ④ natural fabric clothes
⑤ eco-friendly bags

09 영어 듣기 모의고사

1번부터 17번까지는 듣고 답하는 문제입니다.
1번부터 15번까지는 한 번만 들려주고, 16번부터 17번까지는 두 번 들려줍니다.
방송을 잘 듣고 답을 하시기 바랍니다.

01 다음을 듣고, 남자가 하는 말의 목적으로 가장 적절한 것을 고르시오.
① 환경 피해 사례를 조사하려고
② 환경 단체 신입 회원을 모집하려고
③ 환경을 위한 모금 활동을 홍보하려고
④ 다양한 환경 보호 방법을 안내하려고
⑤ 회원들의 적극적인 참여를 독려하려고

02 대화를 듣고, 여자의 의견으로 가장 적절한 것을 고르시오.
① 휴식 없이 운동하는 것은 위험하다.
② 유산소 운동과 근력 운동을 병행해야 한다.
③ 운동할 때는 충분한 수분을 섭취해야 한다.
④ 혼자보다는 여럿이 운동하는 것이 더 효과적이다.
⑤ 부상 예방을 위해서 반드시 준비 운동을 해야 한다.

03 대화를 듣고, 두 사람의 관계를 가장 잘 나타낸 것을 고르시오.
① 경찰관 – 목격자
② 사진사 – 작가
③ 출판사 직원 – 사서
④ 카페 직원 – 손님
⑤ 의상 디자이너 – 모델

04 대화를 듣고, 그림에서 대화의 내용과 일치하지 <u>않는</u> 것을 고르시오.

05 대화를 듣고, 남자가 여자에게 부탁한 일로 가장 적절한 것을 고르시오.
① 배달 물건 받기
② 음식 주문하기
③ 식기류 정리하기
④ 영수증 발급하기
⑤ 고객에게 전화하기

06 대화를 듣고, 남자가 지불할 항공료를 고르시오. [3점]
① $330
② $435
③ $450
④ $465
⑤ $480

07 대화를 듣고, 여자가 취업 결정을 망설이는 이유로 가장 적절한 것을 고르시오.
① 급여가 높지 않아서
② 부모님이 반대하셔서
③ 고향을 떠나기 싫어서
④ 원하던 직업이 아니라서
⑤ 사내 복지 혜택이 좋지 않아서

08 대화를 듣고, Coco Mall에 관해 언급되지 <u>않은</u> 것을 고르시오.
① 위치
② 판매 품목
③ 영업시간
④ 개장 연도
⑤ 주차 시설

09 Waldorf Rose Festival에 관한 다음 내용을 듣고, 일치하지 <u>않는</u> 것을 고르시오.
① 금요일 오전 10시에 시작된다.
② 신입생 환영식으로 시작된다.
③ 어쿠스틱 밴드 콘서트 관람은 입장권이 필요 없다.
④ 점심은 운동장에 있는 야외 식당에서 먹을 수 있다.
⑤ 저녁에 풍등 띄우기 행사가 있다.

10 다음 표를 보면서 대화를 듣고, 여자가 주문할 우산을 고르시오.

Fancy Umbrellas

	Model	Pattern	Size	Foldable	Price
①	A	striped	21 inch	○	$11
②	B	striped	24 inch	○	$9
③	C	solid	26 inch	×	$8
④	D	solid	28 inch	×	$10
⑤	E	polka-dot	25 inch	○	$9

11 대화를 듣고, 남자의 마지막 말에 대한 여자의 응답으로 가장 적절한 것을 고르시오.

① Maybe we will go around the neighborhood.
② We will dress up as heroes or witches.
③ Thank you for coming to our Halloween party.
④ Well, we won't trick-or-treat on that day.
⑤ It's not good for children to eat too many sweets.

12 대화를 듣고, 여자의 마지막 말에 대한 남자의 응답으로 가장 적절한 것을 고르시오.

① Too bad. You'd better fix it soon.
② That's okay. I'll ask someone else.
③ Thanks. I'll return it as soon as possible.
④ No problem. You are welcome to borrow mine.
⑤ Good for you. I hope you will finish it tomorrow.

13 대화를 듣고, 여자의 마지막 말에 대한 남자의 응답으로 가장 적절한 것을 고르시오. [3점]

Man: _____

① Don't nag me. I'm not leaving today.
② Oops. I forgot you are leaving tomorrow.
③ Thank you for helping me. See you when I get back.
④ That's okay. I can withstand the cold weather over there.
⑤ Oh, really? Then, I'll take out some unnecessary clothes.

14 대화를 듣고, 남자의 마지막 말에 대한 여자의 응답으로 가장 적절한 것을 고르시오.

Woman: _____

① Right. I should have brought my laptop.
② I'm afraid I have to check some emails now.
③ Okay. I'll turn off my laptop right now.
④ It's better to go to the beach next time instead of trekking.
⑤ Sure. I don't want you to work during the vacation.

15 다음 상황 설명을 듣고, Samuel이 Jeff에게 할 말로 가장 적절한 것을 고르시오. [3점]

Samuel: _____

① You should have worked harder.
② Thank you for encouraging me.
③ It's not too late to start a business after graduation.
④ Cheer up! Failure is the chance to begin again.
⑤ Your bookstore is becoming more prosperous each day.

[16-17] 다음을 듣고, 물음에 답하시오.

16 여자가 하는 말의 주제로 가장 적절한 것은?

① where sleep disorders come from
② how to promote a good night's sleep
③ various foods to avoid to sleep well
④ importance of eating and sleeping regularly
⑤ misconceptions about preventing sleeplessness

17 언급된 음식이 <u>아닌</u> 것은?

① milk   ② chamomile tea
③ kiwi   ④ bananas
⑤ almonds

1번부터 17번까지는 듣고 답하는 문제입니다.
1번부터 15번까지는 한 번만 들려주고, 16번부터 17번까지는 두 번 들려줍니다.
방송을 잘 듣고 답을 하시기 바랍니다.

01 다음을 듣고, 남자가 하는 말의 목적으로 가장 적절한 것을 고르시오.
① 도서관 건축 비용의 투명한 공개를 요청하려고
② 새롭게 문을 연 도서관을 이용할 것을 권장하려고
③ 새롭게 문을 연 도서관 이용 시 주의 사항을 안내하려고
④ 도서관 건축을 위해 기부한 사람들에게 감사를 표하려고
⑤ 도서관 건축을 위한 모금 행사에 참여할 것을 독려하려고

02 대화를 듣고, 여자의 의견으로 가장 적절한 것을 고르시오.
① 건강을 위해 밤늦게 음식을 먹는 습관을 고쳐야 한다.
② 질병 예방을 위해 건강 검진을 정기적으로 받아야 한다.
③ 콜레스테롤 수치 상승과 수면 시간은 아무런 관계가 없다.
④ 건강과 관련된 가장 나쁜 식습관은 음식을 많이 먹는 것이다.
⑤ 밤에 자기 전과 아침에 일어난 후 물을 마시는 것이 건강에 좋다.

03 대화를 듣고, 두 사람의 관계를 가장 잘 나타낸 것을 고르시오.
① 작가 – 팬　　　　② 감독 – 코치
③ 가이드 – 관광객　　④ 기자 – 배드민턴 선수
⑤ 손님 – 스포츠용품 매장 점원

04 대화를 듣고, 그림에서 대화의 내용과 일치하지 않는 것을 고르시오.

05 대화를 듣고, 여자가 할 일로 가장 적절한 것을 고르시오.
① 거실 청소하기　　　　② 과일 세척하기
③ 오렌지 사러 가기　　　④ 비타민 C 구입하기
⑤ 약국에 약 사러 가기

06 대화를 듣고, 남자가 지불할 금액을 고르시오. [3점]
① $53　② $58　③ $60　④ $63　⑤ $70

07 대화를 듣고, 여자가 ACE Electronics에 지원을 결심한 이유로 가장 적절한 것을 고르시오.
① 월급을 많이 받아서
② 발전 가능성이 높아서
③ 직원 복지 제도가 좋아서
④ 해외 근무 기회가 많아서
⑤ 친구들과 함께 일하고 싶어서

08 대화를 듣고, 마술 동아리에 관해 언급되지 않은 것을 고르시오.
① 설립 시기　② 설립자　③ 정기 공연 횟수
④ 회원 수　　⑤ 회원 가입 방법

09 Phoenix Baseball Camp에 관한 다음 내용을 듣고, 일치하지 않는 것을 고르시오.
① 8월 1일에 시작해서 2주일간 지속된다.
② 작년과 똑같은 장소에서 열린다.
③ 참가 대상자는 9세에서 13세 어린이다.
④ 연령에 따라 세 개의 반으로 나뉜다.
⑤ 등록비에 점심 식사가 포함되어 있다.

10 다음 표를 보면서 대화를 듣고, 두 사람이 임대할 주택을 고르시오.

Rental Houses

	House	Location	Number of Bedrooms	Monthly Rent	Parking Spaces in Garage (car)
①	A	Los Angeles	3	$950	2
②	B	Los Angeles	2	$880	1
③	C	Culver City	3	$930	1
④	D	Santa Monica	2	$810	1
⑤	E	Culver City	4	$1,200	2

11 대화를 듣고, 남자의 마지막 말에 대한 여자의 응답으로 가장 적절한 것을 고르시오.

① Christmas? No, I don't have any special plans yet.
② I'm sorry, but I don't think I can go on a trip. I'm really busy.
③ I'm sure our kids want to go to the sea, not the Grand Canyon.
④ That's right. We have to get some rest during Christmas holidays.
⑤ Yes, I do. I want to see the magnificence of the Grand Canyon.

12 대화를 듣고, 여자의 마지막 말에 대한 남자의 응답으로 가장 적절한 것을 고르시오.

① Should we reschedule our date?
② No problem. I'll order two.
③ Can you order some cake as well?
④ The restaurant is fully booked.
⑤ We need to change the ticket times.

13 대화를 듣고, 남자의 마지막 말에 대한 여자의 응답으로 가장 적절한 것을 고르시오. [3점]

Woman: _____

① Actually, Korean history is not easy to study.
② Absolutely! Take his class, and you won't regret it.
③ Just study hard. You'll become a professor before long.
④ Without your help, I couldn't have finished the class.
⑤ Yes. I'd like to use the audiovisual materials.

14 대화를 듣고, 여자의 마지막 말에 대한 남자의 응답으로 가장 적절한 것을 고르시오.

Man: _____

① Right. I think you really look like your sister.
② Good. When she gets here, I'll get her a new key card.
③ Sure! I really want to work at the restaurant with you.
④ My pleasure. But don't forget that I found the key card.
⑤ I'm hungry, too. Let's go to the restaurant together.

15 다음 상황 설명을 듣고, Rachel이 John에게 할 말로 가장 적절한 것을 고르시오. [3점]

Rachel: _____

① That's right. I'm interested in working as a shop assistant.
② Don't mention it. The long purple coat suits you best.
③ Thank you. I'll definitely come back tomorrow with my wallet.
④ That's a good idea. You'd better get the purple coat mended.
⑤ Without your recommendation, I wouldn't have bought the coat.

[16-17] 다음을 듣고, 물음에 답하시오.

16 여자가 하는 말의 주제로 가장 적절한 것은?

① positive aspects of bats on the ecosystem
② differences between ecosystems and ecology
③ ways of getting rid of pests
④ movies featuring bats
⑤ requirements for maintaining the ecosystem

17 언급된 국가가 <u>아닌</u> 것은?

① England ② France ③ America
④ Thailand ⑤ Brazil

1번부터 17번까지는 듣고 답하는 문제입니다.
1번부터 15번까지는 한 번만 들려주고, 16번부터 17번까지는 두 번 들려줍니다.
방송을 잘 듣고 답을 하시기 바랍니다.

01 다음을 듣고, 여자가 하는 말의 목적으로 가장 적절한 것을 고르시오.
① 애견용 사료를 홍보하려고
② 애완견 입양 절차를 안내하려고
③ 개가 등장하는 이야기를 들려주려고
④ 견주들에게 새 애견 샴푸를 판매하려고
⑤ 애완견 키우기의 이점에 대해 설명하려고

02 대화를 듣고, 남자의 의견으로 가장 적절한 것을 고르시오.
① 직장 내 괴롭힘 문제는 근절되어야 한다.
② 새로운 상사와 일하는 것은 힘든 일이다.
③ 과도한 업무 스트레스는 질병을 유발할 수 있다.
④ 새로운 업무 부여는 직원을 신뢰하고 있다는 증거이다.
⑤ 상사는 직원에게 스트레스를 주지 않도록 노력해야 한다.

03 대화를 듣고, 두 사람의 관계를 가장 잘 나타낸 것을 고르시오.
① 약사 – 고객
② 간호사 – 환자
③ 영양사 – 학생
④ 의사 – 간호사
⑤ 구조대원 – 시민

04 대화를 듣고, 그림에서 대화의 내용과 일치하지 않는 것을 고르시오.

05 대화를 듣고, 남자가 할 일로 가장 적절한 것을 고르시오.
① 파란색 구두 신어 보기
② 지갑에서 자동차 열쇠 찾기
③ 결혼식장까지 갈 택시 부르기
④ 벽장 안에서 자신의 구두 찾기
⑤ 하이힐이 있는지 자동차 안 확인하기

06 대화를 듣고, 여자가 지불할 금액을 고르시오. [3점]
① $68 ② $75 ③ $77 ④ $83 ⑤ $85

07 대화를 듣고, 여자가 팟캐스트를 듣는 이유를 고르시오.
① 재미있어서
② 수업 과제여서
③ 남자가 추천해 주어서
④ 진행자가 지도 교수여서
⑤ 다음 수업을 준비해야 해서

08 대화를 듣고, Seattle Baking Fair에 관해 언급되지 않은 것을 고르시오.
① 날짜
② 장소
③ 입장료
④ 특별 행사
⑤ 참여 제과점 수

09 Riding For a Cause 행사에 관한 다음 내용을 듣고, 일치하지 않는 것을 고르시오.
① 모든 수익은 집이 없는 사람들을 돕는 데 사용된다.
② Hawthorne 대로에서 열린다.
③ 주요 행사는 200킬로미터 경주이다.
④ 지역 밴드의 음악 공연을 관람할 수 있다.
⑤ 자전거 상점에서 표를 구할 수 있다.

10 다음 표를 보면서 대화를 듣고, 남자가 구매할 차를 고르시오.

Cars on Sale

	Model	Price	Type	Fuel Economy (per liter)	Color
①	A	$23,000	Sedan	21 km	Red
②	B	$24,000	Compact	23 km	Black
③	C	$30,000	Sedan	30 km	Green
④	D	$21,000	Compact	18 km	Yellow
⑤	E	$22,000	Compact	22 km	Blue

11 대화를 듣고, 여자의 마지막 말에 대한 남자의 응답으로 가장 적절한 것을 고르시오.

① Not at all. I'll bring them both.
② Of course not. We're out of coffee.
③ Yes. The newspaper wasn't delivered yet.
④ Nope. I'd like some sugar with my coffee.
⑤ Okay. I'd rather watch the news on television.

12 대화를 듣고, 남자의 마지막 말에 대한 여자의 응답으로 가장 적절한 것을 고르시오.

① Okay. I'll see you there after school.
② Yeah. I want to eat dinner after school.
③ Wow! Taking a walk is really nice, isn't it?
④ Sorry. I'm going to be late for our meeting.
⑤ No. Let's borrow the books from the library.

13 대화를 듣고, 여자의 마지막 말에 대한 남자의 응답으로 가장 적절한 것을 고르시오.

Man: _____

① Maybe not. I'd rather drive to Washington.
② Of course. Please book that seat for me.
③ Why not? I would like three seats for that flight.
④ Yes. How long will the flight be to Los Angeles?
⑤ No. Please open the boarding gates on the next flight.

14 대화를 듣고, 남자의 마지막 말에 대한 여자의 응답으로 가장 적절한 것을 고르시오. [3점]

Woman: _____

① Just let me know if you need anything.
② No. Just send the email about the room change.
③ Yeah. I can't wait to see the band play at the party.
④ Yes. I'll talk with the caterers about the food.
⑤ I can bring some extra seats for the meeting.

15 다음 상황 설명을 듣고, Diane이 Jack에게 할 말로 가장 적절한 것을 고르시오. [3점]

Diane: _____

① Since we are a team, we should let everyone play.
② We can't be true champions until we win every game.
③ We need to win this game, so let's have our star players play.
④ The parents would be very happy to see the kids win the game.
⑤ Winning isn't everything so we should lose the game on purpose.

[16-17] 다음을 듣고, 물음에 답하시오.

16 남자가 하는 말의 주제로 가장 적절한 것은?

① features of a new fitness tracker
② reasons for getting a fitness tracker
③ disadvantages of using fitness trackers
④ importance of waterproof fitness trackers
⑤ comparisons of best-selling fitness trackers

17 언급된 기능이 아닌 것은?

① bright screen   ② longer battery life
③ heart rate sensor   ④ waterproof design
⑤ GPS sensor

1번부터 17번까지는 듣고 답하는 문제입니다.
1번부터 15번까지는 한 번만 들려주고, 16번부터 17번까지는 두 번 들려줍니다.
방송을 잘 듣고 답을 하시기 바랍니다.

01 다음을 듣고, 여자가 하는 말의 목적으로 가장 적절한 것을 고르시오.
① 특별 전시회를 안내하려고
② 미술관에 기부를 부탁하려고
③ 미술관의 임시 휴업 결정을 사과하려고
④ 특별 전시관의 공사 일정을 공지하려고
⑤ 아동 미술 교육 프로그램을 안내하려고

02 대화를 듣고, 남자의 의견으로 가장 적절한 것을 고르시오.
① 사용자 후기는 좋은 물건을 고르는 데 도움이 된다.
② 물건을 살 때 환경에 미치는 영향을 고려해야 한다.
③ 가격 대비 기능을 비교하는 것은 현명한 소비 습관이다.
④ 재활용 물품을 구입하는 것이 환경 보호에 도움이 된다.
⑤ 소비를 하기 전에 본인이 갖고 있는 물건을 먼저 확인해야 한다.

03 대화를 듣고, 두 사람의 관계를 가장 잘 나타낸 것을 고르시오.
① 의사 – 환자
② 환자 – 문병객
③ 헬스 트레이너 – 고객
④ 운동선수 – 기자
⑤ 스포츠 의류 점원 – 손님

04 대화를 듣고, 그림에서 대화의 내용과 일치하지 <u>않는</u> 것을 고르시오.

05 대화를 듣고, 남자가 할 일로 가장 적절한 것을 고르시오.
① 조명 점검하기
② 공연 시간표 짜기
③ 음악 파일 받아 오기
④ 예행연습 일정 의논하기
⑤ 음향 시스템 점검하기

06 대화를 듣고, 여자가 지불할 금액을 고르시오. [3점]
① $77 ② $80 ③ $91 ④ $110 ⑤ $130

07 대화를 듣고, 남자가 수강 신청을 포기한 이유를 고르시오.
① 담당 교수님이 변경되어서
② 아르바이트 스케줄과 겹쳐서
③ 필수 과목을 먼저 수강해야 해서
④ 수강이 가능한 학년이 아니어서
⑤ 나중에 친구와 같이 수강하기 위해서

08 대화를 듣고, Community Orchestra에 관해 언급되지 <u>않은</u> 것을 고르시오.
① 입단 자격
② 단원 모집 시기
③ 정기 연습 시간
④ 연습 장소
⑤ 연간 공연 횟수

09 학교 내 지진 대비 훈련에 관한 다음 내용을 듣고, 일치하지 <u>않는</u> 것을 고르시오.
① 내일 5교시 직후로 예정되어 있다.
② 교사의 지도에 따라 중앙 계단 또는 동쪽이나 서쪽 계단을 이용한다.
③ 승강기는 사용하지 않는다.
④ 운동장에서 반별로 모여 인원 점검을 한다.
⑤ 구급대원이 응급 처치 방법을 알려 줄 것이다.

10 다음 표를 보면서 대화를 듣고, 여자가 구매할 로봇 청소기를 고르시오.

Robot Vacuum Cleaners

	Model	Suction Power(Pa)	Run Time(min)	HEPA Filter	Warranty (year)
①	A	560	up to 140	○	1
②	B	680	up to 160	×	2
③	C	730	up to 140	○	1
④	D	770	up to 100	○	2
⑤	E	800	up to 130	×	1

11 대화를 듣고, 남자의 마지막 말에 대한 여자의 응답으로 가장 적절한 것을 고르시오.

① Wonderful. This food tastes really good.
② Sorry. I'll come back on the weekend, then.
③ No thanks. I would like to have a beef steak.
④ Yes, eating vegetables is good for your health.
⑤ Sure. Can you bring the vegetarian menu now?

12 대화를 듣고, 여자의 마지막 말에 대한 남자의 응답으로 가장 적절한 것을 고르시오.

① I'm sorry. I didn't know you have a cold.
② Be careful. Swimming in the sea takes a lot of skill.
③ Sounds good. Let's get some hot chocolate.
④ Don't worry. The weather was sunny yesterday.
⑤ No thanks. I'm too cold.

13 대화를 듣고, 여자의 마지막 말에 대한 남자의 응답으로 가장 적절한 것을 고르시오.

Man: _____

① You're right. People need to think seriously about having a pet.
② That's good news. More people are willing to do volunteer work.
③ Don't worry. I can take good care of your pet while you're gone.
④ Thanks for your understanding. My dog won't cause any trouble.
⑤ I agree. Protecting endangered wild animals is a really important job.

14 대화를 듣고, 남자의 마지막 말에 대한 여자의 응답으로 가장 적절한 것을 고르시오. [3점]

Woman: _____

① Yes. Taking an academic class is very important.
② Not at all. You should follow your teacher's advice.
③ Sure. A little learning every day works wonders.
④ Not really. Working with foreign companies motivates me.
⑤ Absolutely! Driving a car can shorten a long commute time.

15 다음 상황 설명을 듣고, Ella가 Ryan에게 할 말로 가장 적절한 것을 고르시오. [3점]

Ella: _____

① Why don't you buy a laptop as my birthday present?
② Do you know where to get your laptop fixed?
③ Where is the laptop store?
④ Buy the latest laptop and then we'll go home.
⑤ How about buying the present first and then checking out laptops online?

[16-17] 다음을 듣고, 물음에 답하시오.

16 남자가 하는 말의 주제로 가장 적절한 것은?

① how plants remove chemicals from the air
② myths and misconceptions about plants
③ why keeping plants is good for mental health.
④ plants that are easy to grow for beginners
⑤ plants that are good for air purification

17 언급된 식물이 아닌 것은?

① English ivy　　② spider plant
③ rubber tree　　④ bamboo palm
⑤ garden mum

1번부터 17번까지는 듣고 답하는 문제입니다.
1번부터 15번까지는 한 번만 들려주고, 16번부터 17번까지는 두 번 들려줍니다.
방송을 잘 듣고 답을 하시기 바랍니다.

---

01 다음을 듣고, 남자가 하는 말의 목적으로 가장 적절한 것을 고르시오.
① 대중교통 이용을 홍보하려고
② 신설된 주차장 위치를 안내하려고
③ 회사 내 셔틀버스 운행을 공지하려고
④ 주차 구역에 주차할 것을 당부하려고
⑤ 자가용 홀짝제 운행에 참여를 장려하려고

02 대화를 듣고, 여자의 의견으로 가장 적절한 것을 고르시오.
① 상업주의로 밸런타인데이가 변질되었다.
② 마음을 표현할 때 선물의 종류는 중요하지 않다.
③ 때때로 초콜릿을 먹는 것은 긴장 완화에 도움이 된다.
④ 밸런타인데이를 통해서 친구들과 더 가까워질 수 있다.
⑤ 밸런타인데이는 연인에게 고백할 수 있는 절호의 기회이다.

03 대화를 듣고, 두 사람의 관계를 가장 잘 나타낸 것을 고르시오.
① 의사 – 환자   ② 교사 – 졸업생
③ 어머니 – 아들   ④ 변호사 – 의뢰인
⑤ 고객 – 제과점 주인

04 대화를 듣고, 그림에서 대화의 내용과 일치하지 않는 것을 고르시오.

05 대화를 듣고, 남자가 할 일로 가장 적절한 것을 고르시오.
① 풍선 불기   ② 그림 그리기
③ 카드 만들기   ④ 음식 준비하기
⑤ 학생 가르치기

06 대화를 듣고, 여자가 지불할 금액을 고르시오. [3점]
① $45   ② $48   ③ $51   ④ $60   ⑤ $63

07 대화를 듣고, 여자가 전화를 한 이유로 가장 적절한 것을 고르시오.
① 회원권을 등록하려고
② 운동용품을 주문하려고
③ 체육관 위치를 확인하려고
④ 운동 기간을 연장하려고
⑤ 사은품 변경을 요청하려고

08 대화를 듣고, Sunrise Resorts의 프로그램에 관해 언급되지 않은 것을 고르시오.
① 스쿠버 다이빙   ② 스노클링   ③ 불꽃놀이
④ 현지 음식 체험   ⑤ 사우나 하기

09 Vision Language Lab에 관한 다음 내용을 듣고, 일치하지 않는 것을 고르시오.
① Vision 센터 2층에 위치해 있다.
② 20대가 넘는 컴퓨터가 설치되어 있다.
③ 모든 교실에서 영상 녹화가 가능하다.
④ 매주 수요일마다 무료 회화 강좌가 열린다.
⑤ 전화로 수강 신청을 해야 한다.

10 다음 표를 보면서 대화를 듣고, 남자가 구매할 립스틱을 고르시오.

Lipsticks at Ari Cosmetics

	Model	Color	Volume	Price	Bonus Gift
①	A	pink	4 g	$12	lip brush
②	B	purple	4 g	$17	lipstick remover
③	C	purple	5 g	$22	lip liner
④	D	coral	5 g	$19	lip liner
⑤	E	coral	3 g	$17	lipstick remover

11 대화를 듣고, 남자의 마지막 말에 대한 여자의 응답으로 가장 적절한 것을 고르시오.

① You're welcome. He deserves the position.
② Thank you. It'll be a great opportunity for me.
③ Sorry. You have no choice but to accept the job.
④ Sure. It'll be better to move to another company.
⑤ I'm sorry. I should have told you last week.

12 대화를 듣고, 여자의 마지막 말에 대한 남자의 응답으로 가장 적절한 것을 고르시오.

① Hurry up. We'll be late for the party.
② You're right. Let's clear the table first.
③ Of course. We have to give a gift to the hosts.
④ You're kidding. I don't want to go to the party.
⑤ Okay. Let's take a taxi home.

13 대화를 듣고, 여자의 마지막 말에 대한 남자의 응답으로 가장 적절한 것을 고르시오. [3점]

Man: _____

① I'm sorry, but I forgot to bring the receipt.
② In that case, I'll look around for some shirts.
③ Then, I'd like to exchange them for a bigger size.
④ Right, I want these pants in a different color.
⑤ Sure, I like the pants I bought here last weekend.

14 대화를 듣고, 남자의 마지막 말에 대한 여자의 응답으로 가장 적절한 것을 고르시오.

Woman: _____

① Sure. I have a couple of quiet places in mind.
② Yes. You helped me when I moved out.
③ No. I regret moving out of the dormitory.
④ Don't worry. You'll get used to the dormitory.
⑤ Of course. It's best to have a face-to-face conversation with your roommate.

15 다음 상황 설명을 듣고, Rebecca가 Karen에게 할 말로 가장 적절한 것을 고르시오. [3점]

Rebecca: _____

① Thank you. I'm pleased that you like the scarf.
② I appreciate it, but I'm afraid this is not my style.
③ That's great. The scarf really brings out your eyes.
④ You read my mind. It's exactly what I wanted.
⑤ Thank you for helping me choose a gift.

[16-17] 다음을 듣고, 물음에 답하시오.

16 여자가 하는 말의 주제로 가장 적절한 것은?

① benefits of eating organic food
② foods for preventing hypertension
③ secrets to longevity without disease
④ importance of keeping a balanced diet
⑤ newly-discovered causes of adult diseases

17 언급된 음식이 아닌 것은?

① blueberries   ② yogurt   ③ walnuts
④ bananas   ⑤ salmon

1번부터 17번까지는 듣고 답하는 문제입니다.
1번부터 15번까지는 한 번만 들려주고, 16번부터 17번까지는 두 번 들려줍니다.
방송을 잘 듣고 답을 하시기 바랍니다.

01 다음을 듣고, 남자가 하는 말의 목적으로 가장 적절한 것을 고르시오.
① 친환경적인 세차 방법을 소개하려고
② 세차 서비스 전문 업체를 홍보하려고
③ 셀프 세차 시 주의 사항을 안내하려고
④ 열심히 일한 세차장 직원을 칭찬하려고
⑤ 자동차 세차장에서 일할 직원을 모집하려고

02 대화를 듣고, 여자의 의견으로 가장 적절한 것을 고르시오.
① 매일 꾸준히 걸으면 건강을 유지할 수 있다.
② 자신의 건강 상태에 맞추어서 운동을 해야 한다.
③ 판매 보고서 분석은 정확하게 이루어져야 한다.
④ 자신에게 주어진 일은 퇴근 전까지 처리해야 한다.
⑤ 걷기를 시작하기 전에 준비 운동을 반드시 해야 한다.

03 대화를 듣고, 두 사람의 관계를 가장 잘 나타낸 것을 고르시오.
① 비서 – 직장 상사   ② 손님 – 식당 종업원
③ 목격자 – 기자   ④ 노조원 – 노조 간부
⑤ 가이드 – 관광객

04 대화를 듣고, 그림에서 대화의 내용과 일치하지 <u>않는</u> 것을 고르시오.

05 대화를 듣고, 남자가 할 일로 가장 적절한 것을 고르시오.
① 드라마 시청하기
② 파티 음식 만들기
③ 아들에게 전화하기
④ 병원 진료 예약하기
⑤ 학교 학생 상담하기

06 대화를 듣고, 여자가 지불할 금액을 고르시오. [3점]
① $40   ② $45   ③ $80   ④ $90   ⑤ $100

07 대화를 듣고, 여자가 여름 방학 때 하와이에 가려는 이유를 고르시오.
① 서핑을 즐기기 위해
② Robert를 만나기 위해
③ 훌라 댄스를 배우기 위해
④ 자전거 여행을 하기 위해
⑤ 할머니를 도와드리기 위해

08 대화를 듣고, 애완동물 비행기 탑승에 관해 언급되지 <u>않은</u> 것을 고르시오.
① 가격   ② 이동 장 사이즈 규칙
③ 기내 동반 조건   ④ 사료 제공 여부
⑤ 필요 서류

09 Tomato Festival에 관한 다음 내용을 듣고, 일치하지 <u>않는</u> 것을 고르시오.
① 5월 8일에 열려서 5일간 계속된다.
② 약 100여 명의 토마토 재배 농부가 참여한다.
③ 토마토를 이용한 요리 교실이 무료로 진행된다.
④ 시장 가격보다 20% 할인된 가격에 토마토가 판매된다.
⑤ 올해 방문객이 10,000명을 넘을 것으로 예상된다.

10 다음 표를 보면서 대화를 듣고, 남자가 선택할 휴대 전화 요금제를 고르시오.

ABC Telecommunication's Monthly Plans

	Plan	Monthly Fee	Talk Time	Text Messages	Data
①	A	$45	180 minutes	2,000	11 GB
②	B	$55	240 minutes	Unlimited	4 GB
③	C	$45	90 minutes	Unlimited	11 GB
④	D	$35	90 minutes	1,000	11 GB
⑤	E	$35	60 minutes	Unlimited	4 GB

11 대화를 듣고, 여자의 마지막 말에 대한 남자의 응답으로 가장 적절한 것을 고르시오.

① The pizza you brought was really tasty.
② I'd like to recommend spaghetti, not pizza.
③ I don't know which pizza is more expensive.
④ Then the family size would be good for you.
⑤ I'm very hungry now. Let's eat pizza together.

12 대화를 듣고, 남자의 마지막 말에 대한 여자의 응답으로 가장 적절한 것을 고르시오.

① You should have chosen the debate club.
② Don't worry. I'll teach you some debating skills.
③ I don't think joining a club is important for students.
④ You're right. The debate club isn't accepting new members.
⑤ Good! Let's submit our applications to the club tomorrow.

13 대화를 듣고, 여자의 마지막 말에 대한 남자의 응답으로 가장 적절한 것을 고르시오.

Man: _____

① Good idea! Let's have chicken stew this evening.
② Just do as the recipe says, and you'll have a great stew.
③ Sorry, but I can't tell you the recipe. It's a secret.
④ Right. Your mother will text you the recipe.
⑤ Don't worry. I'll make the stew instead of you.

14 대화를 듣고, 남자의 마지막 말에 대한 여자의 응답으로 가장 적절한 것을 고르시오. [3점]

Woman: _____

① Sorry. I have no time to play golf this weekend.
② Right. He'll win easily as you said.
③ No problem. I'm not interested in golf any more.
④ I heard that Gary won't enter the U.S. Open this year.
⑤ I really enjoyed the U.S. Open last week.

15 다음 상황 설명을 듣고, Angela가 Brian에게 할 말로 가장 적절한 것을 고르시오. [3점]

Angela: _____

① I'd like to know why you chose me.
② How many words should I write for the column?
③ Can you tell me when I have to send my writing to you?
④ Don't worry. You can extend the deadline for the column.
⑤ Me too. I'll also subscribe to your magazine from next month.

[16-17] 다음을 듣고, 물음에 답하시오.

16 여자가 하는 말의 주제로 가장 적절한 것은?

① benefits of buying goods at a traditional market
② why large corporations run megastores
③ why people prefer shopping at megastores
④ how to make traditional markets competitive
⑤ similarities between traditional markets and megastores

17 언급된 상품이 아닌 것은?

① carrots　　② onions　　③ oysters
④ shoes　　⑤ T-shirts

1번부터 17번까지는 듣고 답하는 문제입니다.
1번부터 15번까지는 한 번만 들려주고, 16번부터 17번까지는 두 번 들려줍니다.
방송을 잘 듣고 답을 하시기 바랍니다.

01 다음을 듣고, 남자가 하는 말의 목적으로 가장 적절한 것을 고르시오.
① 컴퓨터 수리 및 보급 지연에 대해 사과하려고
② 컴퓨터 파일을 USB에 저장하는 것을 부탁하려고
③ 컴퓨터 바이러스 치료 방법 및 과정을 안내하려고
④ 적절한 컴퓨터 사용 시간 및 휴식 시간을 안내하려고
⑤ 컴퓨터 서버 업그레이드 일정 및 주의 사항을 공지하려고

02 대화를 듣고, 여자의 의견으로 가장 적절한 것을 고르시오.
① 새로운 쇼핑몰은 지역 경제에 도움이 된다.
② 연령별 아이들에게 맞춘 스포츠 교육을 강화해야 한다.
③ 아이들을 위한 야외 공간을 최우선적으로 생각해야 한다.
④ 도시 계획자들은 새로운 일자리 창출을 위해 노력해야 한다.
⑤ 이웃들과 즐길 수 있는 지역 문화 프로그램을 개발해야 한다.

03 대화를 듣고, 두 사람의 관계를 가장 잘 나타낸 것을 고르시오.
① 소방대원 – 신고자   ② 비행기 승무원 – 승객
③ 버스 운전기사 – 승객   ④ 레스토랑 점원 – 손님
⑤ 콜센터 직원 – 문의 고객

04 대화를 듣고, 그림에서 대화의 내용과 일치하지 않는 것을 고르시오.

05 대화를 듣고, 여자가 할 일로 가장 적절한 것을 고르시오.
① 다과 준비하기
② 회의실 예약하기
③ 회의 시간 늦추기
④ 상사에게 직장 동료의 상황 알리기
⑤ 복사실에서 회의 자료 가져다 놓기

06 대화를 듣고, 여자가 지불할 금액을 고르시오. [3점]
① $50   ② $65   ③ $75   ④ $80   ⑤ $95

07 대화를 듣고, 남자가 스웨터를 환불하려는 이유를 고르시오.
① 불량품이라서
② 크기가 맞지 않아서
③ 옷감이 무겁게 느껴져서
④ 색깔이 맘에 들지 않아서
⑤ 알레르기가 있는 재질이어서

08 대화를 듣고, David Hockney 전시회에 관해 언급되지 않은 것을 고르시오.
① 목적   ② 기간   ③ 장소
④ 작품 수   ⑤ 입장료

09 Goodies for Foodies에 관한 다음 내용을 듣고, 일치하지 않는 것을 고르시오.
① 매년 Grant Park에서 개최된다.
② 50대 이상의 푸드 트럭이 참가한다.
③ 유명한 요리사가 요리 시범을 보인다.
④ 행사 기간은 4월 초부터 5월 말까지이다.
⑤ 입장권은 웹 사이트에서 미리 구매할 수 있다.

10 다음 표를 보면서 대화를 듣고, 두 사람이 구입할 수영 튜브를 고르시오.

Swim Tubes

	Model	Sunshade	Price	Handle	Color
①	A	○	$26	1	blue
②	B	○	$27	2	orange
③	C	○	$32	2	orange
④	D	×	$25	2	blue
⑤	E	○	$28	2	blue

11 대화를 듣고, 여자의 마지막 말에 대한 남자의 응답으로 가장 적절한 것을 고르시오.

① Certainly. Please fill out this request form.
② Yes, I think the book is really interesting too.
③ Sorry. I haven't finished reading the book yet.
④ No thanks. I already borrowed it from someone.
⑤ I'm afraid your reservation has been cancelled.

12 대화를 듣고, 남자의 마지막 말에 대한 여자의 응답으로 가장 적절한 것을 고르시오.

① I agree. What we eat makes us who we are.
② That's okay. I'll take a taxi. Thank you, though.
③ Don't mention it. You can treat me to lunch in return.
④ Don't worry. The food was really good and tasty.
⑤ Actually, I really look forward to your cooking.

13 대화를 듣고, 남자의 마지막 말에 대한 여자의 응답으로 가장 적절한 것을 고르시오. [3점]

Woman: _____

① Sure. Eating healthy and fresh food really matters.
② You don't need to cook. Let's eat outside and celebrate.
③ Great! We can save on our grocery bill and our electricity bill!
④ Okay. I'll call customer service to get the refrigerator fixed.
⑤ Really? I didn't know so many people were suffering from lack of food.

14 대화를 듣고, 여자의 마지막 말에 대한 남자의 응답으로 가장 적절한 것을 고르시오.

Man: _____

① Don't worry. I know my hair is a mess and I will cut it soon.
② I agree. Neat hair and clean clothes are very important.
③ I don't think long hair suits you. You're fine as you are.
④ You shouldn't be rude about other people's hairstyles.
⑤ Your hair should be at least 30 cm long and should not be permed.

15 다음 상황 설명을 듣고, Rio가 Mike에게 할 말로 가장 적절한 것을 고르시오. [3점]

Rio: _____

① We really need to study harder when we become second years.
② You should talk with your parents about the subjects you chose.
③ Why don't we study advanced physics and earth science together?
④ How about going on a field trip to NASA for an astronomy project?
⑤ You need to find out what you want to do in the future and study accordingly.

[16-17] 다음을 듣고, 물음에 답하시오.

16 여자가 하는 말의 주제로 가장 적절한 것은?

① types of medicine people take most often
② pros and cons of taking medicine regularly
③ drugs that play a huge role in our lives
④ how drugs are developed by biological chemists
⑤ why we should consult a doctor before taking medicine

17 언급된 약이 아닌 것은?

① penicillin   ② smallpox vaccine
③ insulin   ④ aspirin
⑤ morphine

1번부터 17번까지는 듣고 답하는 문제입니다.
1번부터 15번까지는 한 번만 들려주고, 16번부터 17번까지는 두 번 들려줍니다.
방송을 잘 듣고 답을 하시기 바랍니다.

01 다음을 듣고, 여자가 하는 말의 목적으로 가장 적절한 것을 고르시오.
① 정유 회사의 입장을 전달하려고
② 기름 유출 사고 소식을 전하려고
③ 유가 상승의 원인을 알려 주려고
④ 지역 어업의 문제점을 논의하려고
⑤ 기름 유출이 환경에 미치는 영향을 설명하려고

02 대화를 듣고, 남자의 의견으로 가장 적절한 것을 고르시오.
① 운동을 하면 감기를 예방할 수 있다.
② 의사도 감기의 정확한 원인은 모른다.
③ 감기는 정확한 조기 진단이 가장 중요하다.
④ 차를 마시는 것이 감기 치료에 가장 효과적이다.
⑤ 감기 치료를 위한 민간요법은 효과적이지 않다.

03 대화를 듣고, 두 사람의 관계를 가장 잘 나타낸 것을 고르시오.
① 소방관 – 집주인
② 보험 설계사 – 고객
③ 경찰관 – 용의자
④ 건축가 – 디자이너
⑤ 건물 조사관 – 세입자

04 대화를 듣고, 그림에서 대화의 내용과 일치하지 않는 것을 고르시오.

05 대화를 듣고, 여자가 할 일로 가장 적절한 것을 고르시오.
① 모자 가지러 가기
② 미끼 끼우는 법 배우기
③ 낚시 미끼 가지러 가기
④ 자외선 차단 크림 바르기
⑤ 아이스박스에서 음료수 가져오기

06 대화를 듣고, 남자가 지불할 금액을 고르시오. [3점]
① $240 　② $320 　③ $380 　④ $400 　⑤ $420

07 대화를 듣고, 남자가 새장을 만드는 이유를 고르시오.
① 학교 공예 수업 과제여서
② 주변 공원에 놓기 위해서
③ 학교 박람회에서 팔기 위해서
④ 뒤뜰의 새들에게 집이 필요해서
⑤ 이웃에게 생일 선물로 주고 싶어서

08 대화를 듣고, Boy Scouts Adventure 캠핑 여행에 관해 언급되지 않은 것을 고르시오.
① 캠핑 장소
② 캠핑 시작 날짜
③ 식단과 식사 시간
④ 예정된 활동
⑤ 캠핑 기간

09 People First Food Drive에 관한 다음 내용을 듣고, 일치하지 않는 것을 고르시오.
① 기부 상자는 학교에도 둘 것이다.
② 주최자들은 과일과 채소를 기부해 줄 것을 요청한다.
③ 기부 상자는 8월 내내 놓여 있을 것이다.
④ 기부 식품들은 무료 급식소로 보내질 것이다.
⑤ 자원봉사자들은 급식소에서 사람들에게 음식을 나누어 줄 것이다.

10 다음 표를 보면서 대화를 듣고, 여자가 구매할 노트북 컴퓨터를 고르시오.

Laptop Computers

	Model	Price	Hard Drive	Memory	Processor (GHz)
①	A	$850	SSD	8 GB	3.2
②	B	$800	HDD	4 GB	2.0
③	C	$900	SSD	4 GB	2.5
④	D	$1,100	HDD	8 GB	3.5
⑤	E	$950	SSD	4 GB	3.0

11 대화를 듣고, 남자의 마지막 말에 대한 여자의 응답으로 가장 적절한 것을 고르시오.

① Okay. I'll pick up my car then.
② Sure. The holidays always seem so short.
③ Really? The car is perfect just the way it is.
④ I'll be in tomorrow to collect my things.
⑤ Yeah. I'll drop my car off on Wednesday.

12 대화를 듣고, 여자의 마지막 말에 대한 남자의 응답으로 가장 적절한 것을 고르시오.

① Sure. Let's meet in the park to play.
② No problem. When do you have time?
③ Wow! I want to join the science club, too.
④ Really? Math is much easier than science.
⑤ I'm afraid I'm terrible at all science subjects.

13 대화를 듣고, 여자의 마지막 말에 대한 남자의 응답으로 가장 적절한 것을 고르시오.

Man: _____

① Why not? Please bring me the lobster.
② Of course not! I love vanilla ice cream.
③ Sure. I'd like to order the surf and turf.
④ Certainly. I don't have room for dessert.
⑤ No thank you. That's all for now.

14 대화를 듣고, 남자의 마지막 말에 대한 여자의 응답으로 가장 적절한 것을 고르시오. [3점]

Woman: _____

① Of course. She just loves piñatas.
② Okay. She loves to build sand castles.
③ Yes. I'd like a chocolate ice cream cake.
④ No. The clown is busy that day.
⑤ Absolutely not! My child is terrified of clowns.

15 다음 상황 설명을 듣고, Julie가 Timmy에게 할 말로 가장 적절한 것을 고르시오. [3점]

Julie: _____

① A second-hand machine would be much cheaper.
② Look at all the nice refrigerators in the catalogue.
③ When does the warranty expire on our washing machine?
④ I think we should wait a while before making this purchase.
⑤ Buying a new machine could save money in the long run.

[16-17] 다음을 듣고, 물음에 답하시오.

16 남자가 하는 말의 주제로 가장 적절한 것은?

① importance of writing well
② different types of sentences
③ benefits of having a writing coach
④ common errors made by beginner writers
⑤ necessity of using proper grammar

17 언급된 문장이 아닌 것은?

① compound   ② declarative
③ imperative   ④ interrogative
⑤ exclamatory

17 영어 듣기 모의고사

1번부터 17번까지는 듣고 답하는 문제입니다.
1번부터 15번까지는 한 번만 들려주고, 16번부터 17번까지는 두 번 들려줍니다.
방송을 잘 듣고 답을 하시기 바랍니다.

01 다음을 듣고, 여자가 하는 말의 목적으로 가장 적절한 것을 고르시오.
① 자원봉사 참여를 요청하려고
② 곧 개봉될 영화를 소개하려고
③ 방송국에 대한 기부를 요청하려고
④ 라디오 공개 방송 취소를 알리려고
⑤ 일부 프로그램의 시간 변경을 알리려고

02 대화를 듣고, 남자의 의견으로 가장 적절한 것을 고르시오.
① 달리기는 하이킹보다 더 격렬한 운동이다.
② 사람들과 어울리는 것이 정신 건강에 좋다.
③ 신선한 공기를 마시는 것이 건강에 도움이 된다.
④ 정기적인 운동이 건강을 유지하는 최고의 방법이다.
⑤ 하이킹은 혼자만의 시간을 보내기에 좋은 방법이다.

03 대화를 듣고, 두 사람의 관계를 가장 잘 나타낸 것을 고르시오.
① 소방관 – 시민 ② 간호사 – 환자
③ 영양사 – 부모 ④ 경찰관 – 학생
⑤ 공무원 – 농부

04 대화를 듣고, 그림에서 대화의 내용과 일치하지 않는 것을 고르시오.

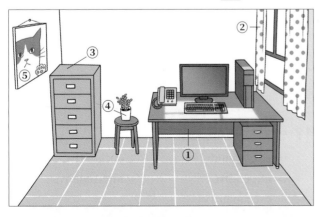

05 대화를 듣고, 남자가 여자에게 부탁한 일로 가장 적절한 것을 고르시오.
① 손 씻고 오기
② 쓰레기 버리기
③ 차에 아이스박스 넣기
④ 차에서 텐트 가방 가져오기
⑤ 야영지에서 텐트 가방 찾아 보기

06 대화를 듣고, 여자가 지불할 금액을 고르시오. [3점]
① $350 ② $360 ③ $400 ④ $440 ⑤ $450

07 대화를 듣고, 남자가 영화를 보러 갈 수 없는 이유를 고르시오.
① 영화 표가 매진이라서
② 자동차 키를 잃어버려서
③ 지난주에 이미 영화를 봐서
④ 자동차 시동이 걸리지 않아서
⑤ 영화에 대한 평이 좋지 않아서

08 대화를 듣고, 청첩장에 언급되지 않은 것을 고르시오.
① 결혼식 날짜 ② 결혼식 장소
③ 결혼식 시간 ④ 축하 선물 목록
⑤ 참석 여부 회답 기한

09 Florida Guitar Festival에 관한 다음 내용을 듣고, 일치하지 않는 것을 고르시오.
① 작년에는 Central Park에서 개최되었다.
② 초보자 대상 기타 만들기 수업이 있다.
③ 유명한 재즈 기타 연주자의 기타 연주 워크숍이 있다.
④ 전설적인 기타 연주자들의 특별 공연이 있다.
⑤ 플로리다 전역에서 노점상들이 와 음식을 제공한다.

10 다음 표를 보면서 대화를 듣고, 여자가 구입할 코트를 고르시오.

Winter Coats

	Model	Price	Waterproof	Insulation	Hood
①	A	$150	×	Down	○
②	B	$165	○	Synthetic	×
③	C	$180	○	Down	○
④	D	$190	○	Down	×
⑤	E	$210	○	Synthetic	○

11 대화를 듣고, 남자의 마지막 말에 대한 여자의 응답으로 가장 적절한 것을 고르시오.

① No problem. I'll be over then.
② Sure. Babysitting is such hard work.
③ I'm afraid I can't. I am free at that time.
④ Of course. I'd love to have dinner with you.
⑤ No. I think Saturday would be better for me.

12 대화를 듣고, 여자의 마지막 말에 대한 남자의 응답으로 가장 적절한 것을 고르시오.

① You're right. That's exactly what I wanted.
② I'm sorry, but I'm full. Why don't we skip the meal?
③ Really? My sister wants a strawberry juice with honey.
④ I'll call my parents to see if they want the same drink.
⑤ Actually, I'm allergic to mangoes. I'll have something else.

13 대화를 듣고, 여자의 마지막 말에 대한 남자의 응답으로 가장 적절한 것을 고르시오. [3점]

Man: _____

① Thank you for your time and effort.
② I would like to start my vacation now.
③ I need to conduct further examinations.
④ I'm available to begin working next week.
⑤ This hospital offers the best care in the city.

14 대화를 듣고, 남자의 마지막 말에 대한 여자의 응답으로 가장 적절한 것을 고르시오.

Woman: _____

① Okay. I'll be expecting your call.
② Yes. I am excited to see my parents this week.
③ Sure. I'd love to have dinner this weekend.
④ Yeah. Teaching has been a real challenge.
⑤ Good. Make sure you write when you go camping.

15 다음 상황 설명을 듣고, Sara가 Tom에게 할 말로 가장 적절한 것을 고르시오. [3점]

Sara: _____

① There's not enough time to take a break.
② Have you ever tried snorkeling in Guam?
③ I'd like it if we spent time relaxing together.
④ Hiking up the mountain sounds fun and relaxing.
⑤ Do you think we really need to sit on the beach?

[16-17] 다음을 듣고, 물음에 답하시오.

16 남자가 하는 말의 주제로 가장 적절한 것은?

① necessity of wireless speakers
② drawbacks of a wireless headset
③ advantages of bluetooth headsets
④ benefits of noise-cancelling headsets
⑤ introduction of a new wireless headset

17 언급된 기능이 <u>아닌</u> 것은?

① noise cancelling   ② sound quality
③ microphone   ④ charging case
⑤ Quick Reality mode

1번부터 17번까지는 듣고 답하는 문제입니다.
1번부터 15번까지는 한 번만 들려주고, 16번부터 17번까지는 두 번 들려줍니다.
방송을 잘 듣고 답을 하시기 바랍니다.

01 다음을 듣고, 남자가 하는 말의 목적으로 가장 적절한 것을 고르시오.
① 졸업하는 선배들에게 축하의 말을 전하려고
② 입지 않는 교복을 기증해 줄 것을 요청하려고
③ 졸업식에서 거행되는 특별 행사를 안내하려고
④ 학생회 주관의 교복 공동 구매 절차를 설명하려고
⑤ 교복 물려 입기 행사의 성공적인 마무리를 자축하려고

02 대화를 듣고, 여자의 의견으로 가장 적절한 것을 고르시오.
① 스마트폰은 친구를 사귈 수 있는 좋은 수단이다.
② 스마트폰을 적극적으로 활용해서 수업을 해야 한다.
③ 교실에서는 학생들의 스마트폰 사용을 금지해야 한다.
④ 날씨가 더워질수록 학생들이 실내에 있는 것을 꺼린다.
⑤ 친구와 대화를 많이 하면 할수록 우정이 더욱 깊어진다.

03 대화를 듣고, 두 사람의 관계를 가장 잘 나타낸 것을 고르시오.
① 의사 – 환자
② 기자 – 증인
③ 손님 – 제과점 주인
④ 경찰 – 목격자
⑤ 승객 – 택시 기사

04 대화를 듣고, 그림에서 대화의 내용과 일치하지 않는 것을 고르시오.

05 대화를 듣고, 여자가 할 일로 가장 적절한 것을 고르시오.
① 카펫 깔기
② 양파와 버섯 사 오기
③ 거실 청소하기
④ 치킨 스튜 요리하기
⑤ 공항으로 마중 나가기

06 대화를 듣고, 여자가 지불할 금액을 고르시오. [3점]
① $60　② $70　③ $80　④ $90　⑤ $100

07 대화를 듣고, 남자가 콘서트를 보러 갈 수 없는 이유를 고르시오.
① 생물 보고서를 써야 해서
② 입장권을 예매하지 못해서
③ 부모님을 마중 나가야 해서
④ 도서관에서 아르바이트를 해야 해서
⑤ 교통사고를 당한 동생을 보러 가야 해서

08 대화를 듣고, 여자의 전기 의류 건조기에 관해 언급되지 않은 것을 고르시오.
① 용량
② 사용 기간
③ 보증 기간
④ 제조사
⑤ 판매 가격

09 Green Jazz Concert에 관한 다음 내용을 듣고, 일치하지 않는 것을 고르시오.
① 옥상에 설치된 특별 무대에서 열린다.
② 7시 정각에 시작해서 약 2시간 동안 계속된다.
③ 5명의 재즈 음악가가 공연을 할 것이다.
④ 20달러 이상의 구매 영수증 소지자는 입장료가 5달러 할인된다.
⑤ 중간 휴식 시간 때 관객에게 음료수를 제공한다.

10 다음 표를 보면서 대화를 듣고, 남자가 선택할 서핑 수업을 고르시오.

Surfing Classes

	Class	Level	Duration	Price	Instructor
①	A	Beginner	1 hour	$50	John
②	B	Beginner	2 hours	$80	Brian
③	C	Beginner	2 hours	$90	Albert
④	D	Intermediate	1 hour	$60	Brian
⑤	E	Beginner	2 hours	$80	John

11 대화를 듣고, 여자의 마지막 말에 대한 남자의 응답으로 가장 적절한 것을 고르시오.

① If you don't take the shuttle bus, you'll be late for the flight.
② That's nice. Let's go to the court and play tennis right away.
③ Can you tell me where I can get a shuttle bus to the airport?
④ Yes. The bus departs every hour on the hour from the front gate.
⑤ I'm sorry. I'm too busy to go with you to the airport right now.

12 대화를 듣고, 남자의 마지막 말에 대한 여자의 응답으로 가장 적절한 것을 고르시오.

① Yes, it's just behind the fire station.
② No problem. Let's have lunch next time.
③ Right. I'm a stranger here myself.
④ Sorry, but I don't want to work in the building.
⑤ Without your help, I couldn't have gone to the restaurant.

13 대화를 듣고, 남자의 마지막 말에 대한 여자의 응답으로 가장 적절한 것을 고르시오.

Woman: _____

① Okay! I'll go on a blind date with your friend.
② Good! I've always wanted to be a fashion model.
③ I don't think so. Actually, you're not as funny as him.
④ It's up to him. He has to decide the time and place.
⑤ Trust me. You won't regret the blind date this weekend.

14 대화를 듣고, 여자의 마지막 말에 대한 남자의 응답으로 가장 적절한 것을 고르시오. [3점]

Man: _____

① Incredible! You're a true language genius.
② Sure! I can make myself understood in Korean.
③ Actually, I'm not interested in K-pop any more.
④ My mistake. I should have studied Korean earlier.
⑤ I don't think so. Your Korean is much better than mine.

15 다음 상황 설명을 듣고, Rebecca가 Lucas에게 할 말로 가장 적절한 것을 고르시오. [3점]

Rebecca: _____

① Can you recommend some good books to read?
② How long does it take to go to work by subway?
③ Do you really want to read books on the subway?
④ Can you tell me why you decided to read books on the subway?
⑤ Why don't you go to work by subway from tomorrow?

[16-17] 다음을 듣고, 물음에 답하시오.

16 남자가 하는 말의 주제로 가장 적절한 것은?

① why people want to keep companion animals
② how to raise companion animals in small spaces
③ considerations about getting companion animals
④ how wild animals can become companion animals
⑤ benefits of keeping companion animals for human beings

17 언급된 동물이 아닌 것은?

① dog
② cat
③ goldfish
④ parrot
⑤ hamster

1번부터 17번까지는 듣고 답하는 문제입니다.
1번부터 15번까지는 한 번만 들려주고, 16번부터 17번까지는 두 번 들려줍니다.
방송을 잘 듣고 답을 하시기 바랍니다.

01 다음을 듣고, 남자가 하는 말의 목적으로 가장 적절한 것을 고르시오.
① 교통사고 발생 시 행동 요령을 안내하려고
② 운전 중 휴대 전화를 사용하지 말 것을 요청하려고
③ 경찰서 교통과에서 자원봉사를 할 사람을 모집하려고
④ 교통사고를 유발하는 다양한 요인에 대해 설명하려고
⑤ 운전 중 휴대 전화 사용을 금지하는 법안에 찬성하려고

02 대화를 듣고, 여자의 의견으로 가장 적절한 것을 고르시오.
① 기업 광고는 기업이 거둔 성과를 보여 주어야 한다.
② 광고는 글자나 숫자로 메시지를 전달하는 것이 좋다.
③ 광고에 한쪽으로 치우친 의견이 들어가서는 안 된다.
④ 기업 광고를 만들 때 감정을 이용하는 것이 효과적이다.
⑤ 기업 이미지 극대화를 위해 상품 홍보는 배제해야 한다.

03 대화를 듣고, 두 사람의 관계를 가장 잘 나타낸 것을 고르시오.
① 의사 – 환자　　　② 교사 – 학생
③ 아버지 – 딸　　　④ 친구 – 친구
⑤ 직장 상사 – 직원

04 대화를 듣고, 그림에서 대화의 내용과 일치하지 <u>않는</u> 것을 고르시오.

05 대화를 듣고, 여자가 남자에게 부탁한 일로 가장 적절한 것을 고르시오.
① 환전하기
② 문자 읽어 주기
③ 기부금 마련하기
④ 지폐를 잔돈으로 바꾸기
⑤ 벼룩시장에서 물건 팔기

06 대화를 듣고, 남자가 지불할 금액을 고르시오. [3점]
① $36　　② $42　　③ $46　　④ $48　　⑤ $50

07 대화를 듣고, 남자가 가려고 했던 식당을 가지 않기로 한 이유를 고르시오.
① 예약이 다 차서
② 식당이 쉬는 요일이어서
③ 종업원 서비스가 좋지 않아서
④ 음식에 대한 평이 좋지 않아서
⑤ 할인 쿠폰의 적용 기한이 지나서

08 대화를 듣고, Busan City Bus Tour에 관해 언급되지 <u>않은</u> 것을 고르시오.
① 출발 장소　　　　② 티켓 구매 방법
③ 티켓 가격　　　　④ 오디오 가이드 제공 여부
⑤ 이용 시 유의점

09 Boston Half Marathon에 관한 다음 내용을 듣고, 일치하지 <u>않는</u> 것을 고르시오.
① 마라톤 행사는 오전 11시에 시작한다.
② 참가 인원은 800명까지 제한한다.
③ 3월 31일에 등록하면 기념품을 제공한다.
④ 마라톤을 완주하면 메달을 받는다.
⑤ 급수대는 출발선에서부터 3킬로미터마다 있다.

10 다음 표를 보면서 대화를 듣고, 두 사람이 구매할 책상을 고르시오.

Children's Desks

	Model	Color	Material	Height Adjustment	Built-in USB Port
①	A	White	Plastic	×	×
②	B	Yellow	Wood	○	○
③	C	Pink	Wood	×	○
④	D	Pink	Plastic	○	×
⑤	E	Yellow	Wood	○	×

11 대화를 듣고, 여자의 마지막 말에 대한 남자의 응답으로 가장 적절한 것을 고르시오.

① Then don't watch TV until tomorrow.
② I'll make sure to deliver the TV today.
③ I'll make sure to be home at that time.
④ This TV is too heavy to carry by myself.
⑤ We should get the TV repaired right away.

12 대화를 듣고, 남자의 마지막 말에 대한 여자의 응답으로 가장 적절한 것을 고르시오.

① If I were you, I would study alone.
② You're really kind. I'm happy you're in my class.
③ Why don't we tell our teacher how difficult it was?
④ The sooner the better. How about this evening?
⑤ I don't want other students in our study group.

13 대화를 듣고, 여자의 마지막 말에 대한 남자의 응답으로 가장 적절한 것을 고르시오. [3점]

Man: _____

① No. I think your argument is off the point.
② Why don't you narrow down the subject first?
③ I disagree with you about artificial intelligence.
④ If it's hard to write the paper, I can help you more.
⑤ Yes. My thoughts are more organized after talking with you.

14 대화를 듣고, 남자의 마지막 말에 대한 여자의 응답으로 가장 적절한 것을 고르시오.

Woman: _____

① Tomato seedlings grow faster than other plants.
② If you visit the flower market, you can see various seedlings.
③ I think a darker room would be better for growing tomatoes.
④ If you spray more soil on the seedlings, they will grow faster.
⑤ How about on the balcony? That's the sunniest place in the house.

15 다음 상황 설명을 듣고, Johns 선생님이 Kevin에게 할 말로 가장 적절한 것을 고르시오. [3점]

Ms. Johns: _____

① You should get out and exercise more.
② Don't be so disappointed at your low grades.
③ Why don't you put aside social media and focus on studying?
④ Social media can be a good way to communicate with others.
⑤ You need to spend more time reviewing what you've learned.

[16-17] 다음을 듣고, 물음에 답하시오.

16 여자가 하는 말의 주제로 가장 적절한 것은?

① disadvantages of alternative energy
② types of eco-friendly energy sources
③ how to cut down on energy consumption
④ misconceptions about fossil-fuel-based energy
⑤ the emergence of environmentally-friendly everyday goods

17 언급된 에너지가 아닌 것은?

① biomass   ② solar energy
③ atomic energy   ④ wind energy
⑤ hydropower

1번부터 17번까지는 듣고 답하는 문제입니다.
1번부터 15번까지는 한 번만 들려주고, 16번부터 17번까지는 두 번 들려줍니다.
방송을 잘 듣고 답을 하시기 바랍니다.

01 다음을 듣고, 여자가 하는 말의 목적으로 가장 적절한 것을 고르시오.
① 공정한 선거 운동을 할 것을 요청하려고
② 경제 상황이 악화된 원인에 대해 발표하려고
③ 시장 선거에서 자신에게 투표할 것을 호소하려고
④ 여론 조사에 적극적으로 참여해 줄 것을 부탁하려고
⑤ 경제 위기에 대한 현 시장의 부적절한 대응을 비판하려고

02 대화를 듣고, 남자의 의견으로 가장 적절한 것을 고르시오.
① 전기 자동차의 판매 가격이 인하되어야 한다.
② 전기 자동차를 충전하는 방식이 쉬워져야 된다.
③ 친환경적인 전기 자동차의 구매 혜택을 늘려야 한다.
④ 전기 자동차 충전소가 좀 더 많이 설치되어야 한다.
⑤ 일반 자동차보다 전기 자동차가 더 인기를 끌 것이다.

03 대화를 듣고, 두 사람의 관계를 가장 잘 나타낸 것을 고르시오.
① 아내 – 남편
② 의사 – 환자
③ 등반 대장 – 등반 대원
④ 산악 구조대원 – 등산객
⑤ 휴대 전화 판매 사원 – 손님

04 대화를 듣고, 그림에서 대화의 내용과 일치하지 <u>않는</u> 것을 고르시오.

05 대화를 듣고, 여자가 남자에게 부탁한 일로 가장 적절한 것을 고르시오.
① 출장 짐 싸 주기
② 항공권 예약하기
③ 해산물 사러 가기
④ 금붕어 먹이 주기
⑤ 점심 식사 사 주기

06 대화를 듣고, 남자가 지불할 금액을 고르시오. [3점]
① $130
② $180
③ $190
④ $360
⑤ $390

07 대화를 듣고, 남자가 Green Market에서 쇼핑을 하지 <u>않으려는</u> 이유를 고르시오.
① 직원이 불친절해서
② 할인 행사를 하지 않아서
③ 농산물이 신선하지 않아서
④ 무료로 배달을 해 주지 않아서
⑤ 아파트에서 멀리 떨어져 있어서

08 대화를 듣고, 은행나무에 관해 두 사람이 언급하지 <u>않은</u> 것을 고르시오.
① 나이
② 높이
③ 지름
④ 열매
⑤ 별명

09 Green Essay Competition에 관한 다음 내용을 듣고, 일치하지 <u>않는</u> 것을 고르시오.
① 환경 보호에 대한 인식을 높이기 위한 행사이다.
② 글쓰기 주제는 '지구를 보호하는 방법'이다.
③ 참가 신청은 학교 웹 사이트에서 이루어진다.
④ 심사 결과는 수상자에게 개별 통보된다.
⑤ 각 학년별로 금메달 수상자가 발표된다.

10 다음 표를 보면서 대화를 듣고, 두 사람이 구입할 커피 머신을 고르시오.

Coffee Machines

	Model	Brand	Water Capacity (liter)	Cafe Latte	Warranty
①	A	ACE	1.0	○	2 years
②	B	Tasty Star	2.0	○	1 year
③	C	Coffee Lover	2.0	○	2 years
④	D	Blue Coffee	2.0	×	2 years
⑤	E	Grace	1.5	×	1 year

11 대화를 듣고, 남자의 마지막 말에 대한 여자의 응답으로 가장 적절한 것을 고르시오.

① I have a reservation for two.
② I had the lobster with salad.
③ Tell them I'm sorry I couldn't make it.
④ I think the movie will be sold out then.
⑤ Fantastic! I'll see you at the restaurant.

12 대화를 듣고, 여자의 마지막 말에 대한 남자의 응답으로 가장 적절한 것을 고르시오.

① I'm sorry, but I can't borrow any of his albums.
② Right. Listen to the song, and you'll love it too.
③ James King? No, I've never heard of that name.
④ Thank you for recommending a good song for me.
⑤ As I told you, I saved enough money to buy his album.

13 대화를 듣고, 여자의 마지막 말에 대한 남자의 응답으로 가장 적절한 것을 고르시오.

Man: _____

① Never mind. I will renovate my house soon.
② Sure! Don't worry about the monthly rental fee.
③ It's up to you. You can live in any house you like.
④ Sounds good. Can I have a look at the house now?
⑤ Right. I didn't know how hard it was to renovate a house.

14 대화를 듣고, 남자의 마지막 말에 대한 여자의 응답으로 가장 적절한 것을 고르시오. [3점]

Woman: _____

① Brian should be in the hospital for a few more days.
② I'm too busy to go to the hospital to see him after work.
③ You shouldn't have used your cell phone while driving.
④ Nobody knows the exact reason for the traffic accident.
⑤ It's sad because those accidents should never have happened.

15 다음 상황 설명을 듣고, Lucy가 Eric에게 할 말로 가장 적절한 것을 고르시오. [3점]

Lucy: _____

① Don't worry. I'll fix the elevator right away.
② From now on, take the stairs instead of elevators.
③ Accidents can happen anytime, anywhere. So we can't avoid them.
④ The elevator breaks down too often. I'll tell the manager about it.
⑤ The repairman is coming in 10 minutes. Then we'll get out of here.

[16-17] 다음을 듣고, 물음에 답하시오.

16 여자가 하는 말의 주제로 가장 적절한 것은?

① positive benefits on kids of playing sports
② the importance of warming up before playing sports
③ how to increase kids' physical strength through sports
④ the difference between individual sports and group sports
⑤ why kids like to play group sports more than individual sports

17 언급된 운동이 아닌 것은?

① soccer　　② baseball　　③ tennis
④ skating　　⑤ swimming

1번부터 17번까지는 듣고 답하는 문제입니다.
1번부터 15번까지는 한 번만 들려주고, 16번부터 17번까지는 두 번 들려줍니다.
방송을 잘 듣고 답을 하시기 바랍니다.

01 다음을 듣고, 남자가 하는 말의 목적으로 가장 적절한 것을 고르시오.
① 아보카도의 대체 과일을 소개하려고
② 아보카도의 효능에 대해서 홍보하려고
③ 아보카도 재배의 문제점을 알려 주려고
④ 아보카도와 잘 어울리는 음식을 소개하려고
⑤ 아보카도를 싸게 살 수 있는 방법을 알려 주려고

02 대화를 듣고, 여자의 의견으로 가장 적절한 것을 고르시오.
① 급격한 체중 증가는 관절에 부담을 준다.
② 불규칙한 식습관은 비만을 초래할 수 있다.
③ 자신의 몸 상태에 맞는 적절한 운동을 해야 한다.
④ 부상을 예방하기 위해 준비 운동을 하는 것이 좋다.
⑤ 유산소 운동과 근력 운동을 병행하는 것이 효과적이다.

03 대화를 듣고, 두 사람의 관계를 가장 잘 나타낸 것을 고르시오.
① 가구점 직원 – 손님
② 화가 – 전시회 관람객
③ 인테리어 업자 – 집주인
④ 건축가 – 부동산 중개인
⑤ 아파트 경비원 – 택배 기사

04 대화를 듣고, 그림에서 대화의 내용과 일치하지 않는 것을 고르시오.

05 대화를 듣고, 여자가 할 일로 가장 적절한 것을 고르시오.
① 내일 날씨 확인하기
② 가스 회사에 전화하기
③ 은행에서 돈 인출하기
④ 승강기 사용 신청하기
⑤ 이삿짐센터에 전화하기

06 대화를 듣고, 남자가 지불할 금액을 고르시오. [3점]
① $54   ② $56   ③ $60   ④ $72   ⑤ $80

07 대화를 듣고, 남자가 Mexico로 출장을 갈 수 없는 이유를 고르시오.
① 출장 기간을 착각해서
② 예약했던 비행편이 취소되어서
③ 중요한 회의가 남아 있어서
④ 축구 경기장 보수 공사를 하기 위해서
⑤ 아들이 출전하는 경기를 보러 가기 위해서

08 대화를 듣고, LED 전구에 관해 언급되지 않은 것을 고르시오.
① 색온도   ② 수명   ③ 소비 전력
④ 설치 비용   ⑤ 발열 수준

09 Typhoon Soulik에 관한 다음 내용을 듣고, 일치하지 않는 것을 고르시오.
① 다음 주에 하와이 섬들에 영향을 줄 것으로 보인다.
② 풍속은 115mph에 달하는데, 이는 3등급 허리케인에 해당하는 풍속이다.
③ 강한 바람이 건물과 벽을 부술 수 있으니 외출하지 않는 것이 좋다.
④ 강한 바람에 비해 비는 많이 오지 않을 것으로 예상된다.
⑤ 다음 주 수요일까지 점차 약해질 것이다.

10 다음 표를 보면서 대화를 듣고, 두 사람이 구매할 선풍기를 고르시오.

Portable Fans

	Model	Price	Charging Time(hour)	Usage Time(hour)	Weight
①	A	$10	4	6	500 g
②	B	$15	6	9	700 g
③	C	$25	2	5	400 g
④	D	$25	7	9	500 g
⑤	E	$40	3	12	400 g

11 대화를 듣고, 남자의 마지막 말에 대한 여자의 응답으로 가장 적절한 것을 고르시오.

① Did you save my phone number in your phone?
② I think saving people's occupations isn't a great idea.
③ It's always difficult for me to remember people's names.
④ You don't have to remember my name and occupation.
⑤ You can also make a note of their physical characteristics.

12 대화를 듣고 여자의 마지막 말에 대한 남자의 응답으로 가장 적절한 것을 고르시오.

① I was told that about 20 minutes ago.
② To be honest, you look very tired today.
③ I think it's difficult to enter the school dormitory.
④ Actually, I don't live too far away from the school.
⑤ I'm happy because I've always wanted to live there.

13 대화를 듣고, 여자의 마지막 말에 대한 남자의 응답으로 가장 적절한 것을 고르시오.

Man: _____

① Yes, it's very simple, so 10 minutes is sufficient.
② The only thing I don't like is its high price.
③ It really helps students to focus on the lessons.
④ But it has a variety of functions.
⑤ Students are very satisfied with the whiteboard.

14 대화를 듣고, 남자의 마지막 말에 대한 여자의 응답으로 가장 적절한 것을 고르시오. [3점]

Woman: _____

① Yes, she's going to be happy with our present.
② Yes. How about buying another present for her?
③ You really helped me to develop good habits.
④ Did she promise you something?
⑤ Yes, I do. I trust her on this.

15 다음 상황 설명을 듣고, Vincent가 학급 친구들에게 할 말로 가장 적절한 것을 고르시오. [3점]

Vincent: _____

① It's good to make our own rules for cleaning our classroom.
② I think we should clean our classroom at least twice a day.
③ I suggest that we should keep our own places clean all the time.
④ How can we keep our classroom neat all the time?
⑤ Cleaning our classroom is more important than anything else.

[16-17] 다음을 듣고, 물음에 답하시오.

16 여자가 하는 말의 주제로 가장 적절한 것은?

① the relationship between rainfall and Malaria
② the introduction of a new vaccine for Malaria
③ the benefits of maintaining a good water supply
④ the demand for investigation of the cause of Malaria
⑤ the solution for the decrease in the amount of rainfall

17 피실험자에 대한 정보로 언급된 것이 아닌 것은?

① gender   ② age   ③ weight
④ job   ⑤ region

1번부터 17번까지는 듣고 답하는 문제입니다.
1번부터 15번까지는 한 번만 들려주고, 16번부터 17번까지는 두 번 들려줍니다.
방송을 잘 듣고 답을 하시기 바랍니다.

01 다음을 듣고, 남자가 하는 말의 목적으로 가장 적절한 것을 고르시오.
① 태양계의 구조에 대해서 설명하려고
② 우주에 관한 다큐멘터리를 홍보하려고
③ 우주 호텔을 예약하는 방법을 안내하려고
④ NASA의 훈련 과정에 대해서 소개하려고
⑤ 우주선을 조종할 우주 비행사를 모집하려고

02 대화를 듣고, 여자의 의견으로 가장 적절한 것을 고르시오.
① 고등학교 교육 과정에서 역사 수업 시간을 늘려야 한다.
② 고등학교 역사 수업 시간은 이미 충분히 확보되어 있다.
③ 고등학교 교육 과정은 장기적인 안목에서 바라봐야 한다.
④ 고등학교 학생들은 평소에 신문 기사를 많이 읽어야 한다.
⑤ 역사만 강조하는 것은 다른 교과와의 형평성에 어긋난다.

03 대화를 듣고, 두 사람의 관계를 가장 잘 나타낸 것을 고르시오.
① 환자 – 의사
② 세입자 – 인구 조사원
③ 보호자 – 요양원 직원
④ 아파트 주민 – 방문 판매원
⑤ 손님 – 건강 관리 센터 직원

04 대화를 듣고, 그림에서 대화의 내용과 일치하지 않는 것을 고르시오.

05 대화를 듣고, 남자가 여자에게 부탁한 일로 가장 적절한 것을 고르시오.
① 빈 상자 버리기
② 설명서 읽어 주기
③ 판자에 나사 끼우기
④ 전동 드라이버 가져오기
⑤ 조립 전문가에게 전화하기

06 대화를 듣고, 남자가 지불할 금액을 고르시오. [3점]
① $1.50   ② $3.50   ③ $5.00
④ $6.50   ⑤ $8.00

07 대화를 듣고, 과학 캠프가 연기된 이유를 고르시오.
① 장소 예약을 못해서
② 장소를 변경해야 해서
③ 초청 강사를 섭외하지 못해서
④ 참가 신청한 학생 수가 적어서
⑤ NASA 방문 일정이 연기되어서

08 대화를 듣고, Louise Safety Theme Park에 관해 언급되지 않은 것을 고르시오.
① 연령 제한   ② 위치
③ 입장료   ④ 수용 인원
⑤ 개장 시간

09 Pacific University Scholarship에 관한 다음 내용을 듣고, 일치하지 않는 것을 고르시오.
① 학생들에게 수여하는 장학금은 두 가지 종류가 있다.
② 성적 장학금을 받으려면 최소 14학점 이상을 듣고, 4.0이상의 평균 점수를 받아야 한다.
③ 도서관이나 실험실에서 일을 하는 학생은 등록금의 절반을 장학금으로 받을 수 있다.
④ 조건을 충족한 학생이라면, 두 종류의 장학금을 한꺼번에 받을 수 있다.
⑤ 학교 규칙을 어긴 학생은 장학금 지급 대상에서 제외될 수 있다.

10 다음 표를 보면서 대화를 듣고, 남자가 구입할 게임기를 고르시오.

Game Consoles

	Model	TV Connection	Maximum Number of Players	Portable	Price
①	A	×	2	○	$140
②	B	○	2	×	$150
③	C	○	4	×	$170
④	D	○	4	○	$200
⑤	E	○	4	×	$250

11 대화를 듣고, 여자의 마지막 말에 대한 남자의 응답으로 가장 적절한 것을 고르시오.

① Great. I arrived just a few minutes ago.
② Okay. I'll leave half an hour earlier next time.
③ No problem. I was supposed to meet you at 3 p.m.
④ You have a point. I forgot to meet you today.
⑤ You're right. I'm tired of heavy traffic jams.

12 대화를 듣고 남자의 마지막 말에 대한 여자의 응답으로 가장 적절한 것을 고르시오.

① Then, I don't need to take my umbrella.
② You'd better pack your raincoat instead.
③ On the way home, I should buy a new bag.
④ Could you check today's weather for me?
⑤ Really? I should change into warmer clothes.

13 대화를 듣고, 여자의 마지막 말에 대한 남자의 응답으로 가장 적절한 것을 고르시오.

Man: _____

① It'll cost less if you buy a used one.
② I just bought a new high-tech computer.
③ Okay. When will you arrive at my house?
④ I recommend you to change your power cable.
⑤ Of course, I'll drop by on my way home.

14 대화를 듣고, 남자의 마지막 말에 대한 여자의 응답으로 가장 적절한 것을 고르시오. [3점]

Woman: _____

① An ultrasound scan costs a lot of money.
② You're right. I'll definitely go and get examined.
③ I agree. You should take care of your health.
④ I'm still waiting for a letter from my client.
⑤ The doctor said that I have a serious health problem.

15 다음 상황 설명을 듣고, Kelly가 Edward에게 할 말로 가장 적절한 것을 고르시오. [3점]

Kelly: _____

① Why don't you return to work again? I'll help you to do this.
② How about trying the business that can develop a new market?
③ I think the proven business guarantees a big profit.
④ Starting a business in these hard times is not as easy as you think.
⑤ Look before you leap! You have to do more market research.

[16-17] 다음을 듣고, 물음에 답하시오.

16 여자가 하는 말의 주제로 가장 적절한 것은?

① the effects of colors on people
② powerful influences on our health
③ the importance of good habits for success
④ ways to control other people's behavior
⑤ the relationship between colors and smells

17 언급된 색이 아닌 것은?

① yellow   ② blue   ③ red
④ black   ⑤ white

1번부터 17번까지는 듣고 답하는 문제입니다.
1번부터 15번까지는 한 번만 들려주고, 16번부터 17번까지는 두 번 들려줍니다.
방송을 잘 듣고 답을 하시기 바랍니다.

01 다음을 듣고, 여자가 하는 말의 목적으로 가장 적절한 것을 고르시오.
① Shakespeare의 대표 작품을 소개하려고
② 라디오 청취의 장점에 대하여 강조하려고
③ 새롭게 시작하는 라디오 코너를 소개하려고
④ 라디오 프로그램의 시간 변경을 공지하려고
⑤ Shakespeare 원작의 연극 공연 일정을 안내하려고

02 대화를 듣고, 남자의 의견으로 가장 적절한 것을 고르시오.
① 아이의 SNS 활동을 부모가 일일이 확인해야 한다.
② 아이가 SNS를 하려는 정확한 이유를 알아야 한다.
③ 아이는 부모의 동의 없이 SNS 계정을 만들면 안 된다.
④ 아이가 SNS상의 정보를 선별할 수 있도록 교육해야 한다.
⑤ 아이가 SNS를 이용하여 친구들과 소통하고 최신 정보를 얻을 수 있어야 한다.

03 대화를 듣고, 두 사람의 관계를 가장 잘 나타낸 것을 고르시오.
① 교통경찰 – 운전자
② 택시 기사 – 승객
③ 회사 사장 – 거래처 직원
④ 비행기 승무원 – 탑승객
⑤ 차량 정비사 – 버스 기사

04 대화를 듣고, 그림에서 대화의 내용과 일치하지 <u>않는</u> 것을 고르시오.

05 대화를 듣고, 남자가 여자에게 부탁한 일로 가장 적절한 것을 고르시오.
① 고기 굽기
② 신고 전화 걸기
③ 창문 열기
④ 가스 밸브 잠그기
⑤ 비눗물 만들기

06 대화를 듣고, 남자가 지불할 금액을 고르시오. [3점]
① $40 ② $45 ③ $50 ④ $54 ⑤ $60

07 대화를 듣고, 남자가 사무실로 들어갈 수 <u>없는</u> 이유를 고르시오.
① 길이 너무 많이 막혀서
② 아들이 있는 병원에 가야 해서
③ 아들의 농구 시합을 보러 가야 해서
④ 고장 난 보일러를 수리해야 해서
⑤ 집을 계약하기 위해 고객과 만나야 해서

08 대화를 듣고, Superhero Festival에 관해 언급되지 <u>않은</u> 것을 고르시오.
① 영웅의 조건
② 접수 방법
③ 접수 마감일
④ 접수 비용
⑤ 투표 기간

09 항공기 AX 120에 관한 다음 내용을 듣고, 일치하지 <u>않는</u> 것을 고르시오.
① 애틀랜타를 출발하여 인천으로 가는 비행기이다.
② 비행기는 지금 날짜 변경선을 넘어서 날짜가 바뀌었다.
③ 비행기의 현재 고도는 11,000미터이고, 속도는 시속 850 킬로미터이다.
④ 도착 예정 시간은 현지 시각으로 오전 10시 반이고, 도착지의 기온은 15°C이다.
⑤ 좌석 주머니에 있는 책은 세금이 붙지 않은 가격으로 구입할 수 있다.

10 다음 표를 보면서 대화를 듣고, 여자가 대여할 장난감을 고르시오.

Toy World

	Toy	Ages	Material	Rental Fee	Place
①	A	3-7	plastic	$5	indoors
②	B	4-7	wood	$5	indoors
③	C	5-8	wood	$10	outdoors
④	D	6-10	wood	$15	indoors
⑤	E	8-12	plastic	$20	outdoors

11 대화를 듣고, 남자의 마지막 말에 대한 여자의 응답으로 가장 적절한 것을 고르시오.

① This library has a lot of interesting materials to read.

② You shouldn't forget to return it by the end of this week.

③ The book tells what happened in this library in the past.

④ The book was just published this month and costs only $10.

⑤ Fill out this application form and submit it with two passport photos.

12 대화를 듣고, 여자의 마지막 말에 대한 남자의 응답으로 가장 적절한 것을 고르시오.

① I think this application is very convenient, but it's not free.

② It calls for heavy rain and strong winds this afternoon.

③ You can simply download this app by touching this button.

④ This app tells you the accurate weather forecast all around the world.

⑤ All you have to do is install this app on your smartphone.

13 대화를 듣고, 남자의 마지막 말에 대한 여자의 응답으로 가장 적절한 것을 고르시오.

Woman: _____

① It is very responsible of you to raise a dog.

② You have to walk and feed the dog every day.

③ I'm sorry, but our apartment has banned pets.

④ You can share the dog pictures with me.

⑤ Training a dog not to bark is more difficult than you think.

14 대화를 듣고, 여자의 마지막 말에 대한 남자의 응답으로 가장 적절한 것을 고르시오. [3점]

Man: _____

① Yes, I found the word "smombie" in the dictionary.

② You're right. I will listen to music and read at the same time.

③ Okay. From now on, I won't use my smartphone while walking.

④ I agree, but what if I bump into a smombie on the street?

⑤ Don't worry. I'll send you the article tomorrow.

15 다음 상황을 듣고, Eriksen이 그의 룸메이트에게 할 말로 가장 적절한 것을 고르시오. [3점]

Eriksen: _____

① Could you help my professor do the project instead of me?

② Can you take my clothes from the washer and put them in the dryer?

③ Would you let me know how to dance like a professional dancer?

④ Would you dance with me at the dance competition tonight?

⑤ Can you lend me your clothes to wear at the dancing competition tonight?

[16-17] 다음을 듣고, 물음에 답하시오.

16 여자가 하는 말의 주제로 가장 적절한 것은?

① amount of disposable products consumed every year

② cases of UFO sightings around the world

③ a future food source for people

④ the lives of two brilliant designers

⑤ a disposable plate that helps to reduce environmental pollution

17 UFO Plates의 재료로 언급된 것이 <u>아닌</u> 것은?

① blended birdseed   ② potato starch

③ guar gum   ④ mustard powder

⑤ seaweed

Part 2 Dictation Test

수능 영어 듣기 모의고사 20+3회 실전

녹음을 다시 한 번 들으면서, 빈칸을 채워 봅시다.

01

M: May I have your attention, students? This is your principal, Mr. Henny. I _____ _____ _____ _____ _____ _____ regarding your gym class. Recently, I have received several emails from our students saying that they feel uncomfortable wearing the school gym shorts during class. Although gym uniforms have been a long tradition at our school, we understand the _____ _____ _____ _____ _____ _____. So, starting next week, students can wear sweatpants or other athletic apparel instead of the gym shorts, _____ _____ _____ _____ _____ _____ by your gym teacher. Keep in mind that you still need to wear your school gym T-shirts. I hope this change will help you have a fun and safe gym class!

02

W: What are you _____ _____ _____ _____, Josh?
M: I'm trying to decide on a pair of sneakers.
W: Do you need any help?
M: Yeah. I _____ _____ _____ _____ _____ between these two pairs.
W: Well, what are you going to be mostly using them for?
M: For moderate to heavy running.
W: Then you should definitely choose this pair. The other one is just for walking.
M: I know, but most of the kids at school are wearing that one.
W: _____ _____ _____. You should buy the pair that _____ _____ _____ _____.
M: But, what if the other kids don't think I'm cool?
W: Grow up, Josh. Your opinion should matter the most, not your friends'.
M: You're right, Sis. Thanks a lot.

03

M: I'm sorry, Judith. Can we do that again?
W: Did I do something wrong? I _____ _____ _____ _____, did I?
M: No, you didn't do anything wrong. It's your watch.
W: My watch? _____ _____ _____ _____?
M: The setting for our movie is the 19th century and that's a digital watch that you're wearing.
W: Oh, I'm so sorry. Did it get caught on film?
M: Yeah. _____ _____ _____ _____ _____ this scene.
W: I didn't realize I had it on. I'll take it off right away.
M: Okay. Just keep doing what you're doing. Your acting was great just now.
W: Thank you. Is my makeup okay?
M: Don't worry about it. It's perfect.
W: Alright. I'm ready to go again now.
M: Then _____ _____ _____ _____ on three. One, two, three.

04

W: Jim, what are you looking at?
M: My school is having a photo contest and I'm _____ _____ _____ _____ _____.
W: Wow! It's beautiful.
M: Thanks. I especially like the romantic message the plane is making in the sky.
W: Yeah. The _____ _____ _____ _____ _____ _____ _____ _____ look like they're enjoying it too.
M: Can you see the man in the sailboat?
W: Which boat? The one with the striped sails on the right, or the spotted sails on the left?
M: The one on the right.
W: He _____ _____ _____ _____ _____ fishing.

M: The three girls playing on the beach at the bottom look so cute.

W: Right. I really like the one in the middle with the tube on.

M: My favorite part is the setting sun on the left side. It completes the picture.

W: I agree. I think you should title it, "A Day at the Beach."

05

W: Whew. _____ _____ _____ _____ _____ _____ to find our luggage.

M: Right. But we're finally here at the destination.

W: Sure. I can't believe we are at an airport in an exotic, foreign country.

M: It's going to be a fantastic trip. Honey, let's get out of this busy airport.

W: I agree. By the way, shall we take a bus or a taxi?

M: Well, we're going to _____ _____ _____ _____ _____ _____ _____. Why don't we just rent a car?

W: I guess that would be _____ _____ _____ _____ _____ _____ for the entire trip.

M: Sure. Oh, there is a rental car booth over there. I'll go rent a car.

W: Okay. While you're doing that, is there anything I should do?

M: Why don't you call the hotel to confirm our reservation?

W: Good idea. I'll do that.

06

[Telephone rings.]

W: Hello. Wally's Water World, the place for your family's water adventure!

M: Hi, I would like to purchase some tickets for this Saturday.

W: Certainly. _____ _____ _____ _____ _____ _____?

M: Four. Two adults and two children.

W: On the weekends, it's $20 for an adult and _____ _____ _____ _____ _____ _____.

M: Both of my children are under 12.

W: Great. Are any of your children under 36 months?

M: Actually, my youngest is 28 months old.

W: I am happy to let you know that the admission for children under 36 months old is free.

M: That's wonderful.

W: Also, if you pay with your credit card over the phone, _____ _____ _____ _____ _____ _____ the total admission price.

M: That sounds great. Let me give you my credit card number.

07

M: Hey, Jules. _____ _____ _____ _____ for you!

W: What is it, Harry?

M: You know how you've always been saying that you wanted to meet people from different countries.

W: Yeah. Of course.

M: Well, there is an International Students Festival coming up at my school.

W: Wow! Sounds like the perfect event for me.

M: Exactly. So, do you want to go with me this Saturday?

W: Oh, no. Any day, but Saturday.

M: Let me guess. You have to babysit your little brother that day.

W: No, it's not that. I promised my mom that I'd go shopping with her.

M: Can't you _____ _____ _____ _____? You can always go another day.

W: I can't. My mom really wants me to go with her and I _____ _____ _____ _____ _____ _____.

M: Oh, well. Maybe next time then.

08

M: It's the weekend! Let's do something fun today, Honey.

W: Sure. How about going to the movies?

M: Perfect. What kind of movie are you _____ _____ _____ _____?

W: How about something light, like a romantic comedy?

M: Okay. Then do you want to catch a movie before or after lunch?

W: Let's _____ _____ _____ _____ at 10 a.m. There will be fewer people at that time.

M: Plus, the ticket price is only $7 for the early showing.

W: Right. Which theater do you want to go to?

M: It _____ _____ _____ _____ _____ _____ as long as it's not too far away.

W: Then, let's go to the theater on 5th street next to the post office.

M: Great! I'll purchase the tickets on my phone right now.

09

W: Dear Students, this is Ms. Greenberg, your vice principal. _____ _____ _____ _____ _____ _____ _____ our annual Queens High School Read-a-thon! For those of you who are new to the Read-a-thon, it is _____ _____ _____ _____ _____ _____ _____ by reading books. Last year, over 500 students participated in the two-week event and raised over $12,000 for children in need. This year, the Read-a-thon period will _____ _____ _____ _____ _____ _____ _____ _____ _____. You can register for the Read-a-thon through the school website. We have exciting prizes for students who raise the most money in each grade. This is a fun and educational event for all and it is _____ _____ _____ _____. I look forward to your active participation!

10

M: Excuse me. _____ _____ _____ _____ _____ here?

W: Yes, we have these five models in stock. _____ _____ _____ _____?

M: Not more than $200.

W: Then, may I recommend this model? It has the highest wattage of the five, so it will purify the air of your car the quickest.

M: That's great but I have _____ _____ _____ _____ _____ _____, so I want one with 30 watts or less.

W: What about Bluetooth connectivity? With it, you can connect your purifier to your smartphone to check the air quality.

M: I don't think I'll be using that feature very often, so _____ _____ _____ _____.

W: Then, that leaves us with two models. Do you want one with a two-filter system or three?

M: I definitely want one with as many filters as possible.

W: Then, this is the model you're looking for.

M: Great. I'll take it.

11

M: Lisa, you weren't in class yesterday. Is everything okay?

W: Oh, hello. Mr. Katz. I _____ _____ _____ _____ _____ _____ _____ all day yesterday.

M: I hope you're feeling better now. Did you go see a doctor?

W: (Not yet. I'm going to the doctor's office after school.)

12

W: The next person in line. *[Pause]* May I help you, sir?

M: Yes. I _____ _____ _____ _____ _____ _____ _____ at your bank.

W: Great. May I see some identification?

M: (No problem. Let me give you my driver's license.)

13

[Cell phone rings.]

M: What's up, Katrina?

W: Hi, Mark. I'm just calling to see how your new blog is doing.

M: It's going okay, I guess. I'm getting about 100 visitors per day.

W: That's a good start.

M: Yeah, but it's been three months and I thought that I'd be attracting a lot more people by now.

W: Well, _____ _____ _____ _____ _____ _____ _____ some advice?

M: Not at all. In fact, _____ _____ _____ _____ .

W: I think the focus of your blog is too broad. You deal with too many different topics.

M: I thought that would attract a wide audience.

W: Maybe at the beginning, but you need to develop a clear identity for your blog _____ _____ _____ _____ _____ _____ .

M: So you are saying that I _____ _____ _____ _____ _____ of my blog.

W: (Exactly. That way your blog can be an authority on that subject.)

14

M: What are you listening to, Josephine?

W: Oh, this is True Boys' new single. It just came out today.

M: It sounds awesome. What's the name of the song?

W: It's called, "No More Lies." It's number one on the charts now.

M: It's a really catchy song. _____ _____ _____ _____ _____ .

W: Yeah. I can't wait to go to their concert next month.

M: How did you get tickets for the concert? I heard the tickets _____ _____ _____ .

W: I was really lucky. I went online _____ _____ _____ _____ _____ _____ and was able to get two tickets.

M: Wow, lucky you! What I wouldn't give to go to that concert!

W: Really? Well, I don't have anyone to go with yet. Will you go with me?

M: (Unbelievable! I can't thank you enough.)

15

M: John is a freshman in high school. He loves playing basketball and wants to play for the school basketball team. The basketball team _____ _____ _____ _____ _____ _____ . John, however, gets really nervous when other people are watching him and doesn't play well. He is very worried and decides to ask Matthew, a sophomore on the school basketball team for advice. After listening to John's dilemma, Matthew realizes that John's problem is _____ _____ _____ _____ . He wants to _____ _____ _____ _____ _____ _____ _____ that no one is watching him during the tryouts and play _____ _____ _____ _____ _____ on the court. In this situation, what would Matthew say to John?

16-17

W: Hello, students. I hope you enjoyed our last lecture on the different color perceptions according to gender. Today, we will talk about some facts _____ _____ _____ _____ _____ _____ .

First, do you know what the most popular color around the world is? It's blue. According to a recent survey, over 40% of people around the world chose it as their favorite color. Next, what is the first color most babies see? The answer is red. Babies, as young as two-weeks old, can see the color red. Here is a question for potential car buyers. What color car _____ _____ _____ _____ _____ a serious accident? If you guessed white, you would be correct. It is the most visible color _____ _____ _____ _____ _____ . Finally, what color is the most relaxing and soothing? In fact, many prisons are painted in this color to reduce the aggressiveness of its prisoners. This relaxing color is pink. Interesting, isn't it? Now, let's look at some photographs with these colors.

녹음을 다시 한 번 들으면서, 빈칸을 채워 봅시다.

01

W: Good morning, and welcome to Housework News. Our top story today is brought to you by our new sponsor, Wave laundry detergent. Wave uses micro-oxygen bubble capsules _____ _____ _____ _____ _____ _____ _____ you'll ever get. Wave's new patented formula will _____ _____ _____ _____ and your darks darker. The new formula is designed to be more concentrated, so you can use less and still have fresh, clean laundry. Wave _____ _____ _____ _____ _____ _____ _____ to fit all your washing needs. You can find Wave in the household cleaning aisle in your local grocery stores. Go to the Housework News website to print out a 10% discount coupon redeemable during check out.

02

M: Hi, Julie. How have you been?
W: Hey, Dan. I've been great. I saw that new movie everyone is talking about.
M: Is that the one about the superheroes?
W: Yeah, it's quite good. There's a lot more to it _____ _____ _____ _____ _____.
M: What do you mean?
W: The plot was well-planned, and the character development was great.
M: I'm _____ _____ _____ _____.
W: Why is that?
M: I think Hollywood producers know they have a sure thing with superhero movies, so they just keep making them.
W: Are you saying that there is _____ _____ _____ _____ _____ these days?

M: Yeah, it seems that most of the movies have something to do with superheroes.
W: You could have a point.

03

W: Mr. Holiday, would you mind taking a look at this?
M: Okay, but I have to warn you that I don't know much about cars.
W: No problem. If you look here, you can see that _____ _____ _____ _____ _____ _____ _____.
M: Does this mean that I should have them changed?
W: In my professional opinion, you should change them now.
M: Is it possible to _____ _____ _____ _____ _____ _____?
W: That depends on how much driving you do from now until then.
M: I don't plan to do all that much driving.
W: If that's the case, I'd say you could wait until next time. But, if you _____ _____ _____ _____ _____, you need to get them changed right away.
M: Alright, thanks.

04

W: Harry, did you finish arranging the living room?
M: Yes, Marge. Come take a look.
W: Wow! I like the way you put the three-person couch in the middle of the room against the wall.
M: Thanks. What do you think about where I put _____ _____ _____ _____ _____ _____ _____?
W: It looks great right above the couch.
M: Good. I put the _____ _____ _____ _____ _____ _____ _____ so you can read there.

W: That's so thoughtful of you. Oh, you put the
   nightstand on the other side of the couch.
M: Yeah. And I put your books in there.
W: Why did you _____ _____ _____ _____
   _____ in front of the couch?
M: I thought it made the room cozier.
W: Okay. I can't wait to invite our friends and family.
M: Me neither.

05

W: Barry, I'm off to _____ _____ _____.
M: Okay, Lisa. What sort of errands?
W: First, I'm going to the cleaners to pick up the dress I
   dropped off last week.
M: I hope they were able to get that coffee stain out.
   Where's your next stop?
W: I'm going to _____ _____ _____ _____ _____
   and pick up some steaks for dinner.
M: That sounds great! You grill the best steaks.
W: After the meat market, I need to _____ _____
   _____ _____ _____ and pick up some envelopes.
M: Is that your last stop?
W: No, I also have to mail some letters at the post office.
M: Sounds like you're going to be busy.
W: Is there anything you need while I'm out?
M: Can you _____ _____ _____ _____ _____
   from the mailbox?
W: Sure thing.

06

M: Welcome to Mohegan Airlines. My name is Frank.
   How may I help you?
W: I'd like a ticket to Crater Lake, please.
M: Okay, that will be $300. _____ _____ _____
   _____ _____ _____?
W: I'd rather fly direct. How much would that be?
M: That would be an additional $100.
W: Oh, that seems expensive. _____ _____ _____
   _____. Also, I'd like to have a vegetarian course for

my in-flight meal.
M: That will be an extra $5.
W: Is it possible to reserve an aisle seat as well?
M: I can do that for you here. Will you be checking in
   any luggage?
W: Yes, I have three suitcases.
M: We _____ _____ _____ _____ _____
   _____, but I'll have to _____ _____ _____
   _____ for the third.
W: That's fine. What's the total for all of this?

07

M: Hi, Allison. What are you watching?
W: Hey, Danny. It's a video clip _____ _____ _____
   _____ _____ _____ _____.
M: Are you planning on cooking one for your husband's
   birthday?
W: No, that was last month. We went out to eat at a
   fancy steakhouse.
M: Did you go to that place I recommended?
W: Yeah, the one you talked about when we were at your
   sister's graduation.
M: So is the video _____ _____ _____ _____
   _____ _____?
W: Not exactly. I won't be making this for my husband.
M: So, why are you watching the video?
W: _____ _____ _____ _____ _____ _____
   _____, and I want to do something special for
   them.
M: That's sweet of you.
W: I hope I don't mess up.
M: Don't worry. You'll do just fine.

08

W: Tim, did you see the flyer for the Summer Seminar?

M: Yeah, Jane. I saw it in the break room.

W: It says we have to _____ _____ _____ _____ _____ _____ _____ .

M: I know. I can't believe I have to give up a Saturday for this.

W: It's not all bad. I'm _____ _____ _____ _____ _____ _____ .

M: That's true. I had fun doing those last year. I especially enjoyed the tug-of-war.

W: The flyer also mentioned that we _____ _____ _____ _____ .

M: Right. We are supposed to go hiking this year.

W: Did the flyer say where we should meet?

M: Yes, _____ _____ _____ _____ _____ _____ , at 9 a.m.

W: How long will the seminar take?

M: I'm not really sure. It doesn't say.

09

M: Good afternoon, podcast listeners. You're listening to Tiny Paws, a podcast that's made for pets and pet owners. I'm your host Gary. Today, I'd like to share with you information about an upcoming gathering _____ _____ _____ _____ _____ . Working with animal shelters and the Veterans Association, the Pets for Vets gathering aims to match homeless cats and dogs with retired service members. Renowned cat trainer, Eddie Cats, will give a short _____ _____ _____ _____ _____ . Also, you and your pet will be able to participate in a Best Trick competition. First prize is _____ _____ _____ _____ _____ _____ . Pets for Vets lasts until the end of the weekend. Please stop by and lend us your support.

10

M: Tina, take a look at this outdoor products catalogue.

W: Look at all the new tents! Should we get one?

M: I was thinking the same thing. Okay, first what's our price range?

W: Let's _____ _____ _____ _____ _____ _____ .

M: Okay. I saw several on the last page that are reasonable.

W: How many people do you think the tent should fit?

M: _____ _____ _____ _____ _____ _____ , especially with our two dogs.

W: These three can fit up to four people.

M: How about the shape? Do you want it a dome or a pyramid?

W: _____ _____ _____ _____ _____ . It feels roomier.

M: Okay, we're down to these two tents.

W: Do you think we need more than one door for the tent?

M: No. I think one is good enough. Let's get this one.

11

[Cell phone rings.]

M: Good afternoon, Ms. Watson. I'm calling to remind you of your appointment tomorrow.

W: I'm glad you called. I'm afraid I need to reschedule my appointment.

M: Not a problem. _____ _____ _____ _____ _____ _____ . Is that okay?

W: (Yes. How does Thursday afternoon sound?)

12

W: Ted, what are you reading so intently?

M: A new mystery novel written by Steven King. It's really interesting.

W: Oh, Steven King is my favorite mystery writer. Can I _____ _____ _____ _____ _____ ?

M: (Of course! I'm sure you'll enjoy it.)

13

W: Look, Dad! It's a new roller coaster.

M: It sure is big, Mia.

W: Can we go on it please?

M: I think we should wait an hour or so before riding it. We just had lunch.

W: Okay, you're right. I don't want to get sick.

M: How about walking over to Monkey Mania Land and seeing if _____ _____ _____ _____ _____ _____ _____?

W: That sounds great. But, before we do that, can we _____ _____ _____ _____ _____? I want to get Mom something nice since she couldn't come with us today.

M: Great idea, Mia. Your mom will be happy that you thought of her.

W: Oh! I think I _____ _____ _____ _____ at the restaurant.

M: Oh, dear. We'd better go back to the restaurant.

W: I hope it's not gone.

M: (Don't worry. I'm sure it's still there.)

14

[Cell phone rings.]

M: Hey, Sue! It's Lucas. Are you ready to enjoy the concert tonight?

W: Oh no! I completely forgot. I don't think I can make it.

M: That's too bad. The bands are going to be amazing. How come you can't go?

W: My parents are coming into town today and they want to have dinner together.

M: Okay, I guess _____ _____ _____ _____. I know how close you are to your family.

W: Why don't you take that girl you met at the coffee shop? She seemed nice.

M: Do you think _____ _____ _____ _____ if I asked?

W: _____ _____ _____ _____ _____ _____. Besides, who wouldn't want to go see this show?

M: You have a point.

W: What do you have to lose?

M: Okay. _____ _____ _____ _____ _____ _____ _____?

W: (Just be yourself and don't overthink it.)

15

W: Jimmy and Sunny are co-owners of a bookstore in their local town. Recently, Jimmy has noticed that a lot of new customers are buying books written by _____ _____. However, Sunny firmly believes that _____ _____ _____ _____ _____ _____ _____. So Sunny wants to stock even more classics. Jimmy and Sunny have to plan a new budget for the books they'll be purchasing over the next year. Jimmy thinks that this is a good time to discuss a way to improve their business. Jimmy wants Sunny to consider _____ _____ _____ _____ _____ _____ _____ _____, to increase sales. In this situation, what would Jimmy most likely say to Sunny?

16-17

M: Hello, you fellow bikers. Welcome back to our channel, Spinning Dreams. Last week, we talked about the advantage of hybrid bikes. Today, I want to tell you about _____ _____ _____ _____, the Phantom G. The Phantom G _____ _____ _____ _____, _____ _____ _____. With a carbon fiber body, the Phantom G weighs in at a reasonable 6.8kg. This light body will have you climbing hills with ease and comfort. Speaking of comfort, the Phantom G comes with an extra-wide seat with a memory foam cushion to make your ride more pleasant. Also a brand-new drive-train is included. Each part of this drive-train is made with precision to make sure you are able to shift gear smoothly and confidently. The Phantom G also comes with puncture resistant 28-inch wheels. Each bike _____ _____ _____ _____ _____ _____ _____. If you're thinking of getting a hybrid bike this year, this is one of the best choices.

녹음을 다시 한 번 들으면서, 빈칸을 채워 봅시다.

01

M: Good afternoon, listeners of Classics for You. This is Nathan Lang. Thank you very much for joining us today. I am very happy to announce that Lisa Donovan will be _____ _____ _____ _____ _____ _____ starting next Monday. As a radio announcer, musician, and arts educator, Lisa Donovan has a wide experience in classical broadcasting. Also, her soft voice and friendly style will _____ _____ _____ _____ _____ _____ Classics for You. Together with Lisa Donovan, Classics for You will continue to help you learn about classical music and have fun, too! If you want to send her a welcome message, _____ _____ _____ _____ _____ at 902-420-2004. We'll be looking forward to your messages!

02

W: Hello, Adam. How are you _____ _____ _____ _____ _____ _____?

M: Hello, Ms. Nam. I'm doing okay. But, I miss my old friends and sometimes feel lonely.

W: I understand. Transferring schools can be quite stressful. Have you made any new friends?

M: Not yet.

W: Well, I think _____ _____ _____ _____ _____ _____ _____ to school better.

M: Do you think so?

W: Sure. If you _____ _____ _____ _____ , school life will become more fun.

M: I guess you're right.

W: Why don't you join one of the student clubs?

M: The student clubs?

W: Yes. Joining a club is a good way to meet new people. And since you like art, you could try joining the cartoon club.

M: That sounds fun. Thank you for your advice.

W: No problem.

03

[Cell phone rings.]

W: Hello?

M: Hello, Ms. Peters. This is Mr. Bales. I heard _____ _____ _____ _____ _____ . Are you all right?

W: Unfortunately, Mr. Bales, my right ankle is broken.

M: Oh, I'm sorry to hear that.

W: The doctor says I need surgery. I'll have to stay at the hospital for about a week.

M: I see. I'll go ahead and _____ _____ _____ _____ _____ _____ _____ your classes.

W: Thank you. Would you ask him to collect the science experiment reports?

M: Of course.

W: And please ask him to put away the experiment equipment.

M: Okay. Is there anything else I can do for you _____ _____ _____ _____ _____ _____ ?

W: No, that's all for now. Thank you very much.

M: You're welcome. Take care and get well soon.

04

M: Honey, take a look at this. It's the new indoor playground opening this weekend.

W: It looks great! Is that a figure of a giraffe on the left corner? It's gigantic!

M: Yes, it looks so real. And look at _____ _____ _____ _____ _____ _____ . It's shaped like an elephant.

W: That's cute. I guess the theme of this place is animals.

M: I guess so. They even have _____ _____ _____ _____ _____ on the ceiling.

W: I like the rock climbing wall shaped like a monkey on the left.

M: Me, too.

W: I can already imagine Mark climbing all over that wall.

M: And look at that _____ _____ _____ _____ _____ _____. Jessie will have a blast in it.

W: Shall we take our kids here this weekend?

M: Sure. I'm sure they'll love it.

05

W: Justin, do you know you can _____ _____ _____ _____ _____ _____?

M: What do you mean?

W: I just wrote a happy birthday message for Mom, but it will be sent later, at midnight.

M: That's convenient! How did you do it?

W: I used an app called Message Scheduler. Do you want me to _____ _____ _____ _____ _____, too?

M: That's okay. I can do that. [Pause] There. It's downloaded.

W: Now you _____ _____ _____ _____ and simply enter the time and date you want.

M: Got it. [Pause] I've written the message, but where do I enter the time and date?

W: Can't you see a blue button on the bottom?

M: No.

W: Maybe you _____ _____ _____ _____ _____ _____.

M: I'm not sure how to do that. Could you help me?

W: Sure.

06

W: Good afternoon. How can I help you?

M: Hello. I'm looking for a rash guard for my daughter. She's seven.

W: Certainly. Come this way, please. _____ _____ _____ _____ _____ and the short-sleeved ones are $20.

M: We'll be swimming outside, so I'll take one long-sleeved rash guard.

W: Okay. We have a special promotion now. If you spend $50 or more, you _____ _____ _____ _____ _____.

M: Great! I also wanted to buy her a pair of aqua shoes. Do you have any?

W: Sure. _____ _____ _____ _____.

M: I'll get one pair in size 12.

W: All right. Do you need anything else?

M: No, that's all.

W: So, one rash guard and _____ _____ _____ _____ _____. After the discount, this is the final price.

M: Okay. I'll pay with my credit card.

07

M: Hey, Lucy. Guess what? I got two tickets for the new musical, *Aladdin*.

W: Really? Didn't you say that all the tickets sold out on the first day?

M: Actually, my parents gave them to me. They can't go because they have to go to their friend's wedding.

W: Lucky you!

M: Do you want to go with me? There's even an opportunity _____ _____ _____ _____ _____ after the show.

W: Sure! When is it?

M: It's next Friday, at 6 p.m.

W: Sorry, I _____ _____ _____ _____ _____.

M: Why not? Do you have dance practice?

W: No, dance practice finished last week.

M: Then, why can't you go?

W: I'm _____ _____ _____ _____ _____ _____. They're having an audition next Friday evening.

M: I see. Well, _____ _____ _____ _____ _____!

W: Thanks. Let's go together another time.

08

W: Tony, are you going to Eco-Friendly Night?

M: Of course! _____ _____ _____ _____ _____ .
   It's this Saturday, right?

W: Yup, Saturday, December 10. And if you want to receive a free souvenir, you have to arrive before 5 p.m.

M: Got it. Do you know what souvenir they're giving out?

W: Well, according to the poster I have, they're _____ _____ _____ _____ _____ _____ _____ .

M: Wow! I guess they got a lot of donations this year.

W: That's right. More than 30 local stores and restaurants are sponsoring the event.

M: Awesome! Is it being held _____ _____ _____ _____ _____ _____ _____ ?

W: No. It's going to be held at Davis Elementary School.

M: Oh, that's really close to my home. I can walk there.

W: Great. I'll see you there, then.

09

W: Attention, residents of Cherrywood Apartments. This is _____ _____ _____ _____ _____ _____ _____ . Please be advised that on March 2nd and 3rd, there will be a fire alarm inspection of all the buildings, including the management office. This will be performed by _____ _____ _____ _____ _____ _____ _____ . During this inspection, alarms will be sounding from time to time, but please do not worry. We will also be using our master key to open each room in your unit, so you don't need to _____ _____ _____ _____ . If you have pets, please put them in your bedrooms. _____ _____ _____ _____ _____ _____ . With your help, we can get the required inspection done with the least inconvenience to you. We would like to thank you in advance for your help and understanding. Have a great day.

10

M: Mom, we need to buy a pet carrier to take Jack on the plane.

W: Right. Let me see the choices. How tall is Jack?

M: He is 29 cm tall.

W: The carrier should _____ _____ _____ _____ _____ _____ _____ . That rules this one out.

M: What about a shoulder strap? It's probably easier to carry Jack with it.

W: I don't think so. It may be unstable for him.

M: Okay. What about ventilation slots? These narrow holes help air flow inside the carrier.

W: Being inside for a long time will be stuffy, so there should _____ _____ _____ _____ _____ _____ _____ _____ .

M: I agree.

W: Also, I don't want Jack to get out of it by any chance. We need a strong door.

M: Right. I think _____ _____ _____ _____ _____ _____ .

W: Good. Let's buy this one.

11

M: Jenny, have you decided to join the school choir?

W: Not yet. I like singing, but I'm a bit shy of _____ _____ _____ _____ _____ _____ .

M: Well, they're having a mini performance tomorrow. Why don't we go see it together before you decide?

W: (Okay. I'll go with you and see what it's like.)

12

W: Dad, look at these pictures. They're from _____ _____ _____ _____ _____ _____ with Grandma.

M: They're really nice! I think Grandma would love to see them, too.

W: I want to print them out and make a photo album for her. Can I use your color printer?

M: (No, I'm afraid you can't. We're out of ink right now.)

13

M: Jasmine, have you finished packing for the summer camp next week?

W: Not yet. Have you?

M: Almost. I just need to _____ _____ _____ _____, and then I'm done.

W: Insect repellent? What for?

M: The place we're going to is near a lake, so there will be lots of mosquitoes.

W: I see. _____ _____ _____ _____ _____ _____.

M: That's right. And they can also spread diseases like malaria and the Zika virus.

W: That sounds scary. So, how can I avoid getting mosquito bites?

M: Well, one of the most effective ways is to _____ _____ _____ _____ _____ _____ _____.

W: In that case, I should buy some as well. Do you know where I can buy some?

M: You can buy them _____ _____ _____ _____ _____ _____.

W: (All right. I'll go to the pharmacy after school and get one.)

14

M: Hello, Ms. Sanders. Do you have a minute?

W: Yes. What's up, Kevin?

M: I want to _____ _____ _____ _____ _____ _____ _____ during the summer vacation.

W: Great. Do you _____ _____ _____ _____ _____?

M: I love animals, so I want to volunteer at the animal hospital.

W: Let's see. *[Pause.]* We have one spot available.

M: That's great!

W: It says they want someone who has experience raising a pet. Have you ever had a pet before?

M: No. Does that mean I can't volunteer there?

W: I'm afraid so. Why don't we look for another program? Is there anything else you're interested in?

M: Well, I guess I'm also interested in _____ _____ _____ _____.

W: Perfect. We _____ _____ _____ _____ the school library. I can sign you up right now.

M: (Thank you. Then, I'll volunteer at the school library.)

15

M: Emma has been good friends with Janice and Fiona since elementary school. She spends most of her free time hanging out with them. However, Janice and Fiona _____ _____ _____ _____ while working on an art project and _____ _____ _____ _____. They need to get together to finish the art project, which is due in one week, but Janice refuses to come to the meeting if Fiona is there. Furthermore, Janice is still very emotional and tells Emma bad things about Fiona. However, Emma thinks Janice also hurt Fiona's feelings and _____ _____ _____ _____ _____. She thinks if Janice calms down and talks to Fiona, they'll _____ _____ _____ _____ _____ _____. In this situation, what would Emma most likely say to Janice?

16-17

W: Good morning, students. Previously, we learned about some interesting English expressions that feature animals. Today, we'll talk about some commonly used idioms that are _____ _____ _____ _____ _____ _____. First, let's look at an expression related to the head. If you say something "off the top of your head," it means that you say it _____ _____ _____ _____ _____. Another phrase using a body part is "play it by ear." When someone says they "played it by ear," it means that they improvised or did something without preparation. There's also _____ _____ _____ _____ _____ _____. When someone says, "You're a sight for sore eyes," it means they are very happy to see you. Lastly, there is _____ _____ _____ _____ _____ _____. When someone says they "have cold feet" right before a big event, it means they are very nervous. Now, let's watch a short video about how these idioms are used in real-life situations.

녹음을 다시 한 번 들으면서, 빈칸을 채워 봅시다.

01

M: Welcome to the leadership seminar! I'm Russell Smith. I'm _____ _____ _____ _____ _____ _____ today. These days, it can be difficult to find skillful and experienced workers in some fields. So, how about hiring "silver workers?" They are senior citizens, people in their sixties and seventies. Many customers feel comfortable with silver workers. They are often kinder than younger workers. Also, they can _____ _____ _____ _____ _____ _____ at work. In fact, a major theater hired dozens of silver workers as ushers last year and the customer satisfaction index improved considerably. Why don't you join this trend and _____ _____ _____ _____ _____? Thank you.

02

M: Jasmine, _____ _____ _____ _____ _____ _____ _____ _____?
W: Sure, I learned about them at school. They mean reading, writing, and arithmetic, right?
M: Well.... You're right, but I'm talking about the Three Rs for the environment.
W: Oh, I got it. You want to talk about _____ _____ _____ _____ _____ to help the environment.
M: Right, but you missed the most important thing.
W: What's that?
M: Well, we produce a lot of waste every day. This waste is a big problem for the environment. So we should reduce waste.
W: _____ _____ _____ _____.
M: Nowadays, the Three R movement is spreading throughout the world. And I think _____ _____ _____ _____.

W: I see your point. I hope that we can conserve resources through the movement.

03

W: Thank you for checking my shop.
M: Not at all. Well, I have a few safety issues to talk to you about.
W: What are they?
M: Above all, you should remove the boxes in front of the fire exit.
W: Oh, I'm sorry. I'll _____ _____ _____ _____.
M: There should not be anything blocking the exits _____ _____ _____ _____ _____.
W: I see. I'll keep that in mind.
M: And remove the dirt on the exit signs above the doors, so that they can be easily seen from a distance.
W: Yes, I will do that today.
M: Finally, I wonder when your employees last received education about fire safety.
W: Last week. We give the training _____ _____ _____ _____.
M: Good. Then, the check-up is finished. Please sign here.

04

M: Emily, what did you do last Sunday?
W: Don't ask. I was very busy because my nephews came to visit. This is a picture I took of them.
M: Oh, there are many children playing in the living room.
W: Yes. Can you _____ _____ _____ _____ _____ _____ _____? That's Scott.
M: He's wearing a baseball cap. So cute. Your child, Paula is playing with blocks on the desk.

W: Right. She likes them. My husband is mopping the floor. _____ _____ _____ _____ _____ _____.

M: He looks tired. Who is the boy playing the piano?

W: That's my nephew, Kevin. He loves playing the piano.

M: Oh my goodness! In the middle of the picture, a boy is drawing a picture on the mat.

W: That's Russell. He draws wherever he can.

M: I see. _____ _____ _____ _____ _____ _____ today.

05

M: Jessica, what are you doing?

W: Oh, Clay. I'm preparing for the camping trip this weekend with my friends.

M: Sounds great. Where are you going?

W: We are going to Lake Mountains. I'm really looking forward to the outdoor barbecue.

M: Sounds wonderful. My family _____ _____ _____ _____ _____ _____ _____ there last month.

W: Oh, so you have been there?

M: Sure. It's one of my favorite places. I will never forget sleeping in a sleeping bag and _____ _____ _____ _____ _____ _____.

W: So you have a sleeping bag?

M: Yes. I bought camping equipment _____ _____ _____ _____ _____ _____ _____ _____ last year.

W: _____ _____ _____ _____, can I borrow your sleeping bag?

M: No problem. Have a great trip and tell me all about it when you get back.

W: Thank you, Clay.

06

M: Excuse me. _____ _____ _____ _____ _____ ?

W: Not yet. I'm looking for a hoodie for this winter.

M: You've come to the right place. There are many kinds of hoodies here.

W: Hmm.... I like this striped one. How much is it?

M: You're in luck. It was originally $40, but it's _____ _____ _____ _____ _____ _____.

W: That's great, but it's still a little expensive.

M: Well, if you buy two of them, we can _____ _____ _____ _____ _____ _____ _____. Of course, the discount applies to the original price of $40.

W: But I can still get the first hoodie for the sale price, right?

M: That's correct.

W: Then do you have the same hoodie in a smaller size? My sister will like it.

M: Sure. Here you are.

W: Okay. I'll buy both of them.

M: Wonderful. _____ _____ _____ _____ _____ over there.

07

[Cell phone rings.]

W: Hi, Ted.

M: Rachel, I heard you caught a cold. How do you feel?

W: Thanks for asking. I got over it. I'm fine now.

M: Good to hear that. Anyway, I'm calling to _____ _____ _____ _____ _____ _____ _____ _____ this weekend.

W: I'd love to, but I can't.

M: Oh, _____ _____ _____. Well, if you're worried about the presentation on Monday, I can give you a hand.

W: That's not why I can't come. I can prepare for it myself.

M: Then, are you _____ _____ _____ _____ _____ this weekend?

W: No. Actually, my parents are moving to another city this weekend.

M: Really? So you have to _____ _____ _____ _____ _____.

W: Yeah. I'll probably have to be with them all weekend.

M: Sure, I understand. See you next time.

08

[Telephone rings.]

M: Hello, Ontario Sheep Farms. How can I help you?

W: Hi. I heard your farm _____ _____ _____ _____ _____ _____.

M: Yes, that's right. We have various events from 10 a.m. to 7 p.m. until Saturday.

W: Can you tell me what kind of events you're having?

M: Sure. We have _____ _____ _____ _____ _____ _____ _____ _____ _____, feeding sheep, and making cheese.

W: Oh, I think my children will like making cheese and shearing wool from sheep. _____ _____ _____ _____ _____ _____?

M: It's $10 for adults and $5 for children.

W: Okay. Is it easy to find your farm?

M: Sure. It's very easy. We're on Malcolm Road, just off Exit 72.

W: Oh, yes. I think I know where you are. We'll visit you tomorrow.

M: Good. See you then.

09

W: Hello, students. This is Jennifer Parker and I'm _____ _____ _____ the Auburn Student Council Election. This year's election _____ _____ _____ _____ on October 7th and 8th. Candidate nominations must be finished _____ _____ _____ _____ _____ _____ _____. All Auburn students can nominate other students for Student Council leadership positions. Self-nomination is not possible. Nominated students are automatically notified of their nominations by email. They _____ _____ _____ _____ _____ _____ by submitting a candidate statement through the school website. The newly elected candidates will work with the current Student Council leaders to become familiar with the general Student Council procedures. New Student Council leaders will take office on January 21st. We encourage all of you to participate in the election process whether as a candidate or a voter. Thank you.

10

W: Eric, have you finished preparing for the trip to Florida?

M: Yes, almost. I just need to choose a sunblock on this website. Could you help me out?

W: Sure. What kind of protection are you looking for in terms of SPF?

M: Well, I don't want extremely high SPF. I heard that products with an SPF of above 30 may be harmful for certain skin types.

W: Okay. Then what about the volume? _____ _____ _____ _____, right?

M: But it would be inconvenient for me to carry a big-sized product in my backpack. I don't want one above 80 ml.

W: I see. How much are you looking to spend?

M: I can _____ _____ _____ _____. Now, there are only two options left, I think.

W: Oh, this product has a high SPF and _____ _____ _____ _____.

M: Yes, it looks perfect. I'll order it.

11

M: Mom, I'm going to Gina's house to discuss the next presentation now.

W: David, it's _____ _____ _____ _____ _____. It's only eight o'clock in the morning.

M: I know, but she told me to stop by at any time.

W: (No way. You'd better call her first before visiting her.)

12

W: Ted, we've almost reached our destination. It's been a long drive.

M: Right. I'm hungry, but I _____ _____ _____ _____ _____ _____ _____.

W: Me, neither. How about going to a drive-through restaurant?

M: (Good idea. Let's get some sandwiches and orange juice.)

13

M: Honey, how was your day? You look tired.

W: You have no idea. It was terrible.

M: What happened?

W: My co-worker, Julia _____ _____ _____ _____ a new project to the clients. But she _____ _____ _____ _____ _____ _____ _____ .

M: So, what did you do?

W: I had to do the presentation instead of her. I was very nervous.

M: But you _____ _____ _____ _____ _____ , right?

W: Yes. I tried to speak as clearly and slowly as I could.

M: Good for you. You're a great public speaker. I'm sure they understood what you said easily.

W: I hope so, but _____ _____ _____ _____ _____ _____ _____ .

M: (Don't be so harsh on yourself. I'm sure you did a good job.)

14

M: Excuse me, ma'am.

W: Yes, what can I do for you?

M: When I put my card through the machine, it says "Invalid Card."

W: Maybe you _____ _____ _____ _____ _____ _____ . May I see it?

M: Sure. Here it is.

W: Let me see. *[Pause]* Yes, _____ _____ _____ _____ _____ . Would you like me to renew it?

M: Yes, please. I want to check out this book for my assignment.

W: Well, here is your new library card. Oh, just a moment. It says _____ _____ _____ _____ _____ on your account.

M: Really? What book is that? I thought I had returned everything on time.

W: Hmm.... Did you take out a book called "Secret Garden?"

M: Ah, I forgot. I left that book in my school locker.

W: (In that case, you can check out the book when you return the overdue one.)

15

M: James likes to watch movies in his leisure time. This weekend, he plans to _____ _____ _____ _____ _____ _____ with his friend, Erin. They are supposed to watch the movie at 7 p.m., but Erin doesn't show up until some time later. She apologizes for her lateness and explains that _____ _____ _____ _____ _____ _____ . When James looks at the time, he realizes that the movie probably hasn't started yet _____ _____ _____ _____ _____ _____ . He thinks they still have enough time to buy tickets and catch the movie. So, he goes to the box office to buy the tickets although he knows they are late. In this situation, what would James most likely say to the clerk?

16-17

W: Good morning, everyone. Last week, we talked about teaching children responsibility through raising pets. Today, I'd like to talk about the _____ _____ _____ _____ _____ _____ . Just imagine the following situation. You come home after a hard day's work. You sit down on your sofa and pet your dog gently. How do you think you would feel? You would feel relaxed and your worries and tension would be relieved. In fact, many studies show that pets give us positive feelings such as constant companionship, love and affection. However, you _____ _____ _____ _____ _____ a specific type of pet. Just looking at fish in a bowl or even touching a pet snake can lower your anxiety level. Of course, if you have a young child, it could be _____ _____ _____ _____ _____ _____ like a guinea pig or a kitten. In a survey of pet owners, most of them reported mental health improvements from having pets in their lives. There are more things pets can give us than we might think. Thank you.

녹음을 다시 한 번 들으면서, 빈칸을 채워 봅시다.

01

M: Hi, everyone! This is your travel columnist, Michael Brown. Nowadays lots of young people want to take a trip somewhere whenever they have free time. But it's not easy to choose a destination and schedule that everyone in your travel party is happy with. Well, I have a simple solution. _____ _____ _____ _____ _____? Many people are afraid of traveling solo, but taking a solo trip can _____ _____ _____ _____ _____ _____. For example, you can experience complete freedom and independence by traveling alone. Whatever you eat, or wherever you go, it's _____ _____ _____ _____. You don't have to worry about anyone. Just take a solo trip when you have a chance! You won't regret it.

02

W: Honey, you don't look well. What's wrong?

M: Well, you know Jack in the marketing department? He _____ _____ _____ _____ _____ _____ during his medical checkup.

W: I'm sorry to hear that. Jack is one of your best friends, isn't he?

M: Right. Yesterday he _____ _____ _____ _____ for three months. He's really depressed now.

W: But you needn't worry too much. Liver cancer has _____ _____ _____ _____ _____ _____ _____ _____ when detected early.

M: Really? Is that true?

W: Absolutely! That's what most doctors say.

M: I really hope you're right.

W: Of course. Don't you remember Uncle Brian?

M: Ah, right. About two years ago, he was diagnosed with liver cancer.

W: Right. But now he's fully recovered, and he's healthier than ever.

03

W: Excuse me, I have a slight toothache. Do you have any painkillers?

M: Yes, we have aspirin. _____ _____ _____ _____ _____ you some?

W: Yes, please. By the way, _____ _____ _____ _____ _____ _____ to get to London?

M: About three more hours. We're supposed to arrive at Heathrow Airport at 11:30 a.m. local time.

W: We still have a long way to go.

M: Why don't you read _____ _____ _____ _____ _____ _____ _____?

W: Do you have mystery novels on board?

M: Yes, we do. We have mystery novels written by James Brown.

W: Oh, James Brown is my favorite author. Could you bring me one?

M: Certainly. I'll be back shortly with your aspirin and book.

W: Thank you.

M: My pleasure. I hope you enjoy the rest of the flight.

04

W: Daddy, look at the painting I drew.

M: What a lovely painting! What's the title?

W: *Animals in the Playground.*

M: You drew a turtle on the top of the slide in the middle. It looks cute.

W: I also drew a kangaroo wearing sunglasses at the bottom of the slide.

M: It _____ _____ _____ _____ _____.

W: What do you think about the elephant on the swing on the left?

M: Wonderful! Who could have imagined an elephant on a swing?

W: Well, my art teacher always tells me that I'm very creative.

M: Sure, you are. _____ _____ _____ _____ _____ the monkey playing in the sand on the right.

W: You know, I drew the monkey for you. It's your favorite animal.

M: Then you _____ _____ _____ _____ _____ playing with a ball next to the monkey for Mom.

W: That's right. Mom loves penguins.

05

M: Jessica, _____ _____ _____ _____ _____ _____ _____ this evening?

W: I'd love to, but I have to attend my club meeting at 6 o'clock.

M: Do you? Where is the meeting taking place?

W: At the Green Restaurant. Have you heard of it?

M: I've been there once. It's near City Hall, isn't it?

W: Right. _____ _____ _____ _____ _____ _____ _____ exactly? I've never been there.

M: Well, it's hard to explain in words. Instead, let me draw a map to the restaurant.

W: Really? I _____ _____ _____ _____.

M: My pleasure. Do you have a pen and a sheet of paper?

W: Yes, here you are.

M: I'm not the best artist but I'll do my best to draw you a map.

W: I _____ _____ _____ _____. You're a big help.

06

W: Excuse me. I'd like to rent a bike.

M: For a mountain bike, it's $5 an hour, and $20 a day.

W: How about a road bike?

M: It's $7 an hour, and $30 a day.

W: I'm going to cycle around the island. Which bike do you think is better?

M: Of course, the road bike. It's _____ _____ _____ _____ _____ _____.

W: I got it. I'll rent the road bike.

M: If you're going to cycle around the island, it will take at least three days.

W: I'm a slow biker. I think I have to rent it for four days.

M: Good choice! Then you can fully _____ _____ _____ _____ of the island.

W: I have a discount coupon from the tourist information center. Can I use it?

M: Yes, you can. With it, you can _____ _____ _____ _____ _____ _____ _____.

07

M: Stella! _____ _____ _____ _____ _____ in the singing contest.

W: Thank you. I got a brand-new tablet PC as a prize.

M: You're so lucky! Are you going to sell the tablet PC you have now?

W: Yes. Daniel, why don't you buy it? It _____ _____ _____ _____ _____ _____ _____ since I bought it.

M: And its design is so cool! How much are you going to sell it for?

W: I can sell it to you for just $200.

M: _____ _____ _____ _____ _____ on it?

W: Two years. It still has about a year and a half left.

M: Good. Its capacity is 64 gigabytes, right?

W: No. It has 32 gigabytes. But it's enough, I think.

M: Sorry, but I can't buy it. I have lots of data to store, so I need one with at least 64 gigabytes of memory.

W: I see. No problem.

08

M: Sunny, have you found an apartment to move into?

W: No. It's not easy to find a good one.

M: Then, how about moving into the Rainbow Apartment Complex? I heard there's an empty apartment there.

W: The Rainbow Apartment Complex? _____ _____ _____ _____ Gold Lake Park?

M: Right. The area is very quiet and peaceful. So you'll be able to live the tranquil life you want.

W: Good. Do you know _____ _____ _____ _____ _____ _____?

M: Yes. It's on the 15th floor. The view from the living room is really fantastic.

W: I'd love to see it. How about the monthly rent?

M: Don't be surprised. It's only $500.

W: Wow! That's really cheap. The monthly rent for a similar apartment elsewhere is at least $700.

M: You're right.

W: Oh, I _____ _____ _____ _____ _____ _____ _____ _____.

09

W: Hi, pet lovers. May I have your attention? I'm going to tell you about the Seattle Pet Fair. The fair is going to be held on May 1st, and it will last for three weeks. The location _____ _____ _____ _____ _____ _____ is the World Convention Center just like last year. More than 100 pet-related companies will take part in the fair, and they will exhibit various pet-related products and services for pet owners. About 200,000 people visited the fair last year, and this year, _____ _____ _____ _____ _____ _____. Unlike last year when the admission fee was free, it's $5 per person this year, and your admission fee _____ _____ _____ _____ _____ _____ _____.

10

M: Cindy, can you help me buy a washing machine?

W: Sure! First, you should decide on the manufacturer.

M: Well, I prefer Queen Electronics or Techno.

W: Good. I heard that Sun Star's washing machines aren't very good. They don't clean the laundry thoroughly.

M: How about the capacity? Do I need a washing machine with more than a 7 kg capacity?

W: Absolutely not! Since you're living alone, a 6 kg washing machine will be best.

M: I see. Then there are two washing machines that _____ _____ _____ _____ so far.

W: Right. _____ _____ _____ _____ _____, the cheaper one or the one with a longer warranty period?

M: Oh, I can't decide. _____ _____ _____ _____, _____ _____ _____ _____?

W: Of course I would take the one with the longer warranty period.

M: Okay, then _____ _____ _____ _____ _____.

11

M: Honey, you haven't forgotten that _____ _____ _____ _____ _____, have you?

W: Of course not. First, we have to clean the bathroom and the living room. Then, we have to organize the garage. It's too messy.

M: Okay. I'll take care of the garage after cleaning the bathroom.

W: (Good. Then I'll be in charge of the living room.)

12

W: Excuse me. I'd like some information about your swimming classes.

M: Sure. Which level are you interested in?

W: I'm _____ _____ _____ _____ _____ _____. How much is the monthly fee?

M: (It's $50 and it includes a personal locker.)

13

[Telephone rings.]

W: Front desk. How can I help you?

M: Hi, I'm staying in room 807. My room is too hot. Is there _____ _____ _____ _____ _____ _____?

W: Of course. You can lower the temperature with the air conditioner remote control.

M: Where is the remote control? I can't find it.

W: It's in the top drawer of the desk next to the television.

M: The top drawer of the desk.... Ah, I found it. Thank you for your help.

W: My pleasure. Is there _____ _____ _____ _____ _____ _____ _____?

M: One more thing. My notebook computer _____ _____ _____ _____ _____.

W: Really? Did you enter the password before connecting to it?

M: Yes, I did. I entered the password in the room manual. It's hotelmoon1997, isn't it?

W: That's right.

M: I think there is a problem in the Wi-Fi network in my room.

W: (Okay. I'll send someone to your room right away.)

14

M: Did you hear that the student union is going to hold a flea market next weekend?

W: No, I didn't. _____ _____ _____ _____ _____ _____ _____?

M: It's being held to help poor children in Africa.

W: That's a great cause. Is there anything I can do to help out?

M: Actually, there are two ways.

W: Two ways? What are they?

M: The first is to work as a volunteer, and _____ _____ _____ _____ _____ _____ _____.

W: I'd like to be a volunteer during the event.

M: Great! They can always use a helping hand.

W: How can I become a volunteer?

M: Go to the student union office and _____ _____ _____ _____ _____ _____.

W: Okay. Hey, why don't you volunteer with me?

M: (Actually, I already registered my name.)

15

M: Brian is a sophomore _____ _____ _____ _____ at Lincoln University, and he hears the news that the Korean Short Story Competition is going to be held by the Korean Embassy. He makes up his mind to _____ _____ _____ _____ _____ _____ and writes a short story in Korean. After a few weeks, he finishes writing the story. He thinks his story is well-organized and very unique. But he is worried that there may be grammatical errors because the competition evaluates _____ _____ _____ _____ _____ _____ in terms of Korean grammar, as well as how good the story is. So he visits Professor Kim, who specializes in Korean grammar. In this situation, what would Brian most likely say to Professor Kim?

16-17

W: Hi, everyone! I'm Amy Jang, the host of "Environment and Human Beings." Today I want to talk to you about electricity. You might know that some methods of producing electricity harm our environment. This means that _____ _____ _____ _____ _____, _____ _____ you can help the environment. So, I'm going to tell you how to save electricity at home. Turn off your computers when you are not using them. If it is too inconvenient to turn the computer off each time, you can just turn off the monitor. For washing machines, _____ _____ _____ _____ _____ _____ several times, do one big load of laundry to consume less electricity. To save electricity on your air conditioners, it is best to set the temperature at a moderate level, rather than at the lowest level. _____ _____ _____ _____ _____ _____ _____ as well. By saving electricity in the ways that I have mentioned, I hope that you will _____ _____ _____ _____ _____ _____ the environment.

녹음을 다시 한 번 들으면서, 빈칸을 채워 봅시다.

01

M: Good morning, students of Maple High School! As you all know, our school has been promoting the importance of eating breakfast. Every student should _____ _____ _____ _____ _____ _____ every day. Previously, we took a look at how students who eat breakfast are physically healthier and _____ _____ _____. Today, as a final project, we are _____ _____ _____ _____ _____ _____. For one week, free breakfast will be available for all students of Maple High School. Simply bring your student ID card and visit the student cafeteria from 7:30 a.m. to 8:20 a.m. We encourage you to eat some healthy food and start your school day with energy!

02

W: Sam, are you ready to visit the job experience center tomorrow?

M: Yes, Ms. Julie. I'm so excited!

W: Good! Have you decided on _____ _____ _____ _____ _____ _____ _____?

M: Not yet. I'm interested in so many jobs.

W: Remember that you can only choose three because of the time limit.

M: I know. What would you advise me to do?

W: Well, I think _____ _____ _____ _____ _____ _____ _____ _____ would help.

M: You mean like sports, medicine, and so on?

W: Yes. Then you can _____ _____ _____ _____ within that field. For example, in the sports field, there are athletic trainers, physical therapists, and so on.

M: That sounds like a good idea. I'll try doing that. Thank you.

W: I'm glad I could help.

03

W: Hello, Mr. Cane. What's the matter?

M: Thanks for coming _____ _____ _____ _____, Ms. Peg. Molly, one of our dolphins, is acting a little strange.

W: Can you be more specific?

M: _____ _____ _____ _____ _____ _____ now, and I have never seen her acting this aggressively.

W: I see. Has she been eating well?

M: No, not much.

W: Okay. May I take a look at her?

M: Of course. This way please.

W: [Pause] Hmm. Her stomach sounds funny. I'd like to run some tests. I'll _____ _____ _____ _____ _____ _____ tomorrow morning.

M: Thank you. Is there anything I should be mindful of?

W: I suggest you stop feeding her until after the tests.

M: All right. I'll do that. I hope she gets better soon.

04

M: Wow! They did an awesome job renovating the children's library!

W: The entrance to the story room is amazing! It looks like an open book!

M: Yes. And that tree-shaped bench makes me want to sit down and read.

W: I like those _____ _____ _____ _____. I heard they were donated by various authors.

M: That's nice of them.

W: I wonder what they're reading at the story room today.

M: I guess it's *The Ugly Duckling*.

W: How do you know that?

M: Can you see _____ _____ _____ _____ _____ _____ _____? There is a picture of a baby swan with some ducks.

W: I see. They also have *The Ugly Duckling* books
_____ _____ _____ _____ _____ _____ .

M: It's a great way to encourage kids to read books.

W: I agree. Let's take a look inside the story room.

05

M: Honey, what are you doing?

W: I'm packing some clothes and blankets I don't need
anymore.

M: Is it _____ _____ _____ _____ _____
already?

W: No. I'm going to send these to Fire Victims
Assistance Agency.

M: Oh, for the people who lost their homes due to the
forest fire?

W: Exactly. It said on the news that they are _____
_____ _____ _____ _____ .

M: That's good of you. Shall I pack some food from the
kitchen?

W: Thanks, but I already packed some canned food.

M: I see. Is there anything I can do to help?

W: Actually, can you _____ _____ _____ _____
_____ _____ ? Then I can finish packing and go to
the post office to send everything.

M: No problem.

06

W: Good afternoon. How can I help you?

M: Hello. I'm looking for a pencil sharpener for my son.

W: Certainly. These pencil sharpeners are popular with
young boys. _____ _____ _____ _____ _____
and the automatic ones are $25.

M: Do the automatic ones come in different colors?

W: I'm afraid we only have gray at the moment. The
manual ones have more choices. They come in
various animation character designs.

M: Oh, my son loves animation characters. I'll _____
_____ _____ _____ with the robot design.

W: Okay. We also _____ _____ _____ _____
_____ if you're interested.

M: That's cute. How much is it?

W: It's normally $10, but we have a special promotion
this week. You can _____ _____ _____ _____
_____ _____ .

M: Great! I'll buy it.

W: All right.

M: I'll pay in cash.

07

W: Hey, Peter. Is that the ad about the one-day cooking
class?

M: Yes, Audrey. Do you want to take one together?

W: You know I'm terrible at cooking.

M: Don't worry. There's a class for beginners, too.

W: In that case, I'd love to. Do I need to prepare
anything?

M: No. It says _____ _____ _____ _____
_____ _____ _____ _____ .

W: Great. When is the class?

M: It's next Thursday at 5 p.m.

W: Oh, I'm really busy next Thursday.

M: Oh, I forgot. You said _____ _____ _____
_____ _____ , right?

W: Yeah, but the appointment will finish before 4 p.m.
Actually, I'm supposed to _____ _____ _____
_____ _____ _____ after that.

M: I see. Well, have a good time, and let's try the cooking
class next time.

08

W: Hey, Jason. Do you want to go to the Book Festival with me?

M: The Book Festival? What's that?

W: It's _____ _____ _____ _____ where you get to meet many well-known authors and participate in various activities.

M: Sounds fun. When is it?

W: It's _____ _____ _____ _____ _____ to 5 p.m.

M: I'm free this Saturday. I'd love to join you. Where is it taking place?

W: _____ _____ _____ _____ _____ _____ _____ _____. Do you know how to get there?

M: Let me check. *[Pause.]* There's a bus near my apartment and it takes only 30 minutes.

W: Great! I'll meet you in front of the statue. And make sure you bring a bottle of water.

M: Okay. Can I bring some snacks, too?

W: No. They don't allow any food or drinks _____ _____ _____.

M: I see. See you this Saturday, then.

09

W: Attention, please. This is Janet from the Queens College Student Committee. I'm excited to announce that Multicultural Day will be held _____ _____ _____ _____ _____ _____ _____.

Multicultural Day is an opportunity to celebrate our diversity and appreciate the contributions of the various multicultural communities to our society.

_____ _____ _____ _____ _____ _____ _____ to encourage student participation in Multicultural Day. Special events include an art exhibition and dance performances from various different cultural communities. _____ _____ _____ _____ _____ _____ thanks to the donations from local shops and restaurants. Multicultural Day is _____ _____ _____ _____, so bring your friends and family. For more information, please contact Tim Cole at tcole@ queens.edu. We look forward to seeing you.

10

M: Good morning. How can I help you?

W: Hi, I'm trying to buy a camping table. Can you recommend some?

M: Sure. First, you should check the weight. The lighter the table, the easier it is to set up.

W: I guess I _____ _____ _____ _____ _____.

M: All right. Do you have any preference on the table top material? We have aluminum and wood.

W: I prefer something that is easy to clean.

M: Then I recommend _____ _____ _____ _____ _____ _____. We have some at reasonable prices.

W: Can you show me the ones that are under $40?

M: Of course. We have this one with two cup holders and that one without cup holders.

W: _____ _____ _____ _____ _____ _____.

M: Then this table is perfect for you.

W: Great. I'll buy it.

11

M: Penny, have you returned the books you borrowed from the library?

W: Not yet. I'm going to return them after school today.

M: In that case, can I _____ _____ _____ _____ _____ _____ _____ _____, too? I have to see Ms. Franklin right after class.

W: (Sure, I can do that for you.)

12

W: Good morning, welcome to Jenny's cafe. What would you like to order, sir?

M: Hello. I'd like a ham and cheese sandwich, please.

W: You can get a cup of coffee for just $1 more. _____ _____ _____ _____ _____ _____?

M: (That's okay. I don't need a drink.)

13

W: Hi, Ned. You don't look very happy today. _____ _____ _____ _____?

M: Well, Lilly _____ _____ _____ _____.

W: Lilly from your music club? I thought you two got along well.

M: We did. We were fine till this morning's practice.

W: What happened?

M: She _____ _____ _____ _____ _____ I made about her new shoes.

W: Really? What did you say?

M: She wore a bright yellow pair of sneakers and I told her they looked like bananas.

W: Ned, that's not very nice of you.

M: But it was just a joke! It's nothing to get upset about.

W: That's what you think. I can understand how it could have hurt her feelings.

M: Really?

W: Yes. Even if you meant it as a joke, I think _____ _____ _____ _____ _____ _____.

M: (All right. I'll apologize to her after school.)

14

W: What are you doing, Liam?

M: I'm thinking of going to the storybook illustration exhibit. I heard it's quite good.

W: The one at the City Art Center? I went there last Sunday.

M: Really? How was it?

W: It was great. There were amazing works from world-famous illustrators.

M: I _____ _____ _____ _____ _____ _____ for myself.

W: Are you planning to take your kids with you?

M: Yes. Do you think they'll like it?

W: Sure. My kids enjoyed it a lot. I especially recommend the family tour.

M: What's that?

W: One of the volunteers _____ _____ _____ _____ _____, and at the end of the tour, you get to participate in creating your own illustrations.

M: That sounds great! Do you know _____ _____ _____ _____ _____ _____ _____?

W: (Yes. You have to make a reservation at the information desk.)

15

W: George is a high school student who is interested in computer programming. He recently found out about a national computer programming competition. He wants to enter it, but he _____ _____ _____ _____ _____ _____ _____ _____. George asks Ms. Teresa, his homeroom teacher, for some advice. Ms. Teresa also thinks that this competition will be a good opportunity _____ _____ _____ _____ _____ _____. But, she also thinks that he should do his best at school. So she wants to suggest that George might ask his history teacher if he could _____ _____ _____ _____ _____ _____ _____. In this situation, what would Ms. Teresa most likely say to George?

16-17

M: Good afternoon. Previously, we discussed about how some animals use camouflage to increase their chances of survival. Today, we'll explore the kinds of camouflage different animal species have developed. First, some animals hide themselves against a background of the same color. For example, the color of the snowy owl is white. This helps it _____ _____ _____ _____ _____ _____ _____. Second, some animals have stripes or patterns that make it difficult _____ _____ _____ _____ _____ _____ from the background. The black and white stripes on zebras make it hard to single out one zebra from the herd. Third, some animals blend in with their surroundings by copying them. For example, the stick insect looks like a stick on a branch in order to hide from its predators. Last, some animals look like other dangerous or poisonous animals. The colors and patterns of the non-poisonous scarlet kingsnake can _____ _____ _____ _____ _____ _____ with other poisonous snakes. Now, let's take a look at some pictures of these animals.

녹음을 다시 한 번 들으면서, 빈칸을 채워 봅시다.

01

W: Good afternoon, Radio One listeners. I'm Patti Smith, and you're listening to Talk of the Town. Today, we'd like to _____ _____ _____ _____ _____ _____ from one of our sister stations. Repair Me is a podcast _____ _____ _____ _____ _____ _____ _____ _____ and how we can cope with it. Hosted by Steve Nicks, Repair Me offers insight into how our routines shape the way stress is managed. Each week a special guest is invited to discuss different ways that stress impacts our lives, and how to cope it. If this sounds like something for you, _____ _____ _____ _____ through your podcast app.

02

W: Honey, I'm worried about Joshua.

M: Joshua? What's wrong?

W: Do you think it's okay that _____ _____ _____ _____ _____ _____ _____?

M: What? He's only four years old.

W: But all the other kids at the kindergarten are beginning to read already.

M: You're overreacting. He'll learn to read when it's time.

W: How can you be so calm about this? What if he _____ _____ _____ _____?

M: Relax. I think there are _____ _____ _____ _____ _____ _____.

W: Benefits? Like what?

M: I think children who read later tend to be more creative.

W: You mean since they can't read the letters, they have to use their imagination more?

M: Exactly. So don't worry. Our kid is doing just fine.

03

W: Mr. Johnson, I enjoyed your talk.

M: Thank you, young lady. It was my pleasure _____ _____ _____ _____ _____ _____.

W: Do you have time to talk? I'd like to ask you a question.

M: Sure, I can spare a few minutes.

W: It's my dream to be a detective. _____ _____ _____ _____ _____?

M: That's a good question. I started by talking to my school guidance counselor.

W: _____ _____ _____. Is there anything else I can do?

M: You need to study various subjects. _____ _____ _____ _____ _____ for 10 years, I can tell you that you need mental abilities as well as physical ones.

W: Okay. I'll study harder from now on.

M: It sounds like you're well on your way. Maybe I'll be working for you one day.

W: Ha ha. I doubt that. Thanks for your time.

04

M: Mom, what's this photo?

W: It's a picture of the room I grew up in.

M: There's _____ _____ _____ _____ _____ in the middle like the one in my room.

W: That's the bed I shared with your aunt. I slept on the bottom bunk. That's my teddy bear _____ _____ _____ _____.

M: What's that to the left of the bed?

W: That's my old desk. On top of the desk is the lamp I used at night.

M: Is that _____ _____ _____ _____ _____ _____ _____ behind the desk?

W: Yes, it is. It was my childhood dream to go to space.

M: What's this in the middle of the room?

W: That's _____ _____ _____ your grandfather got at a yard sale.

M: I really like how your room looked, Mom.

05

M: Rachel, the taxi to the airport is coming in a couple of hours.

W: Okay, Dad. I just finished packing my suitcase.

M: Did you _____ _____ _____ _____ _____ _____?

W: Yeah, I got it. Have you seen the case for my glasses?

M: I think it's next to your bed on the nightstand.

W: Oh, here it is. I found it.

M: Did you make sure to _____ _____ _____ _____ _____ _____ _____ _____?

W: Oh! I almost forgot. What should I write?

M: It should say how many times _____ _____ _____ _____ _____ each day.

W: Yep. Do I need to write anything else?

M: Make sure to mention how long Toby's usual walks are.

W: I'll say that Toby likes to walk in the park, too.

M: That's a great idea.

W: Okay, _____ _____ _____ _____ _____ _____.

06

M: Good evening. How can I help you?

W: I'd like a room, please.

M: How many nights will you be staying with us?

W: Just one night.

M: _____ _____ _____ _____ _____ _____ _____ is $40. But since today is Friday, _____ _____ _____ _____. Will that be okay?

W: Sure. Do you offer any complimentary services?

M: We have a continental breakfast in the cafeteria from 6 to 10 a.m.

W: Great. I seem to have left some of my toiletries at home. Can I purchase some here?

M: _____ _____ _____ _____ _____ _____ _____ _____. So, I have you down for one night at the weekend rate, and one travel kit. Will there be anything else?

W: I have this 10% off coupon.

M: Alright. I can _____ _____ _____ _____ _____ _____ _____. Will that be cash or credit?

W: I'll pay with my credit card.

07

W: Hi, Danny. What are you reading?

M: Hey, Jenny. I'm reading *Crime and Punishment* by Fyodor Dostoevsky.

W: I had no idea you enjoyed reading the classics.

M: To be honest, I'm _____ _____ _____ _____ _____ _____ _____ _____. I prefer reading comics.

W: Then, are you reading for a class assignment?

M: No. Our class assignment was to read *Romeo and Juliet*. I finished that last week.

W: Is your mom making you read another one of her favorites?

M: No, she doesn't like this one. Actually, I _____ _____ _____ _____ _____ _____ _____ _____. So, the teacher told me if I read this, _____ _____ _____ _____ __ _____.

W: Good luck with the book.

M: Thanks. I need all the luck I can get.

W: Let me know how the book ends.

M: Sure. No problem.

08

M: Sweetheart, come take a look at this flyer.

W: Timmy's school is _____ _____ _____ _____ _____ _____ _____.

M: The school is going all out this time. They're holding a pie-eating contest for dads.

W: You do love your pies. Are you going to be able to _____ _____ _____ _____ _____ afterwards?

M: I'll certainly give it a try.

W: The other teams don't stand a chance. There's an arts and crafts activity for moms.

M: We'll all have to get to bed early this Friday since the jamboree begins at 9 a.m.

W: How much are the tickets this year?

M: Students get in for free, and _____ _____ _____ _____.

W: That's double what we paid last year.

M: Yeah. It's going to be a long day. The festivities _____ _____ _____ _____ _____ _____.

09

M: Good morning, everyone. This is Mr. Miller in the administration office. I would like to inform you of the new guidelines for using air conditioners in our school. Since there have been many classrooms with air conditioners left on after school, from today, all air conditioners _____ _____ _____ _____ _____ _____ _____ If you want to use the air conditioners after regular class hours, please let me know one day in advance. The air conditioner temperature is _____ _____ _____ _____ _____ _____ so you can't change it. Also, air conditioner filters are going to be replaced this Saturday so I am sorry to tell you that there _____ _____ _____ _____ _____ _____ that day at the gym. Thank you for your cooperation.

10

W: Rick, Action Sports is having a big sale this month.

M: Great! I need new hiking boots for my trip next week, Barbara.

W: Here. Take a look at the website.

M: Wow! They have a huge selection. Is there _____ _____ _____ _____?

W: Yeah. On the first page of the site. They have four pairs in your price range.

M: Also, I don't want them to be too heavy.

W: They have three pairs that are _____ _____ _____.

M: Are they waterproof?

W: Actually, these two are. You certainly _____ _____ _____ _____ _____.

M: Agreed. It can get pretty wet up in the mountains.

W: All that's left is the color.

M: _____ _____ _____ _____ _____ because of all the dirt and mud.

W: Right! You should get this one then.

11

M: Hi, I'd like to send this package to my daughter in Seoul, Korea by air.

W: Which service would you like? The standard service or the express service?

M: The express service, please. I'd like my daughter to get it _____ _____ _____ _____ _____.

W: (Fine. Please put your package on the scales.)

12

W: Dad, are we going to visit grandma this weekend?

M: I'm sorry dear, she's still on vacation in Hawaii.

W: _____ _____ _____ _____ _____ _____ her trip?

M: (She'll be back in a few days.)

13

W: Mike, this resort is amazing, isn't it?

M: It sure is, Sandy. A great place to spend our honeymoon.

W: So what should we do today?

M: I heard the resort offers a scuba diving tour. The water is supposed to be crystal clear.

W: I'm not sure that's a good idea. The forecast says _____ _____ _____ _____ _____ in the afternoon.

M: I really wanted to look at some exotic fish.

W: _____ _____ _____ _____ _____ _____ next to the resort. We can get the shuttle bus after lunch.

M: That's a great idea, Honey. I totally forgot about the aquarium.

W: Okay. _____ _____ _____. I'm getting a little hungry.

M: Not a problem. Do you _____ _____ _____, _____, _____ _____?

W: Yeah, they're on the coffee table.

M: (Okay, I'm ready. Let's go to lunch.)

14

[Cell phone rings.]

W: Hey, Jake? What's up?

M: Hi, Amy. I wanted to invite you to lunch this afternoon.

W: Oh dear. I'm afraid I can't join you for lunch. How about dinner instead?

M: _____ _____ _____! Where do you want to go?

W: I heard a new Italian restaurant just opened. People say it's really good.

M: I had Italian last night. How about our favorite sushi place?

W: Okay. Let's go there.

M: Great! I'll call ahead and _____ _____ _____ _____ _____ _____ tonight.

W: That sounds perfect. Do you _____ _____ _____ _____ _____ _____ _____?

M: A movie could be fun. Is there anything good playing these days?

W: There's a new romantic comedy that's been getting some good reviews.

M: Okay, you know how I love romantic comedies.

W: (I'll buy two tickets for 9:30 p.m.)

15

W: Gina and Charles are the owners of a popular cafe in the business district of downtown Chicago. Lately, Gina has noticed that _____ _____ _____ _____ _____ _____ _____ for the cafe to handle. She thinks it would _____ _____ _____ _____ _____ _____ _____ _____ with the rush. The new employee would handle the cash register while Gina and Charles make drinks for the customers. On the other hand, Charles thinks that purchasing a new espresso machine would solve the issue. A new espresso machine would allow for Charles and Gina to make double the drinks in half the time. Instead of hiring a new employee, Charles wants to ask Gina _____ _____ _____ _____ _____ _____. In this situation, what would Charles most likely say to Gina?

16-17

M: Good afternoon, developers. Today, I'm excited to talk about Antunes 3.0. As you all know, Antunes is a popular development kit for making apps. Using Antunes 3.0, developers will be able to _____ _____ _____ _____ _____ _____, thanks to new updates. First, Antunes 3.0 has a fast app building feature. Developers should expect to build their apps in half the time. Secondly, memory management has been improved so that the apps are smaller and lighter. Apps developed using Antunes 3.0 will give a 33% reduction in memory usage. Third, Antunes 3.0 comes with a new _____ _____ _____ _____ _____ _____ _____. The new AI, codenamed Terry, offers autocomplete suggestions. Finally, a new option gives developers the ability to view battery consumption. Developers will now be able to _____ _____ _____ _____ _____ _____ by their apps in real time. I will now demonstrate these key features.

녹음을 다시 한 번 들으면서, 빈칸을 채워 봅시다.

01

M: Good morning, Yorkhill Apartments residents. This Wednesday, the day after tomorrow, the _____ _____ _____ to your home will be temporarily _____ _____ _____ _____ an emergency boiler repair. As most of you are aware, we recently installed a new boiler system to save energy, but we have _____ _____ _____ _____ _____ _____ _____. The repair is expected to begin at 7 a.m. and be completed by 5 p.m. As soon as the repair is completed, hot water to your home will be restored. We apologize for this inconvenience and appreciate your understanding in this urgent matter. If you have any questions, please _____ _____ _____ _____ _____ us at 238-9500.

02

W: Hey, Nick. What are you doing?

M: Hey. I am _____ _____ _____ _____ _____ _____ _____ _____.

W: Oh, can I take a look? Wow! Seriously?

M: Why? Is something wrong?

W: Your schedule says you would sleep only for 4 hours a day for the next 3 weeks.

M: Yeah. You know I really need to get good grades this time.

W: But still! You're planning to skip lunch to study? Nick, I don't think this will work.

M: But it was you who advised me _____ _____ _____ _____ _____ _____.

W: I know. But the more important thing is, "Is your schedule realistic?"

M: You mean I should keep in mind _____ _____ _____ _____ _____.

W: That's right. Let's revise the plan. I will help you.

M: Thank you. It's very kind of you.

03

M: Excuse me, Ms. Clancy. Can I ask you about something?

W: Sure. What is it?

M: It's about the cover page of our magazine. Do you have any suggestions?

W: You know this issue is about the plastic island in the Pacific Ocean.

M: Yes. Do you _____ _____ _____ _____ _____ _____ _____ for the cover?

W: Hmm. I want _____ _____ _____ that will draw the readers' attention.

M: Then, how about putting two photos side by side that show the same area 10 years ago and now?

W: That sounds good. It'll also increase awareness about this issue.

M: Okay. Then I'll go there right away and take some pictures. But what about the photo from 10 years ago?

W: I'm sure we have it in our archives. I'll _____ _____ _____ _____ _____.

M: Okay. I'll send you the pictures as soon as I can.

W: Great. Have a safe trip.

04

[Cell phone rings.]

M: Hello.

W: Hello, Mr. Parker. This is Brooks Architecture. I sent you an interior sketch by email.

M: Yes, I am looking at it now.

W: Let me briefly explain. You wanted to change the attic into a cozy place for your children.

M: Yes, I like _____ _____ _____ _____ _____
_____ _____. This will make the room bright.

W: Right. Also there will be bookshelves on both sides
of the window.

M: My children will love reading books in _____
_____ _____ _____ _____ _____ _____. It
looks comfortable.

W: It also gives a cozy atmosphere. A round table will be
placed on the left side.

M: Good, but I think chairs with legs are more practical.

W: Yes, but since the ceiling is low, _____ _____
_____ _____ _____ _____ _____.

M: Okay, then. Let's keep them as they are.

W: I'm glad to hear that.

05

W: Honey, you know _____ _____ _____ _____
_____ _____ this weekend, right?

M: Of course. I've already sent messages to check how
many can come.

W: Did you? Thanks. What kind of food should we
serve?

M: How about pizza and spaghetti with our special
sauce?

W: Good idea. We already have _____ _____ _____
_____ from the last grocery shopping.

M: Then, do we have everything we need?

W: Well... I need to _____ _____ _____ _____
_____ _____.

M: Oh, I just got a message from Amy and Peter. They're
going to bring their children. That means we will have
8 guests total.

W: But we don't have enough plates for 8 guests.

M: I can go to the store and buy more plates.

W: That's okay. I'll pick some up when I shop for
napkins today. Instead, could you _____ _____
_____ _____ _____ from the attic? The children
will want to play them.

M: Okay, I will do that.

06

[Telephone rings.]

M: This is Summerhill Hotel. May I help you?

W: Yes, I would like to book a room for 2 adults for next
Monday.

M: Certainly. You have two options. A double room with
one queen-size bed or _____ _____ _____
_____ _____ _____ _____.

W: How much is each room per night?

M: The _____ _____ _____ _____ for one night.
The twin room costs $70.

W: I'd like to choose the latter one.

M: How many nights are you going to stay?

W: 3 nights.

M: You are in luck. We are running a special promotion
right now. If you _____ _____ _____ _____
_____ _____, your third night only costs $40.

W: Perfect! That would save us a lot of money.

M: Great. Lastly, would you like a room _____ _____
_____ _____? It only costs $10 extra per night.

W: No thanks. That won't be necessary.

07

W: Steve, what are you doing on your phone?

M: I'm checking this weekend's weather. It says it's going
to be sunny.

W: Right. You're visiting Jeju Island this weekend.

M: Actually, I _____ _____ _____ _____ _____.

W: Why? Was the plane ticket too expensive?

M: Not at all. It was a special promotion ticket.

W: Then it must be your school work. You said it was
going to take a lot of time.

M: Luckily, I _____ _____ _____ _____ _____
_____.

W: I don't understand. Why did you cancel your trip to
Jeju Island then?

M: I found out that the Silla Festival is taking place in
Gyeongju this weekend. It seemed interesting _____
_____ _____ _____ _____.

W: I hope you have a great time in Gyeongju.

08

W: Charlie. Look at this ad! The Amateur Chess Tournament is coming to town!

M: Oh, Let me see! I was really looking forward to it.

W: It's going to _____ _____ _____ _____ _____ _____ _____ at City Culture Hall.

M: Good. That's near here.

W: Are you going to participate in it?

M: No. I'm not that good. Besides, you have to be at least 20 years old _____ _____ _____ _____.

W: That's the adult league. You can enter the Junior league.

M: Hmm.... Do you really think I would do well?

W: Sure! You are the chess champion of our school. And if you win, you can _____ _____ _____ _____ _____ for the World Chess Tournament.

M: That would be incredible! Okay. I will do it.

W: _____ _____ _____.

09

W: Attention, students. This is Savina Jean, the school nurse. Today _____ _____ _____ _____ _____ _____ _____ _____. So I'm going to tell you what to do accordingly. Outdoor P.E. classes are cancelled. So if you have a P.E. class today, report to the indoor gym. Our school has air purifier systems so you don't need to _____ _____ _____ _____ _____. Please keep all windows closed. However, in the afternoon, please open the windows _____ _____ _____ _____ _____ _____.

Air purifier systems are working so you don't need to worry when opening the windows. Wash your hands often and gargle with warm water if your throat is sore. If you have itchy eyes, you can _____ _____ _____ at the nurse's office. Thank you for your attention. Have a healthy day.

10

W: Welcome to Camellia's Bakery. May I help you?

M: Yes, I'm looking for a cake for my child.

W: These are the most popular ones. What flavor does your child like? We have chocolate, cheese and fruit.

M: Well, he likes cheese and chocolate.

W: I see. Are you thinking of a specific shape?

M: Well, _____ _____ _____ _____ _____ _____. You know, children want their cakes to look nice and interesting.

W: Of course. What sort of _____ _____ _____ _____ _____ _____?

M: Well, I _____ _____ _____ _____ _____ _____.

W: Then you can choose from these two options.

M: Oh, I'd like the word, "Congratulations!" on the cake.

W: Then this is your only option. We cannot put writing on the other one because it will ruin the shape.

M: Okay, then, I'll take it.

11

W: Dad, you said someone at your work may be able to fix my laptop, right?

M: Yes, I can ask my colleague to take a look at it if he is not busy.

W: Then, _____ _____ _____ _____ _____ _____ tomorrow? It's getting slower and slower.

M: (Sure. It might take a couple of days to fix it.)

12

M: Stella, are you okay? I heard your car broke down on the road.

W: I'm fine, but my car isn't. _____ _____ _____ _____ _____ _____ _____.

M: Oh no. Do you need a ride for a while? You know I don't live very far from you.

W: (That's very kind of you. But I think I'll rent a car.)

13

M: Honey, I need your help over here! I'm in the bedroom.

W: Wow! What are you doing _____ _____ _____ _____?

M: I'm cleaning out the wardrobe. These are clothes that I don't wear anymore.

W: Hmm... what are you going to do with them?

M: I'll throw them away, of course.

W: They still look like they're in good condition, especially the suits. How about donating them to Open Closet?

M: Open Closet? I've never heard of it. Is it a charity?

W: Yes. It _____ _____ _____ _____ _____.

M: Why does it collect only formal clothes?

W: It _____ _____ _____ _____ _____ who cannot afford them for their job interviews.

M: Wow. That's a good idea. How can I give my clothes to the charity?

W: (You can enter our address on its homepage and it will send you a box.)

14

W: Jake, did you know that a new Mexican restaurant has opened on Maple Street?

M: Yes, one of my friends went there. He said the food was great.

W: I'm glad to hear that. It's my friend's restaurant.

M: Wow! _____ _____ _____ _____, she must be a talented cook.

W: How about going there for dinner? I haven't checked it out yet.

M: That sounds good. Let's take a gift _____ _____ _____ _____ _____ _____ _____.

W: Great idea. What kind of gift will be good?

M: How about a painting? She can hang it on the wall of the restaurant.

W: But _____ _____ _____ _____ _____ the decor?

M: Then, _____ _____ _____ _____ _____? She can put it inside or outside the restaurant.

W: That's a good idea! Do you know where to buy one?

M: (Sure. There is a plant shop on the way to Maple Street.)

15

W: Jason is a member of the school broadcasting club and he is very _____ _____ _____ _____ _____. He is in charge of recording school events. Whenever there is a project that requires making movie clips, it is natural for the club members to ask him to do it. However he becomes so busy and feels exhausted and also angry at those who _____ _____ _____ _____ _____. Amelia is Jason's good friend. He tells her about his problem and asks for her advice. Amelia thinks he should tell the club members about his situation and suggest that _____ _____ _____ _____ _____. In this situation, what would Amelia most likely say to Jason?

16-17

M: Hello, class. Last week, we learned about how plastic pollution has become a major threat to our environment and what effects it has on our bodies. Today, I want to talk about how we can reduce plastic in our daily lives. First, you can _____ _____ _____ _____ _____ _____. Plastic bottles are one of the top 3 trash items found in the world's oceans. Carrying your own bottle will decrease the huge amount of plastic trash. Plastic straws are also a major problem, so a lot of coffee shops don't provide them anymore. Instead, smart and thoughtful consumers _____ _____ _____ _____ _____ _____. What we wear can also _____ _____ _____ _____ _____ _____ _____ _____.

For example, buying natural fabric clothes is important because clothes made from synthetic fabric such as polyester make a lot of microplastics when they are washed. Lastly, we can get beautiful eco-friendly bags these days and use them instead of plastic bags.

녹음을 다시 한 번 들으면서, 빈칸을 채워 봅시다.

01

M: Good morning, students. I'm Thomas Smith, the chairman of Saving Us, a student organization for the environment. We focus on the various ways students can _____ _____ _____ _____ _____ _____. Many students support us, taking the bus to school, buying notebooks made from recycled paper, and bringing a reusable water bottle to school. We appreciate your cooperation, but we _____ _____ _____ _____ _____ _____ _____ and help with the activities, campaigns, and fund-raising events. So we are _____ _____ _____ _____ _____ _____. They will play an important role in all the events sponsored by our organization. Why don't you take an active role in protecting our environment? Thank you.

02

W: Hi, Benjamin! Fancy meeting you here!

M: Oh, hi, Gloria. You come here to work out too?

W: Yes, I'm a long-time member here. Oh, you're sweating a lot.

M: Yes, I am. _____ _____ _____ _____ _____ _____ _____ by exercising these days.

W: That's great. But there are some things to remember during workouts.

M: Well, are you going to tell me about the importance of resting? I _____ _____ _____ _____ _____.

W: Not this time. You should remember to drink enough water when you exercise to avoid the danger of dehydration.

M: Really? If I do that, won't it break the flow of my workout?

W: No. In fact, without an adequate supply of water, _____ _____ _____ _____ _____ _____.

M: I see your point. Thank you for your advice.

W: My pleasure. I hope to see you here often.

03

[Cell phone rings.]

M: Hello, Ms. Anderson. How are you?

W: Hi, Mr. Jackson. I just finished writing my new book.

M: Good for you. What is it about this time?

W: It's about criminal investigations. I have focused on the changing psyche of the investigator.

M: That sounds interesting. When will it be published?

W: _____ _____ _____ _____ _____ _____ in a month, so I need a photo for the cover. Can you take my picture?

M: Sure. Do you want a formal portrait photo?

W: Yes. _____ _____ _____ _____ _____ _____.

M: Good. I'm free this afternoon and all day tomorrow. When can you come by my shop?

W: I have a meeting with the editor in chief this afternoon. Can I drop by tomorrow morning?

M: Okay. And I'll _____ _____ _____ _____ _____ _____ _____ _____ after the shoot.

W: You are so kind. See you soon.

04

W: What an interesting picture! _____ _____ _____ _____ _____?

M: Yes. We went to Jeju Island last week and visited a place for riding horses.

W: It looks fun. I notice the banner on the fence saying, "Ride a Horse, Ride a Dream."

M: Right. It was their slogan for the horseback riding course.

W: The girl riding a horse is your sister, Carol, right?

M: Yes. She _____ _____ _____ _____ _____ _____ _____ _____, so my dad is holding the reins for her.

W: What are you doing in the picture?

M: As you can see, I'm carrying some hay to feed the horses.

W: The hay looks heavy.

M: Actually, I could handle it easily. Can you see my mom feeding the horses?

W: Yes, _____ _____ _____ _____ _____ _____. Your family must've had an unforgettable experience there.

M: You can say that again.

05

[Cell phone rings.]

M: Hello, Susan.

W: Hello, Mr. Parker. _____ _____ _____ _____ _____ _____ Green Grocery?

M: It went very well. We'll be provided with more fresh vegetables from next week.

W: Sounds good. Did you meet the client who ordered the catering service?

M: Not yet. I'm waiting for him as we speak.

W: I see. Well, China Dinnerware Company just called and said that the dinnerware sets we ordered will be delivered this afternoon.

M: That sounds good, but I'm not sure _____ _____ _____ _____ _____ _____. Could you receive the delivery instead of me?

W: No problem. I'll be at the restaurant all afternoon.

M: Thank you, Susan. I'll be back as soon as the meeting is over.

W: _____ _____ _____. I will arrange the tables.

M: Okay. See you at the restaurant.

06

W: Welcome to Fly Away Airlines. How may I help you?

M: Hi. _____ _____ _____ _____ _____ _____ from Atlanta to New York.

W: Sure. What date are you traveling?

M: I want to leave on May 3rd. How much is the ticket?

W: Hmm.... It's $150 for an adult.

M: I see. Well, _____ _____ _____ _____ _____ _____?

W: Yes, there is a 10% discount for children under 7. How many people are traveling in your party?

M: Two adults and one 6-year-old child.

W: Okay. Let me see. On that day, the possible departure time is 4 p.m. _____ _____ _____ _____ _____?

M: Yes. Can I reserve the seats beside the emergency exit?

W: Yes. In that case, it will be $10 more per person.

M: Great. I'll take those seats.

07

M: Jessica, I heard you had a job interview last week in New York.

W: Yes, I did. I just got back yesterday.

M: How did it go?

W: Well, it went very well. In fact, they _____ _____ _____ _____ _____ _____.

M: Congratulations. It's what you've always wanted.

W: That's true, but I _____ _____ _____ _____ _____ _____ _____ _____ yet.

M: Really? I don't understand. Was the salary lower than you expected?

W: No, that's not it. The pay would be much higher than what I'm making now.

M: Then, what's the matter? Are the benefits not good?

W: Actually, their benefits are great. It's just that I don't want to leave here. This is _____ _____ _____ _____ _____ _____.

M: I see. It's never easy to start a new life in a new city.

W: Exactly. I don't know what to do.

08

M: Lynn, you look fancy in that sweater today.

W: Thanks. I bought it at Coco Mall on Main Street.

M: What kind of clothes do they sell there?

W: Almost everything, from jackets, pants, and T-shirts, to hats.

M: Wow. I'd love to check it out. The mall opens every day, right?

W: Right, it opens at 10 a.m. and closes at 9 p.m. You should _____ _____ _____ _____ _____ _____ _____ at the latest.

M: I see. _____ _____ _____ _____ _____ _____ _____ there?

W: The prices are pretty good. They're much cheaper than department stores.

M: Sounds great. Are there enough parking spaces?

W: Absolutely. _____ _____ _____ _____ _____ _____ _____. There are always plenty of places to park.

M: Well, if you're not busy, why don't we go there together next time?

W: Why not? It'll be fun.

09

W: Hello, newcomers! I'm Laura Williams, the president of the Waldorf Student Council. The Waldorf Rose Festival you are looking forward to will take place this Friday from 10 a.m. to 9 p.m. We will _____ _____ _____ _____ _____ _____ _____ for you, the incoming freshmen. There will also be great performances, such as a busking show, a magic show, a hip hop dance and an acoustic band concert. _____ _____ _____ _____ _____ _____, you can enjoy all of the performances without an admission ticket. Also, you can have lunch at an outdoor cafeteria in the playground. Last year _____ _____ _____ _____ _____ in the evening, but this year we will have a launching of sky lanterns with your wishes. I hope all of you can come and enjoy this exciting event!

10

M: Good evening. How may I help you?

W: Hi. I'd like to buy some umbrellas. I want to give them as gifts to the guests at my wedding.

M: Oh, congratulations! Here is a brochure showing our umbrellas. Which pattern do you prefer?

W: Hmm.... The polka-dot design is a little loud. The others are okay, I think.

M: Good. How about the size?

W: Well, I don't want anything bigger than 26 inches. A big umbrella is _____ _____ _____ _____.

M: I see. Then, how about foldable umbrellas?

W: I like them. The guests can carry them in their bags.

M: Good choice. All the foldable umbrellas open up with a push of a button. _____ _____ _____ _____?

W: Since I have to buy at least 100 umbrellas, I don't want to _____ _____ _____ _____ _____.

M: Okay. Then, this model is the one for you. If you order today, we'll deliver them to you within three days.

W: Good. I'll place an order today.

11

M: Nancy. What are you going to do for Halloween?

W: I'm going to _____ _____ _____ _____ _____ _____.

M: Sounds exciting! Where are you going to take them?

W: (Maybe we will go around the neighborhood.)

12

W: Hi, Adam. What brings you here?

M: Hi, Karen. _____ _____ _____ _____ _____ this afternoon? Mine isn't working right now.

W: I'm sorry, but I have to finish this term paper today.

M: (That's okay. I'll ask someone else.)

13

W: Mike, why are you packing your suitcase in the middle of the night?

M: I'm sorry, Mom. I didn't _____ _____ _____ you.

W: That's okay. I wasn't asleep.

M: I'm _____ _____ _____ _____ _____ _____ _____ tomorrow. I'm sorry I didn't tell you, but it came up suddenly.

W: I see. Have you finished packing?

M: I'm almost done, but I'm worried about forgetting something.

W: Let me see. Towels, toothbrush and toothpaste, some shirts, pants, two jackets, a coat, and a cardigan. Wow, you're taking a lot of clothes with you.

M: As you know, I'm _____ _____ _____ _____ _____.

W: I know, but it's summer in Australia now.

M: (Oh, really? Then, I'll take out some unnecessary clothes.)

14

M: Honey, we are here on the beach at last. _____ _____ _____ _____ _____ _____ _____.

W: Yeah. I can't remember the last time we were at the beach.

M: Then, why are you still looking at your screen?

W: I'm sorry, Scott. I'm just checking my email.

M: _____ _____ _____ _____. Come on! You need to take a break.

W: I know, but I just want to make sure that my colleagues sent the email about the project.

M: I think they will understand if you don't check your email while you're here.

W: Of course. They told me to enjoy myself and forget about work for a while.

M: _____ _____ _____ _____ _____ _____. It's time to enjoy a real vacation, without your laptop.

W: Well, you're right. We are on a fantastic beach now.

M: You can say that again. _____ _____ _____ _____ _____ _____ in the water?

W: (Okay. I'll turn off my laptop right now.)

15

M: Jeff really likes to read books so he opened up a bookstore downtown after graduating from college. At first, lots of customers came to his store, especially high school students. However, before long, another bookstore opened near his store and the number of customers began to decrease. Jeff _____ _____ _____ _____ _____ _____ _____ _____ _____ _____. Samuel, his college friend, heard this news and visited Jeff. Jeff's _____ _____ _____ _____ _____, and as soon as he saw Samuel, his eyes filled with tears. Samuel thinks the economy is in a terrible situation and many small businesses are experiencing hard times. He wants to console Jeff, _____ _____ _____ _____ _____ _____. In this situation, what would Samuel most likely say to Jeff?

16-17

W: Hello, students. Last lecture, I talked about various _____ _____ _____ _____ _____, sleepwalking, and even bed-wetting. Getting a good sleep is incredibly important for your overall health. So today, I'd like to talk about how to sleep well. First of all, regular exercise during the day relieves the symptoms of sleeplessness. Even light exercise such as walking improves sleep quality. Also, certain foods and beverages like warm milk can _____ _____ _____ _____ _____ _____. A nightly cup of chamomile or peppermint tea can be a perfect relaxing ritual. Eating some fruits like kiwi before bed can increase your sleep duration a little bit. It is reported that eating almonds regularly may help boost sleep quality. Lastly, you should remember that a peaceful bedtime routine sends a powerful signal to your brain that _____ _____ _____ _____ _____ _____ _____ _____ and to get to sleep. Now, let me show you a video clip about creating a good environment for sleeping well.

녹음을 다시 한 번 들으면서, 빈칸을 채워 봅시다.

01

M: Ladies and gentlemen! I'm Robert Brown, the head director of the library. _____ _____ _____ _____ to you today. After almost two years of construction, the library finally opened last Friday. Every student in school can now enjoy reading books and studying in the new library. The five-story building has more than 100,000 books, and can accommodate up to 600 students. It's also _____ _____ _____ _____ _____ _____, and a multi-media center where you can watch a variety of broadcasts and movies. On behalf of the school, I'd really like to _____ _____ _____ _____ _____ _____ _____. The school officials, teachers, and students will always be grateful for your sincere help and kindness.

02

M: Honey, did you get the results of your regular check-up?

W: Yes, I did. Fortunately, everything is good, including the cholesterol level.

M: That's good. _____ _____ _____ _____ _____ _____ recently.

W: Yeah, right. Did you get your results, too?

M: Yes, I did. But they were disappointing. All my results, including the cholesterol level, were poor.

W: Well, I think _____ _____ _____ _____ _____ _____ _____ _____ is mainly responsible for that.

M: Yes. The doctor told me the same thing.

W: If you want to improve your health, _____ _____ _____ _____ _____ _____ _____.

M: You talk as if you were a doctor.

W: I'm serious. If you keep having food late at night, your health will get worse and worse.

M: Okay, okay. I'll _____ _____ _____ _____ _____ _____.

03

W: Hi, nice to meet you, Mr. Jackson! I'm Sally Brown.

M: Hi, Sally! It's nice to meet you too.

W: I heard this isn't your first time visiting Seoul.

M: That's right. I came here last year with my family for sightseeing. We had a really good time.

W: Good. Okay, now let me ask you a question for your fans. _____ _____ _____ _____ _____ _____ _____ this badminton championship?

M: Yes, I am. I've practiced really hard, and _____ _____ _____ _____ _____.

W: I see. Actually, many reporters, including myself, think that you will win.

M: Thank you. _____ _____ _____ _____ _____.

W: Any final words for you fans?

M: Well, I want to say thank you for supporting me. I'll do my best to win the competition.

W: Great! Thank you for your time, and good luck!

04

M: Amber, did you finish the poster outline for the festival?

W: Yes, I did. Please have a look at the monitor.

M: Hmm. You put the festival motto, "Let's Enjoy Outdoor Life!" _____ _____ _____ _____ _____ _____ _____.

W: Yeah. And I put information about when and where the festival is taking place below the motto.

M: Good. Why did you put a palm tree on each side?

W: I wanted to represent nature.

M: I got it. Hmm. You put a girl and a boy _____ _____ _____ _____ _____ _____ _____.

W: Right. I want to encourage the young _____ _____ _____ _____ outdoors.

M: Very good. I'm impressed.

W: Thank you. What do you think about the man riding a skateboard on the right?

M: I like him, too. I think you did a good job.

05

W: Robin, did you go see a doctor today?

M: Yes, Mom. I went to the hospital in the afternoon.

W: Good. What did the doctor say?

M: The doctor said I have flu, and he _____ _____ _____ _____ _____.

W: Make sure you take it all.

M: I will. Ah, _____ _____ _____ _____ _____ _____ _____?

W: No, they've all gone. Why do you ask?

M: Well, the doctor advised me _____ _____ _____ _____ _____ _____ _____ such as oranges or kiwis. She said that vitamin C can help fight the flu.

W: Then, I'll go and buy some oranges right away.

M: Thank you, Mom. I'll clean the living room while you're gone.

W: Don't do that, sweetie. You're sick. Just get some rest.

06

W: Welcome to Grand Trampoline Park. May I help you?

M: Hi! What time do you close today?

W: We close at 10 p.m. on weekdays. But last entry is 8 p.m.

M: Okay. Then I would like to buy tickets for one adult and 5 children.

W: How old are the children? _____ _____ _____ and children under 13 are just $10.

M: Oh, the children are all 12 years old.

W: Okay. Since there are six of you, you _____ _____ _____ _____ _____. You can _____ _____ _____ _____ _____ _____.

M: That's wonderful. Can I also use this $5 coupon?

W: I'm sorry. This coupon can only be used on weekends.

M: That's fine.

W: How would you like to pay? Cash or credit card?

M: I'll pay with my credit card. Here you are.

07

W: Patrick, I heard that you decided to apply to Sydney Bank.

M: Yeah. It _____ _____ _____ _____ _____.

W: Good. I also heard the starting salary is over $50,000.

M: That's another reason. Have you decided which company to apply to?

W: Yes. I'm going to apply to ACE Electronics.

M: ACE Electronics? That's the company Brian and Jennifer applied to.

W: Right. They told me that they applied because of _____ _____ _____ _____ _____ _____.

M: What about you? What made you decide to apply?

W: It was _____ _____ _____ _____ _____. You know I've always dreamed of working abroad.

M: Yes. The company has lots of branches overseas.

W: If I get hired, I'll ask to work in one of the overseas branches.

M: I hope your dream comes true.

08

W: Hi, nice to meet you. I'm Sara Brown, a reporter for the school newspaper.

M: Hi, Sara! I'm honored to be interviewed by the newspaper.

W: Don't mention it. First _____ _____ _____ _____ _____ _____. When was it started?

M: In 1970. Our club has the longest history of the 50 clubs in school.

W: That's really long. I heard that Jim Morrison, _____ _____ _____, _____ _____ _____. Is that true?

M: Right. Every time we do the magic show, he comes to encourage us.

W: Great! _____ _____ _____ _____ _____ _____ _____ _____ the magic show?

M: Twice. Once in summer and once in winter.

W: I got it. Now let's talk about your members. How many members do you have?

M: 23. We meet on Wednesdays and Fridays to practice magic for the show.

W: Great. I'd like to attend a meeting and learn some basic magic skills.

M: Please come along. You are welcome any time.

09

W: Hello, everyone! Please pay attention to me for just a minute. I'm going to introduce an exciting camp to you. It's the Phoenix Baseball Camp. Sponsored by the Seattle Baseball Association, the camp will start _____ _____ _____ _____ _____ _____ _____ _____ _____. The camp will be held in the Rainbow Basketball Center just like last year. The camp is open to all children _____ _____ _____ _____ _____. There are three classes: advanced, intermediate, and beginners, and participants will be placed into them _____ _____ _____ _____ _____, not their age. The registration fee is $150 a child, and it includes lunch and transportation from your house to the camp. I'm sure your children will have a great time at the camp.

10

M: Honey, let's look at the rental house ads and choose one.

W: Okay! Um.... I don't want to move to Santa Monica. It's too far from my office.

M: And it's too crowded. I don't want to live there, either.

W: Then let's choose either Culver City or Los Angeles.

M: Yes. Don't you think _____ _____ _____ _____ _____ _____?

W: Yes. Otherwise, the kids will have to share a room. They won't like that.

M: Okay. How about the monthly rent?

W: Well, I don't think we can afford to spend _____ _____ _____ _____ _____.

M: I agree with you. Now there are two houses left.

W: Why don't we choose the house with the lower rent?

M: But we can park only one car in the garage. We need _____ _____ _____ _____ _____ _____.

W: Ah, right. Okay, let's rent this house.

11

M: Honey, why don't we take a trip to the Grand Canyon with our kids for Christmas?

W: Well, I'm totally _____ _____ _____ _____ _____ _____ _____, but I don't think we should go to the Grand Canyon.

M: Why? Do you have any particular reason you don't want to go there?

W: (I'm sure our kids want to go to the sea, not the Grand Canyon.)

12

[Cell phone rings.]

W: Harry, I'm running a little late for our date.

M: Don't worry, Jessica. I'll go to the cafe and wait for you there.

W: _____ _____ _____ _____ _____ _____ too? I'll have a latte.

M: (No problem. I'll order two.)

13

M: Ellen, you ___ ___ ___ ___ ___ ___ ___, didn't you?

W: That's right. I got an A in that class. Why do you ask?

M: Actually, I'm thinking about taking the class this semester, so I'm getting some information about it.

W: Are you? Then take Professor Lee's class.

M: Did you take his class?

W: Yes, I did. Almost everyone in the class really liked it.

M: Really? Why was that?

W: Well, ___ ___ ___ ___ ___ ___. Whenever we asked him a question, he always answered with ease.

M: Good. What about his way of teaching? Is it boring?

W: No, never. His class was always exciting because he used lots of audiovisual materials.

M: Then ___ ___ ___ ___ ___ ___ ___ during class.

W: (Absolutely! Take his class, and you won't regret it.)

14

W: Excuse me, can I ask you something?

M: Sure! Go ahead.

W: Well, I think I've lost my key card.

M: Don't worry. We can reissue you a key right away. But ___ ___ ___ ___ ___ ___.

W: Is it okay to pay for it when I check out?

M: Of course it is. Can you tell me your room number?

W: I'm staying in 1026.

M: 1026.... Let me check. *[Pause]* It says that ___ ___ ___ ___ ___ Susan Kim. Are you Susan Kim?

W: No, I'm not. I'm Jennifer Kim. Susan Kim is my sister.

M: I'm sorry, but a key card ___ ___ ___ ___ ___ ___ ___ who reserved the room. It's our policy.

W: I got it. Then I'll bring my sister right away. She's at the restaurant on the second floor.

M: (Good. When she gets here, I'll get her a new key card.)

15

M: Rachel is in a clothing store, choosing a long coat to wear this winter. John, a shop assistant, shows her several long coats of various designs. She tries on a simple purple long coat and likes it. But when Rachel tries to take her wallet out of her bag to pay for the coat, she realizes ___ ___ ___ ___ ___ ___. Embarrassed, she tells John this fact. John tells her not to worry, adding that if she really wants to buy this coat, ___ ___ ___ ___ ___ ___ ___ until tomorrow. Rachel ___ ___ ___ ___ and she definitely wants to buy the coat. In this situation, what would Rachel most likely say to John?

16-17

W: Good afternoon, visitors. Welcome to the Bat House at Greenland Zoo. This morning, you have already seen some interesting wild animals here at the zoo. Now, you'll have a chance to observe some bats, the mysterious creatures of the night. Before that, I'm going to tell you some interesting facts about bats. Generally, ___ ___ ___ ___ ___ ___ ___ in European countries such as England or France. You can often see them appear as bad characters in movies. But bats are just victims of being judged by appearance. In fact, bats play an important role ___ ___ ___ ___ and they are actually helpful to human beings. For example, bats are ___ ___ ___ ___ ___. A single bat can catch thousands of pests in a day. Without bats, getting rid of pests would ___ ___ ___ ___ ___ ___ a year. Bats are also important for the ecosystem by acting as a pollinator. Bats in Thailand and Vietnam help plants pollinate so that seeds can grow. Okay! Now, let's go inside to see some baby bats.

녹음을 다시 한 번 들으면서, 빈칸을 채워 봅시다.

01

W: Hi, dog lovers! Do you want your dog to eat healthy food? Then treat your furry little friend with Chew Chew puppy treats. With its new taste that dogs love, your furry friend will do anything to get one bite. Developed to help keep your dog's teeth healthy and clean, Chew Chew treats are _____ _____ _____ _____ _____ _____ _____. Made with organic ingredients, you can be confident your dog is getting the best of the best. Chew Chew treats can _____ _____ _____ _____ _____ _____ _____ _____. Go to the Chew Chew website and _____ _____ _____ _____ _____ _____ to use at the checkout. Give your dog the best.

02

M: Hey, Jill. How's it going today?

W: Good morning, Dale. _____ _____ _____ _____ _____.

M: I'm sorry to hear that. What seems to be the problem?

W: My new boss has been _____ _____ _____ _____ lately.

M: How has he been challenging you?

W: He keeps _____ _____ _____ _____.

M: New assignments might be a good thing.

W: A good thing? How could they be a good thing?

M: New assignments could mean your new boss trusts you.

W: Trust? You're joking. How do these new assignments mean trust?

M: Well, if your boss keeps giving you new assignments, it probably means that he _____ _____ _____ _____ _____ _____.

W: Oh, I guess you could be right. Maybe this is a good thing after all.

03

W: Good morning, Mr. Cooke. You are _____ _____ _____ _____ _____.

M: That's fantastic news. Does this mean that I'm okay now?

W: Yes. You're as good as new.

M: Great. Is there _____ _____ _____ _____ _____ _____ _____?

W: Yes. The doctor told me to _____ _____ _____ _____.

M: What should I do if the wound opens up?

W: That's unlikely. But if it does happen, don't hesitate to come back right away.

M: That's good to know. When is my next appointment?

W: You should come every three days _____ _____ _____ _____ _____, until we take out the stitches.

M: I just want to say thank you to you and the other staff for taking such great care of me.

W: You're very welcome. We were just doing our jobs.

M: Thanks again. I'm ready to go now.

04

M: Wow! Is this picture your bedroom? It's really nice, Kate.

W: Yeah, Ryan. The bed in the middle of the room is so comfortable.

M: It looks great. Is that _____ _____ _____ _____ _____ _____ _____ ?

W: Yes. It makes the room look cozy.

M: You're right. That's a beautiful nightstand to the left of the bed.

W: Yes. My mother gave it to me as a housewarming gift.

M: Is that a real Van Gogh? I mean _____ _____ _____ _____ _____ _____ behind the bed.

W: Of course not. It's a replica of a Van Gogh.

M: That chair in the right corner of the room looks very classic.

W: Doesn't it? I _____ _____ _____ _____ _____ _____ at a garage sale.

M: It looks brand-new. You really have good taste.

W: Thanks for saying so.

05

W: Honey, it's time to go to the wedding. We don't want to be late.

M: Alright, Holly. Have you seen my shoes?

W: They _____ _____ _____ _____ _____ _____ . Could you grab my high heels too?

M: Which ones are you going to wear to the wedding?

W: _____ _____ _____ _____ _____ _____ _____ .

M: I don't see them. Are you sure they're in here?

W: They might be outside in the car. Do you mind taking a look?

M: Okay, one second. Where are the car keys?

W: They are _____ _____ _____ _____ , next to the fruit bowl.

M: I don't see them. Could they be somewhere else?

W: They might be in my purse in the living room.

M: Found them! I'll be right back.

06

[Telephone rings.]

M: Thank you for calling Adventure Tours. This is Rob. How may I help you?

W: Hi, I want to book your whitewater rafting tour.

M: Sure. It's $20 for adults and $15 for children under 13.

W: There are four of us, _____ _____ _____ _____ _____ _____ _____ .

M: Oh, groups of 4 or more can _____ _____ _____ _____ on the tour price.

W: That's wonderful.

M: Have any of you been whitewater rafting before?

W: No, this is our first time.

M: Then I recommend taking our instructional class. _____ _____ _____ _____ _____ and most people find it helpful.

W: I don't think we all need to take it. I'll just _____ _____ _____ _____ for it.

M: Okay. When would you like to take your adventure?

W: Next Saturday.

M: Alright. Let me tell you your total price.

07

M: Hey, Hailey. What are you listening to?

W: Hi, Dylan. I'm listening to a podcast about the importance of creativity.

M: That sounds great. Why are you listening to the podcast?

W: Well, you know I'm taking a summer course at the community college.

M: Right. So this is _____ _____ _____ _____ _____ ?

W: Not exactly. The professor recommended that _____ _____ _____ _____ _____ .

M: Why was that?

W: The professor wants students _____ _____ _____ _____ _____ _____ , which is on creativity.

M: Okay, I'll leave you alone then. Come find me when you're done.

W: Sure. I'll see you after I finish.

08

W: Hey, Eric. I have a great activity for us to do.

M: _____ _____ _____, Pamela. What do you have in mind?

W: I was just reading the newspaper and saw an advertisement for the Seattle Baking Fair.

M: The Seattle Baking Fair? When is it taking place?

W: It's taking place this weekend, _____ _____ _____ _____ _____.

M: Okay. Where is it going to be held this year?

W: It's going to be held in the main building of the Camden Art Center.

M: That's right near my house. How much is _____ _____ _____?

W: Believe it or not, it's only $5.

M: Great! Do you know how many bakeries will be participating in the fair?

W: They say _____ _____ _____ _____ _____ _____ _____.

M: That's wonderful. Let's check it out together this Saturday.

09

M: Now, we turn to local news. The ABC Cycling Club is holding its annual Riding For a Cause event this coming weekend. This year all earnings collected from the event will be _____ _____ _____ _____ _____ _____. The location for the event will be on Hawthorne Boulevard between 25th and 35th street. Food vendors from the local Portland area will be selling food to all visitors. _____ _____ _____ _____ _____ _____ _____ on Saturday, but don't forget to check out the musical performances from local bands. The event starts this weekend, and will continue until Sunday. You can _____ _____ _____ _____ _____ _____ _____ _____ located in the greater Portland area. I hope to see you there.

10

W: Fred, the paper says the local car dealership is having a sale.

M: That's great timing. I need a new car right away.

W: How much are you looking to spend?

M: I don't want to spend more than $25,000.

W: Then you can choose from these four models.

M: My last car was a sedan. _____ _____ _____ _____ _____ _____ _____.

W: They have some compacts for sale. What else are you looking for?

M: I need a car with good fuel economy. It should _____ _____ _____ _____ _____ _____.

W: Well, two of these can do that. What color do you want?

M: Do they have red?

W: No, they have only these two colors.

M: Well, I don't like black so I'll _____ _____ _____ _____ _____.

11

W: Honey, was the newspaper delivered this morning?

M: Yes, dear. Do you want me to get it for you?

W: Yes, please. Also, if it's not too much trouble, do you _____ _____ _____ _____ _____ _____ _____?

M: (Not at all. I'll bring them both.)

12

M: Jenny, can you help me carry my books home after school?

W: Of course. _____ _____ _____ _____ _____, Peter.

M: Great! Let's meet in front of the school by the statue after the last bell.

W: (Okay. I'll see you there after school.)

13

W: May I help you, sir?

M: I am wondering if I am _____ _____ _____ _____ _____ _____.

W: May I have the flight number?

M: It's Flight 802, leaving for Boston.

W: Let me check... I'm afraid _____ _____ _____ _____ _____ on that flight.

M: Oh, no. I was in a terrible traffic jam on the way here.

W: I'm sorry to hear that, but once the gate closes, there is nothing we can do.

M: When is the next flight to Boston?

W: The next flight is in two hours, but _____ _____ _____.

M: How about after that?

W: There is a flight at 7 p.m. and there is one seat left on it. Would you like me _____ _____ _____ _____ _____ _____?

M: (Of course. Please book that seat for me.)

14

[Cell phone rings.]

M: Hi, Susan. _____ _____ _____ _____ _____ _____ for the meeting?

W: I'm almost done, Dan. I just need to call the caterers.

M: Were you able to get the band for the party after the meeting?

W: No, the band was busy. I was only able to get a DJ.

M: That's disappointing, but it will have to do. Any other issues?

W: The room for the meeting had to be changed.

M: How come?

W: There weren't enough seats for everyone. So, we had to _____ _____ _____ _____ _____.

M: Okay, I'll make sure to send out an email _____ _____ _____ _____ _____.

W: That would be a big help. _____ _____ _____ _____ _____ at the moment.

M: Is there anything else I can help you with?

W: (No. Just send the email about the room change.)

15

W: Jack and Diane are coaches for a local baseball team. This weekend is the big championship game. Jack wants to _____ _____ _____ _____ _____ _____ _____ _____ because he feels that the championship game is very important. He thinks they will gain a positive experience from participating in the game. However, Diane wants to make sure that _____ _____ _____ _____ _____ _____ the game. She believes that everyone has earned the right to play in the championship game because they have always _____ _____ _____ _____ _____. Diane wants Jack to consider her point of view, and let everyone on their team play in the big game. In this situation, what would Diane most likely say to Jack?

16-17

M: Welcome to the Fitness Conference, everyone. I'm your speaker, Todd, and I have some news that will revolutionize the way you exercise. I want to _____ _____ _____ _____ _____ _____ _____ that's changing the fitness world. The Fit Master is the latest model on the market. It comes with a bright screen offering easy viewing when you're running, biking, or just going for a walk. With a battery life which lasts up to 7 days, the Fit Master can keep going just as long as you can. This tracker comes _____ _____ _____ _____ _____ _____ so that you know exactly how fast your heart is beating during your exercise. There is also a new design to the wrist band, so it fits all fashion styles. Another notable change to this tracker is _____ _____ _____ _____. Now you can go for quick cool swim and not worry about your Fit Master getting wet. Now, let's talk about why you need a fitness tracker.

녹음을 다시 한 번 들으면서, 빈칸을 채워 봅시다.

01

W: Hello, visitors of Dunparton Art Museum. This is an announcement about this month's special exhibition. Thanks to generous donations from our visitors, we were able to hold an art education program for children in our town. _____ _____ _____ _____ _____ _____ _____ this week and we are showing the children's marvelous drawings in Pine Hall. Pine Hall is located on the 3rd floor and you can enjoy the drawings from tomorrow to the last Friday of this month. _____ _____ _____ _____ _____ _____ _____ how talented our children are. You will also be able to _____ _____ _____ _____ _____ _____ _____. Please don't miss this special occasion. Thank you for visiting our museum and I hope to see you in Pine Hall.

02

M: Honey, have you decided which car to buy?

W: No, but I have _____ _____ _____ _____.

M: What choices do we have?

W: The first one is on a special promotion and is the cheapest. The second one has good consumer reviews and the last one has really high-tech features.

M: Did you _____ _____ _____ _____ and the greenhouse gas emissions of each car?

W: No. Do you think that's necessary?

M: We should check how eco-friendly the car is. Air pollution is a really hot issue these days.

W: You mean we need to be cautious about the environmental impacts of each product?

M: Yes. Let's check how green those cars are.

W: [Clicking sound] Then, we should buy the third one. But it is more expensive than the other two.

M: Don't worry. It _____ _____ _____ _____ _____.

W: Okay. Let's buy it.

03

M: Hello, Ms. Alison. You're here a bit early. How are you feeling today?

W: Hello, Mr. Brown. Actually my back hurts a little bit. _____ _____ _____ _____ _____ _____ do today's session.

M: Oh, what happened?

W: It seems I slept in the wrong position.

M: Let me see. Can you bend forward like this?

W: Yes, I can. But I feel a little pain on the right side of my back.

M: Hmm. It seems that _____ _____ _____ _____.

W: Then, should I skip today's class?

M: No. On the contrary, it's better to do some workouts to release the knots in your back.

W: What kinds of workouts should I do?

M: _____ _____ _____ _____ _____ _____ _____ and use foam rollers to ease muscle tension.

W: Okay. Let me get changed into my gym clothes.

04

W: Mark! You are back! How was your trip?

M: Really good. The hotel I stayed at was terrific!

W: Was it?

M: Let me show you the pictures. This is the hotel lobby.

W: Wow! Look at the curves on the walls. They _____ _____ _____ _____ _____ .

M: You said it! The architect tried to create a scene from nature in the lobby.

W: Then, the ceiling _____ _____ _____ _____ _____ _____ _____ and a moon.

M: Right. Supporting the ceiling are pillars that look like giant trees, and a giant flower lamp is besides the table.

W: Are the flowers on the table real?

M: Yes, they are. Sitting in the lobby, _____ _____ _____ _____ _____ _____ _____ .

W: It looks really nice. I would like to visit there someday.

M: You should. You won't regret it.

05

M: Kate, the school club festival _____ _____ _____ _____ _____ .

W: Right. As members of the school broadcasting club, we still have many things to do.

M: Do we? I though most of the work was done.

W: Well, we have finished checking the audio systems, but not the lights.

M: I can do that after school.

W: I've already _____ _____ _____ _____ _____ _____ . He will do it today.

M: What about the performance timetable?

W: The performance club leaders will decide on it together and let us know.

M: Is there _____ _____ _____ _____ _____ _____ ?

W: We should check each performance club's rehearsal and get music files from the dancing club.

M: Right. I'll collect the music files while you talk with the club leaders about the rehearsal schedule.

W: Okay. That sounds good.

06

M: Ms. Ross. We're going to take students to the movies as a school club activity next Wednesday, right?

W: That's right, Mr. Lewis. I _____ _____ _____ _____ _____ _____ online now.

M: Good. How many students are we going to take?

W: 5 students from your club and 6 students from mine.

M: And how much are the tickets?

W: They cost $10 each.

M: Oh, look. Next Wednesday is culture day, the last Wednesday in the month! We can get a special discount.

W: Right! We can _____ _____ _____ _____ _____ _____ _____ !

M: And don't forget to buy tickets for the two of us, too.

W: Of course not. I already included us on the web page.

M: Okay. _____ _____ _____ .

W: Then, I will pay with a credit card now.

07

W: Hi, Dan. How was Academic English Writing class?

M: Actually, I dropped that class.

W: Why? You seemed excited because your favorite professor was teaching it.

M: I was! I even changed my schedule for that class.

W: I know. You moved your part time job from Monday to Tuesday.

M: Yeah, I also took the Basic English Writing class last semester, _____ _____ _____ _____ _____ _____ .

W: Right. You got A in that class!

M: Well, anyway, I'm going to have to _____ _____ _____ _____ _____ _____ .

W: What happened?

M: Too many students wanted to register for it so the professor only _____ _____ _____ _____ _____ _____ _____ _____ this semester.

W: That class must be really popular. I'd like to take it, too.

M: Let's register for it together next semester.

08

W: Hi, Liam. Where are you going with your violin?

M: Hi, Jean. I'm going to the Community Orchestra practice.

W: Oh. I'd really like to be in the orchestra too.

M: Right! I know you play the flute. You should join!

W: What do I need in order to join?

M: You need _____ _____ _____ _____ _____ _____ _____ _____ _____ _____ and your instrument.

W: How often do you practice?

M: Once a week. We meet on Tuesday nights from 7:30 to 9:30.

W: Okay. _____ _____ _____ _____ _____ _____?

M: We are using a room in Madison Music College. It's not far from here.

W: It sounds perfect. _____ _____ _____ _____ _____ _____?

M: Sure! We have concerts twice a year.

W: Great! I will definitely apply!

09

M: Hello, students, this is Mr. Garcia in the administration office. We are going to _____ _____ _____ _____ _____ just after the 5th period class. _____ _____ _____ _____ _____ _____, follow your teachers' instructions, and in a calm and orderly manner, take the central or west wing stairs to get out of the building. Do not use the east wing staircase because _____ _____ _____ _____ _____ and don't use the elevators. You should never use the elevators in emergency situations. The assembly point is the playground. Please gather according to your class number so that the teachers can check if everyone is there. In the playground, paramedics from the nearby fire station are going to _____ _____ _____ _____ _____ _____. I hope you will participate in this drill sincerely. Thank you for your cooperation.

10

M: Honey, what do you think about buying a robot vacuum cleaner? It will _____ _____ _____ _____ _____ _____ _____ _____.

W: I totally agree with you. Let's decide which model to buy.

M: [Clicking sound] Look at these reviews. How much suction power do we need?

W: Let me see. We need at least 600 pascals.

M: Okay. I think _____ _____ _____ _____ _____ _____ _____ _____ _____.

W: You're right. Hmm, do we need one that comes with a HEPA filter?

M: What does a HEPA filter do?

W: It helps remove fine dust while cleaning, but it is more expensive.

M: We already have an air purifier. I don't think it is necessary.

W: Okay. What about the warranty period?

M: _____ _____ _____ _____.

W: Then, we should buy this one. Let's place an order.

11

M: Sorry for keeping you waiting. May I take your order now?

W: Hmm, I've heard _____ _____ _____ _____ _____ but I can't seem to find it.

M: Oh, I'm sorry. We only offer that menu on weekends. Would you like to order something else?

W: (Sorry. I'll come back on the weekend, then.)

12

W: Wow, look at the view. The sea and the sky look amazing.

M: Yes, it's really great. But the wind is so strong and it's chilly.

W: Then, _____ _____ _____ _____ _____ _____ over there to get warm?

M: (Sounds good. Let's get some hot chocolate.)

13

M: Emily, do you have time this Saturday? Let's go to the movies.

W: Sorry, I do volunteer work in an animal shelter every Saturday.

M: Do you? That's nice of you. What do you do there?

W: I go over adoption applications to _____ _____ _____ _____ _____ _____ _____ taking care of pets.

M: Good. How did you start volunteering there?

W: I once lost my dog and found him there. I was so shocked to see so many dogs and cats there.

M: Are the animals all lost?

W: Some of them are. But _____ _____ _____ _____ _____ because they are old or sick, or even too big.

M: _____ _____ _____ _____ _____ _____ _____? I thought pet owners think of their pets as a family.

W: Most people do. But I think some people can be very irresponsible.

M: (You're right. People need to think seriously about having a pet.)

14

M: Chloe. Can I ask you something?

W: Sure, Jack. What is it?

M: I know you are good at Chinese. Can you give me any tips? I need to be able to _____ _____ _____ _____ _____ _____.

W: Why is that?

M: My new job requires working with Chinese companies. Basic conversation skills will _____ _____ _____ _____ _____ _____ _____.

W: Then, how about _____ _____ _____ _____ _____ _____?

M: I am very busy these days so I don't think I can take classes regularly.

W: Hmm.... You drive to work, right?

M: Yes, I do. Why?

W: How about listening to the radio during your drive? There is a 30-minute Basic Chinese program on the ABC radio station.

M: Sounds good, but do you think that will be enough?

W: (Sure. A little learning every day works wonders!)

15

W: Ryan and Ella are looking for a present for their friend's birthday. Suddenly Ryan wants to go into a laptop store and look around. He promises it won't take long so they go inside. Ryan _____ _____ _____ _____ _____ _____ _____ for a few months so he is excited to see all the latest models. But _____ _____ _____ _____ _____. Ryan _____ _____ _____ _____ _____ _____ _____ _____, but Ella thinks they should leave the store to buy their friend's birthday present. Anyway, Ryan should compare the prices and models more carefully. In this situation, what would Ella most likely say to Ryan?

16-17

M: Hello, students. Previously, we studied about _____ _____ _____ _____ _____ _____ _____ and keep the air clean. So this time we will find out what kinds of indoor plants are _____ _____ _____ _____ _____ _____. First, English ivy. This evergreen climbing plant is commonly found outside but is well adapted to indoors, too. This plant is especially good at removing carbon monoxide from the air. A spider plant is also good at removing certain chemicals and is really easy to grow. It grows quickly and looks great in hanging baskets. Another filtering superstar is bamboo palm. This also gives a healthy dose of moisture into the air, making it _____ _____ _____ _____ _____ _____ _____. Can you guess _____ _____ _____ _____ _____ _____? It's garden mum, the common plant that blooms in the fall. Now, we will go into the greenhouse and see those plants.

녹음을 다시 한 번 들으면서, 빈칸을 채워 봅시다.

01

M: Hello, colleagues. This is Richard Barker, manager of the maintenance department. As you know, we secured a new parking lot behind the building last year for your convenience. Unfortunately, _____ _____ _____ _____ _____ _____ _____, perhaps because of the distance between the office and the parking lot. Instead, many employees are parking outside the main gate and on nearby roads. This kind of careless parking _____ _____ _____ _____ _____ but also affects our safety. The main road around the gate should be clear at all times _____ _____ _____ _____ _____ _____ _____ _____. So starting from next week, cars parked outside the parking area will be towed away. Thank you in advance for your cooperation.

02

M: Rebecca, what are you looking at on the computer?

W: Oh, Greg. I'm choosing some chocolate for my friends. Valentine's Day _____ _____ _____ _____ _____.

M: I know it's a traditional day for people in relationships to express their love to each other.

W: Oh, I'm just buying some sweets for my friends, not my boyfriend.

M: That's very nice of you, but I worry the Valentine's Day _____ _____ _____ _____.

W: Commercialized? In what ways?

M: Nowadays, many companies use Valentine's Day _____ _____ _____ _____ _____ _____ _____ _____ _____.

W: Yes, that's partly true, but I think it's a good opportunity to show your friends that you care for them through giving gifts.

M: Do you really think so?

W: Sure. If you share sweets with friends on that day, your relationships could get closer.

M: You may be right. But as for me, I'm not convinced.

03

W: Blake, how nice to see you!

M: Hello, Ms. Johnson. I'm glad to see you again.

W: I heard you opened a bakery last month. Congratulations!

M: Thank you, ma'am. I'll do my best to make you proud.

W: I'm already proud of you. Well, _____ _____ _____ _____ _____ _____ your other classmates?

M: Yes, I heard that. Jessica is getting a degree in medicine and Scott is in the army.

W: That's good to hear. _____ _____ _____ _____ _____, you were a very creative student.

M: Thank you for saying that. Oh, here is the cake I made for you.

W: Oh, how kind of you! It _____ _____ _____ _____ _____. Thank you.

M: I'm happy you like it. When I was in school, you helped me a lot.

W: It was my pleasure, Blake. And thank you for coming to see me.

04

M: Honey, I'm really looking forward to our trip. As you know, _____ _____ _____ _____ _____.

W: I'm excited, too, but you need to relax. Let's check the boarding pass again.

M: Okay. The flight number and the date are on the right.

W: Exactly. Below that, can you see the logo of Kims Airlines?

M: Yes. It's a simple logo, but it's very eye-catching, I think.

W: I think so, too. On the top left is my name, Linda Mason.

M: _____ _____ _____ _____ _____ _____ _____ is in the center.

W: Yes, we are leaving for Seattle. Hmm.... Where is the gate number for our flight?

M: On the bottom left, it says the gate number is 8.

W: Then, _____ _____ _____ _____ _____ _____ and waiting there?

M: Okay. Let's move.

05

M: You look busy today, Christine. What's up?

W: Oh, I'm just decorating the classroom for a farewell party.

M: A farewell party? For whom?

W: Ms. Guzman, our student teacher.

M: Oh, that's right. _____ _____ _____ _____ _____ _____ this Friday.

W: Uh-huh. Some students thought that it would be nice to _____ _____ _____ _____ _____.

M: That's a great idea. Is there anything I can do to help out?

W: Of course. We need all the help that we can get, Jason. Could you draw some pictures of our classmates on the board?

M: _____ _____ _____ _____. I'm a terrible artist.

W: Okay, then how about blowing up these balloons?

M: It's a deal. I'll get started on it right away.

W: Thanks a million!

06

M: Hello. How can I help you?

W: Hi. Do you have _____ _____ _____ _____ _____, *Digest*?

M: Sure. They are in section B. Please, come this way.

W: Thank you. *[Pause]* Wow! You _____ _____ _____ _____ _____. How much are they?

M: $5 each. But if you buy them in bulk, I can _____ _____ _____ _____ _____ _____ each one.

W: In bulk? Do you mean those bundles?

M: Yes. One bundle has all twelve issues of that year.

W: Good. I'll buy the bundle published last year. Oh, wait! You also have magazines about cycling.

M: Yes. If you are interested in them, I can sell them to you for $3 each.

W: _____ _____ _____ _____. Then, I'll buy last month's issue.

M: I see. Just a minute. I'll put them all in a bag for you.

07

[Telephone rings.]

M: Lion Fitness Center! How may I help you?

W: Hi, I'm Carol Parker. I just registered online for a three-month Lion membership.

M: Thanks for your registration. _____ _____ _____ _____ _____ _____ _____?

W: No, but I've worked out at other fitness centers.

M: I see. We are equipped with state-of-the-art sports equipment and saunas. You'll love working out at our facility.

W: I hope so. Well, I'm _____ _____ _____ _____ _____ _____ _____ _____ _____ I've chosen online.

M: Just a moment, please. *[Typing sound]* You chose a pair of weight-lifting gloves, right?

W: Yes, but I want to change it to a towel, if possible.

M: Let me see. Oh, fortunately, we _____ _____ _____ _____.

W: Good. If I come this evening, can I pick it up?

M: Sure. Just ask for Rob when you come in, and he'll give it to you.

W: Okay. See you this evening.

08

M: Kelly, what are you going to do during the summer vacation?

W: I'm going to go to Sunrise Resorts with my family next week.

M: Really? I've been there before. They have many activities you can enjoy.

W: That's good to hear. _____ _____ _____ _____ _____ _____ scuba diving or snorkeling there.

M: Absolutely. They have programs for both activities. You will _____ _____ _____ _____ _____ _____ _____ _____ _____ _____ .

W: Sounds great.

M: That's not all. It's a great opportunity to taste the local cuisine.

W: Good. We'll stay there for a few days. What kind of activity can we do in the evening?

M: There are many options, but _____ _____ _____ _____ _____ _____ _____ _____ with your family. The water is really good for your skin, they say.

W: I feel relaxed already. Thank you for the helpful information.

09

W: Attention, students. My name is Jennifer Mason and I'm in charge of Vision Language Lab. Our language lab _____ _____ _____ _____ _____ _____ _____ of the Vision Center. We are equipped with 24 desktops and 4 printers for student use. Our area contains 1 drop-in space and 3 classrooms. All classrooms are equipped with a video camera and microphone systems so that the classes can be easily recorded and uploaded. These rooms are used for conversation training sessions held _____ _____ _____ _____ _____ _____ _____ _____ _____ . All students can take this class for free, but they have to _____ _____ _____ _____ _____ _____ _____ through the school website. If you have any questions, please contact the main office. Thank you.

10

W: Brian, what are you looking at?

M: Oh, hi, Sarah. I'm looking for a lipstick for my mother's birthday present. Could you help me choose one?

W: Of course. _____ _____ _____ _____ _____ the color pink. She'll love it.

M: Right, but she already has that color. I want to get her something different.

W: Her skin is pretty fair, so many other colors will be good for her.

M: _____ _____ _____ _____ _____ , which is best?

W: Well, I don't recommend getting the smallest one. It'll run out before you know it.

M: Then, I'll _____ _____ _____ _____ _____ .

W: What price range _____ _____ _____ _____ _____ ?

M: I'm looking to spend somewhere between $15 and $20.

W: Then, there are two options left. How about this one? It comes with a lip liner as a bonus gift.

M: Hmm, not bad. But I think I'll get the other one.

11

M: Janice, you look excited. Do you have some good news?

W: Actually, I was just informed that _____ _____ _____ _____ _____ .

M: Really? Congratulations! You have wanted the position so long.

W: (Thank you. It'll be a great opportunity for me.)

12

W: Honey, it looks like everyone has gone home now.

M: Yes. At last, the party is over. You were a great host.

W: You, too. Now _____ _____ _____ _____ _____ _____ the house.

M: (You're right. Let's clear the table first.)

13

W: Hello, sir. How can I help you?

M: Hi. I bought these pants last weekend, but they don't fit.

W: I'm sorry to hear that. Can I see the receipt?

M: Yes. Here it is.

W: You didn't try them on when you bought them?

M: No. They were my size, so I _____ _____ _____ _____ _____ _____ . I want to exchange them for a bigger size.

W: Let me see. Hmm.... Oh, that's the biggest size we have.

M: Then, I _____ _____ _____ _____ _____ _____ _____ _____ .

W: Oh, I'm so sorry. They were a special sale item, so I can't give you a refund.

M: What? Then what am I supposed to do? I can't wear them.

W: You can _____ _____ _____ _____ to buy other items. Do you need anything else?

M: (In that case, I'll look around for some shirts.)

14

W: Hi, Alex. What's up? You look tired.

M: Hi, Brooke. Actually, I'm not sleeping well these days.

W: I'm sorry to hear that. Do you _____ _____ _____ _____ ?

M: No, but my roommate is _____ _____ _____ . He's a real night owl.

W: That's terrible. Have you tried talking to him about it?

M: Yes, but it didn't help at all. Besides, the halls in the dormitory are always so noisy. People are _____ _____ _____ _____ _____ _____ .

W: I understand how you feel. I moved out of the school dormitory last month for the same reason.

M: Really? I didn't know that.

W: Why don't you move out? It'll help you _____ _____ _____ _____ .

M: Yeah. I'd better move out. Can you help me find a room this weekend?

W: (Sure. I have a couple of quiet places in mind.)

15

M: Rebecca and Karen have been best friends since middle school. They are like sisters and do everything together. They _____ _____ _____ _____ _____ . They have similar tastes in movies, books, music, and even fashion. They _____ _____ _____ _____ they can count on each other. One time, they went shopping together and were very surprised when they _____ _____ _____ _____ _____ _____ _____ _____ _____ . Today is Rebecca's birthday. Karen comes to visit Rebecca to congratulate her and gives her a birthday gift. When Rebecca opens the gift box, she is pleasantly surprised to find the very scarf with flower patterns that she wanted to buy at the mall the other day. In this situation, what would Rebecca most likely say to Karen?

16-17

W: Welcome to the Longevity Healthcare Center. Everyone wants to live a longer, healthier, and happier life free from disease. But as we grow older, it is _____ _____ _____ _____ _____ _____ . The good news is that hypertension can be prevented if we are careful of what we eat. For example, blueberries are rich in natural compounds called flavonoids. According to a study, consuming these compounds can prevent hypertension and help lower blood pressure. Also, eating at least five servings of yogurt per week can _____ _____ _____ _____ _____ _____ _____ _____ . How about eating bananas? Bananas _____ _____ _____ _____ _____ _____ potassium, which is good for lowering blood pressure. Also, you can consider including fish like salmon in your diet. This type of fish is very rich in omega-3 fatty acids, which are effective for controlling blood pressure and reducing inflammation. Changing your lifestyle drastically could _____ _____ _____ and hard to do. However, choosing a better diet can be an easy first step to a healthy life.

녹음을 다시 한 번 들으면서, 빈칸을 채워 봅시다.

01

M: Hi, car lovers! Are you worried about your car's outside condition? Don't worry about it anymore. We, Cleancart, offer a convenient experience to car owners without wasting your valuable time. You don't have to take your car to a car-wash. We come to you. Our ultimate aim is to provide _____ _____ _____ _____ _____ _____ _____ _____. Our services use biodegradable products to _____ _____ _____ _____ _____. For only $150 a month, our professional team will come to your car twice a week and make it _____ _____ _____ _____ _____ _____ you bought it! What's more, if you pay for two months now, the third month is free! Don't miss this wonderful chance and call us right away!

02

M: Oh, I can't work anymore. _____ _____ _____.

W: Are you? What time is it now?

M: It's already 5 p.m. We've been analyzing this sales report for more than two hours.

W: But it's our job. We have to finish it before leaving the office today.

M: Don't you feel tired, Jenny?

W: No, I don't. Why don't you take a break for a while? _____ _____ _____ _____ _____ _____.

M: How can you be so healthy? You don't even go to a fitness center, do you?

W: No, I don't. But I _____ _____ _____ _____ _____ _____.

M: Do you? What is it?

W: I walk for an hour every day. It's my secret for staying healthy.

M: Do you think it's really effective?

W: Absolutely! Rob, just walk steadily every day, and you'll feel different in less than a month.

03

W: Good afternoon, Mr. Brown. How was your lunch?

M: Very good. Thanks to the reservation you made, I had a wonderful lunch.

W: I'm happy to hear that.

M: Now, can you tell me what I have to do this afternoon?

W: First you have an interview with the Sydney Morning Herald at two o'clock.

M: _____ _____ _____ _____ _____ _____?

W: An hour or so. After that, you have to _____ _____ _____ _____ _____ _____ _____.

M: I see. How about the buyers from Korea? When do I see them?

W: Right after the union meeting. They'll be here by 5:30.

M: Okay. Today will be very busy.

W: I think so.

M: You know, I _____ _____ _____ _____ _____ _____ _____.

W: My pleasure. I'm just doing my job.

04

W: Hey, look at the parade!

M: Finally, _____ _____ _____ _____ _____
_____.

W: Mickey and Minnie Mouse are walking in the front.
They're really cute.

M: Yeah. Each of them is _____ _____ _____
_____ _____ _____ "Merry Christmas."

W: Oh, Santa Claus is coming behind them in a horse-
drawn wagon.

M: Can you see a reindeer next to Santa Claus?

W: Yeah. It must be Rudolph. How lovely!

M: Absolutely! Look, there's a parade car behind Santa
Claus.

W: It's gorgeous. There are two children sitting in the car.

M: They're _____ _____ _____ _____ _____
Mickey and Minnie.

W: Yes. I think they're looking at us. Let's wave to them.

W: Okay!

05

W: Honey, you look very happy. _____ _____ _____
_____?

M: Wilson got a role in a TV drama!

W: Really? Our son, Wilson got a role? That's great news!

M: At last, his dream of becoming an actor will come
true.

W: Right. By the way, how did you find this out?

M: He called and told me just a minute ago. He seemed
really excited.

W: Did he say what the drama is about? I'm really
curious.

M: He said it's a medical drama, and that _____
_____ _____ _____ _____ who treats students
with difficulties adjusting to school life.

W: Sounds interesting. Well, why don't we _____
_____ _____ _____ when he comes home?

M: That's a good idea. I'll call him right away and ask
when he can come home.

W: Good! _____ _____ _____ _____ _____
_____ _____ _____ this weekend!

06

[Telephone rings.]

M: Hi, Green Massage Center. Can I help you?

W: Yes, please. I'd like to book a massage at 2 o'clock
this afternoon. Is that time available?

M: Yes, it is. What kind of massage would you like? A
foot massage is $30 for 30 minutes.

W: What about a head massage?

M: It's $20 for 30 minutes.

W: Um... then I'll book _____ _____ _____ _____
_____ _____ _____ _____ for 30 minutes each.

M: I see. _____ _____ _____ _____ _____
_____ for the massage?

W: Two people, please. My husband and me.

M: I got it. Okay, you're booked now.

W: Thank you. Oh, I have a 10% discount coupon that I
got through the mail. Can I use it?

M: Sure, you can. We can _____ _____ _____
_____ _____ _____. See you at 2 o'clock.

07

M: Oh, summer vacation is just around the corner.

W: Right. I heard that you are going on a bicycle trip to
Yosemite National Park with Robert and Eric. Is that
true?

M: Yes. As soon as the vacation starts, we'll leave for
Yosemite.

W: Sounds wonderful!

M: What about you? Are you still going to Hawaii to
enjoy surfing?

W: Well, it's true that I'm going to Hawaii, but I'm not
going for the surfing.

M: Then why are you going there? Are you _____
_____ _____ _____ _____ _____ _____ _____?

W: No. I'm going to Hawaii to help _____ _____
_____ _____ _____.

M: Your grandmother lives in Hawaii? I didn't know
that.

W: Last month, she started to _____ _____ _____
_____. So she wants me to help her this vacation.

M: Oh, you are _____ _____ _____ _____!

08

W: Jerome. I heard you are going to visit England during this summer vacation.

M: Yes, All my family, including my dog, is going.

W: Can you take your dog on an airplane?

M: Yes. There is a 'traveling with pet' option. It costs an extra $100.

W: Then, can you sit with your pet on the airplane?

M: No way. _____ _____ _____ _____ _____ _____ at all times and the carrier has to be big enough for the pet to stand and turn around.

W: Do they _____ _____ _____ _____ _____ _____ _____?

M: That depends. Small dogs under 7 kg can stay in the cabin, but still in pet carriers, under the seat.

W: Then your dog can stay in the cabin.

M: Yes. But I also have to get the document that _____ _____ _____ _____ _____ _____.

W: Wow, there are many things to prepare.

M: Yes, but it's a necessary process.

09

W: Now I'm going to tell you the local news. The Tomato Festival, the most popular festival in Townsville, will be held _____ _____ _____ and _____ _____ _____ _____ _____. About 100 tomato growers will take part in the festival. There will be a variety of programs for visitors, including selecting the most delicious tomatoes and eating tomatoes quickly. A cooking class to make dishes using tomatoes will also _____ _____ _____ _____ _____ _____. During the festival, tomatoes will be sold 20% cheaper than the regular market price. About 7,000 people took part in the festival last year. This year, the number of visitors _____ _____ _____ _____ _____. For more information, please visit the official website, www.townsvilletomato.org.

10

M: Hi, I'd like to _____ _____ _____ _____ _____ _____.

W: I see. Please look at the monthly plans table. How much are you looking to spend a month for your cell phone plan?

M: I don't want to spend more than $50 a month.

W: I got it. Do you talk on the phone a lot?

M: No, I don't. I think _____ _____ _____ _____ _____ _____ of talk time is enough.

W: Okay. Do you send many text messages?

M: Yes, I send a lot. I usually communicate with my friends through text messages.

W: Then you should _____ _____ _____ _____ _____.

M: I couldn't agree more.

W: Now you only have to consider how much data you use.

M: Well, I think on average, I use around 3 gigabytes a month.

W: Then this plan seems perfect for you.

M: Okay, I'll take this one.

11

W: Excuse me, I'd like to order a thin crust pizza.

M: Okay. What size would you like? We have regular, large, and family sizes.

W: Well, it's _____ _____ _____ _____ _____. Which one do you recommend?

M: (Then the family size would be good for you.)

12

M: Lauren, did you _____ _____ _____ _____?

W: Yes, I did. I've made up my mind to join the debate club.

M: The debate club? What a coincidence! Actually, I'm going to join it, too.

W: (Good! Let's submit our applications to the club tomorrow.)

13

M: Lucy, why don't you have some more chicken stew?

W: No, thanks. I'm so full that _____ _____ _____ _____ _____.

M: I see. _____ _____ _____ _____ _____?

W: Wonderful! I've never had such delicious chicken stew in my life.

M: I thought you would say so. Everyone who tries my stew says the same thing.

W: I didn't know you were such a good cook.

M: Well, it's all because of _____ _____ _____ _____ _____ _____ _____.

W: Is your mother a professional cook?

M: No, she isn't. She got the recipe from her mother.

W: Wow! Can you show me the recipe? I'd like to cook that for my family.

M: Sure! The recipe is saved on my smartphone. I'll text it to you.

W: Thank you. I'm _____ _____ _____ _____.

M: (Just do as the recipe says, and you'll have a great stew.)

14

M: Finally, the U.S. Open Championship is going to be held this week.

W: Who do you think will be the champion this year?

M: Gary Smith. I think he'll win the competition easily.

W: _____ _____ _____ _____. He's already won one competition on the PGA Tour this year.

M: Plus, he's _____ _____ _____ _____ _____ _____.

W: Right. So he's more confident than the other players.

M: You know, confidence is one of the most important factors in determining the outcome in golf.

W: Absolutely! It's hard to win without it, _____ _____ _____ _____ _____ _____.

M: I totally agree with you, and Gary has that confidence.

W: (Right. He'll win easily as you said.)

15

M: Angela is a health care professional _____ _____ _____ _____ _____. One day, Brian, a reporter for a health magazine comes to her office. Brian _____ _____ _____ _____ _____ _____ about the mental and psychological pain that teenagers suffer these days. At first, Angela is surprised by the sudden request. After a moment of careful consideration, Angela says to him that she will write it. Brian is very pleased with her positive reply and lets her know that the length of the column is between 1,000 and 1,500 words. After hearing about the length, Angela _____ _____ _____ _____ _____ _____ is for submitting her column to the magazine. In this situation, what would Angela most likely say to Brian?

16-17

W: Hello, listeners. I'm Jackie Robinson, the host of One Minute Simple Economy. Yesterday I talked to you about megastores. Today I'm going to talk to you about traditional markets. Did you know that the traditional market is better than the big megastores _____ _____ _____ _____ _____? At the traditional market, you can buy meat and fruits _____ _____ _____ _____ than in the big megastores. In addition, the traditional market is widely known _____ _____ _____ _____ _____ _____. So if you want to buy vegetables such as carrots and onions or seafood such as oysters, go to a traditional market. Visiting a traditional market is also helpful for your neighbors. Unlike megastores, _____ _____ _____ _____ _____ _____, traditional markets are run by people living in nearby areas. When you buy a pair of shoes from a large megastore, the profit goes to a faceless company. But when you buy a pair of shoes from a traditional market, the profit goes to your neighbors.

녹음을 다시 한 번 들으면서, 빈칸을 채워 봅시다.

01

M: Good morning, everyone. This is Jake from the IT Department. We will be _____ _____ _____ _____ _____ next Tuesday from 9 a.m. to 1 p.m. There will also be _____ _____ _____ _____ _____ _____ from getting access to your computer files. During this time do not save new files on your computer. Also, please _____ _____ _____ _____ _____ _____ _____ to the designated server in advance. I will send the server address through the company messenger. Please do not save the files on personal flash drives. This is _____ _____ _____ _____. This server upgrade procedure is essential and your cooperation will be highly appreciated. We sincerely apologize for any inconvenience. Thank you.

02

W: Hello, Mr. Anderson. Could you take a minute to read this document?

M: Sure, Ms. Allen. What is it?

W: _____ _____ _____ _____ _____ _____ _____ _____ on 5th Avenue.

M: I've heard city planners want to build a new shopping mall there.

W: Yes, but many citizens are against it and _____ _____ _____ _____ on their behalf.

M: May I ask why? The mall will be good for local business.

W: But don't you think providing our children with _____ _____ _____ _____ _____ _____ _____ should be a priority?

M: _____ _____ _____ _____ _____, my son really enjoys playing baseball there.

W: That's what I'm saying.

M: I see your point. I will sign the petition.

W: Thank you, Mr. Anderson.

M: I thank you, Ms. Allen.

03

M: Excuse me, ma'am. Because _____ _____ _____ _____ _____ _____ _____, I have to check a couple of things with you.

W: Oh, okay.

M: First, are you willing to _____ _____ _____ _____ _____ _____ _____?

W: Yes, but could you explain them in more detail?

M: Sure. In case of emergency, please open the emergency exit in accordance with the directions of the crew members and help other passengers exit the aircraft.

W: How can I open the exit door?

M: You pull the handle and turn it down, then push the door outside. It's explained in detail with pictures on this card.

W: Okay. I will read it thoroughly. Oh, and I have a question.

M: Yes, ma'am?

W: I _____ _____ _____ _____ on your website. Could you check if everything is in order?

M: Yes, ma'am. After we take off, I will check and get back to you.

W: Thank you.

04

W: Honey, could you take a look at this picture online?

M: Okay. What's it for?

W: It's for the children's room. How about hanging this picture above their desks?

M: Yes. This world map is interesting and informative.

W: It not only shows the names of the continents and oceans, but also some animals that live there. Look at _____ _____ _____ _____ _____.

M: I like _____ _____ _____ _____

_____ _____ _____.

W: Me too. What about the penguin in Antarctica?

M: Yes, it's cute. Hey, I didn't know that _____ _____

_____ _____ _____ _____.

W: Me neither.

M: I also like the boy and the girl _____ _____

_____ in the bottom left corner. They look like our children.

W: I think so too! So do you think we should buy this picture?

M: Definitely.

05

[Telephone rings.]

W: Hello.

M: Hello, Ellie. This is Peter.

W: Hi, Peter. What's up? Aren't you coming to work today?

M: Yes, I am. But my car broke down on the road so I'm going to be a bit late.

W: Oh, _____ _____ _____ _____ _____

_____. Don't worry.

M: I've already phoned the boss. But could you do something else for me?

W: Sure. What is it?

M: You know we have a meeting this morning. _____

_____ _____ _____ _____ _____ for it.

W: But can you come in time?

M: Yes, I think so. But _____ _____ _____ _____

_____ for the meeting from the copy room?

W: No problem. Do you want me to prepare refreshments for the meeting, too?

M: That's okay. Mia will do it. Thanks a lot. I'll be there soon.

06

M: Welcome to Green Car Services. Can I help you?

W: Hello, I'd like an interior cleaning service.

M: Certainly. We offer a couple of services. Which one would you like?

W: Could you explain the difference?

M: _____ _____ _____ _____ _____ and covers everything from the roof to the carpets, except the seats.

W: Why does it exclude the seats?

M: Because the cost differs depending on the material.

_____ _____ _____ _____ _____ _____

_____ _____.

W: My seats are fabric and I want to get them cleaned. What about the green service?

M: That includes special detergents and steam cleaning. It costs an extra $20.

W: I don't think I need that. Oh, can you get rid of the unpleasant odor coming from the air conditioner?

M: Of course. _____ _____ _____ _____ _____

will take care of that. But it _____ _____ _____

_____.

W: Okay. Please include it. How much is that altogether?

07

W: Noah, this package came for you.

M: Thanks, Mom. It's a sweater I bought online.

W: Check if it's in good condition before you try it on.

M: It looks fine. I'll put it on. [Pause] How do I look?

W: _____ _____ _____ _____ _____. The size is perfect.

M: And even though it's thick, it _____ _____ _____

_____ _____.

W: That's good. Also, _____ _____ _____ _____

_____.

M: Oh dear, Mom. I don't think I can wear it after all.

W: Why? I thought you liked it and it suits you well.

M: My neck is itching. It doesn't feel good. I _____

_____ _____ _____ _____.

W: Let me see. Oh, no. This sweater is made of synthetic fiber. You are allergic to it.

M: What a pity. I'll have to return it for a refund.

08

W: Patrick, did you hear that a David Hockney exhibition is coming to our town?

M: What? A David Hockney exhibition in this small town?

W: Yeah, that's right. It's _____ _____ _____ _____ _____ _____ _____ .

M: Wow. He's my favorite artist. When is it going to be held?

W: It _____ _____ _____ _____ , and _____ _____ _____ _____ .

M: That's about a month away. Where is the exhibition going to take place?

W: At the County Art Museum.

M: Great. That's not far from our school.

W: Right. Why don't we go to the exhibition on the first day?

M: You read my mind. Do you know how many of his paintings will be on exhibition?

W: 133 in all. _____ _____ _____ _____ _____ , including *A Bigger Splash*, _____ _____ _____ _____ .

M: Wonderful! Oh, I can't wait to see them.

09

W: Good morning, listeners. This is Eats and Treats, a podcast for food lovers. I have some exciting news for you all. The annual Goodies for Foodies event is back! _____ _____ _____ _____ _____ _____ , the event aims to bring to you all the exciting new flavors coming out in the culinary world. This year, we will _____ _____ _____ _____ _____ from all around the globe. In addition, there will be a short cooking demonstration from a world-renowned chef. The Goodies for Foodies event _____ _____ _____ and _____ _____ _____ _____ _____ _____ . You can get tickets early by heading to our website. If you order this month, you will receive two free food coupons for any food truck at the event.

10

M: Honey, what are you looking at?

W: I'm trying to order a baby swim tube for Jason online.

M: Let me see. Is that a sunshade attached to the tube? That's awesome.

W: Isn't it? I want to _____ _____ _____ _____ _____ since we're going to an outdoor pool.

M: But it's a bit expensive. Let's find one with a _____ _____ _____ _____ .

W: All right. How about this one?

M: Hmm. It only has one handle. I think the ones _____ _____ _____ _____ _____ _____ .

W: Good point. Then I guess we have two options left.

M: What do you think of that blue one?

W: It's nice, but the blue color _____ _____ _____ once it's in the water.

M: You're right. Then let's get the other one.

W: Okay. I'm sure Jason will like it, too.

11

W: Hello, Mr. Harris. Could you check if the book I asked for has been returned?

M: Sure, Jean. *[Typing sound]* Oh, I'm sorry. It has not.

W: I thought _____ _____ _____ _____ . In that case, can I reserve it?

M: (Certainly. Please fill out this request form.)

12

M: Emma, you really look pale. What's wrong?

W: I'm not sure but I think there was something wrong with the food I ate for lunch.

M: I hope _____ _____ _____ _____ . Do you want me to take you to the hospital?

W: (That's okay. I'll take a taxi. Thank you, though.)

13

M: Honey, when are we going grocery shopping today?

W: Actually, I'm thinking about skipping it this week.

M: Why? Aren't we running out of cheese?

W: I thought so but I found some in the refrigerator. Have you read today's newspaper?

M: Not yet. What does it say?

W: It says Americans have more and bigger refrigerators than citizens of any other countries.

M: Is that a bad thing?

W: I'm afraid so. We buy _____ _____ _____, _____ _____ _____, and then forget about it. This decreases the freshness of the food and increases the electricity bills.

M: Hmm. I know what you mean. We're always saying that there's nothing to eat, but _____ _____ _____ _____ _____.

W: That's just the point.

M: Okay, let's not go to the grocery store. We'll cook something _____ _____ _____ _____ in the refrigerator.

W: (Great! We can save on our grocery bill and our electricity bill!)

14

W: Alex, Can I ask you something?

M: Sure, Abby. What is it?

W: No offence, but _____ _____ _____ _____ _____ _____ _____ _____ so long?

M: Oh, does it seem messy?

W: No, no. I'm just curious. You sometimes complain it's too heavy or too hot, but you never cut your hair.

M: Well, actually I'm waiting until my hair becomes _____ _____ _____ _____.

W: You can donate your hair?

M: Yes, you know, kids who have cancer go through chemotherapy and lose their hair. There is a foundation that _____ _____ _____ _____ _____ for them.

W: That's really great of you. How can I do the same?

M: (Your hair should be at least 30 cm long and should not be permed.)

15

M: Rio and Mike are best friends and they are about to become second-year students in high school. In their school's selective curriculum, second years can _____ _____ _____ _____ _____ _____ _____ _____. Rio's main interest has always been the universe and his dream is to work at NASA someday. So he decides to study advanced physics, astronomy and earth science. Mike keeps asking Rio what subjects he will choose and wants to be _____ _____ _____ _____. Rio knows Mike just wants to study together because they are best friends, but he thinks Mike should seriously _____ _____ _____ _____ _____ _____ in the future. Then he should choose the appropriate subjects. In this situation, what would Rio most likely say to Mike?

16-17

W: Hello, students. Last week, we studied about the development of new drugs and the role of biological chemists. Today, we will find out about some drugs that _____ _____ _____ _____ _____ our daily lives and have saved a lot of people. The first is penicillin, which has become _____ _____ _____ _____ _____. This antibiotic has saved over 80 million lives and without its discovery, 75% of people today would not be alive. The second drug is insulin. Before the discovery of insulin, patients with advanced diabetes were given a near-starvation diet. Insulin also has _____ _____ _____ _____ _____ _____ _____ and saved countless diabetic patients. The next drug is what you take for a headache. Yes, aspirin. This drug is, currently, _____ _____ _____ _____ _____ in the world. The last drug is morphine. Despite the danger of addiction, without this drug, millions of individuals with serious injuries or complicated medical conditions would have been in excruciating pain.

녹음을 다시 한 번 들으면서, 빈칸을 채워 봅시다.

01

W: You're listening to public radio, and I'm your host Elizabeth Banner. _____ _____ _____ _____ _____ _____ off the coast of California. As of now, _____ _____ _____ _____ _____. The accident happened around 5 a.m. this morning. It is still unknown what caused the oil spill. More than 30 million gallons of oil have spilled into the ocean. Experts are saying that the environmental impact will last for 15 to 20 years. As a result, _____ _____ _____ _____ _____ _____ _____ _____ _____. We have contacted the oil company for comment, but they have not responded. We will _____ _____ _____ _____ further developments as this story unfolds.

02

M: Are you okay, Jean? You look really sick.

W: I feel terrible. _____ _____ _____ _____ _____ _____ _____.

M: Have you seen a doctor?

W: I don't need to see a doctor. I have _____ _____ _____ _____ _____ _____ _____.

M: You're kidding, right?

W: No. I'm serious. For example, I drink a lot of ginseng tea when I'm sick.

M: What else do you do?

W: I exercise a lot. I heard that sweating helps you get over a cold.

M: That doesn't sound very scientific. Have these things ever cured your cold?

W: Come to think of it, I'm not really sure.

M: I don't think _____ _____ _____ in fighting a cold. You should just see a doctor.

W: Maybe you're right.

03

M: I have some bad news for you, Mrs. Jones.

W: Was the damage to the house that bad?

M: Yes, _____ _____ _____ _____ _____ _____.

W: My husband and I bought the house 20 years ago.

M: I am very sorry to hear that.

W: Is it safe for me to look around? I'd like to try to find some things.

M: I'm afraid not. _____ _____ _____ _____ _____ _____ _____ at this time.

W: In that case, could you do me a favor, please?

M: Sure. What is it?

W: There's a photo album of the family in the living room.

M: I didn't see it when I was _____ _____ _____ _____, but do you want me _____ _____ _____ _____?

W: If it's not too much trouble. I'd be heartbroken if the fire got that as well.

04

W: What a beautiful view, Mike!

M: This certainly makes up for the long hike.

W: Look at the pine trees on the right. They look majestic.

M: Yeah. Can you see the _____ _____ _____ _____ _____ _____, Kate?

W: Uh-huh. They look like they're searching for food.

M: Do you see the _____ _____ _____ _____ _____?

W: Yes. It's a beautiful cabin. I wonder who lives there.

M: Probably some farmer. Oh, look! There are _____ _____ _____ _____ _____ _____ the cabin.

W: Where? Oh yes, I see them now. They look so cute.

M: _____ _____ _____ _____ _____ must be where they get their water.

W: Right. This looks like something out of a postcard.

M: I couldn't agree more. I would love to live in a place like this someday.

05

W: You promised to teach me how to fish today, Dad.

M: Yes, I did. First, you have to _____ _____ _____ _____ _____ _____.

W: Yuck! You mean I have to touch the worms?

M: I'll show you how to do it the first time, but you'll have to _____ _____ _____ _____ _____ in future.

W: Oh, I don't think I can do it, Dad.

M: It's all a part of fishing. Have you seen the tub of worms we bought?

W: I think it's over by the cooler. Shall I get it?

M: No, I'll get it. _____ _____ _____ _____ _____ like I told you?

W: Yes, I did.

M: What about sunblock? Did you _____ _____ _____ _____ _____?

W: Oh, I forgot. I'll do that now.

06

M: Hi, I would like to hire your moving company.

W: Wonderful. How much stuff do you have?

M: Not much. I _____ _____ _____ _____ _____.

W: Then I think a one-ton truck should be enough.

M: How much would that be?

W: For a studio, we charge $350.

M: That's fine. Is there any extra charge to move the air conditioner?

W: There is no extra charge to move it. But if you want it installed in your new apartment, _____ _____ _____ _____ _____.

M: Okay. Please _____ _____ _____ _____.

W: Alright. Would you be able to move on a weekday? We _____ _____ _____ _____ _____ _____.

M: I was planning to move on a weekend, but a weekday sounds good. How about next Thursday?

W: Great. Let me give you the total.

07

W: Hey, Peter. What are you making?

M: Oh, hi, Sue. I'm making a birdhouse.

W: That's really cool. You must be making it for your backyard. I've seen a lot of birds there.

M: Actually, it's not for me. I already have one in my backyard.

W: Then is it _____ _____ _____ _____ _____ _____ at school?

M: No. It's not an assignment.

W: I got it. You are going to sell it at the school fair next week, right?

M: That's a good guess, but it's not for that either.

W: _____ _____ _____ _____. Why are you making it?

M: My neighbor down the street has a birthday coming up. So, I'm going to _____ _____ _____ _____ _____ _____ _____.

W: That's nice of you. I'm sure she'll love it.

M: I certainly hope so.

08

M: Megan, John just gave me a flyer for his Boy Scouts Adventure Camping Trip.

W: Oh, what does it say?

M: It says they are going to a new camping ground at Lake Eagle.

W: When are they going?

M: It says that the camping trip is _____ _____, _____ _____.

W: That's good. Doesn't your vacation start then?

M: Yeah, so I can accompany John.

W: Do we need to get anything for him before the trip?

M: The flyer says that the boys _____ _____ _____ _____ _____. We should buy some hiking boots for John.

W: That's a good idea. When does the camping trip end?

M: Let me see.... It _____ _____ _____ _____ _____ _____

W: Fantastic! I'll have the whole house to myself for the weekend.

09

M: Hello, everyone. It is time once again for the annual People First Food Drive. The goal of the food drive is to make sure that no one goes hungry in our city. Donation boxes will _____ _____ _____ _____, libraries, and parks. Organizers of the food drive ask that donations be _____ _____ _____ _____ _____ _____ _____. The donation boxes will be out for the entire month of August. At the end of the month, the food will _____ _____ _____ _____ _____ all around our city. If you're not able to donate, please come and volunteer at a meal center to help feed those in need. Every action, no matter how small, will have a great impact on the lives of these people.

10

M: Michele, Best Electronics is having an online sale of their laptop computers.

W: That's great news, James. I really need a new laptop.

M: What's your budget range?

W: I _____ _____ _____ _____ _____ _____.

M: Okay. They have four models you can choose from.

W: What's the difference between SSD and HDD hard drives?

M: SSD stands for Solid State Drive and HDD for Hard Disk Drive. To put it simply, SSD is much faster.

W: Then I'd like a model _____ _____ _____ _____ _____.

M: Alright. How much memory do you want?

W: I don't run any big programs so _____ _____ _____ _____ _____ _____.

M: Then you can choose from these two. All you have to do now is choose the processor.

W: I'll order this one _____ _____ _____ _____ _____.

11

M: Good morning, Ms. Simmons. I'm calling to let you know that _____ _____ _____ _____ _____ _____ _____ _____ _____.

W: Thank you, but I'm unable to get it today. May I come in tomorrow?

M: I'm sorry. We're closed for the holidays. We'll be open again on Wednesday.

W: (Okay. I'll pick up my car then.)

12

W: Mark, is it true that you're really good at science?

M: Well, I don't mean to brag, but I am a member of the school science club.

W: That's good to hear. _____ _____ _____ _____ _____ _____ _____?

M: (No problem. When do you have time?)

13

W: Welcome to Marty's Restaurant. My name is Charlotte. I'll be taking your order today. What will you be having?

M: Hi, Charlotte. Could you tell me about today's special?

W: I'm glad you asked. Our special today is a wonderful surf and turf.

M: Surf and turf? What's that?

W: It's a mouth-watering steak and a juicy lobster served with mashed golden potatoes and steamed carrots.

M: That sounds amazing! I'll have that please.

W: Great choice. _____ _____ _____ _____ _____ _____, sir?

M: I'd like it well done. Also, may I have _____ _____ _____ _____ _____ _____ _____?

W: Sure. Would you like anything to drink with your meal?

M: Could you bring me an orange juice?

W: Right away. _____ _____ _____ _____ _____ _____ _____?

M: (No thank you. That's all for now.)

14

[Telephone rings.]

M: Thank you for calling Birthdays Are Us. This is Jerry. How may I help you?

W: Hi, Jerry. My name is Beth, and I'm _____ _____ _____ _____ _____ _____.

M: You've called the right place! When is the big day?

W: It's on the 10th of this month, but I'd like to have the party on the following weekend.

M: Alright. Is this a party for a special boy or girl?

W: It's for _____ _____, _____ _____ _____ _____.

M: Great! What does your daughter like?

W: She really loves piñatas. Could you bring one?

M: Not a problem. What else does she like?

W: She also likes a lot of colorful balloons.

M: Sure thing. Do you _____ _____ _____ _____ _____ _____ to the party?

W: (Absolutely not! My child is terrified of clowns.)

15

W: Timmy and Julie just moved into a new apartment. They are looking to buy a new washing machine. Timmy wants to _____ _____ _____ _____ from the used appliance store because they have to buy many other things. Also, he thinks it's a waste of money to buy a new washing machine. However, Julie _____ _____ _____ _____ _____ _____ _____ because of the warranty. She fears that _____ _____ _____ _____ _____ _____ at any time. She also feels that a used machine would need professional cleaning before they can use it. Julie wants Timmy to consider buying a new washing machine. In this situation, what would Julie most likely say to Timmy?

16-17

M: Thank you for attending our writing workshop. I'm your writing coach, Sam. This is the second in a series of four classes. In the previous class, we talked about the importance of writing well. This class, we are going to _____ _____ _____ _____ _____ _____ you can use in your writing. The first type is the declarative sentence. It is _____ _____ _____ _____ _____. An example is, "I am your writing coach." The second type is the imperative sentence. It _____ _____ _____ _____ _____ _____, as in the sentence, "Write a sentence on the board." The third type is the interrogative sentence. It is used to ask a question. For example, "Do you write well?" The last type is the exclamatory sentence. It is used to show emotion. The sentence "I love your writing!" is an example. It is important to use these sentences _____ _____ _____ _____ to convey your message well. Now, let's get into groups and do a writing exercise.

17 Dictation Test

녹음을 다시 한 번 들으면서, 빈칸을 채워 봅시다.

01

W: Good morning to all you K-One listeners. I'm your host, Danni Stokes. Before we get back to our regularly scheduled program, I'd like to remind everyone that K-One is _____ _____ _____ _____ _____, and operates thanks to the donations of our listeners. Every show has been made possible because of people like you. On behalf of everyone here at K-One, I'd like to say _____ _____ _____ _____, _____ _____ _____ _____. If you like the stories you hear, please _____ _____ _____ _____ _____ _____ or through your phone. No amount is too small since it will help us bring you the latest stories that you want to hear. Now back to our show.

02

M: Michelle. How are you today?
W: I'm doing good, Dan. _____ _____ _____ _____?
M: Well, nothing much. I recently quit my gym.
W: You love to exercise. Why did you quit?
M: I was _____ _____ _____ _____ _____ all the time.
W: I understand. Sometimes you just need to be outside.
M: Exactly. That's why I am going to start hiking.
W: That's great. What made you decide on hiking? Being one with nature?
M: That's good, but I think the best part of hiking is _____ _____ _____ _____ _____.
W: But you like being with people.
M: I know, but it's sometimes nice to be by myself.
W: I see. I hope I can join you on a hike one of these days.

03

W: Good afternoon, Mr. Smith.
M: Hello, Ms. Roberts. I wanted to _____ _____ _____ _____ _____ _____ _____.
W: Alright. How can I help you?
M: I want to make sure he's eating healthily. Do you have any advice?
W: Oh, I get this question from parents all the time. My advice is _____ _____ _____ _____ _____ _____.
M: Do you mean soda?
W: Yes. Have your son drink more water and less soda and juice.
M: Okay. Is there anything else I should be doing?
W: _____ _____ _____, I can't stress enough the importance of _____ _____ _____ _____ _____ _____.
M: How can I do that? He doesn't like vegetables.
W: Try adding some vegetables to your dishes. For example, blend some carrots and add them to pasta sauce.
M: Thank you. You've been a great help.

04

M: Wow, Hannah. This office looks amazing.
W: Do you really like it?
M: Yeah! I like _____ _____ _____ _____ _____ _____.
W: I put my desk there so I can get some natural light from the window next to it.
M: _____ _____ _____ _____ are cute.
W: Thanks. I put my file cabinet in the left corner. That way I can keep all my important papers close by.
M: I don't see a place for a printer though.
W: I didn't have any room for a printer. So, I put _____ _____ _____ on the small stool instead.

M: It adds a nice touch of green to the room.
W: And over here on the left wall is _____ _____

_____ _____ _____ _____.
M: I've seen that poster before.
W: I know it's very popular, but I find it inspiring.

05

W: Scott, have you _____ _____ _____ _____

_____?
M: Yes, I'm almost finished, Carol. Have you packed the cooler?
W: Yeah, I put that away this morning.
M: Great! Are you doing anything right now?
W: I'm going to go wash my hands. They're a little dirty.
M: Before you go, can you _____ _____ _____

_____ _____?
W: Sure. What do you need me to do?
M: I need you to hold the bag open so I can pack the tent into it.
W: Sure. Where is the bag?
M: I'm not sure. I think I saw it in the back of the car.
W: I didn't see it there when I put the cooler away.
M: Oh. _____ _____ _____ _____ _____ _____

and see if you can find it please?
W: Okay. I will do.

06

M: Alright, ma'am. All the repairs on your car are finished.
W: Great! Could you tell me what work you've done and how much it was?
M: Sure. First, we started with an oil change. That was $25.
W: Right. What else did you do?
M: Your belts were really worn down. _____ _____

_____ _____ _____ _____.
W: Okay. Could you explain this item on the bill?
M: That's the fee for the initial diagnostic test, which was $75.

W: $75 seems a little bit high. Go on, please.
M: The final item on your bill is _____ _____ _____,

_____ _____ _____ _____.
W: Wow. It's a lot more expensive than I thought.
M: Well, I can _____ _____ _____ _____ _____

_____ on the total.
W: That would be much appreciated.

07

[Cell phone rings.]
W: Hey, Larry. Are you going to _____ _____ _____

_____ _____ _____ _____?
M: Hi, Jean. Yeah, I should be there on time.
W: Make sure you're not late. I reserved tickets for the 7 o'clock showing.
M: I promise I'll be there on time. I'm getting into my car right now.
W: I heard so many good things about this movie.
M: Yeah, me too. Everyone keeps talking about how great it is.
W: Did you _____ _____ _____?
M: No. I didn't want to spoil the movie.
W: Sure. I understand what you mean.
M: Jean, I'm _____ _____ _____ _____ _____

_____. It won't start.
W: Oh no! What's wrong?
M: I left the lights on last night. I'm really sorry, Jean. I won't be able to watch the movie today.

08

M: Sweetheart, come take a look. We got a wedding invitation.

W: Who's getting married?

M: My high school friend, James. He's _____ _____ _____ _____ _____ _____.

W: It's about time. When is the wedding?

M: It's on May 5th.

W: That's a good time for a wedding. The weather is not too hot or too cold then. _____ _____ _____ _____ _____?

M: At the church on the corner of 1st and Main.

W: That church is a little small. What time is the wedding?

M: It says here that it starts at 1 p.m.

W: I'm so happy for James.

M: Oh, the invitation says that we need to _____ _____ _____ _____ _____ _____ _____.

W: That's this Friday! Fill it out now so I can mail it tomorrow morning.

09

M: Hello, all you guitar fans. The Florida Guitar Festival is back again, and you don't want to miss it. This annual event will be _____ _____ _____ _____ _____ _____ _____ _____. The festival has many interesting events for the entire family. There will be beginner guitar workshops for anyone who wants to _____ _____ _____ _____ _____ _____. The workshops will be taught by the one and only Lionel Fritz, a world-renowned jazz guitar musician. Also, many legendary guitar musicians will be giving special performances throughout the festival. We shouldn't forget to mention the food. _____ _____ _____ _____ _____ _____ will be serving their delicious dishes throughout the entire event. Bring the whole family, and have a great time.

10

M: Jessica, we got a new catalogue from Everest Sportswear.

W: Great! Are there any winter coats on sale?

M: I saw some on the last page. How much do you want to spend?

W: I don't want to _____ _____ _____ _____ on the coat.

M: You're in luck! They have four on sale for under $200.

W: Wonderful! Which ones _____ _____ _____ _____ _____?

M: These three do. With all the snow we get, the coat should be waterproof.

W: How about the insulation? I want _____ _____ _____.

M: Yeah. Nothing keeps you as warm as down. Both of these coats are down.

W: Alright. Lastly, the coat _____ _____ _____ _____.

M: Only one of these two has a hood.

W: Then that's the one for me.

11

M: Sally, _____ _____ _____ _____ _____ _____ and babysit for us?

W: Sure, Mr. Jones. I'm free then. What time do you need me?

M: My wife and I have a dinner reservation at 7 o'clock, so can you come here by 6 o'clock?

W: (No problem. I'll be over then.)

12

W: Mike. It's so hot. Why don't we _____ _____ _____ _____?

M: Sure. I'm thirsty, too. What kind of drink do you want?

W: I'd like a mango juice. Do you want one too?

M: (Actually, I'm allergic to mangoes. I'll have something else.)

13

W: Mr. House, your qualifications are outstanding.

M: I'm happy to hear that. I feel that I _____ _____ _____ _____ _____ your hospital.

W: Great. Do you have any questions?

M: I _____ _____ _____ _____ _____ _____.
Could you tell me about that?

W: Certainly. As a doctor in our hospital, you will _____ _____ _____ _____. You will also be allowed to purchase stocks once your grace period ends.

M: That's excellent. What about vacations?

W: We have two-weeks paid vacation per year. After seven years, doctors are allowed to take three-months paid leave.

M: How many sick days are available?

W: The hospital _____ _____ _____ _____ _____ in the first year. Every year you work here, you get an additional day.

M: All of this sounds perfect.

W: Okay. So, when can you start?

M: (I'm available to begin working next week.)

14

M: Oh, Lizzy! It's been so long. How have you been?

W: _____ _____ _____ _____. The family is good. Work is steady.

M: Are you still working as a teacher?

W: Yeah. I just started working at the public elementary school next to our place.

M: How is that going? I hear teaching is a very stressful job.

W: It's okay. The staff is great. Everyone is very helpful. The students are excellent too.

M: I have to get going, but we should try to have dinner sometime. I'd like to see the whole family.

W: That sounds fantastic. How about this weekend?

M: This weekend is out for me. I _____ _____ _____ _____ _____.

W: Okay, and next weekend our family is going camping up by the lake.

M: Why don't I just call you? We can _____ _____ _____ _____.

W: (Okay. I'll be expecting your call.)

15

W: Tom and Sara are a married couple and they are planning their first vacation abroad together. After a long discussion, they agree to go to Guam. The problem is they have _____ _____ _____ _____ _____ _____ _____ there. Tom wants to do _____ _____ _____ _____ _____ _____.
He wants to go hiking, surfing and snorkeling. On the other hand, Sara is looking forward to sitting on the beach and spending time with Tom. _____ _____ _____ _____ _____ because this year has been very tough. Sara would like Tom to take a break and relax with her during the vacation. In this situation, what would Sara most likely say to Tom?

16-17

M: Good morning, all you music lovers. You're listening to the Audio Mania podcast, and I'm your host, Jim. Last time, we talked about the advantages of bluetooth speakers. Today, _____ _____ _____ _____ _____ _____ _____. More specifically, a brand-new model called Airpal has just become available. With superb noise cancelling, you can listen to your music on a crowded subway without turning up the volume. Also, due to a new patented technology, the sound quality on the Airpal is _____ _____ _____ _____ _____ _____ currently on the market. These headsets also come with a charging case for convenient charging. Another feature worth mentioning is the Quick Reality mode, which lets you hear outside noise without taking off the headsets. It's great when you are having a quick conversation or ordering coffee at a cafe. _____ _____ _____ _____ _____ _____ _____ _____ of these headsets are turning the heads of music lovers everywhere. Try them out at your local electronics store.

녹음을 다시 한 번 들으면서, 빈칸을 채워 봅시다.

01

M: Good morning! This is Harry Brown, the president of the student council. Now that _____ _____ _____ _____ _____ _____ _____, how do you feel? Next Friday, you will be saying goodbye to our school. At this time, I have something to ask of you. Since _____ _____ _____ _____ _____ _____ _____ _____, why don't you donate them to the student council? If you donate them to us, they'll be cleaned, mended and sorted by size, and finally sent to students who need them. This is your chance to help younger students. From tomorrow to the day before the graduation ceremony, we'll be accepting your uniforms _____ _____ _____ _____ _____. We appreciate your active cooperation. Thank you, seniors.

02

M: Rachel, what did your students do during lunch break today?

W: The usual. Since _____ _____ _____ _____ _____, they don't want to go outside, so they just talked to each other in the classroom.

M: Really? I envy you.

W: You envy me? _____ _____ _____ _____ _____ _____?

M: My students just look at their smartphones in the classroom. They don't even talk to each other.

W: I'm sorry to hear that.

M: Don't your students use their smartphones?

W: They do, but not in the classroom. I don't allow it.

M: Oh, that's good. Why didn't I think of that?

W: I think _____ _____ _____ _____ _____ _____ _____, at least in the classroom. Otherwise they won't do anything else.

M: I totally agree with you. I'll tell my students not to use them, starting tomorrow.

03

W: Hi, it's nice to meet you. I'm Sara Johnson.

M: Hi, I'm Brian Anderson.

W: Thank you for coming. I was beginning to worry that you wouldn't show up.

M: I had to come. I was _____ _____ _____ _____ _____ _____ _____ _____.

W: That's right. So please tell me what you saw in detail.

M: I was walking home from work and suddenly, I heard someone scream. Then a tall guy wearing a blue jacket ran out of the bakery.

W: You must have been very surprised. What did you do next?

M: I ran into the bakery and found a man bleeding. And _____ _____ _____ _____ _____.

W: I got it. Did you see any strange vehicles around the bakery?

M: No. There was a taxi across from the bakery. _____ _____ _____ _____ _____ _____.

W: Okay. What you said will _____ _____ _____ _____ _____. Thank you for your cooperation.

M: I hope you get the criminal as soon as possible.

W: Don't worry, we will.

04

M: Cindy, I heard that you finished arranging the staff lounge.

W: Yes, Mr. Jackson. Have a look, please.

M: Hmm. You put wallpaper with star patterns on the wall as I requested.

W: Yes, and I _____ _____ _____ _____ _____ _____.

M: Good. Oh, there's a world map on the wall.

W: Right. Since our company is _____ _____ _____ _____ _____ _____ all over the world, I thought it would be fitting.

M: That's a very good idea.

W: Thank you. What do you think about the round table in the center?

M: It's _____ _____ _____ _____ _____ _____ we had before.

W: I also hope you like the flower vase on the table.

M: I do. It makes the atmosphere of the lounge more relaxing.

05

W: Daddy, I've finished cleaning the living room.

M: _____ _____ _____ _____ _____, too?

W: Yes, I have.

M: Good! I've also finished cleaning the bathroom and the kitchen.

W: Mom's going to be surprised to see the house so clean.

M: You're right. She _____ _____ _____ _____ _____ _____ how clean the house is.

W: I agree. By the way, what time will Mom arrive home?

M: Um... since _____ _____ _____ _____ _____ _____ at the airport at 5:10 p.m., she'll be home around 7 o'clock.

W: Then she's going to be hungry. Why don't we prepare dinner for her?

M: Good idea. I'll make her favorite, chicken stew.

W: Good. Is there anything I can help you with?

M: Yes, there is. _____ _____ _____ _____ _____ and mushrooms?

W: Sure! I'll go to the grocery store right away.

06

W: Hi, I'd like to _____ _____ _____ _____ _____ _____ _____.

M: We have two kinds of passes. The Gold Pass costs $30, and you can go on every ride in the park with this pass.

W: How about the other pass?

M: That's the Silver Pass, and it's $20. With it, you can go on five rides of your choice.

W: I think the Gold Pass is a better deal.

M: Sure. The Gold Pass is more popular than the Silver Pass.

W: Okay. _____ _____ _____ _____ _____ _____?

M: Do you have any children? Children under 13 pay _____ _____ _____ _____ _____.

W: Yes. Two of the children are under 13.

M: Great. If you pay with an ABC credit card, you can also _____ _____ _____ _____ _____ _____ _____ _____.

W: Great! Here's my ABC credit card.

M: Thank you.

07

[Cell phone rings.]

W: Cindy speaking.

M: Cindy? It's me, Tucker. Can you talk?

W: _____ _____ _____. I'm at the library doing my biology report. What's up?

M: Did you book the tickets for the concert this Friday?

W: Yes, I did. I got us front-row tickets. We can see the performance right in front of the stage.

M: Oh dear! I don't think I can go to the concert with you.

W: Why? Are your parents coming to see you again?

M: No. I just _____ _____ _____ _____ _____ _____ saying that my younger sister _____ _____ _____ _____ this afternoon.

W: Oh, no! Is she alright?

M: Fortunately, nothing is broken and she's okay. But she's in the hospital now so _____ _____ _____ _____ _____ _____ _____.

W: Of course, you should go. When will you come back?

M: Sunday evening. I'm really sorry.

W: No problem. I hope she gets well soon.

08

M: Semi, I heard that you're selling your electric clothes dryer.

W: Right. Are you interested in it?

M: Yeah, the one I'm using now is too small. So I need to buy a bigger one.

W: _____ _____ _____ _____ _____ _____. That's plenty for one person.

M: Good. How long have you used it?

W: I bought it two years ago.

M: Then _____ _____ _____ _____ _____ _____ _____ _____.

W: No. It came with a five-year warranty. So you don't have to worry about that for a while.

M: That's very good. _____ _____ _____ _____ _____, I'd like to buy your dryer.

W: I bought it for $700, but I'll give it to you for $350.

M: Great. You got yourself a deal.

09

W: Attention, shoppers. Thank you for visiting the Rainbow Department Store. We _____ _____ _____ _____ _____ _____. The Green Jazz Concert is going to _____ _____ _____ _____ _____ _____ _____. The concert will start at 7 o'clock this evening, and last for about two hours. Five famous jazz musicians will participate in the concert and perform your favorite jazz titles. _____ _____ _____ _____ _____ _____ _____, but anyone who has a receipt for a purchase over $20 can enjoy the concert for free. During the intermission, the audience will be provided with simple snacks and soft drinks. I hope you jazz lovers will come and enjoy the concert.

10

M: Hi, I'd like to sign up for a surfing class this Saturday.

W: Sure. Have you ever surfed before?

M: No, I haven't. _____ _____ _____ _____.

W: Then we'll put you in the beginner level.

M: Okay. Which class do you recommend?

W: _____ _____ _____ _____ _____. But I'd recommend taking the two-hour class. The one-hour class is not enough for most people.

M: Okay, _____ _____ _____ _____ _____. Hmm.... Why is this class more expensive than the other classes?

W: That's because it includes snacks and drinks during the break time.

M: Well, I don't think I need them.

W: I see. Now you have to choose one of these two instructors. Brian is kind and relaxed, and John is humorous, but a bit strict.

M: I think _____ _____ _____ _____ _____ _____. I'll take this class.

W: You got it.

11

W: Excuse me. Is there a tennis court in the hotel?

M: Yes, there is. It's in the main garden. But you have to make a reservation first.

W: I got it. Thank you. Ah, one more thing. Is there _____ _____ _____ _____ _____ _____ ?

M: (Yes. The bus departs every hour on the hour from the front gate.)

12

M: Excuse me, do you know where the Korean restaurant Arirang is?

W: Arirang? Go straight one block and turn left. Then _____ _____ _____ _____ _____ _____ _____.

M: A big fire station? Is the restaurant close to it?

W: (Yes, it's just behind the fire station.)

13

M: Alice, are you interested in _____ _____ _____ _____ _____ this weekend?

W: A blind date? Do you have someone to introduce to me?

M: Yes, I do. One of my friends saw your picture on my phone, and he wants to meet you.

W: Really? Is he your co-worker?

M: Yes, he is. And he's been _____ _____ _____ _____ _____ _____ _____ _____.

W: Hmm.... Tell me more.

M: He's really handsome. He looks like a fashion model.

W: Hey, appearance isn't everything. It's personality that is important.

M: Don't worry. He's very honest and responsible.

W: Is he? How's his sense of humor? I like _____ _____ _____ _____ _____ _____ _____.

M: He's really funny. He's the funniest guy I know.

W: (Okay! I'll go on a blind date with your friend.)

14

M: Stella, why don't we take the Chinese Conversation class this semester?

W: Sorry, but I already took that class last semester, and I got an A$^+$.

M: Really? I didn't know that. Then which foreign language conversation class are you going to take?

W: French. I've already _____ _____ _____ _____ _____ _____ _____.

M: The Advanced French Conversation class? Can you speak French as well?

W: Yes. I learned basic French when I was in high school.

M: Wow! Are there _____ _____ _____ _____ _____ _____ besides Chinese and French?

W: Sure! I can speak Korean too.

M: Really? Where and how did you learn Korean?

W: Just at home, by myself. _____ _____ _____ _____ _____ _____ _____. So I studied Korean to enjoy K-pop better.

M: (Incredible! You're a true language genius.)

15

W: Recently Rebecca moved to an apartment in Santa Monica. She is satisfied with her new apartment, except that it is far from her job. _____ _____ _____ _____ _____ _____ to get to work from her new apartment. She complains about this to her co-worker, Lucas, adding that the travel to work is very boring. Lucas says that he's in the same situation as Rebecca, and explains that he usually _____ _____ _____ _____ _____ _____ _____ _____. Listening to what Lucas says, Rebecca thinks reading books can be a good way _____ _____ _____ _____ _____ _____. She makes up her mind to follow Lucas's advice, and wants to know which books are good for reading on the subway. In this situation, what would Rebecca most likely say to Lucas?

16-17

M: Hello, everyone! Welcome to Animal World. I'm your host, Adam Brown. Last time, I talked to you about the survival of wild animals such as tigers and wolves. Today, _____ _____ _____ _____ _____ _____ _____. Do you know what you _____ _____ _____ _____ _____ before deciding to get a companion animal? First, you have to think about your personality. If you are not very active, you might _____ _____ _____ _____ _____ _____ instead of a dog, since cats don't need to be taken for a walk each day. Goldfish are another good alternative. Secondly, you should consider how long you can be with your companion animal. A parrot requires much care. So if you are too busy to play with a parrot, you should choose a different animal. The last thing you have to consider is money. A lot of money has to be spent on food, training classes, veterinary care, toys, and other expenses for your companion animals. If this is a problem, please _____ _____ _____ _____ _____ _____ _____.

녹음을 다시 한 번 들으면서, 빈칸을 채워 봅시다.

01

M: Hello, everyone. I'm Gerry Robinson from the Traffic Division of the Greenwich Police Department. Do you know what _____ _____ _____ _____ _____ _____ _____ in our town is? It's _____ _____ _____ _____ _____ _____ _____. In the last three months, about 70 traffic accidents on our roads have been caused by drivers using their cell phones while driving. What's worse, many of the accidents have _____ _____ _____ _____ _____ to almost everyone in the vehicle. It can't be overemphasized that using your cell phone while driving is _____ _____ _____, _____ _____ _____ _____. Therefore, no matter what the circumstance may be, I'd like to ask you not to use your cell phone while operating your vehicle. It's not just for your safety, but for the safety of everyone.

02

W: Clark, how's the corporate advertisement you're in charge of coming along?

M: Okay, I guess. I'm trying to _____ _____ _____ _____ _____ to maximize the company's image.

W: Do you have anything in mind?

M: Well, I'm thinking about listing the company's achievements to let people know its history and tradition.

W: I don't think lists are attractive enough. People won't read them.

M: You have a point. Do you have any other ideas then?

W: These days, I think people are _____ _____ _____ _____ _____ than anything else.

M: Yeah. It seems people are easily swayed by emotional news.

W: That's right. So I think it would be more effective _____ _____ _____ _____ _____ when you make a corporate ad.

M: Hmm.... That makes sense. Okay, let me develop that idea. Thank you for the tip.

W: My pleasure.

03

M: You look pale. What's wrong?

W: I think I'm _____ _____ _____ _____ _____. Last night, I slept with the windows open.

M: What are your symptoms?

W: I have a runny nose as well as a slight fever.

M: Why don't you see the school nurse and tell her your symptoms?

W: _____ _____ _____ _____ _____ _____. Is it okay if I leave early today?

M: Well, let me call your mom first to see if she agrees with your decision.

W: Sure.

M: After getting your mom's permission, I can let you leave early.

W: Thank you.

M: But, if you leave early, you will miss the rest of today's lessons. _____ _____ _____ _____ _____ _____ _____ _____ from your classmates.

W: Okay, I will. Thank you.

04

W: I moved to a new apartment yesterday.

M: Oh, really? Do you like your new place?

W: I love it! Especially the living room. I have a picture of it on my phone.

M: Wow. It's very nice. The first thing that catches my eye is the TV on the center of the wall. It _____ _____ _____ _____ _____ _____ _____.

W: Yeah. I had to _____ _____ _____ _____ _____ _____ to get it mounted on the wall like that.

M: The wall behind the TV is decorated with pictures of fish. Your living room looks like the sea.

W: You got it. I placed a mermaid statue at the bottom left of the TV to go with the wall.

M: Those two round tables _____ _____ _____ _____ _____ _____ are unique.

W: I'm glad you noticed them. I had them made just for my living room.

M: The sofa on the right next to those tables looks so cozy. I am looking forward to visiting your apartment soon.

W: Anytime. You're always welcome.

05

W: Honey, do you remember that I _____ _____ _____ _____ in the flea market?

M: Yeah. I remember.

W: I _____ _____ _____ _____ _____ _____ I can participate in the flea market.

M: Really? That's great news!

W: Yeah. It's a good chance to sell and buy all kinds of used stuff.

M: I hope you make a lot of money there.

W: Actually, all proceeds from the flea market go to charity.

M: I didn't know that. _____ _____ _____ _____!

W: Right. Do you have any stuff that you no longer use, but is still in good condition?

M: I'm sure I can find plenty of things in the garage to sell. Tell me if there's anything else I can do to help.

W: Actually, I need a lot of change. Can you go to the bank and _____ _____ _____ _____ _____ _____?

M: No problem.

06

M: Hello. I want to buy tickets to the Natural History Museum.

W: How many tickets do you want?

M: I want five tickets, including one child. How much is it per person?

W: It's _____ _____ _____ _____ and $6 for a child. How old is your child?

M: My child is 7 years old.

W: 7-year-olds _____ _____ _____ _____ _____ _____.

M: Great. Do you have any other special discounts?

W: If you live in San Diego, you can _____ _____ _____ _____ _____ _____.

M: Two people in my party live in San Diego.

W: Okay. Can you _____ _____ _____ _____ _____?

M: Here you are.

W: Okay, then they can get $2 off.

M: Great. Here's my credit card.

07

M: Honey, why don't we eat out tomorrow evening?

W: Do you have any particular restaurant in mind?

M: How about Henry's Steakhouse?

W: Oh, I love the food there. But don't you think _____ _____ _____ _____ _____ _____?

M: Don't worry. I have a 30% discount coupon for the restaurant.

W: I also have that coupon but I thought that _____ _____ _____ _____. Did you check the expiration date on it?

M: What? Let me see.... Oh, I _____ _____ _____ this coming Saturday.

W: Without it, the dinner will cost a lot.

M: Right. Honey, there's another good steak restaurant near my office.

W: You mean Star Steakhouse?

M: That's right. It _____ _____ _____ _____ _____ _____ _____.

W: Very good. Okay, let's go there tomorrow.

08

[Telephone rings.]

W: Busan City Tour Information Center. How may I help you?

M: Hi. This summer I'm planning to look around Busan.

W: Busan is a very exciting port city. You won't regret visiting it.

M: Good. But I don't know how to get around the city.

W: I recommend using the Busan City Tour Bus. It _____ _____ _____ _____.

M: If I want a one-day ticket, how can I buy one?

W: You can ask the driver when you get on the bus. He can _____ _____ _____ _____ _____.

M: How much is it?

W: It's 5,000 won for an adult and 3,000 won for a child.

M: Good. Is there anything I should keep in mind during the bus tour?

W: The passengers should _____ _____ _____ _____ _____. For example, consumption of food and beverages is not allowed.

M: Thanks a lot.

09

W: Hello, ABC radio listeners. This is Laura Clark, the manager of the Boston Marathon event. We are scheduled to hold the Boston Half Marathon on Sunday, April 14th this year. It starts at 11 a.m. We will _____ _____ _____ _____ _____ _____ _____, so if you want to join our marathon event, register as early as possible. There will be a special souvenir _____ _____ _____ _____ _____. If you register before April 1st, we will present you with a towel with the Boston Marathon logo. If you finish the marathon, you _____ _____ _____ _____ _____ _____ _____. Water stations _____ _____ _____ _____ from the start line. If you have any questions, please email me at manager@bostonmarathon.org. Thank you.

10

M: Honey, this furniture store has a lot of nice children's desks.

W: Wow! Why don't we buy a desk for our daughter's birthday present?

M: Good idea! What color should we get?

W: She likes pink and yellow. Let's choose one of those two colors.

M: Okay. What about the material? I _____ _____ _____ _____.

W: I agree. I think it feels more natural.

M: What about the height adjustment function? She's growing fast every year.

W: Right. _____ _____ _____ _____ _____.

M: Hmm..., what is this slot?

W: That's a USB port. These days, some desks have built-in USB ports.

M: But, then she'll use it to charge her smartphone and send texts instead of studying.

W: Okay. _____ _____ _____ _____ _____. That leaves us with this desk. Let's buy it.

11

W: Frank, the new TV is going to be delivered today.

M: Okay. _____ _____ _____ _____ _____ _____, Claire?

W: The delivery company said that it should be here between 5 and 6 p.m.

M: (I'll make sure to be home at that time.)

12

M: Rebecca, didn't you think today's physics class was too difficult to understand?

W: Definitely. I'm _____ _____ _____ _____ _____ _____. You can join me if you want.

M: Really? That would be really helpful. When should we start?

W: (The sooner the better. How about this evening?)

13

W: How's your report going?

M: I haven't started writing it yet.

W: I heard that your topic is on _____ _____ _____ _____ _____ _____ _____ in the future.

M: You're right. But the topic is so general that I can't organize my thoughts.

W: I think you need to _____ _____ _____ _____.

M: How? Can you give me some tips?

W: For example, do you think artificial intelligence will take away human jobs?

M: Some jobs, but not all of them.

W: Can you give me some examples?

M: Repetitive tasks will be substituted, but artificial intelligence can't do anything creative without human intervention.

W: That's it. I think you're starting _____ _____ _____ _____ _____ _____ _____.

M: (Yes. My thoughts are more organized after talking with you.)

14

M: Mom, I have a flower pot, but I don't know _____ _____ _____ _____ _____ _____ _____.

W: What sort of seedlings are they?

M: Tomato seedlings. Can you give me some tips?

W: First of all, you should water the seedlings regularly.

M: I know. But that's too simple. Any other tips?

W: Tomato seedlings need a lot of strong sunlight.

M: Oh, really? I didn't know that.

W: Then, how were you planning to grow them?

M: Actually, I thought I would _____ _____ _____ _____ _____ _____. I saw my friend grow a seedling that way and it flourished.

W: But that might not have been a tomato seedling.

M: Then, where is _____ _____ _____ _____ _____ _____ in the house?

W: (How about on the balcony? That's the sunniest place in the house.)

15

M: Kevin is a senior in high school. Kevin has been _____ _____ _____ _____ _____ _____ _____, so he wants to consult with his teacher, Ms. Johns. Ms. Johns often _____ _____ _____ _____ during her class, so she also wanted to talk with him. When they talk, she realizes that he is constantly checking his social media. Whenever notifications about new messages go off, he accesses his social media and writes a reply. He admits that even when he studies at home, he is often _____ _____ _____ _____ _____ and goes to sleep late. Ms. Johns thinks that _____ _____ _____ _____ _____ _____ for a while and concentrate on his studies. In this situation, what would Ms. Johns most likely say to Kevin?

16-17

W: Hello, students. Thank you for coming to my lecture today. I'm Sarah Ferguson from the Eco-friendly Energy Institute. Due to _____ _____ _____ _____ _____ _____ _____, the Earth has suffered greatly. The generation of fossil-fuel-based energy causes air pollution, leading to climate change. Today I'll talk about some alternatives to fossil fuel energy. Firstly, biomass is _____ _____ _____ _____ _____, derived from burning animal and plant waste. The organic materials used to produce biomass are infinite, since our society consistently produces waste such as garbage and wood. Secondly, solar energy makes use of the sun's energy and converts it into electricity. It can _____ _____ _____ _____ is cheaper than fossil fuels. Thirdly, energy from wind can be produced through the use of wind turbines, producing zero hazardous waste. Lastly, hydropower is one of the most widely used forms of eco-friendly energy. The use of water as an energy source is _____ _____ _____, _____ _____ _____. Now, let's watch a video of how these four types of energy are being used.

녹음을 다시 한 번 들으면서, 빈칸을 채워 봅시다.

01

W: Hello, everyone. Thank you for coming here despite the heavy rain. I'm Janet Brown and _____ _____ _____ _____ _____. As you all know, our city's economy is in bad shape. Since last year, all economic indicators, including unemployment and inflation, have been at their worst levels ever. I want to overcome this economic crisis. With a Ph.D. in economics, I have taught students at a university, and worked as CEO of a global automobile company. In last week's poll of _____ _____ _____ _____ _____ _____, the overwhelming response was, "the candidate who can solve the economic crisis." That's me, Janet Brown. I hope you won't forget me in the mayoral election next Wednesday. _____ _____ _____ _____ for you and your children, and for Austin City. Thank you.

02

W: Daniel, you have been driving an electric car for almost a month now.

M: Yeah. Time flies.

W: So are you satisfied with the electric car?

M: Well, I'm pretty satisfied, _____ _____ _____ _____.

W: Do you mean its high price?

M: No, it's not that. The problem is _____ _____ _____ _____.

W: Is it difficult to charge at a charging station?

M: No, but it's _____ _____ _____ _____ _____ _____ since there are not so many around.

W: Really? That must be a big problem for electric car owners.

M: Absolutely! I think more charging stations should be installed.

W: Otherwise, electric cars will have _____ _____ _____ _____ _____ _____, even though they are good for the environment.

03

W: Are you Mr. Raymond?

M: Yes, I am. I made _____ _____ _____ _____ _____ _____ half an hour ago. Thank you for coming.

W: No problem. Just doing my job. So could you tell me what happened?

M: I _____ _____ _____ _____ _____ _____ after reaching the summit of the mountain.

W: It seems that you took a heavy fall. Can you stand up?

M: I don't think so. Look, my ankle is swollen. I think I broke my ankle.

W: Don't worry. Two more rescuers are on the way here. _____ _____ _____ _____ _____ _____.

M: Thank you very much.

W: Did you inform your family that you have been injured on the mountain?

M: Yes. I called my wife and told her about the accident. She's also on her way here.

W: Please call her again and let her know that you're safe.

04

M: Honey, I finished decorating the living room for the Christmas party.

W: Oh, you put the Christmas tree next to the fireplace. It's wonderful.

M: And I _____ _____ _____ that says "Merry Christmas" _____ _____ _____ _____.

W: Good. Why did you place the square table in the center of the living room?

M: We can put the gifts on the table, and have the kids choose them as they wish.

W: Really? It'll be exciting since the kids don't know what they'll get.

M: Absolutely! _____ _____ _____ _____ _____

_____ _____ _____.

W: I think so, too. Are those pretty boxes in front of the Christmas tree the presents?

M: That's right. It took almost an hour to wrap them up.

W: You did a great job. Oh, I like _____ _____

_____ _____ _____ _____ _____.

M: I also put some sweets for the kids in the socks.

W: How lovely! You're a really good dad.

05

M: Judith, it's already 12 o'clock. It's time for lunch.

W: Yeah, right. Let's go.

M: Oh, how are your preparations for the business trip to Germany this Friday coming along?

W: Great. I'm done everything, except for one thing.

M: What's that?

W: The goldfish on my desk. I haven't found _____

_____ _____ _____ _____ _____ _____

while I'm on the business trip.

M: Hey, why didn't you ask me to do that? I can take care of it for you.

W: Can you? Oh, thank you, David. You only have to feed it once a day before leaving the office.

M: That's a piece of cake! Don't worry. Your goldfish

_____ _____ _____ _____ _____.

W: I'm so relieved. David, _____ _____ _____

_____ _____ _____ _____ today. Just tell me what you want to have.

M: Um.... How about seafood spaghetti?

W: Okay!

06

M: Hi, I'd like to enroll my twin daughters for one of your sports programs.

W: Sure. What kind of program do you want your children to take?

M: Ballet. How much is the monthly fee?

W: There are two ballet programs. _____ _____

_____ _____ _____ and consists of three lessons a week.

M: What about the other one?

W: It costs $70, and it has two lessons a week.

M: Hmm.... There's a $30 difference between the two programs.

W: Yeah. The intensive program is much more popular.

M: Okay, I'll _____ _____ _____ _____ _____

_____ _____. Oh, is there any discount for registering two children at once?

W: No, there isn't. But you can _____ _____ _____

_____ if you _____ _____ _____ _____

_____ _____.

M: Really? Then I'll pay for two months now.

07

W: Fred, _____ _____ _____ _____ _____.

There's not a single apple left in the fridge.

M: Really? Then why don't we go buy some? We need vegetables, too.

W: Good! Let's go to the Green Market right away.

M: Green Market? You mean, the one just next to our apartment?

W: Yeah. _____ _____ _____ _____ _____ now.

Plus, the staff there are very kind.

M: That's true, but I don't want to go there.

W: How come? They even have a free delivery service for customers.

M: But _____ _____ _____ _____ _____ _____

_____.

W: Then let's go to ABC Market on Maple Street. Their produce is very fresh.

M: Okay. Let me get the car key right now.

W: It's on the table in the kitchen. I put it there after driving to the sports center in the morning.

M: Okay.

08

M: Look at this picture of a tree. It looks awesome.

W: Oh, it's the ginkgo tree in Orange County, Vermont. They say _____ _____ _____ _____ _____ .

M: How do you know about the tree?

W: A few weeks ago, I saw a documentary about it. Can you guess how tall it is?

M: About 30 meters?

W: Actually, it's much taller. It's 62 meters tall. And its diameter is 9 meters.

M: Wow! That's a huge tree. Anyone who sees the tree in person will _____ _____ _____ _____ _____ _____ .

W: Absolutely! So its nickname is "the Great Giant."

M: Oh, I'd like to _____ _____ _____ _____ _____ _____ .

W: Really? Then why don't we go see it this weekend? I also want to see it.

M: That's a good idea.

09

M: Attention, students! The Green Essay Competition has begun. Its aim is to raise awareness about environmental protection. The topic for the competition is "How to Protect the Earth." All students _____ _____ _____ _____ _____ _____ _____ are eligible to participate in the competition. To enter the competition, _____ _____ _____ _____ _____ _____ and register your name on the participants list. You must upload your writing by Earth day, April 22nd. A team of English literature teachers will evaluate your writing, and the results will be posted on the school website on the last day of April. The gold medal _____ _____ _____ _____ _____ _____ _____ , and they will be entitled to participate in the Florida Essay Contest in June as representatives of our school.

10

W: Albert, let's look at this ad and buy a coffee machine for the staff lounge.

M: Okay. Do you have any particular brand in mind?

W: No. But we should avoid Grace. I heard its coffee machines make too much noise while brewing.

M: I heard that, too. What about the water capacity?

W: Well, I think we need one _____ _____ _____ _____ _____ _____ , since more than 20 people will be using the machine.

M: Right. I totally agree with you.

W: Do you think we need one with a cafe latte function?

M: Yes, it'd be _____ _____ _____ _____ _____ _____ .

W: Great! Then we have to order one of these two coffee machines. Which one do you prefer?

M: Of course, this one _____ _____ _____ _____ . What about you?

W: Me too. Okay, let's buy this one.

11

M: Charlotte, _____ _____ _____ _____ _____ _____ ?

W: Yeah, but I'm going to be a little late because of my dental appointment.

M: Not a problem. I'll change the reservation at the restaurant to a bit later.

W: (Fantastic! I'll see you at the restaurant.)

12

W: Brian, what are you listening to now?

M: A new song by James King. The title is *A White Night*. Have you heard it?

W: No, I haven't. But _____ _____ _____ _____ _____ _____ .

M: (Right. Listen to the song, and you'll love it too.)

13

M: Hi, I'd like to rent a house.

W: Sure. Which area are you thinking of?

M: Lakewood. Is there a house with three bedrooms in the area?

W: Yes. There are two houses at the moment.

M: That's great. Can you tell me _____ _____ _____ _____ _____ _____ _____ for those houses?

W: The one on Red Street is $900, and the other one on Blue Street is $1,200.

M: $1,200? Why is this house more expensive than the other one?

W: It _____ _____ _____ _____ _____ _____ _____.

M: Oh, I see. Then all the facilities _____ _____ _____ _____ _____ _____ _____.

W: Definitely! You'll be the first person to live in this house after the renovation if you act quickly.

M: (Sounds good. Can I have a look at the house now?)

14

W: Sam, do you know why Brian is absent today?

M: Didn't you hear that he was in a car accident last night?

W: No, I didn't. Was he seriously injured?

M: Fortunately, he's okay. I heard that the accident was not that serious and he is getting some rest at home.

W: _____ _____ _____! Do you know how the accident happened?

M: Well, he was using his cell phone while driving, and didn't see the other car.

W: Really? I don't understand how he _____ _____ _____ _____ _____.

M: Me neither.

W: You know, using a mobile phone while driving is _____ _____ _____ _____ _____ _____.

M: And I heard that about 40% of traffic accidents last year were caused by drivers who were using their cell phones.

W: (It's sad because those accidents should never have happened.)

15

M: Lucy and Eric _____ _____ _____ _____ _____, which is located on the 27th floor. They step out from their apartment and get in the elevator to go grocery shopping. As they talk about what food to buy, the lights inside the elevator suddenly go out and the elevator stops. Eric becomes very nervous and does not know what to do. He tells Lucy that he _____ _____ _____ _____ _____ _____. To calm him down, Lucy _____ _____ _____ _____ _____ _____ _____ with her smartphone. She sees the emergency telephone on the wall, and picks up the phone to report the situation. The operator says that a repairman will be there in ten minutes. Lucy thinks Eric may feel better when he hears this. In this situation, what would Lucy most likely say to Eric?

16-17

W: Hi, everyone. It's nice to meet you again. I'm Cathy Brown, a sports therapist. Let me ask you a question. Do you let your children play sports? If not, I encourage you to give your child a chance to play sports regularly. Aside from improving their physical strength, _____ _____ _____ _____ _____ _____. First of all, playing group sports such as soccer or baseball can help them _____ _____ _____ _____ _____ _____ _____. Also, while playing group sports with peers, children can _____ _____ _____ _____ _____. Individual sports such as skating or skiing positively affect your child's psychology. A recent study states that children who do these kinds of sports on a regular basis are _____ _____ _____ than children who do not. In the case of swimming, it was found that children who swam regularly were more composed and behaved more calmly in an emergency than children who did not swim. Now take a look at the screen in front of you.

녹음을 다시 한 번 들으면서, 빈칸을 채워 봅시다.

01

M: Hello, everyone. I'm Blake and I work for the Environmentalists' Society. Today, I'd like to talk about a popular fruit, the avocado. Many people like avocados because of their beautiful color and rich nutrients. They have plenty of unsaturated fatty acids, which _____ _____ _____ _____ _____ _____ _____ _____ and skin care. But, it's also _____ _____ _____ _____ _____ _____. Growing one avocado requires nearly 320L of water. To put things into perspective, growing one orange needs 22L of water and growing one tomato, only 5L. The amount of water needed to grow 1kg of avocado can _____ _____ _____ _____ _____ _____ _____ _____. As a result, the more avocados we grow, the faster the earth dries up. So we should not ignore the fact that growing avocados can contribute to water shortages around the world.

02

W: Adam, you don't look very well. What's the matter?

M: Hello, Ms. Nam. _____ _____ _____ _____ _____ _____.

W: Really? Did you injure them?

M: Not that I can remember.

W: Then, have you gained any weight recently?

M: No. I've actually lost some weight. I've been working out every day.

W: Is that so? What kind of workout have you been doing?

M: Well, I've been _____ _____ _____ _____ _____ _____ and two hours of weight training every day.

W: Three hours every day? That's a lot of exercise. Maybe _____ _____ _____ _____ _____.

M: You mean my knees hurt because I exercise too much?

W: Yes. You should exercise moderately according to your body condition.

M: I see. I'll work out less and see if my knees get better. Thank you, Ms. Nam.

03

M: Hello, I'm Asher. Are you Ms. Bronte?

W: Yes, I am. Thank you for coming such a long way.

M: No problem. It was a lovely drive anyway. What kind of help do you need?

W: I have something in mind, but I want to hear your expert opinion.

M: Well, I think the whole house is a little dark.

W: What can be done about that?

M: The walls of the house could be painted in a brighter color, and _____ _____ _____ _____ _____ _____ _____ _____.

W: Good. And I want to _____ _____ _____ _____ _____.

M: Yes, they're quite old. Take a look at this catalogue and _____ _____ _____ _____ _____ _____.

W: I really like the antique designs.

M: Also the windows look too old for the cold winds of winter. They should be changed as well.

W: I agree. When can you start?

M: If you choose a design, I can come with an estimate tomorrow.

04

M: Hello, Kate. What are you doing?

W: Hello, Mr. Brown. I'm _____ _____ _____ _____ _____ _____ _____ _____ for all the students to see.

M: It looks nice. By the way, are you starting a guitar club? I can see a super large guitar in the middle.

W: No. Actually, our band is performing a concert. Do you think I should have drawn other musical instruments?

M: That's all right. People can _____ _____ _____ _____ _____ _____ _____.

W: That's a relief. Can you see the date and place of the concert well?

M: Where are they? Oh, the date is in the top left corner and _____ _____ _____ _____ _____ _____ _____ _____. But I think they are a little too small to read.

W: Yes, you're right.

M: But I really like the letters above the guitar strings.

W: That's the admission fee. Anyway, can you come to the concert?

M: Absolutely.

W: See you this Friday!

05

W: Honey, I can't believe we're moving out tomorrow.

M: Neither can I. I _____ _____ _____ _____ _____ _____.

W: I heard it's going to rain heavily tomorrow. Should we check with the moving service whether we can move out?

M: I already checked. They said _____ _____ _____ _____ _____ _____, but they need two more people.

W: Why do they need more people?

M: They said they can't use the ladder truck because of the bad weather.

W: Then, _____ _____ _____ _____?

M: Of course. I have to withdraw some money for the extra movers.

W: Then on the way to the bank, can you visit the management office to let them know that we're using the elevator tomorrow?

M: Sure.

W: While you're doing that, I'll _____ _____ _____ _____ _____ _____ _____ _____.

M: Good. That's very important.

W: I think we've checked everything, right?

M: I think so.

06

M: Excuse me, is there a bus going to the airport from here?

W: Sure. It comes every thirty minutes. It'll be arriving in five minutes.

M: Good. I have to get to the airport before nine, because my wife is returning from her business trip.

W: Don't worry, there are _____ _____ _____ _____ _____ _____ _____ _____.

M: It's a relief to hear that. What's the price?

W: _____ _____ _____ _____ _____, and $20 for the deluxe express.

M: I'd like to take the express. Can I get a discount if I buy a round-trip ticket?

W: Yes, you can get 10% off.

M: Good. _____ _____ _____ _____ _____ and a one-way ticket for my wife to come back with me.

W: You can _____ _____ _____ _____ _____ if you pay cash.

M: I don't have enough cash. Here's my credit card.

W: Thank you.

07

M: What a busy day!

W: Yes, Mr. Williams. Now you just have one more important meeting left.

M: Okay. What does my schedule look like for tomorrow?

W: You _____ _____ _____ _____ _____ _____ _____ from tomorrow to Saturday.

M: Saturday? I told you I had to go to my son's football game this Friday afternoon.

W: But you said that the game was postponed until next week _____ _____ _____ _____ _____ _____.

M: Didn't I tell you the site of the game has been moved?

W: No, you didn't.

M: Oh, I must have forgotten. The construction is going to take four weeks, so the game has been moved to a nearby stadium.

W: Then, should I cancel your business trip?

M: Definitely. My son will be heartbroken if I don't attend the game.

W: Okay. I'll _____ _____ _____ _____ _____ _____ _____ _____ _____.

08

W: Honey, the lamp in the bedroom is flickering.

M: I can see that. I'll change the light bulb.

W: While you're at it, why don't you change it to an LED light bulb?

M: An LED light bulb? What's that?

W: Its color temperature is about 5,000K, so it's very bright and comfortable to our eyes.

M: Good. Our lamp _____ _____ _____ _____ _____ _____ _____ anyway. How is the life of the LED bulb?

W: It's really long. In fact, it can _____ _____ _____ _____ _____ _____ _____.

M: So using LED bulbs can be economically rewarding.

W: Of course. Also, they only use half as much electricity as regular light bulbs.

M: I can see why many people are switching to LED. Are there any other benefits?

W: Yes, they give off less heat, so they are _____ _____ _____ _____ _____ _____.

M: Then there's no reason not to switch.

09

W: Hello, this is Grace, a weather forecaster at the weather center of Hawaii. It'll be very sunny up to this weekend, but a typhoon will hit Hawaii next week. The 19th typhoon of the season, Typhoon Soulik, will _____ _____ _____ _____ _____ _____ _____ because the wind speed is over 115 mph. That's _____ _____ _____ _____ _____ _____. It can destroy buildings and walls, so be careful _____ _____ _____ _____ _____ when the typhoon hits. Also, it will rain heavily and the ground might be unstable, so do not go near the walls of buildings. The use of planes and boats may be restricted when _____ _____ _____ _____ _____, but it will steadily weaken by next Wednesday.

10

M: We're finally leaving next week.

W: I know. I'm so excited about going to a hot place _____ _____ _____ _____ _____!

M: How about buying a portable fan?

W: Sure. It can get really hot there.

M: Look at this site. *[Clicking sound]*

W: _____ _____ _____ _____ _____ _____. Which one should we buy?

M: I don't want to spend more than $30. And let's get one with a short charging time and a long usage time.

W: But it's hard to _____ _____ _____ _____ _____ _____ _____ at the same time.

M: I see. Then let's get one with the longest usage time. We can charge it during the night.

W: In that case, we can choose one of these two models.

M: I like the lighter one, even though it's more expensive.

W: You're right. Let's order it now.

11

M: I have difficulty _____ _____ _____ _____
_____ _____ _____ because the names are
sometimes very similar.

W: That's why I always write the people's occupations
when I save their numbers on my phone.

M: That's a great idea. Do you have any more tips?

W: (You can also make a note of their physical
characteristics.)

12

W: Hi, Jeff. Where are you going?

M: I'm on my way to school. I was just informed that
_____ _____ _____ _____ _____ _____
_____ .

W: Really? That's great news! How do you feel?

M: (I'm happy because I've always wanted to live there.)

13

W: Honey, how do you like your new school?

M: The other teachers are kind. The students are positive
and active. And, I love my electronic whiteboard.

W: Electronic whiteboard? _____ _____ _____
_____ _____ a regular blackboard?

M: I can use it as a computer screen.

W: Wow! Do you mean you can show your teaching
materials on a large screen?

M: Yes. More surprisingly, _____ _____ _____
_____ _____ _____ _____ , the whole screen
becomes a big touchpad.

W: A touchpad? Can you _____ _____ _____
_____ _____ _____ _____ _____ ?

M: Of course. I can even show a video clip and write
some notes on it.

W: It sounds fantastic. Tell me more.

M: The screen is so bright that you don't need to _____
_____ _____ _____ even during daytime.

W: Great! Is it easy to learn how to use it?

M: (Yes, it's very simple, so 10 minutes is sufficient.)

14

W: Honey, do you have some time tomorrow?

M: Sure. Why are you asking?

W: Can you go with me to buy a smartphone for Olivia?

M: Why does she need one? She's only seven.

W: She wants it as a gift for entering elementary school.

M: I think she's _____ _____ _____ _____ _____ .

W: But we can't follow her around while she's in school.
How can we contact her without it?

M: You might be right.

W: _____ _____ _____ _____ _____ _____ .
What if she gets lost?

M: But I'm worried that she will be _____ _____
_____ _____ _____ .

W: She promised not to spend more than one hour a day
on the phone. And I think she can learn good
screentime habits with our help.

M: You're right, but do you think she can keep her
promise?

W: (Yes, I do. I trust her on this.)

15

M: Today is the first day of the new school year, and
Vincent meets his homeroom teacher and new
classmates for the first time. His teacher _____
_____ _____ _____ _____ _____ the
classroom rules together. _____ _____ _____
_____ _____ _____ , and after talking about
various things, they start to make rules for cleaning
the classroom. One of the students suggests that a
different person _____ _____ _____ _____
each day. Another student suggests that everyone
should clean the classroom twice a day. But Vincent
thinks that _____ _____ _____ _____ _____
_____ _____ _____ all the time. In this
situation, what would Vincent most likely say to his
classmates?

16-17

W: Good afternoon. I'm Amelia, chief researcher at the Virus Research Center in Somalia. I'll explain the result of my study _____ _____ _____ _____

_____ _____ _____ _____ _____ .

They might seem unrelated, but in fact they are strongly connected. I studied 10,000 people who contracted Malaria in five regions of Somalia and I _____ _____ _____ _____ _____ the amount of rain does affect the spread of Malaria. In the data, the basic information of the participants such as gender, age, weight, and region are displayed. As you can see from the data, _____ _____ _____

_____ when it rained a lot. You can guess why this is if you know that mosquitos are the main cause of Malaria. The larvae of mosquitos live in the puddles made by increased rainfall. So we can see that rain and Malaria _____ _____ _____ . Of course, this research is limited, because it was done in only five areas. However, the study shows that we need to remove these puddles whenever possible.

녹음을 다시 한 번 들으면서, 빈칸을 채워 봅시다.

01

M: Hello, everyone. I'm Peter, chief researcher at NASA. I'm sure that you have all _____ _____ _____ _____ _____ _____ _____. Some scientists believe that people will be able to stay in space hotels in just ten years. But you don't have to wait ten years to travel in space. This documentary lets you experience for yourself what it is like to travel in the universe. You will see _____ _____ _____ _____ _____ and videos taken from actual space crafts during their space missions. It's sure to be an opportunity of a lifetime. So _____ _____ _____ _____ _____ _____ _____ _____ at 10 p.m. this Sunday. Don't miss this fantastic trip!

02

W: What are you reading, Honey?

M: I'm reading an article about school curriculum.

W: Can you be more specific?

M: It's about _____ _____ _____ _____ _____ in high school.

W: I think that's a good idea.

M: Really? Students already learn history for three hours per week. Don't you think that's enough?

W: Well, I think understanding history is just as important as learning mathematics or another language.

M: But many people would _____ _____ _____ _____ _____ _____ _____ _____ than history.

W: There is a saying, "A nation that forgets its past has no future." Students need to realize that the _____ _____ _____ _____ _____ _____ _____.

M: You have a point there.

W: Thank you. I think we can never learn enough history.

03

W: Hello, I'm Jean Cruise. I called you yesterday.

M: Oh, nice to meet you, Ms. Cruise. Please have a seat.

W: Thank you. I've been looking for a place for my mother to reside. One of my friends recommended this center to me.

M: You've come to the right place. We have great facilities and an excellent medical staff.

W: _____ _____ _____ _____ _____.

M: Can you explain your mother's condition in more detail?

W: She's 80 years old. She can't digest certain foods well.

M: Don't worry about that. Our nutritionist arranges and provides meals for each patient.

W: That's good. She also suffers from pains in the knee, so she rarely walks. _____ _____ _____ _____ _____ for most of the day.

M: Our therapist will help her exercise for 30 minutes every day. Also, she will _____ _____ _____ _____ _____ and you'll _____ _____ _____ _____ _____.

W: Good. I think I should bring her to this center today.

M: I'm sure she'll love it here.

04

M: Hi, Nancy. How was your vacation?

W: It was great. I went to a beach with my family. Here's a photograph of us all.

M: What a beautiful beach!

W: The person parasailing _____ _____ _____ _____ _____ is me.

M: Fantastic! Oh, _____ _____ _____ _____ _____ in the ocean like the people in the middle.

W: Yes, it's exciting, but you should always use a tube, like them.

M: What's this on the left? It looks like a ship.

W: Actually, it's a restaurant. You can see _____ _____ _____ _____, "Italian Restaurant" next to it.

M: Did you have a chance to eat there?

W: Unfortunately, no. It was closed for renovations.

M: Are your brothers in the photo?

W: Look at the bottom right corner. They're making a big sand castle.

M: Yes, I can see them now.

05

W: Dad, what's in this box?

M: It's a bed frame for your room.

W: But the box doesn't look big enough.

M: _____ _____ _____ _____ a DIY bed frame.

W: A do-it-yourself bed frame? Can you really put it together yourself?

M: Of course. The instructions have pictures that show _____ _____ _____ _____ _____, step-by-step.

W: That sounds easy, but the pictures look pretty complicated. Why don't you get a professional to put it together?

M: Don't worry. I can handle it. I just need to insert some screws in these boards and connect them all together.

W: If you say so. Do you want me to _____ _____ _____ _____ _____?

M: No. I'll clean up after I finish.

W: Is there _____ _____ _____ _____ _____ _____?

M: Sure. Can you insert these screws in the boards?

W: Okay.

06

W: Hi, can I help you?

M: Yes, please. I'd like to _____ _____ _____ _____ _____ _____ _____ _____.

W: Okay. You can get your files printed in black and white or in color. Which do you prefer?

M: Can you tell me how much they are?

W: For black and white, _____ _____ _____ _____ _____ _____, and for color, it costs 50 cents per page.

M: I see. Then please print the science report _____ _____ _____ _____. It consists of 15 pages.

W: I got it. Anything else?

M: There's a history report as well. Please _____ _____ _____ _____ _____.

W: How many pages are there in the history report?

M: Ten pages in all. How much do I have to pay altogether?

W: Wait a second, please. Let me add everything up.

07

W: Ayden, your company is _____ _____ _____ _____ _____ _____, right?

M: We were going to, but the camp was postponed to next month.

W: Huh? I thought you _____ _____ _____ _____ _____ _____ _____ last month.

M: I did. And I was very happy with the location.

W: Then did you have problems getting the guest lecturer from NASA?

M: No. Dr. Luther agreed _____ _____ _____ _____ at the camp.

W: Then what's the problem?

M: Actually, not enough students have _____ _____ _____ _____ _____. We need more time to advertise.

W: I see. A lack of students will cause financial problems.

M: Fortunately Dr. Luther understood our situation and we postponed the camp for one month.

W: That's very fortunate.

08

M: Honey, George's birthday is just around the corner.

W: That's right. How about doing something meaningful for him?

M: Do you _____ _____ _____ _____?

W: He has been talking about going to the Louise Safety Theme Park for months. I heard it has many high-tech facilities.

M: _____ _____ _____ _____ _____ _____ the park?

W: No, it's for all ages.

M: What kinds of things can George do there?

W: Well, he really wants to experience the earthquake activity with 4D simulation.

M: Great! It sounds fun and educational. Where is it?

W: It's a little far from here. It's in Louisville.

M: That will take _____ _____ _____ _____ _____ _____.

W: Right. But the entrance fee is free because the city is managing the park.

M: Good. Let's go this Saturday.

W: It opens at 10 a.m. How about leaving the house at 8?

M: Okay. I'll tell George the good news.

09

W: Hello, everyone. Welcome to Pacific University. I'm Emilia, chief of administration, and I am going to introduce the Pacific University Scholarship system to you. We have two types of scholarships. First, there is one _____ _____ _____ _____ _____ _____. Students who complete at least 14 credits

with a grade point average of over 4.0 receive a full scholarship for the following semester. Second, the other scholarship is for those who work for our school. If students work at the library or the lab for two hours a day, they _____ _____ _____ _____ _____ _____ _____. You can apply for these scholarships during the next two weeks, starting from today. In order to allow as many students as possible to benefit, students can only _____ _____ _____ _____ _____. Lastly, students who break school rules may _____ _____ _____ the scholarships. Thank you.

10

W: Welcome to Power Electronics.

M: Hi, I'm looking for a graduation gift for my son.

W: Game consoles and smartphones are popular these days.

M: I bought him a smartphone last month, so please show me the game consoles.

W: Just _____ _____ _____ _____ _____ _____. We have five models. The prices vary according to their functions.

M: It _____ _____ _____ _____ _____ _____ so that many people can play together. My son likes to play with his friends. I need the machine for four players.

W: How about a portable one? Then he can play games anywhere.

M: No thanks, I don't want him playing all the time.

W: In that case, we have two options.

M: I'll choose the cheaper one. I don't want to spend more than $200.

W: That's a good choice.

M: _____ _____ _____ _____ _____ _____?

W: Of course.

11

W: Mark, why are you so late? The movie has already started.

M: I'm so sorry. There was a heavy traffic jam on the way here.

W: You're always late. _____ _____ _____ _____ _____ _____ _____?

M: (Okay. I'll leave half an hour earlier next time.)

12

M: Have you packed for your school trip tomorrow?

W: I'm almost finished. I just need to check the weather.

M: _____ _____ _____ _____ _____ _____ _____ _____, with no clouds in the sky.

W: (Then, I don't need to take my umbrella.)

13

[Cell phone rings.]

M: Hello, Rachel.

W: Hi, Julian. _____ _____ _____ _____ _____ _____ _____ _____. How's it going?

M: I've been so busy that I haven't been able to _____ _____ _____ _____ _____ _____ _____. I had to prepare for my final exams.

W: Actually, I was calling to ask you for a favor, but I'll understand if you're busy.

M: That's all right. You can ask me.

W: Well, I was watching a video on the Internet, and _____ _____ _____ _____ _____ and wouldn't turn on again.

M: Did you check the power cable?

W: Yes, I did. I also checked the monitor cable. There was nothing wrong with it.

M: Did you try pressing the power button?

W: Yes, I did, but _____ _____ _____.

M: Then, it could be a problem with the main board. I'll have to check it out.

W: I'm really sorry, but do you have time to come to my house?

M: (Of course, I'll drop by on my way home.)

14

M: Honey, a lot of mail came for you today.

W: Thanks, Vincent. I've been waiting for a letter from my client.

M: They're mostly commercial advertisements. But I think this piece of mail looks important.

W: Which one do you mean?

M: This mail from the Ministry of Health.

W: Please open it. What does it say?

M: It says that _____ _____ _____ _____ _____ _____ _____.

W: Already? What examinations _____ _____ _____ _____?

M: You can get various examinations, including a blood test, X-ray, and ultrasound scan. You should _____ _____ _____ _____ _____ _____.

W: I'd like to, but I'm too busy. I have to finish my project by the middle of next month.

M: That's okay. It says that your checkup period is until the end of next month. You can go after completing your project. Being healthy is the most important thing in your life.

W: (You're right. I'll definitely go and get examined.)

15

M: Kelly and Edward are very close colleagues. Recently, Edward quit his job to start his own business. _____ _____ _____ _____, he decides on two businesses. One business is already popular among the young generation. The other business is promising, but completely unfamiliar to Edward. After a long period of consideration, Edward makes up his mind _____ _____ _____ _____ _____ _____ _____ _____ because it is more proven and safe. But Kelly thinks that the market for that business is already full and _____ _____ _____ _____ _____ _____ _____. She wants him to choose the business that has a potential to develop a new market although it may have some challenges. In this situation, what would Kelly most likely say to Edward?

16-17

W: Hello, I'm Margaret from the National Psychology Center. Have you ever felt relaxed or anxious _____ _____ _____ _____? If you have, you may have been affected by the colors around you. Colors are powerful messengers, _____ _____ _____ _____ _____ _____ states or actions. One color may lower blood pressure, and _____ _____ _____ _____ _____ _____. Let's take a close look at the power of colors. Yellow makes us warm and comfortable, but too much can make us highly sensitive. The color blue makes us calm and cool, though sometimes indifferent and cynical. As many people know, red makes us very excited and energetic, so it _____ _____ _____ _____ _____ _____. Last, the color white makes us honest and positive, but we can feel bored and weary when looking at it for a long time. Now, you can control yourself through the power of colors. For example, when you want to analyze something, looking at the color blue can help you. What color do you need most right now?

23 Dictation Test

녹음을 다시 한 번 들으면서, 빈칸을 채워 봅시다.

01

W: Good evening, listeners. I'm Carol, _____ _____ _____ _____ _____ _____, Good Evening Culture, from 7 to 9 p.m. on weekdays. Starting today, we have a new segment called, "Guess Who?" In the new segment, I will mention some facts about _____ _____ _____ _____, and you, the listeners will guess who he or she is. Let's begin to play, "Guess Who?" This person was born on April 26, 1564. He was an English poet and playwright, _____ _____ _____ _____ _____ _____ _____ ever. Can you guess who he is? Okay, let's keep going. His major works include *Hamlet*, *King Lear*, *Macbeth*, and *Romeo and Juliet*. As most of you have guessed by now, the answer is William Shakespeare. I think that this new segment will give you a great chance to test your knowledge about famous people. If you have any suggestions or ideas for this segment, please leave a message on the Q&A board on our website.

02

W: Honey, I think we need to talk.

M: Is there a problem?

W: Grace told me that she wanted to _____ _____ _____ _____ _____, but I didn't know how to respond.

M: Social media? I thought that _____ _____ _____ _____ _____ _____ from making an account.

W: Yes, but an account can be created _____ _____ _____ _____ _____.

M: Why does she want to make one?

W: She wants to post her photos on it. But I worry that she will be exposed to harmful and negative materials on social media.

M: _____ _____ _____ _____ _____ _____ _____ before they happen. I think it's not bad for her to use social media. She can communicate with her friends that way.

W: Do you really think so?

M: Yes. Most children these days communicate with one another using social media, and they get the latest information from it.

W: Now I understand why she wants to open an account.

03

M: Hello. Where to?

W: To the airport, please. Do you take credit cards?

M: Sure. Shall I put your bag in the trunk?

W: Thank you, but please be careful with it. The contents are fragile.

M: Okay. Don't worry.

W: [Pause] How long _____ _____ _____ _____ _____ _____?

M: Less than an hour. Are you in a hurry?

W: I think _____ _____ _____ _____ _____. I have to get on a flight at 11 a.m.

M: Then we can take the highway, but you _____ _____ _____ _____ _____ _____. Is that all right?

W: How much do I have to pay for the tolls?

M: An extra $10.

W: No problem. Just get me there as fast as you can.

M: Fasten your seat belt, and don't worry about being late. There's no traffic jam at this time of day.

W: I really hope so.

04

M: Gloria, look at this picture.

W: Wow, it's very cute. What is it?

M: I took a picture of this room _____ _____ _____ _____ _____ _____.

W: I love it! I want a room just like it.

M: When we move into the new house, I'll make your room just like this.

W: Thank you, Dad. I really like this bed on the right. _____ _____ _____ _____ _____ _____ _____.

M: Yes, it's very unique. Also, through the large window over the bed, you can see the sun every morning.

W: Yes, but it's too bad _____ _____ _____ _____ _____.

M: This closet on the left side is big, so that you can put all your clothes in it.

W: Great. I'm going to change the picture next to the closet with our family portrait.

M: Yes, that'll be better than the mountain picture.

W: Look at the small table between the door and the bed. It's perfect for a vase with flowers, just like in the picture.

M: Yes, I agree.

W: I _____ _____ _____ _____ _____ our new house!

05

M: Honey, I'm back.

W: You're home early today.

M: Yes, I finally finished my project. Um.... What's the smell?

W: I don't smell anything. I roasted some meat for lunch. Maybe it's the smell of barbecue.

M: No, _____ _____ _____ _____ _____. I think it's the smell of gas.

W: What? Leaking gas is very dangerous. Should we call 911?

M: Before we do that, we should _____ _____ _____ _____ _____ _____ _____.

W: How can we do that?

M: First of all, I'll open the windows and _____ _____ _____ _____ _____. It won't be too dangerous if we close the valve.

W: I hope so. I'm so scared.

M: Relax. We should act calmly in this situation. While I'm doing that, you should make some soapy water.

W: Soapy water? To wash your hands?

M: No. I heard that bubbles form when you scrub a leaking gas pipe with soapy water.

W: Okay. I'll make some now.

06

W: Lyon, look at this site!

M: What is it?

W: The online bookstore, Books For You, is holding a special book sale this week.

M: What kind of book sale?

W: You're not going to believe this. _____ _____ _____ _____ _____ _____, regardless of their original prices.

M: Really? This is a great chance to get some expensive books that I couldn't buy before.

W: That's not all. If you buy five books, you _____ _____ _____ _____ _____ _____.

M: Wow! Unbelievable!

W: It says here that there is a limit of ten books per account.

M: I want to order the Compton's Encyclopedia series. It consists of six books.

W: Then you can buy them for the price of five books. Plus, you can _____ _____ _____ _____ _____ the total price if you pay with ABC credit card.

M: Great. I'll buy them right now. I'll pay with my ABC card.

W: Go ahead. Just _____ _____ _____ _____ _____ _____ _____.

M: You bet!

07

[*Telephone rings.*]

W: Hello, this is Diamond Real Estate Office. What can I do for you?

M: Sharon? It's me, John.

W: Hi, John. What's up?

M: I have a meeting _____ _____ _____ _____ _____ _____ _____ this afternoon, but I'm afraid I can't make it. Can you call and change the meeting to tomorrow afternoon?

W: You _____ _____ _____ _____ Mr. Carl at 2 p.m. Can I ask why you can't meet him?

M: The boiler in my basement burst last night. The repairman has just finished fixing it.

W: Well, if you leave now, you can still arrive at the office on time.

M: That's not all. I just got a call from my son's homeroom teacher. My son _____ _____ _____ while playing basketball.

W: Oh, no. Is he okay?

M: It's not serious, but he's going to _____ _____ _____ _____ _____ _____.

W: Don't worry about your meeting. I'll call Mr. Carl right away.

08

M: Irene, what do you think about my cartoon?

W: It looks cool! What's it about?

M: It's a story about a hero saving the world. I'm going to _____ _____ _____ _____ _____ _____ named "Superhero Festival."

W: I haven't heard of the contest, but it sounds really interesting. Does every hero have to have special powers?

M: Yes, every hero has to have at least one superpower. My hero has the ability to control fire with one hand and water with the other.

W: Great! How do you submit your cartoon?

M: You have to _____ _____ _____ _____ _____ _____. It's a world-wide event, so anyone in the world can participate.

W: When is the deadline? I want to enter the contest, too.

M: Today is the last day for submissions.

W: Oh dear! It's too late for me to try.

M: No worries. We can try together next time.

W: Good. I hope people like your cartoon.

M: I hope so, too. There will be online voting for a month, starting from tomorrow.

W: _____ _____ _____ _____ _____ _____ tomorrow.

09

M: Thank you for using Pacific Airlines today. This is the captain of your flight, AX 120 from Atlanta to Incheon, South Korea. The plane _____ _____ _____ _____ _____ _____ _____ _____, so the date is now the 7th of March. The altitude of this plane is 11,000 meters and we are flying _____ _____ _____ _____ 850 km per hour. The expected time of arrival will be _____ _____ _____ _____. It is expected to be very sunny in Incheon and the temperature will be 15°C. If there is anything you need to make your travel more comfortable, please ask our flight attendants. For those of you that want to _____ _____ _____ _____, you can check the catalogue placed in the seat pocket. I hope you enjoy the flight. Thank you.

10

M: Welcome to Toy World. May I help you?

W: I'm looking for a toy for my little girl.

M: _____ _____ _____ _____ _____ _____. We have many toys for rent. We offer special prices this week.

W: That's great.

M: How old is she? It's important to choose a toy _____ _____ _____ _____ _____ _____.

W: She's 6 years old. And I want something that is safe for her to play with.

M: Then how about a wooden toy?

W: Are the wooden toys more expensive than the plastic ones?

M: Actually, the prices are all different.

W: A wooden toy would be best. And I don't want to ___ ___ ___ ___ ___.

M: Okay. Then you can choose one of these two.

W: Well, I want her to play with it inside the house.

M: Good. Then she'll love this one!

11

M: Excuse me. This is ___ ___ ___ ___ ___ ___. How can I borrow this book?

W: You need to get a library card first, and then you can borrow the book.

M: How can I get a card?

W: (Fill out this application form and submit it with two passport photos.)

12

W: Honey, what are you searching for on your phone?

M: I'm checking out the weather with this app. It tells me ___ ___ ___ ___ ___ ___ ___.

W: That sounds like a useful app. What does it say today?

M: (It calls for heavy rain and strong winds this afternoon.)

13

W: Jackson, what are you looking at on your phone?

M: I'm looking at pictures of dogs on social media. Aren't they cute?

W: Yes, they are.

M: Mom, can I get a dog?

W: For the last time, no, you can't.

M: I would really take care of it. Anyway, I feel bored because ___ ___ ___ ___ ___. Please, Mom.

W: That's no reason for getting a dog. And you know I can't stand the sound of barking.

M: I can train the dog not to bark in the house.

W: And have you forgotten that ___ ___ ___ ___ ___?

M: Really? I didn't know that.

W: Besides, raising a dog ___ ___ ___ ___.

M: What kind of responsibilities do you mean?

W: (You have to walk and feed the dog every day.)

14

W: Michael, can't you hear me?

M: Oh, it's you, Linda. I'm sorry. I didn't hear you.

W: I called you at least 10 times. ___ ___ ___ ___ ___ ___ while walking down the street?

M: I was listening to music and reading an article on my favorite soccer team.

W: It's very dangerous to use a smartphone while walking.

M: That's okay. I do it all the time.

W: Do you know that there is a word for people like you?

M: Really? What is it?

W: You are a "smombie."

M: A smombie? What does that mean?

W: It's a combination of the words "smartphone" and "zombie." It's used to describe people who ___ ___ ___ ___ ___ looking at their smartphones.

M: Don't worry. I haven't had an accident yet.

W: But you couldn't hear me just now. ___ ___ ___ ___ ___ into a dangerous situation? This is no laughing matter.

M: (Okay. From now on, I won't use my smartphone while walking.)

15

M: There is a big dance competition tonight, and Eriksen is very excited to take part in it. He has been preparing for it for a month. _____ _____ _____ _____ _____ _____, he washes his most fancy clothes to stand out at the competition. While getting ready, however, he gets a call from his professor, Ms. White. She tells him that he has to _____ _____ _____ _____ _____ _____ or he will fail the class. He hurries to the professor's office to submit his paper, but completely forgets about his laundry. On the way home, he suddenly remembers that his clothes are still in the washing machine. He _____ _____ _____ _____ dry his clothes before the competition starts, so he calls his roommate to ask him to dry the clothes for him. In this situation, what would Eriksen most likely say to his roommate?

16-17

W: Hello, everyone. I'm glad to introduce this amazing invention, the UFO Plate. Do you know _____ _____ _____ _____ _____ _____? According to a survey, the average person uses approximately 100kg of plastic, 420 plastic bags, and 460 disposable cups every year. And as you can guess, they _____ _____ _____ _____ _____ _____. So, two industrial designers in New York, Andrea Ruggiero and Bengt Brummer, made this UFO plate to reduce the usage of disposable products. Of course, it's not a real UFO, but a disposable plate that is thrown away, _____ _____ _____ _____, and returned to nature. It's made from blended birdseed, potato starch, guar gum, and seaweed. It can be used as food for birds or animals when thrown into trees or walls. Because it is non-toxic and completely biodegrades in a month, you don't need to worry about the plates becoming environmental pollution. Why don't you _____ _____ _____ _____ _____?

대학수학능력시험 답안 작성 시 유의 사항 및 작성 요령

▶ 유의 사항

ⓐ 답안지는 시험감독관이 지급하는 컴퓨터용 사인펜만을 사용하여 작성. 펜의 종류와 상관없이 예비 마킹을 할 경우에는 중복 답안 등으로 채점되어 불이익을 받을 수 있음.

ⓑ 답안지는 컴퓨터로 처리되므로 구기거나 이물질로 더럽혀서는 안 됨. 또한, 다른 어떠한 형태의 표시도 하여서는 안 됨.

ⓒ 한 번 표기한 답을 수정하고자 하는 경우에는 흰색 수정테이프만을 사용하여 완전히 지워야 함. (수정액 또는 수정스티커 사용 금지)
- 수정테이프는 수험생이 수정 요구 시 시험감독관이 제공함.
- 수정테이프가 떨어지는 등 불완전한 수정 처리로 인해 발생하는 모든 책임은 수험생에게 있으니 주의 바람.
- 수험생이 희망할 경우 답안지 교체를 할 수 있음.
- 시험실에서 제공하는 것 외의 수정테이프, 컴퓨터용 사인펜을 사용하는 경우 채점 등의 과정에서 불이익을 받을 수 있음.

ⓓ 한 문항에 답을 2개 이상 표기한 경우와 불완전한 표기를 하여 오류로 판독된 경우, 해당 문항을 "0점" 처리함.

ⓔ 기타 답안 작성 및 표기의 잘못으로 인하여 일어나는 모든 불이익은 수험생 본인이 감수하여야 함.

▶ 작성 요령

ⓐ 성명란에는 수험생의 성명을 한글로 정확하게 정자로 기입.

ⓑ 필적확인란에는 컴퓨터용 사인펜으로 문제지 표지에 제시된 문구를 반드시 기입.

ⓒ 수험번호란에는 오른쪽 아래 <수험번호 작성 예시>와 같이 수험번호를 아라비아 숫자로 먼저 기입하고, 수험번호의 숫자 해당란의 숫자에 "●"와 같이 정확하게 표기.

ⓓ 배부 받은 문제지 문형을 확인한 후 해당 문형을 답안지 문형란에 표기.

ⓔ 답안 표기 예시
- 바르게 표기한 것 ○○○○●
- 잘못 표기한 것
  ① ○○●○●○ (2곳에 표기한 것)
  ② ○●○○○● (칼로 긁은 것, 불완전한 수정처리)
  ③ ○○○○○○ (지운 흔적이 있는 것, 불완전한 수정처리)
  ④ ○○○○◖◗ (주위만 표시한 것)
  ⑤ ○○○○○◐ (가운데만 표시한 것)

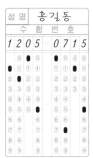

<수험번호 작성 예시>

• 동아출판 홈페이지에서 OMR 카드의 PDF 파일을 제공합니다.
www.bookdonga.com

수프림 수능 영어 듣기 모의고사 실전 답안지

③ 교시 영어 영역

※ 답안지 작성(표기)은 반드시 검은색 컴퓨터용 사인펜만을 사용하고, 연필 또는 샤프 등의 필기구를 절대 사용하지 마십시오.

※ 결시자 확인 (수험생은 표기하지 말것.)

검은색 컴퓨터용 사인펜을 사용하여 수험번호란과 옆란을 표기   ○

※ 문제지 표지에 안내된 필적 확인 문구를 아래 '필적 확인란'에 정자로 반드시 기재하여야 합니다.

필 적 확인란	

성 명	

수 험 번 호

문 형

홀수형 ○

짝수형 ○

※ 문제의 문형을 확인 후 표기

※ 감독관 확인 (수험생은 표기하지 말것.)

본인 여부, 수험번호 및 문형의 표기가 정확한지 확인, 옆란에 서명 또는 날인 | 서 명 또는 날 인

문번	답 란
1	① ② ③ ④ ⑤
2	① ② ③ ④ ⑤
3	① ② ③ ④ ⑤
4	① ② ③ ④ ⑤
5	① ② ③ ④ ⑤
6	① ② ③ ④ ⑤
7	① ② ③ ④ ⑤
8	① ② ③ ④ ⑤
9	① ② ③ ④ ⑤
10	① ② ③ ④ ⑤
11	① ② ③ ④ ⑤
12	① ② ③ ④ ⑤
13	① ② ③ ④ ⑤
14	① ② ③ ④ ⑤
15	① ② ③ ④ ⑤
16	① ② ③ ④ ⑤
17	① ② ③ ④ ⑤
18	① ② ③ ④ ⑤
19	① ② ③ ④ ⑤
20	① ② ③ ④ ⑤

문번	답 란
21	① ② ③ ④ ⑤
22	① ② ③ ④ ⑤
23	① ② ③ ④ ⑤
24	① ② ③ ④ ⑤
25	① ② ③ ④ ⑤
26	① ② ③ ④ ⑤
27	① ② ③ ④ ⑤
28	① ② ③ ④ ⑤
29	① ② ③ ④ ⑤
30	① ② ③ ④ ⑤
31	① ② ③ ④ ⑤
32	① ② ③ ④ ⑤
33	① ② ③ ④ ⑤
34	① ② ③ ④ ⑤
35	① ② ③ ④ ⑤
36	① ② ③ ④ ⑤
37	① ② ③ ④ ⑤
38	① ② ③ ④ ⑤
39	① ② ③ ④ ⑤
40	① ② ③ ④ ⑤

문번	답 란
41	① ② ③ ④ ⑤
42	① ② ③ ④ ⑤
43	① ② ③ ④ ⑤
44	① ② ③ ④ ⑤
45	① ② ③ ④ ⑤

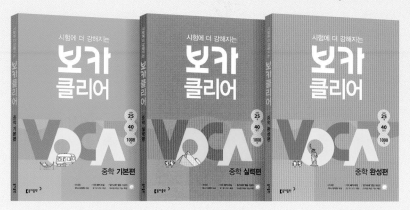
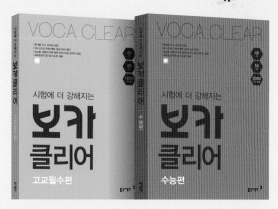

수능·내신 프리미엄 고등 영어 시리즈

Supreme
수프림

정답 및 해설

수능 영어
듣기 모의고사
20+3회 실전

동아출판

영어 듣기 모의고사 20+3회 정답

01 영어 듣기 모의고사 ▶ pp. 06-07

01 ④ 02 ① 03 ② 04 ④ 05 ③ 06 ② 07 ③ 08 ⑤ 09 ⑤
10 ② 11 ④ 12 ② 13 ② 14 ② 15 ③ 16 ① 17 ④

02 영어 듣기 모의고사 ▶ pp. 08-09

01 ③ 02 ⑤ 03 ④ 04 ⑤ 05 ② 06 ③ 07 ⑤ 08 ⑤ 09 ④
10 ⑤ 11 ⑤ 12 ① 13 ③ 14 ② 15 ④ 16 ② 17 ③

03 영어 듣기 모의고사 ▶ pp. 10-11

01 ④ 02 ② 03 ② 04 ⑤ 05 ③ 06 ③ 07 ⑤ 08 ② 09 ⑤
10 ③ 11 ④ 12 ③ 13 ④ 14 ① 15 ⑤ 16 ② 17 ④

04 영어 듣기 모의고사 ▶ pp. 12-13

01 ② 02 ③ 03 ⑤ 04 ⑤ 05 ④ 06 ③ 07 ① 08 ③ 09 ⑤
10 ③ 11 ③ 12 ⑤ 13 ⑤ 14 ④ 15 ⑤ 16 ② 17 ③

05 영어 듣기 모의고사 ▶ pp. 14-15

01 ① 02 ② 03 ④ 04 ⑤ 05 ③ 06 ③ 07 ① 08 ⑤ 09 ④
10 ⑤ 11 ⑤ 12 ② 13 ② 14 ① 15 ① 16 ③ 17 ④

06 영어 듣기 모의고사 ▶ pp. 16-17

01 ① 02 ⑤ 03 ③ 04 ④ 05 ⑤ 06 ② 07 ⑤ 08 ④ 09 ④
10 ③ 11 ② 12 ③ 13 ③ 14 ③ 15 ⑤ 16 ① 17 ③

07 영어 듣기 모의고사 ▶ pp. 18-19

01 ① 02 ⑤ 03 ① 04 ① 05 ⑤ 06 ④ 07 ② 08 ② 09 ⑤
10 ⑤ 11 ① 12 ② 13 ② 14 ② 15 ② 16 ⑤ 17 ⑤

08 영어 듣기 모의고사 ▶ pp. 20-21

01 ④ 02 ③ 03 ③ 04 ⑤ 05 ④ 06 ① 07 ④ 08 ③ 09 ②
10 ② 11 ⑤ 12 ③ 13 ⑤ 14 ④ 15 ⑤ 16 ③ 17 ③

09 영어 듣기 모의고사 ▶ pp. 22-23

01 ② 02 ③ 03 ② 04 ⑤ 05 ① 06 ④ 07 ③ 08 ④ 09 ③
10 ② 11 ① 12 ② 13 ⑤ 14 ① 15 ④ 16 ② 17 ④

10 영어 듣기 모의고사 ▶ pp. 24-25

01 ④ 02 ① 03 ④ 04 ④ 05 ③ 06 ④ 07 ① 08 ⑤ 09 ④
10 ① 11 ③ 12 ② 13 ② 14 ② 15 ③ 16 ① 17 ⑤

11 영어 듣기 모의고사 ▶ pp. 26-27

01 ① 02 ④ 03 ② 04 ⑤ 05 ⑤ 06 ① 07 ⑤ 08 ④ 09 ③
10 ⑤ 11 ① 12 ① 13 ② 14 ② 15 ① 16 ① 17 ⑤

12 영어 듣기 모의고사 ▶ pp. 28-29

01 ① 02 ② 03 ③ 04 ⑤ 05 ③ 06 ③ 07 ④ 08 ② 09 ②
10 ② 11 ② 12 ③ 13 ① 14 ③ 15 ⑤ 16 ⑤ 17 ③

13 영어 듣기 모의고사 ▶ pp. 30-31

01 ④ 02 ④ 03 ② 04 ④ 05 ① 06 ③ 07 ⑤ 08 ③ 09 ⑤
10 ② 11 ② 12 ② 13 ② 14 ① 15 ④ 16 ② 17 ③

14 영어 듣기 모의고사 ▶ pp. 32-33

01 ② 02 ① 03 ① 04 ⑤ 05 ③ 06 ④ 07 ⑤ 08 ④ 09 ③
10 ⑤ 11 ④ 12 ⑤ 13 ② 14 ② 15 ③ 16 ① 17 ⑤

15 영어 듣기 모의고사 ▶ pp. 34-35

01 ⑤ 02 ③ 03 ② 04 ① 05 ⑤ 06 ③ 07 ⑤ 08 ⑤ 09 ④
10 ② 11 ① 12 ③ 13 ③ 14 ⑤ 15 ⑤ 16 ③ 17 ②

16 영어 듣기 모의고사 ▶ pp. 36-37

01 ② 02 ⑤ 03 ① 04 ② 05 ④ 06 ② 07 ③ 08 ③ 09 ②
10 ⑤ 11 ① 12 ③ 13 ④ 14 ⑤ 15 ⑤ 16 ⑤ 17 ①

17 영어 듣기 모의고사 ▶ pp. 38-39

01 ③ 02 ⑤ 03 ③ 04 ② 05 ⑤ 06 ② 07 ④ 08 ④ 09 ②
10 ③ 11 ① 12 ⑤ 13 ④ 14 ① 15 ③ 16 ⑤ 17 ③

18 영어 듣기 모의고사 ▶ pp. 40-41

01 ② 02 ③ 03 ④ 04 ④ 05 ② 06 ② 07 ⑤ 08 ④ 09 ④
10 ② 11 ④ 12 ① 13 ① 14 ① 15 ① 16 ③ 17 ⑤

19 영어 듣기 모의고사 ▶ pp. 42-43

01 ② 02 ④ 03 ② 04 ⑤ 05 ④ 06 ② 07 ⑤ 08 ④ 09 ④
10 ⑤ 11 ③ 12 ④ 13 ⑤ 14 ⑤ 15 ③ 16 ② 17 ③

20 영어 듣기 모의고사 ▶ pp. 44-45

01 ③ 02 ④ 03 ④ 04 ④ 05 ④ 06 ④ 07 ③ 08 ④ 09 ④
10 ③ 11 ⑤ 12 ④ 13 ④ 14 ⑤ 15 ⑤ 16 ① 17 ③

21 영어 듣기 모의고사 [고난도] ▶ pp. 46-47

01 ③ 02 ③ 03 ③ 04 ⑤ 05 ② 06 ② 07 ⑤ 08 ④ 09 ④
10 ④ 11 ⑤ 12 ⑤ 13 ① 14 ⑤ 15 ③ 16 ① 17 ④

22 영어 듣기 모의고사 [고난도] ▶ pp. 48-49

01 ② 02 ① 03 ③ 04 ④ 05 ③ 06 ④ 07 ④ 08 ④ 09 ④
10 ③ 11 ② 12 ① 13 ⑤ 14 ② 15 ② 16 ① 17 ④

23 영어 듣기 모의고사 [고난도] ▶ pp. 50-51

01 ③ 02 ⑤ 03 ④ 04 ⑤ 05 ⑤ 06 ② 07 ② 08 ④ 09 ⑤
10 ② 11 ⑤ 12 ② 13 ② 14 ② 15 ② 16 ① 17 ④

01 ④	02 ①	03 ②	04 ④	05 ③	06 ②
07 ③	08 ⑤	09 ⑤	10 ②	11 ④	12 ②
13 ②	14 ②	15 ③	16 ①	17 ④	

01 ④ 　　　　　　　　　　　　　　　　　　 목적 파악

남: 안내 말씀 드리겠습니다, 학생 여러분. 저는 교장 Henny입니다. 체육 수업에 관해 중요한 발표 사항이 있습니다. 최근에 저는 우리 학생들로부터 체육 수업 중에 입는 학교 체육복 반바지가 불편하다는 내용의 이메일을 여러 통 받았습니다. 체육복이 우리 학교의 오랜 전통이기는 하지만, 시대에 따라 변화할 필요를 이해합니다. 그래서 다음 주부터 학생들은 체육복 반바지 대신에 체육 교사가 승인한 것이기만 하면 트레이닝 바지나 다른 운동복을 입어도 됩니다. 여러분은 여전히 학교 체육복 티셔츠를 입어야 한다는 것을 기억해 주십시오. 이 변화가 여러분이 즐겁고 안전한 체육 수업을 하는 데 도움이 되기를 희망합니다!

문제 해결
남자는 학교 체육복 반바지 대신에 트레이닝 바지나 다른 운동복 바지를 입어도 된다는 학교 체육복 규정 변경을 공지하고 있다.

어휘·표현
announcement 발표, 공고　**regarding** ~에 관하여　**sweatpants** 트레이닝 바지　**athletic apparel** 운동복　**as long as** ~이기만 하면　**approve** 승인하다, 허가하다

02 ① 　　　　　　　　　　　　　　　　　　 주제 파악

여: Josh, 컴퓨터로 뭐하고 있니?
남: 운동화 한 켤레를 고르는 중이야.
여: 도와줄까?
남: 응. 이 두 켤레 중에서 결정하지 못하겠어.
여: 음, 주로 무슨 용도로 사용할 건데?
남: 중간 강도부터 센 강도의 달리기용으로.
여: 그렇다면 넌 확실히 이 운동화를 선택해야 해. 다른 것은 그냥 걷기용이잖아.
남: 알아, 하지만 학교 아이들 대부분이 저것을 신어.
여: 그건 중요하지 않아. 네 용도에 가장 잘 맞는 운동화를 사야지.
남: 그렇지만, 다른 아이들이 내가 멋지다고 생각하지 않으면 어떡해?
여: 철 좀 들어, Josh. 친구들 의견이 아니라 네 의견이 가장 중요해야지.
남: 누나 말이 맞아. 고마워.

문제 해결
여자는 용도에 가장 잘 맞는 운동화를 구입해야 한다고 말하고 있다.

어휘·표현
make up one's mind 결정하다, 결심하다　**moderate** 중간의, 보통의　**definitely** 분명히, 확실히　**Sis** sister의 줄임말로, '누나', '언니'와 같이 직접 부를 때 씀.

03 ② 　　　　　　　　　　　　　　　　　　 관계 추론

남: 미안해요, Judith. 우리 그 장면을 다시 할까요?
여: 제가 뭔가 잘못했나요? 대사를 빠뜨리지는 않았어요, 그렇죠?
남: 아니요. 당신이 잘못한 것은 없어요. 문제는 당신 시계예요.
여: 제 시계요? 뭐가 문제죠?
남: 우리 영화의 배경이 19세기인데 당신이 차고 있는 것은 디지털시계잖아요.
여: 오, 정말 죄송해요. 시계가 필름에 찍혔나요?
남: 네. 그게 이 장면을 다시 하는 이유예요.
여: 시계를 차고 있었던 것을 깜빡했네요. 당장 시계를 뺄게요.
남: 좋아요. 하던 대로 계속 하죠. 방금 당신 연기가 좋았어요.
여: 고맙습니다. 제 분장은 괜찮은가요?
남: 걱정 마세요. 완벽해요.
여: 알겠어요. 저는 지금 다시 할 준비가 되어 있어요.
남: 그러면 셋에 촬영 시작합니다. 하나, 둘, 셋.

문제 해결
남자는 여자의 디지털시계가 필름에 찍혔다는 이유로 장면을 다시 촬영하자고 말하고 있고, 여자는 분장이 괜찮은지 확인을 구하고 있는 것으로 보아 두 사람은 영화감독과 배우의 관계임을 알 수 있다.

어휘·표현
line 대사　**setting** 배경　**redo** 다시 하다　**scene** 장면　**roll the cameras** 촬영을 시작하다

04 ④ 　　　　　　　　　　　　　　　　　　 그림 불일치 파악

여: Jim, 무엇을 보고 있니?
남: 우리 학교에서 사진 대회가 있어. 난 이 사진을 출품하려고 생각 중이야.
여: 와! 아름답다.
남: 고마워. 나는 특히 비행기가 하늘에 만들고 있는 낭만적인 메시지가 마음에 들어.
여: 그렇네. 비행기 오른쪽에 있는 갈매기 세 마리도 그 메시지를 즐기는 것 같이 보여.
남: 요트에 탄 남자가 보이니?
여: 어떤 요트? 오른쪽에 있는 줄무늬 돛을 단 요트, 아니면 왼쪽에 물방울무늬 돛을 단 요트?
남: 오른쪽 요트.
여: 그는 낚시하면서 편안한 시간을 보내고 있는 것처럼 보여.
남: 아래쪽에 해변에서 놀고 있는 세 명의 여자아이들은 아주 귀여워.
여: 맞아. 난 중간에 있는 튜브를 낀 아이가 정말 마음에 들어.
남: 내가 가장 좋아하는 부분은 왼쪽의 석양이야. 그것이 사진을 완성하고 있지.
여: 동의해. 내 생각에는 '해변에서의 하루'라고 제목을 붙이는 게 좋겠어.

문제 해결
튜브를 낀 여자아이가 중간에 있다고 했으므로, ④가 대화의 내용과 일치하지 않는다.

어휘·표현
seagull 비둘기　**striped** 줄무늬　**spotted** 물방울무늬　**relaxing** 편안한, 느긋한　**at the bottom** 바닥에　**setting sun** 석양, 지는 해　**title** 제목을 붙이다

05 ③ 　　　　　　　　　　　　　　　　　　 할 일 파악

여: 휴. 우리 수하물을 찾는 데 생각보다 오래 걸렸어요.
남: 맞아요. 하지만 드디어 우리가 여기 목적지에 도착했어요.

여: 그래요. 우리가 이국적인 외국의 공항에 있다는 것이 믿겨지지 않아요.

남: 멋진 여행이 될 거예요. 여보, 이 분주한 공항을 벗어납시다.

여: 동감이에요. 그런데, 버스를 탈까요 아니면 택시를 탈까요?

남: 음, 우리는 도시 안에 있는 몇몇 관광 명소를 방문할 거예요. 그냥 차를 렌트하는 게 어때요?

여: 전체 여행 동안에 택시를 잡으려고 애쓰는 것보다 그게 더 나을 것 같네요.

남: 물론이에요. 오, 저쪽에 렌터카 부스가 있어요. 내가 차를 빌릴게요.

여: 좋아요. 당신이 그것을 하는 동안, 내가 할 일이 뭐가 있을까요?

남: 호텔에 전화해서 우리 예약을 확인하는 게 어때요?

여: 좋은 생각이에요. 그렇게 할게요.

공항에 도착한 일행 중 남자는 차를 빌리기로 하고, 여자는 호텔에 전화해서 예약을 확인하기로 했다.

luggage 수하물　**exotic** 이국적인　**tourist attraction** 관광 명소　**confirm** 확인하다

06 ②

[전화벨이 울린다.]

여: 안녕하세요. 가족용 수상 모험 장소, Wally's Water World입니다!

남: 안녕하세요. 저는 이번 토요일 표를 구입하고 싶습니다.

여: 알겠습니다. 일행이 몇 명이신가요?

남: 네 명이요. 어른 두 명과 어린이 두 명이요.

여: 주말에는 어른은 20달러이고 12세 미만 어린이는 10달러입니다.

남: 어린이 둘 다 12세 미만이에요.

여: 네. 아이 중 36개월 미만인 아이가 있으신가요?

남: 사실, 막내가 28개월이에요.

여: 36개월 미만 아이는 입장이 무료임을 알려 드리게 되어 기쁘네요.

남: 잘됐네요.

여: 또한, 전화로 신용카드 결제를 하시면 총 입장료에서 10% 할인됩니다.

남: 좋습니다. 제 신용카드 번호를 불러 드릴게요.

입장료가 어른은 $20, 12세 미만 어린이는 $10이다. 일행은 어른 2명, 12세 미만 어린이가 2명인데, 한 아이는 36개월 미만으로 입장료가 무료이므로, 총 입장료는 $50이다. 신용카드 결제 시 10% 할인이 되므로, 남자는 총 $45를 지불할 것이다.

purchase 구입하다　**party** 일행　**admission** 입장

07 ③

남: 안녕, Jules. 널 위한 좋은 소식이 있어!

여: 무슨 소식인데, Harry?

남: 너는 다른 나라 사람들을 만나고 싶다고 항상 이야기해 왔잖아.

여: 응. 물론이지.

남: 국제 학생 축제가 우리 학교에서 열릴 거야.

여: 와! 나에게 꼭 맞는 행사 같은데.

남: 바로 그거야. 그럼 이번 토요일에 나와 함께 갈래?

여: 오, 안 돼. 토요일만 빼고 아무 날이나 되는데.

남: 내가 맞혀 볼게. 그날 남동생을 돌봐야 하는구나.

여: 아니, 그건 아니야. 엄마와 쇼핑을 가기로 약속했어.

남: 약속을 미룰 수 없어? 다른 날 가도 되는 거잖아.

여: 안 돼. 엄마가 정말 내가 함께 가기를 바라셔서 엄마를 실망시키고 싶지 않아.

남: 어, 그래. 그럼 다음번에 가자.

여자는 엄마와 쇼핑을 가야 해서 남자와 함께 축제에 갈 수 없다고 했다.

babysit 아이를 봐 주다　**take a rain check** 다음 기회로 미루다　**let ~ down** ~를 실망시키다

08 ⑤

남: 주말이에요! 여보, 오늘 재미있는 뭔가를 해요.

여: 그래요. 영화를 보는 게 어때요?

남: 좋아요. 어떤 종류의 영화를 보고 싶어요?

여: 로맨틱 코미디 같은 가벼운 거는 어때요?

남: 좋아요. 영화를 점심 전이나 점심 후에 볼까요?

여: 일찍 오전 10시에 상영하는 걸 봐요. 그때가 사람이 적을 거예요.

남: 게다가, 조조 상영은 표 값이 7달러밖에 안 해요.

여: 맞아요. 어느 영화관으로 가고 싶어요?

남: 너무 멀지 않으면 상관없어요.

여: 그럼, 우체국 옆 5번가에 있는 극장에 가요.

남: 좋아요! 지금 바로 전화로 표를 살게요.

장르(로맨틱 코미디), 표 가격($7), 극장 위치(5번가), 상영 시간(오전 10시)에 대해서는 언급했지만, ⑤감독에 대해서는 언급하지 않았다.

in the mood for ~할 기분이 나서　**make much difference** 영향이 있다, 상관이 있다　**as long as** ~이기만 하면　**far away** 멀리 떨어져

09 ⑤

여: 안녕하세요, 학생 여러분. 저는 교감 Greenberg 선생님입니다. 우리의 연례행사인 Queens 고등학교의 독서 마라톤을 소개하게 되어 무척 기쁩니다! 여러분 중 독서 마라톤이 처음인 학생들을 위해 설명하자면, 독서 마라톤은 책을 읽으면서 돈을 모으는 모금 행사입니다. 작년에 500명이 넘는 학생들이 2주간 참여해 도움이 필요한 어린이들을 위해 12,000달러 이상을 모았습니다. 올해는 독서 마라톤 기간이 3월 한 달 동안으로 확대될 것입니다. 여러분은 학교 홈페이지를 통해 독서 마라톤에 등록할 수 있습니다. 각 학년에서 가장 많은 돈을 모은 학생을 위해 멋진 상품이 준비되어 있습니다. 독서 마라톤은 모두에게 재미있고 교육적인 행사이며 좋은 목적을 위한 것입니다. 여러분의 적극적인 참여를 기대합니다!

가장 많은 돈을 모은 학생을 위해 멋진 상품이 준비되어 있다고 했으므로, 책을 가장 많이 모은 학생에게 상품이 주어진다고 한 ⑤는 내용과 일치하지 않는다.

vice principal 부교장, 교감　**read-a-thon** 독서 마라톤　**fundraising** 모금

participate in ~에 참여하다   extend 확대하다, 확장하다   entire 전체의
cause 대의, 목적   look forward to ~을 고대하다, 기대하다

10 ②
도표 정보 파악

남: 실례합니다. 여기서 차량용 공기 청정기를 취급하나요?
여: 네, 이 다섯 가지 모델이 있습니다. 어느 가격대를 생각하고 계신가요?
남: 200달러 이하로요.
여: 그럼, 이 모델을 추천해도 될까요? 다섯 가지 중 가장 전력량이 높아서, 자동차 안 공기를 가장 빨리 정화할 거예요.
남: 그 점은 좋지만 제가 자동차에 많은 장치를 연결해 두어서 30와트나 그 이하면 좋겠어요.
여: 블루투스 연결요? 그게 되면, 청정기와 당신의 스마트폰을 연결해서 공기 질을 확인할 수 있어요.
남: 그 기능을 그렇게 자주 사용할 것 같지 않아서, 그 기능은 넘어갈게요.
여: 그럼 두 가지 모델만 남네요. 필터가 2개인 장치가 좋으세요, 3개인 게 좋으세요?
남: 당연히 가능한 한 많은 필터로 된 것이 좋아요.
여: 그럼, 이 제품이 손님이 찾으시는 모델이에요.
남: 좋아요. 이걸로 할게요.

문제 해결
남자는 가격은 200달러 이하이고, 전력량은 30와트 이하이며, 블루투스 연결 기능은 없고, 필터가 가능한 한 많은 차량용 공기 청정기를 사려고 하므로, 모든 조건에 맞는 남자가 구입할 공기 청정기는 ②이다.

어휘·표현
air purifier 공기 청정기, 공기 정화기   in stock 비축되어, 재고로   price range 가격 범위, 가격대   wattage 전력량   watt 와트(전력의 단위)
Bluetooth 블루투스(전자 기기 간에 데이터를 무선으로 주고받을 수 있는 무선 통신 기술)   connectivity 연결   filter 필터, 여과기

11 ④
짧은 대화의 응답

남: Lisa, 너 어제 수업 때 없던데. 무슨 일 있니?
여: 어, 안녕하세요. Katz 선생님. 저 독감에 걸려서 어제 하루 종일 침대에 누워 있었어요.
남: 지금은 좀 괜찮으면 좋겠구나. 병원에는 갔었니?
여: 아직요. 방과 후에 진찰 받으러 갈 거예요.

문제 해결
독감에 걸렸다는 여자에게 남자가 병원에는 갔었는지 물었으므로, 방과 후에 진찰 받으러 갈 거라고 말하는 ④가 응답으로 가장 적절하다.
① 네. 저는 장래에 의사가 되고 싶어요.
② 죄송해요. 저는 감기에 걸리고 싶지 않아요.
③ 아니요. 저는 지금 막 병원 진료를 받고 돌아왔어요.
⑤ 물론이에요. 제가 내일 수업 시간에 숙제를 제출할 것을 약속해요.

어휘·표현
come down with (병에) 걸리다   appointment 약속, 예약   hand in 제출하다   doctor's office 개인 병원, 의원

12 ②
짧은 대화의 응답

여: 다음 분. [잠시 후] 무엇을 도와드릴까요, 손님?
남: 네. 은행 계좌를 개설하고 싶어요.

여: 알겠습니다. 신분증 좀 보여 주시겠어요?
남: 물론이죠. 운전면허증을 드릴게요.

문제 해결
여자가 신분증을 볼 수 있는지 물었으므로, 운전면허증을 주겠다고 말하는 ②가 남자의 응답으로 가장 적절하다.
① 좋아요. 이번이 우리 은행에 처음 거래하시는 건가요?
③ 물론이죠. 여기서 신분증을 만들 수 있나요?
④ 죄송해요. 손님은 계좌를 만드실 자격이 안 됩니다.
⑤ 저는 제 계좌의 잔고를 확인하는 걸 깜빡했어요.

어휘·표현
bank account 은행 계좌   identification 신분증   license 면허증   bank (특정 은행과) 거래하다   qualified 자격이 있는   balance 잔고, 잔액

13 ②
긴 대화의 응답

[휴대 전화벨이 울린다.]
남: 무슨 일이니, Katrina?
여: 안녕, Mark. 너의 새 블로그가 어떻게 되어 가는지 확인하려고 전화 걸었어.
남: 잘돼 가는 것 같아. 하루에 방문객이 약 100명 정도 돼.
여: 시작이 좋은데.
남: 응, 그렇지만 3개월이 되어 가니까 지금쯤이면 더 많은 사람들을 끌어 모아야 될 것 같아.
여: 음, 내가 조언을 좀 해도 괜찮겠니?
남: 물론이지. 사실 정말 고맙지.
여: 네 블로그의 초점이 너무 넓은 것 같아. 너무 많은 다른 주제를 다루고 있어.
남: 난 그렇게 하는 게 폭넓은 독자층을 끌어 모을 거라고 생각했어.
여: 아마 초반에는 그럴 수 있지만, 핵심적인 구독자 그룹을 끌어들이기 위해서는 너의 블로그를 명확한 독자성을 갖도록 발전시킬 필요가 있어.
남: 그러면 내 블로그의 주제를 좁혀야 한다는 말이구나.
여: 정확해. 그렇게 해야 네 블로그가 그 주제에서 권위를 가질 수 있게 돼.

문제 해결
남자가 여자의 충고가 블로그의 주제를 좁혀야 한다는 말인지를 확인하고 있으므로, 여자의 응답으로 충고한 내용에 대해 보충하는 말을 하는 ②가 가장 적절하다.
① 응. 넌 더 많은 방문객을 끌어들이기 위해 더 많은 광고를 할 필요가 있어.
③ 물론이야. 넓은 범위의 주제를 다루는 것이 언제나 더 재미있어.
④ 맞아. 주의하지 않으면 블로그를 하는 게 공부를 방해할 수 있어.
⑤ 그럼. 매력적인 디자인은 네 블로그의 인기를 더 오래가게 할 거야.

어휘·표현
appreciate 고마워하다   focus 초점   audience 독자(층)   identity 독자성
core group 핵심 그룹   follower 추종자, 팔로어(SNS상의 구독자)   narrow down 좁히다, 줄이다   that way 그와 같이   authority 권위   range 범위
interfere with ~을 방해하다   go a long way 오래가다, 오래 지속되다

14 ②
긴 대화의 응답

남: 무얼 듣고 있니, Josephine?
여: 어, 이건 True Boys의 새 싱글 앨범이야. 오늘 막 나왔어.

남: 멋지다. 노래 제목이 뭐야?

여: 'No More Lies'야. 지금 인기 순위표에서 1위야.

남: 기억하기 쉬운 곡이구나. 그렇게 인기 있는 게 당연해.

여: 응. 난 다음 달에 그들의 콘서트에 가는 게 너무 기대돼.

남: 그 콘서트 표를 어떻게 구했어? 그 콘서트 표가 바로 매진되었다고 들었는데.

여: 정말 운이 좋았어. 판매를 시작한 바로 그때에 온라인에 접속해서 표 2장을 구할 수 있었어.

남: 와, 운이 좋았네! 그 콘서트에 갈 수만 있다면 바랄 게 없을텐데!

여: 정말? 나 아직 함께 가기로 한 사람이 없어. 같이 갈래?

남: <u>이럴 수가! 어떻게 고맙다는 말을 해야 할지 모르겠어.</u>

콘서트에 가고 싶어 하는 남자에게 여자는 콘서트에 함께 가기로 한 사람이 아직 없다며 남자에게 같이 갈 건지 물었다. 이에 대한 남자의 응답으로 고마움을 표현하는 ②가 가장 적절하다.

① 잘됐다! CD를 빌려줘서 고마워.
③ 좋아! 난 그들의 영화를 보는 게 너무 기대돼.
④ 잘됐다! 난 전에 그들에 대해 들어 본 적이 없어.
⑤ 안 돼! 난 콘서트에 여동생을 데려갈 수도 있어.

the charts (음반 판매고에 따른 대중음악 주간) 인기 순위표   catchy 기억하기 쉬운   instantly 즉각, 즉시   exact 정확한, 정밀한   what I wouldn't give to ... ...할 수 있다면 더 이상 바랄 게 없을텐데   unbelievable 믿기 어려울 정도로 좋은

15 ③

남: John은 고등학교 신입생이다. 그는 농구를 매우 좋아해서 학교 농구 팀에서 뛰고 싶다. 농구팀 테스트는 다음 주에 예정되어 있다. 하지만 John은 다른 사람들이 그를 지켜보고 있을 때는 정말 긴장을 해서 잘 뛰지 못한다. 그는 너무 걱정이 되어 학교 농구팀에 있는 2학년생 Matthew에게 충고를 구하기로 한다. John의 딜레마를 들은 후, Matthew는 John의 문제가 신체적인 것이 아니라 심리적인 것이라 는 것을 알게 된다. 그는 John에게 테스트 중에 아무도 그를 보고 있 지 않다고 상상하고 농구장에 그 혼자 있는 것처럼 농구를 해야 한다 고 제안하고 싶다. 이 상황에서, Matthew는 John에게 뭐라고 말할 까?

Matthew가 John에게 아무도 그를 보고 있지 않다고 상상하고 농구를 하라고 제안하려는 상황이므로, ③ '농구장에 있는 사람이 너뿐이라고 상상하고 최선을 다해.'가 John에게 할 말로 가장 적절하다.

① 테스트 때까지 매일 연습하면 넌 잘할 거야.
② 나를 보고 프로답게 농구하는 법을 배워.
④ 농구를 할 만큼 키가 크지 않으니 다른 운동을 시도해 봐.
⑤ 테스트를 받을 때 반드시 코치의 눈을 바라보도록 해.

tryout 테스트, 시험   sophomore 2학년생   dilemma 딜레마   physical 육체의, 신체의   psychological 정신적인, 심리적인   pretend ~이라고 상상하다, ~인 척하다   make sure 반드시 ~하도록 하다

16-17

여: 안녕하세요, 학생 여러분! 성별에 따라서 다른 색채 지각에 관한 지난 강의가 즐거웠기를 바랍니다. 오늘 우리는 여러분이 흥미를 가질 것 같은 색에 관한 어떤 사실들에 대해 이야기할 것입니다. 첫 번째로, 전 세계에서 가장 인기 있는 색이 무엇인지 아시나요? 파란색입니다. 최근 설문 조사에 따르면 전 세계 40% 이상의 사람들이 파란색을 가 장 좋아하는 색으로 선택했습니다. 다음으로, 대부분의 아기들이 보 는 첫 번째 색이 무엇일까요? 정답은 빨간색입니다. 2주가 된 아기들 은 빨간색을 볼 수 있습니다. 여기 잠재적인 자동차 구매자들을 위한 질문이 있습니다. 무슨 색의 자동차가 심각한 교통사고와 관련이 가 장 적을 것 같은가요? 흰색을 추측했다면 맞았습니다. 흰색이 눈을 제 외하고 어떤 기상 조건하에서도 가장 잘 알아볼 수 있는 색입니다. 마 지막으로, 무슨 색이 가장 마음을 느긋하게 해 주고 진정시키는 색일 까요? 사실, 많은 감옥이 수감자들의 공격성을 낮추기 위해서 이 색으 로 페인트칠이 되어 있습니다. 이 마음을 느긋하게 해 주는 색은 분홍 입니다. 흥미롭지 않나요? 자, 이 색들에 관한 사진을 몇 장 보시죠.

perception 지각, 자각   potential 잠재적인   be involved in ~에 개입되다, 관계되다   visible 알아볼 수 있는, 가시적인   soothing 누그러뜨리는, 진정하는   reduce 줄이다, 낮추다   aggressiveness 공격성

16 ①

여자는 가장 인기 있는 색과 아기들이 보는 첫 번째 색 등 색에 관한 여러 가지 흥미로운 사실에 대해 이야기하고 있다.

① 색에 관한 흥미로운 사실
② 색을 감지하기 위한 편한 방법
③ 색이 시력에 미치는 좋은 영향
④ 색이 동물에게 끼치는 놀라운 영향
⑤ 성별에 따른 색채 지각 차이

17 ④

파란색, 빨간색, 흰색, 분홍색에 대한 언급은 있지만, ④ 초록색에 대한 언급은 없었다.

01 ③	02 ⑤	03 ④	04 ⑤	05 ②	06 ③
07 ⑤	08 ⑤	09 ④	10 ⑤	11 ⑤	12 ①
13 ③	14 ②	15 ④	16 ②	17 ③	

01 ③
관심 단어: 목적 파악

여: 좋은 아침입니다, Housework News 청취를 환영합니다. 오늘의 헤드라인은 우리의 새 후원 업체인 Wave 세탁용 세제로 시작합니다. Wave는 여러분이 경험할 수 있는 가장 상쾌하고 깨끗한 세탁을 보장하기 위해 마이크로 산소 거품 캡슐을 사용합니다. Wave의 새로운 특허 기술은 흰색은 더 밝게 하고 어두운 색은 더 어둡게 할 것입니다. 새로운 제조법은 더 농축되도록 고안되어서, 더 적은 양을 사용하고도 여전히 상쾌하고 깨끗한 세탁을 할 수 있습니다. Wave는 여러분 모두의 세탁 요구를 충족시키기 위해 가루형과 액체형 둘 다로 나옵니다. Wave 제품은 지역 식료품점의 가정 청소 제품 코너에서 찾을 수 있습니다. Housework News 홈페이지를 방문하셔서 계산 시 교환할 수 있는 10% 할인 쿠폰을 프린터로 출력하세요.

문제 해결

여자는 후원 업체인 Wave의 세탁용 세제를 홍보하고 있다.

어휘·표현

laundry detergent 세탁용 세제   patented formula 특허 기술
be designed to ~하도록 만들어지다(고안되다)   concentrated 농축된, 응축된
redeemable 교환할 수 있는

02 ⑤
관심 단어: 주제 파악

남: 안녕, Julie. 어떻게 지냈니?
여: 안녕, Dan. 난 잘 지냈어. 나는 모두가 이야기하는 신작 영화를 봤어.
남: 슈퍼 영웅들에 관한 그 영화니?
여: 응, 영화가 꽤 좋았어. 액션과 특수 효과보다 더 많은 것들이 있었어.
남: 무슨 뜻이니?
여: 줄거리가 잘 구성되었고, 캐릭터 변화가 좋았어.
남: 나는 그런 슈퍼 영웅 영화들이 지겨워.
여: 왜 지겨운데?
남: 나는 할리우드의 제작자들이 슈퍼 영웅 영화에 확실한 것이 있다고 알고 있어서 단지 계속해서 그 영화들을 만든다고 생각해.
여: 너는 요즘 영화의 다양성이 부족하다고 말하는 거니?
남: 응, 대부분의 영화들이 슈퍼 영웅과 관련 있어 보여.
여: 일리가 있는 것 같아.

문제 해결

남자는 슈퍼 영웅 영화들만 계속 만들어지고 있어 영화의 다양성이 부족하다고 생각하므로 남자의 의견으로 ⑤가 가장 적절하다.

어휘·표현

special effects 특수 효과   plot 줄거리
have something to do with ~과 관련이 있다

03 ④
관심 단어: 관계 추론

여: Holiday 씨, 여기를 좀 봐 주시겠어요?
남: 네, 그런데 제가 차에 관해서는 잘 알지 못한다는 걸 알려 드려야겠네요.
여: 괜찮습니다. 여기를 보시면, 브레이크 패드가 닳아 있는 것을 볼 수 있어요.
남: 그건 제가 그것들을 교체해야 한다는 것을 의미하나요?
여: 제 전문적인 견해로는 지금 그것들을 교체해야 합니다.
남: 다음 정기 점검까지 기다릴 수 있을까요?
여: 그건 고객님이 지금부터 그때까지 얼마나 운전하는지에 달렸습니다.
남: 그렇게 많이 운전할 계획은 없어요.
여: 그런 경우라면, 다음번까지 기다려도 될 것 같다고 말씀 드릴 수 있겠네요. 하지만 끼익 하는 소리가 들리기 시작한다면 당장 그것들을 교체해야 합니다.
남: 알겠습니다, 감사합니다.

문제 해결

여자는 남자의 차를 보며 브레이크 패드가 닳아서 교체해야 한다고 전문적인 견해를 말하고, 남자는 다음 정기 점검 때 교체해도 되는지 물어 보고 있으므로, 두 사람의 관계로는 ④가 가장 적절하다.

어휘·표현

wear down 마모되다   maintenance 정비, 보수 관리   squeak 끼익 하는 소리를 내다

04 ⑤
관심 단어: 그림 불일치 파악

여: Harry, 거실 정리하는 것을 끝냈나요?
남: 그래요, Marge. 와서 봐요.
여: 와! 전 당신이 3인용 소파를 벽에 기대어 거실 중앙에 둔 게 마음에 들어요.
남: 고마워요. 요트 사진이 담긴 액자가 놓인 곳은 어때요?
여: 소파 바로 위가 보기 좋아요.
남: 잘됐네요. 소파 오른쪽에 스탠딩 램프를 놓아서 당신이 거기서 책을 읽을 수 있어요.
여: 당신 정말 사려 깊네요. 오, 침실용 탁자를 소파의 다른 쪽에 놓았네요.
남: 네. 그리고 당신의 책들을 그 안에 두었죠.
여: 왜 오래된 사각형 양탄자를 소파 앞에 두었어요?
남: 나는 그게 방을 더 아늑하게 만들 거라 생각했어요.
여: 알겠어요. 나는 친구들과 가족을 빨리 초대하고 싶어요.
남: 나도 그래요.

문제 해결

소파 앞에 사각형 양탄자가 있다고 했는데 그림 속 양탄자는 타원형 모양이므로, ⑤가 대화의 내용과 일치하지 않는다.

어휘·표현

arrange 정리하다, 정돈하다   sailboat 요트, 범선   thoughtful 사려 깊은, 배려심이 있는   nightstand 침실용 탁자   rug 깔개, 양탄자   cozy 아늑한

05 ②
관심 단어: 부탁한 일 파악

여: Barry, 나 볼일을 좀 보러 나가요.
남: 알겠어요, Lisa. 어떤 볼일이에요?
여: 먼저, 지난주에 맡겼던 원피스를 찾으러 세탁소에 갈 거예요.
남: 그들이 커피 자국을 빼 주었으면 좋겠네요. 다음 볼일은 어디인가요?
여: 정육점에 들러서 저녁에 먹을 스테이크를 좀 살 거예요.

남: 좋네요! 당신은 최고의 스테이크를 굽잖아요.
여: 정육점 후에는 문구점에 들러서 봉투를 좀 사야 해요.
남: 마지막 장소인가요?
여: 아니요, 나는 우체국에 가서 편지도 부쳐야 해요.
남: 당신 바쁠 것 같네요.
여: 내가 나가 있는 동안 필요한 게 있어요?
남: 우체통에서 조간신문을 가져와 줄래요?
여: 물론이죠.

여러 볼일을 보러 나가는 여자가 남자에게 필요한 게 있는지 묻자 남자는 우체통에서 조간신문을 가져다 달라고 했으므로, 남자가 부탁한 일로 ②가 가장 적절하다.

run an errand 볼일을 보다, 심부름을 하다   cleaners 세탁소   stain 얼룩
swing by (~에) 잠깐 들르다(= stop by)   stationery store 문구점

06 ③

남: Mohegan 항공에 오신 걸 환영합니다. 제 이름은 Frank입니다. 어떻게 도와드릴까요?
여: 저는 Crater Lake로 가는 표를 사고 싶어요.
남: 네, 그건 300달러입니다. 경유해도 괜찮으신가요?
여: 직항이면 좋겠어요. 그건 얼마인가요?
남: 그건 100달러가 더 듭니다.
여: 오, 그건 비싼 것 같네요. 경유를 할게요. 또한, 기내식으로 채식주의자 코스를 주문하고 싶어요.
남: 그건 추가로 5달러가 더 듭니다.
여: 통로 쪽 좌석을 예약하는 것도 가능한가요?
남: 여기서 해 드릴 수 있습니다. 수하물을 부치실 건가요?
여: 네, 저는 여행 가방 세 개가 있어요.
남: 저희는 가방 두 개는 무료로 부쳐 드리지만, 세 번째 가방은 추가 금액 15달러를 지불하셔야 합니다.
여: 괜찮아요. 총 얼마인가요?

Crater Lake로 가는 비행기표를 사려는 여자는 직항은 비싸서 300달러 하는 경유하는 표를 사기로 했고, 5달러 하는 채식주의자 코스 기내식을 추가하였으며, 수하물로 부칠 여행 가방 세 개 중 두 개는 무료이고 세 번째 가방에 15달러를 추가로 지불해야 한다. 따라서 여자가 지불할 총 금액은 320달러이다.

layover 경유   additional 추가의   in-flight meal 기내식   aisle seat 통로
쪽 좌석   luggage 짐, 수하물   complimentary 무료의

07 ⑤

남: 안녕, Allison. 너 뭘 보고 있니?
여: 안녕, Danny. 이건 다섯 가지 코스 요리를 하는 법을 보여 주는 동영상이야.
남: 너는 네 남편의 생일에 그걸 요리할 계획이니?
여: 아니, 남편의 생일은 지난달이었어. 우리는 외출해서 근사한 스테이크 전문 식당에서 먹었어.
남: 내가 추천했던 곳에 갔던 거야?
여: 응, 우리가 네 여동생의 졸업식에 갔을 때 네가 말해 주었던 곳 말야.

남: 그럼 동영상은 남편과의 멋진 식사를 위한 거야?
여: 그렇진 않아. 난 이걸 남편을 위해 만들진 않을 거야.
남: 그럼, 왜 동영상을 보고 있는 건데?
여: 다음 주가 우리 부모님의 30주년 기념일이야. 그래서 난 부모님을 위해 특별한 걸 하고 싶어.
남: 넌 참 다정하구나.
여: 내가 망치지 않았으면 좋겠어.
남: 걱정하지 마. 넌 잘할 거야.

여자는 부모님의 30주년 기념일에 특별한 걸 해 드리고 싶어서 다섯 가지 코스 요리를 하는 법을 보여 주는 동영상을 보고 있다고 했다.

anniversary 기념일   mess up 망치다, 엉망으로 만들다

08 ⑤

여: Tim, 하계 세미나에 관한 전단지 봤어요?
남: 네, Jane. 난 그걸 휴게실에서 봤어요.
여: 거기에 우리가 이번 주 토요일에 세미나에 와야 한다고 쓰여 있었어요.
남: 알아요. 내가 세미나 때문에 토요일을 포기해야 한다는 게 믿기지 않아요.
여: 나쁜 것만은 아니에요. 난 팀워크 활동이 기대돼요.
남: 그건 맞아요. 난 작년에 그걸 하는 게 재미있었어요. 난 특히 줄다리기가 즐거웠어요.
여: 전단지는 우리가 편한 옷을 입어야 한다고도 언급했어요.
남: 맞아요. 올해 우리는 하이킹을 가기로 되어 있어요.
여: 전단지에 어디서 모여야 하는지 쓰여 있었나요?
남: 네, FAB 건물의 302호에서 오전 9시요.
여: 세미나가 얼마나 걸릴까요?
남: 잘 모르겠어요. 그건 쓰여 있지 않아요.

개최 요일(토요일), 활동(하이킹), 옷차림(편한 옷), 모이는 장소(FAB 건물 302호)에 대해서는 언급했지만, ⑤ '토론 주제'에 대해서는 언급하지 않았다.

flyer 전단   break room 휴게실   tug-of-war 줄다리기   mention 언급하다,
말하다

09 ④

남: 팟캐스트 청취자 여러분, 좋은 오후입니다. 여러분은 애완동물과 애완동물의 주인을 위한 팟캐스트, Tiny Paws를 듣고 계십니다. 저는 진행자 Gary입니다. 오늘 저는 이번 주말에 Aloha 경기장에서 하는 다가오는 모임에 관한 정보를 여러분들과 공유하고 싶습니다. 동물 보호소와 재향 군인회와 함께 하는, Pet's for Vets 모임은 유기묘와 유기견을 은퇴한 군인들과 연결하는 것을 목표로 합니다. 유명한 고양이 훈련사 Eddie Cats가 고양잇과 동반자를 기르는 것에 관해 짧은 강연을 할 겁니다. 또한, 여러분과 여러분의 애완동물은 Best Trick 대회에 참가할 수 있습니다. 일등 상은 일년 동안의 애완동물 사료 제공입니다. Pet's for Vets는 주말까지 합니다. 꼭 들러 주셔서 저희에게 힘이 되어 주세요.

문제 해결
모임에서 열리는 대회의 일등 상은 일년 동안의 애완동물 사료 제공이라고 했으므로 ④가 내용과 일치하지 않는다.

어휘·표현

upcoming 다가오는   Veterans Association 재향 군인회   retired 은퇴한
service member 군요원   renowned 유명한, 명성 있는   feline 고양잇과의
companion 동반자

10 ⑤ · 도표 정보 파악

남: Tina, 이 야외 활동 제품 카탈로그를 좀 봐요.
여: 새로 나온 텐트들을 봐요! 우리 하나 살까요?
남: 나도 같은 생각을 하는 중이었어요. 좋아요, 우선 우리 예산 범위가
　　얼마죠?
여: 200달러 넘게는 쓰지 않도록 해요.
남: 그래요. 난 마지막 쪽에서 가격이 적당한 몇 개를 봤어요.
여: 몇 인용에 맞춰야 한다고 생각해요?
남: 우리는 4인용이 필요해요. 특히 우리 두 마리의 개들과 함께 해서요.
여: 이 세 개가 4인용에 맞아요.
남: 모양은 어때요? 돔 모양이 좋겠어요, 아님 피라미드 모양이 좋겠어요?
여: 난 돔 모양이 더 좋아요. 더 널찍하게 느껴져요.
남: 좋아요, 이 두 개의 텐트로 좁혀졌어요.
여: 텐트에 문이 하나보다 더 있어야 한다고 생각해요?
남: 아니요. 하나면 충분하다고 생각해요. 이 텐트를 사도록 하죠.

문제 해결

두 사람은 텐트 카탈로그를 보고 있는데, 200달러가 넘지 않고 4인용에 돔 모양이면서 문은 하나인 텐트를 사려고 하므로, 두 사람이 구입할 텐트로 ⑤가 가장 적절하다.

어휘·표현

price range 가격 폭, 가격대   reasonable (가격이) 너무 비싸지 않은, 적당한
roomy 넓은, 널찍한

11 ⑤ · 짧은 대화의 응답

[휴대 전화벨이 울린다.]
남: 안녕하세요, Watson 씨. 내일 약속을 상기시켜 드리기 위해 전화를
　　드렸습니다.
여: 연락 주셔서 감사합니다. 유감이지만 내일 약속을 다시 조정해야 해
　　요.
남: 문제없습니다. 저는 주 후반에 시간이 됩니다. 괜찮으신가요?
여: 네. 목요일 오후는 어떠신가요?

문제 해결

내일 약속에 대한 사전 확인 연락을 한 남자에게 여자가 약속 조정이 필요하다고 말했고 남자는 주 후반에 시간이 된다며 괜찮은지 물었다. 이에 대한 여자의 응답으로 목요일 오후 시간을 제안하는 ⑤가 가장 적절하다.
① 이번 주 초에 방문하겠습니다.
② 의사가 화를 많이 낼까요?
③ 약속 시간이 거의 다 되었네요.
④ 저는 내일이 딱 좋아요.

어휘·표현

remind A of B A에게 B를 생각나게 하다   appointment 약속

12 ① · 짧은 대화의 응답

여: Ted, 무엇을 그렇게 열심히 읽고 있어?
남: Steven King이 쓴 새로운 추리 소설. 정말로 재미있어.
여: 오, Steven King은 내가 가장 좋아하는 추리 소설 작가야. 네가 다
　　읽으면 그 책을 빌릴 수 있을까?
남: 물론이지! 네가 이 책을 즐길 거라고 확신해.

문제 해결

남자가 Steven King의 신간 소설을 읽고 있다고 하자, 여자는 Steven King은 자신이 가장 좋아하는 작가라고 하면서 그 책을 빌려 달라고 요청하였다. 따라서 책을 빌려 주겠다면서 여자가 이 책을 즐길 것이라고 확신한다고 말하는 ①이 남자의 응답으로 가장 적절하다.
② 걱정하지 마. 난 그 책을 도서관에 반납할 거야.
③ 어떻게 내가 추리 소설 작가가 될 수 있을까?
④ Steven King의 사인을 받는 게 어때?
⑤ 넌 글을 쓰는 데 정말 재능이 있어.

어휘·표현

intently 열심히, 골똘히   mystery novel 추리 소설

13 ③ · 긴 대화의 응답

여: 보세요, 아빠! 새로운 롤러코스터예요.
남: 확실히 크구나, Mia.
여: 저걸 탈 수 있을까요?
남: 그걸 타기 전에 한 시간 정도는 기다려야 할 것 같구나. 우리는 막 점
　　심을 먹었잖아.
여: 그래요, 아빠 말이 맞아요. 속이 안 좋아지고 싶진 않아요.
남: Monkey Mania Land로 걸어가면서 우리가 탈 수 있는 놀이 기구
　　가 있는지 보는 게 어떨까?
여: 좋아요. 하지만 그 전에 선물 가게에 들러도 될까요? 오늘 엄마가 우리
　　와 함께 오지 못했기 때문에 엄마에게 멋진 뭔가를 사 드리고 싶어요.
남: 좋은 생각이구나, Mia. 네가 엄마를 생각해 줘서 엄마는 기뻐할 거야.
여: 오! 저 지갑을 식당에 두고 온 것 같아요.
남: 저런. 식당으로 돌아가는 게 좋겠다.
여: 없어지지 않았으면 좋겠어요.
남: 걱정하지 마렴. 지갑은 여전히 거기에 있을 거라고 확신해.

문제 해결

점심을 먹었던 식당에 지갑을 두고 온 여자가 지갑이 없어지지 않았기를 바란다고 말하므로, 이에 대한 남자의 응답으로 ③ '걱정하지 마렴. 지갑은 여전히 거기에 있을 거라고 확신해.'가 가장 적절하다.
① 서두르렴. 나는 정말 배가 고파.
② 엄마를 위한 선물을 찾았니?
④ 무엇을 주문하고 싶니?
⑤ 모르겠어. 이 롤러코스터는 무섭구나.

어휘·표현

ride 놀이 기구   purse 지갑

14 ② · 긴 대화의 응답

[휴대 전화벨이 울린다.]
남: 안녕, Sue! 나 Lucas야. 오늘 밤 공연을 즐길 준비됐니?
여: 오, 이런! 나 완전히 잊고 있었어. 나 못 갈 것 같아.

남: 유감이야. 밴드들이 멋질 텐데. 왜 못 가니?

여: 부모님께서 오늘 시내에 오셔서 함께 저녁을 먹고 싶어 하셔.

남: 알겠어, 넘어가 줄게. 난 네가 가족과 얼마나 친밀한지 아니까.

여: 커피숍에서 만난 그 여자애를 데려가는 게 어때? 그녀는 괜찮아 보이던데.

남: 넌 내가 물어보면 그녀가 승낙할 거라고 생각하니?

여: 물어보는 걸로 상처 받지는 않을 거야. 게다가, 누가 이 쇼를 보러 가는 걸 원하지 않겠어?

남: 네 말에 일리가 있어.

여: 잃을 게 뭐니?

남: 좋아. 내가 뭘 말해야 할지 조언할 게 있니?

여: 그냥 자연스럽게 행동하고 너무 많이 생각하지 마.

문제 해결
남자와 공연을 보러 함께 가지 못하게 된 여자는 남자가 커피숍에서 만난 여자를 데려가는 것을 제안하고 남자에게 용기의 말을 해 주고 있다. 남자가 뭘 말해야 할지 조언을 구했으므로 이에 대한 여자의 응답으로 ② '그냥 자연스럽게 행동하고 너무 많이 생각하지 마.'가 가장 적절하다.

① 내가 마실 한 잔의 커피를 주문해 줘.

③ 네 부모님께 저녁 식사가 맛있었다고 말씀 드려.

④ 난 너무 기대돼. 오늘 밤 쇼에서 봐.

⑤ 누가 알겠어? 아마 그 밴드는 돌아올 거야.

어휘·표현
completely 완전히, 전적으로   off the hook 곤경을 면한   have a point 일리가 있다   be yourself 자연스럽게 행동하다   overthink 너무 많이(오래) 생각하다

15 ④

여: Jimmy와 Sunny는 그들이 사는 소도시에 있는 서점의 공동 소유자들이다. 최근에, Jimmy는 많은 새로운 고객들이 동시대의 작가들이 쓴 책들을 사고 있다는 것을 인지한다. 그러나, Sunny는 서점의 목록이 주로 고전이어야 한다고 굳게 믿고 있다. 그래서 Sunny는 훨씬 더 많은 고전을 들이고 싶어 한다. Jimmy와 Sunny는 내년에 구입할 책에 대한 새로운 예산을 계획해야 한다. Jimmy는 이번이 그들의 사업을 번창시키기 위한 방법을 논의할 좋은 때라고 생각한다. Jimmy는 Sunny가 매출 증진을 위해 더 새로운 작가들에게 예산을 더 쓰는 것을 고려하기를 원한다. 이런 상황에서, Jimmy는 Sunny에게 뭐라고 말할 것 같은가?

문제 해결
Jimmy는 서점에 고전을 더 갖추고 싶어 하는 Sunny에게 내년 구입 책의 예산을 세울 때 새로운 작가들에게 예산을 더 쓰는 것을 고려하라고 말하고 싶은 상황이므로, Jimmy가 Sunny에게 할 말로 ④ '나는 우리가 더 새로운 작가들에게 더 많은 돈을 써야 한다고 생각해.'가 가장 적절하다.

① 사람들은 요즘 고전 소설을 읽는 것을 정말 좋아해.

② 이 현대 작가는 많은 비평가들의 기분을 상하게 했어.

③ 우리는 재고품을 온라인 상점으로 옮겨야 해.

⑤ 나는 우리가 엄선한 목록에 잡지를 추가하는 것이 우리 매출에 도움이 될 거라고 생각해.

어휘·표현
contemporary author 현대 작가   firmly 굳게, 확고하게   inventory (상품 등의) 목록, 재고품   classic 고전, 명작   stock (물품을) 들여놓다, 비축하다   budget 비용, 예산   selection 선택된 것, 정선품

16-17

남: 안녕하세요, 자전거를 타는 동료 여러분. 채널 Spinning Dreams에 다시 오신 것을 환영합니다. 지난주, 우리는 하이브리드 자전거의 이점에 대해 이야기했습니다. 오늘 저는 새로 나온 하이브리드 자전거 Phantom G에 관해 여러분에게 말하고 싶습니다. Phantom G는 도로, 오솔길, 산에서 탈 수 있습니다. 탄소 섬유로 만들어진 몸체를 가지고 있어, Phantom G는 적당한 6.8킬로그램의 무게가 나갑니다. 이 가벼운 몸체는 여러분이 쉽고 편안하게 언덕을 오르게 해 줄 것입니다. 편안함에 관해 말한다면, Phantom G는 여러분이 달리는 것을 더 쾌적하게 만들기 위해 보통보다 넓은 안장과 메모리 폼 쿠션이 장착되어 있습니다. 또한 완전히 새로운 동력 전달 장치가 포함되어 있습니다. 이 동력 전달 장치의 각 부분은 여러분이 부드럽고 자신감 있게 기어를 이동할 수 있도록 정밀하게 만들어졌습니다. Phantom G는 또한 펑크에 저항력이 있는 28인치 바퀴가 장착되어 있습니다. 각 자전거는 엄격한 품질 관리 검사를 거칩니다. 올해 여러분이 하이브리드 자전거를 구입할 생각이라면, 이것이 최고의 선택 중 하나일 것입니다.

어휘·표현
carbon fiber 탄소 섬유   weigh in at ~로 체중 측정(검사)을 받다   brand-new 아주 새로운, 신품인   drive-train 동력 전달 장치   with precision 정밀하게   shift 이동하다, 위치를 바꾸다   puncture 펑크, 구멍   resistant 저항력이 있는, 잘 견디는   quality control 품질 관리   hazard 위험 (요소)   component 요소, 부품   lightweight 가벼운, 경량의

16 ②

문제 해결
자전거를 타는 사람들을 위한 채널에서 새로 나온 하이브리드 자전거의 특징에 대해 소개해 주고 있으므로, 남자가 하는 말의 주제로 ② '새로 나온 하이브리드 자전거의 특징'이 가장 적절하다.

① 자전거 타기의 건강상의 위험

③ 자전거에 필요한 부품

④ 펑크에 저항력이 있는 타이어의 이점

⑤ 새로운 동력 전달 장치의 이점

17 ③

문제 해결
새로 나온 하이브리드 자전거의 특징을 소개하면서 가벼운 몸체, 편안한 안장, 동력 전달 장치, 펑크에 저항력이 있는 바퀴에 대해서는 언급했지만, 접이식 몸체에 관해서는 언급되지 않았다.

01 ④	02 ②	03 ②	04 ⑤	05 ③	06 ③
07 ③	08 ②	09 ⑤	10 ③	11 ④	12 ③
13 ④	14 ①	15 ⑤	16 ②	17 ④	

01 ④ 　　　　　　　　　　　　　　　　　　　　目的 파악

남: Classics for You 청취자 여러분, 안녕하세요. 저는 Nathan Lang 입니다. 오늘 저희와 함께 해 주셔서 정말 감사합니다. 저는 다음 주 월요일부터 Lisa Donovan이 공동 진행자로서 저희 프로그램에 합류하게 된 것을 알려 드리게 되어 매우 기쁩니다. 라디오 진행자, 음악가, 그리고 예술 교육가로서 Lisa Donovan은 클래식 음악 방송에 폭넓은 경험이 있습니다. 또한, 그녀의 부드러운 목소리와 친근한 스타일로 인해 그녀는 Classics for You에 정말 잘 어울릴 것입니다. Lisa Donovan과 함께 Classics for You는 여러분들이 클래식 음악에 대해 배우고 즐거워할 수 있도록 계속 돕겠습니다! 그녀에게 환영의 메시지를 보내고 싶으시다면 902-420-2004로 마음껏 문자를 보내 주세요. 여러분들의 문자를 기대하고 있겠습니다!

문제 해결

남자는 Classics for You라는 라디오 음악 방송 프로그램에 Lisa Donovan 이 공동 진행자로 합류하게 된 것을 안내하고 있다.

어휘·표현

a perfect fit 완벽하게 맞는 것　**feel free to** 마음껏 ~하다　**look forward to** ~을 기대하다

02 ② 　　　　　　　　　　　　　　　　　　　　主제 파악

여: 안녕, Adam. 새 학교에서의 생활에는 잘 적응하고 있니?
남: 안녕하세요, Nam 선생님. 저는 잘 적응하고 있어요. 하지만 예전 친구들이 그립고 때때로 외로워요.
여: 이해한다. 학교를 옮기는 것은 꽤 스트레스가 될 수 있지. 새 친구들은 사귀었니?
남: 아직요.
여: 음, 내 생각에는 친구들을 사귀는 것이 네가 학교에 더 잘 적응하는 데 도움이 될 것 같구나.
남: 그렇게 생각하세요?
여: 물론이지. 너의 관심사를 함께 나눌 수 있는 사람을 찾는다면 학교생활이 훨씬 즐거워질 거야.
남: 선생님 말이 맞는 것 같네요.
여: 학생 동아리들 중 하나에 가입하는 건 어떠니?
남: 학생 동아리요?
여: 그래. 동아리에 가입하는 건 새로운 사람들을 만날 수 있는 좋은 방법이지. 그리고 네가 미술을 좋아하니까 만화 동아리에 가입하려고 해 볼 수 있겠다.
남: 그거 재미있을 것 같은데요. 조언해 주셔서 감사합니다.
여: 천만에.

문제 해결

여자는 전학 온 학생에게 친구를 사귀는 것이 학교생활에 적응하는 데 도움이 된다고 말하고 있다.

어휘·표현

adjust 적응하다　**transfer** 옮기다, 전학 가다　**stressful** 스트레스가 많은

03 ② 　　　　　　　　　　　　　　　　　　　　관계 추론

[휴대 전화벨이 울린다.]
여: 여보세요?
남: 여보세요, Peters 선생님. 저 Bales 선생입니다. 당신이 계단에서 발을 헛디뎠다고 들었어요. 괜찮은가요?
여: Bales 선생님, 유감스럽게도 제 오른쪽 발목이 부러졌어요.
남: 오, 안됐군요.
여: 의사 말로는 수술해야 한다고 합니다. 저는 일주일 정도 병원에 있어야 할 것 같아요.
남: 알겠습니다. 선생님 수업은 Grey 선생님께서 대신하실 수 있도록 제가 처리할게요.
여: 감사합니다. Grey 선생님께 과학 실험 보고서를 걷어 달라고 부탁해 주시겠어요?
남: 물론이죠.
여: 그리고 실험 도구를 정리해 달라고 부탁드려 주세요.
남: 알겠어요. 학교의 수장으로서 제가 선생님을 위해 해 드릴 수 있는 일이 있나요?
여: 아니요, 지금은 그게 전부예요. 정말 감사합니다.
남: 천만에요. 몸 조심하시고 빨리 회복하세요.

문제 해결

여자가 발목이 부러져서 병원에 일주일 정도 있어야 한다고 말하자 남자는 여자의 수업을 다른 선생님으로 하여금 대체하도록 하겠다고 하였다. 또한 남자가 자신을 '학교의 수장'이라고 말한 것으로 보아, 여자와 남자는 교사와 교장의 관계이다.

어휘·표현

trip 발을 헛디디다　**surgery** 수술　**arrange** (일을) 처리하다
substitute for ~을 대신하다　**experiment** 실험　**put away** (사용 후 원래 있던 장소로) 치우다　**equipment** 장비, 설비　**head** 수장, 교장

04 ⑤ 　　　　　　　　　　　　　　　　　　　　그림 불일치 파악

남: 여보, 이것 좀 봐요. 이번 주말에 개장하는 새로운 실내 놀이터예요.
여: 멋져 보이는데요! 왼쪽 모퉁이에 있는 건 기린 모형인가요? 거대한데요!
남: 맞아요, 정말 진짜 같아 보이네요. 그리고 오른쪽에 있는 미끄럼틀을 봐요. 코끼리 모양으로 생겼어요.
여: 귀엽네요. 이 장소의 테마가 동물인가 보네요.
남: 그런 것 같아요. 심지어 천장에 얼룩말 모양의 전등도 있어요.
여: 난 왼쪽에 있는 원숭이 모양으로 생긴 암벽 등반 벽이 마음에 들어요.
남: 저도요.
여: Mark가 저 벽 곳곳을 올라가는 게 벌써 상상이 되네요.
남: 그리고 중앙에 있는 하마 모양 볼 풀 좀 봐요. Jessie가 저 안에서 아주 즐거운 한때를 보낼 거예요.
여: 이번 주말에 아이들을 여기에 데려갈까요?
남: 좋아요. 아이들이 정말 좋아할 거예요.

문제 해결

중앙에 하마 모양 볼 풀이 있다고 했으므로, 사자 모양 볼 풀인 ⑤가 대화의 내용과 일치하지 않는다.

05 ③

여: Justin, 너 스마트폰에서 메시지를 예약할 수 있는 거 아니?

남: 무슨 소리야?

여: 엄마께 보낼 생일 축하 메시지를 방금 썼는데, 이따 자정에 보내질 거야.

남: 그거 편리하다! 어떻게 한 거야?

여: 난 Message Scheduler라는 앱을 사용했어. 네 스마트폰에도 다운로드해 줄까?

남: 괜찮아. 그건 내가 할 수 있어. [잠시 후] 됐다. 다운로드 됐어.

여: 이제 네 메시지를 입력하고 네가 원하는 시간과 날짜만 기입하면 돼.

남: 알겠어. [잠시 후] 메시지는 작성했는데, 시간과 날짜는 어디에 기입해?

여: 아래쪽에 파란색 버튼 안 보여?

남: 아니.

여: 먼저 네 스마트폰을 업데이트해야 하나 봐.

남: 그건 어떻게 하는지 잘 모르는데. 나를 도와줄 수 있니?

여: 물론이지.

남자는 여자에게 스마트폰 업데이트하는 것을 도와달라고 부탁하였다.

schedule 예약하다, 일정을 잡다   convenient 편리한   app 앱, 응용 프로그램 (application의 줄임말)   type in 입력하다

06 ③

여: 안녕하세요. 무엇을 도와드릴까요?

남: 안녕하세요. 딸이 입을 래시 가드를 찾고 있어요. 그녀는 일곱 살이에요.

여: 알겠습니다. 이쪽으로 오세요. 긴팔 래시 가드는 30달러이고 반팔 래시 가드는 20달러입니다.

남: 저희는 야외에서 수영을 할 거라서, 긴팔 래시 가드를 하나 살게요.

여: 알겠습니다. 저희는 지금 특별 행사 중입니다. 50달러 이상 쓰시면 총 구매 금액의 20%를 할인해 드립니다.

남: 잘됐네요! 딸에게 아쿠아 슈즈도 한 켤레 사 주고 싶었거든요. 아쿠아 슈즈도 있나요?

여: 물론입니다. 한 켤레에 20달러입니다.

남: 사이즈 12로 한 켤레 살게요.

여: 알겠습니다. 다른 것도 필요하신가요?

남: 아니요, 그게 전부예요.

여: 그럼 래시 가드 하나와 아쿠아 슈즈 한 켤레네요. 할인을 받으면, 이게 최종 금액입니다.

남: 알겠습니다. 신용 카드로 계산할게요.

긴팔 래시 가드는 30달러, 아쿠아 슈즈는 20달러이므로 둘을 합한 금액은 50 달러이다. 50달러 이상 구매 시 20% 할인이 된다고 하였으므로, 남자가 지불할 총 금액은 40달러이다.

long/short-sleeved 긴팔/반팔   promotion 홍보, 판촉   discount 할인

07 ③

남: 저기, Lucy. 있잖아, 나 새 뮤지컬 '알라딘' 표가 두 장 생겼어.

여: 정말? 모든 표가 첫날 다 팔렸다고 하지 않았어?

남: 실은, 우리 부모님께서 주셨어. 친구분 결혼식에 가야 해서 못 가게 되셨거든.

여: 너 운 좋다!

남: 나랑 같이 갈래? 심지어 공연 후에 출연진과 사진을 찍을 수 있는 기회도 있어.

여: 좋지! 공연이 언제야?

남: 다음 주 금요일 저녁 6시야.

여: 미안, 금요일은 안 돼.

남: 왜? 춤 연습이 있어?

여: 아니, 춤 연습은 지난주에 끝났어.

남: 그러면 왜 갈 수 없는데?

여: 나 학교 연극에 지원해 보려고. 다음 주 금요일 저녁에 오디션이 있어.

남: 알겠어. 그럼 네 오디션에 행운을 빌게!

여: 고마워. 다음에 같이 가자.

여자는 다음 주 금요일 저녁에 학교 연극 오디션을 봐야 해서 남자와 함께 뮤지컬을 보러 갈 수 없다고 했다.

cast 출연진   make it 성공하다, 해내다   try out for ~에 지원하다

08 ②

여: Tony, 너 Eco-Friendly Night에 갈 거니?

남: 물론이지. 나는 매년 거기에 가. 이번 주 토요일이지, 맞지?

여: 응, 12월 10일 토요일. 그리고 무료 기념품을 받고 싶으면 오후 5시 전에 도착해야 해.

남: 알겠어. 나누어 주는 기념품이 뭔지 알고 있니?

여: 음, 내가 가지고 있는 포스터에 의하면, 500개의 텀블러와 에코 백을 나누어 준대.

남: 와! 올해 기부를 많이 받았나 보다.

여: 맞아. 30개가 넘는 지역 상점들과 음식점들이 이 행사를 후원해.

남: 멋지다! 작년과 똑같은 장소에서 열리는 거야?

여: 아니. Davis 초등학교에서 열릴 거야.

남: 오, 우리 집에서 정말 가깝네. 난 거기에 걸어갈 수 있어.

여: 잘됐다. 그럼 거기에서 보자.

개최 일시(12월 10일), 기념품 종류(텀블러와 에코 백), 후원 업체(지역 상점과 음식점), 개최 장소(Davis 초등학교)에 대해서는 언급했지만, ② 신청 방법에 대해서는 언급하지 않았다.

souvenir 기념품   give out 나누어 주다   donation 기부   sponsor 후원하다

09 ⑤

여: Cherrywood 아파트 주민 여러분께 알려 드립니다. 이 안내는 화재경보기 점검에 관련된 것입니다. 3월 2일과 3일에 관리 사무소를 포함한 모든 건물의 화재경보기 점검이 있을 예정임을 알려 드립니다. 점검은 우리 지역 소방서의 자격을 갖춘 소방관들에 의해 실시될 예

정입니다. 이번 점검 중에 때때로 경보기가 울릴 것이지만 걱정하지 않으셔도 됩니다. 또한 여러분의 가구의 각 방 문을 열기 위해 마스터키를 사용할 것이므로 문을 모두 열어 놓지 않으셔도 됩니다. 애완동물이 있다면 침실에 두시기 바랍니다. 이 점검은 법적으로 요구되는 것입니다. 협조하여 주시면, 불편을 최소화하여 필요한 점검을 마칠 수 있습니다. 여러분들의 협조와 양해에 대해 미리 감사드립니다. 좋은 하루 보내세요.

문제 해결

각 가구의 방 문을 열기 위해 마스터키를 사용할 것이므로 문을 모두 열어 놓지 않아도 된다고 했으므로, 각 방 문을 모두 열어 두어야 한다는 ⑤는 내용과 일치하지 않는다.

어휘·표현

resident 주민, 거주민   inspection 점검, 검사   be advised that ~임을 숙지하다   management office 관리 사무소   certified 자격을 갖춘   unit (아파트 내의) 한 가구   inconvenience 불편   in advance 미리, 사전에

10 ③
도표 정보 파악

남: 엄마, 우리는 Jack을 비행기에 태우기 위해 애완동물 이동 장을 사야 해요.
여: 그렇구나. 선택안을 좀 보여 다오. Jack이 얼마나 크지?
남: Jack은 키가 29센티미터예요.
여: 이동 장은 그보다 적어도 10센티미터는 더 커야 해. 이건 제외하도록 하자.
남: 어깨끈 달린 건 어때요? 그걸로 Jack을 운반하는 것이 아마 더 쉬울 거예요.
여: 그럴 것 같지 않구나. 그렇게 하면 그에게 불안정할 수 있어.
남: 알겠어요. 환풍구 홈은 어떻게 할까요? 이 좁은 홈들은 이동 장 안으로 공기가 흐르는 것을 도와줘요.
여: 그 안에 오랫동안 있는 건 답답할 거야. 그러니까 환풍구 홈은 적어도 3면에 있어야 해.
남: 저도 동의해요.
여: 또한 나는 Jack이 어떤 경우에라도 이동 장 밖으로 나오는 것을 원치 않아. 우리는 튼튼한 문이 필요해.
남: 맞아요. 저는 플라스틱보다 철이 더 낫다고 생각해요.
여: 좋아. 이것을 사도록 하자.

문제 해결

두 사람은 키가 29cm인 애완동물보다 높이가 적어도 10cm는 커야 하고 어깨끈이 없으며 환풍구 홈이 3면에 있고 문이 철로 되어 있는 애완동물 이동 장을 찾고 있다. 따라서 두 사람이 구매할 애완동물 이동 장은 ③이다.

어휘·표현

rule out ~을 제외하다   strap 끈   unstable 불안정한   slot 길고 가는 홈   stuffy 답답한   by any chance 어떤 경우에라도, 혹시라도

11 ④
짧은 대화의 응답

남: Jenny, 너 학교 합창단에 가입하기로 결정했니?
여: 아직. 난 노래하는 것을 좋아하지만 다른 사람들 앞에서 노래하는 것은 좀 내키지 않아.
남: 음, 내일 합창단이 작은 공연을 한대. 네가 결정하기 전에 우리 같이 보러 가는 게 어때?
여: 그래. 너랑 같이 가서 어떤지 볼게.

남자가 합창단 가입을 결정하기 전에 합창단의 공연을 같이 보러 가자고 제안하였으므로, 긍정의 답을 하면서 같이 가서 어떤지 보겠다고 말하는 ④가 여자의 응답으로 가장 적절하다.
① 응. 우리는 동아리 회원이 더 많이 필요해.
② 미안해. 나는 내일 합창단 연습이 있어.
③ 물론이지. 네게 내 새로운 공연을 보여 줄게.
⑤ 괜찮아. 나는 학교 합창단에 이미 가입했어.

어휘·표현

choir 합창단   a bit 조금   have a performance 공연을 하다

12 ③
짧은 대화의 응답

여: 아빠, 이 사진들 좀 보세요. 할머니랑 제주도에서 여름휴가 때 찍은 거예요.
남: 정말 좋구나! 할머니도 그것들을 매우 보고 싶어 하실 것 같구나.
여: 이것들을 출력해서 할머니께 사진 앨범을 만들어 드리고 싶어요. 아빠의 컬러 프린터를 사용해도 돼요?
남: 아니, 유감이지만 그렇게 할 수 없겠다. 지금 잉크가 다 떨어졌거든.

문제 해결

여자가 컬러 프린터를 사용할 수 있는지 물었으므로, 잉크가 다 떨어져서 사용할 수 없다고 하는 ③이 남자의 응답으로 가장 적절하다.
① 물론이지. 우리가 할머니께 새 프린터를 사 드릴 수 있어.
② 괜찮아. 나는 이미 내 사진들을 출력했어.
④ 좋은 생각이다. 할머니와 제주도에 가자.
⑤ 이해한다. 사진 앨범을 만드는 건 쉽지 않지.

어휘·표현

print ~ out ~을 인쇄하다, 출력하다   be out of ~ ~가 다 떨어지다

13 ④
긴 대화의 응답

남: Jasmine, 너 다음 주 여름 캠프에 가져갈 짐은 다 쌌어?
여: 아직. 너는?
남: 난 거의 다 쌌어. 벌레 퇴치제를 사기만 하면 다 끝나.
여: 벌레 퇴치제? 무엇 때문에?
남: 우리가 가려는 곳이 호수 근처니까 모기가 엄청 많을 거야.
여: 그렇구나. 모기에 물리는 건 정말 짜증나지.
남: 맞아. 그리고 모기에 물리는 건 말라리아와 지카 바이러스와 같은 질병을 퍼뜨릴 수도 있어.
여: 그거 겁나는 소린데. 그래, 어떻게 하면 모기에 물리는 것을 피할 수 있어?
남: 음, 제일 효과적인 방법 중 하나가 밖에 나가기 전에 벌레 퇴치제를 바르는 거야.
여: 그렇다면 나도 사야겠다. 어디서 살 수 있는지 아니?
남: 아무 약국이나 동네 슈퍼마켓에서 살 수 있어.
여: 알겠어. 방과 후에 약국에 가서 하나 살게.

문제 해결

모기에 물리는 것을 피할 수 있는 방법 중 하나가 벌레 퇴치제를 바르는 것이라는 말에 여자가 벌레 퇴치제를 어디에서 살 수 있는지 물어보았고, 이에 남자는 약국이나 동네 슈퍼마켓에서 살 수 있다고 응답하였다. 이어질 여자의 말로 방과 후에 약국에 가서 하나 사겠다는 ④가 가장 적절하다.
① 동의해. 우리는 지역 슈퍼마켓을 지지해야 해.

② 문제없어. 우리 캠핑장은 호수에서 멀리 떨어져 있어.
③ 물론이지. 나는 모기에 물리면 엄청 긁어.
⑤ 괜찮아. 이 벌레 퇴치제는 유기농 재료로 만들어졌어.

insect repellent 벌레 퇴치제   mosquito 모기   irritating 짜증나는, 거슬리는
apply (페인트, 크림 등을) 바르다   in that case 그렇다면, 그런 경우에는
pharmacy 약국   ingredient 재료, 성분

14 ①

남: 안녕하세요, Sanders 선생님. 잠깐 시간 되세요?
여: 응. 무슨 일이니, Kevin?
남: 저는 여름 방학 동안 학교 자원봉사 프로그램들 중 하나에 참여하고
    싶어서요.
여: 좋지. 생각해 둔 어떤 구체적인 활동이 있니?
남: 제가 동물들을 아주 좋아해서 동물 병원에서 자원봉사를 해 보고 싶
    어요.
여: 어디 보자. [잠시 후] 한 자리가 가능하구나.
남: 잘됐네요!
여: 여기 보면 애완동물을 길러 본 경험이 있는 사람을 원한다고 하네. 애
    완동물을 길러 본 적이 있니?
남: 아니요. 그럼 저는 그곳에서 봉사할 수 없는 건가요?
여: 미안하지만 그럴 것 같아. 다른 프로그램을 찾아보면 어떨까? 또 관심
    이 가는 것이 있니?
남: 음, 도서관에서 돕는 것도 관심이 있어요.
여: 정말 잘됐다. 학교 도서관에 일손이 필요해. 내가 지금 바로 신청해
    줄 수 있어.
남: 감사합니다. 그럼, 학교 도서관에서 봉사할게요.

남자는 도서관에서 도움을 주는 일에도 관심이 있다고 하였다. 이에 여자가 학교
도서관에 일손이 필요하며 지금 바로 신청해 줄 수 있다고 했으므로, 남자의 응
답으로 고마움과 의사 확인을 표현하는 ①이 가장 적절하다.
② 그거 좋네요. 제가 이 책들을 정리하는 것을 도와주면 돼요.
③ 네. 저는 고양이와 개를 길러 본 경험이 있어요.
④ 동의해요. 우리는 학교 자원봉사 프로그램이 더 많이 필요해요.
⑤ 당신 말이 맞아요. 동물 병원 프로그램에 저를 신청해 주세요.

have ~ in mind ~을 생각하다, 염두에 두다   spot 자리   sign up 신청하다, 등
록하다   organize 정리하다

15 ⑤

남: Emma는 Janice와 Fiona와 초등학교 때부터 좋은 친구이다. 그녀
    는 대부분의 자유 시간을 그들과 어울리는 데 보낸다. 하지만, Janice
    와 Fiona가 미술 프로젝트를 하는 도중에 크게 다투게 되고 사이가
    매우 어색해진다. 그들은 일주일 안에 마감해야 하는 미술 프로젝
    트를 완성하기 위해 함께 모여야 하지만, Janice는 Fiona가 함께 있으
    면 모임에 나오기를 거부한다. 게다가, Janice는 여전히 매우 감정적
    인 상태여서 Emma에게 Fiona에 대한 안 좋은 이야기를 한다. 하
    지만, Emma는 Janice도 Fiona의 마음을 상하게 했다고 생각하며
    어느 편도 들고 싶지 않다. 그녀는 Janice가 진정을 하고 Fiona와 이
    야기한다면 결국 화해를 할 수 있을 것이라고 생각한다. 이 상황에서

Emma가 Janice에게 뭐라고 말할 것 같은가?

Emma는 크게 다툰 두 친구 Janice와 Fiona 중 어느 편도 들고 싶지 않다고
하였고 Janice가 진정을 하고 Fiona와 이야기한다면 결국 화해를 할 수 있을
것이라고 생각하고 있는 상황이므로, Emma가 Janice에게 할 말로 ⑤ '나는
네가 진정을 하고 그녀와 화해를 하려고 노력해야 한다고 생각해.'가 가장 적절
하다.
① 새로운 친구들과 어울려 보는 건 어때?
② 무슨 일이 있더라도 나는 네 편이라는 걸 잊지 마.
③ 그녀가 반대하더라도 넌 네 생각을 고수해야 해.
④ 그녀에게 네 미술 프로젝트를 도와 달라고 하지 그래?

hang out with ~와 시간을 보내다   have an argument 말다툼하다
awkward 어색한   due ~하기로 되어 있는, 예정된   furthermore 더욱이, 게다가
emotional 감정적인   take sides (불화 등이 있는 상황에서) 편을 들다
calm down 진정하다   eventually 결국   make up 화해하다
stick to ~을 고수하다[지키다]

16-17

여: 안녕하세요, 학생 여러분! 지난 시간에, 우리는 동물들을 특징으로 삼
    는 몇몇 흥미로운 영어 표현들에 대해 배웠습니다. 오늘 우리는 흔히
    사용되는 우리의 몸과 관련된 몇몇 관용구에 대해 이야기할 것입니
    다. 첫 번째로, 우리의 머리와 관련된 표현을 살펴봅시다. 여러분이
    '당장 머리에 떠오르는 대로' 말을 한다면 그것은 제대로 생각하지 않
    고 말을 한다는 뜻입니다. 신체 부위를 사용하는 또 다른 문구는 '그
    때그때 봐서 하다'입니다. 누군가가 '그때그때 봐서 했다'고 말하면,
    그것은 뭐든 있는 것으로 처리했거나 준비 없이 무언가를 했다는 뜻
    입니다. 또한 당신의 눈과 관련된 문구도 있습니다. 누군가가 "당신
    은 정말 보기만 해도 즐겁군요."라고 말한다면, 그것은 그들이 당신
    을 보게 되어 정말 기쁘다는 뜻입니다. 마지막으로 당신의 발과 관련
    된 표현이 있습니다. 누군가가 큰 행사를 앞두고 '겁이 난다'고 말하
    면, 그것은 그들이 매우 초조해 한다는 뜻입니다. 이제, 이 관용구들
    이 실제 상황에서 어떻게 사용되는지에 관한 짧은 영상을 보시죠.

feature ~을 특징으로 삼다, 특징   idiom 관용구, 숙어
off the top of your head (깊이 생각하지 않고) 당장 머리에 떠오르는 대로
play it by ear (사전 계획을 세우기보다) 그때그때 봐서 처리하다
improvise (보통 꼭 필요한 것이 없어서) 뭐든 있는 것으로 처리하다
a sight for sore eyes 정말 보기 좋은 것, 보기만 해도 즐거운 것
have cold feet (계획했던 일에 대해) 갑자기 초조해지다, 겁이 나다
real-life situation 실제 상황

16 ②

여자는 흔히 사용되는 우리의 몸과 관련된 몇몇 관용구에 대해 이야기하고 있다.
① 동물들의 흥미로운 특징
② 신체 부위와 관련된 관용구
③ 감정을 표현하는 흔한 방법
④ 신체의 여러 부위들의 기능
⑤ 대화에서 몸짓 언어의 사용

17 ④

문제 해결
관용구에 쓰인 신체 부위로 머리, 귀, 눈, 발에 대해 언급했지만, ④ '팔'에 대해서는 언급하지 않았다.

---

01 ②	02 ③	03 ⑤	04 ⑤	05 ④	06 ③
07 ①	08 ③	09 ⑤	10 ③	11 ③	12 ⑤
13 ⑤	14 ④	15 ⑤	16 ②	17 ③	

01 ② 목적 파악

남: 리더십 세미나에 오신 것을 환영합니다! 저는 Russell Smith입니다. 저는 오늘 기조연설을 맡았습니다. 요즘, 몇몇 분야에서는 숙련되고 경험이 풍부한 직원을 찾기가 어려울 수 있습니다. 그럼 '실버 직원'을 고용하는 건 어떨까요? 그들은 60대, 70대의 노인들입니다. 많은 손님들이 실버 직원과 함께 있을 때 편안함을 느낍니다. 그들은 젊은 직원들보다 흔히 더 친절합니다. 또한 그들은 직장에서 자신의 경험을 활용할 수 있습니다. 실제로, 한 주요 극장이 작년에 안내원으로 수십 명의 실버 직원을 채용하였고, 고객 만족 지수가 상당히 향상되었습니다. 이러한 추세에 동참하여 실버 직원을 채용해 보는 게 어떨까요? 감사합니다.

문제 해결
남자는 숙련되고 경험 많은 직원으로 실버 직원, 즉 고령 직원을 채용하기를 권장하고 있다.

어휘·표현
in charge of ~을 책임지는, 맡고 있는 **keynote speech** 기조연설
skillful 숙련된 **take advantage of** ~을 이용하다 **usher** 안내원, 접수원
considerably 상당히

02 ③ 주제 파악

남: Jasmine, Three Rs에 관해서 들어 본 적 있니?
여: 물론이지, 난 학교에서 배웠어. 읽기, 쓰기, 그리고 산수를 의미하잖아, 맞지?
남: 음…. 네 말도 맞지만, 나는 환경을 위한 Three Rs를 말하는 거야.
여: 오, 알겠다. 너는 환경을 돕도록 일상용품을 재활용하고 다시 쓰는 것에 대해서 얘기하기를 원하는구나.
남: 맞아, 그렇지만 너는 가장 중요한 걸 빠트렸어.
여: 그게 뭔데?
남: 음, 우리는 매일 많은 양의 쓰레기를 배출하잖아. 이 쓰레기가 환경에 큰 문제가 돼. 그래서 우리는 쓰레기를 줄여야만 해.
여: 전적으로 네 말에 동의해.
남: 요즘에, Three Rs 운동이 전 세계적으로 퍼져 나가고 있어. 그래서 나는 '줄이기'가 핵심이라고 생각해.
여: 네 말의 요점을 알겠어. 난 그 운동을 통해 우리가 자원을 보존할 수 있기를 희망해.

문제 해결
남자는 환경 보호를 위해 무엇보다도 쓰레기를 줄이는 것이 중요하다고 강조하고 있으므로, 남자의 의견으로 ③이 가장 적절하다.

어휘·표현
arithmetic 산수 **reduce** 줄이다 **conserve** 보존하다 **resource** 자원

03 ⑤

관계 추론

여: 제 가게를 점검해 주셔서 감사합니다.

남: 아닙니다. 음, 제가 안전에 관해 당신께 몇 가지 말씀드릴 게 있습니다.

여: 어떤 건가요?

남: 무엇보다도, 당신은 비상구 앞에 둔 박스들을 치우셔야 합니다.

여: 오, 죄송해요. 지금 당장 그것들을 치우겠습니다.

남: 비상시를 대비해서 비상구를 막는 어떠한 것도 있어서는 안 됩니다.

여: 알겠습니다. 명심하도록 하겠습니다.

남: 그리고 문 위에 있는 비상구 표시에 쌓인 먼지를 제거하세요. 그래야 멀리서도 잘 보일 수 있습니다.

여: 네, 오늘 그렇게 하겠습니다.

남: 마지막으로, 저는 당신의 직원들이 화재 안전에 관한 교육을 언제 마지막으로 받았는지 궁금합니다.

여: 지난주입니다. 저희는 정기적으로 교육을 시킵니다.

남: 좋습니다. 이제, 점검은 끝났습니다. 여기 서명해 주세요.

문제 해결

여자는 자신의 상점에서 남자에게 답하고 있고, 남자는 화재 안전 점검을 실시하고 있는 것으로 보아 두 사람은 상점 주인과 소방 시설 점검원의 관계임을 알 수 있다.

어휘·표현

remove 제거하다(=get rid of) fire exit 화재 비상구 in case of ~이 발생할 시에는 emergency 비상사태 on a regular basis 정기적으로

04 ⑤

그림 불일치 파악

남: Emily, 지난 일요일에 무엇을 했어요?

여: 말도 마세요. 조카들이 방문해서 아주 바빴어요. 이것이 내가 조카들을 찍은 사진이에요.

남: 오, 거실에서 놀고 있는 많은 아이들이 있네요.

여: 네. 어항을 쳐다보고 있는 남자아이가 보이세요? 그 애는 Scott이에요.

남: 그는 야구 모자를 쓰고 있네요. 정말 귀여워요. 당신 아이 Paula는 책상 위에 있는 블록을 가지고 놀고 있네요.

여: 맞아요. 그녀는 블록을 좋아해요. 제 남편은 바닥을 닦고 있어요. 누군가가 바닥에 물을 흘렸거든요.

남: 그는 피곤해 보이네요. 피아노를 치고 있는 소년은 누구예요?

여: 조카 Kevin이에요. 그는 피아노 치기를 매우 좋아해요.

남: 세상에! 사진 한가운데 있는 소년이 매트에 그림을 그리고 있어요.

여: 그 애가 Russell이에요. 그는 그릴 수 있는 어디에든 그려요.

남: 알겠어요. 당신이 오늘 피곤해 하는 것도 당연하네요.

문제 해결

사진 한가운데 있는 있는 소년은 매트에 그림을 그리고 있다고 했으므로, 간식을 먹고 있는 소년 ⑤가 대화의 내용과 일치하지 않는다.

어휘·표현

nephew 조카 fishbowl 어항 mop 대걸레로 닦다 spill 흘리다, 쏟다

05 ④

부탁한 일 파악

남: Jessica, 무엇을 하고 있어요?

여: 오, Clay. 저는 이번 주에 제 친구들과 함께 갈 캠핑 여행을 준비하고 있어요.

남: 좋겠어요. 어디로 가세요?

여: 우리는 Lake Mountains로 갈 거예요. 야외 바비큐가 정말 기대돼요.

남: 멋지네요. 우리 가족들도 지난달에 거기에서 바비큐를 요리하고 먹으면서 멋진 시간을 보냈어요.

여: 어, 그곳에 가 본 적이 있어요?

남: 물론이죠. 그곳은 제가 제일 좋아하는 장소 중에 하나예요. 침낭에서 잠을 자며 하늘을 가득 채운 별을 본 것은 정말 잊지 못할 거예요.

여: 그럼 침낭을 가지고 계신가요?

남: 네. 저는 작년에 텐트와 침낭과 같은 캠핑 용품을 구매했어요.

여: 괜찮으시다면, 제가 침낭을 빌릴 수 있을까요?

남: 그럼요. 즐거운 여행 보내고 돌아와서 여행에 대해 전부 이야기해 주세요.

여: 고마워요, Clay.

문제 해결

여자는 캠핑에서 사용할 침낭을 남자에게 빌려 달라고 부탁하였다.

어휘·표현

look forward to ~을 고대하다 sleeping bag 침낭 equipment 장비, 용품

06 ③

숫자 정보 파악

남: 실례합니다. 도움을 받고 계신가요?

여: 그렇지 않은데요. 저는 올 겨울에 입을 후드 티를 고르고 있어요.

남: 잘 오셨습니다. 이곳엔 많은 종류의 후드 티가 있습니다.

여: 음…. 저는 이 줄무늬 후드 티가 마음에 드네요. 얼마인가요?

남: 운이 좋으시네요. 원래는 40달러이지만 이번 주간에는 할인해서 30달러입니다.

여: 좋네요. 하지만 여전히 조금 비싸네요.

남: 음, 만약 두 개를 구입하시면 두 번째 품목에 대해 50%를 할인해 드릴 수 있습니다. 물론, 그 할인은 원래의 가격인 40달러에 적용됩니다.

여: 하지만 여전히 첫 번째 후드 티를 세일 가격으로 구입할 수 있는 거죠, 그렇죠?

남: 그렇습니다.

여: 그러면 같은 후드 티의 작은 사이즈가 있나요? 제 동생이 좋아할 것 같네요.

남: 물론이죠. 여기 있습니다.

여: 네. 둘 다 구매하겠습니다.

남: 알겠습니다. 저쪽에서 계산해 드리겠습니다.

문제 해결

첫 번째 후드 티 하나는 할인된 가격 30달러에, 다른 하나는 원래 가격인 40달러에서 50%를 할인하여 구입할 수 있으므로 여자가 지불할 총 금액은 50달러이다.

어휘·표현

hoodie 후드 티 apply 적용하다 ring up 계산하다, 합계를 내다

07 ①

이유 파악

[휴대 전화벨이 울린다.]

여: 안녕, Ted.

남: Rachel, 네가 감기에 걸렸다고 들었는데. 좀 어때?

여: 물어봐 줘서 고마워. 나 다 나았어. 지금은 괜찮아.

남: 그 말 들으니 다행이네. 그런데, 난 이번 주말에 네가 내 생일 파티에

올 수 있는지 물어보려고 전화한 거야.

여: 가고 싶지만 난 못 가.

남: 오, 아쉽다. 음, 만약 네가 월요일에 있는 발표를 걱정한다면, 내가 도와줄 수 있어.

여: 그것 때문에 못 가는 게 아니야. 그건 나 혼자 준비할 수 있어.

남: 그럼, 이번 주말에 아르바이트가 있니?

여: 아니. 사실 이번 주말에 부모님이 다른 도시로 이사를 가셔.

남: 정말? 그래서 네가 도와드려려 하는구나.

여: 맞아. 아마도 나는 주말 내내 부모님과 함께 있어야 할 거야.

남: 그래, 이해해. 나중에 보자.

여자는 이번 주말에 부모님 이사를 도와야 해서 남자의 생일 파티에 갈 수 없다고 하였다.

get over 회복하다   What a shame. 그거 유감이다.

08 ③

[전화벨이 울린다.]

남: 안녕하세요, Ontario 양 농장입니다. 무엇을 도와드릴까요?

여: 안녕하세요. 농장에서 이번 주에 축제를 한다고 들었습니다.

남: 네, 맞습니다. 토요일까지 오전 10시부터 오후 7시까지 다양한 행사를 할 예정입니다.

여: 어떤 종류의 행사를 하는지 말씀해 주시겠어요?

남: 물론이죠. 양털 깎기, 양에게 먹이 주기, 치즈 만들기와 같은 다양한 프로그램이 있습니다.

여: 오, 제 아이들이 치즈를 만들고 양털을 깎는 것을 좋아할 것 같네요. 입장료는 얼마인가요?

남: 성인은 10달러이고 아동은 5달러입니다.

여: 알겠습니다. 농장을 찾기는 쉬운가요?

남: 물론입니다. 아주 쉬워요. 72번 출구로 바로 나와서 Malcolm로에 있습니다.

여: 아, 네. 어디에 있는지 알 것 같아요. 내일 방문하겠습니다.

남: 좋습니다. 그때 뵙겠습니다.

양 농장이 주최하는 행사의 일시, 행사 종류, 입장료, 행사장 위치에 대해서는 언급하고 있으나, 교통편에 대해서는 언급하지 않았다.

feed 먹이다, 먹이를 주다   shear (털을) 깎다, 자르다   admission fee 입장료

09 ⑤

여: 안녕하세요, 학생 여러분. 저는 Auburn 학생회 선거를 책임지고 있는 Jennifer Parker입니다. 올해 선거는 10월 7일과 8일에 온라인으로 치러집니다. 후보자 지명은 선거일 두 달 전에 완료되어야 합니다. 모든 Auburn의 학생들은 학생회 임원직에 다른 학생을 추천할 수 있습니다. 자신을 추천하는 것은 가능하지 않습니다. 지명된 후보에게는 자동적으로 이메일을 통해 지명이 통지됩니다. 지명자는 학교 웹사이트를 통해 후보자 성명서를 제출함으로써 자신의 견해를 표현할 것이 요구됩니다. 새롭게 선출된 후보자들은 전반적인 학생회 절차에 익숙해지기 위해 현 학생회 임원들과 같이 일하게 됩니다. 새 학생회 임원들은 1월 21일에 취임할 것입니다. 여러분 모두가 후보자이

든 투표자이든 간에 선거 절차에 참가하기를 바랍니다. 감사합니다.

새롭게 선출된 후보자들은 현 임원들과 같이 일하다가 1월에 취임한다고 하였으므로, ⑤가 내용과 일치하지 않는다.

in charge of ~을 책임지는   nomination 지명, 추천   prior to ~에 앞서, 먼저
leadership position 지도자의 지위, 요직   automatically 자동적으로
notify (정식으로) 통지하다   current 현재의   take office 취임하다

10 ③

여: Eric, 플로리다로 여행 갈 준비는 다 끝났나요?

남: 네, 거의 끝났어요. 저는 지금 이 사이트에서 자외선 차단 크림을 고르는 중이에요. 저를 좀 도와주실래요?

여: 물론이죠. 자외선 차단 지수와 관련해서는 어떤 제품을 찾고 있나요?

남: 음, 저는 자외선 차단 지수가 매우 높은 것은 원하지 않아요. 자외선 차단 지수가 30이 넘는 제품은 어떤 피부 유형에는 좋지 않을 수 있다고 들었어요.

여: 알겠어요. 그러면 용량은 어떤가요? 클수록 더 좋죠, 그렇죠?

남: 하지만 크기가 큰 제품은 제 가방에 넣고 다니기가 불편할 것 같아요. 저는 80ml가 넘는 것은 원하지 않아요.

여: 알겠어요. 얼마나 지불할 생각인가요?

남: 저는 20달러까지는 쓸 수 있어요. 제 생각엔 이제 두 가지 선택이 남았네요.

여: 오, 이 제품이 자외선 차단 지수가 높고, 배송비도 없네요.

남: 네, 그게 딱 맞는 것 같네요. 그걸로 주문해야겠네요.

남자는 자외선 차단 지수가 30이 넘지 않고, 용량도 80ml가 넘지 않으며, 가격은 20달러 이하인 제품을 고르고 있다. 대화의 마지막에 두 제품 중 SPF가 높고 배송비가 없는 것을 주문하겠다고 한 것으로 보아, 남자가 구매할 자외선 차단 크림으로는 ③이 가장 적절하다.

sunblock (cream) 자외선 차단 크림   SPF 자외선 차단 지수(Sun Protection Factor)   extremely 매우, 극도로   inconvenient 불편한   delivery fee 배달료

11 ③

남: 엄마, 저 지금 다음 발표에 대해 토의하기 위해 Gina의 집으로 갈게요.

여: David, 다른 사람을 방문하기에는 너무 이른 시간이구나. 이제 겨우 오전 8시란다.

남: 알아요, 하지만 그녀가 언제든지 들리라고 말했어요.

여: 안 된다. 그녀를 방문하기 전에 먼저 전화하는 게 낫겠다.

너무 이른 시간에 다른 사람의 집을 방문하려는 남자에게 여자가 할 말로 ③ '안 된다. 그녀를 방문하기 전에 먼저 전화하는 게 낫겠다.'가 가장 적절하다.

① 물론이지. 너무 늦게 다른 사람을 방문하는 것은 무례하단다.

② 난 그렇게 생각지 않아. 그녀는 분명히 아침형 인간일 거야.

④ 넌 지금 그녀를 방문해야 해. 그녀에게 먼저 주소를 물어보렴.

⑤ 무슨 말인지 알겠다. 다음번에는 일찍 일어나야 한다.

presentation 발표   stop by 들르다, 방문하다   morning person 아침형 인간

12 ⑤   짧은 대화의 응답

여: Ted, 우리 거의 목적지에 왔어요. 장기간의 운전이었어요.
남: 맞아요. 배가 고프지만 차 밖으로 나가고 싶지는 않아요.
여: 저도 그래요. 드라이브스루 식당에 가는 게 어때요?
남: 좋은 생각이에요. 샌드위치와 오렌지주스를 사요.

문제 해결

남자는 배가 고프지만 차 밖으로 나가고 싶지 않다고 하였으므로 드라이브스루 식당을 이용하자는 여자의 말에 ⑤ '좋은 생각이에요. 샌드위치와 오렌지주스를 사요.'라고 응답하는 것이 가장 적절하다.
① 좋아요. 요리는 항상 나를 행복하게 해요.
② 좋아요. 우리는 식료품점을 먼저 방문해야 해요.
③ 마침내 목적지에 도착해서 기뻐요.
④ 물론입니다. 그곳은 내가 와 본 최고의 식당이었어요.

어휘·표현

destination 목적지   feel like -ing ~하고 싶은 기분이 들다   drive-through 드라이브스루 (차에 탄 채로 이용할 수 있는 식당들)

13 ⑤   긴 대화의 응답

남: 여보, 오늘 어땠어요? 당신 피곤해 보이네요.
여: 당신은 짐작도 못 할 거예요. 끔찍했어요.
남: 무슨 일이 있었어요?
여: 내 동료, Julia가 고객에게 새로운 프로젝트를 발표하기로 예정되어 있었어요. 그런데 그녀가 미팅에 제시간에 오지 않았어요.
남: 그래서, 당신은 어떻게 했나요?
여: 내가 그녀를 대신해서 발표를 해야만 했어요. 난 너무 긴장했죠.
남: 하지만 당신이 발표를 어쨌든 마친 거네요, 맞죠?
여: 그래요. 나는 내가 할 수 있는 한 분명하고 천천히 말하려고 노력했어요.
남: 잘했어요. 당신은 대중 앞에서 말하는 걸 잘하잖아요. 그들이 당신이 말하는 걸 쉽게 이해했을 거라 확신해요.
여: 그렇기를 바라지만, 내가 프로젝트를 망쳤을까 봐 걱정되네요.
남: 스스로에게 너무 가혹하게 굴지 말아요. 분명히 잘 해냈을 거예요.

문제 해결

갑자기 발표를 한 것에 대해 걱정하고 있는 여자에게 남자는 ⑤ '스스로에게 너무 가혹하게 굴지 말아요. 분명히 잘 해냈을 거예요.'라는 말을 해 주는 것이 가장 적절하다.
① 물론이죠. 그녀는 자신의 발표를 자랑스러워 할 거예요.
② 맞아요. 당신이 그녀를 위해 프로젝트를 발표했어야 해요.
③ 잊어버려요. 다음번에는 회의에 늦지 않도록 노력하세요.
④ 걱정 말아요. 당신이 발표를 잘 하리라고 생각해요.

어휘·표현

co-worker 동료   be supposed to ~하기로 되어 있다   on time 제시간에
manage (어떻게든) ~하다(해내다)   mess up 망치다   harsh 가혹한, 냉혹한

14 ④   긴 대화의 응답

남: 실례합니다, 선생님.

여: 네, 무엇을 도와드릴까요?
남: 제가 카드를 기계에 넣으면, '유효하지 않은 카드'라고 나옵니다.
여: 아마 카드를 갱신할 필요가 있을 것 같습니다. 제가 봐도 될까요?
남: 네. 여기 있습니다.
여: 잠시만요. [잠시 후] 네, 당신의 카드가 지난주에 만료되었어요. 갱신해 드릴까요?
남: 네, 부탁드려요. 제 과제 때문에 이 책을 대출하고 싶어요.
여: 자, 여기 새 도서관 카드가 있습니다. 오, 잠시 만요. 당신 계정에 연체된 책이 한 권 있다고 나오는데요.
남: 정말요? 그게 어떤 책이죠? 전 모두 제때에 반납했다고 생각했는데요.
여: 음…. '비밀의 정원'이란 책을 빌리셨나요?
남: 아, 제가 잊었네요. 학교 사물함에 그 책을 두고 왔네요.
여: 그런 경우라면, 연체된 책을 반납하셔야 책을 대출할 수 있습니다.

문제 해결

반납하지 않아 연체된 책을 학교 사물함에 두고 왔다는 남자의 말에 대한 여자의 응답으로 ④ '그런 경우라면, 연체된 책을 반납하셔야 책을 대출할 수 있습니다.'가 가장 적절하다.
① 너무 늦었네요. 당신은 먼저 도서관 카드를 갱신했어야 합니다.
② 걱정 마세요. 제가 이미 그 책을 읽어서 그것에 관해 이야기할 수 있습니다.
③ 죄송합니다. 대출하고 싶으신 책은 이미 대출 중입니다.
⑤ 문제없습니다. 당신은 카드를 나중에 갱신할 수 있습니다.

어휘·표현

invalid 유효하지 않은   renew 갱신하다   expire 만료되다   overdue (지불·반납 등의) 기한이 지난

15 ⑤   상황에 적절한 말

남: James는 여가 시간에 영화를 보는 것을 좋아한다. 이번 주말에, 그는 친구 Erin과 함께 최근에 개봉한 액션 영화를 볼 계획이다. 그들은 7시에 영화를 보기로 했는데, Erin이 시간이 지날 때까지 나타나지 않는다. 그녀는 자신이 늦은 것에 대해 사과하며 심한 교통 체증이 있었다고 해명한다. James가 시간을 보았을 때, 광고와 예고편 때문에 아마도 영화가 아직 시작되지 않았다는 것을 깨닫는다. 그는 그들이 영화표를 사서 영화를 볼 충분한 시간이 아직 있다고 생각한다. 그래서 그는 자신들이 늦은 것을 알지만 표를 사기 위해서 매표소로 간다. 이러한 상황에서, James는 점원에게 무엇이라 말하겠는가?

문제 해결

상영 시간에 늦었지만 아직 영화가 시작되지 않았다고 생각해 표를 사고 싶어 하는 상황이므로, James가 점원에게 할 말로 ⑤ '늦은 것을 알지만, 7시에 상영하는 영화 표 두 장을 지금 구입할 수 있을까요?'가 가장 적절하다.
① 죄송하지만, 당신은 지금 입장할 수 없습니다.
② 죄송합니다. 이 표를 환불하고 싶어요.
③ 이해합니다. 우리가 다음에 영화를 볼 수 있을 것 같아요.
④ 실례합니다만, 추천해 줄 만한 인기 있는 영화가 있나요?

어휘·표현

released 개봉한   show up 나타나다   apologize for ~을 사과하다
lateness 지각   traffic jam 교통 체증   commercial 광고   preview 예고편
box office 매표소

여: 여러분, 좋은 아침입니다. 지난주, 우리는 애완동물 기르기로 아이들에게 책임감을 가르치는 것에 대해 이야기했습니다. 오늘, 저는 애완동물이 우리에게 주는 긍정적인 효과에 대하여 이야기하려고 합니다. 다음의 상황을 상상해 봅시다. 당신이 힘든 하루 일을 마치고 집에 옵니다. 당신은 소파에 앉아서 당신의 개를 부드럽게 쓰다듬습니다. 기분이 어떨거라 생각되나요? 당신은 편안함을 느끼고 걱정과 긴장감은 풀릴 것입니다. 실제로, 애완동물이 지속적인 교제, 사랑, 애정과 같은 긍정적인 감정을 우리에게 준다고 많은 연구가 증명합니다. 그렇지만 여러분이 특정한 애완동물을 고집할 필요는 없습니다. 그저 어항 속 물고기를 바라보거나 심지어 애완용 뱀을 만지는 것조차 당신의 불안 수준을 줄여 줍니다. 물론, 만약 당신에게 어린 아이가 있다면, 기니피그나 새끼 고양이와 같은 작은 애완동물을 기르는 것이 더 좋은 생각일 수 있죠. 애완동물 주인들을 대상으로 한 조사에서, 대부분의 주인들이 그들의 삶에서 애완동물을 기르는 것으로 인해 정신 건강이 증진되었다고 보고합니다. 애완동물들은 우리가 생각하는 것보다 더 많은 것을 우리에게 제공해 줍니다. 감사합니다.

어휘·표현

responsibility 책임감   pet 애완동물; 쓰다듬다   gently 부드럽게   tension 긴장   relieve (불쾌감·고통 등을) 없애 주다, 덜어 주다   constant 지속적인   companionship 교제   affection 애정   stick to ~을 고수하다   anxiety level 불안 수준

16 ②

문제 해결

여자는 애완동물을 기르는 것이 우리의 정신 건강에 긍정적인 영향을 미친다고 말하고 있으므로, ② '애완동물이 어떻게 우리의 정신 건강에 혜택을 주는지'가 여자가 하는 말의 주제로 가장 적절하다.
① 애완동물을 데려다 기르는 것에 관한 지침
③ 연령에 따라 애완동물을 고르는 것에 대한 조언
④ 애완동물 기르기가 어떻게 아이들을 책임감 있게 만드는지
⑤ 애완동물을 충분히 운동시켜야 하는 것의 중요성

17 ③

문제 해결

애완동물의 종류로 토끼는 언급하지 않았다.

01 ①	02 ②	03 ④	04 ⑤	05 ③	06 ③
07 ①	08 ⑤	09 ④	10 ⑤	11 ⑤	12 ②
13 ②	14 ①	15 ①	16 ③	17 ④	

01 ①

목적 파악

남: 안녕하세요, 여러분! 여행 칼럼니스트 Michael Brown입니다. 요새 많은 젊은 사람들이 자유 시간이 있을 때마다 어디론가 여행을 가고 싶어 합니다. 하지만 함께 여행을 하는 모든 사람들이 좋아하는 목적지와 일정을 선정하는 것은 쉽지 않죠. 자, 저는 한 가지 간단한 해결책을 가지고 있습니다. 혼자 여행을 떠나는 것이 어떠세요? 많은 사람들이 혼자 여행하는 것을 두려워하지만, 혼자 여행하는 것은 여러분에게 아주 많은 혜택을 줄 수 있습니다. 예를 들어, 여러분은 혼자 여행을 함으로써 완전한 자유와 독립을 경험할 수 있습니다. 여러분이 무엇을 먹든 또는 어디를 가든지 간에, 그것은 전적으로 여러분에게 달려 있습니다. 여러분은 그 누구에 대해서도 걱정할 필요가 없습니다. 기회가 있으면 혼자 여행을 떠나십시오! 여러분은 혼자 하는 여행을 후회하지 않을 것입니다.

문제 해결

여행 칼럼니스트인 남자는 혼자 여행을 떠나면 많은 혜택이 있다고 말하면서 혼자 여행을 떠나 볼 것을 제안하고 있으므로, 남자가 하는 말의 목적으로 ①이 가장 적절하다.

어휘·표현

destination 목적지   solo 혼자서; 혼자서 하는   be of benefit 도움이 되다, 유익이다   complete 완전한   independence 독립   absolutely 전적으로

02 ②

주제 파악

여: 여보, 당신 안 좋아 보여요. 무슨 일 있나요?
남: 그게, 마케팅 부서의 Jack 알죠? 그가 건강 검진 중에 간암 초기 진단을 받았어요.
여: 안됐네요. Jack은 당신의 가장 친한 친구 중 한 명이잖아요, 그렇지 않나요?
남: 맞아요. 어제 그가 3개월 병가를 신청했어요. 그는 지금 매우 우울해 하고 있어요.
여: 하지만 너무 많이 걱정할 필요는 없어요. 간암은 조기에 발견하면 완전히 치료될 가능성이 아주 높으니까요.
남: 정말요? 그 말이 사실이에요?
여: 당연하죠! 대부분의 의사들이 하는 말이 그래요.
남: 당신 말이 맞기를 정말로 바라요.
여: 그럼요. 당신 Brian 삼촌 기억 안 나요?
남: 아, 맞아요. 2년 전쯤, 그가 간암 진단을 받았죠.
여: 그래요. 하지만 지금 그는 완벽히 회복해서 그 어느 때보다 더 건강해요.

문제 해결

친한 친구가 간암 초기 진단을 받았다고 하면서 걱정하는 남자에게 여자는 간암은 조기에 발견하면 완전히 치료될 가능성이 높다고 말했다.

be diagnosed with ~로 진단받다   liver 간   apply for ~을 신청하다   sick leave 병가   detect 발견하다

03 ④

여: 여기요, 제가 치통이 약간 있어서요. 진통제가 있나요?

남: 예, 아스피린이 있습니다. 아스피린을 좀 가져다 드릴까요?

여: 네, 부탁합니다. 그런데, London까지 가는 데 얼마나 더 걸릴까요?

남: 약 세 시간 더 걸립니다. 현지 시각으로 오전 11시 30분에 Heathrow 공항에 도착할 예정입니다.

여: 아직도 갈 길이 머네요.

남: 시간을 보내기 위해 추리 소설을 읽어 보는 것이 어떠세요?

여: 기내에 추리 소설이 있나요?

남: 예, 있어요. James Brown이 쓴 추리 소설이 있습니다.

여: 오, James Brown은 제가 좋아하는 작가예요. 한 권 가져다주시겠어요?

남: 그럼요. 아스피린과 책을 가지고 곧 돌아오겠습니다.

여: 고마워요.

남: 천만에요. 남은 비행시간을 즐겁게 보내시길 바랍니다.

문제 해결

여자가 London까지 얼마나 더 걸릴지 묻자, 남자는 Heathrow 공항까지 세 시간 더 가야 한다고 대답했다. 또한, 남자가 여자에게 남은 비행시간을 즐겁게 보내기를 바란다고 한 것으로 보아, 여자는 승객이고 남자는 비행기 승무원임을 알 수 있다.

어휘·표현

painkiller 진통제   be supposed to ~하기로 되어 있다   local time 현지 시각

04 ⑤

여: 아빠, 제가 그린 그림을 보세요.

남: 정말 사랑스러운 그림이구나! 제목이 뭐니?

여: '놀이터에 있는 동물들'이요.

남: 가운데 미끄럼틀 위에 거북이를 그렸구나. 거북이가 귀여워 보여.

여: 미끄럼틀 아래쪽에 선글라스를 끼고 있는 캥거루도 그렸어요.

남: 캥거루가 즐거워하는 것 같구나.

여: 왼쪽에 있는 그네를 타고 있는 코끼리에 대해서는 어떻게 생각하세요?

남: 멋져! 그네를 타는 코끼리를 누가 상상할 수 있었겠어?

여: 음, 제 미술 선생님께서 제가 매우 창의적이라고 항상 저에게 말씀하세요.

남: 그렇고 말고. 내가 가장 마음에 드는 것은 오른쪽에 있는 모래에서 놀고 있는 원숭이야.

여: 있잖아요, 제가 아빠를 위해서 원숭이를 그렸어요. 원숭이는 아빠가 좋아하는 동물이잖아요.

남: 그러면 원숭이 옆에서 공을 가지고 노는 펭귄은 엄마를 위해서 그렸겠구나.

여: 맞아요. 엄마가 펭귄을 정말 좋아하잖아요.

문제 해결

그림 속에서 펭귄은 원숭이와 함께 모래놀이를 하고 있으므로 공놀이를 하고 있다는 대화의 내용과 ⑤는 일치하지 않는다.

어휘·표현

slide 미끄럼틀   swing 그네   must have p.p. ~했음에 틀림없다

05 ③

남: Jessica, 오늘 저녁에 영화 보러 갈래?

여: 그러고 싶은데, 난 6시에 동호회 모임에 참석해야 해.

남: 그래? 모임이 어디서 열리는데?

여: Green 식당에서. 그 식당에 대해 들어 봤어?

남: 그곳에 한 번 가 봤어. 시청 근처에 있잖아, 그렇지 않니?

여: 맞아. 그 식당이 정확히 어디에 있는지 말해 줄래? 나는 그곳에 한 번도 가 본 적이 없거든.

남: 음, 말로는 설명하기 어려워. 대신에, 내가 그 식당으로 가는 지도를 그려 줄게.

여: 정말? 그럼 정말 고맙지.

남: 천만에. 펜과 종이 있니?

여: 응, 여기 있어.

남: 내가 그림을 아주 잘 그리지는 못하지만 최선을 다해서 네게 지도를 그려 줄게.

여: 정말로 고마워. 큰 도움이 될 거야.

문제 해결

Green 식당에 한 번도 가 본 적이 없는 여자를 위해 남자는 그 식당으로 가는 약도를 그려 주겠다고 했으므로, 남자가 여자를 위해 할 일로 ③이 가장 적절하다.

어휘·표현

attend 참석하다   take place (계획된 일이) 개최되다, 일어나다   in word 말로는

06 ③

여: 실례합니다. 저는 자전거를 빌리고 싶어요.

남: 산악자전거는 한 시간에 5달러이고, 하루에 20달러입니다.

여: 로드 자전거요?

남: 한 시간에 7달러이고, 하루에 30달러입니다.

여: 자전거로 섬을 일주하려고 하는데요. 어느 자전거가 더 좋다고 생각하세요?

남: 당연히, 로드 자전거죠. 산악자전거보다 훨씬 더 빠르니까요.

여: 알겠습니다. 로드 자전거를 빌릴게요.

남: 자전거로 섬을 일주하려면, 적어도 3일은 걸릴 거예요.

여: 저는 자전거를 느리게 타요. 제 생각에는 자전거를 4일 동안 빌려야 할 것 같아요.

남: 결정 잘 하셨네요! 그러면 이 섬의 아름다운 풍경을 충분히 즐길 수 있을 거예요.

여: 관광 정보 센터에서 받은 할인 쿠폰이 있어요. 이것을 사용할 수 있나요?

남: 예, 사용하실 수 있습니다. 이 쿠폰으로, 대여 비용에서 10% 할인 받을 수 있습니다.

문제 해결

여자는 하루 대여하는 데 비용이 30달러인 로드 자전거를 4일간 빌리기로 하였는데 할인 쿠폰을 사용하여 10% 할인 받았으므로, 여자가 지불할 금액은 108달러이다.

어휘·표현

rent (사용료를 내고 단기간) 빌리다   fully 완전히, 충분히   scenery 풍경, 경치

07 ①

남: Stella! 노래 경연 대회에서 금메달 받은 걸 축하해.
여: 고마워. 나 상으로 최신형 태블릿 PC를 받았어.
남: 정말 운이 좋구나! 네가 지금 가지고 있는 태블릿 PC는 팔 거니?
여: 그래. Daniel, 네가 내 것을 사는 게 어때? 내가 그것을 산 지 겨우 6개월 정도밖에 안 되었어.
남: 그리고 디자인이 정말로 멋지지! 그것을 얼마에 팔 거니?
여: 너에게는 단돈 200달러에 팔게.
남: 태블릿 PC 보증 기간은 얼마나 기니?
여: 2년. 아직도 1년 반 정도 남았어.
남: 좋아. 용량이 64기가바이트지, 그렇지?
여: 아니. 32기가바이트야. 하지만 그 정도면 충분한 것 같아.
남: 미안하지만, 네 것을 살 수 없어. 나는 저장할 데이터가 많아서 메모리 용량이 최소한 64기가바이트인 것이 필요하거든.
여: 알았어. 괜찮아.

문제 해결

여자가 태블릿 PC의 용량이 32기가바이트라고 말하자, 남자는 자신이 저장할 데이터가 많아서 메모리 용량이 최소 64기가바이트인 것이 필요하다고 말했으므로, 남자가 태블릿 PC를 사지 않는 이유로 ①이 가장 적절하다.

어휘·표현

warranty 보증 capacity 용량

08 ⑤

남: Sunny, 이사 갈 아파트 구했어?
여: 아니. 좋은 아파트를 찾기가 쉽지 않네.
남: 그러면, Rainbow 아파트 단지로 이사를 가는 게 어때? 거기 빈 아파트가 있다고 들었어.
여: Rainbow 아파트 단지? 그 아파트는 Gold 호수 공원 근처에 있지 않아?
남: 맞아. 그 지역은 매우 조용하고 평화로워. 그래서 네가 원하는 평온한 삶을 살 수 있을 거야.
여: 좋은데. 그 아파트가 몇 층에 있는지 알아?
남: 응. 15층에 있어. 거실에서 바라보는 전망이 정말 환상적이야.
여: 그 전망을 보고 싶다. 월 임대료는 어때?
남: 놀라지 마. 겨우 500달러야.
여: 와! 정말로 저렴하구나. 다른 곳에서는 비슷한 아파트의 월 임대료가 적어도 700달러야.
남: 맞아.
여: 오, 그 아파트를 직접 보고 싶어.

문제 해결

남자가 여자에게 권유한 아파트에 관한 내용 중 ⑤ '편의 시설'에 대한 언급은 없다.

어휘·표현

complex (건물) 단지 be located 위치하다 tranquil 평온한 monthly rent 월 임대료 elsewhere 다른 곳에(서) in person 직접

09 ④

여: 안녕하세요, 애완동물을 사랑하는 여러분. 주목해 주시겠습니까? 여러분께 Seattle 애완동물 박람회에 대해 말씀드리겠습니다. 이 박람회는 5월 1일에 열려서 3주일 동안 지속될 것입니다. 박람회가 열리는 장소는 작년과 마찬가지로 World Convention Center입니다. 100개가 넘는 애완동물 관련 회사들이 박람회에 참여하여 애완동물과 관련된 다양한 제품과 서비스를 애완동물을 기르는 사람들을 위해 전시할 것입니다. 작년에 약 200,000명이 박람회를 방문했고, 올해 이 숫자는 두 배가 될 것으로 예상됩니다. 입장료가 무료였던 작년과는 달리, 올해 입장료는 일인당 5달러이며, 여러분의 입장료는 동물 복지를 증진하는 데 사용될 것입니다.

문제 해결

작년 박람회의 입장객 수가 20만 명이었고, 올해 이 숫자는 두 배가 될 것으로 예상한다고 했으므로, ④는 내용과 일치하지 않는다.

어휘·표현

fair 박람회 be held 열리다, 개최되다(=take place) pet-related 애완동물과 관련된 take part in ~에 참가하다 exhibit 전시하다 double 두 배가 되다 admission fee 입장료 promote 촉진하다, 증진하다 welfare 복지

10 ⑤

남: Cindy, 내가 세탁기 사는 것을 도와줄래요?
여: 그럼요! 먼저, 제조사를 결정해야 해요.
남: 음, 나는 Queen 전자 또는 Techno가 더 마음에 들어요.
여: 좋아요. Sun Star의 세탁기는 그리 좋지 않다고 들었어요. 그 세탁기는 빨래를 말끔하게 세탁하지 않는대요.
남: 용량은 어때요? 제가 7kg 용량이 넘는 세탁기가 필요할까요?
여: 절대 아니죠! 당신은 혼자 사니까, 6kg 세탁기가 좋을 거예요.
남: 알았어요. 그러면 지금까지 우리가 말한 것에 알맞은 세탁기가 두 대 있어요.
여: 그렇네요. 어느 것이 더 마음에 들어요? 더 저렴한 것인가요, 아니면 보증 기간이 더 긴 것인가요?
남: 오, 결정할 수가 없어요. 당신이라면, 어떤 것을 사겠어요?
여: 당연히 보증 기간이 더 긴 것을 살 거예요.
남: 좋아요, 그러면 당신의 선택을 따를게요.

문제 해결

Queen 전자 또는 Techno에서 만든 세탁기 중에서 남자는 용량이 6kg이고, 여자의 의견을 따라 보증 기간이 더 긴 것을 살 것이라고 하였으므로, 남자가 구입할 세탁기로는 ⑤가 가장 적절하다.

어휘·표현

manufacturer 제조사, 제조업자 laundry 빨래 thoroughly 완전히, 철저하게 capacity 용량 match 일치하다, 맞다

11 ⑤

남: 여보, 오늘 대청소를 하기로 한 것 잊지 않았죠, 그렇죠?
여: 당연히 잊지 않았죠. 먼저, 우리는 욕실과 거실을 청소해야 해요. 그러고 나서, 차고를 정리해야 해요. 차고가 너무 지저분해요.
남: 알았어요. 내가 욕실을 청소한 다음에 차고를 정리할게요.
여: <u>좋아요. 그러면 내가 거실을 책임질게요.</u>

문제 해결

욕실과 거실을 청소하고 차고를 정리해야 하는 상황에서, 욕실 청소와 차고 정리를 하겠다는 남자의 말에 이어 여자는 자신이 거실을 책임지겠다고 말하는 것이 가장 적절하다.

① 맞아요. 집이 이렇게 깨끗한 줄 몰랐어요.
② 미안하지만, 나는 오늘 집을 청소하는 것을 잊었어요.
③ 그래요. 당신은 차고에 차를 주차하는 게 더 나아요.
④ 물론이죠. 청소 서비스가 매우 편리했어요.

12 ②

여: 실례합니다. 수영 교실에 대한 정보를 얻고 싶은데요.
남: 알겠습니다. 어떤 수준에 관심이 있으세요?
여: 초보자 반을 수강하려고 생각하고 있습니다. 월 수강료가 얼마인가요?
남: 50달러이고 개인용 사물함이 포함됩니다.

문제 해결

수영 초보자 반을 수강하려고 한다는 여자가 월 수강료가 얼마인지 물어보았으므로, '50달러이고 개인용 사물함이 포함된다.'고 말하는 ②가 남자의 응답으로 가장 적절하다.
① 월 수강료가 너무 비싼 것 같아요.
③ 미안하지만, 저는 수영에 관심이 없어요.
④ 월 수강료는 걱정 마세요. 내가 당신에게 50달러를 빌려줄게요.
⑤ 연습을 하면, 당신은 상급 코스로 올라갈 수 있어요.

13 ②

[전화벨이 울린다.]
여: 프런트 데스크입니다. 무엇을 도와드릴까요?
남: 안녕하세요, 저는 807호에 투숙하고 있습니다. 객실이 너무 더워요.
   온도를 낮추는 방법이 있나요?
여: 물론이죠. 에어컨 리모컨을 가지고서 온도를 낮출 수 있습니다.
남: 리모컨은 어디에 있죠? 찾을 수가 없어요.
여: 텔레비전 옆에 있는 책상의 맨 위 서랍에 있습니다.
남: 책상 맨 위 서랍이라…. 아, 찾았어요. 도와주셔서 고마워요.
여: 천만에요. 제가 도와드릴 다른 일이 있나요?
남: 한 가지 더 있어요. 제 노트북 컴퓨터가 와이파이에 연결되지 않아요.
여: 그런가요? 연결하기 전에 비밀번호를 입력하셨나요?
남: 네, 했어요. 객실 매뉴얼에 있는 비밀번호를 입력했어요.
   hotelmoon1997이죠, 그렇지 않나요?
여: 맞습니다.
남: 객실의 와이파이 네트워크에 문제가 있는 것 같은데요.
여: 알겠습니다. 지금 바로 객실로 사람을 보내겠습니다.

문제 해결

프런트 데스크에 전화를 걸어서 자신이 투숙하고 있는 객실의 와이파이 네트워크에 문제가 있다고 하는 남자의 말에 대한 여자의 응답으로 ② '알겠습니다. 지금 바로 객실로 사람을 보내겠습니다.'가 가장 적절하다.
① 걱정 마세요. 당신에게 새 리모컨을 드릴게요.
③ 그것은 당신에게 달려 있습니다. 당신의 비밀번호를 만드세요.
④ 맞아요. 내 컴퓨터를 와이파이에 연결하고 싶어요.
⑤ 당신의 와이파이 네트워크 서비스 덕분에, 내 일을 제시간에 끝냈어요.

14 ①

남: 학생회가 다음 주말에 벼룩시장을 열거라는 소식 들었어?
여: 아니, 못 들었어. 벼룩시장의 목적이 뭔데?
남: 아프리카의 가난한 어린이들을 돕기 위해 열리는 거야.
여: 아주 좋은 목적이구나. 돕기 위해 내가 할 수 있는 일이 있니?
남: 사실, 두 가지 방법이 있어.
여: 두 가지 방법? 그것들이 뭐니?
남: 첫 번째는 자원봉사자로 일하는 것이고, 두 번째는 네 물건을 기증하는 거야.
여: 나는 행사 기간에 자원봉사자가 되고 싶어.
남: 좋아! 학생회에서는 항상 도움의 손길이 필요할 수 있거든.
여: 어떻게 하면 자원봉사자가 될 수 있니?
남: 학생회 사무실에 가서 자원봉사자 목록에 네 이름을 올리면 돼.
여: 알았어. 야, 나랑 같이 자원봉사하는 게 어때?
남: 사실, 난 이미 내 이름을 등록했어.

문제 해결

아프리카의 가난한 어린이를 돕기 위해 열리는 벼룩시장에 자원봉사를 하기로 결심한 여자가 남자에게 함께 자원봉사를 하자고 제안했을 때 남자의 응답으로 ① '사실, 난 이미 내 이름을 등록했어.'가 가장 적절하다.
② 좋아! 지금 바로 아이들을 보러 가자.
③ 간단해! 네가 안 쓰는 물건들을 기증해.
④ 맞아. 자원봉사 경험은 보람 있었어.
⑤ 난 그렇게 생각해. 자원봉사는 생각만큼 쉽지 않아.

15 ①

남: Brian은 Lincoln 대학교에서 한국 문학을 전공하는 2학년 학생이고, 그는 한국 대사관에서 하는 한국어 단편 소설 대회가 개최될 것이라는 소식을 듣는다. 그는 이 대회에 참가하기로 결심하고 한국어로 단편 소설을 쓴다. 몇 주 후, 그는 소설을 다 쓴다. 그는 자신의 소설이 구성이 잘 되어 있고 매우 독특하다고 생각한다. 하지만 대회가 이야기가 얼마나 좋은지뿐만 아니라 소설이 한국어 문법 면에서 얼마나 정확히 쓰였는지를 평가하기 때문에 그는 문법적 오류가 있을까 걱정을 한다. 그래서 그는 한국어 문법 전문인 Kim 교수님을 찾아간다. 이 상황에서, Brian이 Kim 교수에게 뭐라고 말할 것 같은가?

문제 해결

한국어 단편 소설 대회에 참가하기 위해 한국어로 단편 소설을 쓴 Brian이 자신의 소설에 문법적 오류가 있을 것을 걱정하는 상황이므로, Brian이 Kim 교수에게 할 말로 ① '제 소설에 문법적 오류가 있는지 검토해 주시겠어요?'가 가장 적절하다.
② 죄송하지만, 저는 Kim 교수님의 사무실을 방문하고 싶지 않아요.
③ 대회의 심사 위원 중 한 명이 되는 것은 어떠세요?
④ 교수님이 왜 한국어 문법을 전공하기로 결심했는지 궁금합니다.
⑤ 괜찮으시면, 제 소설을 한국 대사관에 제출해 주시겠어요?

sophomore 2학년생   major in ~을 전공하다   literature 문학   embassy 대사관   evaluate 평가하다   accurately 정확히   in terms of ~ 면에서, ~에 관하여

16-17

여: 안녕하세요, 여러분! '환경과 인간'의 진행자 Amy Jang입니다. 오늘 저는 여러분에게 전기에 관해 말씀드리고 싶습니다. 여러분은 아마 전기를 생산하는 일부 방법이 우리의 환경에 해를 끼친다는 것을 아실 겁니다. 이것은 여러분이 전기를 더 많이 아끼면 아낄수록, 환경을 더 많이 보호할 수 있다는 것을 의미합니다. 그래서, 여러분에게 가정에서 전기를 절약할 수 있는 방법을 말씀드리고자 합니다. 컴퓨터를 사용하지 않을 때는 컴퓨터의 전원을 끄십시오. 만약 매번 컴퓨터 전원을 끄는 것이 너무 불편하다면, 그냥 모니터만 꺼도 됩니다. 세탁기의 경우, 적은 양의 빨래를 여러 차례 세탁하기보다는 전기를 덜 소모하기 위해 한 번에 많은 양의 빨래를 하십시오. 에어컨에 쓰이는 전기를 절약하기 위해서, 가장 낮은 수준으로 온도를 설정하기 보다는 적당한 수준으로 온도를 설정하는 것이 제일 좋습니다. 똑같은 규칙이 전기 히터에도 적용됩니다. 제가 말씀드린 방식으로 전기를 절약함으로써, 여러분이 환경을 보호하는 데 커다란 역할을 하기를 바랍니다.

harm 해롭게 하다   inconvenient 불편한   rather than ~보다는, ~하지 말고   load 짐의 양, 한 짐   laundry 빨래   consume 소비하다   moderate 중간의, 적당한, 적정한   apply to ~에 적용되다   play a role in ~에서 역할을 하다   appliances 가전제품   sustainable 지속 가능한   alternative 대체 가능한

16 ③

'환경과 인간'의 진행자인 여자는 가정에서 전기를 절약할 수 있는 방법에 대해 구체적으로 말하고 있으므로, 여자가 하는 말의 주제로 ③ '가정에서 전기를 절약하는 방법'이 가장 적절하다.
① 우리 삶에 전기가 미치는 영향
② 절전용 가전제품의 이점
④ 지속 가능한 대체 에너지에 대한 필요성
⑤ 전기가 환경에 얼마나 해를 끼치는지

17 ④

가전제품으로 텔레비전은 언급되지 않았다.

---

01 ①	02 ⑤	03 ③	04 ④	05 ⑤	06 ②
07 ⑤	08 ④	09 ④	10 ③	11 ②	12 ③
13 ③	14 ③	15 ⑤	16 ①	17 ③	

01 ①

남: Maple 고등학교의 학생 여러분, 좋은 아침입니다! 여러분 모두 알다시피, 우리 학교는 아침을 먹는 것의 중요성에 대하여 홍보해 왔습니다. 모든 학생들은 매일 건강한 아침 식사를 할 수 있어야 합니다. 일전에, 우리는 아침을 먹는 학생들이 얼마나 신체적으로 더 건강하고, 얼마나 더 높은 출석률을 보이는지를 살펴보았습니다. 오늘, 마지막 프로젝트로, 우리는 학교 아침 식사 주간을 공식적으로 선포합니다. 일주일 간, Maple 고등학교의 모든 학생들은 무료로 아침 식사를 할 수 있게 됩니다. 학생증을 가지고 오전 7시 30분에서 오전 8시 20분 사이에 학생 식당을 방문하기만 하면 됩니다. 우리는 여러분이 건강한 음식을 먹고 생기 넘치게 학교 일과를 시작하기를 권합니다!

남자는 교내 무료 아침 식사 프로젝트의 시작과 참여 방법을 안내하고 있다.

promote 홍보하다   have access to ~에 접근할 수 있다   attendance 출석률, 참석   available 구할 수 있는, 이용할 수 있는

02 ⑤

여: Sam, 내일 직업 체험관을 방문할 준비가 되었니?
남: 네, Julie 선생님. 전 정말 신나요!
여: 좋아! 네가 경험해 보고 싶은 어떤 특정 직업을 정했니?
남: 아직요. 저는 너무나 많은 직업들에 관심이 있어요.
여: 시간제한 때문에, 너는 단 세 개만 선택할 수 있다는 것을 명심하렴.
남: 저도 알아요. 제가 무엇을 하면 좋을지 조언해 주실 수 있나요?
여: 음, 나는 네가 가장 관심 있는 분야를 좁혀 보는 것이 도움이 될 거라고 생각해.
남: 스포츠, 의학 등을 말씀하는 거예요?
여: 그래. 그 다음 그 분야에서 구체적인 직업들을 찾아 볼 수 있을 거야. 예를 들면, 스포츠 영역에는 운동선수 트레이너, 물리 치료사 등이 있지.
남: 좋은 생각이네요. 그렇게 해 볼게요. 감사합니다.
여: 도움이 되었다니 기쁘구나.

체험하고 싶은 직업이 너무 많다는 남자에게 여자는 먼저 가장 관심 있는 분야를 좁혀 본 다음 해당 분야에서의 구체적인 직업을 찾아 보는 것이 도움이 될 것이라고 했다.

time limit 시간제한   narrow down 좁히다, 줄이다   athletic trainer 운동선수 트레이너   physical therapist 물리 치료사

03 ③

여: 안녕하세요, Cane 씨. 무슨 일이세요?

남: 갑작스러운 통보에도 와 주셔서 감사해요, Peg 씨. 저희 돌고래 중 하나인 Molly가 좀 이상한 행동을 하고 있어요.

여: 좀 더 구체적으로 말씀해 주실래요?

남: 제가 지금까지 6개월 동안 Molly를 훈련해 오고 있는데, 그녀가 이렇게 공격적으로 행동하는 걸 본 적이 없어요.

여: 그렇군요. 그동안 잘 먹었나요?

남: 아니요, 별로 많이 먹지 않았어요.

여: 알았어요. 제가 그녀를 한 번 볼 수 있을까요?

남: 물론이죠. 이쪽으로 오세요.

여: [잠시 후] 음. 복부에서 이상한 소리가 나네요. 몇 가지 검사를 하고 싶어요. 제가 내일 오전에 제 병원에서 장비를 가지고 올게요.

남: 감사합니다. 제가 주의를 해야 할 부분이 있을까요?

여: 검사가 끝날 때까지 그녀에게 먹이를 주지 않는 게 좋겠어요.

남: 알겠습니다. 그렇게 할게요. 그녀가 금방 좋아지길 바랍니다.

남자는 자신이 훈련하던 돌고래 중 하나가 이상하게 행동한다고 이야기하고 이에 여자는 그런 돌고래를 살펴보고 검사를 위한 장비를 자신의 병원에서 가져올 것이라고 이야기하는 것으로 보아, 여자와 남자는 수의사와 동물 훈련가의 관계임을 알 수 있다.

short notice 촉박한 통보   aggressively 공격적으로   run a test 검사를 하다   kit 장비, 기구   be mindful of ~에 잘 주의하다

04 ④

남: 와! 어린이 도서관 개조를 정말 훌륭하게 했네요.

여: 이야기 방으로 들어가는 입구가 멋져요! 마치 펼쳐진 책 같아요.

남: 맞아요. 그리고 나무 모양의 벤치는 제가 앉아서 책을 읽고 싶게 만드네요.

여: 저는 책 모양의 저 스툴이 좋아요. 그것들은 여러 작가들에게 기증받은 것이라고 들었어요.

남: 참 훌륭하네요.

여: 이야기 방에서 오늘은 무엇을 읽는지 궁금하네요.

남: '미운 오리 새끼' 같은데요.

여: 그걸 어떻게 알아요?

남: 이야기 방 옆에 있는 화면 보여요? 아기 오리들과 함께 있는 아기 백조 그림이 있어요.

여: 그렇군요. 화면 아래에 있는 선반에는 '미운 오리 새끼' 책들도 있어요.

남: 아이들이 책을 읽도록 독려하기에 훌륭한 방법이네요.

여: 저도 동의해요. 같이 이야기 방 안을 한번 살펴보아요.

이야기 방 옆에 있는 화면에 아기 오리들과 아기 백조가 같이 있는 그림이 있다고 했으므로, ④ 고양이 그림은 대화의 내용과 일치하지 않는다.

renovate (낡은 건물·가구 등을) 개조하다   stool (등받이와 팔걸이가 없는) 의자, 스툴   swan 백조

05 ⑤

남: 여보, 뭐하고 있어요?

여: 나한테 더 이상 필요 없는 옷가지들과 담요를 싸고 있어요.

남: 벌써 봄맞이 청소할 때인 거예요?

여: 아니요. 이것들은 화재 피해자 지원 기구에 보낼 거예요.

남: 아, 산불로 집을 잃은 사람들을 위한 거로군요?

여: 맞아요. 뉴스에서 기부금과 생필품을 받고 있다고 했어요.

남: 당신 착하네요. 부엌에서 먹을 것을 좀 포장할까요?

여: 고맙지만 내가 이미 통조림 식품을 좀 쌌어요.

남: 알겠어요. 내가 도울 일이 뭐가 있을까요?

여: 실은, 아이들을 학교에서 데려올 수 있어요? 그러면 나는 포장하는 것을 끝내고 우체국에 가서 전부 보낼 수 있을 거예요.

남: 문제없어요.

여자는 남자에게 아이들을 학교에서 데려와 달라고 부탁하였다.

spring cleaning 봄맞이 대청소   victim 피해자   daily necessities 생활필수품   canned food 통조림 식품

06 ②

여: 안녕하세요. 무엇을 도와드릴까요?

남: 안녕하세요. 저는 제 아들을 위한 연필깎이를 찾고 있어요.

여: 알겠습니다. 이 연필깎이들이 어린 소년들에게 인기가 많습니다. 수동 제품은 15달러이고 자동 제품은 25달러예요.

남: 자동 제품은 다른 색상으로도 나오나요?

여: 유감스럽게도 저희는 현재 회색만 있습니다. 수동 제품은 좀 더 많은 선택권이 있어요. 다양한 만화 캐릭터 디자인으로 나와 있어요.

남: 오, 제 아들은 만화 캐릭터를 정말 좋아해요. 저기 로봇 디자인으로 된 수동 제품을 살게요.

여: 알겠습니다. 혹시 관심 있으시면, 어울리는 필통도 있어요.

남: 그거 귀엽네요. 얼마인가요?

여: 보통 때는 10달러이지만, 이번 주는 특별 행사 기간입니다. 그건 50% 할인을 받을 수 있어요.

남: 잘됐네요! 그걸 살게요.

여: 알겠습니다.

남: 현금으로 지불할게요.

15달러인 수동 연필깎이 한 개와 10달러인 필통 한 개를 사겠다고 했는데, 필통은 50% 할인이 된다고 하였으므로, 남자가 지불할 총 금액은 20달러이다.

manual 수동의   at the moment 현재, 지금   matching 어울리는

07 ⑤

여: 얘, Peter. 저거 일일 요리 강좌에 관한 광고니?

남: 응, Audrey. 하나 같이 들래?

여: 너 나 요리 못하는 거 알잖아.

남: 걱정 마. 초보자를 위한 강좌도 있어.

여: 그런 경우라면, 해 보고 싶어. 무언가 준비해야 하는 거야?

남: 아니. 모든 식재료와 기구들은 제공될 거라고 하는데.

여: 잘됐다. 강좌가 언제야?

남: 다음 주 목요일 오후 5시야.

여: 어, 나 다음 주 목요일은 정말 바쁜데.

남: 아, 깜박했다. 너 치과 예약 있다고 말했었어, 맞지?

여: 응, 하지만 치과 예약은 오후 4시 전에 끝날 거야. 실은 그 후에 할머니의 정원 가꾸는 일을 도와드리기로 했어.

남: 알겠어. 그럼 좋은 시간 보내고, 요리 강좌는 다음에 같이 해 보자.

문제 해결

여자는 치과 예약은 4시 전에 끝나서 5시에 시작하는 요리 강좌를 들을 수 있지만, 이후에 할머니의 정원 가꾸는 일을 도와드리기로 해서 남자와 함께 요리 강좌를 들을 수 없다고 했다.

어휘·표현

one-day class 일일 강좌   ingredient 재료   (cooking) utensils 조리 기구

08 ④
언급 유무 파악

여: 안녕, Jason, 너 나랑 Book Festival 같이 갈래?

남: Book Festival? 그게 뭐야?

여: 그건 많은 유명한 작가들을 만날 수 있고, 다양한 활동에 참여할 수 있는 대형 문학 축제야.

남: 재미있게 들리는데. 언제야?

여: 이번 주 토요일 오전 10시부터 오후 5시까지야.

남: 나 이번 토요일에 한가해. 너랑 같이 가고 싶어. 어디서 열리는 거야?

여: 시청 앞에 있는 광장에서. 거기 어떻게 가는지 아니?

남: 확인해 볼게. [잠시 후] 내 아파트 근처에 버스가 하나 있는데, 30분 밖에 안 걸리네.

여: 잘됐다! 조각상 앞에서 만나자. 그리고 물 한 병 꼭 챙겨 와.

남: 알았어. 간식도 좀 가져가도 될까?

여: 아니. 물을 제외하고는 어떤 음식이나 음료도 허용되지 않아.

남: 알겠어. 그럼 이번 주 토요일에 보자.

문제 해결

행사 일시(이번 주 토요일), 행사 장소(시청 앞 광장), 교통편(버스), 반입 가능 물품(물)에 대해서는 언급했지만, ④ 참가비에 대해서는 언급하지 않았다.

어휘·표현

literary 문학의   well-known 유명한, 잘 알려진   take place (계획된 일이) 개최되다, 열리다   square 광장   statue 조각상   except for ~을 제외하고

09 ④
담화 내용 불일치

여: 안내 말씀 드리겠습니다. 저는 Queens 대학 학생 위원회의 Janet입니다. 이번 주 금요일에 학생회관에서 다문화의 날이 개최될 것이라는 것을 안내하게 되어 매우 기쁩니다. 다문화의 날은 우리의 다양성을 축하하고 여러 다문화 커뮤니티가 우리 사회에 공헌한 것에 대해 감사하는 기회입니다. 다문화의 날에 학생들의 참여를 독려하기 위해 모든 금요일 오후 수업은 취소될 것입니다. 특별 행사에는 여러 다양한 문화 커뮤니티의 예술 전시와 춤 공연이 포함됩니다. 지역 상점과 음식점들의 기부 덕택에 모든 행사는 무료입니다. 다문화의 날은 대중에게 열려 있으니, 여러분들의 가족과 친구들을 데려오세요. 더 많은 정보를 원하시면 Tim Cole에게 tcole@queens.edu로 연락해 주세요. 여러분들을 뵙기를 기대하고 있겠습니다.

문제 해결

지역 상점과 음식점들의 기부 덕택에 모든 행사는 무료라고 했으므로, 행사에 참가하기 위해서 소정의 기부금을 내야 한다는 ④는 내용과 일치하지 않는다.

어휘·표현

committee 위원회   student union 학생회관   multicultural 다문화의

diversity 다양성   appreciate 고마워하다   contribution 공헌, 기여
free of charge 무료로

10 ③
도표 정보 파악

남: 좋은 아침입니다. 무엇을 도와드릴까요?

여: 안녕하세요, 저는 캠핑용 탁자를 사려고 하는데요. 추천 좀 해 주시겠어요?

남: 물론입니다. 우선, 무게를 확인해 봐야 해요. 탁자가 가벼울수록 설치하기가 쉽습니다.

여: 4kg 미만이면 뭐든지 다룰 수 있을 것 같아요.

남: 알겠습니다. 탁자의 상판 재료에 대해서는 선호하는 게 있으신가요? 알루미늄과 원목이 있습니다.

여: 청소하기 쉬운 것을 선호해요.

남: 그렇다면 알루미늄 상판을 가진 모델들을 추천해 드립니다. 우린 합리적인 가격의 모델들이 있습니다.

여: 40달러 이하의 상품을 보여 주시겠어요?

남: 물론이죠. 컵 거치대가 두 개인 이것과 컵 거치대가 없는 저것이 있습니다.

여: 컵 거치대는 꽤 유용할 것 같네요.

남: 그렇다면 이 탁자가 손님께 딱 맞겠네요.

여: 좋아요. 이걸로 살게요.

문제 해결

여자는 무게가 4kg 미만이고, 가격은 40달러 이하이며, 알루미늄 상판에, 컵 거치대가 두 개 있는 탁자를 사려고 하므로, 여자가 구입할 캠핑용 탁자는 ③이다.

어휘·표현

set up 설치하다   handle (기구 등을) 다루다   preference 선호(도), 기호
reasonable 합리적인, 적정한   cup holder 컵 거치대

11 ②
짧은 대화의 응답

남: Penny, 너 도서관에서 빌린 책들 반납했어?

여: 아직. 오늘 방과 후에 반납하려고.

남: 그러면, 날 위해서 이 책도 반납해 줄 수 있니? 난 수업이 끝나면 바로 Franklin 선생님을 뵈러 가야 해.

여: 그래. 내가 그렇게 해 줄게.

문제 해결

남자는 수업 직후 선생님을 뵈러 가야 한다며 여자에게 자기 대신 책을 반납해 달라고 부탁하였으므로, 그렇게 해 주겠다고 말하는 ②가 여자의 응답으로 가장 적절하다.

① 응. 그것들은 네 책이야.

③ 맞아. 내가 그녀에게 네가 온다고 말할게.

④ 아니. 그녀의 사무실은 도서관에서 멀어.

⑤ 안됐다. 도서관은 오늘 문을 열지 않아.

어휘·표현

return 돌려주다, 반납하다

12 ③
짧은 대화의 응답

여: 좋은 아침입니다, Jenny의 카페에 오신 것을 환영합니다. 무엇을 주문하시겠어요, 손님?

남: 안녕하세요. 햄과 치즈 넣은 샌드위치 하나 주세요.

여: 1달러만 더 내시면 커피도 한 잔 드실 수 있어요. 그것도 추가해 드릴까요?

남: <u>괜찮아요. 마실 것은 필요하지 않아요.</u>

샌드위치를 주문한 남자에게 여자가 1달러를 더 내고 커피를 추가하는 것을 원하는지를 물었으므로, 마실 것은 필요하지 않다고 말하는 ③이 남자의 응답으로 가장 적절하다.

① 물론이에요. 내 샌드위치를 먹어도 돼요.

② 괜찮아요. 난 치즈에 알레르기가 있어요.

④ 좋아요. 당신의 음식을 바로 가져다 드릴게요.

⑤ 죄송해요. 저희 커피 머신이 고장이 났어요.

allergic 알레르기가 있는

13 ③

긴 대화의 응답

여: 안녕, Ned. 오늘은 기분이 안 좋아 보이네. 무슨 문제라도 있니?

남: 음, Lilly가 나에게 화가 났어.

여: 음악 동아리에 있는 Lilly 말이야? 너희 둘이 잘 지낸다고 생각했는데.

남: 잘 지냈어. 오늘 아침 연습 때까지만 해도 좋았어.

여: 무슨 일이 있었는데?

남: 내가 그녀의 신발에 대해 한 마디 한 것에 대해 화를 내더라.

여: 정말? 너 뭐라고 했는데?

남: 그녀가 밝은 노란색 운동화를 신었길래 바나나같이 보인다고 했어.

여: Ned, 그건 네가 잘한 일이 아니야.

남: 하지만 그냥 농담이었어! 화를 낼 일은 아니었다고.

여: 그건 네 생각이고. 난 그 일이 어떻게 그녀의 마음을 상하게 했는지 이해되는데.

남: 정말?

여: 응. 넌 농담으로 했을지 몰라도, 그녀에게 미안하다고 말하는 게 좋을 것 같아.

남: 알겠어. 방과 후에 그녀에게 사과할게.

여자는 농담이었지만 상대방의 마음을 상하게 한 남자에게 사과하는 것이 좋겠다고 조언하였으므로, 이에 대한 남자의 응답으로 ③이 가장 적절하다.

① 네 말이 맞아. 그녀는 농담을 무척 좋아해.

② 괜찮아. 나는 노란색 운동화를 좋아하지 않아.

④ 좋은 생각이야. 나는 음악실에서 연습하는 걸 좋아해.

⑤ 잘 모르겠어. 그녀는 바나나를 안 좋아하는 것 같아.

be upset with ~에게 화가 나다   get along well 잘 지내다   make a comment 한 마디 하다, 코멘트를 하다

14 ③

긴 대화의 응답

여: 뭐하고 있어요, Liam?

남: 동화책 삽화 전시에 가는 것에 대해 생각하고 있었어요. 꽤 좋다고 들었거든요.

여: 시립 미술관에서 하는 거 말이죠? 나는 지난 일요일에 다녀왔어요.

남: 정말요? 어땠어요?

여: 정말 멋졌어요. 세계적으로 유명한 삽화가들의 놀라운 작품들이 있었어요.

남: 나도 어서 직접 가서 보고 싶어요.

여: 아이들도 함께 데려갈 계획이에요?

남: 네. 아이들이 좋아할까요?

여: 물론이죠. 우리 아이들도 아주 즐거워했어요. 특히 가족 관람을 추천해요.

남: 그게 뭐에요?

여: 자원봉사자들 중 한 명이 개별 관람을 시켜 주는데, 관람 마지막에는 자기만의 삽화를 만들어 보는 데 참가할 수 있어요.

남: 그거 좋은데요! 어떻게 신청해야 하는지 알아요?

여: 네. 안내 데스크에서 예약을 해야 해요.

전시회에 먼저 다녀온 여자가 남자에게 가족 관람을 추천해 주었고, 남자는 어떻게 신청하는지를 물었다. 이에 대한 여자의 응답으로 안내 데스크에서 예약을 하라고 알려 주는 ③이 가장 적절하다.

① 물론이죠. 모든 자원봉사자들은 미술 전공생이에요.

② 미안해요. 7살 미만의 어린이들은 이 전시를 관람할 수 없어요.

④ 당신이 좋아하는 삽화가의 작품을 전시하길 바라요.

⑤ 확실하지 않지만, 시립 미술관은 매주 일요일에 휴관해요.

illustration (책 등에 실린) 삽화   exhibit 전시(회)   illustrator 삽화가
sign up for ~을 신청하다

15 ⑤

상황에 적절한 말

여: George는 컴퓨터 프로그래밍에 관심이 있는 고등학교 학생이다. 그는 최근에 전국 단위의 컴퓨터 프로그래밍 대회에 대해 알게 되었다. 그는 대회에 참가하고 싶어 하지만, 같은 날 역사 수업 발표가 있다. George는 담임 선생님인 Teresa 선생님께 조언을 구한다. Teresa 선생님 또한 이 대회가 그가 귀중한 경험을 얻을 수 있는 좋은 기회라고 생각한다. 하지만, 그녀는 또한 그가 학교에서 최선을 다해야 한다고 생각한다. 그래서 그녀는 George가 그의 역사 선생님께 그가 대회 전날 미리 발표를 할 수 있는지 물어보라고 조언을 하고 싶어 한다. 이 상황에서, Teresa 선생님은 George에게 뭐라고 말할 것 같은가?

컴퓨터 프로그래밍 대회와 역사 수업 발표 날이 겹친 George에게 Teresa 선생님은 그가 역사 선생님께 대회 전날 미리 발표를 할 수 있는지 물어보도록 조언을 하고 싶어 하는 상황이다. 따라서 ⑤ '역사 선생님께 네가 미리 발표를 할 수 있는지 여쭤 보는 것은 어떠니?'가 George에게 할 말로 가장 적절하다.

① 내가 너라면, 나는 나만의 프로그램을 개발하는 데 집중할 거야.

② 컴퓨터 프로그래밍의 역사를 아는 것은 매우 중요하다고 생각해.

③ 너는 전국 단위 시험을 치름으로써 귀중한 경험을 얻어야 해.

④ 고등학교를 졸업한 후에 대회에 참가하지 그러니?

competition (경연) 대회, 시합   valuable 귀중한   focus on ~에 집중하다, 전념하다

16-17

복합 이해

남: 안녕하세요. 지난 시간에, 우리는 일부 동물들이 생존 확률을 높이기 위해 어떻게 위장을 사용하는지에 대해 논의해 보았습니다. 오늘은, 각기 다른 동물 종이 발달시켜 온 위장의 종류를 살펴보겠습니다. 첫 번째로, 일부 동물들은 배경과 같은 색으로 자기 자신을 숨깁니다. 예

를 들면, 흰올빼미의 색은 흰색입니다. 이것은 흰올빼미가 눈이 오는 환경에 섞여 들어가도록 도와줍니다. 두 번째로, 어떤 동물들은 줄무늬나 무늬를 갖고 있어 포식자들이 그들을 배경과 구별하기 어렵게 만듭니다. 얼룩말의 흑백 줄무늬는 한 마리의 얼룩말을 무리에서 추리는 것을 어렵게 합니다. 세 번째로, 일부 동물들은 자신을 주위 환경과 비슷하게 함으로써 주위 환경에 섞여 듭니다. 예를 들어, 대벌레는 포식자로부터 숨기 위해 나뭇가지의 가지처럼 생겼습니다. 끝으로, 어떤 동물들은 다른 위험하거나 독이 있는 동물들처럼 생겼습니다. 독이 없는 주홍왕뱀의 색과 무늬는 그것의 포식자들이 다른 독사와 혼동하게 합니다. 자, 이러한 동물들의 사진을 살펴보시죠.

어휘·표현

camouflage (보호색이나 형태 등을 통한 동물들의) 위장 species 종(種: 생물 분류의 기초 단위) snowy owl 흰올빼미 blend in with ~와 조화를 이루다 predator 포식자 distinguish 구별하다 single out 뽑아내다, 선발하다 stick insect 대벌레 scarlet kingsnake 주홍왕뱀 confuse *A* with *B* A와 B를 혼동하다 animal kingdom 동물계 natural enemy 천적 evolution 진화

16 ①

문제 해결

남자는 각기 다른 동물 종이 어떤 종류의 위장술을 발달시켜 왔는지에 대해 이야기하고 있다.
① 다양한 종류의 동물 위장술
② 동물계의 천적
③ 야생 동물들의 흔한 행동 양식
④ 환경이 동물의 진화에 미치는 영향
⑤ 자연 위장술과 인공 위장술의 차이점

17 ③

문제 해결

흰올빼미, 얼룩말, 대벌레, 주홍왕뱀에 대해서는 언급했지만, ③ 해마에 대해서는 언급하지 않았다.

01 ①	02 ⑤	03 ①	04 ①	05 ⑤	06 ④
07 ②	08 ②	09 ⑤	10 ⑤	11 ①	12 ②
13 ②	14 ②	15 ②	16 ⑤	17 ⑤	

01 ①　　　　　　　　　　　　　　　　　　　　목적 파악

여: 좋은 오후입니다, Radio One 청취자 여러분. 저는 Patti Smith이고, 여러분은 Talk of the Town을 듣고 계십니다. 오늘, 저희는 자매 방송국들 중 한 곳에서 하는 새로운 팟캐스트에 관해 이야기하려고 합니다. Repair Me는 우리 일상생활의 스트레스와 이를 어떻게 대처할 수 있는지에 초점을 맞춘 팟캐스트입니다. Steve Nicks가 진행을 하는 Repair Me는 우리의 일상이 어떻게 스트레스를 관리하는 방법을 형성하는지에 관한 통찰력을 제공합니다. 매주 특별한 손님이 초대되어 스트레스가 우리의 삶에 영향을 미치는 다양한 방식들과 그것에 대처하는 방식에 관해 토론할 것입니다. 만약 이것이 여러분을 위한 것처럼 들린다면, 팟캐스트 앱을 통해서 그 팟캐스트를 다운로드하세요.

문제 해결

여자는 Repair Me라는 새로운 팟캐스트를 홍보하고 있다.

어휘·표현

brand-new 아주 새로운 cope with ~에 대처하다 insight 통찰력 routine (판에 박힌) 일상 impact 영향을 주다

02 ⑤　　　　　　　　　　　　　　　　　　　　주제 파악

여: 여보, 저는 Joshua가 걱정돼요.
남: Joshua요? 무슨 문제가 있나요?
여: 당신은 그가 아직 읽는 법을 배우지 못했다는 게 괜찮다고 생각해요?
남: 뭐라고요? 그는 아직 네 살이에요.
여: 하지만 유치원의 다른 모든 아이들은 벌써 읽기 시작했어요.
남: 당신이 과잉 반응을 보이고 있네요. 때가 되면 그는 읽는 것을 배울 거예요.
여: 당신은 이것에 대해 어떻게 그렇게 평온할 수 있어요? 만약 그가 또래들보다 뒤떨어지면 어쩌죠?
남: 진정해요. 저는 늦게 읽기를 배우는 데에 이로움이 있다고 생각해요.
여: 이로움이요? 예를 들면요?
남: 저는 늦게 읽는 아이들이 더 창의적인 경향이 있다고 생각해요.
여: 당신 말은 글자를 읽을 수 없기 때문에 그들이 상상력을 더 사용해야 한다는 건가요?
남: 맞아요. 그러니 걱정하지 말아요. 우리 아이는 잘하고 있어요.

문제 해결

아직 글을 읽지 못하는 아들을 걱정하는 여자에게 남자는 늦게 읽는 아이들이 더 창의적인 경향이 있다고 말하고 있으므로, 남자의 의견으로 ⑤가 가장 적절하다.

어휘·표현

overreact 과잉 반응을 보이다 fall behind (~에) 뒤지다, 뒤떨어지다 peer 또래

03 ①

관계 추론

여: Johnson 씨, 강연 재미있었습니다.

남: 고마워요, 어린 숙녀분. 경찰관으로 일하는 것에 대해 이야기하는 것은 제 기쁨이에요.

여: 이야기를 나눌 시간이 있으신가요? 저는 여쭤보고 싶은 게 있어요.

남: 물론이죠, 저는 몇 분 시간을 낼 수 있어요.

여: 저는 형사가 되는 것이 꿈이에요. 제가 어떻게 시작할 수 있을까요?

남: 좋은 질문이네요. 저는 학교 지도 선생님과 이야기하면서 시작했어요.

여: 좋은 조언이에요. 제가 할 수 있는 다른 것은 없나요?

남: 다양한 과목을 공부해야 해요. 제가 10년 동안 경찰관으로 일해 보니, 신체적인 능력뿐만 아니라 지적 능력이 필요하다고 말할 수 있어요.

여: 알겠어요. 지금부터 더 열심히 공부하겠습니다.

남: 당신의 길을 잘 가고 있는 것 같네요. 아마 언젠가 제가 당신을 위해 일하고 있겠네요.

여: 하하. 그렇지 않을 거예요. 시간을 내 주셔서 감사합니다.

문제 해결

여자는 형사가 되기 위해 무엇을 하면 좋을지 남자에게 조언을 구하고 있고, 조언을 해 주는 남자는 경찰관으로 10년을 일했다고 했다. 따라서 두 사람은 학생과 경찰관의 관계임을 알 수 있다.

어휘·표현

the force 경찰   spare (시간 등을) 내다   detective 형사
guidance counselor 지도 교사   mental ability 지적 능력

04 ①

그림 불일치 파악

남: 엄마, 이 사진은 뭐예요?

여: 내가 자란 방의 사진이란다.

남: 제 방의 것처럼 중앙에 벽에 기대어 있는 이층 침대가 있네요.

여: 그건 내가 너의 이모가 함께 썼던 침대란다. 나는 아래쪽 침대에서 잤어. 저것은 내 침대 위에 있는 곰 인형이야.

남: 침대 왼쪽에 있는 것은 뭐예요?

여: 그것은 내 오래된 책상이야. 책상 위에 있는 것은 내가 밤에 사용했던 등이야.

남: 책상 뒤 벽에 있는 건 우주 비행사 포스터인가요?

여: 그래, 맞아. 내 어린 시절 꿈이 우주에 가는 거였단다.

남: 방 중앙에 있는 것은 뭐예요?

여: 그건 너희 할아버지가 벼룩시장에서 사 오신 별 무늬가 있는 깔개야.

남: 저는 엄마 방이 어떻게 생겼었는지 보는 게 정말 좋아요, 엄마.

문제 해결

그림 속에서는 위쪽 침대에 곰 인형이 있으므로, 곰 인형이 여자의 침대인 아래쪽 침대에 있다는 대화의 내용과 ①은 일치하지 않는다.

어휘·표현

bunk 이층 침대   astronaut 우주 비행사   a yard sale 창고 세일, 벼룩시장

05 ⑤

할 일 파악

남: Rachel, 공항으로 가는 택시가 두 시간 정도 후에 올 거야.

여: 알겠어요, 아빠. 저 이제 막 짐 싸는 것을 끝냈어요.

남: 칫솔 챙겼는지 확인했니?

여: 네, 했어요. 제 안경집 보셨어요?

남: 네 침대 옆에 있는 탁자 위에 있는 것 같구나.

여: 오, 여기 있네요. 찾았어요.

남: 도그 시터에게 할 일 목록 남기는 것은 확인했니?

여: 오! 하마터면 잊을 뻔했네요. 무엇을 써야 하죠?

남: Toby가 매일 몇 번 먹이를 먹어야 하는지 써야 해.

여: 네. 또 써야 할 게 있나요?

남: Toby가 평소 얼마나 산책하는지도 꼭 말해 줘.

여: 저는 Toby가 공원에서 산책하는 것을 좋아한다는 것도 쓸래요.

남: 좋은 생각이야.

여: 알겠어요, 지금 목록을 작성할게요.

문제 해결

여자는 도그 시터가 해야 하는 일 목록에 무엇을 적을지 남자와 함께 이야기한 후 지금 목록을 작성하겠다고 했으므로 여자가 할 일로 ⑤가 가장 적절하다.

어휘·표현

nightstand 침실용 탁자   dog sitter 도그 시터, 개의 주인 대신에 개를 돌보는 일을 하는 사람

06 ④

숫자 정보 파악

남: 좋은 저녁입니다. 무엇을 도와드릴까요?

여: 방 하나 부탁합니다.

남: 며칠 밤을 묵으실 건가요?

여: 하룻밤만이요.

남: 하룻밤 표준 가격은 40달러입니다. 하지만 오늘이 금요일이기 때문에, 값은 두 배가 됩니다. 괜찮으신가요?

여: 물론이죠. 무료 서비스가 있나요?

남: 저희는 오전 6시부터 10시까지 식당에서 유럽식 아침 식사를 제공하고 있습니다.

여: 좋네요. 제가 집에 세면도구 몇 개를 두고 온 것 같아요. 여기서 구입할 수 있나요?

남: 10달러짜리 여행용 세면도구 세트가 있습니다. 그러면, 주말 요금으로 하룻밤 숙박과 여행용 세면도구 세트 하나를 하시는 것으로 적어 두겠습니다. 더 필요한 것은 없나요?

여: 저는 10% 할인 쿠폰이 있어요.

남: 알겠습니다. 이 쿠폰은 숙박 요금에만 적용할 수 있습니다. 현금으로 하시겠습니까, 아니면 신용 카드로 하시겠습니까?

여: 신용 카드로 결제할게요.

문제 해결

숙박 요금은 하룻밤에 40달러인데, 주말 요금은 두 배로 적용되므로 80달러이다. 10% 쿠폰은 숙박비에만 적용이 되므로 총 숙박비는 72달러이다. 여기에 10달러짜리 여행용 세면도구 세트를 산다고 했으므로, 여자가 지불할 총 금액은 82달러이다.

어휘·표현

complimentary 무료의   continental 유럽식의   toiletries 세면도구

07 ②

이유 파악

여: 안녕, Danny. 너 뭐 읽고 있니?

남: 안녕, Jenny. 나는 Fyodor Dostoevsky가 쓴 '죄와 벌'을 읽고 있어.

여: 나는 네가 고전 문학 읽는 것을 좋아하는지 몰랐어.

남: 솔직히 말하자면, 나는 고전을 읽는 것에 그렇게 관심이 있진 않아. 나는 만화책 읽는 것을 더 좋아해.

여: 그럼, 숙제 때문에 읽고 있는 거니?

남: 아니야. 우리 수업 과제는 '로미오와 줄리엣'을 읽는 거였어. 나는 지난주에 그걸 끝마쳤어.

여: 너희 어머니가 좋아하는 책들 중 한 권을 너에게 또 읽게 하셨니?

남: 아니야, 그녀는 이 책을 좋아하지 않아. 사실, 나는 내 수업에 가산점이 필요했어. 그래서 선생님이 내가 이 책을 읽으면 내 점수를 올려 주신다고 하셨어.

여: 그 책을 읽는데 행운을 빌어.

남: 고마워. 나는 내가 얻을 수 있는 모든 행운이 필요해.

여: 그 책 결론이 어떻게 되는지 나에게 알려 줘.

남: 그래. 문제없어.

가산점이 필요한 남자에게 선생님이 책 '죄와 벌'을 읽으면 점수를 올려 준다고 해서 남자가 책을 읽고 있으므로, 남자가 책을 읽고 있는 이유로 ②가 가장 적절하다.

assignment 과제, 숙제   extra credit 가산점   bump up ~을 올리다

08 ②

남: 여보, 와서 이 전단지 좀 봐요.

여: Timmy의 학교가 연례 Summer Jamboree를 이번 토요일에 하네요.

남: 이번에 학교가 총력을 기울이고 있어요. 그들은 아빠들을 위해 파이 먹기 대회도 개최할 예정이에요.

여: 당신은 파이 정말 좋아하잖아요. 그 후에 이인삼각 경주에 참가할 수 있는 거죠?

남: 꼭 시도해 볼 거예요.

여: 다른 팀들은 가능성이 없겠네요. 엄마들을 위한 공예 활동도 있어요.

남: jamboree가 오전 9시에 시작하니까 이번 주 금요일에는 우리 모두 일찍 잠자리에 들어야겠어요.

여: 올해 입장료는 얼마예요?

남: 학생들은 무료이고, 학부모들은 각각 5달러예요.

여: 작년에 우리가 지불했던 것의 두 배네요.

남: 네. 긴 하루가 되겠어요. 축제 행사들이 오후 5시까지 끝나지 않네요.

Summer Jamboree가 어디서 열리는지 ② '장소'는 언급되지 않았다.

annual 매년의, 연례의   go all out 전력을 다하다   three-legged race 이인삼각 경주   afterwards 나중에, 그 후에   stand a chance (~을 할) 가능성이 있다   arts and crafts 공예   festivity 축제 행사

09 ⑤

남: 좋은 아침입니다, 여러분. 저는 행정실의 Miller 선생님입니다. 우리 학교에서 에어컨을 사용하기 위한 새로운 규칙을 여러분에게 알려 드리겠습니다. 방과 후에도 에어컨을 켜 놓은 교실이 많았기 때문에, 오늘부터 모든 에어컨은 오후 4시 30분에 자동으로 꺼집니다. 만약 여러분이 정규 수업 시간 후에도 에어컨을 사용하기 원한다면, 하루 전에 미리 저에게 알려 주세요. 에어컨 온도는 중앙 통제에 의해 섭씨 28도로 미리 맞춰져 있어서 여러분이 바꿀 수 없습니다. 또한 에어컨 필터가 이번 주 토요일에 교체될 예정이라서 그날 체육관에서는 스포츠 동아리 활동이 없을 예정이라고 말하게 되어 유감입니다. 여러분

의 협조에 감사드립니다.

이번 주 토요일에 에어컨 필터 교체로 인해 체육관에서 하는 스포츠 동아리 활동은 없을 것이라고 했다.

administration 관리, 행정   guideline 지침   preset 미리 맞춰진

10 ⑤

여: Rick, Action Sports에서 이번 달에 대대적인 세일을 하고 있어.

남: 잘됐다! 난 다음 주 여행에 새 등산화가 필요했어, Barbara.

여: 여기. 이 웹 사이트를 봐.

남: 와! 선택의 폭이 아주 넓구나. 60달러 이하의 물건이 있니?

여: 응. 사이트의 첫 번째 페이지에 있어. 너의 가격 범위 내에서 네 켤레가 있어.

남: 그리고, 등산화가 너무 무겁지 않아야 해.

여: 1킬로그램 이하로는 세 켤레가 있어.

남: 그것들이 방수가 되니?

여: 사실, 이렇게 두 켤레가 돼. 너는 확실히 방수가 되는 것을 원하는구나.

남: 맞아. 산에서 흠뻑 젖을 수 있거든.

여: 남은 건 색상이야.

남: 나는 먼지와 진흙 때문에 신발이 어두운 색인 것이 더 좋아.

여: 그래! 너는 그러면 이것을 사야겠다.

남자는 가격은 60달러 이하이고, 무게는 1kg이 넘지 않아야 하며, 방수가 되는 제품을 고르고 있다. 또한 어두운 색상의 제품을 원하고 있으므로, 남자가 구입할 등산화는 ⑤이다.

hiking boots 등산화   selection 선택 가능한 것들(의 집합)
waterproof 방수의

11 ①

남: 안녕하세요, 한국, 서울에 있는 딸에게 이 소포를 항공으로 보내고 싶은데요.

여: 어떤 배송을 원하시죠? 일반 배송 또는 빠른 배송 중에서요.

남: 빠른 배송이요. 늦어도 이번 주 금요일까지는 딸이 이 소포를 받았으면 좋겠어요.

여: 알겠습니다. 소포를 저울에 올려 주세요.

서울에 있는 딸에게 소포를 항공으로 보내고 싶다는 남자에게 여자가 일반 배송인지 빠른 배송인지 묻자 남자는 빠른 배송으로 보내고 싶다고 말했다. 이에 대한 여자의 응답으로 가장 적절한 것은 ① '알겠습니다. 소포를 저울에 올려 주세요.'이다.

② 소포를 포장하세요. 제가 우체국에 갈게요.

③ 물론입니다. 저는 제 딸이 정말 보고 싶어요.

④ 이번 금요일이요? 배편으로 그걸 보내는 건 불가능합니다.

⑤ 사실, 저는 이번 금요일에 업무 때문에 매우 바빠요.

package 소포   standard 일반적인, 보통의   express 고속의, 급행의
no later than 늦어도 ~까지는

12 ②

여: 아빠, 우리 이번 주말에 할머니 댁에 가요?
남: 미안하구나 애야, 할머니는 아직 하와이에서 휴가를 보내고 계셔.
여: 언제 여행에서 돌아오시나요?
남: 할머니는 며칠 후에 돌아오실 거야.

문제 해결

할머니가 언제 여행에서 돌아오시는지 묻는 여자의 말에 며칠 후에 돌아올 거라고 답하는 ②가 남자의 응답으로 가장 적절하다.
① 이번 주말에 그녀를 보러 가자.
③ 그녀가 탄 비행기는 어제 도착했어.
④ 나도 하와이로 휴가를 가고 싶어.
⑤ 우리는 다음 주에 여행을 하고 있을 거야.

어휘·표현

be on vacation 휴가 중이다   get back 돌아오다

13 ②

여: Mike, 이 리조트 정말 멋있어요, 그렇지 않나요?
남: 맞아요, Sandy. 우리 신혼여행을 보내기에 훌륭한 장소예요.
여: 그럼 우리 오늘은 무엇을 하죠?
남: 나는 리조트에 스쿠버 다이빙 관광이 있다고 들었어요. 물이 수정같이 맑다고 해요.
여: 그건 좋은 생각이 아닌 것 같아요. 날씨 예보에 따르면 오후에 비가 올 가능성이 있대요.
남: 나는 정말 이국적인 물고기들이 보고 싶었어요.
여: 우리는 리조트 옆에 있는 수족관에서 확인해 볼 수 있어요. 점심 식사 후에 셔틀버스를 탈 수 있어요.
남: 좋은 생각이에요, 여보. 수족관을 완전히 잊고 있었어요.
여: 그래요. 밥부터 먼저 먹어요. 배가 고파지고 있어요.
남: 문제없어요. 내 휴대 전화와 지갑, 그리고 열쇠를 봤나요?
여: 네, 탁자 위에 있어요.
남: 알겠어요, 나는 준비됐어요. 점심 먹으러 가요.

문제 해결

두 사람은 수족관에 가기 전에 점심을 먼저 먹기로 했으므로, 휴대 전화와 지갑 등 남자의 물건이 탁자 위에 있다는 여자의 마지막 말에 대한 남자의 응답으로 ② '알겠어요, 나는 준비됐어요. 점심 먹으러 가요.'가 가장 적절하다.
① 안 돼요. 내 커피는 너무 뜨거워요.
③ 이 스쿠버 다이빙 관광은 정말 신이 나요.
④ 수족관이 지금 문 닫을 거예요. 우리는 가야 해요.
⑤ 나는 신혼여행을 가는 것이 너무 신나요.

어휘·표현

be supposed to (일반적으로) ~라고 한다   exotic 이국적인

14 ②

[휴대 전화벨이 울린다.]
여: 안녕, Jake? 무슨 일이니?
남: 안녕, Amy. 나는 오늘 오후 점심 식사에 너를 초대하고 싶었어.
여: 오, 이런. 안타깝지만 나는 점심을 함께 할 수 없어. 대신에 저녁 식사는 어떠니?
남: 저녁이 좋겠다! 어디에 가고 싶니?

여: 나는 새로운 이탈리안 식당이 막 열었다고 들었어. 사람들이 정말 좋다고 하더라.
남: 난 어젯밤에 이탈리안 음식을 먹었어. 우리가 가장 좋아하는 초밥 집은 어떠니?
여: 그래. 그곳으로 가자.
남: 좋아! 내가 먼저 전화해서 오늘 밤 7시로 예약해 놓을게.
여: 그거 좋다. 저녁 식사 후에 영화 보는 게 어때?
남: 영화 재미있겠다. 요즘에 상영하는 좋은 영화 있니?
여: 좋은 평을 받고 있는 새 로맨틱 코미디 영화가 있어.
남: 그래, 내가 로맨틱 코미디를 얼마나 좋아하는지 너도 알잖아.
여: 내가 오후 9시 30분으로 두 장 사 놓을게.

문제 해결

로맨틱 코미디 영화를 보자는 여자의 말에 남자가 로맨틱 코미디를 좋아한다고 하였으므로, 이에 이어질 여자의 말로 ② '내가 오후 9시 30분으로 두 장 사 놓을게.'가 가장 적절하다.
① 저녁 식사가 몇 시니?
③ 점심 식사는 정말 재미있을 거야.
④ 우리 연어를 먹을까, 아니면 참치를 먹을까?
⑤ 나는 오늘 밤 파스타가 정말 기대돼.

어휘·표현

sushi 초밥   review 논평, 비평

15 ②

여: 지나와 Charles는 시카고 시내 상업 지역에서 인기 있는 카페의 주인이다. 최근, 지나는 점심시간에 사람이 너무 많아서 카페에서 처리할 수 없다는 것을 인지한다. 그녀는 이 분주함을 도울 또 다른 직원을 고용하는 것이 가장 좋은 방법일 것이라고 생각한다. 지나와 Charles가 손님들을 위한 음료를 제조할 동안 새로운 직원은 금전 등록기를 다루어야 한다. 반면에, Charles는 새로운 에스프레소 기계를 구입하는 것이 이 문제를 해결할 거라고 생각한다. 새로운 에스프레소 기계가 Charles와 지나가 절반의 시간에 두 배의 음료를 제조할 수 있게 할 것이다. Charles는 새로운 직원을 고용하는 것 대신 에스프레소 기계를 사는 것을 고려해 보라고 지나에게 말하고 싶다. 이러한 상황에서, Charles는 지나에게 무엇이라고 말할 것 같은가?

문제 해결

Charles는 직원을 고용하는 것 대신 새로운 에스프레소 기계를 사고 싶어 하는 상황이므로, Charles가 지나에게 할 말로 ② '그 대신 에스프레소 기계를 사는 게 어때?'가 가장 적절하다.
① 새로운 직원을 고용하는 것은 좋은 생각이야.
③ 우리는 점심시간을 위한 새로운 음료를 개발해야 해.
④ 내가 너에게 에스프레소를 만들어 주길 원하니?
⑤ 아마 우리는 새로운 금전 등록기를 사야 할 거야.

어휘·표현

business district 상업 지역   rush 혼잡, 분주함   cash register 금전 등록기

16-17

남: 좋은 오후입니다, 개발자 여러분. 오늘, 제가 Antunes 3.0에 대해 이야기하게 되어 기쁘네요. 여러분 모두 아시다시피, Antunes는 앱을 만들기 위한 인기 있는 개발 키트입니다. Antunes 3.0을 사용해 개발자들은 새로운 업데이트 덕분에 더욱 쉽고 효율적으로 앱을 만들

수 있을 것입니다. 첫 번째로, Antunes 3.0은 고속 앱 구축 기능을 가지고 있습니다. 개발자들은 절반의 시간으로 그들의 앱이 만들어지길 기대해도 좋습니다. 두 번째로, 메모리 관리가 개선되어 앱이 더 작고 가벼워집니다. Antunes 3.0을 사용해 개발된 앱들은 메모리 사용이 33% 감소될 것입니다. 세 번째로, Antunes 3.0은 개발자들에게 도움을 주는 새로운 AI 도우미를 탑재해 출시됩니다. Terry라고 코드명이 붙은 새로운 AI는 자동 완성 제안을 제공합니다. 마지막으로, 새로운 옵션은 개발자들이 배터리 소모를 볼 수 있게 합니다. 개발자들은 이제 실시간으로 그들의 앱에서 사용되는 배터리의 양을 볼 수 있습니다. 저는 이제 이 핵심 특징들을 시연하겠습니다.

어휘·표현

developer 개발자 reduction 감소 autocomplete 자동 완성
consumption 소비, 소모 demonstrate 설명하다, 보여 주다 novice 초보자
improvement 향상, 개선

16 ⑤

문제 해결

앱을 개발하는 데 사용되는 Antunes의 3.0 버전에 대해 설명하고 있으므로, 남자가 하는 말의 주제로 ⑤ '앱 개발 키트의 개선점들'이 가장 적절하다.
① Antunes를 사용하여 앱을 만드는 방법들
② 앱을 개발할 때 개발자들의 요구
③ 새로운 개발 키트를 사용하는 방법
④ 초보 스마트폰 사용자를 위한 새로운 앱들

17 ⑤

문제 해결

Antunes의 기능으로 User Interface(사용자 인터페이스)는 언급되지 않았다.

01 ④	02 ③	03 ③	04 ⑤	05 ④	06 ①
07 ④	08 ③	09 ②	10 ②	11 ⑤	12 ③
13 ⑤	14 ④	15 ⑤	16 ③	17 ③	

01 ④   목적 파악

남: 안녕하십니까, Yorkhill 아파트 주민 여러분. 이번 주 수요일인 모레에, 긴급 보일러 보수로 인해 여러분의 집에 온수 공급이 일시적으로 중단되겠습니다. 여러분 대부분이 아시다시피, 우리는 최근에 에너지를 절약하기 위해 새 보일러 시스템을 설치했습니다만 보일러실에서 누수를 발견하였습니다. 수리는 오전 7시에 시작되어 오후 5시까지 완료될 것이라 예상됩니다. 수리가 완료되는 대로 여러분의 가정에 온수가 복구될 것입니다. 이러한 불편에 대해 사과드리며 이 긴급한 문제에 대한 여러분의 이해에 감사드립니다. 문의하실 게 있으시면, 주저하지 말고 238-9500으로 연락해 주십시오.

문제 해결

남자는 아파트 주민들에게 긴급 보일러 보수로 인한 온수 공급 중단을 공지하고 있다.

어휘·표현

resident 거주자, 주민 supply 공급(하다) temporarily 일시적으로
shut off 멈추다, 정지하다 due to ~ 때문에 aware 알고 있는, 의식하고 있는
leak 유출, 새다 urgent 긴급한 hesitate 망설이다

02 ③   주제 파악

여: 안녕, Nick. 너 뭐 하고 있니?
남: 안녕. 나 기말고사를 대비해 공부 계획을 짜고 있어.
여: 오, 내가 볼 수 있을까? 와! 진심이야?
남: 왜? 뭐가 잘못되었니?
여: 네 스케줄에 네가 앞으로 3주 동안 하루에 4시간만 잔다고 되어 있어.
남: 그래. 나 이번에 진짜 좋은 성적 받아야 한다는 걸 너도 알잖아.
여: 그렇지만 게다가! 너 공부하기 위해 점심을 거르겠다고 계획하는 거야? Nick, 난 이게 진짜 될 거라 생각하지 않아.
남: 하지만 나한테 공부에 시간을 좀 더 할애하라고 충고한 건 바로 너였어.
여: 나도 알아. 하지만 더 중요한 건, '너의 스케줄이 현실적이냐?'라는 거야.
남: 너는 내가 이 스케줄이 정말 실행 가능한지를 유념해야 한다고 말하는 거구나.
여: 맞아. 계획을 수정해 보자. 내가 도와줄게.
남: 고마워. 넌 정말 친절하구나.

문제 해결

공부 계획을 너무 과도하게 세우고 있는 남자에게 여자가 문제점을 지적하며 스케줄이 실현 가능한지를 생각해 보아야 한다고 하였으므로, 여자의 의견으로 가장 적절한 것은 ③이다.

어휘·표현

allot 할당하다, 분배하다 keep in mind ~을 명심하다 doable 할 수 있는

03 ③

남: 실례합니다, Clancy 씨. 제가 당신에게 뭔가 여쭤봐도 될까요?

여: 그럼요. 무슨 일인가요?

남: 우리 잡지의 표지에 관한 거예요. 제안하실 게 있나요?

여: 이번 호가 태평양의 플라스틱 섬에 관한 것인지는 당신도 알고 있지요.

남: 네. 표지를 위해 제가 그곳의 사진을 찍기를 원하시나요?

여: 음. 전 독자들의 시선을 끌 좀 더 자극적인 것을 원해요.

남: 그러면, 같은 곳의 10년 전과 지금의 2개의 사진을 나란히 배치하는 것은 어떨까요?

여: 그거 좋은 것 같네요. 그것은 이 사안에 대한 경각심도 높일 거예요.

남: 좋아요. 그럼 제가 당장 그곳에 가서 사진을 좀 찍어 올게요. 그런데 10년 전 사진은 어쩌지요?

여: 제가 확신컨대 우리 기록 보관소에서 가지고 있을 거예요. 제가 John 한테 뒤져 보게 할게요.

남: 알겠어요. 제가 가능한 빨리 사진을 보내 드릴게요.

여: 좋아요. 안전하게 다녀 오세요.

문제 해결

이번 호 잡지의 표지에 대해 여자에게 의견을 물어보고 사진을 찍으러 가겠다고 하는 것으로 보아 남자는 잡지사의 사진작가라고 추정할 수 있고, 여자는 잡지의 내용에 따라 표지에 대한 결정을 내리고 John에게 업무를 지시하겠다는 것으로 보아 잡지사의 편집장이라는 것을 알 수 있다.

어휘·표현

issue (정기 간행물의) 호; 주제, 사안   provocative 자극적인, 도발적인
awareness 의식, 인식   archive 기록 보관소   dig up ~에 대해 알아내다, ~을 땅에서 파내다

04 ⑤

[휴대 전화벨이 울린다.]

남: 여보세요.

여: 안녕하세요, Parker 씨. Brooks 건축사입니다. 실내 조감도를 이메일로 보내 드렸는데요.

남: 네, 지금 보고 있습니다.

여: 제가 간단히 설명해 드릴게요. 당신은 다락방을 당신의 아이들을 위한 아늑한 공간으로 바꾸고 싶어 하셨죠.

남: 네, 저는 중앙에 커다란 둥근 창문이 맘에 드네요. 이 창이 방을 밝게 만들겠어요.

여: 맞습니다. 또한 창문 양쪽에 책장이 있게 될 거예요.

남: 제 아이들이 오른쪽에 매달려 있는 소파에서 책 읽는 것을 정말 좋아하겠어요. 그것은 편안해 보이네요.

여: 그것은 또한 분위기를 안락하게 해 줄 거예요. 원형 탁자는 왼쪽 편에 놓일 겁니다.

남: 좋아요. 그런데 저는 다리가 있는 의자가 더 실용적이라고 생각하는데요.

여: 맞습니다, 그런데 천장이 낮아서 다리가 없는 의자가 더 알맞을 겁니다.

남: 그럼 좋습니다. 이대로 하지요.

여: 그렇게 말씀하시는 걸 들으니 다행입니다.

문제 해결

대화에서 천장이 낮아 다리가 없는 의자가 더 알맞다고 했으므로, 그림 속 다리가 있는 의자 ⑤가 대화의 내용과 일치하지 않는다.

어휘·표현

architecture 건축   interior 인테리어, 내부   attic 다락(방)   cozy 안락한
atmosphere 분위기   practical 실용적인   suitable 적합한, 알맞은

05 ④

여: 여보, 이번 주말에 우리 집들이 하는 거 알고 있지요?

남: 그럼요. 나는 이미 몇 명이나 올 수 있는지 확인하려고 메시지를 보냈어요.

여: 그랬어요? 고마워요. 어떤 종류의 음식을 차려야 할까요?

남: 피자와 우리의 특제 소스를 곁들인 스파게티 어때요?

여: 좋은 생각이에요. 우리는 이미 지난번에 장을 봐서 필요한 재료를 다 가지고 있네요.

남: 그러면, 우리는 필요한 게 다 있나요?

여: 음… 식탁에 놓을 새 냅킨을 사야 해요.

남: 오, 방금 Amy와 Peter에게서 메시지를 받았어요. 그들이 아이들을 데려온다는군요. 그럼 우리가 총 8명의 손님을 맞게 될 거라는 말이네요.

여: 하지만 우리는 8명의 손님을 위한 접시가 충분하지 않아요.

남: 내가 가게에 가서 접시를 더 사 올 수 있어요.

여: 괜찮아요. 내가 오늘 냅킨을 사러 갈 때 몇 개 사 올게요. 대신, 당신은 다락에서 보드게임 좀 꺼내 주겠어요? 아이들이 그걸 가지고 놀고 싶어 할 거예요.

남: 알았어요. 그렇게 할게요.

문제 해결

여자가 냅킨을 사러 갈 때 접시도 사 온다고 하면서 남자에게는 다락에서 보드게임을 꺼내 달라고 부탁했다.

어휘·표현

house warming party 집들이   serve (음식을) 제공하다, 차려 주다
ingredient 재료

06 ①

[전화벨이 울린다.]

남: Summerhill 호텔입니다. 도와드릴까요?

여: 네, 저는 다음 주 월요일에 성인 2명을 위한 방을 예약하고 싶습니다.

남: 알겠습니다. 두 개의 선택 안이 있습니다. 퀸 사이즈 침대 하나가 있는 더블 룸 아니면 2개의 싱글 침대가 있는 트윈 룸입니다.

여: 각 방이 하룻밤에 얼마지요?

남: 더블 룸은 하룻밤에 90달러, 트윈 룸은 70달러가 듭니다.

여: 후자를 선택하고 싶습니다.

남: 며칠 밤을 묵을 예정이신가요?

여: 3일 밤이요.

남: 운이 좋으시네요. 저희는 현재 특별 판매를 진행하고 있습니다. 이틀 밤을 연속으로 묵으시면 세 번째 밤은 40달러만 듭니다.

여: 아주 딱이네요! 그렇게 하면 우리 돈을 많이 절약하겠어요.

남: 좋습니다. 마지막으로 바다가 보이는 방으로 하시겠어요? 하룻밤 당 별도의 10달러가 듭니다.

여: 아니요 괜찮습니다. 그건 필요하지 않습니다.

문제 해결

하룻밤에 90달러인 더블 룸과 70달러인 트윈 룸 중 후자를 선택하겠다고 했고, 3일 밤을 묵을 예정인데 특별 행사로 이틀 밤을 묵으면 세 번째 밤은 40달

러만 내면 된다. 바다가 보이는 방은 선택하지 않겠다고 해 추가 금액은 없으므로, 여자가 숙박비로 지불할 총 금액은 180달러이다.

어휘·표현

per ~당, ~마다   latter 후자(의)   in a row 잇달아, 연이어   ocean view 바다가 보이는 전망

07 ④

이유 파악

여: Steve, 전화기로 뭐 하고 있니?
남: 나 이번 주말 날씨 확인하고 있어. 화창할 거라고 하네.
여: 맞다. 너 이번 주말에 제주도에 가지.
남: 사실, 나 제주도 가는 비행편 취소했어.
여: 왜? 비행기표가 너무 비쌌니?
남: 전혀. 그건 특별 판매 표였어.
여: 그러면 너의 학교 숙제 때문이구나. 네가 그거 시간이 많이 걸릴 거라고 했었잖아.
남: 다행히, 나는 시간 안에 그것을 겨우 끝냈어.
여: 이해가 안 돼. 그러면 제주도로 가는 여행은 왜 취소한 거야?
남: 나는 이번 주말에 경주에서 신라 축제가 열리는 걸 알게 됐어. 그게 흥미로워 보여서 계획을 바꿨지.
여: 경주에서 즐거운 시간 보내길 바라.

문제 해결

남자는 제주도행 비행기편을 예매했다가 경주에서 열리는 신라 축제에 가는 것으로 계획을 바꾸어 비행기편을 취소하였다고 했다.

어휘·표현

promotion 판매 촉진   manage to 간신히 ~하다   take place (계획된 일이) 개최되다, 일어나다

08 ③

언급 유무 파악

여: Charlie. 이 광고를 봐! 아마추어 체스 경기가 시내에서 열려!
남: 오, 나 좀 보여 줘! 나 그것을 진짜 기대하고 있었어.
여: 3월 18일부터 28일까지 City Culture Hall에서 열릴 거야.
남: 좋아. 여기서 가깝네.
여: 거기에 참가할 거지?
남: 아냐. 난 그렇게 잘하진 않아. 게다가, 이 경기에 참가하려면 적어도 20살이어야 해.
여: 그건 성인 리그야. 너는 주니어 리그에 출전할 수 있어.
남: 음…. 너는 정말 내가 잘할 거라 생각하니?
여: 물론이지! 너는 우리 학교 체스 챔피언이잖아. 게다가 우승하면, 세계 체스 대회의 참가권과 여행 왕복표를 받을 수 있어.
남: 그거 정말 믿을 수 없네! 좋아. 내가 참가하겠어.
여: 바로 그거야.

문제 해결

아마추어 체스 대회의 개최 기간(3월 18일부터 28일까지), 개최 장소(City Culture Hall), 리그 종류(성인 리그와 주니어 리그), 우승 상품(세계 체스 대회의 참가권과 여행 왕복표)는 언급되었지만, ③ '참가비'는 언급되지 않았다.

어휘·표현

tournament 토너먼트, 승자 진출전   participate in ~에 참가하다   enter (대회 등에) 출전하다, 참가하다   admission 참가, 입장   round-trip 왕복 여행
incredible 믿을 수 없는   That's the spirit. 바로 그거야.(격려의 표현)

09 ②

담화 내용 불일치

여: 주목하세요, 학생 여러분. 보건 선생님인 Savina Jean입니다. 오늘 미세 먼지 수치가 높습니다. 여러분에게 그에 따라서 어떤 행동을 취해야 하는지 알려 주겠습니다. 외부 체육 수업은 취소되었습니다. 그러므로 오늘 체육 수업이 있으면 실내 체육관으로 출석하세요. 우리 학교는 공기 청정 시스템이 갖춰져 있어서 건물 안에서는 마스크를 쓸 필요가 없습니다. 모든 창문을 닫아 두세요. 하지만 오후에 환기를 위해 잠시 동안만 창문을 열어 주세요. 공기 청정 시스템이 작동중이기 때문에 창문을 열 때 걱정할 필요는 없습니다. 손을 자주 씻고 목이 따끔하면 따뜻한 물로 입안을 헹구십시오. 만약 눈이 간지럽다면, 보건실에서 안약을 받을 수 있습니다. 주목해 주어서 고맙습니다. 건강한 하루 되세요.

문제 해결

② 학교 건물에 공기 청정 시스템이 있어서 건물 내에서는 마스크를 쓸 필요가 없다고 하였다.

어휘·표현

fine dust 미세 먼지   accordingly 그에 따라서   report to ~에 출두하다, 출석하다   ventilation 환기   sore 따가운   itchy 간지러운   eye drops 안약

10 ②

도표 정보 파악

여: Camellia 빵집에 어서 오세요. 도와드릴까요?
남: 네, 제 아이를 위한 케이크를 찾고 있어요.
여: 이것들이 제일 인기 있는 것들입니다. 아이가 어떤 맛을 좋아하나요? 우리는 초콜릿, 치즈, 과일 맛이 있습니다.
남: 음, 그 애는 치즈와 초콜릿을 좋아해요.
여: 그렇군요. 특별한 모양이라도 생각하고 계신가요?
남: 음, 둥근 것만 빼고 어느 모양도 괜찮아요. 아시다시피, 아이들은 케이크가 멋지고 재미있어 보이길 원하잖아요.
여: 그럼요. 어느 정도의 가격대를 생각하고 계신가요?
남: 음, 30달러 이상은 쓰고 싶지 않아요.
여: 그러면 이 두 가지 중에 고르실 수 있어요.
남: 오, 케이크 위에 '축하해!'라는 말을 쓰고 싶어요.
여: 그러면 이것이 유일한 선택입니다. 다른 것에는 모양을 망치기 때문에 글자를 쓸 수 없어요.
남: 알겠습니다, 그러면 그것을 살게요.

문제 해결

케이크를 받을 아이가 치즈와 초콜릿 맛을 좋아하고, 케이크는 둥근 모양이 아닌 다른 모양에, 가격은 30달러 이상이 아니어야 하고, 글자를 쓸 수 있는 것을 찾고 있으므로, 남자가 구매할 케이크는 ②이다.

어휘·표현

flavor 맛   price range 가격대   ruin 망치다

11 ⑤

짧은 대화의 응답

여: 아빠, 아빠 직장에 계신 어떤 분이 제 노트북을 고쳐 주실 수도 있다고 말씀하셨어요?
남: 그래, 내 동료에게 너무 바쁘지 않으면 봐 달라고 부탁할 수 있단다.
여: 그러면, 내일 노트북을 직장에 가져가실 수 있나요? 노트북이 점점 느려져서요.
남: 그러마. 그것을 고치는 데 며칠 걸릴 수도 있단다.

남자가 직장 동료에게 노트북을 봐 달라 부탁할 수 있다고 하자 여자가 자신의 노트북을 직장에 가져가 줄 수 있냐고 물었으므로, 그럴 수 있고 노트북을 고치는 데는 며칠 걸릴 수 있다고 말하는 ⑤가 남자의 응답으로 가장 적절하다.

① 아니야. 너는 내 노트북을 가질 수 없단다.
② 미안하지만, 나는 그것을 어떻게 고치는지 모른단다.
③ 그래. 우리는 이번 주말에 새것을 살 수 있어.
④ 좋아. 이게 내가 요청했던 최신 모델이야.

colleague 동료   **latest** 최신의

12 ③

남: Stella, 너 괜찮니? 네 차가 도로에서 고장이 났다고 들었어.
여: 난 괜찮아, 그런데 내 차는 그렇지 않네. 그건 견인되었고 수리가 필요해.
남: 오, 저런. 당분간 차를 태워 줄까? 내가 너랑 멀지 않은 곳에 살잖아.
여: 너 정말 친절하구나. 그런데 난 차를 빌릴까 해.

자가용이 고장 난 여자에게 집이 가까우니 당분간 차를 태워 주겠다고 남자가 제안하고 있다. 이에 대한 여자의 응답으로 그런 말을 한 남자가 정말 친절하지만 당분간 차를 빌릴 생각이라는 ③이 가장 적절하다.

① 그런 건 아냐. 내 차가 아직 그렇게 오래되진 않았어.
② 나도 알아. 부주의한 운전은 정말 위험해.
④ 네 말이 맞아. 때때로 교통 표지판은 참 헷갈려.
⑤ 나도 동의해. 정기적인 차량 점검은 정말 중요해.

break down 고장 나다   **get towed away** 견인되다   **ride** (탈것 따위) 타기, 타고 가기   **rent** (사용료를 내고 단기간) 빌리다   **confusing** 헷갈리는

13 ⑤

남: 여보, 여기 좀 도와줘요! 나 침실에 있어요.
여: 와! 이 옷들로 뭐하고 있는 거예요?
남: 난 옷장을 청소 중이예요. 이것들은 내가 더 이상 안 입는 옷들이에요.
여: 음… 당신은 이걸로 뭐 할 거예요?
남: 당연히 버릴려고 하는데요.
여: 그것들은 여전히 좋은 상태인 것으로 보이는데요. 특히 양복들이요. 그 옷들을 Open Closet에 기부하는 게 어때요?
남: Open Closet이요? 들어 본 적 없어요. 그거 자선 단체예요?
여: 네. 그곳은 정장이나 양복을 모아요.
남: 왜 정장만 모으는 거죠?
여: 그곳은 취업 면접용 정장을 살 여력이 없는 젊은이들에게 정장을 빌려줘요.
남: 와. 정말 좋은 생각이네요. 내 옷을 어떻게 그 자선 단체에 보내죠?
여: 그 자선 단체의 홈페이지에 당신의 주소를 입력하면 거기서 당신에게 상자를 보내 줄 거예요.

남자가 안 입는 옷을 어떻게 자선 단체에 보낼 수 있냐고 물었으므로, 이에 대한 여자의 응답으로 홈페이지에 주소를 입력하면 상자를 보내 줄 거라는 ⑤가 가장 적절하다.

① 당신은 어떤 스타일과 색이 당신에게 어울리는지 알아내야 해요.
② 당신은 중고 가게에서 정장을 사는 것으로 돈을 절약할 수 있어요.
③ 당신은 상황에 따라 적절한 옷을 입어야 해요.
④ 당신은 정장을 입음으로써 사람들에게 전문적인 인상을 줄 수 있어요.

wardrobe 옷장   **suit** 정장; 어울리다   **charity** 자선 단체   **formal** 격식을 차린   **enter** 입력하다, 기입하다   **occasion** 경우, 때   **impression** 인상

14 ③

여: Jake, 너는 Maple 거리에 새 멕시코 식당이 열린 것 알았니?
남: 응, 내 친구 중 한 명이 거기 갔었어. 음식이 훌륭했다고 했어.
여: 그 말을 들으니 좋네. 거기 내 친구의 식당이야.
남: 와! 내가 들은 바로는, 네 친구가 재능 있는 요리사임에 틀림없어.
여: 저녁 먹으러 거기 가 보는 게 어때? 나 아직 가 보지 못했거든.
남: 좋아. 네 친구의 개업을 축하하기 위해 선물을 가져가자.
여: 좋은 생각이야. 어떤 선물이 좋을까?
남: 그림은 어때? 네 친구가 식당 벽면에 그것을 걸 수 있을 거야.
여: 하지만 그것이 실내 장식과 안 어울리면 어쩌지?
남: 그러면, 식물 화분은 어때? 그녀가 식당 안이나 밖에 둘 수 있잖아.
여: 그거 좋은 생각이다! 어디서 살 수 있는지 아니?
남: 물론이지. Maple 거리로 가는 길에 화원이 있어.

식당을 연 친구에게 개업을 축하하는 선물로 화분을 사기로 한 상황에서 화분을 어디서 살 수 있는지 아냐고 물었으므로 ③ '물론이지. Maple 거리로 가는 길에 화원이 있어.'가 응답으로 가장 적절하다.

① 물론이지! 내가 이국적인 음식을 시도하는 걸 좋아하는 거 너도 알잖아!
② 문제없어. 나는 식물을 건강하게 하는 법을 알아.
④ 미안. 나는 네 친구에게 어떤 선물이 좋을지 모르겠어.
⑤ 걱정 마. 새 멕시코 식당은 포장 음식을 제공해.

talented 재능 있는   **decor** 실내 장식   **exotic** 이국적인, 외국의

15 ⑤

여: Jason은 학교 방송부의 일원이고 그는 비디오 영상을 만드는 데 재능이 있다. 그는 학교 행사를 녹화하는 것을 책임지고 있다. 동영상 장면을 만드는 것이 필요한 작업이 있을 때마다, 동아리 부원들이 그에게 그 일을 하도록 부탁하는 것이 자연스럽다. 그러나 그는 너무 바빠지고 지쳤으며 또한 그의 일을 당연하게 생각하는 사람들에게 화가 난다. Amelia는 Jason의 좋은 친구이다. 그는 그녀에게 그의 문제를 이야기하고 그녀에게 도움을 요청한다. Amelia는 그가 동아리 부원들에게 그의 상황에 대해서 이야기하고 그들이 일을 같이 하도록 제안해야 한다고 생각한다. 이러한 상황에서, Amelia는 Jason에게 무엇이라고 말할 것 같은가?

Amelia는 동아리 일이 많아 힘들어하는 Jason이 동아리 부원들에게 자신의 상황을 이야기하고 일을 같이 하자고 말해야 한다고 생각하므로, ⑤ '너는 부원들에게 네 기분이 어떤지를 이야기하고 그들에게 함께 일을 하자고 요청해야 해.'가 Amelia가 Jason에게 할 말로 가장 적절하다.

① 너의 상황에 대해 선생님과 상담해 보는 것은 어때?
② 너는 동아리 활동보다는 공부에 더 집중해야 할 필요가 있어.

③ 너의 재능으로 영화를 제작하는 데서 경력을 쌓는 게 어때?
④ 너는 방송부를 그만두고 네가 하고 싶은 것을 해야 해.

어휘·표현

broadcasting 방송   record 녹화하다   exhausted 기진맥진한
take ~ for granted ~을 당연하게 여기다

16-17 복합 이해

남: 안녕하세요, 학생 여러분. 지난주에 우리는 플라스틱 공해가 어떻게 우리 환경에 주된 위협이 되었고 우리의 몸에 어떤 영향을 미치는지를 배웠습니다. 오늘, 저는 우리가 우리의 일상생활 안에서 어떻게 플라스틱을 줄일 수 있는지 이야기하고 싶습니다. 첫 번째로, 여러분은 자신만의 재사용 가능한 물병을 가지고 다닐 수 있습니다. 플라스틱 병은 세계 바다에서 발견되는 쓰레기의 상위 3위 중 하나입니다. 여러분이 자기 병을 가지고 다니는 것은 엄청난 양의 플라스틱 쓰레기를 줄여 줄 것입니다. 플라스틱 빨대 또한 중대한 문제여서 많은 커피숍들이 더 이상 빨대를 제공하지 않습니다. 대신에, 영리하고 사려 깊은 소비자들은 스테인리스 빨대나 대나무 빨대를 삽니다. 우리가 입는 것 또한 플라스틱 공해를 줄이는 데 중요한 역할을 할 수 있습니다. 예를 들어, 폴리에스테르와 같은 합성 섬유로 만들어진 옷은 세탁할 때 많은 미세 플라스틱을 만들어 내므로, 천연 섬유의 옷을 사는 것이 중요합니다. 마지막으로 요즘 우리는 예쁜 친환경 가방을 사서 비닐봉지 대신에 그것들을 사용할 수 있습니다.

어휘·표현

threat 위협   reusable 재사용할 수 있는   natural fabric 천연 섬유
synthetic 합성의   microplastic 미세 플라스틱

16 ③

문제 해결

플라스틱 공해를 줄이기 위해 우리가 할 수 있는 일을 나열하고 있으므로, 남자가 하는 말의 주제로 ③ '우리가 어떻게 플라스틱 공해를 줄일 수 있는가'가 가장 적절하다.
① 플라스틱 공해가 왜 위험한가
② 미세 플라스틱은 우리의 몸에 어떤 영향을 끼치는가
④ 어떤 종류의 상품이 플라스틱으로 만들어지는가
⑤ 플라스틱 산업은 어떻게 그렇게 성공하게 되었나

17 ③

문제 해결

대나무 빨대는 스테인리스 빨대와 같이 언급되었으나 ③ 대나무 칫솔은 언급되지 않았다.

01 ②	02 ③	03 ②	04 ⑤	05 ①	06 ④
07 ③	08 ④	09 ③	10 ②	11 ①	12 ②
13 ⑤	14 ③	15 ④	16 ②	17 ④	

01 ② 목적 파악

남: 안녕하세요, 학생 여러분. 저는 환경을 위한 학생 단체인 Saving Us의 의장인 Thomas Smith입니다. 우리는 학생들이 환경에 대한 피해를 줄이도록 도울 수 있는 다양한 방법에 집중하고 있습니다. 많은 학생들이 버스를 타서 학교에 오고, 재활용 종이로 만든 공책을 구입하고, 학교에 재사용할 수 있는 물병을 가져옴으로써 우리를 지지하고 있습니다. 여러분의 협조에 감사드리지만, 아직도 활동, 캠페인, 그리고 자금을 모으는 행사를 조직하고 도울 손길이 부족합니다. 그래서 우리의 조직에 새로운 회원을 모집하고 있습니다. 그들은 우리 조직이 후원하는 모든 행사에서 중요한 역할을 할 것입니다. 환경을 보호하는 데 있어서 능동적인 역할을 맡아 보시는 건 어떨까요? 감사합니다.

문제 해결

남자는 환경 단체에서 일할 새로운 회원들을 모집하고 있다.

어휘·표현

organization 조직, 단체   reduce 줄이다   recycled 재활용된   reusable 재사용할 수 있는   cooperation 협조   fund-raising 기금을 모으는   recruit 모집하다   sponsor 후원하다

02 ③ 주제 파악

여: 안녕, Benjamin! 여기서 널 만날 줄 몰랐네!
남: 오, 안녕, Gloria. 너도 운동하러 여기에 오는구나?
여: 그래, 나는 이곳의 오랜 회원이야. 오, 넌 땀을 많이 흘리는구나.
남: 응, 그러네. 난 요즘 운동하면서 체형을 관리하기 위해 열심히 노력하고 있어.
여: 좋아. 하지만 운동할 때 명심해야 할 것이 있어.
남: 음, 휴식의 중요성에 관해 이야기하려고 하니? 난 운동할 때 정기적으로 휴식을 취하고 있어.
여: 이번에는 아니야. 운동할 때 탈수의 위험을 피하기 위해서 충분한 물을 마실 것을 명심해야 해.
남: 정말? 내가 그렇게 하면, 그것이 나의 운동 흐름을 깨지는 않을까?
여: 아니야. 사실, 적절한 물 공급 없이는 너의 근육은 쉽게 피곤해질 수 있어.
남: 무슨 말인지 알겠어. 충고 고마워.
여: 천만에. 여기서 자주 보길 바라.

문제 해결

여자는 운동할 때 충분한 물을 마셔야 한다고 충고하고 있으므로, 여자의 의견으로 ③이 가장 적절하다.

어휘·표현

work out 운동하다   sweat 땀 흘리다   keep in shape 체형을 유지하다
dehydration 탈수   flow 흐름   fatigue 피로케 하다

03 ②
관계 추론

[휴대 전화벨이 울린다.]

남: 여보세요, Anderson 씨. 잘 지내시죠?

여: 안녕하세요. Jackson 씨. 저는 막 새 책의 집필을 마쳤습니다.

남: 잘 됐네요. 이번에는 무엇에 관한 것인가요?

여: 범죄 수사에 관한 거예요. 수사관의 변화하는 마음에 초점을 맞추었어요.

남: 흥미롭게 들리네요. 언제 출판될 예정인가요?

여: 출판업자가 한 달 내에 발간할 거예요. 그래서 전 표지를 위한 사진이 필요해요. 제 사진을 찍어 주시겠어요?

남: 물론이죠. 정식 초상화 사진을 원하세요?

여: 네. 저는 재킷을 입을 거예요.

남: 좋습니다. 전 오늘 오후와 내일 하루 종일 시간이 있습니다. 언제 가게에 들르실 수 있으세요?

여: 오늘 오후에는 편집장과 회의가 있습니다. 내일 오전에 들러도 될까요?

남: 좋습니다. 그리고 촬영 후에 모닝커피 한 잔 대접할게요.

여: 매우 친절하시네요. 곧 뵙겠습니다.

문제 해결

여자는 자신의 새 책 표지에 실릴 사진을 찍으러 남자를 방문하기로 했으므로, 남자와 여자는 사진사와 작가의 관계이다.

어휘·표현

criminal investigation 범죄 수사   psyche 마음, 정신   investigator 수사관   publisher 출판업자   release 발간하다   come by 들르다(=drop by)

04 ⑤
그림 불일치 파악

여: 흥미로운 사진이네요! 당신은 승마하러 갔었나요?

남: 네. 우리는 지난주에 제주도에 가서 말을 탈 수 있는 장소를 방문했어요.

여: 재미있어 보이네요. '말을 타세요, 꿈을 타세요.'라고 쓰인 울타리 위 슬로건이 보이네요.

남: 맞아요. 그것은 승마 코스의 슬로건이었어요.

여: 말을 타고 있는 소녀가 여동생, Carol이군요, 그렇죠?

남: 네. 그녀가 말 타기를 좀 무서워해서, 아빠가 그녀를 위해 고삐를 잡고 있어요.

여: 당신은 사진 속에서 무엇을 하고 있나요?

남: 보다시피, 난 말에게 먹일 건초를 나르고 있어요.

여: 건초가 무거워 보이는데요.

남: 사실, 내가 쉽게 그것을 옮길 수 있었어요. 말에게 먹이를 주고 계신 우리 엄마가 보이시나요?

여: 네, 그녀가 즐거워하시는 것 같군요. 당신 가족은 그곳에서 잊지 못할 경험을 했음에 틀림없군요.

남: 그렇고말고요.

문제 해결

엄마가 말에게 먹이를 주고 있다고 했으나 사진에서는 사진을 찍고 있으므로, ⑤가 대화의 내용과 일치하지 않는다.

어휘·표현

horseback riding 승마   banner 슬로건   rein 고삐   hay 건초

05 ①
부탁한 일 파악

[휴대 전화벨이 울린다.]

남: 안녕하세요, Susan.

여: 안녕하세요, Parker 씨. Green Grocery와의 계약은 어떻게 되었나요?

남: 잘 진행되었어요. 우리는 다음 주부터 더 신선한 채소를 공급받을 거예요.

여: 잘 되었네요. 출장 연회 서비스를 주문한 고객은 만나셨어요?

남: 아직 못 만났어요. 바로 지금 그를 기다리고 있어요.

여: 알겠습니다. 음, China Dinnerware 회사에서 방금 전화해서 우리가 주문한 식기류 세트가 오늘 오후에 배달될 거라고 했어요.

남: 좋아요, 하지만 제가 제 시간에 돌아갈 수 있을지 확실하지 않네요. 저 대신 그 배달을 받아 주시겠어요?

여: 문제없어요. 저는 오후 내내 식당에 있을 거예요.

남: 고맙습니다, Susan. 회의가 끝나면 바로 돌아갈게요.

여: 천천히 하세요. 제가 식탁을 정리할게요.

남: 좋아요. 식당에서 봐요.

문제 해결

남자는 여자에게 오후에 배달되는 식기류를 대신 받아 줄 것을 부탁하였다.

어휘·표현

catering 음식 공급   as we speak 바로 지금   dinnerware 식기류   arrange 정리하다

06 ④
숫자 정보 파악

여: Fly Away 항공사에 오신 것을 환영합니다. 어떻게 도와 드릴까요?

남: 안녕하세요. 애틀랜타에서 뉴욕으로 가는 비행편을 예약하고 싶습니다.

여: 네. 여행하실 날짜가 언제인가요?

남: 5월 3일에 떠나고 싶습니다. 표가 얼마죠?

여: 음…. 성인 한 명당 150달러입니다.

남: 알겠습니다. 음, 아동 할인이 있나요?

여: 네, 7세 미만 아동은 10% 할인됩니다. 여행하시는 일행이 몇 명이신가요?

남: 어른 두 명과 6세 아이 한 명입니다.

여: 좋습니다. 잠시만요. 그날에는 오후 4시가 가능한 출발 시간입니다. 괜찮으시겠습니까?

남: 네. 비상 탈출구 옆 자리로 예약할 수 있을까요?

여: 네. 그 경우에는, 개인당 10달러가 더 듭니다.

남: 좋습니다. 그 좌석으로 예약할게요.

문제 해결

어른 두 명에 300달러, 아동 한 명은 10% 할인된 135달러, 그리고 개인당 10달러씩의 추가 요금이 있으므로, 남자가 지불할 항공료는 총 465달러이다.

어휘·표현

departure time 출발 시간   emergency exit 비상 탈출구

07 ③
이유 파악

남: Jessica, 네가 지난주에 뉴욕에서 취업 면접을 봤다고 들었어.

여: 응, 그랬어. 난 어제 막 돌아왔어.

남: 면접은 어떻게 됐니?

여: 음, 잘 진행되었어. 사실, 그들이 즉석에서 나에게 일자리를 제안했어.

남: 축하해. 그것은 네가 항상 원했던 일이잖아.

여: 사실이야, 하지만 난 아직 그 일자리 제의에 대해 결심을 하지 못했어.
남: 정말? 이해가 안 되는데. 네가 생각했던 것보다 급료가 낮니?
여: 아니, 그것은 아냐. 급료는 내가 지급 받는 것보다 훨씬 높을 거야.
남: 그러면, 뭐가 문제니? 복지가 좋지 않니?
여: 사실, 복지는 훌륭해. 단지 내가 이곳을 떠나고 싶지 않을 뿐이야. 이
 곳은 내가 태어나서 자란 곳이잖아.
남: 알겠다. 낯선 도시에서 새로운 삶을 시작하는 것은 결코 쉽지 않지.
여: 맞아. 난 어떻게 해야 할지 모르겠어.

문제 해결

여자는 태어나서 자란 곳을 떠나고 싶지 않다고 하였으므로, 여자가 취업 결정을
망설이는 이유로 ③이 가장 적절하다.

어휘·표현

on the spot 즉석에서   benefits (회사에서 직원에게 제공하는) 복리 후생

08 ④
언급 유무 파악

남: Lynn, 오늘 그 스웨터를 입으니 멋져 보인다.
여: 고마워. Main가에 있는 Coco Mall에서 그것을 구입했어.
남: 그곳에는 어떤 종류의 옷을 파니?
여: 재킷부터, 바지, 티셔츠, 모자까지 거의 모든 것을 판매해.
남: 와. 나도 그곳에 가 보고 싶다. 그 쇼핑몰은 매일 열지, 그렇지?
여: 맞아, 그곳은 오전 10시에 열고 오후 9시에 닫아. 너는 늦어도 오후 6
 시나 7시까지 거기에 도착해야 해.
남: 알겠어. 그곳의 가격은 어때?
여: 가격은 상당히 괜찮아. 백화점보다 훨씬 저렴해.
남: 좋은데. 주차 공간은 충분하니?
여: 물론이지. 그게 내가 거기에 가는 이유야. 항상 주차 공간이 많이 있어.
남: 음, 바쁘지 않으면 다음번에 그곳에 같이 갈래?
여: 물론이지. 재미있겠다.

문제 해결

Coco Mall의 위치, 판매 품목, 영업시간, 주차 시설에 관한 언급은 있지만, 개
장 연도에 관한 언급은 없다.

어휘·표현

absolutely 물론   plenty of 많은

09 ③
담화 내용 불일치

여: 안녕하세요, 신입생 여러분! 저는 Waldorf 학생회 회장인 Laura
 Williams입니다. 여러분이 고대하던 Waldorf Rose Festival이 이
 번 금요일 오전 10시부터 오후 9시까지 열립니다. 우리는 여러분, 즉
 입학하는 신입생을 위한 환영식으로 축제를 시작할 것입니다. 버스킹
 쇼, 마술쇼, 힙합 댄스, 그리고 어쿠스틱 밴드 콘서트와 같은 멋진 공
 연도 있을 것입니다. 어쿠스틱 밴드 콘서트를 제외하고는, 입장권 없
 이 모든 공연을 즐길 수 있습니다. 또한 여러분은 운동장에 있는 야외
 식당에서 점심을 먹을 수도 있습니다. 작년에는 저녁에 불꽃놀이가
 있었지만, 올해는 여러분의 소망을 담은 풍등을 띄우게 될 것입니다.
 여러분 모두 오셔서 신나는 이 행사를 즐기시기를 바랍니다!

문제 해결

어쿠스틱 밴드 콘서트를 제외한 모든 공연을 입장권 없이 즐길 수 있다는 말은,
어쿠스틱 밴드 콘서트는 입장권이 필요하다는 뜻이다.

어휘·표현

newcomer 신입생   kick off 시작하다   incoming 들어오는
admission ticket 입장권   fireworks display 불꽃놀이   sky lantern 풍등

10 ②
도표 정보 파악

남: 안녕하세요. 어떻게 도와드릴까요?
여: 안녕하세요. 우산을 좀 사려고 하는데요. 제 결혼식에 오실 손님들에
 게 선물로 드리고 싶어서요.
남: 오, 축하드립니다! 여기 우산을 보여 주는 팸플릿이 있습니다. 어떤
 무늬를 선호하세요?
여: 음…. 물방울무늬는 다소 요란하고요. 다른 것은 괜찮은 것 같습니다.
남: 좋습니다. 크기는요?
여: 음, 저는 26인치보다 더 큰 우산은 원하지 않습니다. 큰 우산은 휴대
 하기가 불편해요.
남: 알겠습니다. 그러면, 접는 우산은 어떠신가요?
여: 좋아요. 손님들이 그것을 가방 안에 가지고 다닐 수 있을 거예요.
남: 훌륭한 선택입니다. 모든 접는 우산은 버튼을 누르면 펼쳐집니다.
 가격대는 어느 정도 생각하시나요?
여: 제가 적어도 100개를 구입해야 해서, 개당 10달러를 넘게 쓰고 싶지
 는 않습니다.
남: 좋습니다. 그러면, 이 모델이 손님께 적합하네요. 오늘 주문하시면, 3
 일 이내에 배달해 드리겠습니다.
여: 좋아요. 오늘 주문할게요.

문제 해결

여자는 물방울무늬는 원하지 않고, 26인치보다 작으며, 접을 수 있고, 가격이
10달러 이하의 것을 원하고 있으므로, 여자가 주문할 우산으로 ②가 가장 적절
하다.

어휘·표현

brochure 팸플릿, 소책자   polka-dot 물방울무늬   loud 요란한
inconvenient 불편한   foldable 접을 수 있는   price range 가격대   place
an order 주문하다

11 ①
짧은 대화의 응답

남: Nancy. 핼러윈 때 무엇을 할 거니?
여: 조카딸과 조카를 데리고 trick or treat 놀이를 하러 다닐 거야.
남: 재미있겠는데! 그들을 어디로 데리고 갈 거니?
여: 아마 이웃을 돌아다닐 것 같아.

문제 해결

핼러윈 때 조카들을 데리고 어디를 갈 것인지를 묻는 남자에 말에 대한 여자의
응답으로는 ① '아마 이웃을 돌아다닐 것 같아.'가 가장 적절하다.
② 우리는 영웅이나 마녀처럼 차려입을 거야.
③ 핼러윈 파티에 와 줘서 고마워.
④ 음, 우리는 그날에 trick or treat 놀이를 하지 않을 거야.
⑤ 아이들이 단 것을 너무 많이 먹는 것은 좋지 않아.

어휘·표현

niece 조카딸   nephew 조카   trick-or-treat 핼러윈 데이에 아이들이 괴상한 복
장을 하고 이웃집을 돌아다니며 'trick-or-treat(과자 안 주면 장난칠 테야')'이라고 말하
며 간식류를 얻으러 다니는 놀이   dress up 차려입다   sweet 단 것

12 ②

짧은 대화의 응답

여: 안녕, Adam. 무슨 일로 왔니?
남: 안녕, Karen. 오늘 오후에 네 노트북을 빌릴 수 있을까? 내 것이 지금 작동이 안 돼.
여: 미안하지만, 나는 오늘 이 기말 보고서를 마쳐야 해.
남: 괜찮아. 내가 다른 사람에게 물어볼게.

문제 해결

남자는 여자에게서 노트북을 빌리려고 했으나 여자가 자신도 노트북을 사용해야 한다고 말하고 있으므로, 이에 대한 남자의 응답으로는 ② '괜찮아. 내가 다른 사람에게 물어볼게.'가 가장 적절하다.
① 안됐다. 그것을 빨리 고쳐야겠구나.
③ 고마워. 가능하면 빨리 돌려줄게.
④ 문제없어. 네가 내 것을 빌려가는 건 환영이야.
⑤ 잘됐다. 네가 내일 그것을 마치기를 바랄게.

어휘·표현

laptop 노트북 (컴퓨터)   term paper 학기말 리포트   fix 고치다

13 ⑤

긴 대화의 응답

여: Mike, 왜 한밤중에 여행 가방을 싸고 있니?
남: 죄송해요, 엄마. 깨우려고 했던 것은 아니에요.
여: 괜찮아. 자고 있지 않았어.
남: 저 내일 호주로 출장을 가야 해요. 말씀드리지 않아 죄송하지만, 일정이 갑자기 생겼어요.
여: 알겠다. 짐은 다 꾸렸니?
남: 거의 다 했어요, 하지만 뭔가 잊은 것 같아 걱정돼요.
여: 잠시만. 수건, 칫솔, 치약, 와이셔츠 몇 벌, 바지 몇 벌, 재킷 두 벌, 코트, 그리고 카디건. 와, 넌 정말 많은 옷을 가져가는구나.
남: 아시다시피, 제가 추위에 매우 민감하잖아요.
여: 알지만, 호주는 지금 여름이란다.
남: 오, 정말요? 그러면 불필요한 옷을 좀 빼야겠어요.

문제 해결

남자가 호주 출장 준비로 여행 가방에 재킷, 코트, 카디건 등을 챙겨 넣은 것을 보고 여자는 호주가 지금 여름이라고 알려 주었다. 이에 대한 남자의 응답으로는 ⑤ '오, 정말요? 그러면 불필요한 옷을 좀 빼야겠어요.'가 가장 적절하다.
① 잔소리하지 마세요. 전 오늘 떠나지는 않아요.
② 이런. 당신이 내일 떠나는 것을 깜박했어요.
③ 도와주셔서 감사해요. 돌아오면 봬요.
④ 괜찮아요. 저는 그쪽의 추운 날씨를 견딜 수 있어요.

어휘·표현

suitcase 여행 가방   come up 생기다, 발생하다   sensitive 민감한   nag 잔소리하다   withstand 참다, 견디다

14 ③

긴 대화의 응답

남: 여보, 우리가 마침내 해변에 와 있네요. 우리가 이것을 정말 고대해 왔잖아요.
여: 그래요. 우리가 해변에 있었던 마지막 때가 기억나지 않네요.
남: 그런데, 왜 당신은 아직도 화면을 보고 있어요?
여: 미안해요, Scott. 이메일을 확인하고 있어요.
남: 설마 진심은 아니지요. 이러지 마요! 당신은 휴식이 필요해요.

여: 알아요, 하지만 저는 단지 동료들이 프로젝트에 관해 이메일을 보냈는지 확인하고 싶어요.
남: 내 생각에는 당신이 이곳에 있는 동안에는 이메일을 확인하지 않아도 그들이 이해할 거예요.
여: 물론 그렇죠. 그들은 저에게 즐겁게 보내고 일에 관해서는 잠시 잊으라고 말했어요.
남: 그게 내가 당신에게 말하려는 거예요. 지금은 노트북 없이 진정한 휴가를 즐길 시간이라고요.
여: 음, 당신이 옳아요. 우리는 지금 멋진 해변에 와 있으니까요.
남: 그렇고말고요. 잠시 물에 들어가는 게 어때요?
여: 좋아요. 지금 당장 노트북을 끌게요.

문제 해결

업무에 관해서는 잊고 해변에 왔으니 물에 들어가 보라는 남자의 말에 대한 여자의 응답으로 ③ '좋아요. 지금 당장 노트북을 끌게요.'가 가장 적절하다.
① 맞아요. 나는 노트북을 갖고 왔어야 해요.
② 유감스럽지만 난 지금 몇 통의 이메일을 확인해야 해요.
④ 트레킹 대신에 다음번에는 해변에 가는 게 낫겠어요.
⑤ 물론이죠. 난 휴가 기간에 당신이 일 하는 걸 원치 않아요.

어휘·표현

look forward to ~을 고대하다   colleague 동료   take a dip 잠시 물에 들어가다, 잠깐 수영을 하다

15 ④

상황에 적절한 말

남: Jeff는 독서를 정말 좋아해서 대학을 졸업하고 시내에 서점을 열었다. 처음에는 많은 손님들이 특히, 고등학생들이 서점을 많이 방문했다. 하지만, 얼마 후 그의 서점 근처에 또 다른 서점이 문을 열었고 고객의 숫자가 줄기 시작했다. Jeff는 큰 손실을 보고 사업을 접을 수밖에 없었다. 그의 대학 친구인 Samuel은 이 소식을 듣고 Jeff를 방문했다. Jeff의 얼굴은 실망으로 가득 차 있었고, 그는 Samuel을 보자마자 눈물을 글썽거렸다. Samuel은 경기가 최악의 상황이라 많은 작은 사업체들이 힘든 시기를 겪고 있다고 생각한다. 그는 Jeff를 위로하고, 또 다른 시도를 하도록 그를 격려하고 싶어 한다. 이런 상황에서, Samuel은 Jeff에게 무엇이라고 말할 것 같은가?

문제 해결

Jeff는 서점 문을 닫고 실망해 있으며 Samuel은 그런 Jeff를 격려하려고 하는 상황이므로, Samuel이 할 말로 ④ '힘 내! 실패는 다시 시작할 수 있는 기회야.'가 가장 적절하다.
① 너는 더 열심히 일했어야 했어.
② 나를 격려해 줘서 고마워.
③ 졸업 후에 사업을 시작하는 게 너무 늦은 것은 아니야.
⑤ 너의 서점이 매일 더욱 더 번창하고 있구나.

어휘·표현

before long 머지않아, 얼마 후   be forced to ~할 수밖에 없다
disappointment 실망   console 위로하다   prosperous 번영한, 번창한

16-17

복합 이해

여: 안녕하세요. 학생 여러분. 지난 강의에서 저는 불면증, 몽유병, 그리고 야뇨증과 같은 다양한 수면 장애에 대해 이야기했습니다. 양질의 수면을 취하는 것은 여러분의 전반적인 건강을 위해 굉장히 중요합니다. 그래서 오늘은 여러분에게 숙면하는 방법에 대해 이야기하려고

합니다. 첫 번째로, 낮 동안에 규칙적으로 운동하는 것은 불면증의 증상을 경감시켜 줍니다. 심지어 산책과 같은 가벼운 운동도 수면의 질을 향상시켜 줍니다. 또한, 따뜻한 우유와 같은 특정한 음식과 음료는 사실상 여러분이 좀 더 깊게 잠들 수 있도록 도울 수 있습니다. 밤에 마시는 캐모마일이나 페퍼민트 차 한 잔은 완벽하게 이완시켜 주는 의식일 수 있습니다. 잠들기 전에 키위와 같은 과일을 먹는 것은 여러분의 수면 시간을 다소 늘려 줄 수 있습니다. 아몬드를 규칙적으로 먹는 것은 수면의 질을 증가시키는 데 도움이 될 수 있다고 보고됩니다. 마지막으로, 평화로운 취침 시간의 일상이 이제는 하루의 스트레스를 버리고 잠자리에 들 시간이라고 여러분의 뇌에 강력한 신호를 보낸다는 것을 기억해야 합니다. 이제 숙면을 위한 적절한 환경을 형성하는 것에 관한 비디오 영상을 보여 드리겠습니다.

어휘·표현

sleep disorder 수면 장애   insomnia 불면증(=sleeplessness)
sleepwalking 몽유병   bed-wetting 야뇨증   symptom 증상   ritual 의식
duration 지속, 기간   let go of ~을 놓아 주다   misconception 오해

16 ②

문제 해결

여자는 숙면을 취하는 방법에 대해 이야기하고 있으므로, 여자가 하는 말의 주제로 ② '밤에 숙면을 촉진하는 방법'이 가장 적절하다.
① 수면 장애는 어디에서 오는가
③ 숙면을 위해 피해야 할 다양한 음식
④ 규칙적인 식사와 수면의 중요성
⑤ 불면증 예방에 대한 오해

17 ④

문제 해결

숙면과 관련된 음식으로 바나나는 언급되지 않았다.

---

01 ④	02 ①	03 ④	04 ④	05 ③	06 ④
07 ④	08 ⑤	09 ④	10 ①	11 ③	12 ②
13 ②	14 ②	15 ③	16 ①	17 ⑤	

01 ④   목적 파악

남: 신사 숙녀 여러분! 저는 도서관 수석 관장 Robert Brown입니다. 저는 오늘 여러분께 말하게 되어 영광입니다. 거의 2년 동안의 공사를 거쳐, 마침내 도서관이 지난주 금요일에 문을 열었습니다. 교내의 모든 학생들은 이제 새 도서관에서 독서와 공부를 즐길 수 있습니다. 이 5층 건물은 10만 권이 넘는 책을 소장하고 있고 최대 600명의 학생을 수용할 수 있습니다. 이 도서관은 또한 40개의 개인 어학 실습실과 다양한 방송 및 영화를 볼 수 있는 멀티미디어 센터를 갖추고 있습니다. 학교를 대표하여, 저는 여러분의 아낌 없는 기부에 대해 정말 감사를 표현하고 싶습니다. 학교 당국자들, 교사, 그리고 학생들은 여러분의 진심 어린 도움과 친절을 항상 감사하게 생각할 것입니다.

문제 해결

도서관의 수석 관장인 남자는 학교를 대표하여 도서관을 건설하는 데 기부를 한 사람들에게 감사를 표현하고 싶다고 했으므로, 남자가 하는 말의 목적으로 가장 적절한 것은 ④이다.

어휘·표현

be honored 영광스럽다   construction 공사, 건축   accommodate 수용하다   up to ~까지   be equipped with ~을 갖추고 있다   language lab 어학 실습실   on behalf of ~을 대신해서, ~을 대표하여   appreciation 감사, 고마움   generous 아끼지 않는, 너그러운   contribution 기부, 기여

02 ①   주제 파악

남: 여보, 정기 건강 검진의 결과를 받았나요?
여: 네, 받았어요. 다행히도 콜레스테롤 수치를 포함해서 모든 것이 좋아요.
남: 다행이네요. 당신이 최근 건강에 대해 걱정을 많이 했잖아요.
여: 그래요, 맞아요. 당신도 결과를 받았죠?
남: 네, 받았어요. 하지만 내 결과는 실망스러워요. 콜레스테롤 수치를 포함해서 모든 결과가 나쁘네요.
여: 음, 당신이 밤늦게 음식을 먹는 습관이 주요 원인인 것 같아요.
남: 그래요. 의사가 나에게 똑같은 말을 했어요.
여: 건강을 개선하고 싶다면, 당신은 그 습관을 고쳐야만 해요.
남: 당신 마치 의사처럼 말하는군요.
여: 난 진지하다고요. 당신이 계속해서 밤늦게 음식을 먹는다면, 건강은 점점 더 나빠질 것이에요.
남: 알았어요, 알았어요. 당신이 말한 것을 명심할게요.

문제 해결

건강 검진 결과가 나쁘다는 남자의 말에 여자는 밤늦게 음식을 먹는 습관 때문인 것 같다고 말하면서 남자에게 그 습관을 고쳐야 한다고 말했으므로, 여자의 의견으로 가장 적절한 것은 ①이다.

어휘·표현

regular check-up 정기 건강 검진   including ~을 포함하여

be responsible for ~에 책임이 있다, ~의 원인이다   keep ~ in mind ~을 명심하다

03 ④
관계 추론

여: 안녕하세요, 만나서 반가워요, Jackson 씨! 저는 Sally Brown입니다.
남: 안녕하세요, Sally! 저도 만나서 반가워요.
여: 서울을 방문하신 것이 이번이 처음이 아니라고 들었어요.
남: 맞아요. 관광을 하러 작년에 가족과 함께 여기 왔었어요. 우리는 정말로 좋은 시간을 보냈어요.
여: 다행이군요. 좋습니다, 이제 팬들을 위한 질문을 하겠습니다. 이번 배드민턴 선수권 대회에서 우승할 자신이 있나요?
남: 네, 있습니다. 저는 연습을 정말로 많이 했고, 현재 컨디션이 아주 좋습니다.
여: 알겠습니다. 사실, 저를 포함한 많은 기자들이 당신이 우승할 것이라고 생각합니다.
남: 고맙습니다. 여러분들을 실망시키지 않겠습니다.
여: 팬들에게 할 마지막 말이 있나요?
남: 음, 저를 응원해 주셔서 감사합니다. 대회에서 우승을 하기 위해 최선을 다하겠습니다.
여: 아주 좋습니다! 시간을 내 주셔서 감사하고, 행운을 빕니다!

문제 해결
남자를 인터뷰하는 여자가 자신을 포함한 많은 기자들이 남자가 우승할 거라고 생각한다고 하자, 남자는 고맙다고 하면서 배드민턴 대회에서 우승하기 위해 최선을 다하겠다고 말했다. 이로 보아, 여자는 기자이고, 남자는 배드민턴 선수임을 알 수 있다.

어휘·표현
sightseeing 관광   in condition 건강 상태가 좋은   let ~ down ~를 실망시키다

04 ④
그림 불일치 파악

남: Amber, 축제 포스터의 초안 작성을 끝냈나요?
여: 네, 다 했어요. 모니터를 한번 봐 주세요.
남: 음. 축제 표어인 '아웃도어 라이프를 즐깁시다!'를 포스터의 상단에 놓았군요.
여: 네. 그리고 축제가 언제 어디서 열리는지에 대한 정보를 표어 아래에 놓았어요.
남: 좋아요. 양쪽에 야자수는 왜 넣었죠?
여: 자연을 나타내고 싶었어요.
남: 알겠어요. 음. 왼쪽에 마라톤을 뛰는 소녀와 소년을 넣었군요.
여: 맞습니다. 청소년들이 야외에서 더 활동적이 될 것을 권장하고 싶어서요.
남: 아주 좋아요. 인상적이네요.
여: 고맙습니다. 오른쪽에서 스케이트보드를 타고 있는 남자는 어떠세요?
남: 그 남자도 마음에 들어요. 당신이 일을 잘 한 것 같아요.

문제 해결
왼쪽에 마라톤을 뛰는 소녀와 소년을 넣었다고 말했으므로, 자전거를 타고 있는 아이들인 ④가 대화의 내용과 일치하지 않는다.

어휘·표현
motto 표어, 좌우명   take place (계획된 일이) 개최되다, 일어나다   palm tree

야자수   represent 나타내다   run a marathon 마라톤을 뛰다

05 ③
할 일 파악

여: Robin, 오늘 병원에 갔었니?
남: 네, 엄마. 오후에 병원에 갔었어요.
여: 잘했구나. 의사가 뭐라고 했어?
남: 제가 독감에 걸렸다고 말했고, 약을 처방해 주었어요.
여: 약을 모두 먹는 것을 명심하렴.
남: 그럴게요. 아, 냉장고에 오렌지 남은 것이 있나요?
여: 아니, 다 떨어졌단다. 왜 묻니?
남: 그게, 의사가 오렌지나 키위 같이 비타민 C가 풍부한 과일을 먹으라고 조언해 주었거든요. 비타민 C가 독감을 이기는 데 도움을 줄 수 있다고 말했어요.
여: 그러면, 내가 지금 가서 오렌지를 사 올게.
남: 고마워요, 엄마. 엄마가 가신 동안에 제가 거실을 청소할게요.
여: 청소 안 해도 된다, 얘야. 너는 아프잖니. 그냥 좀 쉬렴.

문제 해결
의사가 비타민 C가 풍부한 과일을 먹는 것이 독감을 이기는 데 도움이 된다고 했다며 남자가 오렌지를 찾자, 여자는 지금 바로 오렌지를 사 오겠다고 했다.

어휘·표현
flu 독감   prescribe 처방하다   fridge 냉장고   rich in ~이 풍부한

06 ④
숫자 정보 파악

여: Grand Trampoline Park에 오신 것을 환영합니다. 무엇을 도와드릴까요?
남: 안녕하세요! 오늘 몇 시에 닫나요?
여: 주중에는 오후 10시에 닫습니다. 하지만 마지막 입장은 오후 8시입니다.
남: 알겠습니다. 그러면 저는 성인 한 명과 어린이 다섯 명의 표를 사려고 합니다.
여: 아이들이 몇 살인가요? 일반 표는 20달러이고 13세 이하 어린이는 10달러만 내시면 됩니다.
남: 오, 아이들은 모두 12살입니다.
여: 좋습니다. 여섯 명이니까, 단체 할인의 자격이 됩니다. 총 금액의 10% 할인을 받을 수 있습니다.
남: 아주 좋네요. 그리고 제가 이 5달러짜리 쿠폰도 쓸 수 있나요?
여: 죄송합니다. 이 쿠폰은 주말에만 사용할 수 있습니다.
남: 괜찮습니다.
여: 어떻게 결제하시겠어요? 현금이요, 아니면 신용 카드요?
남: 저는 신용 카드로 결제하겠습니다. 여기 있어요.

문제 해결
공원 입장료가 어른은 20달러, 13세 이하 어린이는 10달러이다. 총 인원이 여섯 명이라 10% 단체 할인을 받을 수 있으므로, 남자가 지불해야 하는 총 금액은 63달러이다. 할인 쿠폰은 주말에만 쓸 수 있기 때문에 지금은 사용할 수 없다.

어휘·표현
regular 일반적인   qualify 자격을 얻다

07 ④
이유 파악

여: Patrick, 네가 Sydney 은행에 지원하기로 결정했다고 들었어.

남: 그래. 그 회사가 성장 가능성이 아주 크거든.

여: 잘됐어. 그 회사의 초봉이 5만 달러가 넘는다는 이야기도 들었어.

남: 그것은 별개의 이유야. 너는 어떤 회사에 지원할지 결정했어?

여: 응. 나는 ACE 전자에 지원할 거야.

남: ACE 전자? 그곳은 Brian과 Jennifer가 지원한 회사잖아.

여: 맞아. 그들은 나에게 직원에 대한 복지가 좋아서 그 회사에 지원했다고 하더라.

남: 너는 어때? 무엇 때문에 지원하기로 결정했니?

여: 해외에서 일할 수 있는 기회 때문이야. 내가 해외에서 일하는 것을 항상 꿈꿔 왔다는 거 너도 알잖아.

남: 그래. 그 회사는 해외에 지사가 많이 있지.

여: 내가 채용이 되면, 해외 지사 중의 한 곳에서 일하게 해 달라고 요청할 거야.

남: 네 꿈이 실현되기를 바랄게.

문제 해결

ACE 전자에 지원하기로 결정한 이유를 묻는 남자의 물음에 여자는 해외에서 일할 수 있는 기회 때문이라고 말했다.

어휘·표현

apply to ~에 지원하다   potential 가능성   starting salary 초봉   benefits (회사에서 직원에게 제공하는) 복리 후생 급부   branch 지사

08 ⑤   언급 유무 파악

여: 안녕하세요, 만나서 반가워요. 저는 교내 신문 기자 Sara Brown입니다.

남: 안녕하세요, Sara! 교내 신문과 인터뷰를 하게 되어서 영광이에요.

여: 천만에요. 먼저 동아리의 역사에 대해 말씀해 주세요. 동아리가 언제 시작되었죠?

남: 1970년이요. 우리 동아리는 교내에 있는 50개의 동아리 중에서 역사가 가장 길어요.

여: 정말로 오래되었군요. 유명한 마술사인 Jim Morrison이 이 동아리를 설립했다고 들었어요. 사실인가요?

남: 맞아요. 우리가 마술 쇼를 할 때마다, 그분이 오셔서 우리를 격려해 주세요.

여: 멋지네요. 마술 쇼는 일 년에 몇 번이나 하죠?

남: 두 번이요. 여름과 겨울에 한 번씩 합니다.

여: 알겠습니다. 이제 회원들에 대해 이야기를 해 보죠. 동아리에는 회원이 몇 명이나 있나요?

남: 23명이요. 우리는 쇼를 위한 마술을 연습하기 위해서 매주 수요일과 금요일에 모입니다.

여: 대단해요. 저도 그 모임에 참석해서 기본적인 마술 기술 몇 가지를 배워 보고 싶어요.

남: 오세요. 언제나 환영합니다.

문제 해결

마술 동아리의 '회원 가입 방법'에 대해서는 언급되지 않았다.

어휘·표현

found 설립하다, 창립하다   attend 참석하다

09 ④   담화 내용 불일치

여: 안녕하세요, 여러분! 잠시만 저에게 주목해 주십시오. 여러분에게 흥

미로운 캠프를 소개해 드리겠습니다. 그것은 Phoenix 야구 캠프입니다. 시애틀 야구 협회가 후원하는 이 캠프는 8월 1일에 시작해서 2주일 간 계속됩니다. 캠프는 작년과 마찬가지로 Rainbow 야구 센터에서 열릴 것입니다. 이 캠프는 9세에서 13세 사이의 모든 어린이에게 열려 있습니다. 고급, 중급, 그리고 초급 이렇게 세 개의 반이 있고, 참가자는 나이가 아니라 야구 실력에 따라 반에 배정될 것입니다. 등록비는 어린이 한 명당 150달러이고, 점심과 집에서부터 캠프까지의 교통편이 포함되어 있습니다. 여러분의 자녀가 이 캠프에서 아주 즐거운 시간을 보낼 것이라고 저는 확신합니다.

문제 해결

고급, 중급, 초급의 세 반이 있는데, 참가자는 나이가 아니라 야구 실력에 근거해서 반에 배정된다고 했으므로, ④는 내용과 일치하지 않는다.

어휘·표현

sponsor 후원하다   be held 열리다, 개최되다   intermediate 중급의, 중간의   based on ~에 근거해서   registration fee 등록비

10 ①   도표 정보 파악

남: 여보, 임대 주택 광고를 보고 주택 한 채를 골라 봐요.

여: 좋아요! 음…. 나는 Santa Monica로 이사를 가고 싶지는 않아요. 내 사무실에서 너무 멀거든요.

남: 그리고 그곳은 너무 복잡해요. 나도 그곳에서 살고 싶지 않아요.

여: 그러면 Culver City 또는 Los Angeles를 골라요.

남: 그래요. 적어도 침실이 세 개는 있어야 한다고 생각하지 않아요?

여: 맞아요. 그렇지 않으면, 아이들이 방을 함께 써야 할 거예요. 아이들이 그것을 좋아하지 않을 거예요.

남: 알았어요. 월 임대료는 어때요?

여: 음, 우리가 주택에 매달 1,000달러를 넘게 지불할 여유는 없을 것 같아요.

남: 당신 말에 동의해요. 이제 집이 두 채 남았어요.

여: 임대료가 더 낮은 집을 선택하는 게 어때요?

남: 하지만 차고에 자동차를 한 대만 주차할 수 있어요. 우리는 자동차 두 대를 수용하는 차고가 필요해요.

여: 아, 맞아요. 좋아요, 이 집을 임대해요.

문제 해결

Culver City 또는 Los Angeles에 있는 집 중에서 침실이 적어도 세 개 있으며 매달 임대료가 1,000달러를 넘지 않고, 차고에 자동차를 두 대 주차할 수 있는 곳을 임대하기로 했으므로, 두 사람이 임대할 주택은 ①이다.

어휘·표현

rental house 임대 주택   afford to ~할 여유가 있다   garage 차고

11 ③   짧은 대화의 응답

남: 여보, 크리스마스 때 아이들이랑 그랜드 캐니언으로 여행을 가는 게 어때요?

여: 음, 여행을 가는 것은 전적으로 찬성하지만, 우리가 그랜드 캐니언에 가야 할 것 같지는 않아요.

남: 왜요? 거기에 가고 싶지 않은 특별한 이유가 있나요?

여: 아이들이 그랜드 캐니언이 아니라 바다에 가고 싶어 할 거라고 확신하거든요.

문제 해결

여행은 좋지만 그랜드 캐니언에 가야 할 것 같지 않다고 말하는 여자에게 남자가 그 이유를 물었으므로, 아이들이 그랜드 캐니언보다는 바다에 가고 싶을 것이라고 말하는 ③이 여자의 응답으로 가장 적절하다.

① 크리스마스요? 아니요, 나는 아직 특별한 계획이 없어요.
② 미안하지만, 난 여행 못 갈 것 같아요. 정말 바쁘거든요.
④ 맞아요. 우리는 크리스마스 연휴 때 쉬어야 해요.
⑤ 네, 있어요. 난 그랜드 캐니언의 장엄함을 보고 싶어요.

어휘·표현

totally 전적으로   be in favor of ~을 찬성하다   magnificence 장엄, 웅장

12 ②

짧은 대화의 응답

[휴대 전화벨이 울린다.]

여: Harry, 나 우리 데이트에 좀 늦을 것 같아.
남: 걱정하지 마, Jessica. 나 카페에 가서 거기서 너를 기다릴게.
여: 내 음료도 주문해 줄 수 있어? 나는 라테를 마실게.
남: 당연하지. 두 잔 시켜 놓을게.

문제 해결

데이트에 늦을 것 같다는 여자가 카페에서 기다리고 있겠다는 남자에게 자신의 음료도 주문해 줄 수 있는지 물었으므로, 주문해 놓겠다고 말하는 ②가 남자의 응답으로 가장 적절하다.

① 우리 데이트 날을 다시 잡아야 할까?
③ 케이크도 주문해 줄 수 있니?
④ 그 식당은 예약이 꽉 찼어.
⑤ 우리는 표의 시간을 바꿔야 해.

어휘·표현

ran late 늦어지다   wait for ~를 기다리다   order 주문하다   as well ~도, 또한   fully booked 모두 예약된

13 ②

긴 대화의 응답

남: Ellen, 너 지난 학기에 한국사 수업 들었지, 그렇지 않았니?
여: 맞아. 난 그 수업에서 A를 받았어. 왜 물어보는데?
남: 사실, 이번 학기에 그 수업을 들을까 생각 중이어서, 그 수업에 대한 정보를 구하고 있거든.
여: 그래? 그러면 Lee 교수님의 수업을 수강해.
남: 네가 그 수업을 수강했니?
여: 응, 수강했어. 이 수업을 들은 거의 모든 학생들이 그 수업을 좋아했어.
남: 정말? 왜 그런 거야?
여: 음, 그는 한국 역사에 조예가 깊어. 우리가 질문을 할 때마다, 그는 항상 쉽게 대답을 하셨거든.
남: 좋아. 그의 교수법은 어때? 지루하니?
여: 아니, 전혀. 교수님이 많은 시청각 자료를 사용하시기 때문에 그의 수업은 언제나 흥미진진했어.
남: 그러면 수업 시간에 자는 학생이 한 명도 없었겠구나.
여: 물론이지! 그의 수업을 수강하면 후회하지 않을 거야.

문제 해결

남자는 한국사 수업 수강 전에 그 수업을 들어 본 여자에게 수업에 대해 물었고 여자는 해당 수업을 수강할 것을 권유하며, 수업이 언제나 흥미진진했다고 말했다. 이어서 수업시간에 자는 학생이 한 명도 없었을 것 같다는 남자의 말에 여자가 할 말로는 ② '물론이지! 그의 수업을 수강하면 후회하지 않을 거야.'가 가장

적절하다.

① 사실, 한국사는 공부하기에 쉽지 않아.
③ 그냥 열심히 공부해. 너는 머지않아 교수가 될 거야.
④ 네 도움이 없었으면, 난 이 수업을 끝내지 못했을 거야.
⑤ 응. 나는 시청각 자료를 사용하고 싶어.

어휘·표현

semester 학기   be versed in ~에 조예가 깊다   audiovisual material 시청각 자료   absolutely 전적으로, 틀림없이

14 ②

긴 대화의 응답

여: 실례합니다만, 한 가지 물어봐도 될까요?
남: 그럼요! 말씀하세요.
여: 음, 제 카드 키를 잃어버린 것 같아서요.
남: 걱정 마세요. 지금 바로 카드 키를 재발급해 드리겠습니다. 하지만 10달러의 수수료가 있습니다.
여: 체크아웃할 때 그 비용을 내도 될까요?
남: 물론이죠. 객실 번호를 말씀해 주시겠어요?
여: 저는 1026호에 머물고 있어요.
남: 1026…. 확인해 보겠습니다. [잠시 후] 그 객실은 Susan Kim 씨가 예약을 했다고 나와 있네요. Susan Kim 씨인가요?
여: 아니요. 저는 Jennifer Kim입니다. Susan Kim은 제 언니예요.
남: 죄송하지만, 카드 키는 객실을 예약한 분에게만 재발급됩니다. 그것이 저희 방침이에요.
여: 알겠어요. 그러면 지금 언니를 데리고 올게요. 언니가 2층 식당에 있거든요.
남: 좋습니다. 그녀가 여기 오시면, 그녀에게 새 카드 키를 발급해 드릴게요.

문제 해결

카드 키를 재발급 받으려는 여자에게 남자는 호텔 객실을 예약한 사람에게만 카드 키를 재발급해 준다고 한다. 이에 여자는 객실을 예약한 언니가 식당에 있다고 하면서 지금 언니를 데리고 오겠다고 했으므로, 이 말에 대한 남자의 응답으로 ② '좋습니다. 그녀가 여기 오시면, 그녀에게 새 카드 키를 발급해 드릴게요.'가 가장 적절하다.

① 맞아요. 당신은 정말로 언니와 많이 닮은 것 같아요.
③ 물론이죠! 당신과 함께 그 식당에서 정말로 일하고 싶어요.
④ 천만에요. 하지만 제가 카드 키를 찾았다는 것을 잊지 마세요.
⑤ 나도 배가 고파요. 같이 식당에 가요.

어휘·표현

reissue 재발급 하다   reserve 예약하다(=book)   policy 방침, 정책

15 ③

상황에 적절한 말

남: Rachel은 올 겨울에 입을 롱 코트를 고르고 있다. 가게 점원인 John은 그녀에게 다양한 디자인의 롱 코트 몇 벌을 보여 준다. 그녀는 단순한 자주색 롱 코트를 입어 보고는 마음에 들어 한다. 하지만 Rachel이 이 코트 금액을 지불하기 위해서 가방에서 지갑을 꺼내려 했을 때, 그녀는 지갑을 가지고 오지 않은 것을 알아차린다. 당황한 그녀는 John에게 이 사실을 말한다. John은 그녀에게 걱정하지 말라고 하면서 그녀가 정말로 이 코트를 사고 싶다면 자신이 내일까지는 이 코트를 아무에게도 팔지 않겠다고 덧붙인다. Rachel은 이를 고맙게 여기고 이 코트를 꼭 사고 싶어한다. 이러한 상황에서,

Rachel은 John에게 무엇이라고 말하겠는가?

입어 본 코트가 마음에 들어 계산을 하려다 지갑을 가져오지 않은 것을 알게 된 Rachel에게 점원인 Jack은 내일까지 코트를 아무에게도 팔지 않겠다면서 Rachel을 안심시켰다. Rachel은 점원에게 고마워하면서 꼭 코트를 사고 싶어 하는 상황이므로, Rachel이 할 말로 ③ '고마워요. 지갑을 가지고 내일 꼭 다시 올게요.'가 가장 적절하다.

① 맞아요. 나는 가게 점원으로 일하는 것에 관심이 있어요.
② 천만예요. 이 자주색 롱 코트는 당신에게 가장 잘 어울려요.
④ 좋은 생각이에요. 당신은 이 자주색 코트를 수선하는 게 더 나아요.
⑤ 당신의 권유가 없었다면, 나는 이 코트를 사지 않았을 거예요.

embarrassed 당황스러워하는 **be grateful for** ~을 고맙게 여기다
definitely 반드시, 꼭 **suit** (옷·색상 등이) 어울리다 **mend** 수선하다

16-17 [복합 이해]

여: 안녕하세요, 방문객 여러분. Greenland 동물원의 Bat House에 오신 것을 환영합니다. 오늘 아침, 여러분은 이미 이곳 동물원에서 흥미진진한 야생 동물을 보셨습니다. 이제, 여러분은 신비로운 야행성 동물인 박쥐를 관찰할 기회를 가질 것입니다. 그 전에, 여러분에게 박쥐에 대한 몇 가지 흥미로운 사실을 말씀드리겠습니다. 일반적으로, 박쥐는 영국 또는 프랑스와 같은 유럽 국가에서는 불길한 동물로 여겨졌습니다. 여러분은 박쥐가 영화에서 나쁜 캐릭터로 등장하는 것을 종종 볼 수 있습니다. 하지만 박쥐는 단지 외모로만 평가된 피해자일 뿐입니다. 사실, 박쥐는 생태계를 유지하는 데 중요한 역할을 하고 실제로 인간에게 도움을 주기도 합니다. 예를 들어, 박쥐는 해충의 천적입니다. 박쥐 한 마리가 하루에 수 천 마리의 해충을 잡을 수 있습니다. 박쥐가 없다면, 미국의 농부는 해충을 제거하는 데 해마다 수십억 달러가 들 것입니다. 박쥐는 또한 꽃가루 매개자의 역할을 함으로써 생태계에 중요합니다. 태국과 베트남에 있는 박쥐는 씨앗이 자랄 수 있도록 식물이 수분하는 데 도움을 줍니다. 좋습니다! 이제 안으로 들어가서 새끼 박쥐를 보겠습니다.

observe 관찰하다 **be considered** 간주되다, 여겨지다 **victim** 피해자, 희생자
maintain 유지하다 **ecosystem** 생태계 **natural enemy** 천적 **get rid of** 제거하다, 없애다 **pollinator** 꽃가루 매개자 **pollinate** 수분하다

16 ①

여자는 박쥐가 해충을 잡아먹거나 꽃가루 매개자의 역할을 하는 등 생태계를 유지하는 데 중요한 역할을 한다고 했으므로, 여자가 하는 말의 주제로 ① '생태계에 미치는 박쥐의 긍정적인 측면'이 적절하다.

② 생태계와 생태의 차이점
③ 해충을 제거하는 방법
④ 박쥐가 나오는 영화
⑤ 생태계를 유지하는 필요 조건

17 ⑤

여자의 말 속에 브라질은 언급되지 않았다.

11 영어 듣기 모의고사 ▶ pp. 26-27

01 ①	02 ④	03 ②	04 ④	05 ⑤	06 ①
07 ⑤	08 ④	09 ③	10 ⑤	11 ①	12 ①
13 ②	14 ②	15 ①	16 ①	17 ⑤	

01 ① [목적 파악]

여: 안녕하세요, 개를 사랑하는 여러분! 여러분의 개가 건강한 음식을 먹기를 원하시나요? 그렇다면 털로 덮인 여러분의 작은 친구에게 Chew Chew 애견용 사료를 먹이십시오. 개들이 정말 좋아하는 새로운 맛으로, 털로 덮인 여러분의 친구는 한 입을 먹기 위해 무엇이든 할 것입니다. 여러분의 개의 이빨을 건강하고 깨끗하게 유지하는 데 도움이 되도록 개발되어, Chew Chew 사료는 열 명의 수의사 중 아홉 명이 추천합니다. 유기농 재료로 만들어졌기 때문에, 여러분의 개가 최고 중의 최고를 얻고 있다고 자신하실 수 있습니다. Chew Chew 사료는 지역 식료품점에서 찾으실 수 있습니다. Chew Chew 웹 사이트를 방문하셔서 계산 시 교환할 수 있는 10% 할인 쿠폰을 출력하세요. 여러분의 개에게 최고를 주세요.

여자는 Chew Chew 애견용 사료를 홍보하고 있으므로, 여자가 하는 말의 목적으로 ①이 가장 적절하다.

furry 털로 덮인, 부드러운 털의 **veterinarian** 수의사 **ingredient** 재료, 성분

02 ④ [주제 파악]

남: 안녕, Jill. 오늘 어떠니?
여: 좋은 아침이야, Dale. 그다지 좋지는 못해.
남: 그 말을 들어 유감이야. 문제가 뭐니?
여: 새로운 상사가 최근에 나를 많이 힘들게 하고 있어.
남: 그가 너를 어떻게 힘들게 하고 있다는 거야?
여: 나에게 새로운 업무를 계속 줘.
남: 새로운 업무는 좋은 것 같은데.
여: 좋은 거라고? 어떻게 그게 좋은 게 될 수 있니?
남: 새로운 업무는 네 새로운 상사가 너를 신뢰한다는 것을 의미할 수 있어.
여: 신뢰한다고? 농담하는 거지. 어떻게 이런 새로운 업무들이 신뢰를 의미하니?
남: 음, 네 상사가 네게 계속 새로운 업무를 준다면, 그건 아마도 그가 너와 네 능력을 신뢰한다는 의미일 거야.
여: 오, 네 말이 맞을 것 같아. 아마 결국에는 좋은 일이 될 거야.

새로운 상사가 계속 새로운 업무를 줘 힘들다는 여자에게 남자는 그것이 여자를 신뢰한다는 의미라고 말하고 있으므로, 남자의 의견으로 ④가 가장 적절하다.

challenge (상대방에게 도전이 될 일을) 요구하다 **assignment** 과제, 업무, 임무
joke 농담하다 **trust in** ~를 신뢰(신임)하다

03 ②

여: 좋은 아침이에요, Cooke 씨. 퇴원해도 좋을 정도로 몸이 완치되셨네요.

남: 아주 반가운 소식이네요. 그건 지금은 제가 괜찮다는 말이죠?

여: 네. 새 몸처럼 좋으세요.

남: 좋군요. 제가 복용해야 할 약이 있나요?

여: 네. 의사 선생님께서 이 처방전을 드리라고 말씀하셨어요.

남: 만약 상처가 벌어지면 어떻게 해야 하나요?

여: 그럴 가능성은 거의 없어요. 하지만 만약 그렇게 된다면, 주저하지 말고 바로 다시 오세요.

남: 알게 되어 다행이네요. 다음 진료 예약은 언제인가요?

여: 실밥을 뽑을 때까지는 3일마다 오셔서 상처를 소독해야 해요.

남: 당신과 다른 직원분들에게 저를 잘 돌봐 줘서 감사하다는 말을 하고 싶어요.

여: 천만에요. 저희는 저희 일을 하는 것뿐인걸요.

남: 한 번 더 감사드려요. 이제 저는 갈 준비가 됐어요.

여자는 남자에게 퇴원해도 좋다는 소식을 알려 주고 처방전을 전해 주었으며, 남자는 상처에 대해 묻고 다음 예약을 문의하고 있으므로, 두 사람은 간호사와 환자의 관계이다.

discharge 퇴원시키다   medication 약   prescription 처방전   open up (상처가) 벌어지다   hesitate 망설이다, 주저하다   take out the stitches (수술 후에) 실밥을 뽑다

04 ④

남: 와! 이 사진 당신 침실인가요? 정말 좋네요, Kate.

여: 네, Ryan. 방 한가운데에 있는 침대가 아주 편안해요.

남: 좋아 보이네요. 침대 발치에 있는 게 안락의자죠?

여: 네. 이 의자가 방을 아늑해 보이게 해요.

남: 그러네요. 침대 왼쪽에 아름다운 탁자가 있네요.

여: 네. 어머니가 집들이 선물로 제게 주셨어요.

남: 저것은 진짜 반 고흐 작품인가요? 침대 뒤 벽에 있는 꽃 그림을 말하는 거예요.

여: 물론 아니에요. 반 고흐 작품의 복제품이에요.

남: 방 오른쪽 구석에 있는 의자는 매우 클래식해 보여요.

여: 그렇죠? 저는 그것을 차고 세일에서 좋은 가격에 샀어요.

남: 새것 같아 보여요. 당신은 정말 안목이 좋군요.

여: 그렇게 말해 줘서 고마워요.

벽에 반 고흐의 꽃 그림이 있다고 했는데 그림에는 자화상 그림이 있으므로 ④는 대화의 내용과 일치하지 않는다.

armchair 안락의자   at the foot of the bed 침대 발치에   nightstand 침실용 탁자   housewarming 집들이   replica 복제품

05 ⑤

여: 여보, 결혼식에 갈 시간이에요. 늦고 싶지 않아요.

남: 알겠어요, Holly. 내 신발 봤어요?

여: 벽장 안에 있겠죠. 내 하이힐도 꺼내 줄래요?

남: 결혼식에 어떤 하이힐을 신을 거예요?

여: 내 드레스에 맞춰 파란색 하이힐이요.

남: 여기에 파란색 하이힐은 보이지 않아요. 여기 있는 게 확실해요?

여: 바깥에 있는 자동차 안에 있을지도 몰라요. 한번 봐 줄래요?

남: 좋아요, 잠깐만요. 자동차 열쇠는 어디에 있어요?

여: 부엌 조리대 위에 있어요. 과일 그릇 옆이요.

남: 열쇠가 보이지 않아요. 다른 곳에 있을까요?

여: 거실에 내 지갑 안에 있을지도 모르겠어요.

남: 찾았어요! 금방 올게요.

남자는 자동차 안에 파란색 하이힐이 있는지 봐 달라는 여자의 부탁을 듣고 자동차 열쇠를 찾았으므로, 남자는 여자의 하이힐이 있는지 자동차 안을 확인해 볼 것이다.

walk-in closet 큰 벽장   match 어울리다, 맞다   kitchen counter 부엌 조리대

06 ①

[전화벨이 울린다.]

남: Adventure 여행사에 전화해 주셔서 감사합니다. 저는 Rob입니다. 어떻게 도와 드릴까요?

여: 안녕하세요, 급류 래프팅 여행을 예약하고 싶습니다.

남: 네. 성인은 20달러, 13세 미만 어린이는 15달러입니다.

여: 우리는 4명으로, 성인 2명, 13세 미만의 어린이 2명이 있습니다.

남: 오, 4명 이상의 단체는 여행 가격에서 10% 할인을 받을 수 있습니다.

여: 그거 좋네요.

남: 전에 급류 래프팅을 해 보신 적이 있으신가요?

여: 아니요, 이번이 처음입니다.

남: 그럼 교육용 수업을 받으시는 것을 추천합니다. 수업은 1인당 5달러 밖에 안 되며 대부분의 사람들이 도움이 된다고 합니다.

여: 우리 모두가 그 수업을 수강할 필요는 없는 것 같아요. 그냥 남편만 등록하겠습니다.

남: 알겠습니다. 언제로 하시겠습니까?

여: 다음 주 토요일이요.

남: 알겠습니다. 총액을 말씀 드리겠습니다.

래프팅 비용이 어른은 20달러, 13세 미만 어린이는 15달러인데 일행은 어른 2명, 13세 미만 어린이 2명이고, 4인 이상은 10% 할인을 받을 수 있다고 하였다. 거기에 1인당 5달러인 교육용 수업을 한 사람만 등록하였으므로, 여자가 지불할 총 금액은 68달러이다.

whitewater 급류 (타기)   rafting 래프팅   instructional 교육용의   sign up ~에 등록하다

07 ⑤

남: 안녕, Hailey. 너 뭘 듣고 있니?

여: 안녕, Dylan. 나는 창의력의 중요성에 관한 팟캐스트를 듣고 있어.

남: 그거 재미있겠다. 왜 그 팟캐스트를 듣고 있는 거니?

여: 음, 너도 알다시피 내가 지역 대학에서 여름 강좌를 듣고 있잖아.

남: 그렇지. 그래서 이게 그 강좌의 과제니?

여: 그렇진 않아. 교수님이 모두에게 팟캐스트를 들으라고 추천하셨어.

남: 왜 팟캐스트를 듣길 원하셔?

여: 교수님은 학생들이 창의력에 관한 다음 수업을 준비하시길 원하시는 거야.

남: 알겠어. 그럼 널 내버려 둘게. 다 들으면 나를 찾아와.

여: 그래. 내가 다 듣고 보자.

문제 해결

여자는 현재 지역 대학의 여름 강좌를 수강 중인데, 교수님이 창의력에 관한 다음 수업을 학생들이 준비할 수 있도록 추천해 준 팟캐스트를 듣고 있다고 했다. 따라서 팟캐스트를 듣는 이유로 ⑤가 가장 적절하다.

어휘·표현

creativity 창의력, 창조성

08 ④ 언급 유무 파악

여: 안녕, Eric. 우리가 할 수 있는 멋진 활동이 있어.

남: 듣고 있어, Pamela. 어떤 걸 생각하는데?

여: 나 신문을 읽다가 시애틀 제과 박람회에 관한 광고를 봤어.

남: 시애틀 제과 박람회? 언제 열리는데?

여: 이번 주말 3월 5일부터 7일까지 열려.

남: 알겠어. 올해는 어디서 열리는데?

여: Camden 예술 회관의 본관에서 열릴 거야.

남: 우리 집 바로 근처네. 입장료는 얼마야?

여: 믿기 힘들겠지만 단돈 5달러야.

남: 좋아! 너는 얼마나 많은 제과점이 그 박람회에 참여할지 아니?

여: 총 50개의 제과점이 박람회에 참여할 거래.

남: 멋지다. 이번 주 토요일에 함께 확인해 보자.

문제 해결

시애틀 제과 박람회의 날짜(3월 5일~7일), 장소(캠던 예술 회관의 본관), 입장료(5달러), 참여 제과점 수(50개)에 관해서는 언급되었지만, 특별 행사에 관한 언급은 없었다.

어휘·표현

main building 본관   admission fee 입장료

09 ③ 담화 내용 불일치

남: 이제, 지역 소식을 전해 드립니다. ABC 사이클링 클럽이 이번 주말에 Riding For a Cause 연례 행사를 개최합니다. 올해 행사에서 모아지는 모든 수익은 집이 없는 사람들에게 살 곳을 제공하는 것을 돕는 데 기부될 것입니다. 행사 장소는 25가와 35가 사이의 Hawthorne 대로에서 열릴 것입니다. 현지 Portland 지역의 음식 노점상들이 모든 방문객에게 음식을 팔 것입니다. 주요 행사는 토요일에 열릴 100킬로미터 경주이지만, 지역 밴드의 음악 공연을 확인하는 것도 잊지 마세요. 행사는 이번 주말에 시작해서 일요일까지 계속될 것입니다. Portland 지역 일대의 어느 자전거 상점에서든 일찍 표를 받으실 수 있습니다. 여러분을 그곳에서 뵙기를 바랍니다.

문제 해결

③ 주요 행사는 200킬로미터가 아니라 100킬로미터 경주라고 했다.

어휘·표현

annual 연례의, 매년의   house 살 곳을 주다, 거처를 제공하다   boulevard 대로
vendor (거리의) 노점상, 행상인

10 ⑤ 도표 정보 파악

여: Fred, 신문에 지역 자동차 대리점에서 할인을 한다고 쓰여 있네요.

남: 기가 막히게 타이밍이 맞네요. 나는 당장 새 차가 필요해요.

여: 얼마나 쓸 거예요?

남: 25,000달러 이상은 쓰고 싶지 않아요.

여: 그럼 이 네 개의 모델 중 선택할 수 있어요.

남: 지난번 내 자동차가 세단형 자동차였어요. 이번에는 소형차를 갖고 싶어요.

여: 판매하는 소형차들이 있네요. 그 밖에는 뭐를 찾나요?

남: 연비가 좋은 차가 필요해요. 리터당 20킬로미터 이상은 갈 수 있어야 해요.

여: 음, 이들 중 이 두 차가 그렇네요. 어떤 색을 원해요?

남: 빨간색이 있나요?

여: 아니요, 이 두 색밖에 없어요.

남: 음, 나는 검정색을 좋아하지 않으니 다른 색을 선택할게요.

문제 해결

남자는 가격은 25,000달러를 넘지 않고, 소형차이면서 리터당 20킬로미터 이상 갈 수 있고, 검정색이 아닌 다른 색의 차를 사려 하므로, 남자가 구매할 차는 ⑤다.

어휘·표현

dealership 대리점   sedan 세단형 자동차 (4개의 문과 최소 4개의 좌석이 있는 보통의 승용차)   compact 소형의, 소형차   fuel economy 연료 절약, 연비
go for ~을 택하다

11 ① 짧은 대화의 응답

여: 여보, 오늘 아침 신문이 배달되었나요?

남: 그래요, 여보. 내가 당신에게 가져다주길 원해요?

여: 네, 그래 줘요. 또한 괜찮다면, 나에게 커피 한 잔을 가져다줄 수 있을까요?

남: 물론이죠. 둘 다 가져다줄게요.

문제 해결

여자가 남편에게 신문을 가져다달라고 부탁한 후 커피 한 잔 또한 가져다줄 수 있는지 물었으므로, 둘 다 가져다주겠다고 말하는 ①이 남자의 응답으로 가장 적절하다.

② 물론 아니죠. 우리는 커피가 다 떨어졌어요.

③ 네. 신문이 아직 배달되지 않았어요.

④ 아니요. 내 커피에는 설탕이 들어가면 좋겠네요.

⑤ 알겠어요. 나는 차라리 텔레비전으로 뉴스를 보는 게 낫겠어요.

어휘·표현

deliver 배달하다   be out of ~이 떨어지다, 바닥나다   would rather (차라리) ~하겠다

12 ① 짧은 대화의 응답

남: Jenny, 방과 후에 내 책을 집으로 옮기는 걸 도와줄 수 있니?

여: 물론이지. 기꺼이 도와줄게, Peter.

남: 좋아! 마지막 종이 울리면 학교 앞 조각상 옆에서 만나자.

여: 좋아. 방과 후에 거기서 보자.

문제 해결

자신의 책을 집에 같이 옮겨 달라고 도움을 요청한 남자의 부탁을 여자가 기꺼이

수락하자 남자는 마지막 종이 울리면 학교 앞 조각상 옆에서 만나자고 말했다. 따라서, 방과 후에 거기서 보자고 말하는 ①이 여자의 응답으로 가장 적절하다.
② 응. 나는 방과 후에 저녁을 먹고 싶어.
③ 와! 산책하는 거 정말 좋다, 그렇지 않니?
④ 미안해. 나는 우리가 만나기로 한 약속에 늦을 거야.
⑤ 아니. 도서관에서 그 책들을 빌리자.

statue 조각상

13 ②

여: 도와드릴까요, 손님?
남: 제가 제 비행기를 탑승하기엔 너무 늦은 건지 궁금합니다.
여: 비행기 번호를 알려주시겠어요?
남: 보스턴으로 떠나는 802편입니다.
여: 제가 확인해 볼게요. 유감스럽게도 그 비행기의 탑승구가 방금 닫혔습니다.
남: 오, 안 돼. 여기로 오는 길에 교통 체증이 정말 심했거든요.
여: 그 말을 들어 유감이지만, 일단 문이 닫히면 저희가 해 드릴 수 있는 일이 없습니다.
남: 보스턴으로 가는 다음 비행기는 언제인가요?
여: 다음 비행기는 2시간 후에 있지만 예약이 다 찼습니다.
남: 그 다음 비행기는 어떤가요?
여: 저녁 7시 비행기가 한 대 있고 자리 하나가 남아 있습니다. 그 비행기에 이름을 올려 드릴까요?
남: 물론입니다. 그 자리를 예약해 주세요.

남자가 타야 하는 비행기는 이미 탑승구를 닫아 탈 수 없고 바로 다음 비행기도 예약이 다 찬 상황에서, 여자가 저녁 7시 비행기에 한 자리가 남아 있다며 예약을 원하는지 물었다. 이에 대한 남자의 응답으로 ② '물론입니다. 그 자리를 예약해 주세요.'가 가장 적절하다.
① 아마도 아닐 거예요. 저는 워싱턴으로 운전해서 가는 게 낫겠어요.
③ 왜 안 돼요? 저는 그 비행기에서 세 자리를 원해요.
④ 네. 비행기로 로스앤젤레스까지 얼마나 걸릴까요?
⑤ 아니요. 다음 비행기의 탑승구를 열어 주세요.

board 탑승하다, 탑승에 들어가다   boarding gate 탑승구

14 ②

[휴대 전화벨이 울린다.]
남: 안녕하세요, Susan. 회의를 위한 모든 준비가 끝났지요?
여: 거의 다 됐어요, Dan. 출장 요식 업체에 전화만 하면 돼요.
남: 회의 후 파티를 위한 밴드는 구할 수 있었나요?
여: 아뇨, 밴드가 바빴어요. 나는 디제이만 구할 수 있었어요.
남: 그건 실망스럽지만 어쩔 수 없겠네요. 다른 문제들은요?
여: 회의를 위한 방을 바꿔야만 했어요.
남: 왜요?
여: 모든 사람들이 앉을 만한 충분한 의자가 없었어요. 그래서 우리는 더 큰 방으로 바꿔야 했어요.
남: 알겠어요, 내가 사람들에게 변경을 공지하는 메일을 꼭 보내도록 할게요.

여: 그건 큰 도움이 될 거예요. 나는 지금 아주 바쁘거든요.
남: 내가 그 밖에 도와줄 게 있나요?
여: 아뇨. 방 변경에 관한 메일만 보내 줘요.

회의 준비를 하고 있는 여자가 더 큰 방이 필요해 회의실을 바꿨다고 하자 남자는 자신이 메일로 사람들에게 그 변경 사항을 알리겠다고 하였다. 다른 도움이 필요한지 묻는 남자의 말에 대한 여자의 응답으로 ② '아뇨. 방 변경에 관한 메일만 보내 줘요.'가 가장 적절하다.
① 필요한 게 있으면 나에게 알려 줘요.
③ 네. 나는 파티에서 밴드가 공연하는 걸 어서 보고 싶어요.
④ 네. 나는 음식에 관해 출장 요식 업체와 이야기할 거예요.
⑤ 나는 회의에서 사용할 여분의 의자를 가져올 수 있어요.

arrangement 준비   caterer 요리 조달업자, 음식 공급자   switch 바꾸다   notify 알리다, 통보하다   have one's hands full 아주 바쁘다

15 ①

여: Jack과 Diane은 지역 야구팀의 코치들이다. 이번 주말은 챔피언을 결정하는 큰 경기가 있다. Jack은 그 챔피언 결정전이 매우 중요하다고 느끼기 때문에 최고의 선수들이 전 경기를 뛰게 하고 싶다. 그는 그들이 경기에 참여하는 것을 통해 긍정적인 경험을 할 것이라고 생각한다. 하지만, Diane은 모두가 경기에서 뛰게 하고 싶다. 그녀는 그들이 팀으로서 항상 함께 했기 때문에 모두가 챔피언 결정전에서 뛰는 권리를 누려야 한다고 믿는다. Diane은 Jack이 자신의 의견을 고려하길 원하고, 팀의 모두가 그런 큰 경기에서 뛰게 하고 싶다. 이런 상황에서, Diane은 Jack에게 뭐라고 말할 것 같은가?

Diane과 Jack은 지역 야구팀의 코치로, 이번 주말에 챔피언 결정전에 출전할 선수들을 놓고 의견이 다르다. 최고의 선수들로만 뛰게 하고 싶은 Jack과는 달리, Diane은 팀으로 모두가 항상 함께 했기에 모두가 뛰어야 한다고 생각한다. Diane은 이러한 자신의 의견을 Jack이 고려해 주기를 원하므로, Diane이 Jack에게 할 말로 ① '우리는 팀이기 때문에 모두가 뛸 수 있게 해야 해요.'가 가장 적절하다.
② 모든 경기를 이기기 전까지는 우리는 진정한 챔피언이 될 수 없어요.
③ 우리는 이 경기에서 이겨야 하니, 우리의 스타 선수들이 경기하게 해요.
④ 부모님들은 아이들이 경기에서 이기는 걸 보고 기뻐할 거예요.
⑤ 우승이 전부가 아니므로 우리는 일부러 경기에서 져야 해요.

championship game 챔피언 결정전, 결승전   earn (그럴 만한 자격이 되어서) 얻다(받다)   point of view 의견, 견해, 관점   on purpose 일부러, 고의로

16-17

남: 여러분, 신체 단련 학회에 오신 것을 환영합니다. 저는 발표자 Todd입니다. 여러분이 운동하는 방법에 큰 변화를 일으킬 소식이 있습니다. 저는 여러분에게 신체 단련 세계를 바꿀 새로운 신체 단련 추적기에 관해 말씀 드리고 싶습니다. Fit Master는 시장의 최신 모델입니다. 이것에는 여러분이 달리거나 자전거를 타거나 단순히 산책을 할 때 화면을 쉽게 볼 수 있게 해 주는 선명한 스크린이 있습니다. 7일까지 쓸 수 있는 배터리 수명으로, Fit Master는 여러분이 할 수 있는

한 오래 계속 갈 수 있습니다. 이 추적기는 운동하는 중에 여러분의 심장이 얼마나 빨리 뛰는지를 정확히 알 수 있도록 최신의 심박수 센서가 달려 있습니다. 또는 손목 밴드로 하는 새로운 디자인이 있어서 그것은 모든 패션 스타일에 어울립니다. 이 추적기의 또 다른 주목할 만한 변화는 새로운 방수 디자인입니다. 이제 여러분은 빠르게 시원한 수영을 하고 Fit Master가 젖을 것을 걱정하지 않으셔도 됩니다. 이제 여러분에게 왜 신체 단련 추적기가 필요한지 말해 보도록 하죠.

어휘·표현

conference 학회, 회의 revolutionize 대변혁을 일으키다, 큰 변화를 가져오다
tracker 추적기, 추적 장치, 추적자 updated 최신의 heart rate 심박수, 심박
동수 notable 주목할 만한, 눈에 띄는 disadvantage 불편함, 불이익
comparison 비교

16 ①

문제 해결

신체 단련 학회의 발표자가 새로운 신체 단련 추적기의 특징에 대해 소개해 주고 있으므로, 남자가 하는 말의 주제로 ① '새로운 신체 단련 추적기의 특징'이 가장 적절하다.
② 신체 단련 추적기를 가져야 하는 이유
③ 신체 단련 추적기를 사용하는 것의 불편한 점
④ 방수가 되는 신체 단련 추적기의 중요성
⑤ 가장 잘 팔리는 신체 단련 추적기들의 비교

17 ⑤

문제 해결

새로운 신체 단련 추적기의 특징으로 선명한 스크린, 오래 쓸 수 있는 배터리 수명, 심박수 센서, 방수 디자인에 대해서는 언급했지만, GPS 센서에 관해서는 언급하지 않았다.

---

01 ①	02 ②	03 ③	04 ⑤	05 ③	06 ③
07 ④	08 ②	09 ②	10 ②	11 ②	12 ③
13 ①	14 ③	15 ⑤	16 ⑤	17 ③	

01 ①
목적 파악

여: 안녕하세요, Dunparton 미술관 방문객 여러분. 이번 달 특별 전시회에 관한 안내입니다. 우리 방문객들의 후한 기부 덕분에, 우리는 지역 아동을 위한 미술 교육 프로그램을 열 수 있었습니다. 이 프로그램은 이번 주에 종료되며 아이들의 멋진 그림을 Pine Hall에서 전시할 예정입니다. Pine Hall은 3층에 위치하고 있으며 여러분은 내일부터 이번 달 마지막 금요일까지 그림을 감상하실 수 있습니다. 여러분들은 우리 아이들이 얼마나 재능이 있는지를 보고 기분 좋게 놀라실 것입니다. 또한 여러분의 가치 있는 기부의 열매를 직접 확인하실 수 있을 것입니다. 부디 이 특별한 행사를 놓치지 마십시오. 우리 미술관을 방문해 주셔서 감사드리며 Pine Hall에서 여러분을 만날 수 있기를 바랍니다.

문제 해결

여자는 미술 교육 프로그램의 결과물인 아이들의 그림을 선보이는 특별 전시회를 안내하고 있다.

어휘·표현

announcement 공지, 알림 exhibition 전시 donation 기부
marvelous 매우 멋진, 뛰어난 pleasantly 기분 좋게, 즐겁게 talented 재능
있는 witness 목격하다, 보다

02 ②
주제 파악

남: 여보, 어느 차를 살지 결정했어요?
여: 아니요, 하지만 선택지를 좁혔어요.
남: 어떤 선택지가 있는데요?
여: 첫 번째 것은 특별 홍보 기간이라서 가장 싸요. 두 번째 것은 고객 후기가 좋고 마지막 것은 최신 기술을 갖추고 있어요.
남: 각 차의 연료 효율성과 온실 가스 배출량도 확인했어요?
여: 아니요. 그럴 필요가 있다고 생각해요?
남: 우리는 차가 얼마나 환경 친화적인지를 확인해야 해요. 대기 오염이 요즘 정말 뜨거운 논쟁거리잖아요.
여: 우리가 각 제품이 환경에 미치는 영향에 신중할 필요가 있다는 말인가요?
남: 맞아요. 그 차들이 얼마나 친환경적인지 봅시다.
여: [클릭 소리] 그러면, 우리는 세 번째 것을 사야 해요. 하지만 그 차는 다른 두 차보다 더 비싸네요.
남: 걱정 마요. 그만한 돈의 가치가 있을 거예요.
여: 그래요. 그걸로 사죠.

문제 해결

구입할 차를 결정하는 과정에서 남자가 여자에게 차가 얼마나 친환경적인지 확인해야 한다는 말을 하였으므로, 남자의 의견으로 ②가 가장 적절하다.

어휘·표현

narrow down 좁히다, 줄이다 promotion 홍보 efficiency 효율(성)

emission 배출, 배기가스   eco-friendly 친환경적인   cautious 신중한
impact 영향

03 ③
관계 추론

남: 안녕하세요. Alison 씨. 조금 일찍 오셨네요. 오늘 몸 상태는 어떠세요?

여: 안녕하세요, Brown 씨. 사실 제 등이 좀 아프네요. 오늘 수업을 할 수 있을지 모르겠어요.

남: 오. 무슨 일이 있었나요?

여: 제가 잘못된 자세로 잠을 잤나 봐요.

남: 좀 볼게요. 이렇게 앞으로 굽힐 수 있어요?

여: 네, 할 수 있어요. 그런데 등 오른쪽에 통증이 좀 느껴져요.

남: 음. 근육이 뭉친 것 같네요.

여: 그러면, 오늘 수업을 건너뛰어야 할까요?

남: 아니요. 그 반대로, 당신 등의 뭉친 근육을 풀기 위해 운동을 하는 게 더 나아요.

여: 제가 어떤 종류의 운동을 해야 할까요?

남: 우리는 스트레칭을 할 거고, 근육의 긴장을 풀기 위해 폼롤러를 사용할 거예요.

여: 알겠어요. 운동복으로 갈아입을게요.

문제 해결
등이 아프다며 오늘 수업을 못 받을까 봐 걱정하고 있고 여자에게 남자는 여자의 몸 상태를 점검한 후 구체적인 운동 계획을 설명하고 있으므로, 남자와 여자는 헬스트레이너와 고객의 관계이다.

어휘·표현
bend 굽히다   muscle knot 뭉친 근육   workout 운동   release 풀어 주다

04 ⑤
그림 불일치 파악

여: Mark! 너 돌아왔구나! 여행 어땠어?

남: 정말 좋았어. 내가 묵었던 호텔이 정말 멋졌어.

여: 그랬어?

남: 내가 사진을 보여 줄게. 이게 호텔 로비야.

여: 와! 벽에 이 굴곡을 봐. 파도를 연상시키는구나.

남: 맞아! 건축가가 로비에 자연에서 따온 장면을 만들려고 노력했어.

여: 그러면, 이 천장은 별과 달이 달려 있는 하늘이 분명하겠구나.

남: 맞아. 커다란 나무처럼 보이는 기둥이 천장을 지탱하고 있고, 커다란 꽃 모양 램프는 탁자 옆에 있어.

여: 탁자 위에 있는 꽃은 진짜니?

남: 응, 그것들은 진짜야. 로비에 앉아 있으면, 나는 마치 야외에 있는 기분이 들었어.

여: 정말 좋아 보인다. 나도 언젠가 그곳을 방문하고 싶네.

남: 꼭 그렇게 해. 후회하지 않을 거야.

문제 해결
그림에서 탁자 위에 놓여 있는 것은 탁상시계이므로 진짜 꽃이 탁자 위에 놓여 있다는 대화의 내용과 ⑤는 일치하지 않는다.

어휘·표현
terrific 멋진, 뛰어난   curve 곡선, 굴곡   architect 건축가   pillar 기둥

05 ③
할 일 파악

남: Kate. 학교 동아리 축제가 겨우 일주일 남았어.

여: 맞아. 학교 방송부 부원으로서, 우리는 아직 할 일이 많아.

남: 그래? 대부분의 일이 끝났다고 생각했는데.

여: 글쎄, 우리는 음향 시스템 점검하는 것은 끝냈지만, 조명은 아니야.

남: 내가 방과 후에 그 일을 할 수 있어.

여: 내가 이미 Shawn이 그 일을 하도록 했어. 그가 오늘 그 일을 할 거야.

남: 공연 시간표는 어때?

여: 공연 동아리 회장들이 같이 결정하고 우리에게 알려 줄 거야.

남: 그 밖에 해야 될 다른 일이 있어?

여: 우리는 각 공연 동아리의 예행연습을 확인하고 댄스 동아리로부터 음악 파일을 받아야 해.

남: 맞아. 네가 동아리 회장들과 예행연습 일정에 대해 얘기하는 동안 내가 음악 파일을 받아 올게.

여: 그래. 그게 좋겠다.

문제 해결
여자가 동아리 회장들과 예행연습 일정을 의논하는 동안 남자는 음악 파일을 받아 오기로 했다.

어휘·표현
broadcasting 방송   arrange (일을) 처리하다   performance 공연
rehearsal 리허설, 예행연습

06 ③
숫자 정보 파악

남: Ross 선생님. 우리 다음 주 수요일에 학교 동아리 활동으로 학생들을 영화관에 데리고 가는 거 맞지요?

여: 맞아요. Lewis 선생님. 제가 막 온라인으로 표를 살 참이었어요.

남: 좋아요. 우리가 학생들 몇 명을 데리고 가죠?

여: 선생님 동아리에서 5명 그리고 제 동아리에서 6명이요.

남: 그리고 표가 얼마인가요?

여: 하나에 10달러예요.

남: 오, 보세요. 다음 주 수요일이 문화의 날인 마지막 주 수요일이네요. 우리는 특별 할인을 받을 수 있어요.

여: 맞네요! 우리는 각 표당 30% 할인을 받을 수 있어요.

남: 그리고 우리 두 사람의 표를 사는 것도 잊지 마세요.

여: 당연히 잊지 않죠. 제가 이미 웹 페이지에 우리도 포함시켰어요.

남: 좋아요. 모든 게 정확해 보이네요.

여: 그럼, 제가 지금 카드로 지불할게요.

문제 해결
표 하나에 10달러라고 했는데, 문화의 날이라 30%를 할인받아 표 하나에 7달러이다. 동아리 학생 6명과 5명을 합하면 11명에, 교사 2명을 포함하면 총 13명이므로, 지불해야 할 총 금액은 91달러이다.

어휘·표현
be about to 막 ~하려는 참이다   include 포함시키다

07 ④
이유 파악

여: 안녕, Dan. 학술적 영어 작문 수업 어땠니?

남: 사실, 나 그 수업 취소했어.

여: 왜? 넌 네가 가장 좋아하는 교수님이 가르치신다고 신나 보였는데.

남: 나 신났었어! 심지어 그 수업 때문에 내 스케줄까지 바꿨다고.

여: 알아. 너 아르바이트를 월요일에서 화요일로 옮겼잖아.

남: 그래, 게다가 학술적 영어 수업 전 필수 과목인 기본 영어 작문 수업

도 지난 학기에 수강했어.

여: 맞아. 너 그 수업에서 A를 받았잖아!

남: 어쨌든, 나는 다음 학기에 학술적 작문 수업을 수강 신청해야 할 것 같아.

여: 무슨 일이 있었는데?

남: 너무 많은 학생들이 그 수업에 등록하고 싶어 해서 교수님이 이번 학기엔 2학년생만 수업을 수강하도록 하셨어.

여: 그 수업 진짜 인기 있는 게 틀림없구나. 나도 그 수업 듣고 싶다.

남: 다음 학기에 같이 수강 신청하자.

남자는 학술적 영어 작문 수업을 수강하기 위해 아르바이트 시간도 바꾸고 필수 과목도 들었지만 교수님이 2학년생만 수업을 수강하도록 해서 수업을 취소했다고 했으므로, 수강 신청을 포기한 이유로 ④가 가장 적절하다.

drop 그만두다   required 필수의   register for ~에 등록하다, 수강 신청을 하다

08 ②

여: 안녕, Liam. 너 바이올린 들고 어디 가니?

남: 안녕, Jean. 나 지역 오케스트라 연습에 가는 중이야.

여: 오, 나도 그 오케스트라에 정말 들고 싶어.

남: 맞아! 난 네가 플루트를 연주하는 걸 알고 있어. 너도 꼭 들어와!

여: 들어가려면 뭐가 필요해?

남: 네가 지역 주민이라는 걸 보여 주는 거주 증명서와 너의 악기가 필요해.

여: 얼마나 자주 연습하니?

남: 일주일에 한 번. 우리는 매주 화요일 밤 7시 30분부터 9시 30분까지 만나.

여: 그렇구나. 연습은 어디서 하니?

남: Madison 음대의 강의실을 사용하고 있어. 그곳은 여기서 멀지 않아.

여: 정말 완벽한 것 같다. 콘서트도 여니?

남: 그럼! 우리는 일 년에 두 번 콘서트를 열어.

여: 멋지다! 나 꼭 지원할 거야!

Community Orchestra의 단원을 모집하는 시기는 언급하지 않았다.

community 지역 사회, 공동체   proof 증명(서)   take place (계획된 일이) 개최되다, 열리다   as well 또한   definitely 분명히, 꼭, 절대로   apply 지원하다

09 ②

남: 안녕하세요, 학생 여러분. 행정실의 Garcia 선생님입니다. 내일 5교시 수업 직후에 지진 대비 훈련이 있을 예정입니다. 알람 소리를 듣는 순간, 교사의 지시에 따라 차분하고 질서 있는 태도로 중앙 또는 서쪽 계단을 이용하여 건물 밖으로 나가십시오. 동쪽 계단은 아직 보수 중이기 때문에 사용하지 말고 승강기를 사용하지 마십시오. 긴급 상황 시에는 절대 승강기를 사용해서는 안 됩니다. 집합 장소는 운동장입니다. 교사가 모두 있는지를 확인할 수 있도록 반별로 모여 주십시오. 운동장에서는 근처 소방서에서 오신 구급대원이 여러분에게 응급 처치 방법을 가르쳐 주실 것입니다. 여러분들이 이 훈련에 진지하게 참여하기를 바랍니다. 여러분의 협력에 감사를 표합니다.

동쪽 계단은 보수 중이라 사용하지 말라고 했으므로 ②가 내용과 일치하지 않는다.

drill 훈련, 연습   instruction 지시   orderly 질서 있는   under repair 보수 중인   assembly 집결   paramedic 구급대원, 응급 의료 요원   cooperation 협력, 협조

10 ②

남: 여보, 로봇 진공청소기를 사는 것에 대해 어떻게 생각해요? 그것은 우리가 집안일에 시간을 덜 쓰도록 도와줄 거예요.

여: 나도 전적으로 동의해요. 어떤 모델을 살지 결정해 봐요.

남: [클릭 소리] 이 후기들을 봐요. 어느 정도의 흡입력이 필요할까요?

여: 어디 봐요. 우리는 적어도 600파스칼은 필요해요.

남: 그래요. 내 생각에 작동 시간은 2시간 이상은 돼야 해요.

여: 맞아요. 음, HEPA 필터가 있는 게 필요할까요?

남: HEPA 필터가 무슨 용도인데요?

여: 그건 청소 동안에 미세 먼지를 제거하는 걸 도와줘요. 하지만 더 비싸네요.

남: 우리는 이미 공기 청정기가 있잖아요. 나는 그것이 필요하다고 생각하지 않아요.

여: 좋아요. 보증 기간은요?

남: 길수록 좋아요.

여: 그러면, 우리는 이걸 사야겠네요. 주문하죠.

두 사람은 흡입력은 적어도 600파스칼이 되어야 하고 작동 시간은 2시간 이상이 되어야 하며, HEPA 필터는 필요 없고, 남은 것 중 보증 기간이 더 긴 청소기를 찾고 있다. 따라서 구매할 로봇 청소기는 ②이다.

vacuum cleaner 진공청소기   chore 가사, 집일   suction 흡입   pascal 파스칼 (압력의 국제단위)   fine dust 미세 먼지   warranty 보증   place an order 주문하다

11 ②

남: 기다리게 해서 죄송합니다. 지금 주문하시겠어요?

여: 음, 제가 여기 채식주의 메뉴가 있다고 들었는데 찾을 수가 없네요.

남: 오, 죄송해요. 저희는 주말에만 그 메뉴를 제공합니다. 다른 것을 주문하시겠어요?

여: 미안합니다. 그러면 주말에 다시 올게요.

채식주의 메뉴를 찾는 여자에게 남자가 채식 메뉴는 주말에만 제공한다고 했으므로, 여자의 응답으로 주말에 다시 오겠다는 ②가 가장 적절하다.

① 훌륭해요. 이 음식은 맛이 정말 좋군요.

③ 괜찮아요. 저는 쇠고기 스테이크를 먹을게요.

④ 네, 야채를 먹는 것은 건강에 좋습니다.

⑤ 물론이죠. 이제 채식 메뉴를 가져다주시겠어요?

vegetarian 채식주의자, 채식주의의   offer 제공하다

12 ③
짧은 대화의 응답

여: 와, 경치 좀 봐. 바다와 하늘이 멋있게 보인다.

남: 그래, 정말 멋지다. 그런데 바람이 너무 강하고 쌀쌀해.

여: 그럼, 몸을 따뜻하게 하러 저기 카페테리아에 가는 게 어때?

남: 좋아. 핫초코를 마시자.

문제 해결

경치는 좋지만 춥다는 남자의 말에 여자가 카페테리아에 가서 몸을 녹이자고 제안하고 있으므로, 남자의 응답으로 그 제안에 동의하며 따뜻한 음료를 마시자는 내용의 ③이 가장 적절하다.

① 미안해. 나는 네가 감기에 걸린 줄 몰랐어.

② 조심해. 바다에서 수영하는 것은 많은 기술이 필요해.

④ 걱정하지 마. 어제 날씨는 화창했어.

⑤ 고맙지만 사양할게. 난 너무 추워.

어휘·표현

view 경치 chilly 쌀쌀한, 추운

13 ①
긴 대화의 응답

남: Emily, 이번 주 토요일에 시간 있니? 영화 보러 가자.

여: 미안, 나 매주 토요일마다 동물 보호소에서 봉사 활동을 해.

남: 그래? 너 진짜 착하다. 거기서 무슨 일을 하니?

여: 나는 지원자들이 애완동물을 돌보는 데 적합한지를 보기 위해 입양 신청서를 검토해.

남: 멋지다. 어쩌다 거기서 봉사활동을 시작하게 되었어?

여: 내가 한번은 개를 잃어버린 적이 있었는데 거기서 찾았어. 난 그곳에서 너무 많은 개와 고양이를 보고 무척 충격을 받았지.

남: 그 동물들은 다 잃어버린 애들이니?

여: 몇몇은 그래. 그런데 많은 동물들이 늙었거나 아프거나 심지어 너무 크다고 버려진 거야.

남: 사람들이 어떻게 그런 짓을 할 수 있지? 나는 애완동물이 있는 사람들은 애완동물을 가족으로 생각한다고 알았는데.

여: 대부분의 사람들은 그래. 그런데 내 생각에 몇몇 사람들은 너무 무책임할 수 있어.

남: 네 말이 맞아. 사람들은 애완동물을 키우는 것에 대해 진지하게 생각해야 해.

문제 해결

몇몇 사람들이 애완동물을 버리는 것에 대해 너무 무책임하다는 여자의 의견에 대한 남자의 응답으로, ① '네 말이 맞아. 사람들은 애완동물을 키우는 것에 대해 진지하게 생각해야 해.'가 가장 적절하다.

② 그거 좋은 소식이네. 더 많은 사람들이 기꺼이 자원봉사를 할 거야.

③ 걱정하지 마. 네가 없는 동안 내가 너의 애완동물을 잘 돌볼 수 있어.

④ 이해해 줘서 고마워. 내 개가 말썽을 피우진 않을 거야.

⑤ 나도 동의해. 멸종 위기 야생 동물을 보호하는 것은 정말 중요한 일이야.

어휘·표현

go over 검토하다 adoption 입양 application 지원(서), 신청(서)
suitable 적절한 abandon 버리다 irresponsible 무책임한

14 ③
긴 대화의 응답

남: Chloe, 제가 뭘 물어봐도 될까요?

여: 그럼요, Jack. 무엇인가요?

남: 당신이 중국어를 잘한다는 걸 알고 있어요. 제게 조언을 해 줄 수 있을까요? 제가 중국어로 간단한 대화를 할 수 있었으면 해요.

여: 왜요?

남: 제 새로운 업무에 중국 회사와 일하는 것이 필요해요. 기본적인 대화 기술이 좋은 관계를 맺는 데 도움이 될 거예요.

여: 그러면, 어학원에서 수업을 듣는 게 어때요?

남: 제가 요즘 너무 바빠서 수업을 정기적으로 들을 수 있을 것 같지 않네요.

여: 음…. 당신은 회사 올 때 운전을 하죠, 그렇죠?

남: 네, 그래요. 왜 그러세요?

여: 운전하는 동안 라디오를 듣는 게 어때요? ABC 라디오 방송에 30분짜리 기초 중국어 프로그램이 있어요.

남: 괜찮겠는데요. 그런데 그걸로 충분할 거라 생각하세요?

여: 그럼요. 매일 하는 적은 학습이 기적 같은 효과를 낳을 거예요.

문제 해결

중국어를 배우고 싶은데 너무 바빠서 어학원 수업을 들을 시간은 없다는 남자의 말에 여자는 운전하는 동안 기초 중국어 라디오 방송을 들을 것을 조언하고 있다. 그것으로 충분하겠냐는 남자의 물음에 대한 여자의 응답으로 ③ '그럼요. 매일 하는 적은 학습이 기적 같은 효과를 낳을 거예요.'가 가장 적절하다.

① 맞아요. 학원 수업을 듣는 것이 매우 중요해요.

② 전혀요. 당신은 선생님의 충고를 따라야 해요.

④ 그렇진 않아요. 외국 회사와 일하는 것은 저에게 동기를 부여합니다.

⑤ 당연하죠! 차를 운전하는 것은 통근 시간을 줄여 줄 수 있어요.

어휘·표현

academy 학원 regularly 정기적으로 motivate 동기를 부여하다
commute time 통근 시간

15 ⑤
상황에 적절한 말

여: Ryan과 Ella는 친구의 생일 선물을 찾고 있다. 갑자기 Ryan은 노트북 상점에 들어가서 둘러보고 싶어 한다. 그가 오래 걸리지 않을 것이라 약속해서 그들은 안으로 들어간다. Ryan은 몇 달 동안 노트북을 사고 싶어 했어서 최신 모델을 보면서 매우 신나 한다. 그러나 예상한 것보다 시간이 오래 걸린다. Ryan은 가장 비싼 노트북을 사려는 참이지만, Ella는 그들이 친구의 생일 선물을 사기 위해 이 상점을 나가야 한다고 생각한다. 어쨌든 Ryan은 가격과 모델을 더 신중하게 비교해야 한다. 이런 상황에서, Ella는 Ryan에게 뭐라고 말할 것 같은가?

문제 해결

Ryan이 가장 비싼 노트북을 사려는 것을 말리고 친구의 생일 선물을 사러 가자고 해야 하는 상황에서 Ella가 할 말로 ⑤ '선물을 먼저 사고 노트북은 인터넷으로 확인해 보는 건 어때?'가 가장 적절하다.

① 내 생일 선물로 노트북을 사는 게 어때?

② 네 노트북을 어디서 고칠 수 있는지 아니?

③ 노트북 상점이 어디에 있니?

④ 최신 노트북을 산 다음 집에 갈 거야.

어휘·표현

latest 최신의

16-17
복합 이해

남: 안녕하세요, 학생 여러분! 이전에, 우리는 식물이 실내의 해로운 화학

물질을 제거하고 공기를 깨끗이 하는 데 어떻게 작용하는지를 공부했습니다. 이 시간에 우리는 어떤 종류의 실내 식물이 공기를 깨끗하게 유지하는 데 특별히 좋은지를 알아볼 것입니다. 첫 번째는 서양담쟁이덩굴(English ivy)입니다. 이 사시사철 푸른 덩굴 식물은 야외에서 흔하게 볼 수 있으며 실내에도 잘 적응합니다. 이 식물은 특히 공기 중의 일산화탄소를 제거하는 데 아주 좋습니다. 자주달개비(spider plant) 또한 특정 화학 물질을 제거하는 데 좋고 키우기가 정말 쉽습니다. 그것은 빨리 자라고 매달린 바구니에 멋지게 어울립니다. 또 다른 공기 정화 슈퍼스타는 관음죽(bamboo palm)입니다. 이것은 또한 공기 중에 건강한 약간의 수분을 주어 건조한 겨울 기간 동안 더욱 환영받습니다. 어떤 식물이 공기를 정화하는 데 가장 뛰어날지 추측할 수 있나요? 그것은 가을에 피는 흔한 식물인 국화(garden mum)입니다. 이제 온실로 들어가서 그 식물들을 보도록 하죠.

어휘·표현

function 작동하다 기능하다   toxic 해로운, 독성의   chemical 화학물질
carbon monoxide 일산화탄소   filter 거르다   dose 약간
welcome addition 환영받는 존재   misconception 오해
purification 정화, 정제

16 ⑤

문제 해결

실내 공기 청정에 좋은 식물의 종류를 열거하며 소개하고 있으므로, 남자가 하는 말의 주제로 ⑤ '공기 청정에 좋은 식물'이 가장 적절하다.
① 식물이 공기 중의 화학 물질을 제거하는 방법
② 식물에 관한 미신과 오해
③ 식물을 기르는 것이 정신 건강에 좋은 이유
④ 초보자가 기르기 쉬운 식물

17 ③

문제 해결

실내 공기 청정 식물의 종류로 고무나무(rubber tree)는 언급하지 않았다.

01 ④	02 ④	03 ②	04 ④	05 ①	06 ③
07 ⑤	08 ③	09 ⑤	10 ②	11 ②	12 ②
13 ②	14 ①	15 ④	16 ②	17 ③	

01 ④   목적 파악

남: 안녕하세요, 동료 여러분. 저는 관리부서의 책임자인 Richard Barker입니다. 아시다시피, 여러분의 편리를 위해 우리는 작년에 건물 뒤에 새로운 주차장을 확보했습니다. 아마도 사무실과 주차장과의 거리 때문에, 유감스럽게도 많은 직원들이 그곳에 주차하지 않고 있습니다. 그 대신, 많은 직원들은 정문 바깥쪽이나 근처 도로에 주차하고 있습니다. 이러한 부주의한 주차는 보행자의 통행을 방해할 뿐만 아니라 우리의 안전에도 영향을 미칩니다. 입구 근처의 주도로는 화재와 같은 긴급 상황에 대비하여 항상 비워져 있어야 합니다. 그래서 다음 주부터 주차 구역 밖에 주차된 차량은 견인될 것입니다. 여러분의 협조에 미리 감사드립니다.

문제 해결

주차 구역 외에 주차된 차량은 견인될 것이라며 지정된 주차장을 이용할 것을 당부하고 있다.

어휘·표현

maintenance (점검·보수하는) 유지   secure 확보하다   nearby 근처의
interrupt 방해하다   pedestrian 보행자   in case of ~에 대비하여   tow away 견인하다

02 ④   주제 파악

남: Rebecca, 컴퓨터로 무엇을 보고 있니?
여: 오, Greg. 난 친구들을 위해 초콜릿을 고르고 있어. 밸런타인데이가 바로 코앞이잖아.
남: 그날은 교제 중인 사람들이 서로에게 사랑을 표현하는 전통적인 날이라고 알고 있어.
여: 오, 나는 남자 친구가 아니라 친구들을 위해 사탕을 좀 사려는 것 뿐이야.
남: 매우 친절하구나, 하지만 나는 밸런타인데이가 너무 상업화되는 것이 걱정이 되는데.
여: 상업화가 된다고? 어떤 면에서?
남: 요즘, 많은 회사들이 수많은 사탕과 초콜릿을 판매하는 수단으로 밸런타인데이를 이용해.
여: 응, 부분적으로는 사실이지만, 선물을 주면서 친구들에게 좋아한다고 표현할 수 있는 좋은 기회라고 생각해.
남: 정말 그렇게 생각하니?
여: 물론이지. 그날에 친구들과 사탕을 나눈다면, 관계가 더 가까워질 수 있어.
남: 네가 맞을 수도 있어. 하지만 나로서는 수긍은 못하겠어.

문제 해결

여자는 밸런타인데이에 선물을 주면서 친구들과 더 가까워질 수 있다고 말하고 있다.

be around the corner 목전에 닥치다, 곧 오다   sweets 사탕, 단 것
commercialize 상업화하다

03 ②
관계 추론

여: Blake, 만나게 돼서 정말 반갑구나!
남: 안녕하세요. Johnson 선생님. 다시 뵙게 되어 기뻐요.
여: 지난달에 네가 제과점을 열었다는 소식을 들었어. 축하한다!
남: 감사합니다, 선생님. 선생님이 자랑스러워하실 수 있도록 최선을 다할 거예요.
여: 난 이미 네가 자랑스럽단다. 음, 다른 급우들 소식은 들었니?
남: 네, 들었어요. Jessica는 의학에서 학위를 받게 되고 Scott은 군대에 있어요.
여: 소식 듣게 되어 기쁘구나. 생각해 보니, 넌 매우 창의적인 학생이었단다.
남: 그렇게 말씀해 주시니 감사해요. 오, 여기 선생님을 위해 만든 케이크예요.
여: 오, 정말 자상하구나! 이 케이크는 먹기에는 너무나 훌륭하구나. 고마워.
남: 좋아하시니 저도 기뻐요. 제가 학교에 있을 때, 선생님은 저를 많이 도와주셨어요.
여: 천만에, Blake. 나를 만나러 와 주다니 고맙구나.

문제 해결
학교를 졸업하고 제과점을 개업한 남자가 선생님을 방문하여 인사를 나누는 상황이므로, 여자와 남자는 교사와 졸업생의 관계이다.

어휘·표현
get a degree 학위를 받다   medicine 의학   come to think of it 생각해 보니, 그러고 보니

04 ④
그림 불일치 파악

남: 여보, 난 우리 여행이 정말 기대돼요. 알다시피, 난 이번이 첫 해외여행이잖아요.
여: 나도 흥분돼요, 하지만 당신은 좀 진정할 필요가 있어요. 탑승권을 다시 확인해 봐요.
남: 좋아요. 항공편 번호와 날짜는 오른쪽에 있어요.
여: 맞아요. 그 아래에 Kims 항공사의 로고가 보이죠?
남: 그래요. 그건 단순한 로고지만, 매우 눈길을 끄는 것 같아요.
여: 나도 그렇게 생각해요. 왼쪽 상단에 내 이름, Linda Mason이 있어요.
남: 출발지와 목적지 도시에 관한 정보는 중앙에 있어요.
여: 그래요, 우리는 시애틀로 갈 거예요. 음…. 탑승을 위한 출입구 번호가 어디에 있지요?
남: 왼쪽 아래에, 출입구 번호가 8이라고 쓰여 있어요.
여: 그러면, 그 출입구 쪽으로 가서 거기서 기다리는 게 어때요?
남: 좋아요. 이동합시다.

문제 해결
여자는 시애틀로 갈 거라고 했으므로, 보딩패스에서 목적지를 표시하는 ④는 대화의 내용과 일치하지 않는다.

어휘·표현
boarding pass 탑승권   flight number 항공편 번호   eye-catching 눈길을 끄는   departure 출발   destination 목적지

05 ①
할 일 파악

남: 오늘 바빠 보이는구나, Christine. 무슨 일이야?
여: 아, 송별회 때문에 교실을 장식하고 있어.
남: 송별회? 누구 송별회?
여: 우리 교생 선생님인 Guzman 선생님.
남: 아, 맞다. 이번 금요일이 우리 학교에 계시는 선생님의 마지막 날이지.
여: 응. 몇몇 학생들이 그녀를 위해 환송 파티를 열어 주면 좋겠다고 생각했어.
남: 좋은 생각이다. 내가 도울 일이 뭐 있니?
여: 물론이지. 우리는 얻을 수 있는 모든 도움이 필요해, Jason. 칠판에 우리 반 친구들 그림을 그려 줄 수 있어?
남: 그림 그리는 건 빼고. 난 그림은 형편없거든.
여: 알겠어. 그러면 이 풍선 좀 불어 줄래?
남: 좋아. 바로 시작할게.
여: 정말 고마워!

문제 해결
남자는 그림을 그리는 것 대신 풍선을 불어 주기로 했다.

어휘·표현
farewell party 송별회   throw a going-away party 환송 파티를 열다
blow up (풍선 등에) 공기를 주입하다   get started (어떤 일을) 시작하다

06 ③
숫자 정보 파악

남: 안녕하세요. 무엇을 도와드릴까요?
여: 안녕하세요. Digest 잡지 헌 책이 있나요?
남: 물론입니다. 그것들은 섹션 B에 있습니다. 이쪽으로 오세요.
여: 감사합니다. [잠시 후] 와! 정말 많은 과월호가 있네요. 그것들은 얼마인가요?
남: 각각 5달러입니다. 하지만 대량으로 구입하시면 각각 1달러씩 할인해 드릴 수 있습니다.
여: 대량으로요? 저 묶음을 말씀하시는 건가요?
남: 네. 한 묶음이 그해의 12개호 전부입니다.
여: 좋습니다. 작년에 출판된 묶음을 구입하겠습니다. 오, 잠시만요! 사이클링에 관한 잡지도 있네요.
남: 그렇습니다. 그것에 관심이 있으시면 각각 3달러에 드릴 수 있습니다.
여: 괜찮은 거래네요. 그러면, 지난달 호를 구입하겠습니다.
남: 알겠습니다. 잠시만요. 봉지에 전부 넣어 드리겠습니다.

문제 해결
Digest 잡지 12권을 각각 4달러에 구입하며, 추가로 사이클링 잡지 한 권을 3달러에 구입하고 있으므로 여자가 지불할 금액은 51달러이다.

어휘·표현
secondhand 중고의   issue 판, 호, 발행   in bulk 대량으로   bundle 묶음, 꾸러미   deal 거래

07 ⑤
이유 파악

[전화벨이 울린다.]
남: Lion Fitness Center입니다! 무엇을 도와드릴까요?
여: 안녕하세요, 저는 Carol Parker입니다. 온라인으로 방금 세 달치 라이온 회원권에 등록했습니다.
남: 등록해 주셔서 감사합니다. 이전에 우리 체육관을 이용해 보신 적이

있나요?

여: 아뇨, 하지만 작년에 다른 피트니스 센터에서 운동했었습니다.

남: 알겠습니다. 우리 센터는 최신 장비와 사우나를 갖추고 있습니다. 우리 시설에서 운동하시는 것을 매우 좋아하실 겁니다.

여: 그러길 바랍니다. 음, 제가 온라인에서 선택한 사은품을 변경할 수 있을지 물어 보려고 전화했습니다.

남: 잠시만 기다려 주세요. *[타이핑 소리]* 웨이트 트레이닝 장갑을 선택하셨네요, 맞지요?

여: 네, 그런데 가능하면 그것을 수건으로 바꾸고 싶습니다.

남: 잠시만요. 오, 다행히 남은 수건이 몇 장 있습니다.

여: 다행이네요. 오늘 저녁에 가면, 그것을 받을 수 있을까요?

남: 물론이죠. 오셨을 때 Rob을 찾으시면, 그가 드릴 겁니다.

여: 알겠습니다. 저녁에 뵙겠습니다.

문제 해결

여자는 사은품으로 선택한 장갑을 수건으로 바꿀 수 있는지 문의하고 있으므로 여자가 전화를 건 이유로 ⑤가 가장 적절하다.

어휘·표현

register 등록하다   state-of-the-art 최신식의   be equipped with ~을 갖추다   equipment 장비   facility 시설

08 ③   언급 유무 파악

남: Kelly, 여름 방학에 뭐 할 거니?

여: 다음 주에 가족들과 함께 Sunrise Resorts에 갈 거야.

남: 정말? 난 전에 거기에 가 본 적이 있어. 네가 즐길 수 있는 많은 활동이 있을 거야.

여: 반가운 소식이야. 거기에서 스쿠버 다이빙이나 스노클링을 할 수 있을지 궁금한데.

남: 물론이지. 두 가지 활동에 대한 프로그램이 있어. 넌 아름다운 산호초의 숨 막히는 광경을 결코 잊지 못할 거야.

여: 근사하게 들린다.

남: 그게 다가 아니야. 현지 요리를 맛볼 수 있는 좋은 기회가 될 거야.

여: 좋다. 우리는 거기서 며칠 머무를 거야. 저녁에 우리가 할 수 있는 어떤 활동이 있을까?

남: 선택할 수 있는 것들이 많지만 가족들과 함께 사우나에 가는 것을 추천하고 싶어. 물이 정말 피부에 좋다고 하더라고.

여: 이미 편안한 느낌이 든다. 도움이 되는 정보를 줘서 고마워.

문제 해결

Sunrise Resorts 프로그램 중 '불꽃놀이'에 대한 언급은 없었다.

어휘·표현

breathtaking 숨이 (턱) 막히는[멎는 듯한]   coral reef 산호초   cuisine 요리   option 선택

09 ⑤   담화 내용 불일치

여: 주목해 주세요, 학생 여러분. 제 이름은 Jennifer Mason이고 Vision 어학실을 책임지고 있습니다. 우리 어학실은 비전 센터의 2층에 위치해 있습니다. 학생 사용을 위해 24대의 데스크톱 컴퓨터와 4대의 프린터를 갖추고 있습니다. 우리 공간은 잠시 들르는 공간과 3개의 교실을 포함하고 있습니다. 모든 교실은 비디오 카메라와 마이크 시설을 갖추고 있어서 수업이 쉽게 녹화되고 업로드될 수 있습니다. 이 교실들은 매주 수요일에 정기적으로 열리는 회화 교육을 위해

사용됩니다. 모든 학생들은 이 수업을 무료로 들을 수 있지만 학교 웹 사이트를 통해서 먼저 수업에 등록해야 합니다. 질문이 있으면, 중앙 사무실에 연락 주세요. 감사합니다.

문제 해결

수강 신청은 학교 웹 사이트를 통해서 해야 한다고 안내하고 있으므로, ⑤가 담화의 내용과 일치하지 않는다.

어휘·표현

language lab 어학실   be equipped with ~을 갖추다   drop-in (예약 없이) 잠시 들르는   on a regular basis 정기적으로   register for ~에 등록하다   in advance 먼저, 미리

10 ②   도표 정보 파악

여: Brian, 무엇을 보고 있니?

남: 오, 안녕, Sarah. 엄마 생일 선물로 립스틱을 찾고 있어. 내가 고르는 것을 좀 도와줄래?

여: 물론이지. 분홍색을 고르면 전혀 문제가 없을 거야. 엄마가 그것을 매우 좋아하실 거야.

남: 맞아, 하지만 엄마는 이미 그 색깔을 갖고 계셔. 나는 그녀에게 다른 색깔을 드리고 싶어.

여: 그녀 피부가 꽤 흰 편이라서, 많은 다른 색깔이 그녀에게 어울릴 것 같다.

남: 용량에 대해서라면, 어느 것이 가장 좋을까?

여: 음, 가장 적은 것은 추천하고 싶지 않아. 그것은 순식간에 다 쓰게 될 거야.

남: 그러면, 3g짜리는 제외시켜야겠다.

여: 어떤 가격대를 고려하고 있니?

남: 나는 15달러에서 20달러 사이에서 쓰려고 생각 중이야.

여: 그러면, 두 가지 선택이 남았네. 이것은 어때? 사은품으로 립 라이너를 같이 주네.

남: 음, 나쁘진 않아. 하지만 다른 것을 주문해야겠다.

문제 해결

분홍색과 3g짜리를 제외하고, 15달러에서 20달러 사이의 립스틱을 고르고 있다. 마지막으로 사은품이 립 라이너가 아닌 다른 것을 원하므로 남자가 구매할 립스틱은 ②이다.

어휘·표현

go wrong (일이) 잘못되다, 문제를 겪다   fair 흰 피부의   when it comes to ~에 대해서라면   run out 다 떨어지다, 부족하다   leave out 제외시키다

11 ②   짧은 대화의 응답

남: Janice, 너 신나 보인다. 좋은 소식이라도 있니?

여: 사실, 내가 관리자로 승진된다고 방금 연락받았어.

남: 정말? 축하해! 넌 오랫동안 그 자리를 원했잖아.

여: **고마워. 나에게 좋은 기회가 될 거야.**

문제 해결

여자가 승진한다는 소식을 듣고 축하하는 남자의 말에 대한 여자의 응답으로 ② '고마워. 나에게 좋은 기회가 될 거야.'가 가장 적절하다.

① 천만에. 그는 그 자리를 맡을 자격이 있어.

③ 미안해. 넌 그 일을 수락할 수밖에 없어.

④ 물론이지. 다른 회사로 옮기는 게 나을 거야.

⑤ 유감이다. 내가 네게 지난 주에 말했어야 했는데.

promote 승진하다   deserve ~을 받을 만하다, 누릴 자격이 있다
have no choice but to ~할 수 밖에 없다

12 ②

여: 여보, 모든 사람들이 이제 집에 간 것 같아요.
남: 그래요. 마침내 파티가 끝났어요. 당신은 훌륭히 해냈어요.
여: 당신도요. 이제 집 청소를 시작할 시간이에요.
남: 맞아요. 식탁을 먼저 치웁시다.

문제 해결

파티가 끝나고 집 청소를 하자는 여자의 말에 대한 남자의 응답으로 ② '맞아요.
식탁을 먼저 치웁시다.'가 가장 적절하다.
① 서둘러요. 파티에 늦겠어요.
③ 물론이죠. 우린 그 파티의 집주인에게 선물을 줘야 해요.
④ 농담하지 말아요. 난 파티에 가고 싶지 않아요.
⑤ 좋아요. 집에 택시를 타고 갑시다.

어휘·표현

clean up 청소하다   clear 치우다

13 ②

여: 안녕하세요, 손님. 무엇을 도와드릴까요?
남: 안녕하세요. 지난주에 이 바지를 샀는데요, 잘 맞지가 않네요.
여: 그런 말씀을 듣게 되어 유감입니다. 영수증을 볼 수 있을까요?
남: 네. 여기 있습니다.
여: 그것을 구입하실 때 입어 보시지 않았나요?
남: 입어 보지 않았습니다. 그것은 제 사이즈라서 잘 맞을 것을 의심하지
   않았어요. 저는 그것을 더 큰 사이즈로 교환하고 싶어요.
여: 잠시만요. 음…. 오, 그것이 저희가 가지고 있는 가장 큰 사이즈입니
   다.
남: 그러면, 환불을 받을 수밖에 없네요.
여: 오, 정말 죄송합니다. 그것은 특별 할인 제품이라서, 환불이 안 됩니다.
남: 뭐라고요? 그러면 제가 어떻게 해야 하나요? 전 그것을 입을 수가 없
   어요.
여: 다른 상품을 구매할 수 있는 상품권을 받으실 수 있습니다. 그 밖에
   다른 것이 필요하신가요?
남: 그런 경우라면, 셔츠 좀 둘러볼게요.

문제 해결

환불이 불가능해서 다른 상품을 구입할 수 있는 상품권을 줄 수밖에 없다는 여
자의 말에 대한 남자의 응답으로 ② '그런 경우라면, 셔츠 좀 둘러볼게요.'가 가
장 적절하다.
① 죄송합니다만, 영수증을 가져오는 것을 잊었습니다.
③ 그러면, 그것을 더 큰 사이즈로 교환하고 싶습니다.
④ 맞아요, 전 이 바지를 다른 색깔로 구입하고 싶어요.
⑤ 물론이죠, 저는 지난 주말에 여기에서 구입한 바지가 마음에 듭니다.

어휘·표현

have no choice but to (do) ~할 수 밖에 없다   get a refund 환불받다
store credit 상품권

14 ①

여: 안녕, Alex. 무슨 일 있니? 너 피곤해 보인다.
남: 안녕, Brooke. 사실 난 요즘 잠을 잘 자지 못하고 있어.
여: 그런 말을 들어서 유감이구나. 불면증 같은 것이 있는 거니?
남: 그건 아니고, 내 룸메이트가 나를 미치게 해. 그는 정말 밤잠이 없는
   사람이야.
여: 끔찍하구나. 그것에 관해 그에게 이야기해 보았니?
남: 응, 하지만 전혀 도움이 되지 않았어. 게다가 기숙사 복도는 늘 시끄
   러워. 사람들이 때를 안 가리고 돌아다녀.
여: 어떤 기분인지 알겠다. 나도 같은 이유로 지난달에 학교 기숙사에서
   나왔어.
남: 정말? 그것을 미처 몰랐네.
여: 기숙사에서 나오는 게 어떠니? 그것이 네가 학업에 집중하는 데 도움
   이 될 거야.
남: 그래. 나오는 게 낫겠어. 이번 주말에 내가 방을 찾는 것을 도와줄래?
여: 물론이지. 몇몇 조용한 장소가 생각이 나네.

문제 해결

이번 주말에 방을 찾는 것을 도와달라는 남자의 말에 대한 여자의 응답으로 ①
'물론이지. 몇몇 조용한 장소가 생각이 나네.'가 가장 적절하다.
② 응. 내가 이사할 때 네가 도움이 되었어.
③ 아니. 난 기숙사를 나온 것이 후회돼.
④ 걱정 마. 넌 기숙사에 적응하게 될 거야.
⑤ 물론이지. 네 룸메이트와 얼굴을 맞대고 대화하는 게 최선이야.

어휘·표현

insomnia 불면증   night owl 밤잠이 없는 사람   dormitory 기숙사
at all hours 때를 가리지 않고   concentrate on ~에 집중하다

15 ④

남: Rebecca와 Karen은 중학교 때부터 가장 친한 친구이다. 그들은 자
   매처럼 모든 것을 함께 한다. 그들은 공통점이 많다. 그들은 영화, 책,
   음악, 그리고 심지어 패션에 이르기까지 비슷한 취향을 갖고 있다. 그
   들은 서로를 의지할 수 있는 것에 항상 감사한다. 한번은, 그들이 같
   이 쇼핑하러 가서 동시에 같은 옷을 집어서 매우 놀라기도 했다. 오늘
   은 Rebecca의 생일이다. Karen은 그녀를 축하하려고 Rebecca를
   방문해서 그녀에게 생일 선물을 준다. Rebecca가 선물 상자를 열자,
   그녀는 요전 날에 쇼핑몰에서 자신이 사고 싶었던 바로 그 꽃무늬 스
   카프를 발견하고는 유쾌하게 놀란다. 이런 상황에서 Rebecca는
   Karen에게 무엇이라고 말할 것 같은가?

문제 해결

자신이 사고 싶었던 스카프를 선물 상자에서 발견한 상황이므로 Rebecca가
Karen에게 할 말로 ④ '네가 내 마음을 읽었구나. 그것은 바로 내가 원했던 거
야.'가 가장 적절하다.
① 고마워. 네가 스카프를 마음에 들어 해서 기쁘다.
② 고마워, 하지만 유감스럽게도 이것은 내 스타일이 아니야.
③ 좋아. 그 스카프는 네 눈을 돋보이게 한다.
⑤ 내가 선물을 고르는 것을 도와줘서 고마워.

어휘·표현

grateful 감사하는   count on 의지하다   pull out 집다, 뽑다   outfit 옷, 의상
bring out 눈에 띄게 만들다

16-17

여: 장수 건강 관리 센터에 오신 것을 환영합니다. 모든 사람들은 질병 없이 더 길고, 건강하고, 행복한 삶을 살길 원합니다. 그러나 우리가 나이가 들어가면서, 고혈압을 겪는 것을 피하는 것은 어렵습니다. 좋은 소식은 우리가 먹는 것을 주의한다면 고혈압을 예방할 수 있다는 것입니다. 예를 들어, 블루베리는 플라보노이드라고 불리는 자연 화합물이 풍부합니다. 한 연구에 따르면, 이러한 화합물을 섭취하는 것은 고혈압을 예방하고 혈압을 낮추는 데 도움이 될 수 있습니다. 또한, 일주일에 적어도 다섯 번 요거트를 먹는다면 고혈압 발병의 위험을 낮출 수 있습니다. 바나나 섭취는 어떻습니까? 바나나는 혈압을 낮추는 데 유효한 칼륨이 풍부하다고 알려져 있습니다. 또한, 여러분은 식단에 연어와 같은 생선을 포함시킬 것을 고려해 볼 수 있습니다. 이러한 종류의 생선은 오메가 3 지방산이 매우 풍부한데, 이것은 혈압을 조절하고 염증을 줄이는 데 효과적입니다. 생활 방식을 급격하게 바꾸는 것은 다소 부담스럽고 실천하기 어려울 수 있습니다. 하지만 더 나은 식단을 선택하는 것은 건강한 삶으로의 쉬운 첫 번째 발걸음이 될 수 있습니다.

어휘·표현

longevity 장수   free from ~이 없는   hypertension 고혈압   compound 화합물, 혼합물   consume 섭취하다   serving 한 그릇의 음식, 1인분   potassium 칼륨   inflammation 염증   drastically 급격하게   burdensome 부담스러운

16 ②

문제 해결

여자는 고혈압 예방에 좋은 음식을 소개하고 있으므로, 여자가 하는 말의 주제로 ② '고혈압을 예방하기 위한 음식'이 가장 적절하다.
① 유기농 음식을 섭취하는 것의 장점
③ 질병 없는 장수의 비결
④ 균형 잡힌 식단을 유지하는 것의 중요성
⑤ 새롭게 발견된 성인병의 원인

17 ③

문제 해결

고혈압 예방에 좋은 음식으로 walnuts(호두)은 언급되지 않았다.

---

01 ②	02 ①	03 ①	04 ⑤	05 ③	06 ④
07 ⑤	08 ④	09 ③	10 ⑤	11 ④	12 ⑤
13 ②	14 ②	15 ③	16 ①	17 ⑤	

01 ②

남: 안녕하세요, 자동차를 사랑하는 여러분! 여러분의 자동차 외관의 상태가 걱정되나요? 더 이상 걱정하지 마십시오. 저희 Cleancart가 자동차 소유주분들께 소중한 시간을 낭비하지 않는 편리한 방법을 제공해 드립니다. 여러분은 세차장에 갈 필요가 없습니다. 여러분에게 저희가 갑니다. 저희의 궁극적인 목표는 여러분의 생활을 더 쉽게 만드는 세차 서비스를 제공하는 것입니다. 저희 서비스는 여러분의 차량이 더 오래 깨끗한 상태가 유지되도록 자연 분해성 제품을 사용합니다. 한 달에 단 150달러의 비용으로, 저희의 전문 팀이 일주일에 두 번 여러분의 자동차를 찾아가서 자동차를 구입한 첫날만큼 깨끗하게 만들어 드릴 것입니다! 게다가, 지금 두 달 비용을 지불하시면, 세 번째 달은 무료입니다! 이 멋진 기회를 놓치지 마시고 지금 바로 우리에게 전화를 걸어 주세요.

문제 해결

남자는 직접 찾아가 세차를 해주는 세차 서비스 전문 업체를 홍보하고 있다.

어휘·표현

convenient 편리한   car-wash 세차장   ultimate 궁극적인   biodegradable 자연 분해성의

02 ①

남: 오, 난 더 이상 일 못 해. 완전히 지쳤어.
여: 그래? 지금 몇 시야?
남: 벌써 5시야. 우리는 두 시간 넘게 이 판매 보고서를 분석하고 있어.
여: 하지만 그게 우리 일이야. 오늘 퇴근하기 전에 이 일을 끝내야 해.
남: 넌 피곤하지 않니, Jenny?
여: 아니. 너는 잠시 쉬는 게 어때? 내가 네 부분을 처리할게.
남: 넌 어떻게 그렇게 건강할 수 있어? 심지어 너는 헬스클럽도 안 가잖아, 그렇지?
여: 그래, 안 가. 하지만 나는 건강을 유지하는 나만의 방법이 있어.
남: 그래? 그게 뭔데?
여: 나는 매일 한 시간씩 걸어. 그게 내가 건강을 유지하는 비결이야.
남: 그게 정말로 효과가 있다고 생각해?
여: 당연하지! Rob, 꾸준히 매일 걷기만 해 봐. 그러면 너는 한 달도 안돼서 다른 점을 느낄 거야.

문제 해결

헬스클럽도 다니지 않는 여자는 매일 한 시간씩 꾸준히 걷는 것이 건강을 유지하는 비결이라고 말했으므로, 여자의 의견으로 가장 적절한 것은 ①이다.

어휘·표현

completely 완전히   exhausted 지친   analyze 분석하다   stay fit 건강을 유지하다   steadily 꾸준히

03 ①
관계 추론

여: 좋은 오후입니다, Brown 씨. 점심 식사는 어떠셨나요?

남: 아주 좋았어요. 당신이 예약을 해 준 덕분에, 훌륭한 점심 식사를 했어요.

여: 그 말을 들으니 기쁘네요.

남: 이제 오늘 오후에 내가 무엇을 해야 할지 말해 줄래요?

여: 먼저 Sydney Morning Herald와 2시에 인터뷰가 있습니다.

남: 그 인터뷰는 얼마나 오래 걸리죠?

여: 한 시간 정도요. 그 후, 노조에서 주최하는 회의에 참석하셔야 합니다.

남: 알겠습니다. 한국에서 온 바이어들은요? 그들을 언제 만나나요?

여: 노조 회의 직후에요. 바이어들은 5시 30분까지 여기 올 거예요.

남: 좋아요. 오늘도 매우 바쁘겠군요.

여: 저도 그렇게 생각합니다.

남: 당신도 알겠지만, 당신이 없으면 난 이 바쁜 스케줄을 해 나갈 수 없어요.

여: 천만에요. 저는 그저 제 일을 할 뿐입니다.

문제 해결

남자가 오후에 할 일을 알려 달라고 하자, 여자는 신문사 인터뷰, 회의 참석, 바이어 만남 등의 스케줄이 있다고 말한다. 이로 보아, 여자와 남자는 비서와 직장 상사의 관계이다.

어휘·표현

attend 참석하다 buyer 바이어, 구매자 as usual 평상시처럼
handle 처리하다, 다루다

04 ⑤
그림 불일치 파악

여: 야, 이 퍼레이드를 봐!

남: 드디어 크리스마스가 여기에 온 것 같아.

여: 미키 마우스와 미니 마우스가 앞에서 걷고 있어. 정말 귀여워.

남: 그래. 둘 다 '메리 크리스마스'라고 쓰인 하트 모양의 풍선을 들고 있어.

여: 오, 산타클로스가 말이 끄는 마차를 타고 그들 뒤에서 오고 있어.

남: 산타클로스 옆에 순록이 보이니?

여: 그래. 루돌프가 틀림없어. 예쁘다!

남: 당연하지! 봐, 산타클로스 뒤에는 퍼레이드 차가 있어.

여: 멋지다. 차에 두 명의 어린이가 앉아 있어.

남: 어린이들도 미키와 미니가 들고 있는 것과 똑같은 풍선을 들고 있어.

여: 그래. 어린이들이 우리를 쳐다보는 것 같아. 그들에게 손을 흔들어 주자.

남: 좋아!

문제 해결

차 안에 앉아 있는 두 명의 어린이가 미키 마우스와 미니 마우스가 들고 있는 것과 똑같은 풍선을 들고 있다고 하였으므로, 대화의 내용과 ⑤는 일치하지 않는다.

어휘·표현

parade 퍼레이드, 행진, 행렬 horse-drawn 말이 끄는 wagon 마차
absolutely 전적으로, 틀림없이 gorgeous 아주 멋진

05 ③
할 일 파악

여: 여보, 당신 정말 기분 좋아 보이네요. 좋은 일이 있었나요?

남: Wilson이 텔레비전 드라마에서 배역을 얻었어요!

여: 정말이요? 우리 아들, Wilson이 배역을 얻었다고요? 정말 좋은 소식이네요!

남: 마침내 배우가 되겠다는 아들의 꿈이 실현될 거예요.

여: 맞아요. 그런데 이것을 어떻게 알았어요?

남: 그가 방금 전에 전화해서 나에게 말해 주었어요. 그가 정말로 흥분해 있는 것 같았어요.

여: 그가 드라마가 어떤 것에 대한 것인지도 말했나요? 정말로 궁금해요.

남: 의학 드라마이고, 학교생활 적응에 어려움을 겪는 학생들을 치료하는 정신과 의사 역할을 할 거라고 말했어요.

여: 재미있게 들리네요. 음, 그가 집에 오면 파티를 하는 게 어때요?

남: 좋은 생각이에요. 내가 지금 바로 그에게 전화를 해서 언제 집에 올지 물어볼게요.

여: 좋아요! 그가 이번 주말에 집에 오면 좋을 것 같아요.

문제 해결

드라마에서 역할을 맡은 아들을 축하하기 위해 파티를 열자고 여자가 제안하자 남자는 좋은 생각이라고 하면서 자신이 지금 바로 아들에게 전화를 해서 언제 집에 올지 물어보겠다고 했다. 따라서 남자가 할 일로는 ③이 가장 적절하다.

어휘·표현

come true 이루어지다, 실현되다 psychiatrist 정신과 의사
adjust to ~에 적응하다 throw a party 파티를 열다

06 ④
숫자 정보 파악

[전화벨이 울린다.]

남: 안녕하세요, Green 마사지 센터입니다. 도와드릴까요?

여: 네. 오늘 오후 2시에 마사지를 예약하고 싶습니다. 그 시간이 가능한가요?

남: 네. 어떤 마사지를 원하시나요? 발 마사지는 30분에 30달러입니다.

여: 머리 마사지는요?

남: 30분에 20달러입니다.

여: 음… 그러면 발 마사지와 머리 마사지 둘 다 30분씩 예약할게요.

남: 알겠습니다. 몇 명을 예약하시겠습니까?

여: 두 명이요. 남편이랑 저요.

남: 알겠습니다. 됐습니다. 예약되셨습니다.

여: 고마워요. 오, 우편으로 받은 10% 할인 쿠폰이 있어요. 사용할 수 있나요?

남: 그럼요. 그 쿠폰은 총액에 적용될 것입니다. 2시에 뵙겠습니다.

문제 해결

30분에 30달러인 발 마사지와 30분에 20달러인 머리 마사지를 모두 30분씩 두 명 예약했는데 10% 할인 쿠폰을 사용하기로 했으므로, 여자가 지불할 총 금액은 90달러이다.

어휘·표현

book 예약하다 available 이용 가능한 apply 적용하다

07 ⑤
이유 파악

남: 오, 여름 방학이 코앞으로 다가왔어.

여: 그래. 네가 Robert와 Eric과 함께 Yosemite 국립 공원으로 자전거 여행을 갈 거라고 들었어. 사실이야?

남: 그래. 방학 시작하자마자, 우리는 Yosemite로 떠날 거야.

여: 멋지다!

남: 너는? 여전히 서핑을 즐기러 하와이에 갈 거니?

여: 음, 내가 하와이에 가는 것은 맞지만, 서핑을 하러 가는 것은 아니야.
남: 그럼 하와이에 왜 가? 훌라 댄스를 배울 생각이야?
여: 아니. 하와이에 계시는 할머니를 도와드리러 갈 거야.
남: 할머니가 하와이에 사신다고? 그건 몰랐어.
여: 지난달에, 할머니가 작은 게스트 하우스 운영을 시작하셨어. 그래서 할머니가 내가 이번 방학에 도와주길 원하셔.
남: 오, 너는 정말로 착한 손녀구나.

문제 해결

여자는 지난달 작은 게스트 하우스를 운영하기 시작한 할머니를 도와드리러 하와이에 가는 것이라고 말했다.

어휘·표현

be around the corner 코앞으로 다가오다   run (사업체 등을) 운영하다

08 ④

여: Jerome, 나는 네가 이번 여름 방학 동안 영국을 방문한다고 들었어.
남: 맞아. 내 개를 포함해서 우리 가족 모두가 가.
여: 개를 비행기에 태울 수 있어?
남: 응. '애완동물과 여행하기' 선택권이 있어. 추가로 100달러가 들어.
여: 그러면, 너는 비행기에서 애완동물과 앉을 수 있니?
남: 어림도 없지. 애완동물은 항상 애완동물 이동 장에 있어야만 해. 그리고 그 이동장은 동물이 서 있고 몸을 돌 수 있을 정도로 충분히 커야만 해.
여: 동물들이 비행 동안 항공기 화물칸에 머물러 있니?
남: 상황에 따라 달라. 7키로 미만의 작은 개만 기내에, 하지만 여전히 좌석 아래의 이동장 안에서만 있을 수 있어.
여: 그러면 너의 개는 기내에 있을 수 있구나.
남: 응. 하지만 난 내 개가 완전히 예방 접종이 되었다는 것을 증명하는 서류도 받아야만 해.
여: 와, 준비할 게 많구나.
남: 응, 하지만 필요한 절차야.

문제 해결

'애완동물과 여행하기' 선택안이 100달러가 추가 되며(가격) 이동장이 애완동물이 서 있고 돌 수 있을 정도로 커야 한다는 사이즈 규칙을 이야기했다. 작은 개만 기내 동반이 가능하며 예방접종을 증명할 서류도 필요하다. 사료 제공 여부는 거론되지 않았다.

어휘·표현

cargo hold 비행기 화물칸   cabin (비행기의) 여객실   vaccinate 예방 접종을 하다

09 ③

여: 이제 지역 뉴스를 말씀드리겠습니다. Townsville에서 가장 인기 있는 축제인 토마토 축제가 5월 8일에 열려서 5일간 계속됩니다. 약 100명의 토마토 재배 농부들이 축제에 참가할 것입니다. 가장 맛있는 토마토 고르기와 토마토 빨리 먹기를 포함하여 다양한 프로그램이 방문객들을 위해 준비되어 있습니다. 토마토를 사용해서 음식을 만드는 요리 교실 또한 적은 요금으로 방문객들에게 제공될 것입니다. 축제 기간 동안, 일반적인 시장 가격보다 20% 저렴한 가격으로 토마토가 판매될 것입니다. 작년에 약 7,000명이 이 축제에 참가했었는데요. 올해, 방문객의 숫자는 10,000명이 넘을 것으로 예상됩니다. 더 많은 정보를 원하시면, 공식 웹사이트 www.townsvilletomato.org를 방

문해 주십시오.

문제 해결

토마토를 사용해서 음식을 만드는 요리 교실이 적은 요금으로 방문객들에게 제공될 것이라고 했으므로, 무료로 진행된다는 ③은 내용과 일치하지 않는다.

어휘·표현

run (얼마의 기간 동안) 계속되다   take part in ~에 참가하다   select 고르다, 선발하다   charge 요금   exceed 넘다, 초과하다

10 ⑤

남: 안녕하세요, 제 휴대 전화 월 요금제를 바꾸고 싶어요.
여: 알겠습니다. 월 요금제 표를 봐 주세요. 한 달에 휴대 전화 요금으로 얼마를 쓸 계획이세요?
남: 한 달에 50달러 넘게 쓰고 싶지는 않아요.
여: 알았습니다. 휴대 전화로 통화를 많이 하시나요?
남: 아니요. 60분 또는 90분 통화 시간이면 충분한 것 같아요.
여: 알겠습니다. 문자 메시지는 많이 보내시나요?
남: 네, 많이 보내요. 보통 친구들이랑 문자 메시지를 통해서 대화를 하거든요.
여: 그러면 무제한 문자 메시지가 있는 요금제를 고르셔야 해요.
남: 맞네요.
여: 이제 데이터를 얼마나 많이 사용할지만 생각하시면 돼요.
남: 음, 평균적으로 저는 한 달에 3기가바이트 정도를 쓰는 것 같아요.
여: 그러면 이 요금제가 손님에게 딱 맞는 것 같아요.
남: 좋아요, 이것으로 할게요.

문제 해결

남자는 요금으로 한 달에 50달러 넘게 쓰고 싶지 않고, 60분 또는 90분의 통화 시간을 제공하는 요금제 중에서 문자 메시지 무제한 사용과 3기가바이트 정도의 데이터를 쓸 수 있는 요금제를 택하기로 했으므로, 남자가 선택한 휴대 전화 요금제로 ⑤가 적절하다.

어휘·표현

unlimited 무제한의   consider 고려하다, 생각하다   on average 평균적으로

11 ④

여: 실례합니다, 씬 크러스트 피자를 주문하고 싶은데요.
남: 알겠습니다. 어떤 사이즈를 원하시나요? 레귤러, 라지, 그리고 패밀리 사이즈가 있습니다.
여: 음, 저를 포함해서 네 명이 먹을 거예요. 어떤 사이즈를 추천하시나요?
남: 그러면 패밀리 사이즈가 손님에게 좋을 것 같습니다.

문제 해결

레귤러, 라지, 패밀리 사이즈의 피자가 있다는 말에 여자가 네 명이 먹을 거라고 하면서 어떤 사이즈의 피자를 추천하는지 물었으므로, 패밀리 사이즈의 피자가 좋을 거라고 말하는 ④가 남자의 응답으로 가장 적절하다.
① 당신이 가져온 피자는 정말 맛있었어요.
② 저는 피자가 아니라 스파게티를 추천하고 싶습니다.
③ 어떤 피자가 더 비싼지 모르겠어요.
⑤ 저는 지금 배가 무척 고파요. 함께 피자를 먹읍시다.

어휘·표현

crust 빵 껍질   including ~을 포함하여

12 ⑤

남: Lauren, 너 어떤 동아리에 가입할지 결정했어?
여: 응. 나는 토론 동아리에 가입하기로 결정했어.
남: 토론 동아리? 우연의 일치구나! 사실, 나도 그 동아리에 가입할 거야.
여: 잘됐다! 내일 그 동아리에 우리 지원서를 제출하자.

문제 해결

토론 동아리에 가입하기로 결정했다는 여자의 말에 남자가 자신도 그 동아리에 가입할 것이라고 했으므로, 동아리에 지원서를 함께 제출하자고 말하는 ⑤가 여자의 응답으로 가장 적절하다.
① 넌 토론 동아리를 선택했어야 했어.
② 걱정하지 마. 내가 토론 기술을 가르쳐 줄게.
③ 난 동아리에 가입하는 것이 학생들에게 중요하다고 생각하지 않아.
④ 네 말이 맞아. 토론 동아리는 신규 회원을 받지 않아.

어휘·표현

debate 토론 coincidence 우연의 일치 submit 제출하다
application 지원(서), 신청(서)

13 ②

남: Lucy, 치킨 스튜를 더 먹는 게 어때요?
여: 아니요, 괜찮아요. 너무 배가 불러서 한 입도 더 먹을 수가 없어요.
남: 알았어요. 치킨 스튜 어땠어요?
여: 훌륭했어요! 내 인생에서 이렇게 맛있는 치킨 스튜는 먹어 본 적이 없어요.
남: 당신이 그렇게 말할거라 생각했어요. 내 치킨 스튜를 먹어 본 사람들 모두가 같은 말을 하거든요.
여: 당신이 이렇게 요리를 잘하는지 몰랐어요.
남: 음, 이게 다 어머니가 나에게 준 요리법 덕분이에요.
여: 어머니가 직업 요리사인가요?
남: 아니요. 어머니는 할머니께 그 요리법을 받았어요.
여: 와! 그 요리법을 나에게 보여 줄래요? 우리 가족을 위해서 치킨 스튜를 만들고 싶어요.
남: 물론이죠! 요리법은 내 스마트폰에 저장되어 있어요. 문자로 요리법을 보내 줄게요.
여: 고마워요. 그 요리법이 기대가 되네요.
남: 그냥 요리법에 쓰인 대로만 하면, 당신은 아주 맛있는 스튜를 먹게 될 거예요.

문제 해결

맛있는 치킨 스튜의 비법이 엄마의 요리법이라는 남자의 말에 여자는 그 요리법을 알려 달라고 말하고, 남자는 요리법을 문자로 알려 주겠다고 말한다. 이에 여자가 고맙다고 하면서 그 요리법이 기대가 된다고 했으므로, 이에 대한 남자의 응답으로는 ② '그냥 요리법에 쓰인 대로만 하면, 당신은 아주 맛있는 스튜를 먹게 될 거예요.'가 가장 적절하다.
① 좋은 생각이에요! 오늘 저녁에는 치킨 스튜를 먹어요.
③ 미안하지만, 그 요리법을 말해 줄 수 없어요. 비밀이거든요.
④ 맞아요. 당신의 어머니가 당신에게 그 요리법을 문자 메시지로 보낼 거예요.
⑤ 걱정 마요. 당신 대신에 내가 스튜를 만들 거예요.

어휘·표현

recipe 요리법 text 문자 메시지를 보내다 look forward to ~를 기대하다

14 ②

남: 드디어, U.S. Open Championship이 이번 주에 열려.
여: 올해는 누가 우승할 것 같아?
남: Gary Smith. 그가 쉽게 우승할 거라고 생각해.
여: 나도 동의해. 그는 이미 올해 PGA 투어에서 우승을 한 번 했으니까.
남: 게다가, 그는 이 대회의 작년도 우승자야.
여: 맞아. 그래서 그는 다른 선수들보다 더 자신 있어 하지.
남: 너도 알다시피, 골프에서 결과를 결정하는 데 자신감이 가장 중요한 요소 중의 하나야.
여: 당연하지! 아무리 잘해도, 자신감이 없으면 우승하기는 어려워.
남: 네 말에 전적으로 동의해. 그리고, Gary는 그 자신감을 가지고 있다고.
여: 맞아. 네가 말한 대로 그가 쉽게 우승할 거야.

문제 해결

남자와 여자 둘 다 U.S. Open Championship에서 Gary Smith가 우승할 거라고 말했는데, 계속해서 남자가 골프에서 중요한 것은 자신감이고 Gary Smith는 그 자신감을 갖고 있다고 말했으므로, 이에 대한 여자의 응답으로 ② '맞아. 네가 말한 대로 그가 쉽게 우승할 거야.'가 가장 적절하다.
① 미안. 나는 이번 주말에 골프를 칠 시간이 없어.
③ 괜찮아. 나는 더 이상 골프에 관심이 없어.
④ 나는 Gary가 올해 U.S. Open에 참가하지 않을 거라고 들었어.
⑤ 나는 지난 주 U.S. Open 대회를 정말 즐겼어.

어휘·표현

defending champion 작년 대회 우승자 factor 요소, 요인 determine 결정하다 outcome 결과 no matter how 아무리 ~일지라도

15 ③

남: Angela는 청소년 건강을 전공으로 하는 건강 관리 전문가이다. 어느 날, 건강 잡지의 기자인 Brian이 그녀의 사무실에 온다. Brian은 Angela에게 요새 청소년이 겪는 정신적이고 심리적인 고통에 대해 신문 칼럼을 써 줄 것을 요청한다. 처음에, Angela는 급작스런 요청에 놀란다. 잠시 신중하게 생각한 후에, Angela는 자신이 칼럼을 쓰겠다고 그에게 말한다. Brain은 그녀의 긍정적인 답변에 기뻐하면서 그녀에게 칼럼의 길이가 1,000 단어에서 1,500 단어 사이라는 것을 알려 준다. 길이에 대해서 들은 후에, Angela는 칼럼을 잡지사에 제출해야 하는 마감일이 언제인지 알고 싶어 한다. 이 상황에서, Angela가 Brian에게 뭐라고 말할 것 같은가?

문제 해결

Brian으로부터 칼럼을 써 줄 것을 부탁받은 Angela가 칼럼의 제출 마감일이 언제인지 알고 싶어 하는 상황이므로, Angela가 Brian에게 할 말로 ③ '내가 당신에게 언제 글을 보내 주어야 하는지 말해 주시겠어요?'가 가장 적절하다.
① 왜 나를 선택했는지 알고 싶어요.
② 내가 몇 단어로 칼럼을 써야 하나요?
④ 걱정 마세요. 칼럼 마감일을 연장할 수 있어요.
⑤ 나도 그래요. 저도 다음 달부터 당신네 잡지를 구독할게요.

어휘·표현

specialize in ~을 전문으로 하다 adolescent 청소년(의) mental 정신적인
psychological 심리적인 consideration 숙고, 고려 length 길이
extend 연장하다 subscribe 구독하다

16-17

복합 이해

여: 안녕하세요, 청취자 여러분. 저는 '1분 간단 경제'의 진행자 Jackie Robinson입니다. 어제 저는 여러분에게 초대형 상점에 대해 말씀드렸습니다. 오늘은 전통 시장에 대해 말씀드리겠습니다. 가격 경쟁력 측면에서 전통 시장이 초대형 상점보다 더 우위에 있다는 것을 알고 계셨나요? 전통 시장에서 여러분은 고기와 과일을 초대형 상점에서보다 훨씬 더 낮은 가격에 구입할 수 있습니다. 게다가, 전통 시장은 신선한 채소와 해산물을 판매하는 것으로 널리 알려져 있습니다. 그러므로 여러분이 당근과 양파와 같은 채소 또는 굴 같은 해산물을 구입하길 원한다면, 전통 시장으로 가십시오. 전통 시장을 방문하는 것은 또한 여러분의 이웃에게도 도움이 됩니다. 대기업이 운영하는 초대형 상점과는 달리, 전통 시장은 근처 지역에서 살고 있는 사람들에 의해 운영이 됩니다. 여러분이 초대형 상점에서 신발 한 켤레를 구입하면, 그 이익은 얼굴 없는 회사로 들어갑니다. 하지만 여러분이 전통 시장에서 신발 한 켤레를 구입하면, 그 이익은 여러분의 이웃에게로 갑니다.

어휘·표현

megastore 초대형 상점   **traditional market** 전통시장   **in terms of** ~의 측면에서   **price competitiveness** 가격 경쟁력   **commodity** 생필품, 상품   **oyster** 굴   **profit** 이익

16 ①

문제 해결

1분 간단 경제의 진행자인 여자는 초대형 상점보다 전통 시장이 상품을 저렴한 가격에 판매하고 전통 시장에서 판매되는 채소와 해산물이 신선하다는 등의 내용을 이야기하고 있으므로, 여자가 하는 말의 주제로 ① '전통 시장에서 물건을 구입하는 것의 이점'이 가장 적절하다.
② 대기업이 초대형 상점을 운영하는 이유
③ 사람들이 초대형 상점에서 쇼핑하는 것을 선호하는 이유
④ 전통 시장을 경쟁력 있게 만드는 방법
⑤ 전통 시장과 초대형 상점의 유사한 점

17 ⑤

문제 해결

여자의 말에서 티셔츠는 언급되지 않았다.

---

01 ⑤	02 ③	03 ②	04 ①	05 ⑤	06 ③
07 ⑤	08 ⑤	09 ④	10 ②	11 ①	12 ②
13 ③	14 ⑤	15 ⑤	16 ③	17 ②	

01 ⑤

목적 파악

남: 좋은 아침입니다. 여러분. 저는 IT 부서의 Jake입니다. 우리는 다음 주 화요일 오전 9시부터 오후 1시까지 컴퓨터 서버 업그레이드를 실시할 예정입니다. 여러분의 컴퓨터 파일에 바이러스가 접근하는 것을 막기 위한 보안 업데이트도 있을 것입니다. 이 시간 동안 여러분의 컴퓨터에 새로운 파일을 저장하지 마십시오. 또한, 여러분의 컴퓨터의 모든 데이터를 미리 지정된 서버에 올려 주십시오. 서버 주소는 회사 메신저로 보내 드리겠습니다. 개인 플래시 드라이브에 파일을 저장하지 마십시오. 이것은 우리의 보안 정책에 어긋나는 것입니다. 이 서버 업그레이드 과정은 필수적이므로 여러분의 협조에 매우 감사드리겠습니다. 불편을 드려서 진심으로 사과드립니다. 감사합니다.

문제 해결

남자가 회사 서버 업그레이드 및 보안 업데이트의 일정을 공지하면서 미리 해야 할 일과 하지 말아야 할 일에 대해 이야기하고 있다. 따라서 남자가 하는 말의 목적으로 ⑤가 가장 적절하다.

어휘·표현

perform 수행하다, 실시하다   **company-wide** 회사 전반의   **designated** 지정된   **in advance** 미리   **policy** 정책, 방침   **inconvenience** 불편

02 ③

주제 파악

여: 안녕하세요, Anderson 씨. 이 문서를 읽을 시간을 잠시 내 주실 수 있을까요?
남: 물론이죠, Allen 씨. 그것은 무엇인가요?
여: 이건 5번가에 있는 공원을 유지하기 위한 청원서예요.
남: 저는 도시 계획자들이 거기에 새로운 쇼핑몰을 짓고 싶어 한다고 들었어요.
여: 맞아요, 하지만 많은 시민들이 반대하고 있고 제가 그들을 대신해서 서명을 모으고 있어요.
남: 왜 그렇게 하는지 물어도 될까요? 쇼핑몰은 지역 경제에 좋을 텐데요.
여: 하지만 당신은 우리의 아이들에게 야외 활동을 즐기기 위한 안전한 장소를 제공하는 것이 우선 사항이라고 생각하지 않으세요?
남: 그러고 보니, 제 아들도 거기서 야구 하는 것을 정말 즐거워하네요.
여: 제가 말씀드리는 점이 그거예요.
남: 무슨 말인지 알겠어요. 청원서에 서명할게요.
여: 고맙습니다, Anderson 씨.
남: 제가 고맙죠, Allen 씨.

문제 해결

여자는 쇼핑몰을 건설할 계획인 공원 부지를 지켜야 한다고 청원서 서명을 받으면서 남자에게 아이들이 야외 활동을 즐길 수 있는 공간이 우선이 아니냐고 말하고 있다. 따라서 여자의 의견으로 ③이 가장 적절하다.

어휘·표현

petition 청원(서)   **citizen** 시민   **on one's behalf** ~을 대신하여

priority 우선 사항, 더 중요한 것   come to think of it 그러고 보니, 생각해 보니

informative 유익한, 정보를 주는   continent 대륙   adorable 사랑스러운
the Atlantic Ocean 대서양   Antarctica 남극 대륙

03 ②

남: 실례합니다, 부인. 당신이 비상구 통로에 앉으셨기 때문에 당신과 몇 가지를 확인하고 싶습니다.

여: 오, 좋습니다.

남: 첫 번째로, 당신은 이 카드에 적힌 의무 사항을 수행하실 의향이 있습니까?

여: 네, 그런데 더 자세히 설명해 줄 수 있을까요?

남: 물론이죠. 비상 상황 시, 승무원의 지시에 따라 비상구를 열어 주시고 다른 승객들이 항공기를 빠져나가는 것을 도와주십시오.

여: 비상구는 어떻게 열지요?

남: 손잡이를 당겨서 아래로 돌린 후, 문을 바깥쪽으로 밀면 됩니다. 이 카드에 그림과 함께 자세히 설명되어 있습니다.

여: 알겠습니다. 제가 그것을 꼼꼼히 읽어 볼게요. 오, 그리고 질문이 있습니다.

남: 네, 부인.

여: 제가 당신 항공사의 웹 사이트에서 채식 기내식을 요청하였습니다. 모든 것이 제대로 되었는지 확인해 줄 수 있을까요?

남: 네, 부인. 이륙한 후에 제가 확인하고 당신께 돌아오겠습니다.

여: 고맙습니다.

항공기의 비상구 줄에 앉은 여자에게 남자는 비상 시에 여자가 해야 할 일을 설명해 주었다. 또한 여자는 남자에게 자신의 기내식이 채식으로 준비되었는지 확인을 부탁하였으므로, 남자와 여자는 비행기 승무원과 승객임을 알 수 있다.

row 줄   in accordance with ~에 따라서   crew member 승무원
thoroughly 철저히

04 ①

여: 여보, 온라인의 이 그림 좀 봐 주겠어요?

남: 알았어요. 이것은 뭘 위한 건가요?

여: 우리 아이들 방을 위한 거예요. 이 그림을 아이들 책상 위에 거는 게 어때요?

남: 그래요. 이 세계 지도는 재미있고 유익하네요.

여: 그것은 대륙과 대양의 이름을 보여 줄 뿐 아니라 그곳에 사는 동물도 보여 줘요. 호주에 있는 이 사랑스러운 코알라를 봐요.

남: 나는 대서양에 있는 고래와 돌고래가 마음에 들어요.

여: 나도 그래요. 남극 대륙의 펭귄은 어때요?

남: 네, 귀여워요. 어, 나는 남아메리카 위쪽 지역에 원숭이가 산다는 것을 몰랐어요.

여: 나도 몰랐어요.

남: 나는 또한 하단 왼쪽 모서리에 탐험복을 입고 있는 소년과 소녀도 마음에 들어요. 마치 우리 아이들처럼 보이네요.

여: 나도 그렇게 생각했어요! 그래서 우리가 이 그림을 사야 한다고 생각해요?

남: 당연하죠.

대화에서는 호주에 있는 코알라를 언급했지만 그림에는 캥거루가 그려져 있으므로, 대화 내용과 일치하지 않은 것은 ①이다.

05 ⑤

[전화벨이 울린다.]

여: 여보세요.

남: 여보세요, Ellie. 저 Peter예요.

여: 안녕하세요, Peter. 무슨 일이예요? 오늘 직장에 안 오나요?

남: 아니요, 가요. 그런데 내 차가 도로에서 고장이 나서 제가 좀 늦을 거예요.

여: 오, 내가 상사에게 알릴게요. 걱정 마요.

남: 제가 이미 상사에게 전화했어요. 그런데 날 위해 다른 걸 해 줄 수 있을까요?

여: 물론이죠. 뭔데요?

남: 우리 오늘 아침에 회의 있는 거 당신도 알잖아요. 내가 이미 그것 때문에 회의실을 예약해 두었어요.

여: 그런데 당신은 시간 안에 올 수 있겠어요?

남: 네, 그럴 것 같아요. 그런데 회의 때 쓸 보고서를 복사실에서 가져다 놓아줄 수 있을까요?

여: 문제없어요. 내가 다과도 준비하길 원하나요?

남: 괜찮아요. 그건 Mia가 할 거예요. 정말 고마워요. 곧 갈게요.

차가 고장이 나 출근이 늦게 된 남자는 상사에게 이야기하는 것과 회의실 예약을 이미 다 했다고 했다. 다과 준비는 Mia가 할 거라며 남자는 여자에게 복사실에서 회의 때 쓸 보고서를 가져다 달라고 부탁했다.

conference 회의   refreshments 다과, 간식

06 ③

남: Green Car Service에 어서 오세요. 도와드릴까요?

여: 안녕하세요, 차 내부 세차 서비스를 받고 싶은데요.

남: 알겠습니다. 우리는 여러 가지 서비스를 제공해 드립니다. 어떤 것을 원하시나요?

여: 차이점을 설명해 주실 수 있나요?

남: 기본 서비스는 50달러가 들고 지붕부터 카펫까지 좌석을 제외한 모든 것을 포함합니다.

여: 왜 좌석은 제외하나요?

남: 재료에 따라 가격이 다르기 때문이죠. 천은 15달러가 추가로 들고 가죽은 25달러가 추가됩니다.

여: 제 좌석은 천이에요. 그리고 저는 그것들을 세탁하길 원합니다. green 서비스는 무엇인가요?

남: 그것은 특별 세제와 증기 세차를 포함합니다. 20달러가 추가되죠.

여: 저는 그게 필요할 것 같진 않네요. 오, 에어컨에서 나오는 불쾌한 냄새도 제거해 주실 수 있나요?

남: 물론이죠. 차량 환풍 시스템을 청소하면 그 문제가 해결될 것입니다. 그런데 추가로 10달러가 듭니다.

여: 좋아요. 그것을 포함시켜 주세요. 모두 얼마인가요?

여자는 50달러 하는 기본 세차 서비스에, 15달러 하는 천으로 된 좌석 청소를

추가했다. 거기에 특별 세제와 증기 청소가 포함된 green 서비스는 선택하지 않았고, 10달러 하는 차량 환풍구 청소를 추가했으므로, 여자가 지불할 총 금액은 75달러이다.

interior 내부   exclude 제외하다   detergent 세제   odor 냄새
ventilation system 환기 장치, 통풍 장치   take care of ~을 처리하다

07 ⑤ 이유 파악

여: Noah, 너에게 이 소포가 왔다.
남: 고마워요, 엄마. 그건 내가 온라인으로 산 스웨터네요.
여: 네가 입어보기 전에 괜찮은 상태인지 확인해 보렴.
남: 괜찮아 보여요. 입어 볼게요. [잠시 후] 저 어때 보여요?
여: 너한테 정말 잘 어울리는구나. 크기가 딱 맞네.
남: 그리고 두꺼운데도 전혀 무겁게 느껴지지 않아요.
여: 좋구나. 또한 녹색이 너의 눈을 더욱 돋보이게 하는구나.
남: 오, 이런. 엄마. 저 결국은 이 옷 못 입을 것 같아요.
여: 왜? 네가 마음에 들어 한다고 생각했고 너한테 정말 잘 어울리는데.
남: 목이 간지러워요. 느낌이 좋지 않아요. 발진이 올라오는 게 느껴져요.
여: 내가 좀 보자. 오 이런. 이 스웨터는 합성 섬유로 만들어졌구나. 너는 합성 섬유에 알레르기가 있잖니.
남: 유감이네요, 저는 이거 환불을 위해 반품해야겠어요.

남자가 주문한 스웨터는 상태도 괜찮고, 크기도 딱 맞는 데다 가볍고 남자의 눈을 돋보이게 만들어 주었지만, 남자가 합성 섬유에 알레르기가 있어서 환불해야겠다고 했다.

bring out 돋보이게 하다   rash 발진   synthetic 합성의   allergic 알레르기가 있는

08 ⑤ 언급 유무 파악

여: Patrick, David Hockney 전시회가 우리 도시에서 열린다는 소식 들었어?
남: 뭐라고? 이 작은 도시에 David Hockney 전시회라고?
여: 그래, 맞아. 현대 예술에 대한 대중의 관심을 끌어올리기 위한 것이래.
남: 와. 그는 내가 좋아하는 화가야. 전시회가 언제 열리니?
여: 6월 1일에 시작해서, 두 달 동안 계속 돼.
남: 약 한 달 정도 남았구나. 전시회가 어디서 열리는데?
여: County Art Museum에서.
남: 잘됐다. 그곳은 우리 학교에서 멀지 않아.
여: 맞아. 우리 전시회 첫날에 갈래?
남: 내 생각을 읽었구나. 전시회에 그의 그림 몇 점이 전시되는지 알아?
여: 전부 133점. '더 큰 첨벙'을 포함해서 대표적인 그의 그림 대부분이 전시될 거야.
남: 멋지다! 오, 그의 그림을 빨리 보고 싶어.

David Hockney 전시회에 관해 ⑤ '입장료'는 언급되지 않았다.

exhibition 전시회, 전시   raise 올리다   contemporary art 현대 미술
take place (계획된 일이) 개최되다, 일어나다   representative 대표하는, 대표

splash 첨벙 하는 소리, 첨벙거리다

09 ④ 담화 내용 불일치

여: 안녕하세요. 청취자 여러분. 음식 애호가들을 위한 팟캐스트 Eats and Treats입니다. 여러분들 모두를 위한 흥미로운 소식이 있습니다. 연례 Goodies for Foodies 행사가 돌아왔습니다! 매년 Grant Park에서 열리는 이 행사는 여러분 모두를 요리 세상으로 나오는 흥미롭고 새로운 맛들로 이끄는 것을 목표로 하고 있습니다. 올해, 전 세계에서 50대 이상의 푸드 트럭이 올 것입니다. 게다가, 세계적으로 유명한 요리사가 짧은 요리 시범을 보일 것입니다. Goodies and Foodies 행사는 5월 1일에 시작해서 6월 말까지 계속될 겁니다. 저희 웹 사이트에 가서 입장권을 미리 구입하세요. 만약 이번 달에 구입하시면, 그 행사의 푸드 트럭 무료 음식 쿠폰 두 장을 받으실 거예요.

행사는 5월 1일에 시작해서 6월 말까지 이어진다고 하였으므로 ④는 내용과 일치하지 않는다.

foodie 식도락가, 미식가   culinary 요리[음식]의   demonstration (시범) 설명, 실연

10 ② 도표 정보 파악

남: 여보, 무엇을 보고 있어요?
여: Jason을 위한 유아용 수영 튜브를 온라인에서 주문하려고 하고 있어요.
남: 어디 봐요. 저것은 튜브에 부착된 햇빛 가리개예요? 멋진데요.
여: 그렇죠? 야외 수영장에 갈 거라서 햇빛 가리개가 있는 것으로 사고 싶었어요.
남: 하지만 좀 비싸네요. 햇빛 가리개가 있는 것으로 30달러 이하로 찾아봅시다.
여: 알겠어요. 이건 어때요?
남: 음. 손잡이가 하나밖에 없네요. 손잡이가 두 개 있는 것이 더 안정적인 것 같아요.
여: 좋은 지적이에요. 그러면 우리에겐 두 가지 선택이 남은 것 같네요.
남: 저 파란색 튜브는 어때요?
여: 좋긴 한데, 물에서는 파란색이 눈에 띄지 않을 거예요.
남: 당신 말이 맞아요. 그럼 다른 것으로 합시다.
여: 그래요. Jason도 분명 좋아할 거예요.

햇빛 가리개가 있고, 가격은 30달러 이하이며, 손잡이가 두 개에 파란색이 아닌 튜브를 사려고 하므로, 두 사람이 구입할 수영 튜브는 ②이다.

sunshade 햇빛 가리개   stable 안정적인   stand out 눈에 띄다, 두드러지다
once ~할 때, ~하자마자

11 ① 짧은 대화의 응답

여: 안녕하세요, Harris 씨. 제가 요청했던 책이 반납되었는지 확인해 주실 수 있을까요?
남: 그럼, Jean. [타이핑 소리] 오, 미안하구나. 아직 반납이 안 되었네.
여: 어제가 기한이라고 생각했는데요. 그렇다면, 제가 그 책을 예약할 수

있나요?

남: 물론이지. 이 요청서를 작성해 주렴.

문제 해결

아직 반납이 안 된 책을 미리 예약할 수 있냐고 물었으므로, 그에 대한 응답으로
① '물론이지. 이 요청서를 작성해 주렴.'이 가장 적절하다.
② 그래, 나도 그 책이 정말 재미있다고 생각한다.
③ 미안하구나. 나는 그 책을 읽는 것을 아직 끝내지 못했단다.
④ 고맙지만 괜찮다. 나는 그것을 이미 다른 사람에게 빌렸단다.
⑤ 네가 했던 예약이 취소되어 유감이구나.

어휘·표현

return 반납하다　due 예정인, 기한의　fill out 기입하다　request 요청(서)

12 ②　〔짧은 대화의 응답〕

남: Emma, 당신 진짜 창백해 보여요. 뭐가 잘못 됐나요?
여: 확실하진 않은데 내 생각에 점심으로 먹은 음식이 뭔가 잘못된 것 같아요.
남: 식중독이 아니길 빌어요. 내가 당신을 병원에 데려다 주길 원하나요?
여: 괜찮아요. 나는 택시를 탈게요. 아무튼 고마워요.

문제 해결

남자가 아픈 여자에게 병원에 데려다 주길 원하는지 물었고, 그에 대한 응답으로
② '괜찮아요. 나는 택시를 탈게요. 아무튼 고마워요.'가 가장 적절하다.
① 나도 동의해요. 우리가 먹는 것이 우리가 누구인지를 만들죠.
③ 괜찮아요. 답례로 당신이 나에게 점심을 사 주면 돼죠.
④ 걱정하지 마세요. 음식은 정말 좋고 맛있었어요.
⑤ 사실, 당신이 요리하는 것이 저는 정말 기대돼요.

어휘·표현

pale 창백한　food poisoning 식중독　in return 답례로

13 ③　〔긴 대화의 응답〕

남: 여보, 오늘 언제 식료품 사러 갈까요?
여: 사실, 나는 이번 주는 식료품 사는 것을 건너뛸까 생각 중이에요.
남: 왜요? 우리 치즈가 떨어져 가지 않아요?
여: 나도 그렇게 생각했는데 냉장고에서 치즈를 발견했어요. 당신 오늘 신문 읽어 봤어요?
남: 아직요. 신문에 뭐라고 나왔는데요?
여: 신문에 미국인이 세계 어느 나라의 도시인들보다 더 많고 더 큰 냉장고를 가지고 있다고 나왔어요.
남: 그게 나쁜 건가요?
여: 유감이지만 그래요. 우리는 많은 음식을 사서 그것을 저장해 놓고는 잊어버리는 거죠. 그건 음식의 신선도를 떨어뜨리고 전기세도 올라가게 해요.
남: 음. 무슨 말인지 알겠어요. 우리는 항상 먹을 게 없다고 말하지만 우리 냉장고는 항상 가득히 차 있어요.
여: 바로 그 점이 문제예요.
남: 알겠어요. 식료품 가게에 가지 말아요. 냉장고에 있는 것으로 뭔가를 요리해 봅시다.
여: 좋아요! 우리는 식료품비와 전기세를 아낄 수 있어요!

문제 해결

여자가 많은 음식물을 냉장고에 저장해 놓고 잊어버리는 것을 문제점으로 지적

했고, 남자가 이에 동의하여 식료품을 새로 사지 말고 냉장고에 있는 것으로 요리를 하자고 한 상황이다. 따라서 이어질 여자의 말로 ③ '좋아요! 우리는 식료품비와 전기세를 아낄 수 있어요!'가 가장 적절하다.
① 물론이죠. 건강하고 신선한 음식을 먹는 것이 정말 중요해요.
② 요리할 필요 없어요. 외식하며 축하합시다.
④ 좋아요. 냉장고 수리를 받기 위해 내가 고객 서비스에 전화를 걸게요.
⑤ 정말요? 나는 그렇게 많은 사람들이 음식 부족으로 고통 받는 줄 몰랐어요.

어휘·표현

grocery 식료품점　run out of ~이 다 떨어지다　matter 중요하다
suffer from ~으로 고통 받다　lack 부족

14 ⑤　〔긴 대화의 응답〕

여: Alex, 내가 뭔가를 물어봐도 될까?
남: 물론이지 Abby. 뭔데?
여: 기분 나쁘게 하려는 건 아닌데 네가 머리카락을 왜 그렇게 길게 기르는지 물어 봐도 될까?
남: 오, 그게 지저분하게 보이니?
여: 아냐, 아냐. 그냥 내가 궁금해서 그래. 너는 가끔 그게 너무 무겁다거나 덥다고 불평하는데, 절대 머리카락을 자르지 않잖아.
남: 어, 사실 나는 내 머리가 기부하기에 충분히 길어질 만큼 기다리고 있는 중이야.
여: 머리카락을 기부할 수 있다고?
남: 응, 너도 알다시피, 암에 걸린 아이들은 화학 치료를 겪고는 머리카락이 빠지잖아. 그들을 위해 기증받은 머리카락으로 가발을 만드는 재단이 있어.
여: 너 정말 대단하다. 나도 어떻게 같은 일을 할 수 있니?
남: 너의 머리카락은 최소한 30센티미터 길이여야 하고 파마가 되어서는 안 돼.

문제 해결

암 치료로 머리카락이 빠진 아이들을 위해 기부하려고 머리를 기른다는 남자의 말을 듣고 여자가 같은 일을 어떻게 할 수 있는지 묻고 있으므로, 방법을 알려 주는 ⑤ '너의 머리카락은 최소한 30센티미터 길이여야 하고 파마가 되어서는 안 돼.'가 남자의 응답으로 가장 적절하다.
① 걱정하지 마. 나는 내 머리가 지저분하다는 걸 알고 있고 곧 머리카락을 자를 거야.
② 나도 동의해. 단정한 머리와 깨끗한 옷은 매우 중요해.
③ 나는 긴 머리가 너에게 어울린다고 생각하지 않아. 너는 있는 그대로가 좋아.
④ 너는 다른 사람의 머리 모양에 대해 무례해서는 안 돼.

어휘·표현

no offence (내 말·행동에) 기분 나빠 하지 말아라　messy 지저분한, 엉망인
go through ~을 겪다　chemotherapy 화학 요법　foundation 재단

15 ⑤　〔상황에 적절한 말〕

남: Rio와 Mike는 가장 친한 친구 사이이고 그들은 곧 고등학교 2학년이 될 참이다. 그들 학교의 선택 교육 과정에서, 2학년은 그들이 공부하고 싶은 과목을 선택할 수 있다. Rio의 주요 관심사는 항상 우주였고 그의 꿈은 언젠가 NASA에서 일하는 것이다. 그래서 그는 심화 물리학, 천문학, 그리고 지구 과학을 공부하기로 결정한다. Mike는

Rio에게 그가 무슨 과목을 선택할 것인지 계속 묻고 같은 수업을 듣고 싶어 한다. Rio는 Mike가 그들이 단지 가장 친한 친구이기 때문에 같이 공부하고 싶어 한다는 것을 알지만, Mike가 미래에 무엇을 하고 싶은지 진지하게 고려해야 한다고 생각한다. 그런 다음 그는 적절한 과목을 선택해야 한다. 이러한 상황에서, Rio는 Mike에게 무엇이라고 말할 것 같은가?

문제 해결

자신의 흥미나 꿈과는 상관없이 친한 친구와 같은 수업을 들으려는 Mike를 보고, Rio는 Mike가 하고 싶은 것이 뭔지 고려하고 그것에 적절한 과목을 선택해야 한다고 생각하는 상황이다. 따라서 Rio가 Mike에게 할 말로 ⑤ '너는 네가 미래에 무엇을 하고 싶은지 찾아서 그것에 맞춰 공부해야 해.'가 가장 적절하다.
① 2학년이 되면 우리는 정말 더 열심히 공부할 필요가 있어.
② 너는 너의 부모님과 네가 선택한 과목에 대해 이야기를 나눠야 해.
③ 우리 같이 심화 물리학과 지구 과학을 공부하는 게 어때?
④ 천문 프로젝트를 위해 NASA로 견학 가는 거 어때?

어휘·표현

selective 선택의　**physics** 물리학　**astronomy** 천문학　**accordingly** 그에 따라, 그에 맞춰

16-17　복합 이해

여: 안녕하세요, 학생 여러분. 지난주에 우리는 신약 개발과 생물 화학자들의 역할에 대해 공부했습니다. 오늘, 우리는 우리의 일상생활에 큰 영향을 끼치고 많은 사람들을 살린 몇 가지 약에 대해 알아볼 것입니다. 첫 번째는 페니실린으로, 그것은 생명을 살리는 데 가장 효과적인 항생제가 되었습니다. 이 항생제는 8천만 명이 넘는 생명을 살려 왔고, 그것의 발견이 없었다면 오늘날 사람들의 75%는 살아 있지 못할 것입니다. 두 번째 약은 인슐린입니다. 인슐린의 발견 전에는 심한 당뇨병이 있는 환자는 거의 굶는 것과 같은 식단만을 받았습니다. 인슐린은 또한 호르몬 대체 치료법의 길을 닦아 왔고 셀 수 없이 많은 당뇨병 환자를 구해 왔습니다. 다음 약은 여러분이 두통으로 인해 먹는 것입니다. 네, 아스피린입니다. 이 약은 현재 세계에서 가장 흔하게 사용되는 진통제입니다. 마지막 약은 모르핀입니다. 중독의 위험성에도 불구하고, 이 약 없이는, 심각한 부상 또는 복잡한 의학적 질환 상태인 수백만의 사람들이 극도의 고통에서 지냈을 것입니다.

어휘·표현

biological chemist 생물 화학자　**impact** 영향　**antibiotic** 항생제　**diabetes** 당뇨　**starvation** 굶주림　**pave the way for** ~을 위해 길을 열다　**replacement** 대체　**therapy** 치료법　**pain-reliever** 진통제　**addiction** 중독　**excruciating** 극심한, 몹시 고통스러운　**pros and cons** 장단점

16 ③

문제 해결

우리의 일상생활에 큰 영향을 끼치고 많은 사람들을 살린 약을 열거하고 있으므로, 여자가 하는 말의 주제로 ③ '우리의 삶에 큰 역할을 하는 약들'이 가장 적절하다.
① 사람들이 가장 자주 먹는 약의 종류들
② 약을 정기적으로 먹는 것의 장점과 단점
④ 약이 생물 화학자에 의해 어떻게 개발되는가
⑤ 왜 우리는 약을 먹기 전 의사와 상담해야 하는가

17 ②

문제 해결

smallpox vaccine(천연두 백신)에 대해서는 언급되지 않았다.

01 ②	02 ⑤	03 ①	04 ②	05 ④	06 ②
07 ⑤	08 ③	09 ②	10 ⑤	11 ①	12 ②
13 ⑤	14 ⑤	15 ⑤	16 ②	17 ①	

01 ② 　　　　　　　　　　　　　　　　　　　　　　목적 파악

여: 여러분은 공영 라디오 방송을 듣고 계시고, 저는 진행자 Elizabeth Banner입니다. 캘리포니아 연안에서 대형 기름 유출 사고가 발생했습니다. 지금까지 사망자는 보고되지 않았습니다. 사고는 오늘 오전 5시경에 발생했습니다. 기름 유출의 원인이 무엇인지는 아직까지 알려지지 않았습니다. 3천만 갤런 이상의 기름이 바다로 유출되었습니다. 전문가들은 환경에 미치는 영향이 15년에서 20년은 갈 것이라 말하고 있습니다. 그 결과, 지역 어업은 심각한 영향을 받게 되었습니다. 저희는 입장을 듣기 위해 정유 회사에 연락을 시도했지만 그들은 응답하지 않고 있습니다. 이 이야기가 전개됨에 따라 추가되는 내용들은 계속 여러분에게 알려 드리도록 하겠습니다.

문제 해결

라디오 진행자인 여자는 새벽에 캘리포니아 연안에서 발생한 대형 기름 유출 사고를 전하고 있으므로, 여자가 하는 말의 목적으로 ②가 가장 적절하다.

어휘·표현

oil spill 기름 유출　occur 발생하다, 일어나다　fatality 사망자
environmental impact 환경에 미치는 영향　further 더 이상의, 추가의
unfold 전개되다, 펼쳐지다

02 ⑤ 　　　　　　　　　　　　　　　　　　　　　　주제 파악

남: 괜찮아요, Jean? 당신은 정말 아파 보여요.
여: 아주 안 좋아요. 하루 종일 재채기와 기침을 했어요.
남: 의사의 진찰을 받았어요?
여: 의사를 만날 필요는 없어요. 감기가 낫는 저만의 방법이 있어요.
남: 농담이죠?
여: 아니요. 진심이에요. 예를 들어, 나는 아플 때 인삼차를 많이 마셔요.
남: 또 뭘 해요?
여: 운동을 많이 해요. 땀을 흘리는 것이 감기가 낫는 데 도움이 된다고 들었어요.
남: 그건 과학적이지 않은 것 같아요. 이러한 것들이 감기를 치료한 적이 있어요?
여: 생각해 보니, 확실하지는 않네요.
남: 민간요법이 감기를 치료하는 것에 효과적인 것 같지는 않아요. 당신은 의사에게 진찰을 받아야 해요.
여: 아마 당신 말이 맞을 거 같군요.

문제 해결

여자가 감기 치료를 위해 시도하는 민간요법에 대해서 남자는 민간요법이 감기 치료에 효과적인 것 같지 않다고 말하고 있으므로, 남자의 의견으로는 ⑤가 가장 적절하다.

어휘·표현

sneeze 재채기하다　get over ~을 회복하다　ginseng 인삼　folk remedy 민간요법

03 ① 　　　　　　　　　　　　　　　　　　　　　　관계 추론

남: 당신에게 안 좋은 소식이 있어요, Jones 씨.
여: 집에 손상이 그렇게 심한가요?
남: 네, 집의 대부분이 파괴되었네요.
여: 남편과 저는 20년 전에 이 집을 샀어요.
남: 그 말을 들으니 매우 유감이군요.
여: 제가 둘러보는 건 안전한가요? 뭔가를 좀 찾고 싶어서요.
남: 유감이지만 안 됩니다. 지금은 집으로 들어가는 게 안전하지 않습니다.
여: 그렇다면 부탁 하나만 들어주실 수 있을까요?
남: 물론입니다. 무엇인가요?
여: 거실에 가족 앨범이 있어요.
남: 제가 불을 끄고 있을 때는 그것을 보지 못했는데, 제가 한번 더 살펴봐 드릴까요?
여: 너무 실례가 되지 않는다면요. 그것마저도 불에 타 버렸다면 저는 비통할 것 같아요.

문제 해결

20년 전에 남편과 집을 샀고 거실에 가족 앨범이 있다고 말한 것으로 보아 여자는 집주인이고, 불을 끌 때 가족 앨범을 보지 못했다고 말하는 것으로 보아 남자는 소방관임을 알 수 있다.

어휘·표현

put out (불을) 끄다　heartbroken 비통한

04 ② 　　　　　　　　　　　　　　　　　　　　　　그림 불일치 파악

여: 정말 아름다운 경치야, Mike!
남: 이 경치가 오랜 시간의 하이킹을 확실히 보상해 주네.
여: 오른쪽에 있는 소나무들을 봐. 아주 장엄해 보여.
남: 응. 나무들 위로 빙글빙글 돌고 있는 두 마리의 독수리가 보이니, Kate?
여: 그래. 그들은 먹이를 찾고 있는 것처럼 보여.
남: 왼편에 나무로 된 오두막집이 보이니?
여: 응. 아름다운 오두막집이네. 거기에 누가 사는지 궁금해.
남: 아마도 어떤 농부일 거야. 오, 봐! 오두막 오른쪽에 양들이 있어.
여: 어디? 어, 그래. 이제 보이네. 양들이 아주 귀여워 보인다.
남: 중앙에 있는 저 우물은 양들이 물을 먹는 곳일 거야.
여: 맞아. 이건 엽서에서 나온 것 같아.
남: 전적으로 동감해. 언젠가 이런 곳에서 정말 살고 싶어.

문제 해결

두 사람은 오랜 하이킹 후 경치를 보고 있는데 소나무 위로 두 마리의 독수리가 빙글빙글 돌고 있다고 했다. 그림의 ②는 두 마리의 독수리가 소나무 위에 앉아 있으므로 대화의 내용과 일치하지 않는다.

어휘·표현

make up for ~에 대해 보상하다　pine tree 소나무　majestic 장엄한, 웅장한

05 ④ 　　　　　　　　　　　　　　　　　　　　　　할 일 파악

여: 오늘 저에게 낚시하는 법을 가르쳐 주시기로 약속했었죠, 아빠.
남: 응, 그랬지. 먼저, 낚싯바늘에 미끼를 끼워야 한단다.
여: 윽! 제가 벌레를 만져야 한다는 건가요?
남: 처음은 내가 너에게 어떻게 하는지 보여 주겠지만, 그 뒤에는 네 스스

로 해야 한단다.

여: 오, 전 못할 것 같아요, 아빠.

남: 그것도 전부 낚시의 일부야. 우리가 산 벌레 통을 봤니?

여: 그건 아이스박스 옆쪽에 있는 것 같아요. 가져다 드릴까요?

남: 아니, 내가 가지러 가마. 내가 네게 말한 대로 모자는 가져왔니?

여: 네, 가져왔어요.

남: 자외선 차단 크림은? 그걸 바르는 건 기억했지?

여: 오, 깜빡했어요. 지금 바를게요.

아빠와 낚시를 온 여자는 자외선 차단 크림을 발랐는지 묻는 아빠에게 깜빡했다며 지금 바르겠다고 하였으므로, 여자가 할 일로 ④가 가장 적절하다.

어휘·표현

bait 미끼 **yuck** 윽 (역겨울 때 내는 소리) **tub** 통 **worm** 벌레 **cooler** 아이스박스, 냉장고

06 ②
언급 유무 파악

남: 안녕하세요, 저는 여기 이삿짐 회사를 이용하고 싶은데요.

여: 좋습니다. 짐이 얼마나 되시나요?

남: 많지는 않아요. 저는 오피스텔형 아파트에 살고 있어요.

여: 그럼 1톤 트럭이면 충분할 것 같네요.

남: 그건 얼마인가요?

여: 오피스텔형이라면, 350달러를 청구합니다.

남: 괜찮네요. 에어컨을 옮기는 데 추가 비용이 드나요?

여: 옮기는 건 추가 비용이 없어요. 하지만 새 아파트에 설치를 원하신다면 추가로 50달러를 받습니다.

남: 좋아요. 에어컨을 설치해 주세요.

여: 알겠습니다. 평일에 이사하는 게 가능하신가요? 평일에 이사하시면 20%를 할인해 드립니다.

남: 주말에 이사하려고 계획하고 있었는데, 평일이 좋겠네요. 다음 주 목요일 어떤가요?

여: 좋습니다. 총액을 알려 드릴게요.

문제 해결

남자는 이삿짐 회사를 통해 이사를 가려 하는데, 오피스텔형 아파트 이사에 350달러, 새 아파트에 에어컨 설치를 하는 데 추가로 50달러가 든다. 주말에 이사를 하려다가 평일에 20% 할인을 해 준다고 해서 평일에 하려고 하므로, 남자가 지불할 총 금액은 400달러에서 20%가 할인된 320달러이다.

어휘·표현

moving company 이삿짐 회사 **studio apartment** 오피스텔형(원룸형) 아파트 **install** 설치하다 **weekday** 평일

07 ⑤
이유 파악

여: 안녕, Peter. 너 뭘 만들고 있니?

남: 오, 안녕, Sue. 나는 새장을 만들고 있어.

여: 정말 멋지네. 뒷마당에 두려고 만들고 있는 거로구나. 거기서 많은 새들을 봤거든.

남: 사실 이건 나를 위한 게 아냐. 내 뒷마당에는 이미 하나가 있어.

여: 그럼 그건 학교 공예 수업의 과제니?

남: 아니. 과제는 아니야.

여: 알겠다. 다음 주 학교 박람회에서 그것을 팔려는 거야, 그렇지?

남: 좋은 추측이지만, 그 또한 아니야.

여: 더 이상 생각이 안 나. 왜 만들고 있는 거야?

남: 길 아래편에 사는 이웃의 생일이 다가오고 있어. 그래서 그녀에게 선물로 주려고 해.

여: 넌 정말 사려 깊구나. 그녀가 아주 좋아할 거라고 확신해.

남: 나도 정말 그러길 바라.

문제 해결

남자는 곧 생일인 이웃에게 생일 선물로 주기 위해 새장을 만들고 있다고 했다.

어휘·표현

backyard 뒤뜰, 뒷마당 **assignment** 과제, 숙제

08 ③
언급 유무 파악

남: Megan, John이 나에게 Boy Scouts Adventure 캠핑 여행 전단지를 주었어요.

여: 오, 뭐라고 쓰여 있나요?

남: 그들이 Eagle 호수에 있는 새로운 야영지로 갈 거라고 쓰여 있네요.

여: 언제 가는데요?

남: 캠핑 여행이 3월 1일 금요일이라고 쓰여 있어요.

여: 잘됐네요. 당신 휴가도 그때 시작하지 않나요?

남: 맞아요, 그래서 나는 John과 함께 갈 수 있어요.

여: 여행 전에 그를 위해 뭘 사야 할까요?

남: 전단지에는 소년들이 하이킹을 하고 수영을 할 거라고 하네요. 우리는 John에게 하이킹 부츠를 사 줘야겠어요.

여: 좋은 생각이에요. 캠핑 여행은 언제 끝나요?

남: 내가 볼게요…. 일요일 오후 6시에 끝나요.

여: 좋네요! 주말 동안 집 전체가 내 차지네요.

문제 해결

캠핑 장소(Eagle 호수), 캠핑 시작 날짜(3월 1일), 활동(하이킹, 수영), 캠핑 기간(금요일~일요일)에 관해서는 언급했지만, 식단과 식사 시간에 관해서는 언급하지 않았다.

어휘·표현

flyer (광고·안내용) 전단 **camping ground** 야영지 **accompany** 동반하다, 동행하다

09 ②
담화 내용 불일치

남: 안녕하세요, 여러분. 연례 People First Food Drive가 다시 한 번 돌아왔습니다. food drive의 목적은 우리 도시의 그 누구도 배고프지 않게 하는 것입니다. 기부 상자는 학교, 도서관, 그리고 공원에 놓일 것입니다. food drive의 주최자들은 기증품이 잘 부패하지 않는 건조 식품이나 통조림 식품이어야 한다고 부탁합니다. 기부 상자는 8월 내내 놓여 있을 것입니다. 그달 말에, 모인 음식은 우리 도시 전체의 무료 급식소로 배급될 것입니다. 여러분이 기부할 수 없다면, 급식소에 오셔서 도움이 필요한 사람들에게 음식을 나누어 주는 걸 돕는 자원봉사를 해 주세요. 모든 행동은 그것이 얼마나 작던 간에, 이 사람들의 삶에 커다란 영향을 미칠 것입니다.

문제 해결

주최자들은 건조 식품이나 통조림 식품을 기부해 줄 것을 요청한다고 하였으므로, ②는 내용과 일치하지 않는다.

어휘·표현

food drive 음식을 모으는 자선 행사 **organizer** 주최자, 조직자

non-perishable 잘 부패하지 않는   dry goods 마른 식품들, 건물류(곡물 등 물기 없는 식품들)   canned food 통조림 식품   distribute 나누어 주다, 분배하다
soup kitchen 무료 급식소

10 ⑤
도표 정보 파악

남: Michele, Best Electronics가 노트북 컴퓨터를 온라인에서 할인하고 있어.
여: 좋은 소식이다, James. 나는 새 노트북이 정말 필요해.
남: 예산 범위가 어떻게 돼?
여: 난 1,000달러 이상은 쓰고 싶지 않아.
남: 좋아. 네가 선택할 수 있는 네 가지 모델이 있어.
여: SSD와 HDD 하드 드라이브의 차이는 뭐야?
남: SSD는 Soild State Drive를 의미하고 HDD는 Hard Disk Drive를 의미해. 간단히 말하면, SSD가 훨씬 더 빨라.
여: 그럼 난 더 빠른 하드 드라이브를 가진 모델을 살래.
남: 좋아. 메모리는 얼마나 되었으면 좋겠니?
여: 나는 대용량 프로그램은 사용하지 않아서 8기가바이트가 꼭 필요하진 않아.
남: 그럼 넌 이 두 가지 중에서 선택할 수 있어. 이제 네가 할 일은 프로세서를 선택하는 거야.
여: 난 프로세서 속도가 더 높은 것을 주문할래.

문제 해결
여자는 가격이 1,000달러가 넘지 않고, SSD 하드 드라이브를 가지고 있으며, 8기가바이트가 아닌 노트북 컴퓨터 중 프로세서 속도가 더 높은 것을 주문한다고 했다. 따라서 여자가 구매할 노트북은 ⑤이다.

어휘·표현
electronics 전자 장치, 전자 기기   budget range 예산 범위
to put it simply 간단히 말하면   processor (컴퓨터의) 프로세서, 처리기

11 ①
짧은 대화의 응답

남: 좋은 아침입니다, Simmons 씨. 고객님의 차를 가져가셔도 된다고 알려 드리려고 전화드렸습니다.
여: 감사합니다만 오늘은 가져갈 수 없네요. 내일 가도 될까요?
남: 죄송합니다. 저희가 휴일에는 문을 닫아서요. 저희는 수요일에 문을 다시 열 예정입니다.
여: 알겠습니다. 그때 제 차를 가져갈게요.

문제 해결
차를 가져가라는 연락을 받은 여자가 내일 가도 되는지 묻자, 남자는 휴일이라 문을 닫고 수요일에 다시 연다고 했으므로, 그날 가겠다고 말하는 ①이 여자의 응답으로 가장 적절하다.
② 물론이죠. 휴일은 항상 짧은 것 같아요.
③ 정말요? 차는 지금 그대로 완벽해요.
④ 제 물건들을 가지러 내일 갈게요.
⑤ 네. 저는 수요일에 차를 인계할 거예요.

어휘·표현
unable ~할 수 없는, ~하지 못하는

12 ②
짧은 대화의 응답

여: Mark, 네가 과학을 정말 잘한다는 게 사실이야?

남: 음, 자랑하고 싶진 않지만, 난 학교 과학 동아리 부원이야.
여: 잘됐다. 네가 나를 가르쳐 줄 수 있을까?
남: 문제없어. 언제 시간이 되니?

문제 해결
과학을 잘하고 과학 동아리의 부원이라는 남자에게 여자가 자신을 가르쳐 줄 수 있는지 물었으므로, 문제없다며 언제 시간이 되는지 묻는 ②가 남자의 응답으로 가장 적절하다.
① 물론이지. 공원에서 만나서 놀자.
③ 와! 나도 과학 동아리에 가입하고 싶어.
④ 정말? 수학이 과학보다 훨씬 더 쉬워.
⑤ 유감이지만 나는 모든 과학 과목들을 정말 못해.

어휘·표현
brag (심하게) 자랑하다, 떠벌리다   tutor 가르치다, 개인 교습을 하다

13 ⑤
긴 대화의 응답

여: Marty의 식당에 오신 것을 환영합니다. 제 이름은 Charlotte입니다. 제가 오늘 고객님의 주문을 받을 예정입니다. 무엇을 드시겠습니까?
남: 안녕하세요, Charlotte. 오늘의 특별 요리를 말해 주겠어요?
여: 물어 보셔서 기쁩니다. 오늘의 특별 요리는 근사한 surf and turf입니다.
남: surf and turf요? 그게 뭔가요?
여: 군침이 돌게 하는 스테이크와 육즙 풍부한 바닷가재에 으깬 황금빛 감자와 찐 당근이 곁들여져 나옵니다.
남: 환상적으로 들리네요! 그걸 먹을게요.
여: 탁월한 선택이십니다. 손님, 스테이크는 어떻게 해 드릴까요?
남: 완전히 익혀 주세요. 또한 식초와 기름이 섞인 드레싱을 뿌린 샐러드를 주문할 수 있나요?
여: 물론입니다. 식사와 함께 할 음료를 드시겠습니까?
남: 오렌지주스를 가져다주시겠어요?
여: 바로 가져다 드리겠습니다. 후식 메뉴를 보시겠습니까?
남: 아니요, 괜찮아요. 이제 충분합니다.

문제 해결
식당에서 음식을 주문한 남자에게 여자가 후식 메뉴를 보겠냐고 물었으므로, 이에 대한 남자의 응답으로 ⑤ '아니요, 괜찮아요. 이제 충분합니다.'가 가장 적절하다.
① 왜 안 되겠어요? 제게 바닷가재를 가져다주세요.
② 물론 아니죠! 저는 바닐라 아이스크림을 정말 좋아해요.
③ 물론이에요. 저는 surf and turf를 주문할게요.
④ 당연하죠. 저는 후식을 먹을 배가 없네요.

어휘·표현
surf and turf 바닷가재나 새우 등의 해산물과 육류가 함께 나오는 요리
mouth-watering 군침이 돌게 하는   mashed potato 으깬 감자   vinegar 식초

14 ⑤
긴 대화의 응답

[전화벨이 울린다.]
남: Birthdays Are Us에 전화해 주셔서 감사합니다. 저는 Jerry입니다. 어떻게 도와 드릴까요?
여: 안녕하세요, Jerry. 제 이름은 Beth이고 생일 행사를 예약하려고 전화했습니다.

남: 제대로 전화하셨습니다! 생일이 언제입니까?

여: 이번 달 10일이지만 그 다음 주말에 파티를 하고 싶습니다.

남: 알겠습니다. 파티의 주인공이 소년인가요, 아니면 소녀인가요?

여: 열두 살이 되는 딸을 위한 파티입니다.

남: 좋아요! 딸은 무엇을 좋아합니까?

여: 제 딸은 piñata를 정말 좋아해요. 하나를 가져올 수 있나요?

남: 문제없습니다. 다른 건 무엇을 좋아합니까?

여: 그녀는 형형색색의 풍선이 많은 것을 좋아합니다.

남: 네. 파티에 광대를 보내 드릴까요?

여: 절대 안 돼요! 우리 아이는 광대를 무서워해요.

문제 해결

여자는 생일 파티 이벤트 업체에 전화를 걸어 딸의 생일 파티 이벤트를 예약하고 있다. 파티에 광대를 보내 줄지 묻는 말에 대한 여자의 응답으로 ⑤ '절대 안 돼요! 우리 아이는 광대를 무서워해요.'가 가장 적절하다.

① 물론이에요. 그녀는 piñata를 아주 좋아해요.

② 알겠어요. 그녀는 모래성을 쌓는 것을 아주 좋아해요.

③ 네. 초콜릿 아이스크림 케이크를 주세요.

④ 아니요. 광대는 그날 바빠요.

어휘·표현

piñata 피냐타(장난감과 사탕이 가득 든 통으로, 미국에서 아이들이 생일 파티 때 눈을 가리고 막대기로 쳐서 깨뜨리곤 한다.)   clown 광대   terrified 무서워하는

15 ⑤   상황에 적절한 말

여: Timmy와 Julie는 방금 새 아파트로 이사했다. 그들은 새 세탁기를 사려고 보고 있다. Timmy는 다른 많은 물건을 사야 하므로 중고 가전제품 상점에서 중고 세탁기를 구입하려고 한다. 또한 그는 새 세탁기를 구입하는 것이 돈 낭비라고 생각한다. 그러나 Julie는 보증 기간 때문에 새로 나온 세탁기를 사고 싶다. 그녀는 중고품은 언제든지 고장 날 수 있어 염려스럽다. 그녀는 또한 중고품은 사용하기 전에 전문적인 청소가 필요하다고 생각한다. Julie는 Timmy가 새 세탁기 구입을 고려하기를 원한다. 이런 상황에서, Julie는 Timmy에게 뭐라고 말할 것 같은가?

어휘·표현

Timmy는 중고 세탁기를 사려고 하고, Julie는 고장과 청소 비용 등을 감안해서 새 세탁기 구입을 원하는 상황이므로, Julie가 Timmy에게 할 말로 ⑤ '길게 보면 새 제품을 사는 것이 돈을 절약할 수 있어요.'가 가장 적절하다.

① 중고품이 훨씬 더 저렴할 거예요.

② 카탈로그에 실린 근사한 냉장고들을 봐요.

③ 우리 세탁기의 보증 기간이 언제 만료되나요?

④ 우리는 이 구매를 하기 전에 잠시 보류해야 할 것 같아요.

어휘·표현

appliance store 가전제품 상점   warranty 품질 보증   break down 고장 나다   expire 만료되다   in the long run 결국에는

16-17   복합 이해

남: 작문 워크숍에 참석해 주셔서 감사합니다. 저는 글쓰기 코치, Sam입니다. 이것은 일련의 네 수업 중 두 번째입니다. 이전 수업에서, 우리는 글쓰기의 중요성에 대해 이야기했습니다. 이번 수업에서는 작문에 사용할 수 있는 여러 유형의 문장에 대해 이야기할 것입니다. 첫 번째 유형은 평서문입니다. 평서문은 정보를 서술하는 데 사용됩니다. 예

를 들면, '저는 당신의 글쓰기 코치입니다.'와 같은 문장입니다. 두 번째 유형은 명령문입니다. '칠판에 한 문장을 쓰시오.' 같은 문장처럼 명령 또는 요청을 말합니다. 세 번째 유형은 의문문입니다. 질문하는 데 사용됩니다. 예를 들어, '글을 잘 쓰십니까?'입니다. 마지막 유형은 감탄문입니다. 감정을 나타내는 데 사용돼요. '나는 당신의 글이 정말 좋아요!'라는 문장이 그 예입니다. 여러분의 메시지를 잘 전달하기 위해 이 문장들을 적절한 상황에서 사용하는 것이 중요합니다. 이제 그룹을 지어 글쓰기 연습을 해 봅시다.

어휘·표현

a series of 일련의   declarative 평서문의   state 말하다, 진술하다
imperative 명령을 나타내는   command 명령   interrogative 질문 형태의, 의문문에 쓰이는   exclamatory 감탄을 나타내는   convey 전달하다
compound 합성의 (cf. compound sentence 중문)

16 ②

문제 해결

글쓰기 코치가 작문에 사용할 수 있는 여러 유형의 문장에 대해 설명하고 있으므로, 남자가 하는 말의 주제로 ② '여러 유형의 문장'이 가장 적절하다.

① 글을 잘 쓰는 것의 중요성

③ 글쓰기 코치를 두는 것의 이점

④ 글쓰기 초급자들이 범하는 흔한 오류

⑤ 올바른 문법 사용의 필요성

17 ①

문제 해결

여러 유형의 문장에 대해 설명하면서 평서문, 명령문, 의문문, 감탄문에 대해서는 언급했지만, ① '중문'에 관해서는 언급하지 않았다.

01 ③	02 ⑤	03 ③	04 ②	05 ⑤	06 ②
07 ④	08 ④	09 ②	10 ③	11 ①	12 ⑤
13 ④	14 ①	15 ③	16 ⑤	17 ③	

01 ③
목적 파악

여: K-One 청취자 여러분 안녕하세요. 저는 진행자인 Danni Stokes 입니다. 정규 방송에 들어가기에 앞서, 여러분들께 K-One이 무료 공공 라디오 방송이며 청취자분들의 기부 덕분에 운영된다는 사실을 상기시켜 드리고자 합니다. 모든 쇼는 여러분 같은 분들 덕분에 가능했습니다. 여기 K-One의 모든 사람을 대신하여, 여러분의 청취와 지원에 대해 감사드립니다. 여러분이 청취하시는 이야기들이 마음에 드신다면, 우리 웹 사이트를 통해 또는 전화로 기부해 주십시오. 여러분이 듣고자 하는 최신 이야기를 전달해 드리는 데 도움이 되므로 어떤 금액도 적지 않습니다. 이제 우리 쇼로 들어가겠습니다.

문제 해결
여자는 K-One 공공 라디오 방송이 청취자들의 기부 덕분에 운영된다고 말하면서 청취자들에게 방송을 위한 기부를 요청하고 있다.

어휘·표현
regularly 정기적으로 operate 운영되다 on behalf of ~을 대신하여, ~을 대표하여

02 ⑤
주제 파악

남: Michelle. 오늘 기분 어때?
여: 좋아, Dan. 뭐 새로운 일 있니?
남: 별로. 나 최근에 헬스클럽을 그만뒀어.
여: 너 운동하는 걸 아주 좋아하잖아. 왜 그만뒀어?
남: 항상 실내에 갇혀 있는 게 지겨워졌어.
여: 이해해. 때로는 바깥에 나갈 필요가 있지.
남: 맞아. 그게 내가 하이킹을 시작하려고 하는 이유야.
여: 그거 좋은데. 뭐 때문에 하이킹으로 결정했어? 자연과 하나가 되려고?
남: 그것도 좋지만, 내 생각에 하이킹의 가장 좋은 점은 다른 사람들에게서 떨어져 있는 거야.
여: 하지만 너 사람들과 함께 있는 걸 좋아하잖아.
남: 알아, 하지만 가끔은 혼자서 있는 게 좋아.
여: 그렇구나. 조만간에 너 하이킹 갈 때 내가 함께 갈 수 있길 바라.

문제 해결
남자는 하이킹의 좋은 점이 사람들과 떨어져 혼자서 있을 수 있다는 것이라고 말하고 있으므로, 남자의 의견으로 가장 적절한 것은 ⑤이다.

어휘·표현
stuck 움직일 수 없는, 갇힌 indoors 실내에서

03 ③
관계 추론

여: 안녕하세요. Smith 씨.
남: 안녕하세요. Roberts 씨. 제 아들의 식단에 대해서 당신과 이야기를 나누고 싶어요.

여: 알겠어요. 무엇을 도와드릴까요?
남: 제 아들이 건강하게 먹으면 좋겠어요. 조언해 주실 게 있으신가요?
여: 아, 저는 부모님들에게서 항상 이 질문을 받는답니다. 제 조언은 설탕이 든 음료를 끊으라는 것이에요.
남: 탄산음료를 말씀하시는 건가요?
여: 네. 아드님이 물을 더 마시고 탄산음료와 주스를 덜 마시도록 하세요.
남: 알겠어요. 제가 해야 할 다른 게 있나요?
여: 영양사로서, 식단에 더 많은 채소를 포함시키는 것의 중요성은 아무리 강조해도 지나치지 않아요.
남: 어떻게 그렇게 할 수 있을까요? 제 아들은 채소를 좋아하지 않거든요.
여: 음식에 채소를 첨가하려고 해 보세요. 예를 들어, 당근을 갈아서 파스타 소스에 넣는 식으로요.
남: 고맙습니다. 큰 도움이 됐어요.

문제 해결
남자는 아들이 건강하게 먹게 하려면 어떻게 할지 조언을 구하고 있고, 여자는 탄산음료와 주스 대신 물을 마시게 하고, 더 많은 채소를 먹게 하라는 조언을 하고 있다. 이로 보아, 여자와 남자는 영양사와 부모의 관계임을 알 수 있다.

어휘·표현
cut back on ~을 줄이다 sugary 설탕이 든 nutritionist 영양사 stress 강조하다

04 ②
그림 불일치 파악

남: 와, Hannah. 이 사무실 멋져 보이네요.
여: 정말 마음에 들어요?
남: 그럼요! 난 오른쪽 구석에 있는 책상이 마음에 들어요.
여: 책상을 거기에 두어 옆에 있는 창문을 통해 자연 채광을 받을 수 있어요.
남: 당신이 달아 놓은 저 별무늬 커튼이 귀엽네요.
여: 고마워요. 난 왼쪽 구석에 파일 캐비닛을 놓았어요. 그렇게 하면 중요한 서류를 모두 가까이에 둘 수 있어요.
남: 그래도 프린터를 놓을 자리가 보이지 않네요.
여: 프린터를 놓을 공간이 없었어요. 그래서, 대신 작은 스툴 의자 위에 멋진 식물을 두었어요.
남: 그 식물이 방에 녹색 기운을 잘 더했네요.
여: 여기 왼쪽 벽에는 고양이 포스터가 있어요.
남: 전에 그 포스터를 본 적이 있어요.
여: 매우 인기 있는 포스터라는 것을 알고 있지만 저는 이 포스터에서 영감을 얻어요.

문제 해결
창문에 별무늬 커튼이 달려 있다고 했으므로, 그림 속 물방울무늬 커튼인 ②가 대화의 내용과 일치하지 않는다.

어휘·표현
close by 가까이에 inspire 영감을 주다

05 ⑤
부탁한 일 파악

여: Scott, 텐트를 다 걷었나요?
남: 네, 거의 끝나가요, Carol. 아이스박스는 챙겼어요?
여: 네, 오늘 아침에 치웠어요.
남: 좋아요! 지금 뭔가를 할 거예요?
여: 손을 씻으러 가려고요. 손이 지저분해요.

남: 가기 전에, 내가 이 텐트 치우는 것 좀 도와줄 수 있어요?

여: 물론이죠. 내가 뭘 하면 돼요?

남: 내가 텐트를 안에 넣을 수 있도록 가방을 좀 열고 있어 줬으면 해요.

여: 알겠어요. 가방은 어디 있어요?

남: 모르겠네요. 차 뒷자석에서 봤던 것 같은데요.

여: 내가 아이스박스를 넣으러 갔을 때 거기에서 보지 못했어요.

남: 아. 야영지를 둘러보며 가방을 찾아 봐 줄 수 있어요?

여: 알겠어요. 찾아 볼게요.

문제 해결

텐트를 넣어야 할 가방이 보이지 않자 남자는 여자에게 야영지를 둘러 보며 가방을 찾아 봐 달라고 부탁했으므로, 남자가 부탁한 일로 ⑤가 가장 적절하다.

어휘·표현

take down (구조물을 해체하여) 치우다　**cooler** 아이스박스, 냉장고
put away 치우다, 넣다　**campsite** 야영지, 캠프장

06 ②

숫자 정보 파악

여: 네, 손님. 차에 대한 모든 수리가 끝났습니다.

남: 좋아요! 무엇을 작업했고 그게 얼마인지 알려 주시겠어요?

여: 물론입니다. 먼저 엔진 오일 교환을 했어요. 그건 25달러입니다.

남: 알겠어요. 또 뭐를 했나요?

여: 벨트가 정말 닳아서 못 쓰게 되었더군요. 그걸 교체하는 게 100달러였습니다.

남: 알겠어요. 청구서의 이 항목을 설명해 주시겠어요?

여: 그건 75달러인 초기 진단 검사 비용입니다.

남: 75달러는 좀 비싼 것 같군요. 계속 하세요.

여: 청구서의 마지막 항목은 부품과 인건비로, 200달러가 나왔습니다.

남: 와. 제가 생각했던 것보다 훨씬 더 비싸네요.

여: 음, 총액에서 관리자 재량으로 10퍼센트 할인해 드릴 수 있어요.

남: 그렇게 해 주신다면 더 감사하겠어요.

문제 해결

차 수리비로 엔진 오일 교환이 25달러, 벨트 교체가 100달러, 초기 진단 검사 비용이 75달러, 부품과 인건비가 200달러가 나왔는데, 총액에서 10퍼센트를 할인해 준다고 했으므로, 여자가 지불할 총 금액은 360달러이다.

어휘·표현

oil change (자동차의) 엔진 오일 교환　**wear down** 마모시키다, 마모되다
initial 초기의　**diagnostic test** 진단 검사　**parts** 부품　**labor** 일, 업무, 노동, (자동차 수리비 중의) 기술료

07 ④

이유 파악

[휴대 전화벨이 울린다.]

여: 이 봐, Larry. 영화 시간에 맞춰 올 수 있는 거니?

남: 안녕, Jean. 응, 시간 맞춰 도착할 거야.

여: 꼭 늦지 마. 나는 7시 상영 표를 예매했어.

남: 제시간에 가겠다고 약속할게. 지금 내 차에 타고 있어.

여: 이 영화에 대해 좋은 말을 아주 많이 들었어.

남: 응, 나도 그래. 모든 사람들이 그 영화가 얼마나 훌륭한지 계속 이야기하더라.

여: 그 영화 예고편을 봤니?

남: 아니. 영화 내용을 미리 알고 싶지 않았어.

여: 그래. 네가 무슨 말을 하려는지 알겠어.

남: Jean, 내 자동차에 문제가 있어. 시동이 안 걸려.

여: 오! 무슨 일이야?

남: 어젯밤에 라이트를 켜 놓았었어. 정말 미안해, Jean. 난 오늘 영화를 볼 수 없겠어.

문제 해결

남자는 자동차 시동이 걸리지 않아서 영화를 볼 수 없다고 했다.

어휘·표현

trailer 예고편　**spoil** 망치다, 버려 놓다, 못쓰게 만들다

08 ④

언급 유무 파악

남: 여보, 한번 봐요. 청첩장을 받았어요.

여: 누가 결혼하는데요?

남: 내 고등학교 친구인 James요. 그가 마침내 결혼을 하네요.

여: 할 때가 되었죠. 결혼식이 언제예요?

남: 5월 5일이에요.

여: 결혼하기에 좋은 때네요. 그때는 날씨가 너무 덥지도 춥지도 않을 때죠. 결혼식을 어디에서 하나요?

남: 1번가와 Main가가 만나는 모퉁이에 있는 교회에서요.

여: 그 교회는 조금 작은데요. 결혼식이 몇 시죠?

남: 청첩장에는 오후 1시에 시작한다고 쓰여 있어요.

여: James가 결혼하게 되어 너무 기뻐요.

남: 아, 초대장에는 우리가 이달 말일까지 참석 여부를 회답해야 한다고 쓰여 있어요.

여: 이달 말일이면 이번 주 금요일이네요! 내일 아침에 우편으로 보낼 수 있도록 지금 작성하도록 해요.

문제 해결

결혼식 날짜(5월 5일), 결혼식 장소(1번가와 Main가가 만나는 모퉁이에 있는 교회), 결혼식 시간(오후 1시), 참석 여부 회답 기한(이달 말일)에 대해서는 언급했지만, ④ 축하 선물 목록에 대해서는 언급하지 않았다.

어휘·표현

tie the knot 결혼을 하다　**RSVP** (파티 등의 초대에) 참석 여부를 회답하다

09 ②

담화 내용 불일치

남: 안녕하세요, 기타 팬 여러분. Florida 기타 페스티벌이 다시 돌아왔으니 놓치지 마십시오. 이 연례행사는 작년과 마찬가지로 Central Park에서 개최됩니다. 이 축제에는 온 가족을 위한 흥미로운 다양한 행사들이 열립니다. 기타 연주법을 배우고 싶은 사람을 위한 초보자 기타 워크숍이 열립니다. 이 워크숍은 세계적으로 유명한 재즈 기타 연주가인 Lionel Fritz가 진행합니다. 또한 많은 전설적인 기타 연주가들이 축제 내내 특별한 공연을 펼칠 것입니다. 음식을 말씀드리는 것을 빠뜨려선 안 되겠죠. 플로리다 전역에서 온 노점 음식점들이 행사 내내 맛있는 요리를 제공할 것입니다. 온 가족이 함께 오셔서 멋진 시간을 보내십시오.

문제 해결

초보자 대상 기타 연주법 배우기 워크숍이 열릴 것이라고 했으므로, ②가 내용가 일치하지 않는다.

어휘·표현

the one and only 유일한, 유명한　**world-renowned** 세계적으로 유명한
legendary 전설적인　**vendor** 노점상, 행상인

10 ③

도표 정보 파악

남: Jessica, Everest Sportswear에서 새 카탈로그를 받았어요.
여: 좋아요! 판매 중인 겨울 코트가 있나요?
남: 마지막 장에서 몇 개 봤어요. 얼마를 지출하려고 하나요?
여: 코트에 200달러 이상은 쓰고 싶지 않아요.
남: 운이 좋네요! 200달러 이하로 4벌의 코트를 판매하고 있어요.
여: 잘됐네요! 어느 것이 방수 외피가 있죠?
남: 이 세 개가 방수예요. 여기 내리는 눈이면, 코트는 방수여야 해요.
여: 단열 처리는 어때요? 저는 다운재킷을 원해요.
남: 그래요. 다운(깃털)만큼 따뜻하게 해 주는 것은 없죠. 이 두 코트가 다 다운이네요.
여: 알겠어요. 마지막으로, 코트에 후드가 있어야 해요.
남: 이 두 개 중 하나에만 후드가 있어요.
여: 그럼 그게 나에게 맞는 것이에요.

문제 해결

여자는 가격이 200달러가 넘지 않고, 방수가 되며, 다운재킷이면서 후드가 달려 있는 코트를 구입하고 싶어 한다. 따라서 여자가 구입할 코트는 ③이다.

어휘·표현

waterproof 방수의 **shell** 외피 **insulation** 단열 처리 **down** (새의) 부드러운 털 **hood** (외투 등에 달린) 모자

11 ①

짧은 대화의 응답

남: Sally, 이번 주 금요일에 와서 아이 좀 봐 줄 수 있니?
여: 물론이죠, Jones 씨. 저 그때 한가해요. 몇 시에 필요하세요?
남: 아내와 내가 7시에 저녁 식사 예약이 되어 있어서, 6시까지 여기 올 수 있겠니?
여: 문제없어요. 그때 갈게요.

문제 해결

여자는 금요일에 한가해서 아이를 돌봐 줄 수 있다고 말했고, 이에 남자가 6시까지 올 수 있는지 물었으므로, 여자의 응답으로 문제없다고 말하는 ①이 가장 적절하다.
② 물론이죠. 아기 돌보기는 정말 힘든 일이에요.
③ 안 되겠어요. 저는 그 시간에 한가해요.
④ 물론이죠. 당신과 저녁 식사를 정말 하고 싶어요.
⑤ 아니요. 제게는 토요일이 더 나을 것 같아요.

어휘·표현

babysit (부모가 외출한 동안) 아이를 봐 주다

12 ⑤

짧은 대화의 응답

여: Mike. 너무 더워요. 우리 뭐 좀 마시면 어때요?
남: 좋아요. 저도 목이 말라요. 당신은 어떤 종류의 음료수를 마시고 싶어요?
여: 저는 망고 주스요. 당신도 하나 원해요?
남: 사실, 저는 망고 알레르기가 있어요. 저는 다른 것으로 할게요.

문제 해결

목이 말라서 음료수를 선택해야 하는 상황에서, 망고 주스를 마시려는 여자가 남자에게 같은 주스를 원하는지를 물었다. 이에 대한 남자의 응답으로 망고 알레르기가 있다며 망고 주스를 거절하는 ⑤가 가장 적절하다.
① 당신 말이 맞아요. 그것이 바로 제가 원했던 거예요.

② 미안하지만, 저는 배가 불러요. 우리 식사를 거르는 게 어때요?
③ 정말로요? 제 여동생은 꿀을 넣은 딸기 주스를 원해요.
④ 부모님이 같은 음료수를 원하시는지를 확인하고자 부모님께 전화해 볼게요.

어휘·표현

allergic to ~에 알레르기가 있는

13 ④

긴 대화의 응답

여: House 씨, 당신의 자격 요건이 훌륭하군요.
남: 그 말을 들으니 기쁩니다. 제가 당신의 병원에 큰 보탬이 될 것 같습니다.
여: 좋아요. 질문하실 게 있나요?
남: 보수가 궁금합니다. 그것에 대해 말씀해 주시겠습니까?
여: 물론입니다. 저희 병원의 의사로서 귀하는 완벽한 의료 보험 혜택을 누리게 됩니다. 유예 기간이 끝나면 주식을 구매할 수도 있습니다.
남: 훌륭합니다. 휴가는 어떻습니까?
여: 매년 2주간의 유급 휴가가 있습니다. 7년 후, 의사는 3개월의 유급 휴가를 받을 수 있습니다.
남: 병가는 며칠이 가능합니까?
여: 병원은 첫해에 7일의 병가를 제공합니다. 여기서 일하면 매년 하루씩 더 추가됩니다.
남: 모든 게 완벽한 것 같군요.
여: 네. 그럼, 언제부터 시작할 수 있습니까?
남: 다음 주에 근무를 시작할 수 있습니다.

문제 해결

남자는 여자에게 복리 후생에 관한 설명을 들은 후, 모든 게 완벽하다고 말하며 조건에 만족을 표했다. 따라서 언제부터 시작할 수 있냐는 여자의 물음에 대한 남자의 응답으로 ④ '다음 주에 근무를 시작할 수 있습니다.'가 가장 적절하다.
① 시간을 내 주시고 수고해 주셔서 감사합니다.
② 저는 지금 휴가를 시작하고 싶습니다.
③ 저는 추가 검사를 받을 필요가 있습니다.
⑤ 이 병원은 그 도시에서 최고의 치료를 제공합니다.

어휘·표현

qualifications 자격 요건 **outstanding** 뛰어난, 두드러진 **compensation package** (급여와 복리 후생을 포함한) 보수 **health benefits** 의료 보험 **grace period** 유예 기간 **conduct** 수행하다 **further** 더 이상의, 추가의

14 ①

긴 대화의 응답

남: 오, Lizzy! 너무 오랜만이야. 어떻게 지냈어?
여: 늘 똑같아. 가족들은 잘 지내고, 일은 꾸준해.
남: 아직도 선생님으로 일하고 있어?
여: 응. 나는 우리 집 옆에 있는 공립 초등학교에서 일하기 시작했어.
남: 어떠니? 가르치는 것이 매우 스트레스가 많은 일이라고 하던데.
여: 괜찮아. 직원들은 훌륭해. 모두가 많은 도움을 줘. 학생들도 훌륭해.
남: 나 가 봐야 하는데 언젠가 저녁을 먹자. 온 가족을 보고 싶어.
여: 정말 좋겠다. 이번 주말은 어때?
남: 이번 주말은 내가 안 돼. 부모님이 오시거든.
여: 알겠어, 다음 주말에 우리 가족은 호수 옆에서 캠핑을 할 거야.
남: 그냥 내가 전화하면 어때? 우린 나중에 뭔가를 계획할 수 있을 거야.

여: 좋아. 네 전화 기다리고 있을게.

문제 해결

각자의 일정으로 저녁을 함께 먹을 날짜를 정하지 못한 상황에서 남자가 '그냥 내가 전화하면 어때?'라고 말하면서 나중에 계획을 하자고 말했다. 이에 대한 여자의 응답으로 ① '좋아. 네 전화 기다리고 있을게.'가 가장 적절하다.

② 응. 이번 주에 우리 부모님을 뵙게 돼서 신나.

③ 물론이야. 이번 주말에 저녁 식사를 하면 정말 좋겠어.

④ 그래. 가르치는 일은 정말 도전이었어.

⑤ 좋아. 캠핑 가서 나에게 꼭 편지를 써.

어휘·표현

steady 꾸준한   expect 기대하다, 예상하다

15 ③

상황에 적절한 말

여: Tom과 Sara는 결혼한 부부이며 그들은 첫 해외 휴가를 함께 계획 중이다. 오랜 토론 끝에 그들은 Guam에 가는 것에 동의한다. 문제는 그곳에서 시간을 보내는 방법에 대한 생각이 다르다는 것이다. Tom은 가능한 한 많은 야외 활동을 원한다. 그는 하이킹, 서핑, 스노클링을 하러 가기를 원한다. 반면, Sara는 해변에 앉아서 Tom과 함께 시간을 보내길 고대하고 있다. 그녀는 올해 매우 힘들었기 때문에 휴가 중에 휴식을 취하고 싶다. Sara는 휴가 동안 Tom이 휴식을 취하고 그녀와 함께 느긋이 있기를 원한다. 이런 상황에서, Sara는 Tom에게 뭐라고 말할 것 같은가?

문제 해결

Sara는 휴가 기간 동안 Tom과 함께 편안히 쉬고 싶어 하므로, Sara가 할 말로 ③ '우리가 함께 편안히 시간을 보내면 좋겠어.'가 가장 적절하다.

① 휴식을 취할 시간이 충분하지 않아.

② Guam에서 스노클링을 해 본 적이 있니?

④ 산에 올라가는 것은 재미있고 편안할 거 같아.

⑤ 우리가 정말 해변에 앉아 있을 필요가 있다고 생각해?

어휘·표현

relax 휴식을 취하다, 느긋이 쉬다   tough 힘든

16-17

복합 이해

남: 안녕하세요. 음악 애호가 여러분들. 여러분은 팟캐스트 Audio Mania를 듣고 계십니다. 저는 진행자 Jim입니다. 지난 시간에는 블루투스 스피커의 장점에 대해 이야기했습니다. 오늘은 무선 헤드셋에 대해 이야기하고 싶습니다. 보다 구체적으로, Airpal이라는 새로운 모델이 막 출시되었습니다. 탁월한 소음 방지 기능으로, 볼륨을 높이지 않고도 혼잡한 지하철에서 음악을 들을 수 있습니다. 또한 새로운 특허 기술로 인해 Airpal의 음질은 현재 시중에 나와 있는 다른 헤드셋보다 훨씬 우수합니다. 이 헤드셋에는 편리한 충전을 위한 충전 케이스가 함께 제공됩니다. 언급할 가치가 있는 또 다른 기능은 헤드셋을 벗지 않고도 외부 소음을 들을 수 있는 '빠른 현실' 모드입니다. 짧은 대화를 나누거나 카페에서 커피를 주문할 때 아주 좋습니다. 이 헤드셋의 탁월한 음질과 풍부한 기능은 도처에 있는 음악 애호가의 상당한 관심을 끌고 있습니다. 가까운 전자 제품 매장에서 사용해 보십시오.

어휘·표현

superb 최상의, 대단히 훌륭한   noise cancelling 소음 방지

patented technology 특허 기술   be superior to ~보다 더 뛰어나다
turn heads 관심을 끌다, 시선을 끌다   electronics store 전자 제품 매장
drawback 결점, 문제점

16 ⑤

문제 해결

남자는 새로운 무선 헤드셋의 우수성과 기능에 대해 이야기하고 있으므로, 남자가 하는 말의 주제로 ⑤ '새로운 무선 헤드셋 소개'가 가장 적절하다.

① 무선 스피커의 필요성

② 무선 헤드셋의 결점

③ 블루투스 헤드셋의 장점

④ 소음 방지 헤드셋의 장점

17 ③

문제 해결

소음 방지, 음질, 충전 케이스, 빠른 현실 모드에 대해서는 언급했지만, ③ 마이크에 대해서는 언급하지 않았다.

01 ②	02 ③	03 ④	04 ④	05 ②	06 ②
07 ⑤	08 ④	09 ④	10 ②	11 ④	12 ①
13 ①	14 ①	15 ①	16 ③	17 ⑤	

01 ②
목적 파악

남: 안녕하세요! 저는 학생회장 Harry Brown입니다. 졸업식이 불과 1주일 밖에 남지 않았는데, 여러분은 기분이 어떠신가요? 다음 주 금요일, 여러분은 학교에 작별 인사를 할 것입니다. 이때에, 저는 여러분에게 부탁할 것이 있습니다. 졸업을 하면 여러분은 교복이 더 이상 필요하지 않으니, 교복을 학생회에 기증하는 것이 어떠세요? 여러분이 교복을 저희에게 기증하면, 교복을 세탁하고 수선해서 크기별로 분류한 후에 마지막으로 그 교복을 필요로 하는 학생들에게 보낼 것입니다. 이것은 여러분이 후배 학생들을 도울 기회입니다. 내일부터 졸업식 전날까지, 우리는 학생회실에서 여러분의 교복을 받겠습니다. 우리는 여러분의 적극적인 협조에 감사드립니다. 고맙습니다, 선배님들.

문제 해결
학생회장인 남자는 졸업을 1주일 앞둔 선배들에게 교복을 학생회에 기증할 것을 요청하고 있다.

어휘·표현
graduation ceremony 졸업식   mend 수선하다, 수리하다   senior 상급자

02 ③
주제 파악

남: Rachel, 오늘 점심시간에 당신의 학생들은 무엇을 했나요?
여: 평소에 하던 것이요. 점점 더 추워지고 있어서, 학생들은 밖으로 나가려 하지 않고 교실에서 그냥 서로 이야기를 했어요.
남: 정말이요? 부럽네요.
여: 나를 부러워한다고요? 그게 무슨 뜻이죠?
남: 내 학생들은 교실에서 그저 스마트폰만 보고 있거든요. 그들은 심지어 서로 이야기도 하지 않아요.
여: 안타깝네요.
남: 당신의 학생들은 스마트폰을 사용하지 않나요?
여: 사용하죠. 하지만 교실에서는 안 해요. 제가 사용하지 못하게 해요.
남: 오, 그거 좋은데요. 내가 왜 그 생각을 못 했을까요?
여: 적어도 교실에서는 학생들이 스마트폰을 사용하는 것을 허락해서는 안 된다고 생각해요. 그렇지 않으면 학생들은 다른 어떤 것도 하지 않을 거예요.
남: 완전히 동의해요. 내일부터 학생들에게 스마트폰을 사용하지 말라고 해야겠어요.

문제 해결
여자는 교실에서 스마트폰 사용이 허락되면 학생들이 다른 어떤 것도 하지 않을 것이라고 하면서 교실에서는 학생들의 스마트폰 사용이 허락되어서는 안 된다고 했다. 따라서 여자의 의견으로 ③이 가장 적절하다.

어휘·표현
envy 부러워하다   otherwise 그렇지 않으면

03 ④
관계 추론

여: 안녕하세요, 만나서 반가워요. 저는 Sara Johnson입니다.
남: 안녕하세요, Brian Anderson입니다.
여: 와 주셔서 감사합니다. 당신이 오지 않을까 걱정되기 시작했거든요.
남: 와야만 했어요. 지난밤 현장에 있었던 유일한 사람이 저였으니까요.
여: 맞습니다. 그러니 목격하신 것을 자세히 말씀해 주십시오.
남: 일을 끝내고 집에 가는 길이었는데, 갑자기 누군가 비명을 지르는 것을 들었어요. 그때 파란색 재킷을 입은 키가 큰 남자가 빵집에서 뛰어 나왔어요.
여: 매우 놀라셨겠군요. 다음에는 무엇을 하셨나요?
남: 빵집으로 뛰어 들어가서 한 남자가 피를 흘리는 것을 발견했어요. 그리고 즉시 경찰에 전화했습니다.
여: 알겠습니다. 빵집 주위에서 이상한 차량을 보셨나요?
남: 아니요. 빵집 건너편에 택시 한 대가 있었어요. 이것이 지난밤 제가 본 전부입니다.
여: 알겠습니다. 당신이 말씀해 주신 것은 우리가 범인을 잡는 데 도움이 될 것입니다. 협조해 주셔서 감사합니다.
남: 가능한 한 빨리 범인을 잡길 바랍니다.
여: 걱정하시 마세요, 그렇게 하겠습니다.

문제 해결
지난밤에 목격한 것을 자세히 말해 달라는 여자의 말에 남자는 자신이 본 것을 자세하게 설명하였고 이에 여자는 남자의 증언이 범인을 잡는 데 도움이 될 것이라고 말했다. 이로 보아, 여자와 남자는 경찰과 목격자의 관계이다.

어휘·표현
show up 나타나다, 등장하다   in detail 자세히   scream 비명 지르다, 외치다
bleed 피를 흘리다   criminal 범인

04 ④
그림 불일치 파악

남: Cindy, 당신이 직원 휴게실 정리하는 것을 끝냈다고 들었어요.
여: 네, Jackson 씨. 한번 보세요.
남: 음. 내가 요청한대로 별 무늬가 있는 벽지를 벽에 발랐군요.
여: 네, 그리고 창문 옆에 냉장고를 놓았어요.
남: 좋아요. 오, 벽에 세계 지도가 있군요.
여: 맞습니다. 우리 회사가 전 세계에서 사업을 하는 무역 회사이기 때문에, 그것이 어울린다고 생각했거든요.
남: 아주 좋은 생각이에요.
여: 고맙습니다. 중앙에 있는 둥근 탁자는 어떠세요?
남: 우리가 전에 가지고 있었던 직사각형 탁자보다 훨씬 더 좋네요.
여: 탁자 위에 있는 꽃병도 마음에 드시기를 바라요.
남: 마음에 들어요. 휴게실 분위기를 더 편안하게 해 주네요.

문제 해결
중앙에 둥근 탁자가 있다고 했으므로, 대화의 내용과 일치하지 않는 것은 ④이다.

어휘·표현
lounge 휴게실   wallpaper 벽지   request 요청하다   refrigerator 냉장고
trading company 무역 회사   fitting 어울리는, 적합한
rectangular 직사각형의   atmosphere 분위기

05 ②
할 일 파악

여: 아빠, 거실 청소를 다 했어요.

남: 카펫도 진공청소기로 청소했니?

여: 네, 했어요.

남: 잘했다! 나도 욕실과 부엌 청소를 끝냈단다.

여: 집이 이렇게 깨끗해진 것을 엄마가 보면 놀랄 거예요.

남: 네 말이 맞구나. 엄마는 집이 얼마나 깨끗한지 꿈에도 상상하지 못할 거야.

여: 맞아요. 그런데, 엄마가 몇 시에 집에 와요?

남: 음… 엄마가 탄 비행기가 오후 5시 10분에 공항에 도착할 예정이니까, 엄마는 7시쯤 집에 올 거야.

여: 그러면 엄마가 배가 고플 거예요. 엄마를 위해서 우리가 저녁을 준비하는 게 어때요?

남: 좋은 생각이구나. 엄마가 좋아하는 치킨 스튜를 만들어야겠어.

여: 좋아요. 제가 도와드릴 것이 있나요?

남: 있지. 양파와 버섯을 사다 줄래?

여: 물론이죠! 지금 바로 식료품 가게에 갈게요.

문제 해결

치킨 스튜를 요리하려는 남자가 여자에게 양파와 버섯을 사다 달라고 부탁하자 여자가 지금 바로 식료품 가게에 가겠다고 했으므로, 여자가 할 일로 ②가 가장 적절하다.

어휘·표현

vacuum 진공청소기로 청소하다   in one's wildest dream 꿈에도, 전혀
be supposed to ~하기로 되어 있다   grocery store 식료품 가게

---

06 ②   숫자 정보 파악

여: 안녕하세요, 놀이공원 이용권을 구입하고 싶은데요.

남: 두 종류의 이용권이 있습니다. Gold 이용권은 30달러인데, 이 이용권으로 놀이공원에 있는 모든 놀이 기구를 탈 수 있습니다.

여: 다른 이용권은요?

남: Silver 이용권으로, 가격은 20달러입니다. Silver 이용권으로는 다섯 개의 놀이 기구를 골라서 탈 수 있습니다.

여: Gold 이용권이 더 좋은 것 같군요.

남: 그럼요. Gold 이용권이 Silver 이용권보다 훨씬 더 인기가 많습니다.

여: 좋아요. Gold 이용권 네 장 주시겠어요?

남: 어린이가 있나요? 13세 이하의 어린이는 성인 입장권 가격의 절반만 지불하시면 됩니다.

여: 네. 2명의 어린이가 13세 이하입니다.

남: 좋습니다. ABC 신용 카드로 결제하시면, 또한 총액에서 20달러를 할인받을 수 있습니다.

여: 잘됐네요! 제 ABC 신용 카드 여기 있습니다.

남: 고맙습니다.

문제 해결

여자는 30달러인 Gold 이용권 4장을 구입하려 하는데 그 중 2장은 13세 이하 어린이 할인을 받아 절반만 지불하면 된다. 또한 ABC 신용 카드로 결제하면 총액에서 20달러를 할인받는다고 했다. 따라서 여자가 지불할 총 금액은 70달러이다.

어휘·표현

pass 이용권   amusement park 놀이공원   go on a ride 놀이 기구를 타다

---

07 ⑤   이유 파악

[휴대 전화벨이 울린다.]

여: Cindy입니다.

남: Cindy? 나야, Tucker. 이야기할 수 있어?

여: 오래는 못해. 나 도서관에서 생물 보고서를 쓰고 있거든. 무슨 일이야?

남: 이번 주 금요일 콘서트 입장권을 예매했니?

여: 응, 했어. 앞줄 입장권을 구했지. 우리는 무대 바로 앞에서 공연을 볼 수 있어.

남: 오, 이런! 너랑 같이 콘서트에 갈 수 없을 것 같아.

여: 왜? 부모님이 또 너를 보러 오시니?

남: 아니. 방금 부모님께 전화를 받았는데 오늘 오후에 여동생이 자동차 사고를 당했대.

여: 오, 이런! 동생은 괜찮아?

남: 다행히도, 부러진 곳은 없고 괜찮아. 하지만 지금 동생이 병원에 있어서 동생을 보러 가고 싶어.

여: 당연히 가야지. 넌 언제 돌아올 거야?

남: 일요일 저녁. 정말로 미안해.

여: 괜찮아. 동생이 빨리 낫기를 바랄게.

문제 해결

남자는 여동생이 교통사고를 당했다는 소식을 부모님께 들었다고 하면서 병원에 있는 동생을 보러 가고 싶다고 말했으므로, 남자가 콘서트를 보러 갈 수 없는 이유로 ⑤가 가장 적절하다.

어휘·표현

biology 생물학   fortunately 운 좋게도

---

08 ④   언급 유무 파악

남: Semi, 난 네가 전기 의류 건조기를 팔려고 한다고 들었어.

여: 그래. 너 관심이 있니?

남: 응, 내가 지금 사용하고 있는 것은 너무 작거든. 그래서 나는 더 큰 것을 사야 해.

여: 내 의류 건조기는 용량이 9kg이야. 한 사람이 쓰기에는 충분하지.

남: 좋아. 너는 그 의류 건조기를 얼마 동안 썼니?

여: 2년 전에 샀어.

남: 그러면 무료 수리 보증 기간이 만료되었겠구나.

여: 아니. 이 제품의 보증 기간은 5년이야. 그러니까 보증 기간에 대해서는 당분간 걱정하지 않아도 돼.

남: 아주 좋은데. 가격이 적당하면, 난 네 것을 사고 싶어.

여: 내가 이것을 700달러에 샀는데, 네게는 350달러에 팔게.

남: 아주 좋아. 그렇게 하자.

문제 해결

여자의 전기 의류 건조기에 관해서 ④ '제조사'는 언급되지 않았다.

어휘·표현

electric clothes dryer 전기 의류 건조기   capacity 용량
warranty 품질 보증(서)   expire 만료되다, 유효 기간이 끝나다   deal 거래, 합의

---

09 ④   담화 내용 불일치

여: 집중해 주십시오, 쇼핑객 여러분. Rainbow 백화점을 방문해 주셔서 감사합니다. 여러분의 관심을 끌 만한 안내 말씀을 드리겠습니다. 옥상에 설치된 특별 무대에서 Green 재즈 콘서트가 열릴 것입니다. 이 콘서트는 오늘 저녁 7시에 시작하여 약 2시간 동안 계속될 것입니다. 다섯 명의 유명한 재즈 음악가들이 공연에 참가해서 여러분이 좋아하

는 재즈 곡을 공연할 것입니다. 입장료는 1인당 5달러이지만, 20달러가 넘는 구매 영수증이 있는 사람이면 누구나 무료로 콘서트를 즐길 수 있습니다. 중간 휴식 시간 동안, 관객은 간단한 스낵과 음료수를 제공받을 것입니다. 재즈를 사랑하는 여러분들이 오셔서 콘서트를 즐기시기를 바랍니다.

문제 해결

콘서트 입장료는 1인당 5달러이지만, 20달러 이상의 구매 영수증을 가지고 있는 사람이면 누구나 무료로 콘서트를 즐길 수 있다고 했으므로, ④가 내용과 일치하지 않는다.

어휘·표현

rooftop 옥상　participate in ~에 참가하다　purchase 구매
intermission 중간 휴식 시간

10 ②
도표 정보 파악

남: 안녕하세요, 이번 주 토요일 서핑 수업을 등록하고 싶은데요.
여: 알겠습니다. 전에 서핑을 해 본 적이 있나요?
남: 아니요, 없습니다. 완전한 초보예요.
여: 그러면 초보 수준에 당신을 편성하겠습니다.
남: 알겠습니다. 어떤 수업을 추천하나요?
여: 사람마다 다릅니다. 하지만 2시간 수업을 수강할 것을 권장합니다. 대부분의 사람들에게 한 시간의 수업은 충분하지 않거든요.
남: 알겠습니다. 두 시간짜리 수업을 수강할게요. 음…. 왜 이 수업은 다른 수업보다 더 비싼가요?
여: 이 수업은 휴식 시간에 제공하는 스낵과 음료수를 포함하기 때문에 그렇습니다.
남: 음, 나는 그것들은 필요한 것 같지 않습니다.
여: 알겠습니다. 이제 이 두 명의 강사 중 한 명을 고르셔야 합니다. Brian은 친절하고 관대하고, John은 유머러스하지만 다소 엄격합니다.
남: 친절한 강사가 제게 적합할 것 같아요. 이 수업을 수강할게요.
여: 알겠습니다.

문제 해결

이전에 서핑을 해 본 적이 없어서 초보 수준에 편성된 남자는 2시간 동안 이루어지는 수업을 듣겠다고 하였고, 스낵과 음료를 제공하는 더 비싼 수업은 선택하지 않았으며, 두 강사 중 친절한 강사 Brian이 진행하는 수업을 수강하겠다고 했다. 따라서 남자가 선택할 서핑 수업으로 ②가 가장 적절하다.

어휘·표현

sign up for 등록하다　complete 완전한　instructor 강사
relaxed 느긋한, 여유 있는, 관대한　fit 적합하다, ~에 알맞다

11 ④
짧은 대화의 응답

여: 실례합니다. 호텔에 테니스 코트가 있나요?
남: 네, 있습니다. 주 정원 안에 있습니다. 하지만 먼저 예약을 하셔야 합니다.
여: 알겠어요. 고마워요. 아, 한 가지 더요. 공항으로 가는 셔틀버스가 있나요?
남: 네. 호텔 정문에서 매시 정각에 버스가 출발합니다.

문제 해결

공항으로 가는 셔틀버스가 있는지 여자가 물었으므로 호텔 정문에서 매시 정각

에 버스가 출발한다고 말하는 ④가 남자의 응답으로 가장 적절하다.
① 셔틀버스를 타지 않으면, 당신은 비행기 시간에 늦을 거예요.
② 좋아요. 지금 같이 테니스 코트에 가서 테니스를 쳐요.
③ 공항으로 가는 셔틀버스를 어디에서 탈 수 있는지 말해 주시겠어요?
⑤ 미안해요. 지금은 너무 바빠서 당신과 함께 공항에 갈 수 없어요.

어휘·표현

make a reservation 예약하다　depart 떠나다, 출발하다
every hour on the hour 매시 정각에

12 ①
짧은 대화의 응답

남: 실례합니다, 한국 식당 '아리랑'이 어디에 있는지 아세요?
여: '아리랑'이요? 한 블록 직진해서 좌회전하세요. 그러면 커다란 소방서가 보일 거예요.
남: 커다란 소방서요? 식당이 소방서 가까이에 있나요?
여: 네. 소방서 바로 뒤에 식당이 있어요.

문제 해결

식당의 위치를 물어보는 남자에게 여자가 직진해서 좌회전하면 커다란 소방서가 보인다고 했다. 이에 남자가 소방서 가까이에 식당이 있는지 물었으므로, 소방서 바로 뒤에 식당이 있다고 말하는 ①이 여자의 응답으로 가장 적절하다.
② 괜찮아요. 다음에 같이 점심을 먹어요.
③ 맞아요. 저도 이곳이 처음입니다.
④ 미안하지만, 나는 그 건물에서 일하고 싶지 않아요.
⑤ 네 도움이 없었으면, 나는 그 식당에 갈 수 없었을 거야.

어휘·표현

fire station 소방서

13 ①
긴 대화의 응답

남: Alice, 이번 주말에 소개팅을 하는 거에 관심 있어?
여: 소개팅? 나에게 소개시켜 줄 누군가가 있어?
남: 그래, 있어. 내 친구 중의 한 명이 내 전화에 있는 네 사진을 봤는데 너를 만나고 싶어 해.
여: 정말? 그가 네 직장 동료니?
남: 그래. 그리고 그는 고등학교 때부터 가장 친한 내 친구들 중 한 명이야.
여: 음…. 더 자세히 말해 봐.
남: 그는 정말로 잘생겼어. 그는 패션모델 같아.
여: 야, 외모가 전부는 아니야. 중요한 건 성격이지.
남: 걱정 마. 그는 매우 정직하고 책임감이 있어.
여: 그래? 유머 감각은 어때? 나는 유머 감각이 풍부한 사람이 좋거든.
남: 그는 정말로 재미있어. 그는 내가 알고 있는 가장 재미있는 사람이야.
여: 좋아! 네 친구랑 소개팅을 할게.

문제 해결

남자가 자신의 친구와 소개팅을 시켜 주겠다고 하자 여자는 그 친구에 대해 자세히 알려 달라고 말한다. 이에 남자가 그 친구가 잘생겼고 정직하며 책임감이 있고 재미있는 사람이라고 말했으므로, 이어질 여자의 말로 ① '좋아! 네 친구랑 소개팅을 할게.'가 가장 적절하다.
② 좋아! 나는 늘 패션모델이 되고 싶었어.
③ 난 그렇게 생각하지 않아. 사실, 너는 그 사람만큼 재미있지 않아.
④ 그에게 달렸어. 그가 시간과 장소를 정해야만 해.
⑤ 날 믿어. 너는 이번 주말 소개팅을 후회하지 않을 거야.

어휘·표현

go on a blind date 소개팅을 나가다   co-worker 동료   appearance 외모
personality 성격   responsible 책임감 있는   sense of humor 유머 감각

14 ①

남: Stella, 이번 학기에 중국어 회화 수업을 수강하는 게 어때?
여: 미안하지만, 나는 이미 지난 학기에 그 수업을 수강해서, A⁺를 받았
　어.
남: 정말? 그건 몰랐어. 그러면 너는 어떤 외국어 회화 수업을 수강할 거
　니?
여: 프랑스어. 프랑스어 고급 회화반을 이미 등록했어.
남: 프랑스어 고급 회화반? 너 프랑스어도 할 줄 알아?
여: 응. 고등학교 때 프랑스어 기초를 배웠거든.
남: 와! 중국어와 프랑스어를 제외하고 네가 할 수 있는 또 다른 외국어가
　있니?
여: 물론이지! 나는 한국어도 할 수 있어.
남: 정말? 한국어는 어디서 어떻게 배웠는데?
여: 그냥 집에서 나 혼자. 작년에 내가 케이팝에 정말로 푹 빠져 있었잖아.
　그래서 케이팝을 더 잘 즐기려고 한국어를 공부했거든.
남: 믿을 수 없어! 너는 진정한 언어 천재야.

문제 해결

중국어와 프랑스어를 할 줄 아는 여자가 한국어도 할 수 있다고 하자 남자는 놀
라면서 한국어를 어디서 어떻게 배웠는지 묻고 여자는 집에서 혼자 공부했다고
말했으므로, 이어질 남자의 말로 ① '믿을 수 없어! 너는 진정한 언어 천재야.'가
가장 적절하다.
② 물론이지! 나는 한국어로 의사소통을 할 수 있어.
③ 사실, 나는 케이팝에 더 이상 관심이 없어.
④ 내 실수야. 나는 더 일찍 한국어를 공부했어야 했어.
⑤ 나는 그렇게 생각하지 않아. 네 한국어 실력이 나보다 훨씬 더 나아.

어휘·표현

semester 학기   register for ~에 등록하다   besides ~ 외에, ~을 제외하고
be into ~을 좋아하다, ~에 관심이 많다   incredible 믿을 수 없는, 믿기 힘든
genius 천재   make oneself understood 자기 의사를 제대로 전달하다

15 ①

여: 최근에 Rebecca는 Santa Monica에 있는 아파트로 이사를 했다.
　그녀는 자신의 직장에서 멀다는 점만 제외하면, 새 아파트에 만족한
　다. 그녀가 자신의 아파트에서 지하철로 직장까지 가는 데는 한 시간
　이 걸린다. 그녀는 동료인 Lucas에게 이것에 대해 불평을 하면서, 통
　근하는 것이 매우 지루하다고 덧붙인다. Lucas는 자신도 Rebecca
　와 같은 상황이라고 말하고, 자신은 시간을 보내기 위해서 보통 책을
　읽는다고 설명한다. Lucas가 하는 말을 듣고, Rebecca는 책을 읽는
　것이 출근 시간을 의미 있게 보낼 수 있는 좋은 방법이 될 수 있겠다
　고 생각한다. 그녀는 Lucas의 조언을 따르기로 결심하고, 어떤 책이
　지하철에서 읽기에 좋은 책인지 알고 싶어 한다. 이런 상황에서,
　Rebecca는 Lucas에게 뭐라고 말할 것 같은가?

문제 해결

지하철로 한 시간이 걸리는 출근 시간에 Lucas가 하는 대로 책을 읽기로 결심
한 Rebecca가 어떤 책이 읽기에 좋은 책인지 알고 싶어 하는 상황이므로, ①
'읽기에 좋은 책을 추천해 줄 수 있니?'가 Rebecca가 Lucas에게 할 말로 가장

적절하다.
② 지하철로 출근하는 데 얼마나 오래 걸려?
③ 너는 정말로 지하철에서 책을 읽고 싶니?
④ 네가 왜 지하철에서 책을 읽기로 결심했는지 말해 줄래?
⑤ 내일부터 지하철로 출근하는 게 어때?

어휘·표현

except that ~을 제외하고   pass the time 시간을 보내다(때우다)
commute time 통근 시간   meaningfully 의미 있게

16-17

남: 안녕하세요, 여러분! '동물의 세계'에 오신 것을 환영합니다. 저는 진
　행자, Adam Brown입니다. 지난 시간, 저는 여러분에게 호랑이와
　늑대 같은 야생 동물의 생존에 대해 이야기했습니다. 오늘 저는 반려
　동물에 대해 말하고자 합니다. 여러분이 반려동물을 키우기로 결정하
　기 전에 고려해야 할 사항을 알고 있습니까? 먼저, 여러분은 여러분의
　성격에 대해 생각해야 합니다. 만약 여러분이 그다지 활동적이지 않
　다면, 여러분은 개보다는 고양이를 선택하는 것이 더 좋은데, 이는 고
　양이는 매일 산책시킬 필요가 없기 때문입니다. 금붕어는 다른 좋은
　대안입니다. 두 번째로, 여러분은 반려동물과 얼마나 오래 함께 할 수
　있는지도 고려해야 합니다. 앵무새는 많은 돌봄을 필요로 합니다. 따
　라서 여러분이 앵무새와 놀아 주기에 너무 바쁘다면, 여러분은 다른
　동물을 선택해야 합니다. 여러분이 고려해야 할 마지막 것은 돈입니
　다. 먹이, 훈련 교실, 동물 병원 치료, 장난감, 그리고 반려동물을 위
　한 다른 비용에 많은 돈이 쓰입니다. 만약 이것이 문제라면, 반려동물
　을 키우는 것에 대해 재고해 주세요.

어휘·표현

companion animal 반려동물   take ~ into consideration ~을 고려하다
be better off (~하는 것이) 더 낫다   alternative 대안   parrot 앵무새
veterinary 수의과의   think twice 재고하다, 숙고하다

16 ③

문제 해결

남자는 반려동물을 키우기로 결정하기 전에 고려해야 할 사항이 몇 가지 있다고
하면서 이에 대해 구체적으로 이야기하고 있으므로, 남자가 하는 말의 주제로
③ '반려동물을 기르는 것에 대해 고려해야 할 사항'이 가장 적절하다.
① 사람들이 반려동물을 키우고 싶어 하는 이유
② 작은 공간에서 반려동물을 기르는 방법
④ 야생동물이 어떻게 반려동물이 될 수 있는가
⑤ 인간에게 주는 반려동물 기르기의 이로움

17 ⑤

문제 해결

남자가 예를 들어 설명한 여러 동물 중 햄스터는 언급되지 않았다.

효과적이라고 이야기하였다. 따라서 여자의 의견으로 가장 적절한 것은 ④이다.

어휘·표현

corporate 기업의, 회사의   be in charge of ~을 담당하다   come up with
~을 생각해 내다   maximize 극대화하다   achievement 업적, 성취한 것
responsive 즉각 반응하는   sway 흔들리다

19 영어 듣기 모의고사 ▶ pp. 42-43

01 ②	02 ④	03 ②	04 ④	05 ④	06 ②
07 ⑤	08 ④	09 ④	10 ⑤	11 ③	12 ④
13 ⑤	14 ⑤	15 ③	16 ②	17 ③	

01 ②   목적 파악

남: 안녕하세요 여러분. 저는 Greenwich 경찰서 교통과의 Gerry
Robinson입니다. 여러분은 우리 마을의 교통사고의 첫 번째 원인이
무엇인지 아십니까? 그것은 운전하는 동안 휴대 전화를 사용하는 것
입니다. 지난 3개월 동안, 우리 도로에서 약 70건의 교통사고가 운전
중 휴대 전화를 사용하는 운전자들에 의해 일어났습니다. 심지어, 많
은 사고가 차량 안의 거의 모든 사람들에게 심각한 신체적 손상을 입
혔다는 것입니다. 운전 중 휴대 전화 사용은 불법적일 뿐만 아니라 또
한 위험하다는 것은 아무리 강조해도 지나치지 않습니다. 그러므로,
상황이 어떠하든지간에, 저는 여러분들이 차를 운행하는 중에는 휴대
전화를 사용하지 않기를 당부하고 싶습니다. 그것은 여러분의 안전뿐
만이 아니라 모든 사람들의 안전을 위한 것입니다.

문제 해결
경찰서 교통과 경찰인 남자는 교통 사고의 제일의 원인으로 운전 중 휴대 전화
사용을 들면서 운전 중 휴대 전화를 사용하지 말 것을 당부하고 있으므로, 남자
가 하는 말의 목적으로는 ②가 가장 적절하다.

어휘·표현

division 부서   result in ~을 낳다, 야기하다   significant 중요한
overemphasize 지나치게 강조하다   no matter what 비록 무엇이 ~일지라도
circumstance 상황

02 ④   주제 파악

여: Clark, 당신이 맡고 있는 기업 광고는 어떻게 진행되고 있나요?
남: 제가 생각하기엔 괜찮아요. 저는 회사의 이미지를 극대화시킬 아이디
어를 생각해 내려고 하는 중이에요.
여: 생각해 둔 것 있어요?
남: 글쎄요. 저는 사람들이 회사의 역사와 전통을 알게끔 회사의 업적들
을 열거하는 것에 대해 생각하고 있어요.
여: 저는 업적 열거가 충분히 매력적이라고 생각하지 않아요. 사람들은
그것들을 읽지 않을 거예요.
남: 일리 있는 말이네요. 그럼 당신에게는 다른 아이디어가 있나요?
여: 요즘에, 사람들이 어떤 다른 것보다 감정에 훨씬 더 반응하는 것 같아
요.
남: 그래요. 사람들은 감정적인 소식에 쉽게 흔들리는 것 같아요.
여: 맞아요. 그래서 저는 당신이 기업 광고를 만들 때 감정을 사용하는 것
이 더욱 효과적일 거라고 생각해요.
남: 흠…. 말이 되네요. 좋아요, 제가 그 생각을 발전시켜 볼게요. 조언 감
사합니다.
여: 천만에요.

문제 해결
회사의 이미지를 극대화시킬 기업 광고에 대해 고민하는 남자에게 여자는 사람
들이 감정에 더 반응하고 쉽게 흔들리므로 광고에 감정을 사용하는 것이 더욱

03 ②   관계 추론

남: 너 창백해 보이는구나. 어디가 안 좋니?
여: 감기에 걸린 것 같아요. 지난밤에 창문을 열어 놓고 잤거든요.
남: 증상이 어떠니?
여: 미열과 함께 콧물이 나요.
남: 양호 선생님께 가서 너의 증상을 말해 보는 게 어떠니?
여: 저는 제 담당 의사에게 가 봤으면 해요. 제가 오늘 조퇴해도 괜찮을까
요?
남: 음, 너의 결정에 동의하는지를 확인해 보고자 먼저 너의 어머니께 전
화해 볼게.
여: 네.
남: 너의 어머니의 허락을 얻은 후에, 너를 일찍 보내 줄 수 있어.
여: 감사합니다.
남: 하지만 만약 네가 조퇴하면, 너는 오늘 수업의 나머지 부분을 놓칠 거
야. 꼭 학급 친구들에게서 필기와 과제를 받도록 하렴.
여: 네, 그렇게 할게요. 감사합니다.

문제 해결
여자는 감기 증상 때문에 일찍 조퇴하려고 하고, 남자는 여자의 어머니에게 전화
를 해서 허락을 받은 뒤 조퇴시켜 주겠다고 하고 학급 친구들에게서 필기와 과
제를 받아 놓을 것을 여자에게 당부하는 것으로 보아, 남자와 여자는 교사와 학
생의 관계임을 알 수 있다.

어휘·표현

coming down with (병에) 걸리다   symptom 증상   regular 단골의, 정해진
assignment 과제

04 ④   그림 불일치 파악

여: 나는 어제 새 아파트로 이사했어.
남: 오, 정말? 새로운 곳이 마음에 드니?
여: 정말 좋아! 특히 거실이. 내 핸드폰에 거실 사진이 있어.
남: 와. 정말 좋구나. 내 시선을 사로잡은 첫 번째 것은 벽 한가운데에 있
는 TV야. 그것은 벽에 내재되어 있는 것처럼 보이네.
여: 그래. 나는 그처럼 TV를 벽에 고정시키기 위해 엄청난 돈을 들여야
만 했어.
남: TV 뒤의 벽은 물고기 사진들로 장식되어 있네. 너의 거실은 바다처
럼 보여.
여: 맞아. 나는 벽과 잘 어울리도록 하기 위해 TV 왼쪽 하단에 인어 조각
상을 놓았지.
남: 방 한가운데에 있는 두 개의 둥근 탁자들은 독특하네.
여: 네가 그것들을 알아봤다니 기쁜걸. 나는 내 거실만을 위해 그것들을
주문 제작했어.
남: 그 탁자들 바로 옆 오른쪽에 있는 소파는 정말 아늑해 보인다. 내가
조만간 너의 아파트를 방문하기를 기대할게.
여: 언제든지. 너는 언제나 환영이야.

방 한가운데에 둥근 모양의 탁자가 두 개 있다고 하였으므로, 그림 속 삼각형 모양의 두 개의 탁자인 ④는 대화의 내용과 일치하지 않는다.

pay an arm and a leg 엄청난 돈이 들다 **mount** 끼우다, 고정시키다
mermaid 인어 **go with** ~와 어울리다

05 ④ 부탁한 일 파악

여: 여보, 내가 벼룩시장에 지원했던 거 기억나요?
남: 그래요. 기억나요.
여: 내가 벼룩시장에 참가할 수 있다는 문자 메시지를 받았어요.
남: 정말요? 좋은 소식이네요!
여: 네. 그것은 모든 종류의 중고품을 사고팔 수 있는 좋은 기회예요.
남: 당신이 거기서 돈을 많이 벌었으면 좋겠네요.
여: 사실 벼룩시장에서 나오는 모든 수익금은 자선 단체로 가요.
남: 그건 몰랐네요. 정말로 가치 있는 일이군요!
여: 맞아요. 당신은 더 이상 사용하지는 않지만 여전히 상태가 좋은 물건이 있어요?
남: 분명히 차고에서 팔만한 많은 것들을 찾을 수 있을 거예요. 내가 도울 수 있는 또 다른 일이 있다면 나에게 말해 줘요.
여: 사실, 나는 잔돈이 많이 필요해요. 은행에 가서 이 지폐들을 잔돈으로 바꿔 줄 수 있어요?
남: 문제없어요.

벼룩시장에 참여하려는 여자는 남자에게 은행에 가서 지폐를 잔돈으로 바꿔 달라고 부탁하였다.

apply for ~을 지원(신청)하다 **flea market** 벼룩시장 **proceeds** 수익금
charity 자선 단체 **worthwhile** 가치 있는 **cause** 대의, 목적

06 ② 숫자 정보 파악

남: 안녕하세요. 자연사 박물관 입장권을 구매하고자 합니다.
여: 몇 장의 표를 원하시나요?
남: 아이 한 명을 포함하여 다섯 장의 표를 원합니다. 일인당 표 값이 얼마죠?
여: 어른은 10달러, 아이는 6달러입니다. 아이가 몇 살인가요?
남: 제 아이는 7살입니다.
여: 7살은 어린이 표를 받을 수 있습니다.
남: 좋습니다. 다른 특별 할인이 있나요?
여: 만약 당신이 San Diego에 사신다면, 당신은 원래 가격에서 2달러 할인을 받을 수 있습니다.
남: 제 일행 중 두 사람이 San Diego에 삽니다.
여: 좋아요. 저에게 주소 증명서를 보여 줄 수 있나요?
남: 여기 있습니다.
여: 좋습니다, 그러면 그들은 2달러씩 할인을 받을 수 있습니다.
남: 잘됐네요. 여기 제 신용 카드 있습니다.

어른은 10달러, 아이는 6달러 하는 자연사 박물관 입장료를 남자는 어른 4장, 아이 1장을 사려고 한다. San Diego에 거주하는 두 명은 2달러씩 할인을 받을 수 있으므로, 남자가 지불할 입장료는 총 42달러이다.

eligible for ~에 자격이 있는 **party** 일행 **proof** 증명(서)

07 ⑤ 이유 파악

남: 여보, 내일 저녁에 외식하는 게 어때요?
여: 염두에 둔 특정 레스토랑이 있어요?
남: Henry's Steakhouse 어때요?
여: 오, 나는 거기 음식을 정말 좋아해요. 그런데 가격이 좀 비싸다고 생각하지 않아요?
남: 걱정 마요. 나에게 그 레스토랑 30% 할인 쿠폰이 있어요.
여: 나도 그 쿠폰이 있는데 내 생각으로는 그 쿠폰은 지난주 토요일에 기한이 만료되었어요. 당신은 그 쿠폰의 유효 기한을 확인해 봤어요?
남: 뭐라고요? 한번 볼게요…. 어, 내가 그 날짜를 이번 주 다가오는 토요일로 착각했어요.
여: 그 쿠폰이 없다면, 저녁 식사 비용이 상당히 많이 들 거예요.
남: 맞아요. 여보, 내 사무실 근처에 또 다른 좋은 스테이크 레스토랑이 있어요.
여: 당신 Star Steakhouse 말하는 거죠?
남: 맞아요. 거기는 합리적인 가격에 좋은 품질의 스테이크를 제공해요.
여: 아주 좋네요. 좋아요, 내일 거기에 가요.

남자는 비싼 식당에서 사용하려고 했던 할인 쿠폰의 기한이 만료되었기 때문에 가격이 상대적으로 합리적인 식당으로 바꾸었다. 따라서, 가려고 했던 식당을 가지 않기로 한 이유로 ⑤가 가장 적절하다.

expire (기한이) 만료되다 **expiration date** 유효 기한 **quality** 고급의, 양질의 **reasonable** 합리적인

08 ④ 언급 유무 파악

[전화벨이 울린다.]
여: 부산시 관광 안내소입니다. 무엇을 도와드릴까요?
남: 안녕하세요. 저는 이번 여름에 부산을 둘러볼 계획입니다.
여: 부산은 매우 흥미진진한 항구 도시죠. 그곳을 방문한 것을 후회하지 않으실 거예요.
남: 좋습니다. 그런데 저는 도시를 어떻게 돌아다녀야 할지를 모르겠어요.
여: 저는 부산시 관광버스를 이용할 것을 추천합니다. 그것은 부산역에서 출발합니다.
남: 만약에 제가 1일 티켓을 원한다면, 어떻게 살 수 있죠?
여: 버스를 탈 때 운전사에게 요청할 수 있어요. 그 운전사가 당신에게 1일 티켓을 줄 수 있어요.
남: 1일 티켓은 얼마인가요?
여: 어른은 5,000원이고 아이는 3,000원입니다.
남: 좋습니다. 버스 투어 기간 중에 제가 명심해야 할 것이 있나요?
여: 승객들은 기본적인 대중교통 예절을 지켜야 합니다. 예를 들면, 음식과 음료수의 섭취는 허용되지 않습니다.
남: 대단히 감사합니다.

여자가 설명하는 부산시 버스 투어에 관해서 ④ '오디오 가이드 제공 여부'는 언급되지 않았다.

depart 출발하다   etiquette 예절   beverage 음료

09 ④

여: 안녕하세요, ABC 라디오 청취자 여러분. 저는 보스턴 마라톤 행사 운영자인 Laura Clark입니다. 저희들은 올해 4월 14일 일요일에 보스턴 하프 마라톤을 개최할 예정입니다. 행사는 오전 11시에 시작합니다. 참가자의 수는 800명까지로 제한할 것이므로, 만약 저희 마라톤 행사에 참가하기를 원한다면, 가능하면 일찍 등록해 주세요. 일찍 등록하는 참가자들에게는 특별 기념품이 있겠습니다. 4월 1일 이전에 등록하시는 분들에게 보스턴 마라톤 로고가 새겨진 수건을 증정할 것입니다. 마라톤을 완주하면, 당신은 완주 증명서를 받게 될 것입니다. 급수대는 출발선에서부터 매 3km마다 위치해 있습니다. 질문이 있으시면 manager@bostonmarathon.org로 제게 이메일을 보내 주세요. 감사합니다.

마라톤을 완주하면 완주 증명서를 받는다고 했으므로 ④는 내용과 일치하지 않는다.

participant 참가자   register 등록하다   certificate 증명서

10 ⑤

남: 여보, 이 가구점에 좋은 어린이 책상들이 많이 있네요.
여: 와! 우리 딸 생일 선물로 책상 하나 사는게 어때요?
남: 좋은 생각이에요! 어떤 색깔을 사야 할까요?
여: 그녀는 분홍색과 노란색을 좋아해요. 그 두 가지 색깔 중에 하나를 고르죠.
남: 좋아요. 재질은 어때요? 나는 플라스틱보다는 나무가 더 좋아요.
여: 나도 동의해요. 나무가 더욱 자연스러운 느낌이 있는 것 같아요.
남: 높이 조절 기능은 어때요? 우리 딸은 매년 빠르게 성장하고 있어요.
여: 맞아요. 책상이 그러한 기능을 가지고 있어야만 해요.
남: 음… 이 구멍은 뭐죠?
여: 그것은 USB 포트예요. 요즘 일부 책상들에는 내장된 USB 포트가 있어요.
남: 하지만, 그러면 그녀는 그것을 스마트폰 충전하는 데 사용하고 공부하는 대신 문자 메시지를 보낼 거예요.
여: 좋아요. USB 포트 없는 책상을 사죠. 그러면 이 책상을 구입하면 되겠어요. 그것을 사요.

딸아이가 좋아하는 분홍색과 노란색인 책상 중에서 나무 재질에 높이 조절 기능이 있지만, USB 포트는 없는 책상을 찾고 있으므로, 두 사람이 구입할 책상으로는 ⑤가 가장 적절하다.

adjustment 조절, 조정   slot 구멍   charge 충전하다

11 ③

여: Frank, 오늘 새 TV가 배달될 거예요.
남: 알겠어요. 몇 시에 배달될까요, Claire?

여: 배달 회사 말로는 TV가 오후 5시에서 6시 사이에 여기 도착할 거래요.
남: 그 시간에 집에 있어야겠네요.

여자가 오후 5시에서 6시 사이에 TV가 배달될 거라고 했으므로, 그 시간에 집에 있어야겠다고 말하는 ③이 남자의 응답으로 가장 적절하다.
① 그럼 내일까지 TV를 보지 마세요.
② 오늘 TV를 반드시 배달할게요.
④ 이 TV는 너무 무거워서 나 혼자 나를 수 없어요.
⑤ 우리는 당장 TV 수리를 맡겨야 해요.

deliver 배달하다   repair 수리하다

12 ④

남: Rebecca, 너는 오늘 물리 수업이 이해하기에 너무 어려웠다고 생각하지 않아?
여: 물론이야. 나는 스터디 그룹을 만들 계획이야. 만약 원한다면 너도 나와 함께 할 수 있어.
남: 정말? 그거 정말 도움이 되겠다. 우리 언제 시작해야 할까?
여: 빠르면 빠를수록 좋아. 오늘 저녁 어때?

물리 수업이 어렵다는 남자는 스터디 그룹을 만들 거라는 여자에게 스터디 그룹을 언제부터 시작할지를 물어보았으므로, 빠를수록 좋다며 오늘 저녁부터 시작할 것을 제안하는 ④가 여자의 응답으로 가장 적절하다.
① 내가 너라면, 나는 혼자 공부할 거야.
② 너는 정말로 친절하구나. 네가 우리 반에 있어서 나는 기뻐.
③ 우리 선생님께 수업이 얼마나 어려웠는지를 말해 보는 게 어떨까?
⑤ 나는 우리 스터디 그룹에 다른 학생들을 원치 않아.

physics 물리학

13 ⑤

여: 리포트는 잘돼 가니?
남: 난 아직 쓰는 것을 시작도 안 했어.
여: 나는 너의 주제가 미래에 인공 지능이 사회에 미치는 영향이라고 들었어.
남: 맞아. 그런데 그 주제가 너무 일반적이어서 내 생각들을 정리할 수가 없어.
여: 내 생각에는 너는 주제를 좀 더 좁힐 필요가 있어.
남: 어떻게? 나에게 조언 좀 해 줄래?
여: 예를 들면, 너는 인공 지능이 인간의 직업을 빼앗아 갈 것이라고 생각해?
남: 어떤 직업은 그렇겠지만, 모든 직업이 다 그렇지는 않을 거야.
여: 나에게 예를 좀 들어 줄 수 있어?
남: 반복적인 작업은 대체되겠지만, 인공 지능은 인간의 개입 없이는 창의적인 것은 할 수 없어.
여: 바로 그거야. 나는 네가 리포트의 방향을 잡기 시작하고 있다고 생각해.
남: 응. 너와 이야기를 나눈 후 내 생각이 더 정리되고 있어.

문제 해결

리포트 주제가 일반적이어서 생각을 정리할 수 없다는 남자에게 여자는 해당 주제에 대해 이야기를 나누고는 남자가 논문의 방향을 잡기 시작하고 있다고 말하였다. 이에 대한 남자의 말로 가장 적절한 것은 ⑤ '응. 너와 이야기를 나눈 후 내 생각이 더 정리되고 있어.'이다.

① 아니. 나는 너의 주장이 논점을 벗어난다고 생각해.
② 먼저 그 주제를 좁혀보는 게 어때?
③ 나는 인공 지능에 대한 너의 의견에 동의하지 않아.
④ 리포트 쓰기가 어렵다면 내가 너를 더욱 도와줄 수 있어.

어휘·표현

artificial intelligence 인공 지능 **organize** 정리하다 **narrow down** 좁히다
repetitive 반복적인 **substitute** 대체하다 **intervention** 개입
off the point 논점에서 벗어난

14 ⑤ ───────── 긴 대화의 응답

남: 엄마, 저 화분이 있는데, 이 어린 묘목을 어떻게 돌봐야 할지를 모르겠어요.
여: 그것들이 어떤 종류의 묘목인데?
남: 토마토 묘목이에요. 저에게 조언 좀 해 주실래요?
여: 우선, 묘목에 정기적으로 물을 줘야지.
남: 저도 알아요. 하지만 그것은 너무 단순해요. 다른 조언은 없으세요?
여: 토마토 묘목은 강한 햇빛이 많이 필요하단다.
남: 아, 정말요? 저는 그건 몰랐어요.
여: 그렇다면, 그것을 어떻게 재배할 계획이었는데?
남: 사실, 저는 흙을 촉촉하게 유지할 생각이었어요. 제 친구가 그런 식으로 묘목을 재배하는 것을 보았는데 묘목이 잘 자랐어요.
여: 그런데 그것이 토마토 묘목이 아닐지도 모르겠구나.
남: 그렇다면, 이 집에서 토마토 식물을 재배하기에 가장 좋은 장소는 어디예요?
여: 발코니가 어떠니? 거기가 이 집에서 햇볕이 가장 잘 드는 곳이야.

문제 해결

토마토 묘목에 햇빛이 많이 필요하다는 조언을 받은 남자는 여자에게 집에서 어디가 토마토 묘목을 재배하기에 가장 좋은 장소일지 물었다. 이에 대한 여자의 응답으로 가장 적절한 것은 ⑤ '발코니가 어떠니? 거기가 이 집에서 햇볕이 가장 잘 드는 곳이야.'이다.

① 토마토 묘목은 다른 식물보다 더 빨리 자란다.
② 꽃 시장을 방문하면, 너는 다양한 묘목을 볼 수 있어.
③ 나는 더 어두운 방이 토마토를 재배하는 데에 더욱 낫다고 생각해.
④ 만약 묘목에 더욱 많은 흙을 뿌리면, 그것들은 더욱 빠르게 자랄 거야.

어휘·표현

flower pot 화분 **seedling** 묘목 **moist** 촉촉한 **flourish** 번창하다, 잘 자라다

15 ③ ───────── 상황에 적절한 말

남: Kevin은 고등학교 3학년이다. Kevin은 최근 자신의 성적 하락에 대해 걱정하고 있어서, 그는 그의 선생님 Johns 선생님과 상담을 하기를 원한다. Johns 선생님은 종종 그가 그녀의 수업 시간 중에 졸고 있는 것을 발견했고, 그래서 그녀 또한 그와 이야기를 하기를 원했다. 그들이 대화할 때, 그녀는 그가 끊임없이 소셜 미디어를 확인하고 있는 것을 알아챈다. 새로운 메시지에 대한 알림이 울릴 때마다, 그는 그의 소셜 미디어에 접속해서 답장을 쓴다. 그는 심지어 그가 집에서

공부할 때에도, 종종 소셜 미디어 메시지에 정신이 분산되곤 하고 늦게 잠을 잔다고 인정한다. Johns 선생님은 그가 당분간 소셜 미디어 사용을 중단하고 공부에 집중해야 한다고 생각한다. 이러한 상황에서, Johns 선생님은 Kevin에게 뭐라고 말할 것 같은가?

문제 해결

Johns 선생님은 성적이 떨어져 상담을 하는 Kevin에게서 소셜 미디어에 계속 접속해서 공부에 집중력이 떨어지는 모습을 발견하고 이에 대한 적절한 조언을 해 주어야 하는 상황이므로, Johns 선생님이 Kevin에게 할 말로 가장 적절한 것은 ③ '소셜 미디어를 제쳐 두고 공부에 집중하는 것이 어때?'이다.

① 너는 나가서 운동을 더 해야 해.
② 낮은 성적에 그렇게 실망하지 마.
④ 소셜 미디어는 다른 사람들과 의사소통할 수 있는 좋은 방법일 수 있어.
⑤ 너는 배운 것을 복습하는 데에 더 많은 시간을 보낼 필요가 있어.

어휘·표현

doze off 잠이 들다, 졸다 **constantly** 끊임없이 **notification** 알림, 통지
go off (경보기 등이) 울리다 **distract** (정신이) 산만하게 하다
put ~ aside ~을 한쪽으로 치우다

16-17 ───────── 복합 이해

여: 학생 여러분, 안녕하세요. 오늘 제 강의에 와 주셔서 감사합니다. 저는 친환경 에너지 연구소에서 온 Sarah Ferguson입니다. 화석 연료 에너지의 끊임없는 사용 때문에, 지구는 크게 피해를 입어 왔습니다. 화석 연료에 기반한 에너지의 생산은 대기 오염을 일으키고 기후 변화를 초래합니다. 오늘 저는 화석 연료 에너지에 대한 대안에 대해 이야기를 할 것입니다. 첫 번째로, 바이오매스는 동물과 식물 폐기물을 태우는 것에서 나오는 재생 가능한 에너지원입니다. 바이오매스를 생산하는 데에 사용된 유기물은 무한한데, 이는 우리 사회가 지속적으로 쓰레기와 나무와 같은 폐기물을 생산하기 때문입니다. 두 번째로, 태양 에너지는 태양의 에너지를 사용하고 전기로 전환합니다. 그것은 우리의 생태학적 발자국을 줄일 수 있고 화석 연료보다 더 저렴합니다. 세 번째로, 풍력 에너지는 풍력 터빈의 사용으로 생산될 수 있는데, 해로운 폐기물을 생산하지 않습니다. 마지막으로, 수력 발전은 친환경 에너지의 가장 널리 사용되는 형태 중 하나입니다. 에너지원으로서 물을 사용하는 것은 가격이 저렴할 뿐만이 아니라 매우 신뢰할만 합니다. 이제, 이 네가지 형태의 에너지가 어떻게 사용되고 있는지에 대한 영상을 보시겠습니다.

어휘·표현

eco-friendly 환경 친화적인 **fossil fuel** 화석 연료 **generation** 발생
alternative 대안 **renewable** 재생 가능한 **derive from** ~에서 유래하다
infinite 무한한 **consistently** 지속적으로 **convert** 전환시키다
ecological 생태학의 **hazardous** 위험한 **hydropower** 수력 전기
reliable 믿을 수 있는
cut down on ~을 줄이다 **misconception** 오해 **emergence** 출현
atomic 원자의, 원자력의

16 ②

문제 해결

친환경 에너지 연구소에서 온 강연자는 화석 연료 에너지의 문제점을 지적하면서 화석 연료 에너지의 대안인 친환경 에너지에 대해 구체적으로 설명하고 있

다. 따라서 여자가 하는 말의 주제는 ② '친환경 에너지원의 유형들'이다.
① 대체 에너지의 단점
③ 에너지 소비를 줄이는 방법
④ 화석 연료에 기반한 에너지에 대한 오해
⑤ 환경 친화적인 일상용품의 출현

17 ③

친환경 에너지로 ③ '원자력 에너지'는 언급하지 않았다.

20 영어 듣기 모의고사 ▶ pp. 44-45

01 ③	02 ④	03 ④	04 ③	05 ④	06 ④
07 ③	08 ④	09 ④	10 ③	11 ⑤	12 ②
13 ④	14 ⑤	15 ⑤	16 ①	17 ③	

01 ③ — 목적 파악

여: 안녕하세요, 여러분. 폭우에도 불구하고 이곳에 와 주셔서 감사합니다. 저는 Janet Brown이고 시장 선거에 출마했습니다. 여러분 모두 아시다시피, 우리 시의 경제는 불황입니다. 지난해부터, 실업률과 인플레이션을 포함해 모든 경제 지표가 최악의 수준에 이르고 있습니다. 저는 이 경제 위기를 극복하고 싶습니다. 경제학 박사 학위가 있는 저는 대학에서 학생들을 가르쳤고, 전 세계적인 자동차 회사의 CEO로 일했습니다. 누가 다음 시장이 되어야 하는지에 대한 지난주 여론조사에서, 압도적인 반응은 '이 경제 위기를 해결할 수 있는 후보자'였습니다. 그 사람은 저, Janet Brown입니다. 저는 여러분이 다음 주 수요일 시장 선거에서 저를 잊지 않으시기를 바랍니다. 여러분과 여러분의 자녀를 위해서, 그리고 Austin 시를 위해서 저에게 투표해 주십시오. 감사합니다.

다음 주 수요일에 열리는 시장 선거에 출마한 여자는 자신이 현 경제 위기를 책임질 적임자라고 하면서 자신에게 투표할 것을 요청하고 있으므로, 여자가 하는 말의 목적으로 가장 적절한 것은 ③이다.

run for ~에 출마하다   mayor 시장   in bad shape 불황인   indicator 지표
overwhelming 압도적인

02 ④ — 주제 파악

여: Daniel, 너 거의 한 달 동안 전기 자동차를 운전했지.
남: 그래. 시간이 빨리 간다.
여: 그래 전기차에 만족하니?
남: 음, 한 가지만 제외하고는 상당히 만족해.
여: 높은 가격을 말하는 거니?
남: 아니, 그건 아니야. 문제는 내 전기 자동차를 충전하는 거야.
여: 충전소에서 충전하는 것이 어렵니?
남: 아니, 하지만 주위에 충전소가 많지 않아서 충전소를 찾는 것이 꽤 어려워.
여: 정말? 그건 전기 자동차 소유자에게 커다란 문제임에 틀림없어.
남: 물론이지! 난 더 많은 충전소가 설치되어야 한다고 생각해.
여: 그렇지 않으면, 전기 자동차가 환경에 좋다고 할지라도, 주류의 인기를 얻는 데 고전을 면치 못할 거야.

전기 자동차에 대해 만족하는지 묻는 여자의 말에 남자는 전기 자동차 충전소가 많지 않다고 하면서 더 많은 충전소가 설치되어야 한다고 말했다.

except for ~을 제외하고는   charge 충전하다   charging station 충전소
install 설치하다   mainstream 주류, 대세

03 ④

관계 추론

여: Raymond 씨인가요?

남: 네, 맞습니다. 제가 30분 전에 구조 센터에 전화를 했어요. 와 주어서 고마워요.

여: 괜찮습니다. 제 일을 할 뿐입니다. 그래 무슨 일이 일어났는지 말씀해 주시겠어요?

남: 산의 정상에 도달한 후에 비탈길을 내려오다가 미끄러졌어요.

여: 심하게 떨어지신 것 같습니다. 일어서실 수 있겠어요?

남: 아니요. 보세요, 제 발목이 부어올랐어요. 발목이 부러진 것 같아요.

여: 걱정 마세요. 구조대원이 두 명 더 여기로 오고 있습니다. 우리가 산 아래로 당신을 데리고 갈 거예요.

남: 정말 고맙습니다.

여: 산에서 부상을 당했다고 가족들에게 알렸나요?

남: 네. 아내에게 전화를 해서 사고에 대해 말했어요. 아내도 여기로 오는 길입니다.

여: 아내분에게 다시 전화하셔서 당신이 안전하다고 말씀해 주세요.

문제 해결

산 정상에서 내려오다가 비탈길에서 미끄러져서 부상을 당한 남자가 구조 센터에 구조 요청을 하였고 이에 구조대원인 여자가 와서 남자를 안심시키고 있는 상황이므로, 여자와 남자는 산악 구조대원과 등산객의 관계이다.

어휘·표현

rescue center 구조 센터   slip 미끄러지다   slope 비탈길   summit 정상
take a fall 넘어지다, 떨어지다   swollen 부어오른   break one's ankle 발목
이 부러지다

04 ③

그림 불일치 파악

남: 여보, 크리스마스 파티를 위한 거실 장식을 끝냈어요.

여: 오, 벽난로 옆에 크리스마스트리를 놓았군요. 멋져요.

남: 그리고 벽난로 위쪽 높이 'Merry Christmas'라고 쓴 현수막을 걸었어요.

여: 좋아요. 거실의 가운데 왜 사각 탁자를 놓았어요?

남: 우리는 이 탁자 위에 선물을 올려놓고 아이들로 하여금 원하는 대로 선물을 고르게 할 수 있어요.

여: 정말요? 아이들이 무엇을 받을지 모르기 때문에 흥미진진하겠는데요.

남: 그럼요! 아이들은 분명히 좋은 시간을 보낼 거예요.

여: 나도 그렇게 생각해요. 크리스마스트리 앞에 있는 상자들이 선물인가요?

남: 맞아요. 이것들을 포장하는 데 거의 한 시간이 걸렸어요.

여: 아주 잘했어요. 오, 벽난로에 걸려 있는 양말 세 개가 마음에 드네요.

남: 아이들을 위해서 양말 안에 사탕도 좀 넣어 놓았지요.

여: 멋져요! 당신은 정말 좋은 아빠예요.

문제 해결

여자가 거실 가운데에 사각 탁자가 있다고 했으므로, ③이 대화의 내용과 일치하지 않는다.

어휘·표현

fireplace 벽난로   wrap 포장하다, 싸다

05 ④

부탁한 일 파악

남: Judith, 거의 12시에요. 점심을 먹을 때에요.

여: 그래요, 맞아요. 가요.

남: 오, 이번 주 금요일 독일 출장 준비는 어때요?

여: 아주 잘 되고 있어요. 한 가지만 제외하고는 다 했어요.

남: 그게 뭐죠?

여: 내 책상에 있는 금붕어요. 내가 출장 가는 동안 금붕어를 돌봐 줄 사람을 찾지 못했어요.

남: 여기요, 왜 나에게 그 일을 해 달라고 부탁하지 않았어요? 내가 당신을 위해서 금붕어를 돌봐 줄 수 있어요.

여: 그래요? 오, 고마워요, David. 퇴근하기 전에 하루에 한 번 금붕어에게 먹이만 주면 돼요.

남: 정말로 쉽네요! 걱정 말아요. 금붕어는 잘 돌봄을 받을 거예요.

여: 정말로 안심이 되네요. David, 오늘 내가 점심을 살게요. 먹고 싶은 거 말만 하세요.

남: 음…. 해산물 스파게티 어때요?

여: 좋아요!

문제 해결

여자가 출장을 가는 동안에 자신의 책상 위에 있는 금붕어를 돌봐 줄 사람을 찾지 못했다고 하자, 남자는 자신이 금붕어를 돌봐 주겠다고 한다. 이에 여자는 남자에게 고맙다고 하면서 퇴근하기 전에 금붕어에게 먹이를 한 번씩 줄 것을 부탁했다.

어휘·표현

in good hands 안심할 수 있는, 잘 관리되는   relieved 안도하는, 다행으로 여기는

06 ④

숫자 정보 파악

남: 안녕하세요, 제 쌍둥이 딸들을 이 스포츠 프로그램 중의 한 개에 등록하고 싶어요.

여: 알겠습니다. 자녀가 어떤 종류의 프로그램을 수강하길 바라시나요?

남: 발레요. 월 회비가 얼마죠?

여: 두 개의 발레 프로그램이 있습니다. 집중 프로그램은 100달러이고, 일주일에 세 번 수업을 합니다.

남: 다른 것은요?

여: 70달러이고, 일주일에 두 번 수업이 있습니다.

남: 음…. 두 프로그램 사이에 30달러의 차이가 있군요.

여: 그렇습니다. 집중 프로그램이 훨씬 더 인기가 있습니다.

남: 좋아요, 딸들을 위해서 집중 프로그램을 수강할게요. 어, 두 자녀를 한 번에 등록하는 경우 할인이 있나요?

여: 아니요, 없습니다. 하지만 두 달 수강료를 미리 지불하시면 10% 할인을 받으실 수 있습니다.

남: 정말요? 그러면 지금 두 달 수강료를 지불할게요.

문제 해결

쌍둥이 딸들을 위해서 한 달 수강료가 100달러인 발레 집중 프로그램을 신청하려는 여자는 직원에게서 두 달 수강료를 미리 내면 10% 할인받을 수 있다는 정보를 듣고 두 달 수강료를 한 번에 내기로 했다. 따라서 여자가 지불할 총 금액은 360달러이다.

어휘·표현

enroll 등록하다   intensive 집중적인   consist of ~로 구성되다
in advance 미리

07 ③

이유 파악

여: Fred, 과일이 다 떨어졌어요. 냉장고에 사과 한 개도 없어요.

남: 정말이요? 그러면 좀 사러 가는 게 어때요? 우리는 채소도 필요해요.

여: 좋아요! 지금 Green Market에 가요.

남: Green Market이요? 우리 아파트 바로 옆에 있는 거 말하는 건가요?

여: 그래요. 지금 그곳에서 대대적인 세일을 하고 있거든요. 게다가, 그곳의 직원들이 아주 친절해요.

남: 그건 맞지만, 나는 거기에 가고 싶지 않아요.

여: 어째서요? 그곳은 소비자를 위해서 무료 배송 서비스도 해 주잖아요.

남: 하지만 그곳에서 판매하는 농산물은 신선하지 않아요.

여: 그러면 Maple 거리에 있는 ABC Market에 가요. 그곳의 농산물은 아주 신선해요.

남: 좋아요. 지금 바로 자동차 열쇠를 가지고 올게요.

여: 자동차 열쇠는 부엌 식탁 위에 있어요. 오전에 스포츠 센터에 차를 몰고 다녀온 후에 자동차 열쇠를 그곳에 놓았거든요.

남: 알았어요.

문제 해결

Green Market에 가고 싶지 않다는 남자에게 여자가 이유를 묻자 남자는 그곳의 농산물이 신선하지 않다고 말했다.

어휘·표현

run out of ~이 떨어지다 fridge 냉장고 plus 게다가, 또한 produce 농산물

08 ④ ·········· 언급 유무 파악

남: 이 나무 사진을 봐. 멋져 보이지.

여: 오, 이 나무는 Vermont 주의 Orange County에 있는 은행나무야. 사람들이 그러는데 이 나무가 500년이 더 넘었대.

남: 이 나무에 대해 어떻게 알아?

여: 몇 주 전에, 이 나무에 관한 다큐멘터리를 봤어. 이 나무가 얼마나 큰지 맞춰 볼래?

남: 약 30미터?

여: 사실 훨씬 더 커. 62미터야. 그리고 지름이 9미터야.

남: 와! 거대한 나무구나. 이 나무를 직접 본 사람이면 누구나 이 나무의 규모 자체에 압도당하겠다.

여: 당연하지! 그래서 이 나무의 별명이 '위대한 거인'이야.

남: 오, 내 눈으로 이 나무를 보고 싶어.

여: 정말? 그러면 우리 이번 주말에 이 나무 보러 갈래? 나도 이 나무를 보고 싶거든.

남: 좋은 생각이야.

문제 해결

은행나무의 ④ '열매'는 언급되지 않았다.

어휘·표현

ginkgo tree 은행나무 diameter 지름 overwhelm 압도하다, 제압하다
sheer 순전한

09 ④ ·········· 담화 내용 불일치

남: 학생 여러분, 집중해 주세요! Green Essay 대회가 시작되었습니다. 이 대회의 목적은 환경 보호에 대한 인식을 높이는 것입니다. 대회 주제는 '지구를 보호하는 방법'입니다. 학년에 관계없이 우리 학교에 다니는 학생 모두가 대회에 참가할 자격이 있습니다. 대회에 참여하기 위해서는 학교 웹사이트에 접속해서 참가자 목록에 여러분의 이름을 등록하십시오. 지구의 날인 4월 22일까지 여러분의 글을 올려야 합니다. 영문학 교사 팀이 여러분의 글을 심사할 것이고 결과는 4월 마

지막 날 교내 웹 사이트에 게시될 것입니다. 학년별로 금메달 수상자가 발표될 것이고, 이들은 학교 대표로 6월에 열리는 Florida Essay 대회에 참가할 자격이 주어질 것입니다.

문제 해결

심사 결과가 4월 마지막 날 교내 웹 사이트에 게시될 것이라고 했으므로, ④는 내용과 일치하지 않는다.

어휘·표현

awareness 인식 regardless of ~에 관계없이 eligible 자격이 있는
(=entitled) log in to ~에 접속하다 evaluate 심사하다, 평가하다
representative 대표

10 ③ ·········· 도표 정보 파악

여: Albert, 이 광고를 보고 직원 휴게실에 놓을 커피 머신을 사요.

남: 좋아요. 마음에 두고 있는 브랜드가 있나요?

여: 아니요. 하지만 Grace는 피해야 해요. 이 브랜드의 커피 머신은 커피를 끓일 때 너무 시끄러운 소리가 난다고 들었어요.

남: 나도 그것을 들었어요. 물 용량은 어때요?

여: 음, 20명 이상이 커피 머신을 사용할 것이기 때문에 적어도 2리터 용량인 것을 사야 할 것 같아요.

남: 맞아요. 당신 말에 전적으로 동의해요.

여: 카페라테 기능이 있는 것을 사야 할까요?

남: 네, 카페라테를 선택할 수 있으면 좋을 것 같아요.

여: 아주 좋아요! 그러면 이 두 커피 머신 중에서 한 개를 주문해야 해요. 어느 것이 더 마음에 들어요?

남: 당연히, 보증 기간이 더 긴 이것이요. 당신은 어때요?

여: 나도 그래요. 좋아요. 이것을 사요.

문제 해결

Grace 브랜드가 아닌 커피 머신 중에서, 물 용량이 최소 2리터이고 카페 라테 기능이 있으며 보증 기간이 더 긴 커피 머신을 구입하기로 했으므로, 두 사람이 구입할 커피 머신은 ③이다.

어휘·표현

staff lounge 직원 휴게실 brew (커피를) 끓이다 capacity 용량
function 기능 warranty 보증

11 ⑤ ·········· 짧은 대화의 응답

남: Charlotte, 오늘 밤에 저녁 먹기로 한 거 맞지?

여: 응, 그런데 난 치과 예약 때문에 조금 늦을 것 같아.

남: 괜찮아. 내가 식당 예약을 조금 늦게 변경해 놓을게.

여: <u>좋아! 식당에서 보자.</u>

문제 해결

약속 시간에 조금 늦는다는 여자를 위해 식당 예약 시간을 변경하겠다는 남자의 말을 듣고, 여자는 좋다면서 식당에서 보자고 답하는 것이 가장 적절하다.

① 나는 두 사람 예약을 했어.

② 나는 샐러드와 바닷가재를 먹었어.

③ 그들에게 내가 못 가서 미안하다고 말해 줘.

④ 나는 그때 영화가 매진될 거라고 생각해.

어휘·표현

dental appointment 치과 예약 lobster 바닷가재

12 ②

여: Brian, 지금 뭐 듣고 있어?
남: James King의 신곡. 제목이 A White Night야. 이 노래 들어봤니?
여: 아니, 못 들어 봤어. 하지만 사람들이 나에게 이 노래가 정말로 좋다고 말했어.
남: 맞아. 이 노래를 들어 보면, 너도 정말 좋아할 거야.

문제 해결

James King의 신곡을 듣고 있는 남자에게 여자는 사람들이 그 노래가 좋다고 말했다고 하였다. 이에 대한 남자의 응답으로 가장 적절한 것은 ②이다.
① 유감이지만, 나는 그의 앨범 중 어느 것도 빌릴 수 없어.
③ James King? 아니, 나는 그 이름을 들어 본 적이 없어.
④ 나에게 좋은 노래를 추천해 주어서 고마워.
⑤ 네게 말한 것처럼, 나는 그의 앨범을 사려고 돈을 충분히 모았어.

어휘·표현

title (노래 등의) 제목

13 ④

남: 안녕하세요, 집을 빌리고 싶은데요.
여: 알겠습니다. 어느 지역을 생각하세요?
남: Lakewood요. 그 지역에 침실이 세 개인 집이 있나요?
여: 네. 현재 두 채 있어요.
남: 잘됐네요. 그 집의 월 임대료가 얼마인지 말해 주시겠어요?
여: Red 거리에 있는 집은 900달러이고, Blue 거리에 있는 다른 집은 1,200달러예요.
남: 1,200달러요? 이 집은 왜 다른 집보다 더 비싼가요?
여: 불과 두 달 전에 완전히 수리를 했거든요.
남: 오, 그렇군요. 그러면 모든 시설이 새것이고 상태가 좋겠어요.
여: 물론이죠! 당신이 빠르게 행동한다면 이 집을 수리한 이래로 당신이 이 집에서 사는 첫 번째 사람이 될 거예요.
남: 좋은데요. 지금 그 집을 둘러볼 수 있을까요?

문제 해결

남자가 임대료가 더 비싼 이유를 묻자, 여자는 두 달 전에 집을 완전히 수리했다고 하면서 남자가 빨리 행동하면 집을 수리한 이후로 첫 번째로 이 집에 사는 사람이 될 것이라고 말했다. 이 말에 대한 남자의 응답으로 가장 적절한 것은 ④ '좋은데요. 지금 그 집을 둘러볼 수 있을까요?'이다.
① 걱정하지 마세요. 나는 곧 내 집을 수리할 거예요.
② 물론이죠! 월 임대료는 걱정하지 마세요.
③ 당신에게 달려 있어요. 당신은 마음에 드는 어떤 집에서도 살 수 있어요.
⑤ 맞아요. 나는 집을 수리하는 것이 얼마나 힘든지 몰랐어요.

어휘·표현

at the moment 현재, 지금   rental fee 임대료   renovate 수리하다
facility 시설

14 ⑤

여: Sam, Brian이 오늘 왜 결근했는지 알아요?
남: Brian이 지난밤에 교통사고를 당했다는 소식 못 들었어요?
여: 아니요, 못 들었어요. 그가 심각하게 다쳤나요?
남: 다행히도, 괜찮아요. 사고가 그다지 심각하지 않아서 그가 집에서 안

정을 취하고 있다고 들었어요.
여: 천만다행이에요! 사고가 어떻게 났는지 알아요?
남: 음, 그가 운전을 하면서 휴대 전화를 사용하는 바람에 다른 차를 못 봤대요.
여: 정말요? 어째서 그가 그렇게 부주의한 행동을 할 수 있었는지 이해가 안 돼요.
남: 나도 그래요.
여: 알다시피, 운전 중 휴대 전화 사용은 운전자의 주의를 분산시키는 가장 큰 요인 중의 하나예요.
남: 그리고 작년 교통사고의 약 40%가 휴대 전화를 사용하는 운전자 때문이라고 들었어요.
여: 그 사고들은 일어나지 말았어야 했는데 안타까워요.

문제 해결

작년에 발생한 교통사고의 40%가 운전자의 휴대 전화 사용 때문이라고 한 남자의 말에 대한 여자의 응답으로 ⑤ '그 사고들은 일어나지 말았어야 했는데 안타까워요.'가 가장 적절하다.
① Brian은 며칠 더 병원에 있어야 해요.
② 나는 너무 바빠서 퇴근 후에 그를 보러 병원에 갈 수가 없어요.
③ 당신은 운전 중에 휴대 전화를 사용하지 말았어야 했어요.
④ 그 교통사고에 대한 정확한 이유를 아무도 몰라요.

어휘·표현

relief 안도, 안심   distraction 주의를 분산시키는 것

15 ⑤

남: Lucy와 Eric은 고층 아파트에 살고 있는데, 아파트는 27층에 위치해 있다. 그들은 자신들의 아파트에 나와서 식료품 쇼핑을 하기 위해 엘리베이터에 탄다. 그들이 어떤 음식을 살지 이야기를 할 때, 엘리베이터 내부의 불이 갑자기 꺼지고 엘리베이터가 멈춘다. Eric은 매우 긴장해서 무엇을 해야 할지 모른다. 그는 Lucy에게 자신이 폐쇄 공포증이 있다고 말한다. 그를 진정시키기 위해서, Lucy는 자신의 스마트폰으로 엘리베이터의 내부를 밝힌다. 그녀는 벽에 있는 비상 전화를 보고, 전화를 들어 이 상황을 알린다. 엘리베이터 관리인은 수리 기사가 10분 안에 그곳에 갈 것이라고 말한다. Lucy는 Eric이 이 소식을 들으면 기분이 나아질 것이라고 생각한다. 이 상황에서, Lucy는 Eric에게 뭐라고 말할 것 같은가?

문제 해결

엘리베이터에 갇힌 상황에서, Lucy는 비상 전화를 걸어 수리 기사가 10분 안에 도착할 것이라는 이야기를 들었고, Eric에게 이 소식을 전달하면 그의 기분이 나아질 것이라고 생각하고 있다. 이러한 상황에서 Lucy가 Eric에게 할 말로 가장 적절한 것은 ⑤ '수리 기사가 10분 안에 올 거예요. 그러면 우리는 이곳을 나갈 거예요.'이다.
① 걱정하지 말아요. 내가 지금 바로 엘리베이터를 고칠게요.
② 이제부터, 엘리베이터 대신에 계단을 이용해요.
③ 사고는 언제 어디서나 일어날 수 있어요. 그러니 우리는 사고를 피할 수 없어요.
④ 엘리베이터가 너무 자주 고장이 나요. 이것에 대해서 관리자에게 이야기할게요.

어휘·표현

high-rise 고층의   a fear of small spaces 폐쇄 공포증   light up ~를 환하게 밝히다   emergency 비상   repairman 수리 기사

16-17

복합 이해

여: 안녕하세요, 여러분. 다시 만나게 되어서 반가워요. 저는 스포츠 치료사 Cathy Brown입니다. 여러분에게 질문을 하나 할게요. 여러분은 자녀가 스포츠를 하게 하나요? 만약 그렇지 않다면, 저는 여러분이 자녀에게 스포츠를 할 기회를 정기적으로 줄 것을 권합니다. 체력을 향상시키는 것뿐만 아니라, 스포츠를 하는 것은 많은 이점을 가져다줍니다. 무엇보다도, 축구 또는 야구와 같은 단체 스포츠를 하는 것은 어린이들이 협력과 책임감의 의미를 배우도록 도와줍니다. 또한, 또래 친구들과 단체 스포츠를 하면서, 어린이들은 팀워크를 키워 나갈 수 있습니다. 스케이트 또는 스키와 같은 개인 스포츠는 자녀의 심리에 긍정적으로 영향을 끼칩니다. 최근의 연구에 따르면 정기적으로 이러한 종류의 스포츠를 하는 어린이가 그렇지 않은 어린이보다 심리적으로 더 안정적이라고 합니다. 수영의 경우, 정기적으로 수영을 한 어린이들은 그렇지 않은 어린이들보다 비상 상황에서 더 차분했고 더 침착하게 행동했다는 것이 밝혀졌습니다. 이제 여러분 앞에 있는 스크린을 보아 주십시오.

어휘·표현

therapist 치료사 **regularly** 정기적으로, 규칙적으로 **aside from** ~ 외에는, ~을 제외하고 **beneficial** 유익한, 이로운 **cooperation** 협력, 협동 **psychology** 심리 **on a regular basis** 정기적으로 **stable** 안정적인 **composed** 차분한, 침착한

16 ①

문제 해결

스포츠 치료사인 여자는 자녀에게 정기적으로 스포츠를 할 기회를 주라고 말하면서, 스포츠를 하면 자녀의 신체적인 힘이 향상되는 것뿐만 아니라 협력과 책임감을 키워 주고 또 자녀의 심리에도 긍정적으로 영향을 끼친다고 했다. 따라서 여자가 하는 말의 주제로 가장 적절한 것은 ① '스포츠를 하는 것이 어린이에게 미치는 긍정적인 이로움'이다.
② 운동을 하기 전 준비 운동의 중요성
③ 운동을 통해 어린이의 체력을 향상시키는 방법
④ 개인 스포츠와 단체 스포츠의 차이
⑤ 어린이가 개인 스포츠보다 단체 스포츠를 더 좋아하는 이유

17 ③

문제 해결

축구, 야구, 스케이트, 수영에 대한 언급은 있지만, ③ '테니스'에 대한 언급은 없었다.

---

21 영어 듣기 모의고사 [고난도] ▶ pp. 46-47

01 ③	02 ③	03 ③	04 ⑤	05 ②	06 ②
07 ⑤	08 ④	09 ④	10 ④	11 ⑤	12 ⑤
13 ①	14 ⑤	15 ③	16 ①	17 ④	

01 ③

목적 파악

남: 안녕하세요, 여러분. 저는 Blake이고, Environmentalists' Society에서 일합니다. 오늘, 저는 인기 있는 과일인 아보카도에 대해서 말하려고 합니다. 많은 사람들이 아름다운 색깔과 풍부한 영양 때문에 아보카도를 좋아합니다. 아보카도에는 불포화 지방산이 많은데, 그것은 다이어트와 피부 관리에 좋다고 알려져 있습니다. 그러나, 아보카도는 물 부족의 원인이기도 합니다. 아보카도 한 개를 재배하는 데는 거의 320L의 물이 필요합니다. 넓게 보면, 오렌지 한 개를 재배하는 데는 22L의 물이 필요하고, 토마토 한 개를 재배하는 데는 겨우 5L가 필요합니다. 아보카도 1kg을 재배하기 위해 필요한 물의 양으로 사람 한 명에게 거의 16개월 동안 수분을 공급할 수 있습니다. 결론적으로, 우리가 더 많은 아보카도를 재배할수록, 지구는 더 빨리 말라갑니다. 그러니 우리는 아보카도를 재배하는 것이 전 세계적으로 물 부족의 원인이 될 수 있다는 사실을 간과해서는 안 됩니다.

문제 해결

남자는 사람들이 즐겨 먹는 아보카도를 재배하는 것이 사실은 전 세계적인 물 부족 현상의 원인이 될 수 있음을 알려 주고 있다.

어휘·표현

environmentalist 환경 운동가 **nutrient** 영양분 **unsaturated fatty acid** 불포화 지방산 **shortage** 부족 **perspective** 관점 **hydrate** 수화(水化)시키다, 수분을 공급하다 **ignore** 무시하다

02 ③

주제 파악

여: Adam, 너 안 좋아 보이는구나. 무슨 일 있니?
남: 안녕하세요, Nam 선생님. 최근에 무릎이 아팠어요.
여: 정말? 무릎을 다쳤니?
남: 잘 기억나지 않아요.
여: 그러면, 최근에 체중이 늘었니?
남: 아니요. 사실 살이 약간 빠졌어요. 저는 매일 운동하고 있거든요.
여: 그래? 어떤 운동을 하고 있는데?
남: 음, 저는 매일 한 시간 동안 유산소 운동과 두 시간 동안 근력 운동을 하고 있어요.
여: 하루에 세 시간? 그건 너무 많은 운동이야. 아마도 그것이 네 무릎이 아픈 이유일 거야.
남: 제가 운동을 너무 많이 해서 무릎이 아프다는 말씀이세요?
여: 그래. 네 몸 상태에 따라서 적당히 운동해야 해.
남: 알겠습니다. 운동을 덜 하고 무릎이 좋아지는지 볼게요. 감사합니다, Nam 선생님.

문제 해결

여자는 너무 많이 운동을 하는 것이 오히려 몸을 아프게 할 수 있다면서, 남자에게 몸 상태에 따라서 적당히 운동할 것을 조언하고 있다.

어휘·표현

injure 부상을 입다   work out 운동하다   cardio exercise 유산소 운동
weight training 근력 운동   moderately 적당히

03 ③
관계 추론

남: 안녕하세요. 저는 Asher입니다. 당신이 Bronte 씨인가요?
여: 네, 접니다. 이렇게 먼 길을 와 주셔서 감사합니다.
남: 전혀 문제 없습니다. 게다가 아름다운 운전 길이었습니다. 어떤 도움이 필요하신가요?
여: 제가 생각해 둔 게 있지만, 당신의 전문적인 의견을 듣고 싶습니다.
남: 음, 저는 집 전체가 약간 어둡다고 생각합니다.
여: 그것에 대해서 무엇을 할 수 있을까요?
남: 집의 벽을 더 밝은 색으로 칠할 수 있습니다. 그리고 전등을 더 밝은 것들로 바꿀 수 있고요.
여: 좋습니다. 그리고 저는 부엌과 화장실을 새로 고치고 싶습니다.
남: 네, 그것들은 상당히 오래되었네요. 이 카탈로그를 보시고 마음에 드시는 디자인을 골라 주세요.
여: 저는 이 고풍스러운 디자인이 정말 마음에 들어요.
남: 그리고 창문도 겨울의 찬 바람을 생각하면 너무 낡아 보입니다. 그것들도 역시 바꿔야 합니다.
여: 맞아요. 언제 시작할 수 있나요?
남: 디자인을 고르시면, 내일 견적서를 들고 오겠습니다.

문제 해결

남자는 여자에게 벽을 더 밝은 색으로 칠하고, 전등을 더 밝은 것으로 바꾸며, 창문이 오래되어서 바꿔야 한다고 말하고 있고, 여자는 남자에게 부엌과 화장실을 새로 고치고 싶고, 고풍스러운 디자인이 좋다고 말하고 있다. 이를 통해, 두 사람은 인테리어 업자와 집주인의 관계임을 알 수 있다.

어휘·표현

renew 새로 교체하다   antique 고대의, 고풍스러운   estimate 견적서

04 ⑤
그림 불일치 파악

남: 안녕, Kate. 뭐하고 있어?
여: 안녕하세요, Brown 선생님. 저는 이 포스터를 모든 학생들이 볼 수 있도록 게시판에 붙이고 있어요.
남: 멋져 보이는구나. 그런데, 기타 동호회를 시작하려고 하니? 중앙에 엄청 큰 기타가 보이네.
여: 아니에요. 사실, 우리 밴드가 콘서트를 하려고 해요. 제가 다른 악기들을 그렸어야 했다고 생각하시나요?
남: 괜찮아. 사람들이 기타에 있는 이 큰 글씨들을 볼 수 있을 거야.
여: 다행이네요. 콘서트의 날짜와 장소는 잘 보이시나요?
남: 그것들이 어디에 있어? 아, 날짜는 왼쪽 구석 상단에 있고, 장소는 오른쪽 구석 아래쪽에 있구나. 그런데 그것들이 읽기에는 좀 작은 것 같아.
여: 네, 선생님 말씀이 맞아요.
남: 하지만 나는 기타 줄 위에 있는 이 글자들이 정말 마음에 들어.
여: 그것은 입장료예요. 그건 그렇고, 콘서트에 오실 수 있나요?
남: 그럼.
여: 이번 주 금요일에 봬요!

문제 해결

남자는 입장료에 대한 공지가 기타 줄 위에 있다고 했는데, 그림에서는 기타 줄

아래 부분에 있으므로 ⑤는 대화 내용과 일치하지 않는다.

어휘·표현

put up 게시하다   bulletin board 게시판   musical instrument 악기
relief 안심, 안도   admission fee 입장료

05 ②
할 일 파악

여: 여보, 나는 우리가 내일 이사 가는 것이 믿어지지 않아요.
남: 나도 믿어지지 않아요. 저는 정말 이 집에 정 들어 있었어요.
여: 내일 비가 엄청 올 거라고 들었어요. 우리는 이삿짐센터에 우리가 이사 갈 수 있는지를 확인해야 할까요?
남: 내가 이미 확인했어요. 그들은 우리가 예정한 대로 이사 갈 수 있다고 했어요. 그런데 그들은 두 사람이 더 필요하대요.
여: 왜 사람들이 더 필요하대요?
남: 날씨가 안 좋아서 사다리 차를 쓸 수가 없다고 했어요.
여: 그러면 비용이 더 들까요?
남: 물론이지요. 나는 추가로 짐 나르는 사람들 몫의 돈을 좀 뽑아야겠어요.
여: 그러면 은행 가는 길에, 관리 사무소에 들러서 우리가 내일 승강기를 사용한다는 것을 알려 줄래요?
남: 그럼요.
여: 당신이 그 일을 하는 동안, 나는 가스 회사에 전화해서 서비스를 끊어 달라고 할게요.
남: 좋아요. 그건 매우 중요하지요.
여: 우리가 모든 것을 확인한 것 같아요, 그렇지요?
남: 그런 것 같아요.

문제 해결

남자가 돈을 뽑으러 은행에 가는 길에 관리 사무소에 들러서 승강기 사용을 신청하는 동안 여자는 가스 회사에 전화해서 가스 서비스 종료 요청을 하겠다고 했다.

어휘·표현

be attached to ~에 애착을 갖다   ladder truck 사다리 차   withdraw (돈을) 인출하다   management office 관리 사무소   terminate 끝내다, 종료하다

06 ②
숫자 정보 파악

남: 실례합니다, 여기에서 공항으로 가는 버스가 있나요?
여: 물론이지요. 30분마다 옵니다. 5분 안에 도착할 거예요.
남: 잘됐네요. 아내가 출장에서 돌아오고 있기 때문에 9시 전에 공항에 도착해야 하거든요.
여: 걱정마세요. 이 시간에는 교통 체증이 없어요.
남: 그 말을 들으니 안심이 됩니다. 가격은 얼마인가요?
여: 일반 버스는 10달러이고, 우등 고속버스는 20달러입니다.
남: 저는 고속으로 사겠습니다. 왕복 표를 사면 할인을 받을 수 있나요?
여: 네, 10% 할인받을 수 있습니다.
남: 좋습니다. 왕복 표 한 장과 아내가 저와 함께 돌아올 편도 표 한 장 주세요.
여: 현금으로 지불하시면 추가 5% 할인을 받을 수 있습니다.
남: 저는 현금을 충분히 갖고 있지 않아요. 여기 제 신용 카드 있습니다.
여: 감사합니다.

문제 해결

남자는 우등 고속버스 왕복 표 한 장과 편도 표 한 장을 사려고 한다. 총 금액은

60달러지만, 왕복 표는 10% 할인을 받을 수 있기 때문에 남자가 지불해야 하는 총액은 56달러이다. 신용 카드로 지불하였으므로 현금 할인은 받지 못한다.

어휘·표현

relief 안심   regular 보통의   deluxe 고급의   express 고속의, 급행의
discount 할인   round-trip 왕복의   one-way 편도의   additional 추가적
인

07 ⑤ 이유 파악

남: 정말 바쁜 날이네요!
여: 그렇네요, Williams 씨. 이제 중요한 회의 하나만 남았습니다.
남: 알겠어요. 내일 제 일정은 어떻게 되나요?
여: 내일부터 토요일까지 멕시코로 5일 동안 출장이 있습니다.
남: 토요일이요? 제가 이번 금요일 오후에 제 아들의 축구 경기에 가야 한
다고 말했는데요.
여: 하지만 그 경기가 경기장 수리 때문에 다음 주로 미뤄졌다고 말씀하
셨는데요.
남: 제가 경기 장소가 옮겨졌다고 얘기하지 않았나요?
여: 네, 안 하셨어요.
남: 아, 제가 잊었나 보네요. 공사가 4주 걸릴 거라서, 경기가 근처의 경
기장으로 옮겨졌어요.
여: 그러면, 출장을 취소해야 할까요?
남: 물론이지요. 제가 경기에 가지 않으면, 제 아들은 몹시 슬퍼할 거예요.
여: 알겠습니다. Kim 씨에게 대신 갈 수 있는지 확인하겠습니다.

문제 해결

남자는 아들의 경기가 연기되지 않고 다른 경기장에서 진행되기 때문에, 그 경기를 보러 가기 위해서 출장을 취소하겠다고 했다.

어휘·표현

postpone 연기하다   construction 건설, 공사   definitely 틀림없이
heartbroken 비통해 하는, 마음이 찢어지는

08 ④ 언급 유무 파악

여: 여보, 침실의 등이 깜빡이고 있어요.
남: 나도 보여요. 전구를 교체할게요.
여: 이왕 하는 김에, 그것을 LED 전구로 바꾸는 건 어때요?
남: LED 전구요? 그게 뭔데요?
여: LED 전구의 색온도가 5,000K이어서, 매우 밝고 우리 눈에 편안해
요.
남: 좋네요. 게다가 우리 등은 책을 읽기에는 약간 어두웠어요. LED 전
구의 수명은 어떤가요?
여: 정말 길어요. 실제로, 10년까지 사용할 수 있어요.
남: 그러면 LED 전구를 사용하는 것이 경제적으로 가치가 있네요.
여: 물론이지요. 또한, 일반 전구보다 절반의 전기만 사용해요.
남: 왜 사람들이 LED로 바꾸는지 알겠어요. 다른 이점도 있나요?
여: 열을 덜 발산해서, 불을 덜 나게 할 것 같아요.
남: 그러면 바꾸지 않을 이유가 없네요.

문제 해결

LED 전구의 색온도(5,000K), 수명(10년까지 가능), 소비 전력(일반 전구의 절반), 발열 수준(적은 발열)은 언급되었지만, ④ 설치 비용은 언급되지 않았다.

어휘·표현

flicker 깜빡이다   light bulb 전구   temperature 온도   economically 경
제적으로   rewarding 가치가 있는, 보람 있는   switch 바꾸다   benefit 혜택,
이득

09 ④ 담화 내용 불일치

여: 안녕하세요, 저는 Hawaii 기상 센터의 기상 예보관인 Grace입니다.
이번 주말까지는 매우 맑겠습니다만, 다음 주에 태풍이 Hawaii를 강
타하겠습니다. 이번 시즌 19호 태풍인 Typhoon Soulik은 풍속이
115mph 이상이어서 섬들에 엄청난 영향을 끼칠 것입니다. 이 풍속
은 3등급 허리케인과 맞먹는 것입니다. 태풍이 건물과 벽을 파괴할
수 있기 때문에, 태풍이 강타할 때에는 밖에 다니지 않도록 주의하시
기 바랍니다. 또한, 비가 많이 내릴 것이고 지반은 불안정할 수 있기
때문에, 건물 벽 근처에 가지 마시기 바랍니다. 태풍이 절정에 도달할
때 비행기와 배의 사용이 제한될 수 있습니다만, 다음 주 수요일까지
태풍은 점점 약해질 것입니다.

문제 해결

19호 태풍 Soulik은 바람이 매우 강하며, 비도 많이 올 것이라고 하였으므로,
비가 많이 오지 않을 것이라는 ④는 내용과 일치하지 않는다.

어휘·표현

forecaster 기상 요원, 예보관   typhoon 태풍   enormous 엄청난, 거대한
equivalent 동등한, 맞먹는   unstable 불안정한   restrict 제한하다   peak 절
정   steadily 꾸준하게   weaken 약화되다

10 ④ 도표 정보 파악

남: 우리가 드디어 다음 주에 떠나.
여: 맞아. 나는 한겨울에 더운 곳에 가는 것이 너무 흥분돼.
남: 휴대용 선풍기를 사는 게 어때?
여: 좋아. 거기는 정말 더울 수 있어.
남: 이 사이트를 봐봐. [클릭 소리]
여: 다섯 개 제품이 할인 중이네. 어떤 것을 사야 할까?
남: 나는 30달러 이상을 쓰고 싶지는 않아. 그리고 충전 시간은 짧고 사용
시간은 긴 것을 사자.
여: 그렇지만 충전과 사용 시간 조건을 동시에 만족시키는 것은 어려워.
남: 알았어. 사용 시간이 제일 긴 것으로 사자. 밤 동안 충전할 수 있잖아.
여: 그렇다면, 우리는 이 두 개의 제품 중에서 하나를 고를 수 있어.
남: 나는 더 비싸더라도 더 가벼운 것이 좋아.
여: 맞아. 이것을 지금 주문하자.

문제 해결

두 사람은 30달러를 넘지 않고 사용 시간이 제일 긴 휴대용 선풍기 중에서 더
가벼운 모델을 사려고 하고 있기 때문에, 두 사람이 구입할 휴대용 선풍기는 ④
이다.

어휘·표현

portable 휴대용의   charging time 충전 시간   usage 사용, 이용

11 ⑤ 짧은 대화의 응답

남: 저는 이름들이 때론 매우 비슷해서, 전화기의 주소록에 있는 사람이
누구인지를 기억하기가 어려워요.
여: 그것이 제가 항상 전화기에 사람들을 저장할 때 그들의 직업을 적는

이유예요.

남: 좋은 생각이네요. 조언이 더 있을까요?

여: <u>그들의 신체적인 특징도 적을 수 있어요.</u>

사람들의 이름을 더 잘 기억할 수 있는 방법에 대해서 언급하는 ⑤가 여자의 응답으로 가장 적절하다.

① 당신의 휴대 전화에 제 전화번호를 저장했나요?

② 저는 사람들의 직업을 저장하는 것이 좋지 않다고 생각해요.

③ 저는 사람들의 이름을 기억하는 것이 항상 어려워요.

④ 제 이름과 직업을 기억하실 필요 없어요.

occupation 직업 make a note 메모하다, 기록하다 characteristic 특징

12 ⑤

여: 안녕, Jeff. 어디 가고 있어?

남: 나는 학교에 가는 길이야. 나 방금 학교 기숙사에서 살 수 있다고 통지받았어.

여: 정말? 좋은 소식이구나! 기분이 어때?

남: 난 항상 거기에서 살고 싶었기 때문에 기뻐.

기숙사에 살 수 있다는 통지를 받은 사람에게 기분이 어떤지 물었으므로 그 응답으로 가장 적절한 것은 ⑤이다.

① 나는 약 20분 전에 그것을 들었어.

② 솔직히 말하면, 너는 오늘 매우 피곤해 보여.

③ 나는 학교 기숙사에 들어가는 것이 힘들다고 생각해.

④ 사실, 나는 학교에서 너무 멀리 떨어져 살고 있지 않아.

dormitory 기숙사 to be honest 솔직히 말하자면

13 ①

여: 여보, 새로운 학교는 어때요?

남: 다른 선생님들은 친절해요. 학생들은 긍정적이고 적극적이에요. 그리고, 저는 전자 화이트보드가 정말 마음에 들어요.

여: 전자 화이트보드요? 그건 보통의 칠판과는 어떻게 다른가요?

남: 칠판 전체를 컴퓨터 화면으로 사용할 수 있어요.

여: 와! 큰 화면에 당신의 교육용 자료를 보여 줄 수 있다는 말인가요?

남: 네. 더 놀라운 것은, 간단히 버튼 한 번만 누르면, 전체 화면이 큰 터치 패드가 돼.

여: 터치 패드요? 칠판을 누르기만 하면 파일을 열 수 있어요?

남: 물론이지요. 심지어 동영상도 보여 주고, 그 위에다 필기를 할 수도 있어요.

여: 환상적이네요. 더 얘기해 줘요.

남: 화면이 매우 밝아서 낮에도 불을 끌 필요가 없어요.

여: 멋지네요! 어떻게 사용하는지 배우는 건 쉽나요?

남: <u>네, 매우 간단해서, 10분이면 충분해요.</u>

여자가 전자 화이트보드 사용법을 배우는 것이 쉬운지 물어봤으므로, 남자의 응답으로 ① '네, 매우 간단해서 10분이면 충분해요.'라고 답하는 것이 가장 적절하다.

② 내 마음에 들지 않는 유일한 것이 그것의 높은 가격이에요.

③ 그건 정말 학생들이 수업에 집중하는 데 도움이 돼요.

④ 하지만 그건 다양한 기능이 있어요.

⑤ 학생들은 그 화이트보드에 매우 만족하고 있어요.

electronic 전자의 teaching material 교육용 자료 click (마우스를) 클릭하다, 누르다 video clip 동영상 sufficient 충분한

14 ⑤

여: 여보, 내일 시간 좀 있어요?

남: 물론이지요. 왜 물어봐요?

여: Olivia를 위해 스마트폰을 사러 같이 갈 수 있어요?

남: 그녀가 그게 왜 필요해요? 그녀는 겨우 7살이잖아요

여: 그 아이가 초등학교 입학 선물로 그것을 원해요.

남: 저는 그녀가 그것을 갖기에는 너무 어리다고 생각해요.

여: 하지만 그녀가 학교에 있는 동안에 우리가 그녀를 따라다닐 수는 없어요. 그것이 없다면 우리가 그녀와 어떻게 연락을 할 수 있어요?

남: 당신 말이 맞을 수도 있겠네요.

여: 나는 비상 상황에 대해서도 걱정이에요. 그녀가 길을 잃는다면 어떻해요?

남: 하지만 나는 그녀가 스마트폰을 너무 많이 할까 봐 걱정이에요.

여: 그녀는 스마트폰을 하루에 한 시간 이상 쓰지 않겠다고 약속했어요. 그리고 나는 그녀가 우리의 도움으로 좋은 스마트폰 이용 습관을 배울 수 있다고 생각해요.

남: 당신 말이 맞아요. 하지만 그녀가 약속을 지킬 수 있다고 생각해요?

여: <u>네. 나는 그 점에서 그녀를 믿어요.</u>

남자가 딸이 스마트폰을 하루에 한 시간만 사용할 것이라는 약속을 지킬 것이라고 생각하는지 아내에게 묻고 있으므로, 여자의 응답으로 ⑤ '네. 나는 그 점에서 그녀를 믿어요.'가 가장 적절하다.

① 네, 그녀는 우리 선물을 좋아할 거예요.

② 네. 그녀에게 다른 선물을 사 주는 건 어때요?

③ 당신은 제가 좋은 습관을 들이는 것을 많이 도와주셨어요.

④ 그녀가 당신에게 뭔가를 약속했나요?

contact 연락하다 be concerned about ~을 염려하다
emergency 비상(사태)

15 ③

남: 오늘은 새 학년의 첫날이고, Vincent는 담임 선생님과 새로운 학급 친구들을 처음으로 만난다. 그의 선생님은 학생들 모두가 학급 규칙을 함께 만들자는 제안을 한다. 다양한 의견들이 나오고, 많은 것들에 대해 이야기를 나눈 후에, 그들은 교실 청소에 대한 규칙을 만들기 시작한다. 학생들 중 한 명이 매일 다른 사람이 교실을 청소하자고 제안한다. 다른 학생은 모두가 교실을 하루에 두 번씩 청소하자고 제안한다. 그러나 Vincent는 모두가 자신들의 책상과 주변을 항상 깨끗하게 해야 한다고 생각한다. 이 상황에서, Vincent가 학급 친구들에게 뭐라고 할 것 같은가?

Vincent가 학급 친구들에게 자신이 생각하는 청소 방법을 제안하고 싶어하므

로, Vincent가 할 말로 ③ '나는 우리가 자기 자리를 항상 깨끗하게 해야 한다고 제안해.'가 가장 적절하다.

① 우리 교실을 청소하기 위한 규칙을 만드는 게 좋아.
② 나는 적어도 하루에 두 번씩 우리가 교실을 청소해야 한다고 생각해.
④ 어떻게 우리가 항상 교실을 깨끗하게 유지할 수 있을까?
⑤ 교실을 청소하는 것은 다른 어떤 것보다 더 중요해.

어휘·표현
surroundings 환경, 주변   neat 깔끔한

16-17
복합 이해

여: 좋은 오후입니다. 저는 소말리아에 있는 Virus Research Center의 수석 연구원인 Amelia입니다. 저는 말라리아와 강수량의 관계에 대한 제 연구 결과를 설명하겠습니다. 관련 없어 보이겠지만, 그것들은 사실 강하게 연결되어 있습니다. 저는 소말리아의 5개 지역에서 말라리아에 걸린 10,000명의 사람들을 연구했고, 강수량이 말라리아 확산에 영향을 준다는 결론에 도달했습니다. 데이터에, 성별, 나이, 체중, 지역 같은 참가자들에 대한 기본 정보가 나타나 있습니다. 여러분께서 데이터에서 보시듯이, 비가 많이 왔을 때 더 많은 사람들이 말라리아에 걸렸습니다. 여러분이 모기가 말라리아의 주요 원인이라는 것을 아신다면, 왜 그런지를 추측할 수 있을 것입니다. 모기의 유충은 증가된 강우량으로 만들어진 물웅덩이에서 삽니다. 그래서 우리는 비와 말라리아가 상관관계가 높다는 것을 알 수 있습니다. 물론, 이 연구는 다섯 개의 지역에서만 행해졌기 때문에 제한적입니다. 그러나 연구는 우리가 가능하다면 이 물웅덩이를 제거할 필요가 있다는 것을 보여 줍니다.

어휘·표현
rainfall 강우   unrelated 관련이 없는   contract (병에) 걸리다   region 지역
conclusion 결론   display 전시하다, 보여 주다   puddle 물웅덩이
correlate 연관성[상관관계]이 있다

16 ①
문제 해결
여자는 모기의 유충이 물웅덩이에서 살기 때문에 강우량과 말라리아가 상관관계가 높다고 말하고 있으므로, 여자의 말의 주제로 ① '강우와 말라리아의 관련성'이 가장 적절하다.
② 새로운 말라리아 백신 소개
③ 충분한 물 공급 유지의 혜택
④ 말라리아의 원인을 조사하라는 요구
⑤ 강수량 감소의 해결책

17 ④
문제 해결
데이터에는 피실험자의 성별, 나이, 체중과 지역에 대한 정보가 나와 있다고 했지만, 직업에 대해서는 언급하지 않았다.

01 ②	02 ①	03 ③	04 ④	05 ③	06 ④
07 ④	08 ④	09 ④	10 ③	11 ②	12 ①
13 ⑤	14 ②	15 ②	16 ①	17 ④	

01 ②
목적 파악

남: 안녕하세요, 여러분. 저는 NASA의 수석 연구원, Peter입니다. 저는 여러분 모두가 우주 여행 가는 것을 꿈꿔 왔다고 확신합니다. 어떤 과학자들은 단지 10년 안에 사람들이 우주 호텔에서 머무를 수 있을 것이라고 믿고 있습니다. 하지만 여러분은 우주로 여행을 가기 위해서 10년을 기다릴 필요가 없습니다. 이 다큐멘터리는 여러분이 직접 우주를 여행하는 것 같은 경험을 하게 합니다. 여러분은 우주 임무를 수행 중인 실제 우주선들이 찍은 믿을 수 없는 사진들과 영상들을 많이 보게 될 것입니다. 이것은 일생의 기회가 될 것이라 확신합니다. 그러니 이번 주 일요일 오후 10시에 7번 채널을 꼭 틀어 주세요. 이 환상적인 여행을 놓치지 마세요!

문제 해결
남자는 이번 주 일요일 저녁 채널 7번에서 하는 다큐멘터리를 사람들에게 홍보하고 있다.

어휘·표현
chief researcher 수석 연구원   a number of 많은   incredible 믿을 수 없는, 믿기 힘든   space craft 우주선   tune in 채널을 맞추다, (라디오·텔레비전 프로를) 청취(시청)하다

02 ①
주제 파악

여: 뭘 읽고 있어요, 여보?
남: 학교 교육 과정에 관한 기사를 읽고 있어요.
여: 좀 더 구체적으로 말해 줄래요?
남: 고등학교에서 역사 수업을 늘려야 할지에 대한 거예요.
여: 난 그게 좋은 아이디어라고 생각해요.
남: 정말요? 학생들은 이미 매 주마다 세 시간씩 역사를 배워요. 그것이 충분하다고 생각하지 않아요?
여: 음, 나는 역사를 이해하는 것이 수학이나 다른 언어를 배우는 것만큼 중요하다고 생각해요.
남: 하지만 많은 사람들은 역사보다는 문학이나 수학을 더 중요하게 여기곤 해요.
여: 이런 속담이 있잖아요. '과거를 잊은 민족에게 미래는 없다.' 학생들은 현재가 과거의 결과라는 것을 알 필요가 있어요.
남: 당신 말이 맞아요.
여: 고마워요. 나는 우리가 아무리 해도 역사를 충분히 배울 수 없다고 생각해요.

문제 해결
여자는 역사를 이해하는 것이 중요하다며 역사 수업을 늘려야 한다고 말하고 있다.

어휘·표현
curriculum 교육 과정   mathematics 수학   literature 문학

renovation 수리

여: 안녕하세요, 저는 Jean Cruise입니다. 어제 전화드렸어요.

남: 아, 만나서 반갑습니다, Cruise 씨. 자리에 앉으세요.

여: 감사합니다. 저는 저희 어머니가 지낼 장소를 찾고 있습니다. 제 친구들 중 하나가 저에게 이 센터를 소개했어요.

남: 제대로 찾아오셨습니다. 저희는 좋은 시설과 훌륭한 의료진을 갖추고 있습니다.

여: 그 말을 들으니 안심이 되네요.

남: 어머니의 상태를 좀 더 자세하게 설명해 주시겠어요?

여: 어머니는 80세입니다. 특정 음식은 잘 소화하지 못하세요.

남: 그건 걱정하지 마세요. 저희 영양사는 각 환자에 맞게 식사를 준비해서 제공합니다.

여: 좋네요. 그녀는 또한 무릎 통증으로 고생하고 있어서, 거의 못 걸으십니다. 거의 하루 종일 침대에 누워 계세요.

남: 저희 치료사가 그녀로 하여금 매일 30분씩 운동하도록 도울 겁니다. 또한, 그녀는 매달 건강 검진을 받을 것이고, 당신께 결과를 알려 드리겠습니다.

여: 좋습니다. 오늘 이 센터로 어머니를 모시고 와야겠습니다.

남: 틀림없이 여기 계시는 것을 좋아하실 겁니다.

문제 해결
여자는 어머니가 지낼 곳을 찾고 있다고 했고, 남자는 센터의 시설과 의료진에 대해서 설명하며, 여자의 어머니의 상태를 자세하게 확인하고 있다. 마지막에 여자가 어머니를 모시고 오겠다고 하고 있는 것으로 보아, 두 사람은 보호자와 요양원 직원의 관계이다.

어휘·표현
reside 살다, 거주하다   facility 시설   relieve 안심하게 하다   digest 소화하다   nutritionist 영양사   arrange 준비하다, 마련하다   be confined to ~에 틀어박혀 있다, 갇혀 있다   therapist 치료사   medical checkup 건강 검진   notify 알리다

남: 안녕, Nancy. 방학 어땠어?

여: 좋았어. 나는 가족들과 해변에 갔어. 여기 우리 사진이야.

남: 아름다운 해변이네!

여: 오른쪽 위에서 패러세일링을 하는 사람이 나야.

남: 멋지다! 아, 나는 중앙에 있는 사람들처럼 바다에서 수영하고 싶어.

여: 응, 재미있지. 하지만 너는 그들처럼 항상 튜브를 사용해야 해.

남: 왼쪽에 있는 이건 뭐야? 배처럼 생겼어.

여: 사실, 그건 식당이야. 옆에 '이탈리아 식당'이라고 써 있는 간판이 보이지.

남: 거기에서 먹어 봤어?

여: 안타깝게도, 못 먹어 봤어. 수리하느라 문을 닫았거든.

남: 네 남동생들이 이 사진에 있어?

여: 오른쪽 아래를 봐. 그들은 큰 모래성을 만들고 있어.

남: 응, 이제 그들이 보이네.

문제 해결
대화에서 식당 옆에 '이탈리아 식당'이라고 쓰인 간판이 있다고 했으므로, 그림 속 '프랑스 식당'이라고 쓰인 간판은 대화와 일치하지 않는다.

어휘·표현
parasail 패러세일링을 하다, (모터보트 등으로 끄는) 낙하산을 타다

여: 아빠, 이 상자에 뭐가 있어요?

남: 그건 네 방에 넣을 침대 틀이야.

여: 하지만 이 상자는 충분히 커 보이지 않는데요.

남: 내가 DIY용 침대 틀을 주문해서 그래.

여: 직접 조립하는 침대 틀이요? 정말 그것을 직접 조립하실 수 있으세요?

남: 물론이지. 설명서에 단계별로 어떻게 조립하는지를 보여 주는 사진들이 있어.

여: 쉬운 것 같지만, 사진이 상당히 복잡해 보여요. 전문가를 불러서 조립하는 게 어때요?

남: 걱정 마라. 내가 할 수 있어. 이 판들에다가 나사들을 몇 개 끼우고 모두 연결하기만 하면 돼.

여: 그렇게 말씀하시면요, 뭐. 제가 빈 상자들을 버릴까요?

남: 아냐. 끝내고 나서 내가 치울게.

여: 제가 도와드릴 일이 있을까요?

남: 물론이지. 판자에 이 나사들을 끼워 줄래?

여: 알겠어요.

문제 해결
남자는 여자에게 판자에 나사를 끼워 달라고 부탁하였다.

어휘·표현
frame 틀   put together 조립하다   instruction 설명서   step-by-step 단계별의   handle 처리하다   insert 끼우다   screw 나사   throw away 버리다

여: 안녕하세요, 도와드릴까요?

남: 네. 제 플래시 드라이브에 있는 파일을 출력하고 싶어요.

여: 알겠습니다. 파일을 흑백 또는 컬러로 출력할 수 있습니다. 어느 것을 더 선호하시나요?

남: 비용이 얼마인지 말씀해 주시겠어요?

여: 흑백은 쪽당 10센트이고, 컬러는 쪽당 50센트입니다.

남: 알겠습니다. 그러면 과학 보고서를 흑백으로 출력해 주세요. 보고서는 15페이지입니다.

여: 알겠습니다. 다른 것은요?

남: 역사 보고서도 있어요. 그 보고서는 컬러로 출력해 주세요.

여: 역사 보고서는 몇 쪽이죠?

남: 모두 10쪽입니다. 모두 얼마를 지불해야 하나요?

여: 잠시만 기다려 주세요. 제가 전부 합산해 보겠습니다.

문제 해결
쪽당 가격이 10센트인 흑백 출력을 15쪽, 쪽당 가격이 50센트인 컬러 출력을 10쪽 해 달라고 하였으므로, 남자가 지불할 총 금액은 6달러 50센트이다. 100센트는 1달러이다. ($1=￠100)

어휘·표현
flash drive 플래시 드라이브   consist of ~로 이루어지다   add up 합산하다

여: Ayden, 네 회사에서 다음 주 금요일에 과학 캠프를 여는 게 맞지?

남: 그러려고 했지만, 그 캠프는 다음 달로 연기되었어.

여: 어? 나는 네가 지난 달에 그 캠프 장소를 예약했다고 생각했는데.

남: 했었지. 게다가 난 그 장소가 너무 좋았어.

여: 그러면 NASA에서 초청 강사를 부르는 데 문제가 있었어?

남: 아냐. Luther 박사는 캠프에서 강의를 하겠다고 했어.

여: 그러면 뭐가 문제였어?

남: 사실, 캠프를 신청한 학생의 수가 충분하지 않았어. 우린 홍보할 시간이 더 필요해.

여: 그래. 학생 수가 부족하면 재정적인 문제가 생길 거야.

남: 다행히도 Luther 박사가 우리 상황을 이해해 주었고, 우린 캠프를 한 달 연기했어.

여: 정말 다행이다.

문제 해결

남자는 신청한 학생 수가 부족해 신청 인원을 채울 수 있도록 캠프를 홍보할 시간이 필요해 캠프를 연기했다고 했다.

어휘·표현

postpone 연기하다   reservation 예약   guest lecturer 초청 강사
advertise 광고하다, 홍보하다   financial 재정의   fortunate 운이 좋은

08 ④
언급 유무 파악

남: 여보, 이제 곧 George의 생일이에요.

여: 맞아요. 그를 위해 뭔가 의미 있는 것을 하는 게 어때요?

남: 뭐라도 생각한 게 있나요?

여: 그는 몇 달 동안 Louise Safety Theme Park에 가고 싶다고 얘기해왔어요. 그곳이 많은 첨단 시설들을 갖추고 있대요.

남: 그 공원은 나이 제한이 있나요?

여: 아니요, 전 연령 입장 가능해요.

남: George가 거기서 어떤 종류의 것들을 할 수 있어요?

여: 그게, 그는 4D 시뮬레이션으로 지진 활동을 정말로 체험하고 싶어해요.

남: 좋네요! 재미있고 교육적일 것 같아요. 그 공원은 어디에 있나요?

여: 여기에서는 좀 멀어요. Louisville에 있어요.

남: 적어도 차로 2시간은 걸리겠네요.

여: 맞아요. 하지만 도시에서 그 공원을 운영하고 있기 때문에 입장료가 무료예요.

남: 잘됐네요. 이번 토요일에 갑시다.

여: 그곳은 오전 10시에 열어요. 8시에 집에서 출발하는 게 어때요?

남: 그래요. 내가 George에게 좋은 소식을 전할게요.

문제 해결

테마파크의 연령 제한(전 연령 가능), 위치(Louisville 내), 입장료(무료), 개장 시간(오전 10시)에 대해서는 언급했지만, 수용 인원에 대해서는 언급하지 않았다.

어휘·표현

age limit 나이 제한   earthquake 지진   entrance fee 입장료
manage 운영하다

09 ④
담화 내용 불일치

여: 안녕하세요, 여러분. Pacific 대학에 오신 것을 환영합니다. 저는 행정 부장인 Emilia입니다. 저는 여러분에게 Pacific 대학의 장학금 제도를 소개하려고 합니다. 우리는 두 가지 종류의 장학금이 있습니다.

첫째, 높은 성적을 유지한 학생들을 위한 것입니다. 4.0 이상의 평균 점수를 받고 최소 14학점을 마친 학생들은 다음 학기에 전액 장학금을 받게 됩니다. 둘째, 다른 장학금은 학교를 위해 일한 사람들을 위한 것입니다. 학생들이 도서관이나 실험실에서 하루에 두 시간 동안 일한다면, 그들은 등록금의 절반에 해당하는 장학금을 받게 됩니다. 여러분은 오늘부터 시작하여 2주 동안 이 장학금들을 신청할 수 있습니다. 최대한 많은 학생들이 이 혜택을 받을 수 있도록, 학생들은 한 종류의 장학금만 받을 수 있습니다. 마지막으로, 학교 교칙을 어긴 학생들은 장학금에서 제외될 수 있습니다. 감사합니다.

문제 해결

최대한 많은 학생들이 장학금 혜택을 받을 수 있도록 학생들은 한 종류의 장학금만 받을 수 있다고 했으므로, 두 종류의 장학금을 한꺼번에 받을 수 있다고 한 ④는 내용과 일치하지 않는다.

어휘·표현

administration 행정, 관리   scholarship 장학금   maintain 유지하다
full scholarship 전액 장학금   lab 실험실   tuition 수업료, 등록금   exclude
제외하다

10 ③
도표 정보 파악

여: Power Electronics에 오신 것을 환영합니다.

남: 안녕하세요, 저는 아들에게 줄 졸업 선물을 찾고 있습니다.

여: 요즈음엔 게임기와 스마트폰이 인기 있습니다.

남: 저는 지난달에 그에게 스마트폰을 사 줬기 때문에, 게임기를 보여 주세요.

여: 그러면 이 카탈로그를 보세요. 저희는 다섯 개의 모델을 갖고 있습니다. 그것들의 기능에 따라 가격은 다양합니다.

남: 많은 사람들이 함께 하려면 텔레비전과 연결해야 합니다. 제 아들은 친구들하고 게임하는 것을 좋아해요. 4인용 게임기가 필요해요.

여: 휴대용 게임기는 어떻습니까? 그럼 어디에서도 게임을 할 수 있지요.

남: 아니요, 괜찮아요. 저는 그가 내내 게임을 하길 원하진 않아요.

여: 그런 경우라면, 우리에게는 두 가지 선택이 있네요.

남: 저는 더 싼 것을 고르겠어요. 200달러 이상을 쓰고 싶지는 않아요.

여: 선택 잘 하셨습니다.

남: 그것을 포장해 주실 수 있나요?

여: 물론이지요.

문제 해결

남자는 텔레비전과 연결할 수 있고 4명이 함께 할 수 있지만 휴대는 할 수 없으며, 가격이 200달러 이하의 게임기를 사려고 하므로, 남자가 구입할 게임기는 ③이다.

어휘·표현

game console 게임기   catalogue 카탈로그, 목록   function 기능
vary 서로 다르다   portable 휴대할 수 있는   wrap up 포장하다, 싸다

11 ②
짧은 대화의 응답

여: Mark, 왜 이렇게 늦었어? 영화가 이미 시작했잖아.

남: 정말 미안해. 여기 오는 길에 심한 교통 체증이 있었어.

여: 너는 항상 늦잖아. 더 일찍 나오는 게 어때?

남: 알았어. 다음에는 30분 일찍 출발할게.

약속 시간에 항상 늦는 남자에게 여자가 더 일찍 나올 것을 제안하고 있으므로, 앞으로는 30분 일찍 나오겠다고 말하는 ②가 남자의 응답으로 가장 적절하다.

① 좋아. 나는 바로 몇 분 전에 도착했어.

③ 문제 없어. 나는 너를 오후 3시에 만나기로 했잖아.

④ 네 말이 맞아. 나는 오늘 널 만나는 것을 잊어버렸어.

⑤ 맞아. 나는 심한 교통 체증에 질렸어.

어휘·표현

traffic jam 교통 체증   **be supposed to** ~하기로 되어 있다
have a point 일리가 있다

12 ①

남: 내일 수학여행 짐은 쌌니?

여: 거의 다 했어요. 날씨만 확인하면 돼요.

남: 일기 예보에서 하늘에 구름 한 점 없이 화창할 거라고 하더라.

여: 그러면, 우산을 챙길 필요는 없네요.

문제 해결

남자가 날씨가 맑을 것이라고 했으므로, 우산을 챙길 필요가 없겠다고 말하는 ①이 여자의 응답으로 가장 적절하다.

② 대신 비옷을 챙기는 게 낫겠어요.

③ 집에 오는 길에 새 가방을 사야겠어요.

④ 저를 위해 오늘의 날씨를 확인해 주시겠어요?

⑤ 정말이요? 좀 더 따뜻한 옷으로 바꿔야겠어요.

어휘·표현

pack (짐을) 싸다   **weather forecast** 일기 예보

13 ⑤

[휴대 전화벨이 울린다.]

남: 안녕, Rachel.

여: 안녕, Julian. 너를 본 지 오래 되었구나. 어떻게 지냈어?

남: 나는 너무 바빠서 한동안 독서 동아리에 나갈 수 없었어. 난 기말고사 를 준비해야 했거든.

여: 사실 나는 너에게 부탁을 하려고 전화한 건데, 바쁘다면 괜찮아.

남: 괜찮아. 부탁해도 돼.

여: 음, 내가 인터넷으로 동영상을 보고 있었는데, 갑자기 컴퓨터가 꺼지 더니 다시 켜지지 않아.

남: 전원 선은 확인해 봤어?

여: 응, 했어. 그리고 모니터 선도 확인했어. 잘못된 것이 없었어.

남: 전원 버튼은 눌러 봤어?

여: 응, 했지만, 소용없었어.

남: 그러면, 그건 메인보드의 문제일 수 있어. 내가 가서 확인해야겠다.

여: 정말 미안한데, 우리 집에 올 시간이 있어?

남: 물론이지. 내가 집에 가는 길에 들를게.

문제 해결

남자가 여자의 컴퓨터를 점검하기 위해 직접 가서 봐야겠다고 했으므로, 시간이 있는지 묻는 여자의 말에 집에 가는 길에 들르겠다고 말하는 ⑤가 응답으로 가장 적절하다.

① 네가 중고를 사면 더 쌀 거야.

② 나는 새로운 첨단 컴퓨터를 방금 샀어.

③ 알았어. 언제 우리 집에 도착해?

④ 나는 네가 전원 선을 교체하는 걸 추천해.

어휘·표현

power cable 전원 선   **work** 효과가 있다   **drop by** 들르다

14 ②

남: 여보, 당신에게 오늘 많은 우편물이 왔어요.

여: 고마워요, Vincent. 나는 고객으로부터 편지를 기다리고 있는 중이 었어요.

남: 그것들은 대부분 상업용 광고들이에요. 하지만 저는 이 우편물이 중 요해 보인다고 생각해요.

여: 어떤 걸 말하는 거예요?

남: 보건부에서 온 우편이요.

여: 열어 봐 줘요. 뭐라고 써 있어요?

남: 당신이 정기 건강 검진을 받아야 할 때래요.

여: 벌써요? 어떤 검사들을 받을 수 있어요?

남: 혈액 검사, X-ray, 그리고 초음파 검사 같은 다양한 검사들을 받을 수 있어요. 당신은 이번에 검사를 받아 봐야 해요.

여: 그러고 싶지만, 너무 바빠요. 다음 달 중순까지 프로젝트를 마무리해 야 해요.

남: 괜찮아요. 당신의 검진 기간은 다음 달 말까지라고 적혀 있어요. 프로 젝트를 끝내고 나서 갈 수 있어요. 건강한 것이 당신의 삶에서 가장 중요한 거예요.

여: 당신 말이 맞아요. 꼭 가서 검사받을게요.

문제 해결

너무 바빠서 건강 검진을 받을 수 없다는 여자에게 남자는 건강이 가장 중요하 다며 건강 검진 받을 것을 권하고 있다. 따라서 여자의 응답으로 꼭 가서 검진을 받겠다는 ②가 가장 적절하다.

① 초음파 촬영은 돈이 많이 들어요.

③ 동의해요. 당신은 건강을 챙겨야 해요.

④ 저는 아직도 고객으로부터의 편지를 기다리고 있어요.

⑤ 제게 심각한 건강상의 문제가 있다고 의사가 말했어요.

어휘·표현

client 의뢰인   **mostly** 대개   **commercial** 상업적인   **advertisement** 광고
ministry (정부의 각) 부처   **regular** 정기적인   **examination** 검사   **eligible**
~을 할 수 있는   **ultrasound** 초음파   **definitely** 틀림없이

15 ②

남: Kelly와 Edward는 매우 가까운 동료이다. 최근에, Edward는 자신 의 사업을 시작하기 위해 직장을 그만두었다. 시장 조사를 한 후에, 그는 두 개의 사업을 정한다. 한 사업은 젊은 세대에서 이미 인기 있 다. 다른 사업은 전도유망하지만, Edward에게는 완전히 낯선 사업 이다. 오랜 시간 고심한 끝에, Edward는 더 검증되었고 안전하기 때 문에 젊은 세대를 겨냥한 사업을 하기로 결심한다. 그러나 Kelly는 그 사업의 시장이 이미 포화 상태이고 더 이상 큰 이익을 만들어 내지 못할 것이라고 생각한다. 그녀는 그에게 어려움이 있더라도 새로운 시장을 개척할 잠재력이 있는 사업을 선택하게 하고 싶어 한다. 이 상 황에서, Kelly가 Edward에게 뭐라고 할 것 같은가?

문제 해결

Kelly는 Edward에게 시장이 포화되어 더 이상 이익을 내기 어려운 사업보다 는 어려움이 있더라도 새로운 시장을 개척할 잠재력이 있는 사업을 선택하라고

제안하려고 하므로, ② '새로운 시장을 개척할 수 있는 사업을 해 보는 게 어때?'가 Edward에게 할 말로 가장 적절하다.

① 다시 직장으로 돌아가는 건 어때? 내가 그걸 할 수 있도록 도울게.
③ 나는 검증된 사업이 큰 이익을 보장해 준다고 생각해.
④ 이렇게 어려운 시기에 사업을 시작하는 것은 네 생각만큼 쉽지 않아.
⑤ 잘 생각해 보고 행동해! 너는 시장 조사를 더 많이 해야 해.

어휘·표현

colleague 동료 generation 세대 promising 전도유망한
consideration 심사숙고 proven 입증된 profit 이익 potential 가능성이
있는, 잠재적인 challenge 도전, 어려움

16-17   복합 이해

여: 안녕하세요, 저는 국립 심리 센터의 Margaret입니다. 여러분은 특별한 이유 없이 편안하거나 불안함을 느낀 적이 있습니까? 만약 있다면, 당신은 주변의 색깔들에 영향을 받은 것일 수 있습니다. 색깔들은 강력한 전달자들이어서, 기분뿐만 아니라 상태나 행동에도 영향을 미칩니다. 어떤 색깔은 혈압을 낮출 수도 있고, 다른 색깔은 당신의 바이오리듬을 높일 수도 있습니다. 색의 힘에 대하여 자세하게 알아봅시다. 노란색은 우리를 따뜻하고 편안하게 만듭니다. 그렇지만 너무 지나치면 우리를 매우 예민하게 만들 수도 있습니다. 파란색은 우리를 차분하고 침착하게 만들지만 때때로 무관심하거나 냉소적으로 만듭니다. 많은 사람들이 알고 있듯이, 빨간색은 우리를 매우 흥분되고 활동적으로 만들기 때문에, 우리가 목표에 집중하도록 돕습니다. 마지막으로, 하얀색은 우리를 솔직하고 긍정적으로 만들지만, 너무 오랫동안 볼 때에는 지루하고 지칠 수 있습니다. 이제, 여러분은 색의 힘을 통해 여러분 자신을 통제할 수 있습니다. 예를 들면, 여러분이 무언가를 분석하고 싶을 때, 파란색을 보는 것이 도움이 될 수 있습니다. 여러분은 바로 지금 어떤 색깔을 가장 필요로 하나요?

어휘·표현

psychology 심리 messenger 전달자 blood pressure 혈압 sensitive
예민한 cool 침착한 indifferent 무관심한 cynical 냉소적인 weary 지친
analyze 분석하다

16 ①

문제 해결

여자는 색이 사람들의 기분, 상태, 행동 등에 미치는 영향에 대하여 이야기하고 있다.
① 색이 사람들에게 미치는 영향
② 건강에 대한 강력한 영향
③ 성공을 위한 좋은 습관들의 중요성
④ 다른 사람들의 행동을 통제하는 방법들
⑤ 색과 냄새 사이의 관계

17 ④

문제 해결

여자는 노란색, 파란색, 빨간색, 하얀색에 대해 언급했지만, 검은색에 대해서는 언급하지 않았다.

---

23 영어 듣기 모의고사 고난도 ▶ pp. 50-51

01 ③	02 ⑤	03 ②	04 ⑤	05 ⑤	06 ②
07 ②	08 ④	09 ⑤	10 ②	11 ⑤	12 ②
13 ②	14 ③	15 ②	16 ⑤	17 ④	

01 ③   목적 파악

여: 좋은 저녁입니다, 청취자 여러분. 저는 주중 저녁 7시부터 9시까지 하는 라디오 프로그램, Good Evening Culture의 진행자 Carol입니다. 오늘을 시작으로, '누구인지 맞혀 보세요'라는 새 코너를 합니다. 새 코너에서, 저는 문화적으로 중요한 유명 인사에 대한 몇 가지 사실들을 언급할 것입니다. 그러면 여러분, 청취자들이 그 또는 그녀가 누구인지 맞히면 됩니다. '누구인지 맞혀 보세요'를 시작해 보겠습니다. 이 사람은 1564년 4월 26일에 태어났습니다. 그는 영국의 시인이자 극작가로, 역사상 가장 위대한 작가들 중의 한 사람으로 널리 평가받습니다. 누구인지 맞힐 수 있겠나요? 좋아요. 계속하죠. 그의 주요 작품들로는 'Hamlet', 'Lear왕', 'Macbeth', 그리고 'Romeo와 Juliet'이 있습니다. 여러분 대부분이 지금 짐작한 것처럼, 정답은 William Shakespeare입니다. 저는 이 새 코너가 여러분에게 유명한 사람들에 대한 지식을 시험하는 좋은 기회를 줄 것이라고 생각합니다. 이 코너에 대한 어떤 제안이나 생각이 있으시다면, 우리 웹사이트의 질의응답 게시판에 메시지를 남겨 주세요.

문제 해결

여자는 '누구인지 맞혀 보세요'라는 새로운 코너를 소개하며, 청취자들에게 문제도 내고, 해당 코너에 대한 제안이 있으면 게시판에 남겨 달라고 부탁하고 있다. 따라서 여자가 하는 말의 목적으로 ③ '새롭게 시작하는 라디오 코너를 소개하려고'가 가장 적절하다

어휘·표현

host 진행자 segment 부분, 조각 mention 언급하다 culturally 문화적으로 significant 중요한 celebrity 유명 인사 playwright 극작가

02 ⑤   주제 파악

여: 여보, 나는 우리가 얘기할 필요가 있다고 생각해요.
남: 무슨 문제가 있나요?
여: Grace가 내게 소셜 미디어 계정을 만들고 싶다고 얘기했지만, 나는 어떻게 응답해야 할지 모르겠어요.
남: 소셜 미디어요? 나는 법으로 14세 미만의 어린이들이 계정을 만드는 것을 금지시켰다고 생각했어요.
여: 맞아요. 그런데 부모의 동의가 있으면 계정을 만들 수 있어요.
남: 그녀는 왜 그것을 만들고 싶어 하나요?
여: 그녀는 거기에 자신의 사진들을 올리고 싶어 해요. 하지만 나는 그녀가 소셜 미디어상의 해롭고 부정적인 자료들에 노출될까 봐 걱정이에요.
남: 그런 것들이 일어나기 전에 걱정해 봤자 소용없어요. 나는 그녀가 소셜 미디어를 사용하는 게 나쁘지 않다고 생각해요. 그런 방식으로 친구들과 소통할 수 있잖아요.
여: 정말 그렇게 생각해요?
남: 그래요. 요새는 대부분의 아이들이 소셜 미디어를 사용해서 서로 소통하고 그것으로부터 최신 정보들을 얻어요.

여: 이제야 그녀가 계정을 만들려는 이유를 이해하겠어요.

요즘 아이들이 소셜 미디어를 통해 친구들과 서로 대화하고 최신 정보를 얻는다고 하는 말에서 남자가 딸이 소셜 미디어 계정을 만드는 것의 필요성을 알고 이해하고 있음을 알 수 있다.

account 계정   **ban** 금지하다   **consent** 동의   **expose** 노출시키다
latest 최신의

03 ② 관계 추론

남: 안녕하세요. 어디로 가시나요?
여: 공항으로 가 주세요. 신용 카드를 받으시나요?
남: 물론이지요. 당신의 가방을 트렁크에 넣어 드릴까요?
여: 감사합니다만, 조심해 주세요. 속에 든 것들이 깨지기 쉬워요.
남: 알겠습니다. 걱정하지 마세요.
여: [잠시 후] 공항까지 얼마나 오래 걸릴까요?
남: 한 시간이 안 걸릴 겁니다. 급하신가요?
여: 약간 늦을 것 같아요. 저는 오전 11시에 비행기를 타야만 합니다.
남: 그러면 우리는 고속 도로를 탈 수 있습니다. 하지만 통행료에 대한 추가금은 지불하셔야 합니다. 괜찮으신가요?
여: 통행료로 얼마를 내야 하나요?
남: 추가금이 10달러예요.
여: 문제 없어요. 할 수 있는 한 가장 빠르게 갈 수 있게 해 주세요.
남: 안전벨트를 매시고 늦는 것은 걱정하지 마세요. 이 시간에는 교통 체증이 없습니다.
여: 그러기를 정말 바라요.

남자는 트렁크에 여자의 짐을 실어 주고, 목적지까지의 소요 시간을 알려 주었으며, 여자는 공항으로 가 달라고 했고, 시간이 늦을까 봐 추가금을 내더라도 고속 도로로 갈 것을 요청하였다. 이로 보아, 남자와 여자는 택시 기사와 승객의 관계이다.

fragile 깨지기 쉬운, 부서지기 쉬운   **in a hurry** 급히   **highway** 고속 도로
extra 추가의   **toll** 통행료

04 ⑤ 그림 불일치 파악

남: Gloria, 이 사진을 봐.
여: 와, 정말 귀여워요. 그게 뭐예요?
남: 내가 모델 하우스를 둘러보던 중에 이 방의 사진을 찍은 거란다.
여: 제 마음에 쏙 들어요! 저는 이것 같은 방을 갖고 싶어요.
남: 우리가 새집으로 이사 갈 때, 내가 네 방을 딱 이것 같이 만들어 줄게.
여: 감사해요, 아빠. 저는 오른쪽에 있는 이 침대가 정말 좋아요. 이전에는 하트 모양의 침대를 본 적이 없어요.
남: 그래, 그건 매우 독특하구나. 게다가, 침대 위쪽의 큰 창문을 통해, 너는 매일 아침 해를 볼 수 있어.
여: 그러네요. 하지만 커튼이 없어서 너무 아쉬워요.
남: 왼쪽에 있는 벽장은 커서 안에 네 옷 전부를 넣을 수 있을 거야.
여: 좋아요. 저는 벽장 옆에 있는 사진을 우리 가족 사진으로 바꿀 거예요.
남: 그래, 그것이 산 사진보다 더 낫겠구나.
여: 문과 침대 사이에 있는 작은 테이블을 보세요. 딱 사진에서처럼 꽃이

꽂힌 꽃병을 놓기에 완벽해요.
남: 맞아, 동의해.
여: 어서 우리의 새집으로 이사 가고 싶어요!

여자는 사진에서처럼 문과 침대 사이에 있는 작은 테이블이 꽃병을 놓기에 완벽하다고 했지만, 그림에서는 꽃병이 아니라 전등이 있으므로 ⑤가 대화의 내용과 일치하지 않는다.

model home 모델 하우스   **closet** 벽장   **family portrait** 가족 사진

05 ⑤ 부탁한 일 파악

남: 여보, 저 돌아왔어요.
여: 오늘은 일찍 왔네요.
남: 네, 나는 드디어 프로젝트를 끝냈어요. 음…. 무슨 냄새죠?
여: 나는 아무 냄새도 안 나는데요. 점심으로 고기를 구웠어요. 아마도 바비큐 냄새일 거예요.
남: 아니에요, 그런 종류의 냄새가 아니에요. 가스 냄새인 것 같아요.
여: 뭐라고요? 가스가 새는 것은 매우 위험하잖아요. 911을 불러야 하나요?
남: 그러기 전에, 우리는 가스가 진짜로 새고 있는지 확인하도록 해요.
여: 우리가 어떻게 그걸 할 수 있죠?
남: 우선, 내가 창문을 열고 가스 밸브를 잠글게요. 우리가 밸브를 잠그면 많이 위험하진 않을 거예요.
여: 그러길 바라요. 난 너무 겁이 나요.
남: 진정해요. 우리는 이런 상황에서 침착하게 행동해야 해요. 내가 그 일을 하고 있는 동안에, 당신은 비눗물을 좀 만들어 줘야 해요.
여: 비눗물이요? 손을 씻으려고요?
남: 아니에요. 나는 비눗물로 새는 가스관을 문지르면 거품이 생긴다고 들었어요.
여: 알겠어요. 지금 만들게요.

남자는 창문을 열고 가스 밸브를 잠그겠다고 하였고, 그 동안 여자에게 비눗물을 만들어 달라고 부탁하였다.

roast 굽다   **leak** 새다   **shut off** 차단하다   **valve** 밸브   **calmly** 침착하게
soapy water 비눗물   **bubble** 거품

06 ② 숫자 정보 파악

여: Lyon, 이 사이트를 봐!
남: 그게 뭔데?
여: 온라인 서점인 Books For You가 이번 주에 특별 책 할인 판매를 하고 있어.
남: 어떤 종류의 책 할인 판매인데?
여: 너는 이걸 믿지 못할 거야. 원래 가격과는 상관 없이, 모든 책이 각각 10달러밖에 안 해.
남: 정말? 이건 이전에 살 수 없었던 비싼 책들을 살 수 있는 좋은 기회구나.
여: 그게 다가 아니야. 다섯 권을 산다면, 공짜로 한 권을 더 받아.
남: 와! 믿을 수 없어!
여: 계정당 책 10권의 제한이 있다고 써 있어.

남: 나는 Compton 백과사전 시리즈를 주문하고 싶어. 그것은 여섯 권으로 구성되어 있어.

여: 그러면 너는 다섯 권의 가격으로 그것들을 살 수 있어. 게다가, ABC 카드로 결제하면 총액의 10%를 추가 할인받을 수 있어.

남: 잘됐다. 나는 지금 바로 살래. ABC 카드로 결제할 거야.

여: 어서 해. 네 계정으로 로그인해서 주문하면 돼.

남: 물론이지.

온라인 서점 할인 판매 행사로 책 한 권당 10달러에 살 수 있는데 남자는 여섯 권으로 구성된 백과사전을 사고 싶어 한다. 다섯 권을 사면 한 권을 공짜로 주기 때문에 다섯 권의 금액인 50달러를 지불해야 하는데, ABC 카드로 결제하면 추가 10% 할인을 받을 수 있으므로, 남자가 지불해야 하는 총 금액은 45달러이다.

regardless of ~에 상관없이   account 계정   encyclopedia 백과사전
consist of ~로 구성되다   additional 추가적인   log into ~에 접속하다

07 ②
이유 파악

[전화벨이 울린다.]

여: 여보세요, 여기는 Diamond 부동산 중개소입니다. 무엇을 도와드릴까요?

남: Sharon? 저, John이에요.

여: 안녕하세요, John. 무슨 일이에요?

남: 제가 오늘 오후에 계약을 하기 위해서 고객과 만나기로 했는데, 갈 수 없을 것 같아요. 당신이 전화를 해서 약속을 내일 오후로 바꿔 주시겠어요?

여: 당신이 오후 2시에 Carl 씨와 만나기로 되어 있네요. 왜 그와 만날 수 없는지 물어봐도 될까요?

남: 지하실에 있는 보일러가 어젯밤에 터졌어요. 수리공이 이제 막 다 고쳤어요.

여: 음, 당신이 지금 출발하면, 아직은 제 시간에 사무실에 도착할 수 있어요.

남: 그게 다가 아니에요. 저는 막 제 아들의 담임 선생님으로부터 전화를 받았어요. 제 아들이 농구를 하다가 다른 선수와 부딪혔대요.

여: 오, 이런. 그는 괜찮나요?

남: 심각하지는 않지만, 이마에 몇 바늘 꿰매야 할 거래요.

여: 약속에 대해서는 걱정하지 마세요. 제가 바로 Carl 씨에게 전화할게요.

남자는 보일러가 터져서 수리하느라 사무실로 늦게 출발하게 되었는데, 학교로부터 아들이 농구를 하다가 다쳤다는 전화를 받아서 사무실에 들어갈 수 없다고 말하고 있다.

real estate 부동산   close a contract 계약을 맺다   burst 터지다, 파열하다
collide 충돌하다, 부딪치다   stitch (수술로 기운) 바늘   forehead 이마

08 ④
언급 유무 파악

남: Irene, 내 만화에 대해서 어떻게 생각해?

여: 멋지다! 뭐에 대한 거야?

남: 그건 세상을 구하는 영웅에 대한 이야기야. 나는 'Superhero

Festival'이라는 만화 대회에 그 만화로 참가하려고 해.

여: 나는 그런 대회는 들어 본 적이 없지만, 정말 재미있을 것 같다. 모든 영웅이 특별한 능력을 갖고 있어야 해?

남: 응, 모든 영웅은 적어도 한 가지의 초능력을 가져야 해. 내 영웅은 한 손으로는 불을, 다른 한 손으로는 물을 통제할 수 있는 능력을 가지고 있어.

여: 멋지다! 만화를 어떻게 제출해?

남: 이메일 주소로 그것을 보내야 해. 세계적인 행사여서, 전 세계에 있는 누구라도 참가할 수 있어.

여: 언제가 마감일이야? 나도 대회에 참가하고 싶다.

남: 오늘이 제출 마지막 날이야.

여: 이런! 내가 시도해 보기에는 너무 늦었네.

남: 걱정하지 마. 우리는 다음에 함께 도전할 수 있어.

여: 좋아. 사람들이 네 만화를 좋아해 주기를 바랄게.

남: 나도 그랬으면 좋겠어. 내일부터 시작해서 한 달 동안 온라인 투표가 있을 거야.

여: 내일 너를 위해 꼭 투표할게.

만화 대회 참가와 관련하여 영웅의 조건(하나 이상의 초능력), 접수 방법(이메일), 접수 마감일(오늘), 투표 기간(내일부터 한 달간)에 대해서는 언급했지만, ④ '접수 비용'에 대해서는 언급하지 않았다.

cartoon 만화   enter 참가하다, 출전하다   submit 제출하다
deadline 마감일   submission 제출

09 ⑤
담화 내용 불일치

남: 오늘 Pacific 항공사를 이용해 주셔서 감사합니다. 저는 애틀랜타에서 한국의 인천까지 가는 항공기, AX 120의 기장입니다. 비행기는 지금 막 국제 날짜 변경선 위를 날고 있습니다. 그래서 날짜는 이제 3월 7일입니다. 이 비행기의 고도는 11,000미터이고 우리는 시속 850km로 날고 있습니다. 도착 예상 시간은 현지 시간으로 오전 10시 30분입니다. 인천의 날씨는 매우 맑을 것으로 예상되고, 온도는 15도입니다. 여러분의 여행을 더 편하게 하기 위해서 필요한 것이 있으시다면, 저희 승무원들에게 문의하시기 바랍니다. 면세 쇼핑을 원하시는 분들께서는 좌석 주머니에 놓여진 카탈로그를 확인하실 수 있습니다. 즐거운 비행이 되기를 바랍니다. 감사합니다.

면세 쇼핑을 원하는 승객들은 좌석 주머니에 있는 카탈로그를 확인할 수 있다고 했으므로, 책을 세금이 붙지 않은 가격으로 살 수 있다고 한 ⑤는 내용과 일치하지 않는다.

captain 기장   International Date Line 국제 날짜 변경선   altitude 고도
flight attendant 승무원

10 ②
도표 정보 파악

남: Toy World에 오신 것을 환영합니다. 무엇을 도와드릴까요?

여: 저는 어린 딸을 위한 장난감을 찾고 있습니다.

남: 제대로 오셨습니다. 저희는 많은 대여용 장난감을 갖고 있습니다. 이번 주에 특가를 제공합니다.

여: 좋네요.

남: 그녀는 몇 살인가요? 나이에 적절한 장난감을 고르는 것이 중요합니다.

여: 그녀는 6살입니다. 그리고 저는 그녀가 갖고 놀기에 안전한 장난감을 원합니다.

남: 그러면 나무 장난감은 어떠신가요?

여: 나무 장난감들이 플라스틱 장난감들보다 더 비싼가요?

남: 사실, 가격들은 모두 다릅니다.

여: 나무 장난감이 좋겠어요. 그리고 저는 대여에 10달러보다 더 쓰고 싶지는 않습니다.

남: 알겠습니다. 그러면 이 두 개 중에서 하나를 고르실 수 있습니다.

여: 음, 저는 그녀가 집 안에서 그것을 갖고 놀게 하고 싶습니다.

남: 좋습니다. 그녀는 이것을 좋아할 겁니다!

문제 해결

여자는 6살짜리 딸에게 나무로 된 장난감 중에서 가격이 10달러를 넘지 않고, 실내에서 갖고 놀 수 있는 장난감을 대여하고 싶어 하므로, 여자가 대여할 장난감은 ②이다.

어휘·표현

rent 대여   suitable 적절한, 적합한   wooden 나무로 된   rental 대여, 대여료

11 ⑤ 짧은 대화의 응답

남: 실례합니다. 저는 도서관에 처음 왔어요. 제가 이 책을 어떻게 빌릴 수 있을까요?

여: 도서관 카드를 먼저 만드셔야 합니다. 그런 후에 책을 빌릴 수 있어요.

남: 카드를 어떻게 만드나요?

여: 이 신청서를 작성하시고 여권용 사진 두 장과 함께 제출하세요.

문제 해결

남자가 도서관 카드를 만드는 방법에 대해서 물었으므로, 그에 대한 응답으로 신청서를 제출하라는 ⑤가 가장 적절하다.

① 이 도서관에는 읽을 만한 흥미로운 자료들이 많이 있습니다.

② 이번 주말까지 그것을 반납하는 것을 잊지 않으셔야 합니다.

③ 그 책은 이 도서관에서 과거에 무슨 일이 있었는지를 알려 줍니다.

④ 그 책은 바로 이번 달에 출판되었고, 가격은 10달러밖에 안 합니다.

어휘·표현

application form 신청서   submit 제출하다

12 ② 짧은 대화의 응답

여: 여보, 전화기로 뭘 찾고 있어요?

남: 나는 이 앱으로 날씨를 확인하고 있는 중이에요. 이 앱은 매일 아침마다 날씨가 어떤지 알려 줘요.

여: 참 유용한 앱인 것 같네요. 오늘은 뭐라고 해요?

남: 오늘 오후에 비가 많이 내리고 강한 바람이 분대요.

문제 해결

날씨 앱을 확인 중인 남자에게 여자가 오늘의 날씨를 물었으므로, 비와 바람이 심할 거라고 날씨를 알려 주는 ②가 남자의 응답으로 가장 적절하다.

① 나는 이 앱이 매우 편리하다고 생각하지만, 공짜는 아니에요.

③ 이 버튼을 누르면 이 앱을 간단히 내려받을 수 있어요.

④ 이 앱은 전 세계의 정확한 날씨 예보를 당신에게 알려 줘요.

⑤ 당신이 해야 하는 일은 이 앱을 스마트폰에 설치하는 것이에요.

어휘·표현

app(=application) 앱   call for 예보하다   accurate 정확한

forecast 예보   install 설치하다

13 ② 긴 대화의 응답

여: Jackson, 전화기로 뭘 보고 있니?

남: 소셜 미디어에서 개들의 사진들을 보고 있어요. 귀엽지 않나요?

여: 그래, 그렇구나.

남: 엄마, 제가 개를 입양할 수 있을까요?

여: 마지막으로 얘기하는데, 안 돼!

남: 제가 정말 돌볼게요. 어쨌든, 저는 형제자매가 없어서 따분하단 말이에요. 제발이요, 엄마.

여: 그게 개를 입양하는 이유는 안 돼. 그리고 너는 내가 개 짖는 소리를 못 견딘다는 것을 알잖니.

남: 개가 집에서 짖지 않도록 제가 훈련시킬 수 있어요.

여: 그리고 우리 아파트에는 애완동물 금지 정책이 있다는 사실 잊었니?

남: 정말이요? 저는 그걸 몰랐어요.

여: 게다가, 개를 키우는 것에는 많은 책임이 따라.

남: 어떤 종류의 책임을 말씀하시는 거예요?

여: 너는 매일 개를 산책시키고 먹이를 줘야 해.

문제 해결

여자는 개를 키우는 것에는 책임이 따른다고 말하고 있고, 남자는 어떤 책임을 말하는지를 확인하고 있기 때문에, 여자의 응답으로는 책임의 구체적인 종류를 말하는 ②가 가장 적절하다.

① 네가 개를 기르다니 매우 책임감이 있구나.

③ 유감이지만, 우리 아파트는 애완동물을 금지한단다.

④ 너는 그 개 사진들을 나와 나눌 수 있어.

⑤ 짖지 않도록 개를 훈련시키는 것은 네가 생각하는 것보다 더 어려워.

어휘·표현

stand 견디다   bark 짖다   policy 정책   besides 게다가
responsibility 책임   feed 먹이를 주다

14 ③ 긴 대화의 응답

여: Michael, 내 말 안 들리니?

남: 아, 너구나, Linda. 미안해. 못 들었어.

여: 내가 너를 적어도 열 번은 불렀어. 길을 걸으면서 뭐에 그렇게 빠져 있어?

남: 나는 음악을 들으면서 내가 좋아하는 축구 팀에 대한 기사를 읽고 있었어.

여: 걸으면서 스마트폰을 사용하는 것은 매우 위험해.

남: 괜찮아. 나는 항상 그렇게 해.

여: 너 같은 사람들을 말하는 단어가 있다는 것을 너는 알고 있니?

남: 정말? 그게 뭔데?

여: 너는 'smombie'야.

남: smombie? 그게 무슨 뜻이야?

여: 그것은 '스마트폰'과 '좀비'라는 단어의 조합이야. 그건 스마트폰을 보느라 고개를 숙인 채 걷는 사람들을 묘사하는 데 쓰여.

남: 걱정하지 마. 나는 아직까지 사고 난 적이 없어.

여: 하지만 너는 지금 막 내 말을 못 들었잖아. 네가 위험한 상황으로 걸어가고 있었으면 어땠겠어? 이건 웃을 만한 문제가 아니야.

남: 알았어. 이제부터는, 걸으면서 스마트폰을 사용하지 않을게.

걸으면서 스마트폰을 사용하는 남자에게 여자가 위험하다고 주의를 주고 있으므로, 남자의 응답으로 다시는 길을 걸으며 스마트폰을 사용하지 않겠다고 다짐하는 ③이 가장 적절하다.

① 그래, 나는 사전에서 'smombie'란 단어를 찾았어.
② 네 말이 맞아. 나는 음악을 들으면서 동시에 읽을 거야.
④ 네 말에 동의하지만, 내가 길에서 smombie와 부딪힌다면 어떻게 하지?
⑤ 걱정 마. 내가 내일 너에게 그 기사를 보내 줄게.

어휘·표현

be absorbed in ~에 열중하다, ~에 빠져 있다   **article** 기사
combination 조합   **describe** 묘사하다

15 ②
상황에 적절한 말

남: 오늘 밤 대규모 춤 경연 대회가 있고, Eriksen은 대회에 참가하는 것에 매우 흥분해 있다. 그는 한 달 동안 대회를 준비해 오고 있다. 1등을 하기를 바라면서, 그는 대회에서 눈에 띄기 위해 그의 가장 화려한 옷을 세탁한다. 그러나 준비하는 동안에, 그는 그의 교수인 White 교수님으로부터 전화를 받는다. 그녀는 그가 오늘 기말 보고서를 제출해야 하고, 그렇지 않다면 그 과목에서 낙제하게 될 것이라고 말한다. 그는 보고서를 제출하기 위해서 교수님의 사무실로 서둘러 갔으나, 그의 빨래에 대해서 완전히 잊어버린다. 집에 가는 길에, 그는 갑자기 그의 옷이 여전히 세탁기 안에 있다는 것이 기억난다. 그는 대회가 시작하기 전까지 옷을 말릴 시간이 없기 때문에, 그의 룸메이트에게 전화를 걸어 그를 위해 옷을 말려 달라고 부탁해야 한다. 이 상황에서, Eriksen은 그의 룸메이트에게 뭐라고 할 것 같은가?

문제 해결

Ericksen은 급하게 보고서를 제출하고 오는 길이라 대회에 입고 나갈 옷을 직접 말릴 시간이 없어서 그의 룸메이트에게 건조를 부탁해야 하는 상황이므로, ② '내 옷을 세탁기에서 꺼내서 건조기에 넣어 주겠니?'가 룸메이트에게 할 말로 가장 적절하다.

① 나 대신 교수님이 프로젝트를 하시는 것을 도와줄 수 있어?
③ 전문 무용수처럼 춤추는 방법을 나에게 알려 주겠니?
④ 오늘 밤 춤 경연 대회에서 나와 같이 춤출래?
⑤ 오늘 밤 춤 경연 대회에서 입을 옷을 내게 빌려 주겠니?

어휘·표현

competition 대회   **stand out** 눈에 띄다   **hand in** 제출하다   **laundry** 빨래
dryer 건조기

16-17
복합 이해

여: 안녕하세요, 여러분. 제가 이렇게 놀라운 발명품인 UFO 접시를 소개하게 되어서 기쁩니다. 여러분은 우리가 얼마나 많은 일회용품을 사용하는지 아시나요? 조사에 따르면, 평균적으로 한 사람이 매년 대략 100kg의 플라스틱, 420개의 비닐 봉지, 그리고 460개의 일회용 컵을 사용합니다. 그리고 여러분들이 짐작할 수 있듯이, 그것들은 많은 환경 오염을 만들어 냅니다. 그래서, 뉴욕에 있는 두 명의 산업 디자이너들인 Andrea Ruggiero와 Bengt Brummer가 일회용품 사용을 줄이기 위해 이 UFO 접시를 만들었습니다. 물론, 그것은 진짜 UFO가 아니라, 버려지고, 작은 조각들로 부숴지며, 자연으로 돌아가는 일회용 접시입니다. 그것은 혼합된 새 모이, 감자 녹말, 구아 검,

그리고 해초로 만들어집니다. 그것은 나무나 벽에 던져져서 새들이나 동물들의 먹이로 사용될 수 있습니다. 그것은 무독성이고 한 달 안에 완벽하게 자연 분해되기 때문에, 환경 오염이 되지 않을까 걱정할 필요가 없습니다. 이 접시를 한번 사용해 보시지 않겠습니까?

어휘·표현

disposable 일회용의   **survey** 조사   **approximately** 대략   **industrial**
산업의   **blended** 혼합된   **birdseed** 새 모이   **starch** 녹말   **seaweed** 해초
non-toxic 무독성의   **biodegrade** 자연 분해되다   **give ~ a try** ~을 한번 해
보다

16 ⑤

문제 해결

여자는 새들과 동물들의 먹이가 될 수 있고 자연적으로 분해도 되어 환경을 보호할 수 있는 UFO 접시에 대해 소개하고 있으므로, 여자가 하는 말의 주제로 ⑤ '환경 오염을 줄이는 데 도움이 되는 일회용 접시'가 가장 적절하다.

① 매년 소비되는 일회용품의 양
② 전 세계적으로 UFO를 목격한 사례들
③ 사람들을 위한 미래의 음식 재료
④ 두 명의 훌륭한 디자이너들의 삶

17 ④

문제 해결

친환경적인 UFO 접시의 재료로 혼합된 새 모이, 감자 녹말, 구아 검, 그리고 해초는 언급되었지만, ④ '머스타드 가루'에 대한 언급은 없었다.

01 have an important announcement to make / need to change with the times / as long as it is approved

02 doing on the computer / can't make up my mind / That doesn't matter / best fits your use

03 didn't miss a line / What's wrong with it / That's why we need to redo / let's roll the cameras

04 thinking of entering this picture / three seagulls to the right of the plane / looks like he's having a relaxing time

05 It took longer than we thought / visit some tourist attractions in the city / better than trying to catch cabs

06 How many are in your party / $10 for a child under 12 / there is a 10% discount on

07 I've got good news / take a rain check / don't want to let her down

08 in the mood for / catch an early showing / doesn't make much difference to me

09 It gives me great pleasure to introduce / a fundraising event where you raise money / be extended for the entire month of March / for a great cause

10 Do you carry car air purifiers / What price range do you have in mind / many devices connected to my car / I'll skip that one

11 had a bad cold and stayed in bed

12 would like to open a bank account

13 do you mind if I give you / I'd really appreciate it / to attract a core group of followers / should narrow down the focus

14 No wonder it's so popular / sold out instantly / at the exact second they went on sale

15 tryouts are scheduled for next week / not physical but psychological / suggest to John that he should pretend / as if he were alone

16-17 about colors that you might find interesting / is least likely to be involved in / under any weather condition except snow

01 to ensure the freshest and cleanest wash / get your whites brighter / comes in both powder and liquid form

02 than action and special effects / tired of those superhero movies / less variety in the movies

03 your brake pads are worn down / wait until my next scheduled maintenance / start to hear some squeaking

04 the framed picture of the sailboat / standing lamp to the right of the couch / put the old square-shaped rug

05 run some errands / swing by the meat market / stop by the stationery store / bring in the morning paper

06 Do you mind having a layover / I'll take the layover / offer complimentary check-in for two bags / charge an extra $15

07 showing how to cook a five-course meal / for great dinner with your husband / Next week is my parents' 30th anniversary

08 come in this Saturday for a seminar / looking forward to the team-building exercises / should wear comfortable clothing / in the FAB building room 302

09 this weekend at Aloha Stadium / lecture on raising your feline companion / a year's supply of pet food

10 try not to spend more than $200 / We need one for four people / I prefer a dome shape

11 I'm available later in the week

12 borrow the book when you are done

13 there are any rides we can handle / look in the gift shop / left my purse back

14 you're off the hook / she would say yes / It wouldn't hurt to ask / Any advice on what I should say

15 contemporary authors / the store inventory should be mainly classics / spending more of the budget on newer authors

16-17 a new hybrid bicycle / is intended for roads / trails and mountains / goes through a strict quality control check

01 joining our program as the co-host / make her a perfect fit for / feel free to text us

02 adjusting to your new school life / making some friends can help you adjust / find someone who shares your interests

03 you tripped on the stairs / arrange for Mr. Grey to substitute for / as the head of the school

04 the slide on the right side / a zebra shaped light bulb / hippo-shaped ball pool in the middle

05 schedule your messages on your smartphone / download it on your smartphone / type in your message / need to update your smartphone first

06 The long-sleeved ones are $30 / get 20% off your total purchase / They're $20 a pair / a pair of aqua shoes

07 to take pictures with the cast / can't make it on Friday / trying out for the school play / good luck on your audition

08 I go there every year / giving out 500 tumblers and eco bags / at the same place as last year

09 an announcement regarding the fire alarm inspection / certified officers from our community fire station / unlock all the doors / This inspection is required by law

10 be at least 10 cm bigger than him / be ventilation slots on at least 3 sides / steel will be better than plastic

11 singing in front of other people

12 our summer vacation in Jeju Island

13 buy an insect repellent / Mosquito bites sure can be irritating / apply insect repellent before you go outside / at any pharmacy or local supermarket

14 join one of the school volunteer programs / have anything specific in mind / helping out at the library / need extra hands at

15 have a big argument / things get very awkward / doesn't want to take sides / eventually be able to make up

16-17 related to parts of our body / without really thinking about it / a phrase related to your eyes / an expression that involves your feet

01 in charge of the keynote speech / take advantage of their own experience / give silver workers a try

02 have you ever heard about the Three Rs / recycling and reusing daily products / I couldn't agree more / "reducing" is at the core

03 get rid of them right away / in case of an emergency / on a regular basis

04 see the boy looking at the fishbowl / Somebody spilled water on it / No wonder you are so tired

05 had a great time cooking and eating barbecues / looking up at the star-filled sky / such as a tent and a sleeping bag / If you don't mind

06 Is someone helping you out / on sale this week for $30 / give you a 50% discount on the second one / Let me ring it up

07 ask whether you can come to my birthday party / what a shame / working at your part-time job / lend them a helping hand

08 is having a festival this week / a variety of programs such as cutting sheep's wool / How much is the admission fee

09 in charge of / will be held online / two months prior to the election date / are requested to express their opinions

10 The bigger the better / spend up to $20 / has no delivery fee

11 too early to visit someone

12 don't feel like getting out of the car

13 was supposed to present / didn't come to the meeting on time / managed to finish the presentation / I'm afraid I messed up our project

14 need to renew your card / your card expired last week / there is an overdue book

15 watch a newly released action movie / there was a terrible traffic jam / because of the commercials and previews

16-17 positive effects pets can have on us / don't have to stick to / a better idea to have a small pet

01 Why don't you go alone / be of great benefit to you / absolutely up to you

02 was diagnosed with early liver cancer / applied for sick leave / a very high chance of being completely cured

03 Would you like me to bring / how much longer will it take / some mystery novels to pass the time

04 looks like it's having fun / What I like most is / must have drawn the penguin

05 why don't we go see a movie / Can you tell me where it is / would really appreciate that / can't thank you enough

06 much speedier than the mountain bike / enjoy the beautiful scenery / get a 10% discount on the rental

07 Congratulations on the gold medal / has only been about half a year / How long is the warranty

08 Isn't it located near / what floor the apartment is on / can't wait to see the apartment in person

09 where the fair will take place / the number is expected to double / will be used to promote animal welfare

10 match what we've said / Which one do you prefer / If you were me, what would you buy / I'll go with your choice

11 it's spring cleaning day today

12 thinking about taking the beginner class

13 any way to lower the temperature / anything else I can help you with / can't connect to your Wi-Fi

14 What's the purpose of the flea market / the second is to donate your stuff / put your name on the volunteer list

15 majoring in Korean Literature / take part in the competition / how accurately the novel is written

16-17 the more electricity you save, the more / rather than washing small amounts of clothing / The same rule applies to electric heaters / play a big role in protecting

01 have access to a healthy breakfast / have better attendance / officially announcing the School Breakfast Week

02 which specific jobs you want to experience / narrowing down the field you're most interested in / search for specific jobs

03 on such short notice / I've been training her for six months / bring the kit from my hospital

04 stools shaped like books / the screen next to the story room / on the shelves under the screen

05 time to start spring cleaning / accepting donations and daily necessities / pick up the kids from school

06 The manual ones are $15 / buy that manual one / have a matching pencil case / have a 50% discount on it

07 all cooking ingredients and utensils will be provided / you have a dental appointment / help my Grandma with her gardening

08 a huge literary festival / this Saturday from 10 a.m. / At the square in front of City Hall / except for water

09 this Friday at the Student Union Building / All Friday afternoon lectures will be canceled / All events are free of charge / open to the public

10 can handle anything under 4 kg / the models with aluminum table tops / The cup holders seem quite useful

11 ask you to return this book for me

12 Would you like to add that

13 Is something the matter / is upset with me / got upset about a comment / you should say sorry to her

14 can't wait to go see it / gives you a private tour / how I can sign up for that

15 has a history presentation on the same day / for him to gain valuable experience / do his presentation the day before the competition

16-17 to blend in with the snowy environment / for their predators to distinguish them / cause its predators to confuse it

07 Dictation Test 정답 ▶ pp. 78-81

01 tell you about a brand-new podcast / focusing on the stress of our daily lives / please download the podcast

02 he hasn't learned how to read yet / falls behind his peers / benefits of learning to read later

03 talking about working on the force / How can I get started / That's great advice / Working as a police officer

04 a bunk bed against the wall / on top of my bed / a poster of an astronaut on the wall / the star-patterned rug

05 make sure to pack your toothbrush / leave a to-do list for the dog sitter / Toby needs to get fed / I'll write the list right now

06 The standard rate for a single night / it will be double / We have travel kits for $10 / apply this toward your room rate only

07 not all that interested in reading old books / needed some extra credit in my class / she'd bump my grades up

08 having its annual Summer Jamboree this Saturday / run in the three-legged race / parents pay $5 each / don't end until 5 p.m.

09 will automatically shut off at 4:30 p.m. / preset at 28°C by central control / will be no sports club activities

10 anything for under $60 / under a kilogram / want them to be waterproof / I prefer my shoes dark

11 no later than this Friday

12 When does she get back from

13 there's a chance of rain / We could check out the aquarium / Let's eat first / see my phone / wallet / and keys

14 Dinner sounds great / make a reservation for 7 p.m. / want to see a movie after dinner

15 the lunch time crowd is too large / be best to hire another employee to help / to consider buying an espresso machine

16-17 create apps more easily and efficiently / AI helper to offer assistance to developers / see the amount of battery used

08 Dictation Test 정답 ▶ pp. 82-85

01 hot water supply / shut off due to / discovered a leak in the boiler room / do not hesitate to contact

02 making a study plan for the final exam / to allot more time to studying / whether this schedule is really doable

03 want me to take photos of it / something more provocative / have John dig it up

04 the big round window in the middle / the hanging sofa on the right side / chairs without legs may be more suitable

05 we're having a house warming party / all the necessary ingredients / buy new napkins for the table / get the board games out

06 a twin room with two single beds / double room costs $90 / stay two nights in a row / with an ocean view

07 cancelled the flight to Jeju / managed to finish it in time / so I changed my plans

08 be held from March 18th to 28th / to enter the tournament / get admission and round-trip tickets / That's the spirit

09 we have a high level of fine dust / wear masks inside the building / for a short while for ventilation / get eye drops

10 any shape but the round one / price range are you thinking of / don't want spend more than $30

11 could you take it to work

12 It got towed away and needs repairing

13 with all these clothes / collects formal clothes or suits / lends suits to young adults

14 From what I heard / to congratulate your friend on the opening / what if it doesn't fit / how about a potted plant

15 talented at making video clips / take his work for granted / they do the work together

16-17 carry your own reusable water bottle / buy stainless steel or bamboo straws / have an important role in reducing plastic pollution

01 help reduce damage to the environment / are still short of hands to organize / recruiting new members to our organization
02 I'm trying hard to keep in shape / take regular rests during workouts / your muscles can easily be fatigued
03 The publisher will release my book / I'm supposed to wear a jacket / treat you to a cup of morning coffee
04 Did you go horseback riding / was a little afraid of riding a horse / it looks like she's enjoying it
05 How did the contract go with / I can make it back in time / Take your time
06 I'd like to book a flight / is there any discount for children / Would that be all right
07 offered me a job on the spot / haven't made up my mind about the job offer / where I was born and raised
08 get there by 6 or 7 p.m. / What do you think about the prices / That's the reason why I go there
09 kick off the festival with a welcome ceremony / Except for the acoustic band concert / there was a fireworks display
10 too inconvenient to carry / What's your price range / spend more than $10 each
11 take my nieces and nephews trick-or-treating
12 May I borrow your laptop
13 mean to wake / going on a business trip to Australia / very sensitive to the cold
14 We've been really looking forward to it / You can't be serious / That's what I'm telling you / Why don't you take a dip
15 was forced to close his business with a great loss / face was full of disappointment / encouraging him to take another chance
16-17 sleep disorders such as insomnia / actually help you sleep more soundly / it's time to let go of the day's stresses

01 I'm honored to speak / equipped with 40 private language labs / express my appreciation for your generous contributions
02 You've been worried about your health / your habit of eating food late at night / you have to fix that habit / keep what you said in mind
03 Are you confident that you will win / I'm in great condition now / I won't let you down
04 on the upper part of the poster / running a marathon on the left / to be more active
05 prescribed some medicine for it / are there any oranges left in the fridge / to eat fruits rich in vitamin C
06 Regular tickets are $20 / qualify for a group discount / get 10% off the total price
07 has great potential for development / the good benefits for the employees / the chance to work abroad
08 tell me about your club's history / the famous magician / founded the club / How many times a year do you perform
09 on August 1st and last for two weeks / from ages 9 to 13 / based on their baseball skills
10 we need at least three bedrooms / more than $1,000 every month on housing / a garage that holds two cars
11 in favor of going on a trip
12 Could you order me a drink
13 took the Korean history class last semester / he's well versed in Korean history / there must have been no one sleeping
14 there is a $10 fee / the room was booked by / can be reissued only to the guest
15 she didn't bring it with her / he won't sell it to anyone else / is grateful for this
16-17 bats have been considered to be unlucky / in maintaining the ecosystem / natural enemies of harmful pests / cost farmers in America billions of dollars

01 recommended by nine out of ten veterinarians / be found in your local grocery stores / print out a 10% discount coupon

02 Things aren't going so well / challenging me a lot / giving me new assignments / trusts in you and your abilities

03 all clear to be discharged / any medication that I need to take / give you this prescription / to have your wound cleaned

04 an armchair at the foot of the bed / the flower painting on the wall / got a great deal on it

05 should be in the walk-in closet / The blue ones that match my dress / on the kitchen counter

06 2 adults and 2 children under 13 / receive a 10% discount / It's only $5 per person / sign my husband up

07 an assignment for your course / everyone listen to the podcast / to prepare for the next lesson

08 I'm all ears / from March 5th to the 7th / the admission fee / 50 bakeries in total will be there

09 donated to help house the homeless / The main event is a 100 km race / get your tickets early at any bicycle store

10 I want a compact car this time / do more than 20 km per liter / go for the other one

11 mind bringing me a cup of coffee

12 I'm happy to help you

13 too late to board my flight / the boarding gates just closed / it's fully booked / to put you on that plane

14 Have all the arrangements been made / switch to a larger room / notifying people of the change / I have my hands full

15 have their best players play the entire game / everyone gets to play in / worked together as a team

16-17 talk to you about a new fitness tracker / with an updated heart rate sensor / the new waterproof design

01 The program is coming to an end / You will be pleasantly surprised to see / witness the fruits of your valuable donations

02 narrowed down the choices / check the fuel efficiency / will be worth the money

03 I'm not sure if I can / you have muscle knots / We are going to do some stretching

04 remind me of sea waves / must be the sky with hanging stars / I felt as if I were outdoors

05 is only one week away / arranged for Shawn to do it / anything else that needs to be done

06 was just about to buy tickets / get a 30% discount on each ticket / Everything seems correct

07 the required class before Academic Writing / register for Academic Writing next semester / allowed second year students to take the class

08 proof of address to show you are a community member / Where does the practice take place / Do you hold concerts as well

09 have an earthquake drill tomorrow / The moment you hear the alarm / it is still under repair / teach you how to do first aid

10 help us spend less time on household chores / the run time should be more than 2 hours / The longer the better

11 you have a vegetarian menu

12 how about going into the cafeteria

13 see if the applicants are suitable for / many of them are abandoned / How could people do such a thing

14 have a simple conversation in Chinese / be helpful in making a good relationship / taking a class at a language academy

15 has been wanting to buy a laptop / it takes longer than expected / is about to buy the most expensive laptop

16-17 how plants function to remove toxic chemicals indoors / especially good for keeping the air clean / a welcome addition in dry winter months / which plant is the air-purifying champion

01 not many employees have been parking there / not only interrupts pedestrian traffic / in case of an emergency such as fire

02 is right around the corner / has become very commercialized / as a means of selling lots of candy and chocolate

03 have you heard any news from / Come to think of it / looks too good to eat

04 it's my first trip overseas / Information about the departure and destination cities / how about heading toward the gate

05 It's her last day at our school / throw her a going-away party / Anything but drawing pictures

06 secondhand copies of the magazine / have so many back issues / give you a one-dollar discount on / That's a great deal

07 Have you ever used our gym before / calling to ask if I can change the free gift / have some towels left

08 I wonder if I can try / never forget the breathtaking view of the beautiful coral reefs / I'd like to suggest going to the sauna

09 is located on the 2nd floor / on a regular basis on Wednesday of each week / register for the class in advance

10 You can't go wrong with / When it comes to volume / leave out the 3 g product / do you have in mind

11 I'm getting promoted to manager

12 it's time to start cleaning up

13 had no doubt they would fit / have no choice but to get a refund / receive a store credit

14 have insomnia or something / driving me crazy / coming and going at all hours / concentrate on your studies

15 have a lot in common / are always grateful that / pulled out the same outfit at the same time

16-17 difficult to avoid suffering from hypertension / lower the risk of developing high blood pressure / are known to be rich in / be a little burdensome

01 a car wash service that makes your lives easier / keep your vehicle clean longer / as clean as the first day

02 I'm completely exhausted / I'll take care of your part / have my own way of staying fit

03 How long will the interview last / attend a meeting held by the union / couldn't handle the busy schedule without you

04 it feels like Christmas is here / holding a heart-shaped balloon that says / holding the same balloons as

05 Has something good happened / he would play a psychiatrist / throw him a party / It would be wonderful to have him home

06 both a foot massage and a head massage / How many people will you book / apply it to the total price

07 thinking of learning how to hula dance / my grandmother who lives there / run a small guesthouse / such a great granddaughter

08 Pets must be in pet carriers / stay in the cargo hold during the flight / proves my dog is fully vaccinated

09 on May 8th / will run for five days / be offered to visitors for a small charge / is expected to exceed 10,000

10 change my mobile phone's monthly plan / either 60 minutes or 90 minutes / take one with unlimited texts

11 for four people including me

12 decide which club to join

13 I can't eat another bite / How did you like it / the recipe that my mother gave me / looking forward to it

14 I couldn't agree more / the defending champion of this competition / no matter how good you are

15 who specializes in adolescent health / asks Angela to write a newspaper column / wants to know when the deadline

16-17 in terms of price competitiveness / at much lower prices / for selling fresh vegetables and seafood / which are run by large corporations

01 performing company-wide computer server upgrades / a security update to prevent viruses / upload all the data in your computer / against our security policy

02 It is a petition to keep the park / I am collecting signatures / a safe space to enjoy outdoor activities / Come to think of it

03 you are in an emergency exit row / perform the duties listed on this card / requested vegetarian in-flight meals

04 this adorable koala in Australia / the whale and dolphin in the Atlantic Ocean / monkeys live in upper South America / in explorer's clothes

05 I will let the boss know / I've already booked the conference room / could you bring the reports

06 The basic service costs $50 / Fabric costs an extra $15 and leather $25 / Cleaning your car's ventilation system / costs an extra $10

07 It looks great on you / doesn't feel heavy at all / green brings out your eyes / feel a rash coming on

08 to raise public interest in contemporary art / starts on June 1st / lasts for two months / Most of his representative paintings / will be on display

09 Held every year at Grant Park / have over 50 food trucks / starts May 1st / continues until the end of June

10 get one with a sunshade / sunshade that's under $30 / with two handles seem more stable / won't stand out

11 it was due yesterday

12 it's not food poisoning

13 lots of food / store it away / our refrigerator is always full / from what we have

14 Can I ask why you grow your hair / long enough to donate / makes wigs with donated hair

15 choose the subjects they want to study / in the same classes / consider what he wants to do

16-17 have had big impacts on / the most effective life-saving antibiotic / paved the way for hormone replacement therapies / the most commonly used pain-reliever

01 A major oil spill has occurred / no fatalities have been reported / the local fishing industry will be heavily impacted / keep you updated on

02 I've been sneezing and coughing all day / my own way of getting over a cold / folk remedies are effective

03 most of the house is destroyed / It isn't safe to enter the house / putting out the fire / to take another look

04 two eagles circling above the trees / wooden cabin on the left / some sheep to the right of / That well in the middle

05 put a bait on your hook / do it on your own / Did you bring your hat / remember to put some on

06 live in a studio apartment / we charge an additional $50 / install the air conditioner / give a 20% discount on weekdays

07 an assignment for your craft class / I'm out of ideas / give it to her as a gift

08 on Friday, March 1st / will be hiking and swimming / ends on Sunday at 6 p.m.

09 be placed at schools / non-perishable dry goods or canned food products / be distributed to soup kitchens

10 don't want to spend over $1,000 / with the faster hard drive / I don't really need 8 gigabytes / with the higher processor speed

11 your car is ready for you to pick up

12 Do you think you could tutor me

13 How would you like your steak / a salad with vinegar and oil dressing / Would you like to see the dessert menu

14 calling to schedule a birthday event / my daughter / who is turning twelve / want me to send a clown

15 purchase a second-hand machine / wants to get a brand-new washing machine / a used machine could break down

16-17 talk about different types of sentences / used to state some information / states a command or a request / in the proper situations

01 a free public radio station / thank you for listening, and for your support / make a donation through our website

02 What's new with you / tired of being stuck indoors / being away from other people

03 talk to you about my son's diet / to cut back on sugary drinks / As a nutritionist / including more vegetables in one's meals

04 the desk in the right corner / Those star-patterned curtains you put up / a nice plant / a poster of a cat

05 finished taking the tent down / help me with the tent / Can you look around the campsite

06 It was $100 to change them / parts and labor / which came to $200 / give you a 10% manager's discount

07 make it in time for the movie / watch the trailer / having a problem with my car

08 finally going to tie the knot / Where are they having it / RSVP by the end of the month

09 held in Central Park just like last year / learn how to play the guitar / Vendors from all over Florida

10 spend more than $200 / have a waterproof outer shell / a down jacket / should have a hood

11 could you come over this Friday

12 get something to drink

13 would be a great addition to / was curious about your compensation package / have full health benefits / offers seven days sick leave

14 The same as usual / have my parents coming over / work something out later

15 different ideas on how to spend their time / as many outdoor activities as possible / She'd like to relax on her vacation

16-17 I'd like to talk about wireless headsets / far superior to any other headset / The excellent sound quality and rich features

01 the graduation ceremony is only a week away / you won't be needing your uniforms after graduation / at the student union office

02 it's getting colder and colder / What do you mean by that / we shouldn't allow students to use smartphones

03 the only person at the scene last night / I called the police immediately / That's all I saw last night / help us catch the criminal

04 placed the refrigerator next to the window / a trading company that does business / much better than the rectangular table

05 Have you vacuumed the carpet / couldn't imagine in her wildest dreams / her flight is supposed to arrive / Can you buy some onions

06 buy a pass to the amusement park / Can I have four Gold Passes / half of the adult price / get a $20 discount from the total price

07 Not for long / got a phone call from my parents / had a car accident / I want to go and see her

08 My dryer has a capacity of 9 kg / the warranty for free repairs must have expired / If the price is reasonable

09 have an exciting announcement for you / be held on the special rooftop stage / The entrance fee is $5 per person

10 I'm a complete beginner / It depends on the person / I'll take the two-hour class / a kind instructor will fit me

11 a shuttle bus to the airport

12 you will see a big fire station

13 going on a blind date / one of my best friends since high school / people with a good sense of humor

14 registered for the Advanced French Conversation class / any other languages you can speak / I was really into K-pop last year

15 It takes her an hour by subway / reads a book to pass the time / to spend the commute time meaningfully

16-17 I'd like to talk about companion animals / have to take into consideration / be better off choosing a cat / think twice about getting a companion animal

01 the number one cause for traffic accidents / using of cell phone while driving / resulted in significant physical damage / not only illegal / but dangerous as well

02 come up with an idea / much more responsive to emotions / to make use of emotions

03 coming down with a cold / I'd rather see my regular doctor / Make sure you get the notes and assignments

04 looks like it's built into the wall / pay an arm and a leg / in the middle of the room

05 applied for a spot / got a text message saying that / What a worthwhile cause / change these bills into small change

06 $10 for an adult / are eligible for the child ticket / get $2 off the original price / show me proof of address

07 the prices are a bit expensive / it expired last Saturday / mistook it for / serves good quality steaks at reasonable prices

08 departs from Busan Station / give you a one-day ticket / keep basic public transportation etiquette

09 limit the number of participants to 800 / for those who register early / will be given a certificate of completion / are positioned every 3 km

10 prefer wood over plastic / It should have that function / Let's get one without it

11 What time will it be delivered

12 planning to make a study group

13 the impact of artificial intelligence on society / narrow down the subject / to find the direction of your report

14 how to look after these young seedlings / try to keep the soil moist / the best place to grow tomato plants

15 concerned about his recent drop in grades / found him dozing off / distracted by social media messages / he should stop using social media

16-17 the constant use of fossil fuel energy / a renewable source of energy / reduce our ecological footprint / not only cheap / but highly reliable

01 I am running for mayor / who should be the next mayor / Please vote for me

02 except for one thing / charging my electric car / quite hard to find a charging station / a tough time gaining mainstream popularity

03 a call to your rescue center / slipped while walking down the slope / We'll carry you down the mountain

04 put the banner / high above the fireplace / They are sure to have a great time / the three socks hanging from the fireplace

05 anyone to take care of the goldfish / will be in good hands / let me take you out to lunch

06 The intensive program costs $100 / take the intensive program for my daughters / get a 10% discount / pay for two months in advance

07 we've run out of fruits / They're having a big sale / the produce they're selling is not fresh

08 it's over 500 years old / be overwhelmed by its sheer size / see it with my own eyes

09 who attend our school regardless of grade / log in to the school website / winners will be announced for each grade

10 with at least two liters capacity / nice to have the latte option / with the longer warranty

11 are we still on for dinner tonight

12 people have told me it's really good

13 how much the monthly rental fee is / was fully renovated just two months ago / must be new and in good condition

14 What a relief / could have acted so carelessly / one of the biggest distractions to drivers

15 live in a high-rise apartment / has a fear of small spaces / lights up the inside of the elevator

16-17 playing sports has many beneficial effects / learn the meaning of cooperation and responsibility / develop a sense of teamwork / more psychologically stable

01 are known to be good for our diet / a cause of water shortage / keep one person hydrated for almost 16 months

02 My knees have been hurting lately / doing one hour of cardio exercise / that's why your knees hurt

03 the lamps could be changed for brighter ones / renew the kitchen and bathroom / pick out a design you like

04 putting up this poster on the bulletin board / see the big letters on the guitar / the place is in the bottom right corner

05 was really attached to this house / we can move out as scheduled / will it cost more / call the gas company to terminate the service

06 no traffic jams at this time of day / $10 for the regular bus / Give me a round-trip ticket / get an additional 5% discount

07 have a five-day business trip to Mexico / because of repairs to the gym / check if Mr. Kim can go in your place

08 was a little dark for reading books / be used for up to 10 years / less likely to cause a fire.

09 have an enormous effect on the islands / equivalent to a Category three hurricane / not to walk around outside / the typhoon reaches its peak

10 in the middle of winter / Five models are on sale / satisfy both charging and usage time conditions

11 remembering who's in my phone address book

12 I could live in the school dormitory

13 How is that different from / with the simple touch of a button / open your files by just touching the board / turn off the lights

14 too young to have one / I'm also concerned about emergency situations / on her smartphone too much

15 suggests that all the students make / A variety of opinions come up / should clean the classroom / everyone should keep their desks and surroundings clean

16-17 on the relationship between Malaria and the amount of rainfall / came to the conclusion that / more people contracted Malaria / are highly correlated

01 dreamed of going on a space trip / a number of incredible pictures / make sure to tune in to channel 7

02 whether to increase history classes / consider literature and mathematics to be more important / present is the result of the past

03 I'm relieved to hear that / She's confined to her bed / get a monthly medical checkup / be notified of the results

04 in the top right corner / I wish I could swim / a sign that says

05 That's because I ordered / you how to assemble it / throw away the empty boxes / anything I can help you with

06 have some files from my flash drive printed / it costs 10 cents per page / in black and white / print that report in color

07 holding a science camp next Friday / made a reservation for the camp location / to give a lecture / signed up for the camp

08 have anything in mind / Is there an age limit for / at least two hours by car

09 for students who maintain high grades / receive a scholarship for half the tuition / receive one type of scholarship / be excluded from

10 take a look at this catalogue / has to connect to the television / Can you wrap it up for me

11 Why don't you just try leaving earlier

12 The weather forecast says that it'll be sunny

13 I haven't seen you for a long time / attend the reading club for a while / suddenly my computer turned off / it didn't work

14 it's time for your regular medical checkup / am I eligible for / get yourself checked out this time

15 After conducting market research / to try the business for the young generation / will not make a big profit anymore

16-17 for no specific reason / influencing not only feelings but also / another color can increase your biorhythm / helps us focus on our goals

01 the host of the radio program / a culturally significant celebrity / widely regarded as one of the greatest writers

02 make a social media account / the law bans children under 14 / with the consent of the parents / There's no use in worrying about things

03 will it take to the airport / I'm running a bit late / have to pay extra for tolls

04 while looking around a model home / I've never seen a heart-shaped bed before / that there are no curtains / can't wait to move into

05 it's not that kind of smell / check if the gas is really leaking / shut off the gas valve

06 All books are just $10 each / get one more book for free / get an additional 10% off / log into your account and place an order

07 with a client to close a contract / are supposed to meet / collided with another player / need some stitches in his forehead

08 enter it in a cartoon contest / send it to their email address / I will definitely vote for you

09 has just flown over the International Date Line / at the speed of / 10:30 a.m. local time / do some duty-free shopping

10 You've come to the right place / that is suitable for her age / spend more than $10 rental

11 my first time in a library

12 what the weather is like every morning

13 I have no brothers or sisters / our apartment has a no-pet policy / comes with many responsibilities

14 What are you so absorbed in / walk with their heads down / What if you were walking

15 Hoping to win the first prize / hand in his final report today / has no time to

16-17 how many disposable products we use / create a lot of environmental pollution / broken into smaller pieces / give these plates a try

MEMO

수능 영어
듣기 모의고사
20+3회 실전

Supreme수프림

수능과 내신을 한 번에 잡는,

수능 프리미엄 고등 영어 시리즈

'수프림(supreme)': 최고의, 가장 뛰어난

수능과 내신을 한 번에 잡는
프리미엄 고등 영어 수프림 시리즈

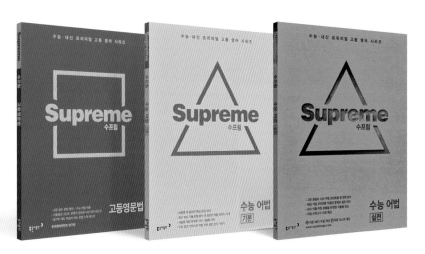

문법 어법

Supreme 고등영문법

쉽게 정리되는 고등 문법 / 최신 기출 문제 반영 /
문법 누적테스트

Supreme 수능 어법 기본

수능 어법 포인트 72개 / 내신 서술형 어법 대비 /
수능 어법 실전 테스트

Supreme 수능 어법 실전

수능 핵심 어법 포인트 정리 / 내신 빈출 어법 정리 /
어법 모의고사 12회

독해

Supreme 구문독해

독해를 위한 핵심 구문 68개 / 수능 유형 독해 /
내신·서술형 완벽 대비

Supreme 유형독해

수능 독해 유형별 풀이 전략 / 내신·서술형 완벽 대비 /
미니모의고사 3회

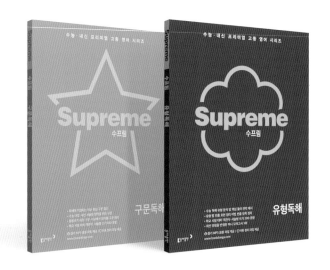

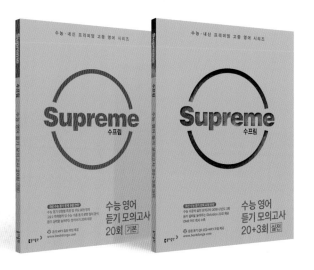

듣기

Supreme 수능 영어 듣기 모의고사 20회 기본

14개 듣기 유형별 분석 / 수능 영어 듣기 모의고사 20회 /
듣기 대본 받아쓰기

Supreme 수능 영어 듣기 모의고사 20+3회 실전

수능 영어 듣기 모의고사 20회+고난도 3회 /
듣기 대본 받아쓰기